POLEMICAL ENCOUNTERS

IEE

IBERIAN ENCOUNTER AND EXCHANGE, 475–1755

SERIES EDITORS
Erin Kathleen Rowe
Michael A. Ryan

The Iberian Peninsula has historically been an area of the world that fostered encounters and exchanges among peoples from different societies. For centuries, Iberia acted as a nexus for the circulation of ideas, people, objects, and technology around the premodern western Mediterranean, Atlantic, and eventually the Pacific. Iberian Encounter and Exchange, 475–1755 combines a broad thematic scope with the territorial limits of the Iberian Peninsula and its global contacts. In doing so, works in this series will juxtapose previously disparate areas of study and challenge scholars to rethink the role of encounter and exchange in the formation of the modern world.

ADVISORY BOARD
Paul H. Freedman
Richard Kagan
Marie Kelleher
Ricardo Padrón
Teofilo F. Ruiz
Marta V. Vicente

OTHER TITLES IN THIS SERIES:
Thomas W. Barton, *Contested Treasure: Jews and Authority in the Crown of Aragon*

POLEMICAL ENCOUNTERS

CHRISTIANS, JEWS, AND MUSLIMS IN IBERIA AND BEYOND

EDITED BY
MERCEDES GARCÍA-ARENAL
AND GERARD WIEGERS

THE PENNSYLVANIA STATE UNIVERSITY PRESS
UNIVERSITY PARK, PENNSYLVANIA

Library of Congress Cataloging-in-Publication Data

Names: García-Arenal, Mercedes, editor. | Wiegers, Gerard Albert, 1959– editor.
Title: Polemical encounters : Christians, Jews, and Muslims in Iberia and beyond / Mercedes García-Arenal and Gerard Wiegers, editors.
Other titles: Iberian encounter and exchange, 475–1755.
Description: University Park, Pennsylvania : The Pennsylvania State University Press, [2018] | Series: Iberian encounter and exchange, 475–1755 | "Most of the chapters collected here were presented as papers at the conference 'Polemical Encounters: Polemics between Christians, Jews, and Muslims in Iberia and Beyond,' which took place at the Consejo Superior de Investigaciones Científicas (CSIC) in Madrid in October 2014 . . . Other chapters included here were presented afterward at the monthly CORPI seminar and added to the volume."—Acknowledgements. | Includes bibliographical references and index.
Summary: "A collection of essays exploring the polemical encounters in the fields of religion and culture that took place among Jews, Christians, and Muslims in the Iberian Peninsula between the late Middle Ages and the seventeenth century"—Provided by publisher.
Identifiers: LCCN 2018036210 | ISBN 9780271081212 (cloth : alk. paper)
Subjects: LCSH: Christianity and other religions—Iberian Peninsula—Islam—History—Congresses. | Christianity and other religions—Iberian Peninsula—Judaism—History—Congresses. | Islam—Relations—Christianity—History—Congresses. | Islam—Relations—Judaism—History—Congresses. | Judaism—Relations—Christianity—History—Congresses. | Judaism—Relations—Islam—History—Congresses. | Iberian Peninsula—Civilization—Congresses. | Polemics—Congresses.
Classification: LCC BP172 .P655 2018 | DDC 201/.50946-dc23
LC record available at https://lccn.loc.gov/2018036210

Printed in the United States of America
Published by The Pennsylvania State University Press,
University Park, PA 16802-1003

The Pennsylvania State University Press is a member of the Association of University Presses.

It is the policy of The Pennsylvania State University Press to use acid-free paper. Publications on uncoated stock satisfy the minimum requirements of American National Standard for Information Sciences—Permanence of Paper for Printed Library Material, ANSI Z39.48-1992.

Contents

LIST OF ILLUSTRATIONS vii

ACKNOWLEDGMENTS ix

Introduction 1

PART I THE MEDIEVAL IBERIAN WORLD

1 "When I Argue with Them in Hebrew and Aramaic":
Tathlīth al-waḥdānīyah, Ramon Martí, and Proofs of Jesus's Messiahship 25
Thomas E. Burman

2 Qur'ānic Quotations in Latin: Translation,
Tradition, and Fiction in Polemical Literature 45
Antoni Biosca i Bas and Óscar de la Cruz

3 The Mudejar Polemic *Ta'yīd al-Milla* and Conversion between
Islam and Judaism in the Christian Territories of the Iberian Peninsula 53
Mònica Colominas Aparicio

4 "Sermo ad conversos, christianos et sarracenos":
Polemical and Rhetorical Strategies in the Sermons of
Vincent Ferrer to Mixed Audiences of Christians and Muslims 71
Linda G. Jones

PART II AROUND THE FORCED CONVERSIONS

5 Jewish Anti-Christian Polemics in Light of
Mass Conversion to Christianity 103
Daniel J. Lasker

6 Theology of the Laws and Anti-Judaizing Polemics in Hernando de Talavera's *Católica impugnación* 117
Davide Scotto

7 The Double Polemic of Martín de Figuerola's *Lumbre de fe contra el Alcorán* 155
Mercedes García-Arenal

8 Art of Conversion? The Visual Policies of the Jesuits, Dominicans, and Mercedarians in Valencia 179
Borja Franco Llopis

9 Marcos Dobelio's Polemics against the Authenticity of the Granadan Lead Books in Light of the Original Arabic Sources 203
Pieter Sjoerd van Koningsveld and Gerard Wiegers

PART III MEDITERRANEAN AND EUROPEAN TRANSFERS

10 Prisons and Polemics: Captivity, Confinement, and Medieval Interreligious Encounter 271
Ryan Szpiech

11 The *Libre de bons amonestaments* by ʿAbd Allāh al-Tarjumān: A Guidebook for Old and New Christians 305
John Dagenais

12 Poetics and Polemics: Ibrahim Taybili's Anti-Christian Polemical Treatise in Verse 331
Teresa Soto

13 Torah Alone: Protestantism as Model and Target of Sephardi Religious Polemics in the Early Modern Netherlands 357
Carsten Wilke

BIBLIOGRAPHY 377

NOTES ON CONTRIBUTORS 414

INDEX 419

Illustrations

8.1. Miguel del Prado, *Saint Vincent Ferrer Preaching in Valencia* 185

8.2. José Orient, *San Pedro Pascual* 194

9.1. *Book of the Outstanding Qualities and Miracles of Our Lord Jesus and of His Mother the Holy Virgin Mary* 222

10.1. The "Códice rico" of the *Cantigas de Santa María* 279

10.2. Ramon Llull, *Disputatio Raimundi christiani et Homeri saraceni* 285

10.3. Alonso de Espina, *Fortalitium fidei* 290

Acknowledgments

Most of the chapters collected here were presented as papers at the conference "Polemical Encounters: Polemics between Christians, Jews, and Muslims in Iberia and Beyond," which took place at the Consejo Superior de Investigaciones Científicas (CSIC) in Madrid in October 2014. This conference was organized by the editors of this volume under the auspices of the European Research Council's Advanced Grant project, European Union's Seventh Framework Programme (FP7/2007–13) / ERC Grant Agreement 323316, project CORPI ("Conversion, Overlapping Religiosities, Polemics, Interaction: Early Modern Iberia and Beyond"), led by Principal Investigator Mercedes García-Arenal. Other chapters included here were presented afterward at the monthly CORPI seminar and added to the volume. Another collection of essays that grew out of the same conference has been published as a special issue of the journal *Medieval Encounters* (vol. 24, 2018) dedicated to "Interreligious Encounters in Polemics between Christians, Muslims and Jews in Iberia and Beyond" and is complementary to the present volume: for this issue, we chose the essays dedicated to the dialogical aspects of polemics, while in the present book, we focus on aggressive texts that aim at rising barricades between religious groups. CORPI has produced another book that also deals, in part, with polemics: *After Conversion: Iberia and the Emergence of Modernity*, edited by Mercedes García-Arenal and published in Leiden by Brill in 2016.

We want to acknowledge here the contributions, through discussion and debates, of all those who participated in the conference, including those who participated orally and contributed neither to this volume nor to the special issue of *Medieval Encounters*: Alex Novikoff, Harvey J. Hames, Piero Capelli, Samir Kaddouri, Nuria Gómez Llauger, Raul Platas Romero, Cándida Ferrero Hernández, Joan-Pau Rubiés, Claude B. Stuczynski, and Emanuele Colombo. We also gratefully mention the invaluable work done by our American editor, Deirdre Casey, and Teresa Madrid Álvarez-Piñer, who compiled the bibliography and indexes. And last, our heartfelt thanks to the two anonymous readers who suggested changes and corrections.

INTRODUCTION

This book focuses on polemical encounters in the field of religion and culture that took place in the Iberian Peninsula between the late Middle Ages and the seventeenth century. *Polemic* was not a term used in the Middle Ages; it only begins to appear in the sixteenth century to denote a particular kind of writing dedicated to debate between competing (religious or philosophical) ideas.[1] This fact poses an analytical problem: we need to explain in which sense we are using a label (*polemicus, polemica*) that did not exist in premodern times and nowadays covers different literary genres. By using the term *polemical encounters,* we allude to a certain type of interaction between religious communities mediated usually—but not only—through learned discourse. This interaction is considered here under the aspect of its verbal and rhetorical aggression toward the religious other, aiming to prove him wrong, to challenge his truth claims, or to exclude him from salvation. At the same time, this interaction affects the polemicizing person because he must learn about the other in order to argue against him. Not less importantly, many times the polemical encounter was in fact a rhetorical one, from the well-orchestrated public disputation to the erudite text geared to internal consumption. In this last case, the polemical encounter is mostly an encounter with oneself. By attacking the other, the aggressor defines his own boundaries. We are interested in this two-sided dynamic of the phenomenon. In that sense, the term *polemical encounters* will serve to shift our attention away from the singularity of the historical case and the specificity of the genre of religious dispute (*disputatio, apologia, confutatio,* humanist dialogues, martyrologies, Counter-Reformation sermons, the spiritual autobiographies of converts, devotional images, and many others that are discussed in the different chapters of this book). Instead, our focus on the polemical encounter will draw our view to the larger cultural and intellectual dynamics of the conflicts that marked relations among Jews, Christians, and Muslims in Iberia in its Mediterranean context. We want to approach these polemical conflicts in a comparative perspective and consider polemics not only as part of a theological discourse but also as a form of social practice that carried with it real consequences for interreligious relations.

Our comparative approach brings us to consider here not merely attacks by Christians on Jews or Muslims followed by counterattacks against Christians. Jews and Muslims also wrote polemics on their own initiative against Christianity and against each other. We say *attacks* because texts of polemics are aggressive and vituperative in nature. Medieval and early modern polemical texts are produced within the framework of exclusive prophetic religions. Each of the three religions played a persistent role in the entangled sacred histories and apologetic discourses of the others, challenging or establishing some "salvation histories" as superior. We need not insist on what Jan Assman has defined as the exclusive and polemical stance of monotheism. Monotheisms vindicate the superiority of their own prophecies and assert the supremacy and uniqueness of one revelation, which could itself be presented as a polemical text.[2]

All polemical texts analyzed here offer examples that express both implicitly and explicitly the understanding of their authors and readers that they are members of distinct communities of faith—they are, in the words of Ryan Szpiech, "polemical communities."[3]

This book will pay close attention to how the three religions each affected the development of the others over time and will focus on polemical social, cultural, and political fields as factors in the way the three religious communities interacted in the many diverse regions of the peninsula. This is because, as this book argues, the polemic usually serves not to convince an opponent but rather to erect religious and social barriers between the group to which the polemicist belongs and the group or groups from which the polemist deems it necessary to demarcate his own. This book reveals the permeability of boundaries in interconfessional apologetics, challenging our notions of religious homogeneity. A point made in most of the chapters in this collection is that many of these polemics and disputations are addressed by Christians to Christians, not to Jews, Muslims, or converts from Islam or Judaism—or at least as much to the former as to the latter. Inter- and intra-Christian religious polemic was an important factor in defining Spanish Catholicism up to and including the seventeenth century. We also find that theological debates took place not only among Christians but also within Jewish and Muslim communities and were translated into polemics against others.

Recent historiography about polemical writings has oscillated in a debate about whether interreligious polemics were produced for internal consumption or external conversion. Alex Novikoff has mediated in this debate, suggesting that the emergence of a "public sphere" in the thirteenth century conditioned by the rise of universities and itinerant preachers is a more profitable place to situate the increasing number of polemical texts.[4] In the same line of thought, Harvey Hames's work on Ramon Martí has shown that it was written for Christian consumption, particularly in a university setting as an attempt to reconcile reason and faith. The purpose of the use of rabbinic materials and Muslim texts was to provide new textual evidence for establishing the truth of Christianity for doubting Christians.[5] We will follow in the paths of these two scholars, whose participation in the conference from which this book grew up was of crucial importance, and will consider the polemical material not so much from the point of view of their intended aim—which is to mark boundaries, to reach self-definition though the other—but to attend to unintended effects. This book will show how, at times, dialectical exchange with the other religion also entailed a knowledge, a recognition, and even an ethnographic consideration of the adversary. Religious polemics are often characterized, as we have said, by truth claims, doctrinal clarity, and an explicit articulation of the boundaries between groups. But many scholars of polemics have for too long privileged clear-cut definitions and fixed categories. Polemicists and apologists really did try to define and maintain the religious, social, and legal positions of their groups, and because of this, highly diversified and indistinct religious cultures were pigeonholed. But the sources that document the forced conversions in Iberia bring to life people who did not fit these categories. Therefore, we are especially interested in identifying and analyzing this diversity, ambiguity, and indeterminacy both in the texts and the authors who wrote them as well as in the sociohistorical context that they reflect. Where polemical texts deal in binary distinctions, many chapters in this book show the blurred and complex contexts in which the texts were produced. Our intention is to make clear how the focus on the three religions obscures the diversity—both religious (rationalist, reformist, illuminist) and cultural (language, dress, food)—within the Christian, Jewish, and Muslim communities in the Iberian Peninsula as well as among the growing ranks of skeptics and outright unbelievers, who can only with difficulty be categorized as belonging to one of those communities. The more Christians, Muslims, and Jews challenged each other polemically, the more they challenged their own identities. And the more they sought to define and defend identity, the more open to reform their own religious hierarchies became.

That is why we reflect on the compartmentalization that, due to polemics, has become a methodological problem in contemporary historiography. Thus the present book asks the following questions: Has scholarship, by adopting the clear separation between religious cultures expressed in polemical works, created the illusion of a multiplicity of well-defined and different cultures inside a dominant one, where in reality, there was no such compartmentalization? Has this clear separation obscured the different currents and versions inside each alleged group? And is it possible that the very absence of clear religious categories might explain, in part, the large number of polemical works produced in Iberia?

*

The chapters in this book transcend not only disciplinary limits but also the frontiers of Iberia, taking into account in particular the Mediterranean and Northern European contexts and considering the influence of problems traditionally associated with Iberia in other parts of Europe and the Mediterranean. We will discuss the question of how the Iberian polemical context works when transferred to other settings, particularly after the expulsion of Jews (1492) and forcibly converted Muslims (Moriscos, many of whom continued to practice their previous religions in secret) from Spain between 1609 and 1614. Therefore, this book will cover a long period of time—namely, from the twelfth century to the end of the seventeenth.

Religious conversion is very much at the core of religious polemics. Religious conversion necessarily implies the articulation of religious or communal boundaries; it forces the parties concerned to conceive of the kind of transformations that were supposed to be taking place.[6] In fact, from the late Middle Ages onward, a culture developed in Iberia that was heterogeneous and continually involved in debate, a culture that can itself be seen as polemical in its diversity.

During the Middle Ages, the Iberian Peninsula was divided into separate territories under Islamic or Christian rule, with Jewish minorities living in both. This fact set Iberia apart from other regions of Europe. The borders between Islamic and Christian territories were slowly shifting over the course of the Middle Ages. Conquest, emigration, internal political strife—all contributed to the existence on both sides of the Islamic-Christian border of minority communities: Muslims in Christian territories, Christians in Muslim territories, and Jews in both. These religious minorities were legally recognized in accordance with a system of religious and legal pluralism in which the king was the ultimate arbiter and protector. This political order was challenged by the emergence in the twelfth century of what some historians have called "the dream of conversion" (in the words of R. I. Burns or of John Tolan),[7] shared by Christians and Muslims in Iberia. Thus we have the appearance of the orders of Mendicant preachers and their large-scale campaigns on one side and the Almohads and their policies of forced conversion on the other. The thirteenth century was also important: it witnessed four crusades and saw the Mongols defeat the Abbasid Caliphate. It was as if the end of Islam was at hand. It is also the century of the great territorial expansion of the Iberian Christian kingdoms, which conquered most of Islamic Spain. It was in this century that Franciscans and Dominicans started to fully apply their ideas of conversion to Jews and Muslims.

The end of the fourteenth century witnessed a more radical change in the treatment of minorities in Iberia. The work and preaching of Vincent Ferrer was of singular importance. His declaration that "the neighbor of a Jew will never be a good Christian" fundamentally changed the general attitude toward cohabitation in medieval Iberia and provoked a series of pogroms and forced conversions, targeting mainly Jews. The civil war and succession struggle that marked the life of Castile in the 1460s and the violence against Jews and converts erupted in several urban centers. The situation escalated up to the time of the expulsion of the Jews in 1492, which was followed in 1502 by the first decree of conversion of the Muslims. As a consequence, there was growing debate in the sixteenth century about heterodoxy, Christianization, and conversion, reflecting how entangled political challenges, theological considerations, and interreligious contact had become a triad peculiar to Iberia.

The forced conversions that took place between the end of the fourteenth century and the first decades of the sixteenth coincided with the final Christian conquest of Islamic territories in Iberia. The Kingdom of Granada ended the same year as the expulsion of the Jews was decreed. The evangelization of Granadan Muslims, the forced conversions that gave rise to crypto-Muslim and crypto-Jewish groups, were the base of an early modern wave of polemical texts and images. Widespread conversion created new forms not only of otherness but also of familiarity, of intimacy. Christian society had to redefine itself through confrontation with and rejection of what it considered to be the religious and cultural characteristics of the other religious groups. Moreover, defining Spanish Catholicism meant distinguishing it from other local forms of Christianity. This redefinition was undertaken with an ongoing commitment to polemical confrontation and self-assertion. From the fifteenth century onward, the *converso* problem—in the sense of not only how to regard converts but also how to be a convert, what to retain from the old religion—was of primary importance. Converts often gave little thought to the precise limits between their old and new religions, and even Christians sometimes had doubts about the boundaries or the tenets of their own religion when faced with large numbers of converts or with, for example, the Hebrew Bible, which was the sacred text of a rival religion but also contained part of the revealed truth according to Christianity. In different historical moments, it is clear that here were similarities among the three groups' religious and philosophical thought, as is shown in the chapters of this book. Due to ambivalence and to the fact that some converts continued to practice their original religion in secret, differentiating between religious affiliations was difficult. What becomes evident from the chapters in this book is that polemics against Islam and Judaism provided an opportunity for Catholics to clarify their own doctrines vis-à-vis those of competing Christian groups and for those who would reform the Church and society to express their reform agendas disguised as a struggle against Judaism or Islam.

*

This book is also concerned with exploring the connections between polemics, on the one hand, and the origins of Arabic/Islamic and Hebrew/Judaic studies, on the other, as well as the relationship between polemics and the production of knowledge about the other. Beginning with the remarkable attempts of thirteenth-century Dominican Arabists to read the Qur'ān, the Hadith and Qur'ānic exegesis, and in the same century, Ramon Martí's use of rabbinic materials, languages were learned by many apologists and polemicists, sacred texts were translated, and grammars and dictionaries were in high demand. Thomas E. Burman has already highlighted the ambivalence between polemic and philology in the translation of the Qur'ān.[8] The polysemy of ancient and revealed texts such as the Bible or the Qur'ān displays many possibilities of translation and makes the boundaries between misreading, manipulation, and interpretation blurry. Polemicists used the polysemy of a revealed text to create narratives of ignorance and accuse the other religion of all kinds of unbelievable or barbaric beliefs. Readers of polemics in turn could find new meanings to create their own personal narratives.[9] How did the learning of another language and the effort of translation and dealing with polysemy affect the way in which the apologists or polemicists thought about their own scriptures? We will follow this thread from Ramon Martí up to the seventeenth century with the polemical work of an Eastern Christian in Spain, Marcos Dobelio, showing that the philological approach to these texts also needs to be analyzed within its own context, especially in the case of outstanding scholars, which Dobelio certainly was. Polemicists also deal with contradictions and paradoxes that they search for in the scripture of the religion they want to attack. Did this quest affect the way in which they dealt with their own scripture?

Comparativism is inherent to polemical works that aim to study the religion of the opponent through the latter's eyes, as the later works considered in this book do. We attempt to explore this aspect further and try to understand how, within polemics, knowledge of Islam, Judaism, and—in the case of Jewish and Muslims polemics—Christianity influenced not only the birth of the comparative study of religions and cultures but also the concept of religious tolerance among European elites, without overlooking the fact that a prodigious, centuries-old tradition of religious polemics, hagiographies, sermons, religious tracts, and so on existed in order to incite anti-Judaism, anti-Islamism, and anti-Christian ideas throughout Europe, the effects of which are still being felt today. As an example of the influence of Iberian polemics and their long discussion of different scriptures, we would point to the Sephardi philosopher Baruch Spinoza, whose criticism of scriptures as divine in origin in his *Tractatus Theologico-politicus* influenced Enlightenment thought.[10] We therefore focus on religious polemics in a framework of shifting identities, languages, and both religious and scholarly knowledge. This book also brings into focus the important role played by converts in writing polemics and as sources of erudition because of their knowledge of the texts and the hermeneutics of their previous religions. It highlights the lesser-known role of captives as authors of polemical texts, whose captivity constituted a badge of authority. We will consider the relationship that each polemicist had with political power: the Christian rulers in Spain on the one hand and the Muslim rulers in Iberia and across the Mediterranean in North Africa on the other. Their policies with respect to one another are inextricable, which implies that religious polemics in Iberia should be studied within the complex political and legal frameworks that existed in and between Christendom and Islam.

*

The book is divided into three parts. Part 1, "The Medieval Iberian World," begins in the twelfth century, a century that brought about so many profound changes. In the first chapter of this book, Thomas E. Burman traces the surprising parallels between the anonymous *Tathlīth al-waḥdānīya*, a Christian apologetic work from Iberia, and Ramon Martí's Trinitarian argument in his *Pugio fidei*, including the extensive citation of Hebrew and Aramaic texts. The *Pugio fidei* has long been seen as the culmination of the mission to the Jews and was central to the thirteenth century and to the work of the Mendicant orders. Not only do both the Arab-Christian author of the *Tathlīth al-waḥdānīya* and Martí argue that it is possible to demonstrate on the basis of the Hebrew Bible alone that the Messiah had come in the figure of Jesus, but they both actually quote biblical passages in Hebrew and in one case in

Aramaic before translating it to Arabic, something that only Martí did in the Latin Christian world. All this suggests, according to Burman, that *Tathlīth al-waḥdānīya* is a product of Dominican missionizing activity, perhaps even the work of Martí himself. Latin Scholasticism engaged very differently with Islam than with Judaism, according to Burman. He argues that the Dominican order did not address or consider Islam and its scriptures in depth, while Judaism and its Talmud were central to their missionizing efforts. Arab philosophy was important for Latin theology and philosophy, but Islam as a religion was not considered important, despite the twelfth-century translation of the Qurʾān by Robert of Ketton and even though Arabic Qurʾānic manuscripts circulated among Dominicans in this period. Burman contends that there was no place within Scholastic education for the Qurʾān.

The second chapter, by Antoni Biosca i Bas and Óscar de la Cruz, is dedicated to Latin Qurʾānic quotations in polemical literature, mainly in works by such scholars as Pedro Alfonso, Ramon Martí, and Alonso Buenhombre. The authors have chosen examples from their database Fragmenta Alcoranica Latina. Anti-Islamic polemical literature in Latin frequently used quotations from the Qurʾān to describe the rival religion. Occasionally, these Qurʾānic quotations, as the authors show, were taken from earlier Latin texts and exhibited the distortions of their own textual tradition, differing greatly from the Arabic original. Buenhombre claimed to have translated the texts from Arabic and passed off as Muslim ideas drawn from Ramon Martí or Nicholas de Lyra. This chapter points to the importance for Dominican polemicists to appeal to "authentic" Jewish and Muslim sources. These two first chapters introduce the questions of "authenticity" and "authority" conveyed by translations of sacred texts. The authors analyze how translation, tradition, and fiction can be detected in the Qurʾānic quotations, reflecting different levels of knowledge about the Qurʾān among the polemicists. Knowledge does not entail a tolerant or positive attitude. Polemical writers did not hesitate to create false quotations with the intention of supporting their arguments against Islam. As John Tolan has reminded us, the intellectual effort of the Dominicans in their conversionist discourse eventually expressed itself also as a political issue with practical consequences.[11]

During this period, Judaism became a compelling subject. Jeremy Cohen has argued that for Dominicans, the Jews of their time were not only incapable of understanding the Bible in a correct way but unwilling to do so.[12] In the eyes of these Dominicans, this put the Jews in the same category as Christian heretics, who should no longer have a place within Christian society. And at the same time, Christians were very conscious that the Hebrew texts, though corrupted, contained a part of Christian truth. Differentiation from (or identification with) Judaism was crucial for Christian self-definition from the beginnings of Christianity, and this continues to be the case up through the period we are dealing with. It was also a compelling subject for Muslims, as is demonstrated in chapter 3 by Mònica Colominas Aparicio on Muslim polemics against Judaism. Events in Christian Iberia and in Almohad and post-Almohad al-Andalus produced waves of Jewish converts to Islam both among people in Islamic territories and, interestingly, among those who had immigrated to Christian territories. According to Colominas Aparicio, the permeability between Judaism and Islam in the Christian kingdoms accounts for the success among Mudejar communities (Muslims living in Christian lands) of Muslim polemics against Judaism, mainly *Kitāb taʾyīd al-milla* and *Kitāb al-Mujādala maʿa al Yahūd wa-l-Naṣārā*. The first of these works was copied, revised, abridged, and even transmitted for many generations in *aljamiado* (Spanish written in Arabic script) between the fourteenth and the seventeenth centuries. This long period of transmission raises many questions, such as who the audience of those texts was. They were surely addressed to converts from Judaism but possibly also to Muslim communities destabilized by conversions or by the increasing need to keep a clear separation between the different religious groups. The second work is directed against not only Judaism but also Christianity, and the much greater stress on Christians testifies to the fact that Muslims in the kingdoms of Castile and Aragon found it necessary to respond to Christian missionary efforts as well. The combined response to Judaism and Christianity may even indicate that we are dealing in this work with some sort of "contagion" by Christian society's increasing anti-Judaism. In any case, Christian authorities dealt harshly with conversions to religions other than Catholicism.

In the fourth chapter, Linda G. Jones analyzes the polemical and rhetorical strategies of the Dominican preacher and polemicist Vincent Ferrer (1350–1419), focusing on sermons that, Jones suggests, were delivered in front of mixed audiences of Christians and Muslims and not, as many of Ferrer's better-known sermons were, to Jews alone. Jones nuances if not challenges Burman's argument about the Dominicans' lack of engagement with Islam and Muslims. Ferrer's sermons demonstrate that he targeted Jews and Muslims for proselytization and not merely for religious polemics, while his primary concern was always the salvation of Christians.

In the second part of the book, "Around the Forced Conversions," the shifting dynamics of medieval coexistence is studied in the context of assimilation, resistance, the imminent threat of forced conversion, and expulsion.

Part 2 begins with a chapter by Daniel J. Lasker on polemics against Christianity written by prominent rabbis and figures in Jewish philosophy at the end of the Middle Ages. These figures and their works are analyzed in the context of another important political period in Christian-Jewish relations in Iberia, including the second half of the fifteenth century. Lasker discusses the impact of events such as the pogroms of 1391 or the Disputa de Tortosa of 1413 and of the growing number of converts on Jewish polemical literature, comparing it with Jewish anti-Christian polemics before those events. He reaches the conclusion that though it appears that Jewish thinkers in late medieval Iberia were motivated by the Christian threat and the growing numbers of converts to Christianity, the message and arguments were the same as those of earlier Jewish polemicists who were not threatened by Christian pressure. Other scholars have argued that works written in the late fourteenth and fifteenth centuries revealed new emphases and lines of thought.[13] Conversely, Lasker concludes that the genre has its own apologetical motives that register little variation. It changes, according to Lasker, more in response to internal philosophical developments, just as Christian theologians and polemicists also had to revise their views and use the new Aristotelian terminology that became influential in this period. The main argument of the Jewish polemicists nevertheless continued to be that Jesus was not the anticipated Messiah of the Torah and that Christianity is a false religion.

The chapter by Davide Scotto is dedicated to polemics against Judaism or, more precisely, against converts who believed they could retain elements of Judaism after their conversion to Christianity. He provides a close reading of several chapters of the *Católica impugnación* by Hernando de Talavera (1428–1507), where Talavera's strict interpretation of Christian faith and practices serves to counter the threat of a heterodox Judaizing wave. Confessor of Queen Isabella, bishop of Avila, and first archbishop of Granada after the conquest of the capital city, Hernando de Talavera has been mainly considered by scholars for his role in the evangelization of Muslims in late fifteenth-century Granada. Much less attention, however, has been paid to his long-standing reflection on Jewish converts. Before Granada, Scotto shows, Talavera had been preaching in Seville and delivering sermons dedicated to demonstrating the superiority of the Gospels with respect to the "old" Law, a "dead law" whose commandments, ceremonies, opinions, and precepts had ceased to be valid after Jesus came into the world. This argument, which first appears in Talavera's sermons, was later developed in the *Católica impugnación*, revealing its ultimate polemical nature. The *Católica impugnación* makes manifest the political dimension of the Judaizing deviation and the role of theology in shaping a society in transition.

Among Jewish-Christian polemics in fifteenth-century Iberia, Talavera's refutation can be compared to Alonso de Cartagena's *Defensorium unitatis christianae*, Juan de Torquemada's *Tractatus contra Madianitas et Ismaelitas*, and Alonso de Oropesa's *Lumen ad revelationem gentium*, three works that deal with Paul's view on the role of the Jews in Christian salvation history. Though they are marked by different theological sensitivities, all these works provide apologetic arguments in favor of *converso* communities under attack after the Toledo riots of 1449 and oppose exclusivist views such as those expressed in Alonso de Espina's *Fortalitium fidei*. Talavera's exegetical thinking is equally indebted to Paul's view of the two Laws as outlined especially in the epistles to the Romans and the Galatians. What is more, Talavera looks at Paul as the most authoritative source for the debate on conversion and for its spiritual implications. Talavera's polemics make use of the subtle doctrinal distinction between apostasy and heresy in order to distinguish a gradation between biblical Jews, contemporary Jews, Jewish converts, and Judaizers in the specific context of late medieval Iberia. Writing after 1478, he was perfectly aware that he was making an accusation of heresy against a group of Jewish converts in Seville in the aftermath of a thorny debate about the establishment of the Inquisition in Castile. To avoid external pressure from the Crown in possible rulings against heretics, he felt the need to underline that, according to canon law, the identification and persecution of heretics fell exclusively within ecclesiastical jurisdiction.

Martín de Figuerola was a near contemporary of Hernando de Talavera, but his activities were directed at Muslims rather than Jews. His treatise *Lumbre de fe* (1519) is the focus of the chapter by Mercedes García-Arenal.

Figuerola belonged to a group of missionary preachers organized by Bishop Martín García, who had been requested to do so by the Catholic Monarchs. Figuerola preached in the villages around Zaragoza and was accompanied, among others, by a man called Juan Gabriel, a convert who had been the *alfaquí* of Teruel. With the help of Juan Gabriel (the same Ioannes Gabrielis who collaborated afterward with Cardinal Egidio da Viterbo on his translation of the Qur'ān), Martín de Figuerola wrote his *Lumbre de fe*. In it, he disputed different suras of the Qur'ān that he included in Arabic in his work, along with a phonological transcription and translation into Spanish. But he also—and this is the focus of the chapter—wrote a sort of diary about his missionary travels in Aragon. His efforts were directed at two groups: on the one hand, at the Aragonese *aljamas*; on the other, at the Aragonese authorities and nobility, whom he tried to convince of the need to decree the conversion of Muslims as had already been done in Castile and Navarre. García-Arenal discusses Martín García's polemical strategies, his arguments, and his way of addressing the nobility and the Muslim population. The chapter describes Figuerola's campaigns in the *morerías*, analyzing his ideology and his insistence on "blasphemy" and "indirect compulsion" in the context of the discussion about forced conversion, which was being carried out at the time in Iberia, and its relation with contemporary events. It is important to remark that he finished writing his work in Valencia in November 1519. At the beginning of 1519, just a few months after Charles V had left Spain to be crowned emperor in Germany, the revolt of the *Germanías* began in Valencia, led by the city's guilds of craftsmen and traders. During that year, the city of Valencia was the scene of violent riots. During the summer of 1521, thousands of Muslims were led to baptism by the *Agermanados*—in some cases under threat of death, in other cases out of panic or through the indirect pressure exerted by local authorities who sought to preempt an attack by the rebels. After the rebellion was suppressed, Charles V decided that the baptisms administered by the *Agermanados* were irrevocable and that all Muslims living in the Crown of Aragon had to convert to Catholicism.

Borja Franco Llopis's chapter is also about the Mudejars and Moriscos of Aragon and Valencia. He analyzes the visual policies of the orders dedicated to their evangelization—Dominicans, Mercedarians, and Jesuits—and shows how these visual policies, which were translated into artistic artifacts, grew out of debates within these orders regarding the question of the Moriscos' assimilation or expulsion. In their artistic depictions of Moriscos in Valencia during the sixteenth and seventeenth centuries, Jesuits, Dominicans, and Mercedarians responded in diverse ways to the political and religious situation surrounding them and constructed a visual discourse steeped in controversy and nuance. All three orders defended the educational use of art in theory but used it in practice in different ways—for example, the creation of policies that required visual representations to be emblems of Christianity and the creation of an iconography that depicted Muslims as vanquished. The Dominican order created images with strong apologetic content. Interestingly, none of the three used a decidedly hostile depiction of Muslims until after the expulsion, when there were no longer any Muslims in Iberia.

The chapter by Pieter Sjoerd van Koningsveld and Gerard Wiegers also deals with the Moriscos, converted Muslims, this time from Granada. They address the late sixteenth- and seventeenth-century controversy in Spain about to the so-called Lead Books of the Sacromonte, which were discovered in the outskirts of Granada at the end of the sixteenth century. The twenty-one Lead Books included texts in Arabic that purported to be from early Christian times and described the life and beliefs of a group of Arabic-speaking Christians who had arrived in Spain in the company of St. James in the first century and were martyred at the hands of the Romans. The authenticity of the books became the subject of a debate between defenders and critics. The critics maintained that the authors of the Lead Books were Moriscos and their contents tainted by Islamic ideas. Van Koningsveld and Wiegers focus on the polemical works of one of the most important and learned critics, known in Spain as Marcos Dobelio (an Eastern Christian and perhaps a convert to Christianity), who was summoned from Rome to translate the Lead Books. He wrote, as they show, two important polemical texts against the Lead Books that were later used by the Vatican to anathematize the documents after they had been sent to Rome. In an appendix, they publish for the first time a critical edition of the original Arabic text of the Lead Book that served as the basis for Dobelio's critique, along with an English translation. The Italian and Eastern connection in this last chapter establishes a nexus with the final part of the collection.

Part 3, "Mediterranean and European Transfers," is dedicated first of all to the Mediterranean world and the frontier with Muslim North Africa, with chapters authored by Ryan Szpiech, John Dagenais, Teresa Soto, and Carsten Wilke.

Ryan Szpiech considers the role of captivity in medieval Christian polemical writings, not only as a social and political reality that affected many individuals and often placed them in dire circumstances, but also as a literary topos and a symbol. Szpiech considers cases in which captivity facilitated the transfer of linguistic skills and of knowledge. He analyzes a number of examples in which captivity or slavery defined the context of polemical writing, most importantly the case of Ramon Llull (ca. 1232–1316), who not only learned Arabic and Islam from his own Muslim slave but also depicted himself as a captive while debating with a Muslim. Szpiech argues that captivity is not only a circumstance that facilitates interreligious contact; it is also a symbol of (Christian) resistance to conversion and a rejection of alternative sacred histories. Claiming captivity is a means of authorizing the captive to speak with knowledge about the other, a symbol of resistance and redemption, almost a kind of martyrdom. It is a badge of knowledge or a proof of the authenticity of one's claims. Finally, he proposes, captivity can be considered a metaphor for polemical writing itself, which involves a "conquest" and a "taking captive" of the histories and scriptures of Muslim opponents through translation and interpretation.

Like Szpiech, John Dagenais moves back and forth across the Mediterranean, between the shores of Catalonia, the Balearic Islands, and the Maghreb. His subject is the Mediterranean legacy of the Franciscan friar Anselm Turmeda (1355–1423), who converted to Islam in about 1390, adopting the name ʿAbd Allāh al-Tarjumān, and went to live in Tunisia as a translator for the sultan. Turmeda wrote a famous polemical Islamic treatise in Arabic against Christianity, titled *Tuḥfat al-adīb fī al-radd ʿalā ahl al-ṣalīb*, in which his own religious experience and conversion are an important part of the polemical argument. Dagenais, however, focuses on another, later work by Anselm Turmeda, *Libre de bons amonestaments*, or *Book of Good Counsel* (1398). It is a book of Christian religious instruction, of Christian teachings written in a language simple enough for children to understand and in a verse form that made it easy to memorize. The work remained very influential in the education of young children in Catalonia until the nineteenth century. Dagenais's close reading of this text takes into account the problems it faced with the Inquisition in the late sixteenth century because of its justification of lying in cases of necessity, which critics argued might excuse dissimulation in the context of the North African and Southern European frontier, where many people lived their lives trying to avoid conflict with different religious authorities. He suggests that the *Book of Good Counsel* was written for people who had to be prepared to demonstrate at least some knowledge of Catholicism before the Inquisition or other authorities. It was written for people who lived in the Mediterranean space and had to change their religion several times, adopting Islam or Catholicism as circumstances demanded. This Mediterranean world was made up of individuals, maybe even an entire society, for whom these binaries, no matter how loudly they were declared, disguised the much more complex situation of the people caught between them. John Dagenais's reading of Turmeda's work sheds light on many polemical treatises and on many issues analyzed elsewhere in this book and helps us reflect on the polemical treatise as a pedagogical tool in complex situations in which people were obliged to choose among clear-cut options.

John Dagenais's chapter is closely related to Teresa Soto's study of a polemical treatise in verse, written in Spanish, against Christianity, by a Morisco exiled in Tunis whose name was Ibrahim Taybili. It was written at least two decades after the expulsion of the Moriscos, in about 1628, and it is surprising because, as Soto shows, Spanish verse is being used as a vehicle for an Islamic message. It is also surprising because Taybili copies freely from the Spanish poet Juan de Valdivieso, using the *a lo divino* technique, and draws from the anti-Trinitarian writings of another Morisco polemicist, Muhammad Alguazir (ca. 1611). Here again we find another complex context that produced individuals who are difficult to classify using clear-cut or binary distinctions. In any case, we are faced with Muslim and Jewish individuals who were permeated by Christian concepts that they had thoroughly internalized. Their texts show an intimate acquaintance with Christian literature, rhetoric, poetry, and theology.

Soto's chapter also looks at the case of exiled Moriscos in terms of issues that have so far been explored mainly in relation to the Sephardic "New Jews" of Amsterdam. To them, the chapter by Carsten Wilke is dedicated. Wilke takes us to Northern Europe, focusing on the effects that the schisms and internal controversies of the Western Church had on Jewish intellectual self-awareness. During the period he studies, Northern Europe underwent a process that has been called "confessionalization," characterized by the expansion of religions and an identification of religion with early nationhood. According to Wilke, it is this development toward unprecedented religious pluralization that obliges Jewish authors to develop strategies of doctrinal self-definition and polemical self-defense, especially against Catholicism. How did Portuguese New Christians, turned Jews, see the new multiplicity of Christian churches? Wilke's chapter shows that the Jews were surprisingly active in the confessionalization process. He argues that the Sephardic polemical writings he analyzes are evidence not of adaptation to the secularization of the public sphere in Dutch society but rather of Judaism's expanding role along confessional lines, siding with Protestantism, which was dominant in the Republic of the United Provinces, against Catholicism. Whether we are dealing with Portuguese or Morisco polemics in the Diaspora, this anti-Catholic element appears to be a common feature. But the same may hold true for confessionalization, which implied the importance of a diversity of religious credos in social life, but most importantly, it envisioned a political-religious order characterized by pluralism. Jewishness is no longer the social experience of exile among the nations; rather, it is understood in theological terms as one set of dogmas, texts, memories, and rituals among a multiplicity of religious communities in Northern Europe. As Wiegers has argued elsewhere, Morisco polemical writings from Tunis (where Taybili wrote) can be seen as evidence of a similar confessionalization process taking place in the Ottoman territories of North Africa[14] (see also the recent work of Tijana Krstić, quoted by Wilke).[15]

As is one of the main tenets of this book, Wilke argues that Jewish ideas on Christianity do not hinge on theological principles; they largely reflect the two communities' changing relations and internal apologetics needs. Although he agrees (e.g., with Daniel J. Lasker)[16] that the bulk of their exegetical, philosophical, and historical arguments follow those of the medieval predecessors, he demonstrates that the sixteenth and seventeenth centuries produced significant innovations on the levels of literary culture, rhetorical expression, and ideological content.[17] Since the early seventeenth century, writings on and against Christianity used Spanish and Portuguese for polemical and other texts destined for internal Jewish consumption. The authors adopted literary models from the Christian environment. Jewish apologists seek, at least rhetorically, to gain proselytes. Once in exile, theological distinction from Christianity became increasingly important for affirming Jewish identity.

Wilke's chapter on Sephardic Jews in Amsterdam and Soto's on the Morisco from Toledo—Taybili, who lived in Tunis—show a clear historical and literary connection for strikingly new phenomena common to Moriscos and Jewish converts in exile: a new theological self-definition expressed in the clandestine vernacular texts of the Portuguese Jewish writers and, in the Morisco case, expressed in the Romance vernacular written with the Latin alphabet, whereas in the peninsula, they had been writing in *aljamía* (vernacular in the Arabic alphabet). Also, and most importantly, both show a remarkable receptiveness toward and adaptation of Spanish (Christian) literary models, a process of borrowing across boundaries to the point of what we would nowadays call plagiarism: they construct a Jewish or Muslim polemical text from Christian Spanish texts that apparently influenced them and that acquire a new religious context in the appropriation process.

*

Polemics, this study shows, serve to shape external social relations and strengthen internal cohesion. They contribute importantly to the construction of the religious definition of the group to which the polemicist belongs through attacks on the ideas or beliefs of outsiders, but they are also vehicles of criticism and correction addressed to those within their own communities who are regarded as heretics. The questions of heresy and apostasy, even of blasphemy, underlie many of the chapters collected here. Polemical concepts such as the idea of the corruption of previous scriptures (the Islamic accusation of *taḥrīf* charges Christianity and Judaism with intentional corruption of true revelation, while Christians and Jews charge the other religions with corrupting or falsifying true revelation), the various types of theology of substitution, the dogma of exclusive salvation, or the rejection of the cult of images or oral confession were all used by the different groups against one another in a process that has been termed *heresy transfer*.[18] Michel de Certeau's term *heterology* also provides a useful way to understand the construction by dominant Spanish Christianity of a single category to encompass everything considered unorthodox according to the tenets of Catholicism and attribute it to Islam or to Judaism. It is a "discourse that is other and of the other," in the words of Michel de Certeau—like a negative image of the orthodox discourse that was constantly being produced by the institutional Church.[19]

This book shows, we hope, that it is of great importance for the study of religious polemics in Christian Iberia to observe that reform movements had started questioning dominant Catholic ideas from the fifteenth century onward. These reform movements, culminating in what has become known as the Reformation, had started to question and deny the intermediary role of the Church as well as the infallibility of many of its teachings (e.g., regarding the sacrament of penitence and the religious authority of the Church, the role of the saints, and images). Catholic religious authorities in Iberia were very sensitive to this issue and always sought to reinforce it. The authority of the Church impinged on some of the aspects that are transversal to many contributions in this book—namely, reflections on faith, certainty, doubt, heresy, conversion, and apostasy—and it also impinged on authenticity and falsification, authenticity becoming a new source of authority (Burman, Biosca and Cruz, Szpiech). With the division among the Christians and the challenge to the Church's mediating function by Protestants, many Catholic theologians started to think about faith mainly in terms of a struggle against heresy. The Catholic Church being the promoter and the guardian of faith (the Church being infallible), heresy became the subject of much critical reflection during the sixteenth century and after. In the sixteenth century, the distinction was clearly established between formal heresy, which consisted of professing a misconception with full knowledge and obstinacy, and inquisitorial heresy, which covered opinions and behaviors that the Inquisition defined as falling within the crime of heresy. The notions of both heresy and apostasy were connected to blasphemy, a notion so present in many polemical texts (García-Arenal, Scotto).

Also important for reflecting on the propositions and ideological attitudes of the polemical texts considered here is that until the seventeenth century, the separation between theology and canonical law was not yet complete. Reflection on faith, doubt, and heresy was not purely speculative but aimed to determine whether the doubter was guilty not only before God but also in the eyes of the civil authorities, the Church, and the Inquisition. And what was the difference between apostasy and heresy? Many people of *converso* origins were accused by the Inquisition of remaining Jewish or Muslim. Did that make them apostates or heretics? Simulation and dissimulation became key issues, as well as the coming into being of identities that were less fixed and static than official religious doctrine would have it (Dagenais, Wilke).

The resurfacing of heresiology in late medieval Castile raises intriguing questions about the possibilities of "syncretism," the missionary purpose and the controversial capacity of Christian theology to confront historical challenges emerging from shifting interreligious scenarios.[20] While Talavera struggled with Jewish converts who still interacted in various ways with their former coreligionists, sixteenth-century Granadan authorities wrestled with the customs and usages of the Muslims converts who spoke Arabic and cherished all sorts of cultural and religious customs and practices. It was these Moriscos who found an eloquent spokesperson in Don Francisco Núñez Muley, who famously defended them as cultural usages in his *Memorial*.[21] They were spokespersons for diversity, if not pluralism, the pluralism that had existed during the Middle Ages and into the early modern centuries, a pluralism that never included the skeptical relativism combined with mutual civil respect and equality that we name tolerance but that was contemporary to the French *politiques* who advocated liberty of conscience in the midst of the religious struggle between Catholics and Protestants that shook the country. Similar Spanish *políticos* advocated in their own way for the "libertad de conciencia" to be accorded to Moriscos.[22]

We suggest that we stop considering, as this book insists that we do, any religious activity or stance in religious dissidence in early modern Iberian Catholicism as originated in Judaism and Islam and instead consider the whole diversity of religions in the perspective of "heterologies," bringing to the surface the voices of neglected minorities within the majorities and the agency of hitherto muted cultural minorities. The result will be a totally different and much richer panorama of religious and cultural diversity from what is generally considered in extant historiography.

But the culturally diverse situation we have dealt with above proved, as we know, instable in itself and was accompanied by political and cultural repression, persecution, and eventually expulsion. Massive forced migrations transported the polemical issues to other regions and into other political constellations: Ottoman Tunis, Sa'did Morocco, and the Dutch Republic, where Iberian migrants of Muslim and Jewish descent continued to discuss similar themes—namely, cultural (language), political, and religious, as the late Louis Cardaillac and Miriam Bodian have shown.[23] Yet not everything was continuity. Wilke shows that even though the polemical themes are the same, they functioned in a new framework of confessionalization. The hitherto unexplored role of internal criticisms within the Roman Catholic Church, culminating in the Reformation in the Iberian context for the interactions among Christianity, Judaism, and Islam, may perhaps contribute to a better insight into the problematic framework of a three-partite interaction.[24]

Notes

The research leading to these results has received funding from the European Research Council under the European Union Seventh Framework Programme (FP7/2007–13) / ERC Grant Agreement number 323316, project CORPI, "Conversion, Overlapping Religiosities, Polemics, Interaction: Early Modern Iberia and Beyond." We want to thank Yonathan Glazer-Eytan and Deirdre Casey, who discussed with us previous drafts of this introduction.

1. Szpiech, "Introduction," 9.
2. Assmann, *Of God and Gods.*
3. Szpiech, "Introduction," 13.
4. Novikoff, *Medieval Culture of Disputation.*
5. Hames, "Reason and Faith"; and Hames, "Rethinking the Dynamics."
6. Fox and Yisraeli, *Contesting Inter-religious Conversion*, 17.
7. Burns, "Christian-Islamic Confrontation"; Tolan, *Sarracens.*
8. Burman, *Reading the Qur'ān.*
9. Tommasino, "Textual Agnogenesis," 172.
10. Wilke, "That Devilish Invention."
11. Tolan, "Royal Policy," 96–110.
12. Cohen, *Living Letters.*
13. Bodian, *Dying in the Law*; Kozodoy, *Secret Faith.*
14. Wiegers, "Polemical Transfers," 229–50.
15. Krstić, *Contested Conversions.*
16. Lasker, *Jewish Philosophical Polemics*; Lasker, "Jewish Anti-Christian Polemics."
17. See Carsten Wilke's excellent introduction to his edition of *The Marrakesh Dialogues.*
18. Mulsow, "Socinianism, Islam."
19. Certeau, *Heterologies*, 18.
20. It is Joel Robbins who has reminded us that the study of Christianity has so far lacked a clear conceptual framework for those who, once converted, do not neatly fit the categories of Christianity nor those of their previous religions. See Robbins, "Crypto Religion"; and see also Albera, "Why Are You Mixing?"
21. See Barletta, *Memorandum for the President.*
22. Márquez Villanueva, *Personajes y temas*, 277.
23. Cardaillac, *Morisques et Chrétiens*; Bodian, *Hebrews of the Portuguese*; and Bodian, *Dying in the Law*, 58.
24. As noticed and addressed by our late and regretted colleague Olivia Remie Constable and her colleague Belen Vicens in their 2013 conference devoted to "Rethinking Medieval Iberia: Beyond the Land of the Three Cultures." See the website at https://mediberia.wordpress.com/.

I

THE MEDIEVAL IBERIAN WORLD

I

"WHEN I ARGUE WITH THEM IN HEBREW AND ARAMAIC"

Tathlīth al-waḥdānīyah, Ramon Martí, and Proofs of Jesus's Messiahship

Thomas E. Burman

In 1239, the Dominican friar Peter of Ferrand (d. ca. 1254) reworked the earliest account of the history of his order—that of Jordan of Saxony from some ten years previous—into a narrative called *Legenda Sancti Dominici*, a text that, for the most part, played up St. Dominic as the saintly model of his order.[1] It contains, however, a curious episode that makes us wonder what role Dominic thought his order should have in confronting Islam. When the Order of Preachers was still very new, Peter tells us, Dominic decided to institute an administrative innovation (which did not, in fact, endure long), asking his followers to choose one from among themselves to serve as abbot. After they selected Brother Matthew, Dominic then sent his followers out to preach, variously to Spain, Paris, and Bologna. Peter points out that the occasion for this structural change was that Dominic himself had desired to go to the *terra Sarracenorum* to preach and was even preparing for departure by growing a beard "for a certain time"—*aliquanto tempore*.[2] Strikingly, however, for all we can tell from Peter of Ferrand's account, Dominic immediately abandoned that venture, and directly afterward, we find Dominic wending his way to Bologna—his scratchy new beard apparently shaved off, his mission to Muslims forgotten.[3]

I mention this puzzling episode—really a nonevent, but one recounted by two different Dominican historians[4]—at the outset of this chapter about the relationship between Ramon Martí's works and a problematic, fragmentary Arab-Christian text because that relationship, whatever it may have been, should raise a similar question in our minds. Why do we find thirteenth-century Spanish Dominicans—and Dominic, Peter of Ferrand, and Ramon Martí were all Spaniards—gesturing toward Islam and then turning decisively away from it? On Peter's telling, Dominic seemed quite aware of the need to preach the gospel—the very duty of his young order—to the vast number of Muslims who rejected Catholic teaching, and he indeed took steps toward doing so himself but immediately redirected his course away from the Arab-Islamic world toward Bologna, one of the great intellectual centers of Latin Christendom. Dominic never, as far as we know, preached to Muslims, and the thirteenth-century makers of Dominican history never portray Dominicans preaching to Muslims either.[5]

We see the same gesturing toward and turning away from Islam in the life and works of Ramon Martí. After writing one short—though very learned—treatise against Islam in the late 1250s, Martí, the thirteenth-century Dominican order's most learned scholar of Arabic and Islam, directed all his considerable erudition entirely toward Judaism for the remaining decades of his life, scarcely giving another thought to the religion of the Prophet. But his disengagement from Islam looks even more puzzling in the light of the intriguing parallels between his works against Judaism and the anonymous text called *Tathlīth al-waḥdānīyah* (Trinitizing the unity [of the Godhead]), written somewhere in Iberia, probably in about 1220. I have elsewhere discussed a kalāmic argument for the Trinity that we find in both this text and Martí's immense anti-Jewish opus, *Pugio fidei*,[6] and in what follows, I will examine a second, very different but equally striking parallel: the Arab-Christian author of *Tathlīth al-waḥdānīyah* not only argues that it is possible to demonstrate on the basis of the Hebrew Bible alone that the Messiah has come in the form of Jesus but—and this is something quite exceptional in Arab-Christian polemic and theology—actually quotes a series of biblical passages in Hebrew and, in one case, in Aramaic before translating them into Arabic, a procedure associated almost exclusively with Martí in the Latin world.

As we will see, it is not at all clear what to make of these remarkable parallels. Did Martí know the *Tathlīth al-waḥdānīyah* and adopt its argumentation? Was he possibly its author? Are the common features entirely independent developments in two different linguistic worlds? Whatever the exact relationship, it is clear that someone in Spain thought it made sense to preach Catholic Christianity to Muslims in their language and, indeed, was making arguments in Arabic to Muslims that are just like the ones Martí was making in Latin against Jews. Yet like Dominic in Peter of Ferrand's *Legenda*, the Dominican preacher Martí, after motioning in that direction, turned definitively away from it.

Both Dominic's and Martí's gestures toward Islam and ensuing, resolute marches away seem, I will be suggesting here, much stranger to us than they would have in their time. While modern scholars have often taken the Dominican order's supposed goal of preaching the gospel to the whole world[7] at face value[8] and have assumed that early Friars Preachers must have been as committed to preaching to Muslims as to Jews or any other non-Christian group, this was clearly not the case. As Robin Vose has persuasively shown, for example, Dominicans in the Crown of Aragon in the thirteenth century had little interest in engaging Islam in any direct way.[9] Moreover, if the early histories of the Dominican order repeatedly depict Dominic and his brethren choosing paths that led away from the House of Islam, those same paths, as often as not, took them directly to the centers of Latin Scholastic culture, such as Paris and Bologna.[10] That the Dominican order zealously embraced Scholasticism is, of course, well known. What has not been appreciated, it seems to me, is that in doing so, the Order of Preachers assumed a culture of education and inquiry in which Islam and its books were virtually invisible and unspeakable, while Judaism and its Talmud, Targumim, and midrashim were increasingly familiar and compelling topics that could be approached from within core disciplines and genres of the movement. In turning his back on Islam and immersing himself for two decades in the postbiblical literature of Judaism, Martí was, therefore, fundamentally replicating thirteenth-century Latin Scholasticism's very different engagements with Christianity's fellow Mediterranean monotheisms.

The Arab-Christian treatise that is the focus of much of my attention here—which survives only fragmentarily and is difficult to date, points I will return to later—takes its name, *Tathlīth al-waḥdānīyah*, from the first of its three parts, which advances a rationalist argument for the Trinity based on kalāmic thought.[11] In the second part, the anonymous author defends the doctrine of the Incarnation. It is part 3, though, that will concern us here.

Entitled (somewhat misleadingly, as we will see) "The Argument of the Three Religions" ("Iḥtijāj al-thalāt milal"), this portion of the Arab-Christian text begins with an intriguing discussion of disputation among the three religions of medieval Iberia. Men of all three faiths—Jews, Christians, and Muslims—assert, we are told, that their own religion is the only true faith, generally doing so for worldly reasons and without knowledge of the rules of logical argument. Moreover, if a pagan (*majūsī*) came to this land, he would find a thoroughly confusing religious situation: while the faithful of all three religions believe that the Jewish prophets are true messengers of God, Christians argue that the Gospels abrogate the Jewish scriptures, and Muslims contend that the Qur'ān invalidates the Christian scriptures, with the Jews adamantly maintaining that no scriptures other than their own are valid at all. In such circumstances, convincing a *majūsī* of the rightness of one's faith requires Christians to present evidence from the Jewish scriptures that demonstrates that the Messiah awaited by Jews has already come, and Muslims must demonstrate that the prophethood of Muḥammad is foretold in the Bible. Whoever can do so is a believer in the true faith.[12]

In the ensuing sections of part 3 of *Tathlīth al-waḥdānīyah*, therefore, the Christian author argues first that it is clear from the Jewish scriptures alone that the Messiah has come. He cites Hosea 3:4, for example ("For many days the Children of Israel will abide without king and without prince"), and Genesis 49:10 ("Ruling power [*mulk*] will not disappear from Judah, nor the legislator from between his feet until the Messiah comes, and to him the nations will give obedience") to make the standard Christian argument that since Jews lack political power, and their own scriptures say that this will happen with the coming of the Messiah, the Messiah must have come.[13] Remarkably, the anonymous author quotes these verses in Hebrew (and in one case Aramaic as well) in Arabic script before translating them into Arabic. He presents the Hosea passage, for example, as follows: "The prophet Hosea son of Beeri, peace be upon him, speaks the following in Hebrew speech: Ki yamim rabi yshebu bene yisra'el 'en melekh we-'en ṣar. Its translation: 'For many days the Children of Israel will endure without king and without leader.' Now when the Jewish infidel is asked if among [the Jews] there is a king or a leader, he will have no answer except to say, 'we have no king and no leader.'"[14]

Having argued in this way that the Hebrew Bible alone demonstrates that Jesus was the Messiah awaited by the Jews, the Christian author then demands that his Muslim interlocutors similarly demonstrate that Muḥammad was foretold by the Bible, but he then rather forecloses that possibility by asserting that Christians will not accept such arguments in any case, since they do not recognize the authority of the Qurʾān, which contains such objectionable content as marriage laws encouraging adultery.[15]

That the Hebrew Bible alone is sufficient to demonstrate the messiahship of Jesus is an argument that cannot but make us think of Martí. The *Capistrum iudaeorum* (ca. 1267), the first of his two lengthy works against Judaism, is, as he describes it, "a collection of certain authoritative passages from the Old Testament by which the advent of the Christ is proved,"[16] while in the second of the three books of his *Pugio fidei*, "the advent of the Messiah" is likewise demonstrated on the basis of the Hebrew scriptures alone.[17] In both these works, Martí does something that the Arab-Christian author of *Tathlīth al-waḥdānīyah* does not do, however: he cites an enormous range of postbiblical Jewish sources alongside the Hebrew Bible as he advances this argument. The principle, though, is the same: Christians can show that authoritative Jewish texts by themselves demonstrate that Jesus of Nazareth was the Messiah.

Moreover, both the author of *Tathlīth al-waḥdānīyah* and Martí offer their readers much the same explanation for why they cite these Jewish texts in their original languages. "Notice," the former comments, "that I have written down for you in the Hebrew language and the Aramaic language some of the scriptural evidences of the prophets sent by God from the books in their (i.e., the Jews') hands, and that the Jews are not able [therefore] to deny a word of them when I advance [these scriptural evidences] in argument with them in Hebrew and Aramaic."[18] In the preface to the *Pugio fidei*, Martí likewise explained,

> When citing in Hebrew authoritative passages of the text, from wherever [in the text] derived, I will not follow the Septuagint or any other translation, and—what might appear to be even more presumptuous—I will not pay obeisance to Jerome or even avoid somewhat improper Latin, in order to translate the truth of whatever the Hebrews have [in their scriptures] word for word whenever it is possible to do so. For by this means, a wide and spacious way of escape is closed off for the lying Jews, since they are entirely unable

to say that [the text] is not thus among them, since the truth will be cited by us against them, with me as the translator.[19]

Leaving aside for the moment the messy question of the dating of the Arabic text, when we read it alongside Martí's works, a series of arresting similarities and differences compete for our attention. At times, we feel that Martí could in fact have been the author of the Arab-Christian treatise (an outside possibility, as we will see below), though at others, very different minds seem to be at work. On the one hand, of the eight[20] biblical passages the Arab-Christian author offers in their original languages—Hosea 3:4, Genesis 49:10, Lamentations 2:3, Jeremiah 15:1–2, Jeremiah 31:31–32, Jeremiah 3:14, Jeremiah 3:15, Jeremiah 3:16—five appear in both of Martí's works against Judaism: Hosea 3:4, Genesis 49:10, Lamentations 2:3, Jeremiah 31:31–32, Jeremiah 3:14.[21] But on the other hand, the respective Arabic and Latin translations of these verses are often quite different. In Genesis 49:10, for example, the Hebrew *mehoqeq*, "a prescriber (of laws)," becomes the very literal *rāsim*, "inscriber, drawer," in Arabic, while Martí gives us the rather more suitable *legumlator* and *legumdator*, "giver of laws."[22] The Arab-Christian author, furthermore, abbreviates and paraphrases Jeremiah 31:31–32, while Martí translates this passage literally but only partially. The Hebrew text in full reads as follows: "See, a time is coming—declares the Lord—when I will make a new covenant with the House of Israel and the House of Judah. It will not be like the covenant I made with their fathers, when I took them by the hand to lead them out of the land of Egypt."[23]

In *Tathlīth al-waḥdānīyah*, the whole Hebrew text appears followed by this abridged version in Arabic: "God says, I have established a new covenant for the House of Israel and Judah, not like the covenant which I spoke to their father on the day upon which I led them from the house of servitude."[24] In Martí's two Latin versions—in the *Capistrum iudaeorum* and the *Pugio fidei*—on the other hand, only the first part of this passage appears, but without abbreviation or paraphrase (quoting the former version here with the *Pugio fidei*'s variations in brackets): "I will make a new pact [new law] for the House of Israel and the House of Judah, not like the pact [berith (in transliteration)] which I made with their fathers on the day on which I took [strengthened] their hand in order to lead them from Egypt."[25]

And there are still other notable differences. Martí translates the Hebrew *karati . . . berith hadasha* (I will cut a new covenant) rather slavishly as *scindam . . . foedus novum / legem novam* (I will cut a new pact / new law), where the Arabic is less literal: *uthbitu . . . ʿahdan jadīdan* (I have established a new covenant). Moreover, the Arabic paraphrases "the land of Egypt" as "the house of servitude," while in Latin, it becomes simply "Egypt."

But it is not just the translations that differ. Martí discusses these passages at far greater length than the author of the *Tathlīth al-waḥdānīyah* does, even though their argumentative use is the same. The Christian author of the latter work quotes the Hebrew and Arabic versions of Lamentations 2:3 ("In blazing anger He has cut down all the might of Israel") prefaced by the explanation that "God spoke on the tongue of Jeremiah the prophet about the cutting off of [the Jews'] ruling authority in Hebrew speech as follows," with no other comment of any kind.[26] In both the *Capistrum iudaeorum* and the *Pugio fidei,* Martí surrounds his quotation of this verse with a discussion of a lengthy midrash on it, the whole running to more than fifty lines of text in the earliest manuscript of the *Pugio.*[27]

Nevertheless, there are striking parallels here that go beyond the fact that, as in the *Pugio fidei,* the Hebrew/Aramaic passages appear in transliteration in *Tathlīth al-waḥdānīyah* as well as in translation. While there are differences in detail between the respective Arabic and Latin versions, in general, the translations into both languages carefully follow the Hebrew text—the respective Arabic and Latin versions of Hosea 3:4, for example, hew closely to the Hebrew word order.[28] Furthermore, Martí's interpretations of these verses are sometimes highly reminiscent of those offered in the *Tathlīth al-waḥdānīyah.* In introducing his quotation of Jeremiah 3:14, the author of *Tathlīth al-waḥdānīyah* asserts that the "new covenant" described later in Jeremiah 31:31–32 is specifically the faith of Jesus's disciples and those who follow them: "Just as God said in another passage on the tongue of Jeremiah the prophet about the disciples. . . . Its translation: 'Return, O sons of stubbornness, for I have become master over you. I will take you, one from a city, and two from a clan, and I will introduce you into Zion [Jer. 3:14].' And thus [Jesus] took the disciples, one from a city and two from a clan."[29]

In both the *Capistrum iudaeorum* and the *Pugio fidei,* Martí quotes this verse as it appears in a passage from tractate Sanhedrin (111a) that he argues indicates that only a small number of Jews will be saved. In the *Pugio fidei,* however, he lingers over this verse, connecting it explicitly with Jesus's disciples as well, for "our Lord Jesus Christ had saved Jews, one from a city, such as blessed Paul of Tarsus in Cilicia, and two from a family, such as blessed Peter and Andrew, who were brothers, and James and John who were also brothers."[30]

Moreover, the selection of verses itself is telling. While some of the five passages quoted in both *Tathlīth al-waḥdānīyah* and the works of Martí are so commonplace in Christian works *adversus judaeos*—Jeremiah 31:31–32 and, especially, Genesis 49:10—that the coincidence by itself means nothing, others appear far more rarely in this literature, such as Jeremiah 3:14. Isidore of Seville used it centuries earlier in his *De fide catholica ex veteri et novo testamento contra judaeos*, but I know of no other cases. One passage—Lamentations 2:3, "He [God] will cut off all the horn of Israel," which *Tathlīth al-waḥdānīyah* says refers to "the cutting off of [the Jew's] ruling authority,"[31] and Martí reads likewise—appears nowhere else in Christian attacks on Judaism that I have examined. In these cases, the fact that the passage appears in both works suggests a far closer connection, perhaps even common authorship.

The evidence from part 3 of the *Tathlīth al-waḥdānīyah* discussed up to this point, therefore, is something of a muddle. Some passages are handled quite differently: in some cases, there are striking parallels in translation or interpretation (some aspects of both works are so typical of the *adversus judaeos* genre that no conclusions can be drawn from their inclusion in these works); in other places, we are in the presence of highly suggestive coincidence.

In the one instance in which the author of *Tathlīth al-waḥdānīyah* gives us both the Hebrew *and* the Aramaic versions of a verse—when he takes up Genesis 49:10—we find the same conflicting evidence. Having quoted the verse initially in Hebrew, he then translates the key word *Shiloh* as "Messiah" in accordance with the ubiquitous Christian interpretation of this verse that goes back to Justin Martyr: *Lā yantaqidu al-mulk min Yahūda . . . ḥattá ya'tá al-Masīḥ* (The king will not disappear among the Jews . . . until the Messiah comes). This being the case, he observes, addressing the Jews directly, "Since you do not have ruling authority . . . the Messiah has come."[32]

But after an intervening discussion of Jeremiah 15:1–2, the Christian author surprisingly returns to the Genesis passage, this time presenting it in the Aramaic translation of the Targum Onkelos followed by an Arabic translation of that version: "Then God (He is exalted!) said on the tongue of Jacob the excellent Prophet in the Aramaic (*suryānī*) language as follows: *Lo ya'ede shuleṭan mi-dabet Yehuda we-safra mi- bane banohi 'ad* 'alama' *'ad dayete Mashiha dadileh ḥi' malkhutha wa-leh yishtama'on, 'amamaya'*. And this is the translation of it . . . 'ruling authority will not disappear from Judah, and the scribe from his sons, until *Mashīḥā* comes, which is the Messiah who has ruling authority, and the nations will be obedient to him.'"[33] The Arab-Christian author's point in quoting the Targum here is that it gives a seemingly Christian interpretation to the Hebrew *Shiloh* by translating it as "Messiah," *Mashīḥā*. Martí likewise often presented both the Hebrew original of a verse and its Aramaic translation when the amplified version of the Targum seemed particularly susceptible to Christian interpretation. Indeed, his handling of Genesis 49:10 in both the *Capistrum iudaeorum* in the 1260s and the *Pugio fidei* in the 1270s is identical with what we find in *Tathlīth al-waḥdānīyah*. In the *Pugio*, he quotes the verse first in Hebrew and then gives us his Latin translation, which follows the Hebrew closely. After asserting that "no one among [the Jews] presumes to contradict" the Aramaic version of the Hebrew Bible, which was translated long before the coming of the Messiah, he then quotes it, followed by an amplified translation of his own into Latin: "The fact or action of power or royal dominion will not disappear from the House of Judah . . . until the Messiah comes."[34] So here we have Genesis 49:10 quoted in both Hebrew and Aramaic, with the Aramaic version from Targum Onkelos being used for exactly the same purpose for which the author of *Tathlīth al-waḥdānīyah* used it: to justify the interpretation of the Hebrew *Shiloh* as "Messiah."

Though Martí does not present the original Hebrew and Aramaic versions of Genesis 49:10 in his earlier *Capistrum iudaeorum* but only Latin translations of them (and this is his normal procedure in that work), his handling of this verse in that work is in some ways even more similar to what we find in *Tathlīth al-waḥdānīyah*. Here, having cited Genesis 49:10 and having discussed the meaning of the Hebrew term *gōyim* ("that is," he explains, "the nations"), he then emphasizes that "likewise in the Targum [there is what is necessary] for proving that *Shiloh* in the above verse is Messiah."[35] He then gives us a Latin translation of the Aramaic that differs from what he later presents in the *Pugio fidei*: "Non praeteribit actio soldani de domo Yehuda, et scriba de filiis filorum eius usque in saeculum, donec quod veniat Messiha, cui est regnum, et ei obedient populi." (The action of ruling will not disappear from the house of Judah, and the scribe from his sons until the end of the age, until Messiha comes, who possesses ruling power, and the people will obey him.)[36]

The corresponding Arabic version of this Aramaic verse that we find in *Tathlīth al-waḥdānīyah* reads as follows: "Lā yantaqiḍu qaḍīb al-mulk min yahuda wa-rāsim min ibnāʾihi ḥattá an yaʾtī mashiḥā alladhī huwa al-Masīḥ wa-la-hu taṭūʿu al-umam." (The staff of ruling authority will not disappear from Judah and the scribe from among his sons until mashiḥā who is the Messiah, and the nations obey him.)[37] There are clear differences in approach here: Martí's Latin retains the Aramaic's *shuleṭan* (ruling power) for the Hebrew "scepter" by means of the Latin *soldanus* ("sultan," "ruling power"—ultimately derived from that Aramaic term through Arabic), while the Arabic stays somewhat closer to the original Hebrew, with *qaḍīb al-mulk* (staff of ruling authority). But the parallels are just as striking: not only does the Aramaic *Mashīḥā*—and that word only—appear in transliteration in both versions, but in both versions, the Aramaic *dadileh hī malkhūta* (to him is ruling authority) is translated with dative-of-possession constructions that scrupulously adhere to the original (*cui regnum est / wa-lahu al-mulk*); indeed, the Latin and Arabic versions could easily be translations of each other.

Once again, therefore, we have remarkable parallels as well as equally remarkable differences, making it difficult to draw convincing conclusions about the relationship between *Tathlīth al-waḥdānīyah*'s Hebrew Bible arguments for Jesus's messiahship and those developed at great length by Martí. We might well see *Tathlīth al-waḥdānīyah's* and Martí's recourses to these methods as unrelated, parallel developments of a kind that do sometimes occur. Indeed, the view to which I once subscribed, that the author of *Tathlīth al-waḥdānīyah* was a Jewish convert to Christianity, could well make sense of all this, for he thus would have had the linguistic means and traditional Jewish learning necessary to quote the Hebrew and Aramaic versions of Genesis 49:10 before translating them into Arabic.[38] On that interpretation, there would be no need to assume any connection at all between the Arab-Christian author and the learned Dominican polemicist.

But looked at more broadly, it is hard not to see the parallels as potential signs of a close relationship between the anonymous Arab-Christian text and Martí's writings against Judaism. First of all, while the Hebrew Bible did play a key role in intra-Christian discussions in the Arab world,[39] it was always problematic to argue on the basis of it or the Christian Bible with Muslims because, as Barbara Roggema has put it, Muslims were "generally eager to point out that the text of the Bible was corrupt"[40]—likely, that is, to invoke the well-known doctrine of *taḥrīf*, the Muslim belief that Jews and Christians had gravely distorted their scriptures. While not all Muslim intellectuals agreed that this had occurred,[41] the majority held that both Jews and Christians had removed important passages from their scriptures and forged other material that they added to them, making them largely unreliable. In the eleventh century, al-Juwaynī in the east and Ibn Ḥazm in the west, for example, had rehearsed at great length the contradictions in the Bible that they took as evidence of this corruption.[42] Not surprisingly, the Muslim scholar al-Qurṭubī, whose work preserves the *Tathlīth al-waḥdānīyah*, responds to the latter's citation of the eight Hebrew Bible verses with a substantial chapter entitled "Concerning the Imperfection That Has Overtaken the Torah and That It Was Not Handed Down in an Unbroken Succession, So It Therefore Is Not Preserved from Error and Mistake,"[43] in which many of the standard Muslim arguments are trotted out.[44]

Such attacks on its validity did not, of course, keep Muslims from citing other passages of the Hebrew Bible as authoritative predictions of the coming of Muḥammad—any more than Christian attacks on the Qurʾān kept Christians from using it to argue in favor of the Trinity—and this is something that al-Qurṭubī also does at great length later in the *Iʿlām*.[45] It is also true that, as Sabine Schmidtke has shown, Jews who had converted to Islam, especially in the Ottoman period, were known to quote passages of the Hebrew Bible, in both Hebrew and in Arabic transliteration, that they believed demonstrated the prophethood of Muḥammad, much as the author of *Tathlīth al waḥdānīyah* did.[46] But I know of no precedent in Arab-Christian literature for the citation of Hebrew and Aramaic biblical passages in disputation against Muslims, and this would have been especially unlikely after Muslim arguments for the corruption of the Bible became more common beginning in the eleventh century.[47]

More to the point, while Christians had long used Old Testament passages in disputation with Jews to argue that the Messiah had come, there is something distinctly odd about a Christian making this argument to Muslims because, in a very real sense, they already believed it. One of Jesus's most common Qur'ānic titles is, after all, "Jesus the Messiah," and he was regularly referred to in Muslim texts as simply *al-Masīḥ*, "the Messiah." What Muslims did not believe was that this Messiah was also divine and the second person of the Trinity, something the first two parts of *Tathlīth al-waḥdānīyah* attempted to prove. Arguing that the Hebrew Bible demonstrates that the Messiah has come is, in point of fact, very unusual in Christian apologetic directed at Islam.

Now, it is true that the author of *Tathlīth al-waḥdānīyah* refers to this third section of his work—as we have seen—as "the argument of the three religions," and thus we might view this portion as intended primarily for Jewish readers who knew Arabic. Yet this is clearly not what he has in mind. Indeed, he stresses that the argument is strictly between Christians and Muslims. If the former can demonstrate convincingly that the Messiah has come on the basis of the Jewish scriptures, they are believers in the true faith; if Muslims can demonstrate that Muḥammad was prophesied by the Bible, they are the true believers.[48] And certainly, al-Qurṭubī read this section as directed only at Muslims, as is readily apparent in his attack on the Jewish scriptures that immediately followed.

Part 3 of the Andalusī *Tathlīth al-waḥdānīyah*, therefore, appears to be entirely exceptional in the Arabic tradition of Christian polemic against Islam. Its core argument, moreover, shares a great deal in common with arguments for Jesus as the Messiah advanced in Christian Spain by Ramon Martí, who, as I have shown elsewhere, also made the same Trinitarian argument that *Tathlīth al-waḥdānīyah* offers in its first part.[49] Had Martí—whose Arabic was exceptionally good—been reading *Tathlīth al-waḥdānīyah* or other Arab-Christian texts like it? Could he, on the other hand, actually be the author of *Tathlīth al-waḥdānīyah*? Or were the author of *Tathlīth al-waḥdānīyah* and Martí working from common sources?

I have thus far avoided discussing the date of *Tathlīth al-waḥdānīyah* but can obviously do so no longer. Here also, we are faced with messy uncertainty, though recent, painstaking work by Samir Kaddouri has clarified the picture somewhat. The only manuscripts of *Al-I'lām bi-mā fī dīn al-Naṣārā min al-fasād*—the Muslim work that preserves this Christian treatise fragmentarily—attribute it to one "Imam al-Qurṭubī," the Cordoban *imām*, a vague identifier indeed in the context of medieval al-Andalus. As a result, there were a number of proposed datings for this lengthy text (nearly five hundred pages in the modern edition). Kaddouri, however, was able to identify this Cordoban *imām* definitively as Aḥmad ibn ʿUmar ibn Ibrāhīm ibn ʿUmar al-Anṣārī al-Qurṭubī, a traditionist who died in 626/1258. Moreover, while it is difficult to be certain when in his lifetime this scholar wrote *Al-Iʿlām*, Kaddouri has made a fairly persuasive if not fully convincing argument that he must have written it before about 1220.[50]

Tathlīth al-waḥdānīyah, a work preserved only in fragments quoted in that Muslim refutation of Christianity, must therefore have been written before 1258 and very likely before 1220. If Kaddouri is wrong about the latter point, and Aḥmad ibn ʿUmar al-Qurṭubī's *Al-Iʿlām bi-mā fī dīn al-Naṣārā min al-fasād* and possibly, therefore, *Tathlīth al-waḥdānīyah* were written not long before the death of al-Qurṭubī, then we would be justified in seeing *Tathlīth al-waḥdānīyah* as potentially a work of Martí or his circle of Arabic-, Hebrew-, and Aramaic-educated friars. Indeed, 1258 is likely the year when Martí completed his only real Latin work against Islam, the brief *De secta Mahometi*. If, on the other hand, Kaddouri is correct in his dating of about 1220 for the Muslim work that contains it, then it seems likely, as I have recently suggested, that *Tathlīth al-waḥdānīyah* was written not long before by someone connected to the court of Archbishop Rodrigo Jiménez de Rada (1170–1247), where the Trinitarian argument was also being deployed (this time against Jews) and where we also find an interest in making Christian arguments in Arabic against Muslims.[51] Of course, earlier dates for *Tathlīth al-waḥdānīyah* are possible as well, though I have reiterated in even stronger terms my view of twenty years ago that it had to have been written after about 1150.[52]

But whatever the case, we find ourselves in much the same position as when we pondered St. Dominic's shaved beard and disengagement from Muslims. For whether Martí was the author of *Tathlīth al-waḥdānīyah* (possible but unlikely), or it was a work of Archbishop Rodrigo's court (which seems probable to me), or even if it was written at a still earlier date and perhaps even entirely unconnected with Martí's writings—the respective Arabic and Latin works being independent in their origins (highly unlikely)—what is certain is that a prominent Muslim traditionist and scholar who died when Martí was a young man refuted Christian arguments remarkably similar to the ones that Martí would begin to direct at Jews in Latin soon after. Someone was using a theological vocabulary just like Martí's to preach the gospel in Arabic to the Muslims.

Martí, like St. Dominic, took steps in the direction of doing likewise: learning the Arabic language as thoroughly as he did Hebrew and Aramaic and writing one very learned, but rather short, work against Islam in Latin. But in the next paragraph of Peter of Ferrand's *Legenda*, St. Dominic headed instead toward the lively Latin intellectual center of Bologna, and in the next paragraph of his career, Martí immediately pivoted away from Islam, never to write meaningfully against it for the rest of his career. But in the intellectual world of Latin Scholasticism, this would not have been surprising. The attractive myth, advanced since the fourteenth century, that Thomas Aquinas wrote the *Summa contra gentiles* as a handbook for Dominican preachers to Muslims has been definitively debunked by the modern Dominican René-Antoine Gauthier,[53] though it should have been clear enough to anyone reading that great work that it in no way engaged Islam as a religion—its few hostile references to Muḥammad and his religion, in fact, making clear to readers that real Muslims were not even worthy of the author's consideration.[54] Not only does Aquinas never meaningfully address Islam and its beliefs or practices, but neither do any other leading Scholastic theologians or philosophers, with the exception of William of Auvergne (d. 1249), though the four chapters of his *De legibus* hardly amount to a systematic refutation of a feared rival.[55] There were, of course, a few thirteenth-century Latin works written against Islam, but they are brief works by marginal figures in the Scholastic world—men like Martí and his fellow Dominicans, Riccoldo da Monte di Croce and William of Tripoli.[56] However, things were quite different in the Islamic world, where Christianity was subject to extended scrutiny and refutation not just by relatively unknown scholars such as Aḥmad ibn ʿUmar al-Qurṭubī, author of the text that preserves *Tathlīth al-waḥdānīyah*, but by such seminal figures as al-Ghazālī (d. 1111) and Ibn Taymīyah (d. 1328), the latter of whom authored what is perhaps the longest work in all of Christian-Muslim controversial literature, a full six volumes in a recent scholarly edition.[57] Despite how important Arab philosophy was to Latin theology and philosophy, Islam as a religion scarcely registered.

On the other hand, writing about Judaism (often on the basis of intimate knowledge of postbiblical Jewish writings) was, if not at the core of Latin Scholasticism, nevertheless a well-established and lively intellectual enterprise, especially in England and France, by Martí's lifetime. Gilbert Dahan, among others, has shown that scores of works engaging Jewish belief, Jewish books, and the Hebrew Bible were being produced in the Scholastic period. These ranged from the *correctoria* that offered emendations of the Vulgate based on the Hebrew Bible, to biblical commentaries that (beginning in the twelfth century) drew on Jewish exegetical experts such as Rashi to expound the *Hebraica veritas* of the Old Testament, to the massive Dominican project of the 1240s to translate excerpts of the Talmud for polemical use.[58]

Judaism, of course, had always been unavoidably visible to (though often ignored by) Christian scholars because 80 percent of the Christian Bible is Jewish. But certain aspects of the Scholastic project ensured that Jews and their books would occupy an especially important place in the thirteenth century. The compulsion, for example, to ground Christian allegorizing of the Hebrew Bible in its literal, historical meaning inspired commentators from at least as early as Andrew of St. Victor (d. 1175) and Nicholas of Lyra (1270–1349) not only to scrutinize the Hebrew text of the Bible but to seek out the contemporary Jewish interpretation of it, often in the form of Rashi's commentaries.[59] This meant that the Hebrew Bible and postbiblical Jewish books were already being cited in one of the most important genres of Latin-Christian writing: biblical commentaries.

The Qur'ān was, it is true, fairly widely available in Latin Europe, especially in Robert of Ketton's twelfth-century Latin translation, and indeed we possess clear evidence of not only this version but even copies of the Arabic Qur'ān circulating among the Dominicans themselves in this period.[60] But there was no place within Scholastic education or scholarly production for the Qur'ān, let alone any other Muslim books, to be drawn into conversation. And its absence from the Scholastic syllabus finds its parallel in the absence of Islam—and the nearest lands where it thrived—from at least some highly influential Scholastic visions of the world. Ramon Martí's older Dominican confrere, Vincent of Beauvais (d. 1264), for example, compiled the largest encyclopedia of the Middle Ages, the *Speculum majus*, fully 6.5 million words long.[61] The largest of its three parts is the *Speculum historiale*, an enormous universal history of mankind from creation to Vincent's lifetime. While he does present one of the most ample accounts of Muḥammad's life and the history of Islam available in Latin,[62] it is located in book twenty-three of his universal history, which treats the reign of Heraclius, and thereafter we hear surprisingly little of Islam again. While we meet Saracens, of course, when Vincent describes the Crusades, the flourishing of Islam in North Africa and al-Andalus go virtually unmentioned, and Spain itself—both Christian and Muslim—scarcely exists in this Dominican's conception of geography and history.[63] Overlooked in Scholastic visions of the world, Islam and its books were very hard to hear or see within the intellectual movement that the Dominicans so zealously embraced.

It is noteworthy that when Vincent of Beauvais narrates the history of his own order within this vast chronicle, he repeats the curious story of Dominic's inchoate mission to Islam—beard shaven, the Dominican founder heads for Bologna, not Bougie—in this account as well.[64] But given how little both Spain and Islam figure in Vincent's view of history, Dominic's change of course makes much better sense, and Martí's still more so. A brilliant Semitic linguist—equally capable in Hebrew, Aramaic, and Arabic—he could have continued to engage Islam as he had done in his brief *De secta Mahometi*, but this would have meant applying his impressive skills to a field of endeavor on the periphery of the intellectual currents that dominated his scholarly culture and against a religion that scarcely registered in the minds of its leading thinkers. While the surviving fragments of *Tathlīth al-waḥdānīyah* make clear that he or, more likely, someone else in Iberia thought polemical approaches just like those he later used against Judaism could be deployed against Islam, even a Spaniard like Martí living in the still-very-Islamic Iberian Peninsula must have found the much ampler space available in Scholastic culture for engaging Judaism and its vast postbiblical literature simply too difficult to resist.

Notes

1. On the thirteenth-century Dominican histories of the Dominican order, see Engen, "Dominic and the Brothers."
2. "Hoc autem faciebat vir sanctus disponens adire terram Sarracenorum et eis verbum fidei predicare; unde etiam barbam aliquanto tempore nutriebat." Peter of Ferrand, *Legenda Sancti Dominici*, 32, p. 232.
3. Ferrand, 32–33, pp. 232–33.
4. The great Dominican encyclopedist Vincent of Beauvais also recounts this curious episode. See Burman and Walker, "Spain, Islam."
5. Burman and Walker.
6. See Burman, "Ramon Martí."
7. As articulated, for example, in the following comment attributed to St. Dominic by Jordan of Saxony in the earliest account of the history of order: "Et invocato sancto spiritu convocatisque fratribus dixit hoc esse sui propositum, ut omnes eos licet paucos per mundum transmitteret, nec iam ibi diutius insimul habitarent." Saxony, "Libellus de principiis ordinis praedicatorum," 48.
8. For an insightful discussion of this, see Vose's excellent *Dominicans, Muslims, and Jews*, 3–10.
9. Vose.

10. As, for example, Jordan of Saxony made clear in his "Libellus de principiis ordinis praedicatorum" (pp. 49–51, 52, 54–55).
11. See Burman, "*Via impugnandi*"; and Burman, *Religious Polemic*, 157–89. On *Tathlīth al-waḥdānīyah* in general, see, most recently, Burman, "Riccoldo da Monte di Croce"; and Potthast's extremely learned *Christen und Muslime im Andalus*, 327–38 (see pp. 537–50 for a German translation).
12. Anonymous, *Tathlīth al-waḥdānīyah* (hereafter cited as *TW*), fragments of which survive only in al-Qurṭubī, *Kitāb al-I'lām*, 163–65. On this Muslim work, see Monferrer Sala, "Al-Imām al-Qurṭubī."
13. "Inna ayyāman kathīrah yuqīmū banī [*sic*] Isrā'īl dūna mulk wa-dūna muqaddim"; "Lā yuntiqaḍū al-mulk min Yahūdā wa-rāsim min bayna rijlayhi ḥattá ya'tī al-Masīḥ wa-la-hu taṭawwa'u al-umam." *TW*, in al-Qurṭubī, *Kitāb al-I'lām*, 181. The Christian author has translated the Hebrew *Shiloh* as "Messiah" (*al-Masīḥ*) in a Christological reading of the passage.
14. "Qāla al-nabī Hoshi'a ibn Bi'īrī . . . hakadhā bi-kalām 'ibrānī: 'ki yamīm rabīm yeshebū bene isra'īl [*sic*] 'en melekh (?) we-'en ṣār;' tafsīruhu: 'Inna ayyāman kathīrah yuqīmū banī [*sic*] Isrā'īl dūna mulk wa-dūna muqaddim. Fa-idhā su'ila al-Yahūdī al-jāḥid in kāna la-hum malik aw muqaddim, fa-lā yakūnu jawābuhu illá an yaqūla 'laysa 'inda-nā malik wa-lā muqaddim." *TW*, in al-Qurṭubī. I quote the transliterated Hebrew from Monferrer Sala's better edition of these passages in his "Siete citas hebreas," 396.
15. *TW*, in al-Qurṭubī, 215–17.
16. "Incipit collectio quarumdam auctoritatum Veteris Testamenti, quibus probabitur, primo ac principaliter, adventus Christi." Martí, *Capistrum iudaeorum*, 1:54.
17. "Incipit pars secunda ubi probabitur aduentum [*sic*] messie." Martí, *Pugio fidei*, MS 1405, Bibliothèque Sainte-Geneviève, Paris, fol. 32r (on this manuscript, see that library's online catalog at http://www.calames.abes.fr/pub/bsg.aspx#details?id=BSGB10365); cf. the early modern edition, Martí, *Pugio fidei adversus*, 260 (hereafter cited as Leipzig ed.).
18. "I'lām annī katabtu la-ka bi-al-'ibrānī wa-al-suryānī min shahādāt al-anbiyā' 'an Allāh min al-kutub allatī bi-aydīhim wa-anna al-yahūd lā yaqdirūna 'alá inkār ḥarfin min-hā aḥtajju ma'a-hum bi-al- al-'ibrānī wa-al-suryānī." *TW*, in al-Qurṭubī, *Kitāb al-I'lām*, 185.
19. "Ceterum. inducendo auctoritates textus. ubicumque ab ebraico fuerit deriuatum (ut vid.) non .lxx. sequar nec interpretem alium. et quod maioris presumptionis uidebitur; non ipsum etiam in hoc reuerebor ieronimum. nec tolerabilem latine linque uitabo improprietatem; uero que apud hebreos sunt; ex uerbo in uerbum quocienscumque seruari hoc poterit; transferam ueritatem. Per hoc enim iudei falsiloquis lata ualde spaciosaque subterfugiendi precludetur uia. cum minime poterunt dicere. non sic haberi apud eos; ut a nostris contra ipsos me interprete ueritas induceretur." Martí, *Pugio fidei* proemium, Sainte-Geneviève MS 1405, fol. 3r; Leipzig ed., 4.
20. Monferrer Sala learnedly discussed seven quotations of the Hebrew Bible in this work, but there is an eighth—Jer. 15:1–2—that he passed over. See his "Siete citas hebreas"; and *TW*, in al-Qurṭubī, *Kitāb al-I'lām*, 181–82.
21. *TW*, in al-Qurṭubī, 181–85. Martí's quotations: Hosea 3:4 (*Capistrum iudaeorum*, 2.7.9 [2:236]; *Pugio fidei* 3.3.21, Sainte-Geneviève MS 1405, fol. 424v; Leipzig ed., 953); Gen. 49:10 (*Capistrum iudaeorum* 1.2.3 [1:72]; *Pugio fidei* 2.4.1–3, Sainte-Geneviève MS 1405, fol.46r; Leipzig ed., 312); Lam. 2:3 (*Capistrum iudaeorum* 2.7.15, 17 [2:254–58]; *Pugio fidei* 2.14, Sainte-Geneviève MS 1405, fol. 110r; Leipzig ed., 454–55); Jer. 31:31–32 (*Capistrum iudaeorum* 1.3.23 [1:122]; *Pugio fidei* 2.4, Sainte-Geneviève MS 1405, fol. 54r; Leipzig ed., 328); Jer. 3:14 (*Capistrum iudaeorum* 2.1.11–12 [2:38–40]; *Pugio fidei* 2.11, Sainte-Geneviève MS 1405, fol. 83v; Leipzig ed., 405).

22. *TW*, in al-Qurṭubī, *Kitāb al-I'lām*, 181. In *Capistrum iudaeorum*, we have *legumlator* (1.2.3 [1:72]); in *Pugio fidei*, we have *legumdator vel lator* (2.4.1–3, Sainte-Geneviève MS 1405, fol. 46r; Leipzig ed., 312).
23. Here and below, I use New Jewish Publication Society of America, *Tanakh*, for extended quotations of the Hebrew Bible in English.
24. "Yaqūlu Allāh: wa-athbattu li-bayt Isrā'īl wa-Yahūdā 'ahd jadīd laysa ka-al-'ahd alladhī qultu li-ābā'ihim fī al-yawm alladhī akhrajtu-hum min arḍ Miṣr min bayt al-'ubūdīyah." *TW*, in al-Qurṭubī, *Kitāb al-I'lām*, 182–83; cf. Monferrer Sala, "Siete citas hebreas," 397.
25. "Scindam domui Israel et domui Iuda foedus novum, non sicut foedus quod scidi cum patribus in die qua apprehendi manum eorum ut educerem eos de terra Aegypti." Martí, *Capistrum iudaeorum* 1.3.23 (1:122). "Scindam domui israel et domui iuda. berith nouam id est legem vnde subdit; non sicut berith quam scidi cum patribus eorum in die qua confortaui manum eorum, ut educerem eos de terra egipti." Martí, *Pugio fidei* 2.4, Sainte-Geneviève MS 1405, fol. 54r; Leipzig ed., 328.
26. "Qāla Allāh . . . 'alá lisān Irmīyā' al-nabī fī inqiṭā' mulkihim bi-kalām 'ibrānī hakadhā." *TW*, in al-Qurṭubī, *Kitāb al-I'lām*, 182.
27. Martí, *Capistrum iudaeorum* 2.7.15, 17 (2:254–58); Martí, *Pugio fidei* 2.14, Sainte-Geneviève MS 1405, fols. 110r–111v; Leipzig ed., 454–56.
28. "Quia diebus multi sedebunt vel habitabunt vel morabuntur filii israel sine rege, et sine principe." Martí, *Capistrum iudaeorum* 2.7. 9 (2:246). "Diebus enim multis. morabuntur filii Israel. sine rege. et sine principe." Martí, *Pugio fidei* 3.3.21, Sainte-Geneviève MS 1405, fol. 424v; Leipzig ed., 953.
29. "Kamā qāla Allāh fī mawḍū' ākhar 'alá lisān Irmīyā' al-nabī bi-lisān 'ibrānī 'an al-imān al-ḥawārīyūn . . . tafsīruhu: 'Irja'ū yā awlād al-lajājah fī-innī sudtu 'alaykum wa ākudhukum wāḥidan min madīnah wa-ithnayn min 'ashīrah wa-adkhulukum ilā ṣahyūn.' Wa-ka-dhalika ākhadu al-ḥawārīyūn wāḥidan min madīnah wa-ithnayn min 'ashīrah." *TW*, in al-Qurṭubī, *Kitāb al-I'lām*, 183; cf. Monferrer Sala, "Siete citas hebreas," 398.
30. "Cum igitur dominus noster ihesus christus. saluauerit iudeos. unum de ciuitate. ut beatum paulum de tarso cilicie, et duos de cognatione. ut petrum et andream qui fuerunt fratres. iacobum et iohannem; qui similiter fuerunt fratres." Martí, *Pugio fidei* 2.11, Sainte-Geneviève MS 1405, fol. 83v; Leipzig ed., 405; cf. Martí, *Capistrum iudaeorum* 2.1.11–12 (2:38–40).
31. Chapter 3, PL 83 505b–506a.
32. "Fa-yuqālu la-hum: idh laysa la-kum mulk . . . fa-qad jā'a al-Masīḥ." *TW*, in al-Qurṭubī, *Kitāb al-I'lām*, 181.
33. "Thumma qāla Allāh ta'āla 'alá lisān Ya'qūb al-nabī al-fāḍil bi-lisān suryāni hakadhā: '*Lo ya'ede shuleṭan mi-dabet Yehuda we-safra mi-bane banohi 'ad* 'alama' *'ad dayete Mashiha dadileh ḥi' malkhutha wa-leh yishtama'on, 'amamaya'.'* Wa-hadhā tafsīruhu . . . 'lā yantaqiḍu qaḍīb al-mulk min Yahūda wa-rāsim min abnā'ihi ḥattá an ya'tī *Mashiha* alladhī huwa al-Masīḥ alladhī la-hu al-mulk wa-la-hu taṭū' al-umam." *TW*, 182. For the Aramaic, I have followed Monferrer Sala, "Siete citas hebreas," 400.
34. "Quod autem eiusmodi translatio <Latina> premissorum . . . sit fidelis; ostenditur per targum id est translationem caldaicam . . . quae inter iudeos eos tantam auctoritatem obtinet; quod a nullo eorum sibi presumitur contradici . . . factum uel actio. sultan. potestatis uel dominii regii. middebeth yehuda. de domo uel familia iude . . . áád deyethe . . . usquequo ueniat. messihá. messias uel christus." Martí, *Pugio fidei* 2.4.1–3, Sainte-Geneviève MS 1405, fol. 46r; Leipzig ed., 312. Here Martí, after quoting the Aramaic in the Hebrew Aramaic alphabet, also transliterates it as he paraphrases.
35. "Idem in Targum ad probandum quod šilōh in praedicta auctoritate est Messias." Martí, *Capistrum iudaeorum* 1.2.3 (1:72).
36. Martí.

37. *TW*, in al-Qurṭubī, *Kitāb al-I'lām*, 182.
38. See Burman, *Religious Polemic*, 76–77.
39. See, for example, in Keating, "Ḥabīb ibn Khidma," the *Shahādāt min qawl al-Tawrāt wa-al-anbiyā' wa-al-qiddīsīn*, a collection of eighty Hebrew Bible passages of use in arguing for the Trinity or Incarnation, in Thomas and Roggema, *Christian-Muslim Relations*, 1:576–77.
40. See Roggema, "To Mār Naṣr, Letter 36," 1:530–31.
41. See Lazarus-Yafeh, "Taḥrīf."
42. See al-Juwaynī, *Shifā' al-ghalīl*; and Ibn Ḥazm, *Kitāb al-Fiṣal*.
43. "Faṣl fī ba'ḍ mā ṭara'a fī al-tawrah min al-khalal wa-anna-hā lam tanqul naqlan mutūwātiran fa-<lam> taslam li-ajlihi min al-khaṭa' wal-zalal." *TW*, in al-Qurṭubī, *Kitāb al-I'lām*, 188.
44. *TW*, 188–202.
45. *TW*, 263–68.
46. See, for example, Schmidtke, "Rightly Guiding Epistle," 442.
47. See, for example, Griffith, "Arguing from Scripture."
48. *TW*, in al-Qurṭubī, *Kitāb al-I'lām*, 215–17.
49. See Burman, "Ramon Martí, the Trinity."
50. Kaddouri, "Identificación de 'al-Qurṭubī"; and Kaddouri, "Riḥlāt Aḥmad." On this work in general, see Monferrer Sala, "Al-Imām al-Qurṭubī."
51. See Burman, "*Via impugnandi*."
52. Burman.
53. Gauthier, *Introduction à la Somme*, 126–27.
54. See Aquinas, *Opera omnia iussu*, 17.
55. Aquinas's brief and hastily written response to some questions put to a fellow Dominican by anonymous Muslims scarcely amounts to a serious engagement either, since it consists mostly of material borrowed directly from the *Summa contra gentiles*. See Aquinas, *Opera omnia iussu*, 161–89; Murphy, "William of Auvergne."
56. See Burman, "Riccoldo da Monte di Croce"; and Burman, "William of Tripoli."
57. Ibn Taymīyah, *Al-Jawāb al-ṣaḥīḥ*. As anti-Christian polemicists in general, see El-Kaisy-Friemuth, "Al-Ghazālī"; and Hoover, "Ibn Taymīyah."
58. Dahan, *Intellectuels chrétiens*, 271–308, 361–422.
59. The bibliography here is vast, but for a recent overview, see Sapir Abulafia, "Bible in Jewish-Christian Dialogue," 629–33.
60. See Burman, *Reading the Qur'ān*; and Burman, "Italian Friar."
61. For an excellent overview and introduction to the *Speculum*, including references to a broad range of relevant scholarship, see Paulmier-Foucart and Duchenne, *Vincent de Beauvais*.
62. On which, see, most recently, Emilio Platti, "L'image de l'Islam."
63. See Burman and Walker, "Spain, Islam."
64. "Hoc autem faciebat vir sanctus disponens adire terram Saracenorum, & eis verbum Domini praedicare, propter quod etiam barbam aliquanto tempore nutriebat." Vincent of Beauvais, *Speculum historiale*, 30:67, edited by Balthazar Bellère as *Bibliotheca Mundi*, 4:1257a.

2

QUR'ĀNIC QUOTATIONS IN LATIN

Translation, Tradition, and Fiction in Polemical Literature

Antoni Biosca i Bas and Óscar de la Cruz

At least ten Latin translations of the Qur'ān are known to have been produced between the twelfth and the seventeenth centuries: the translations of Robert of Ketton (1142–43), Mark of Toledo (ca. 1210), and John of Segovia (1456); the partial translation of Raymond of Moncada (ca. 1480); the collaborative translation by Egidio da Viterbo, Gabrielis Terrolensis, and Joannes Leo Africanus (1518); the translations by Guillaume Postel (1544) and Ignazio Lomellini (1622); and the ones attributed to Cyril Lucaris (ca. 1630), Herman of Silesia (ca. 1650–69), and Ludovico Marracci (1698). We might also include other Orientalist scholars who published partial translations of the Qur'ān as part of studies or for their chrestomathies, such as Guillaume Postel (1539) or Thomas Erpenius (1617).

Each one of these translations responded to its own nature and tradition. They were cultural indicators of different phases in the relationship between Christianity and Islam, evidence of an intellectual approach to the Islamic world opposed to violence. The most influential translations may be Robert of Ketton's,[1] widely disseminated thanks to Bibliander's edition of 1543,[2] and to a lesser degree Mark of Toledo's, which was especially well known in Italy.[3]

Anti-Islamic polemical literature is vast—more than a hundred authors and works of refutation are known from the Middle Ages.[4] In them, it is common to find Qur'ānic quotations with no correlation to the Latin translations. These translations are scarcely cited in later works and thus seem to have exercised little influence on them. However, there are numerous quotations from and direct references to authors who preceded the translation of Robert of Ketton. In this regard, both Dominique Millet-Gérard[5] and Franz R. Franke[6] concur that the quotation of Qur'ān 33:37 by Eulogius Cordubensis (d. 859) was the first to occur in Christian polemical literature of the Mozarab period: "[Muḥammad] commanded that she [sc. Zaynab] should be included in his law, like the voice of the Lord: 'And as that woman displeased Zeit's eyes and he rejected her, he gave her in marriage to his prophet, which was an example for the others, so that in the future it was no sin for the faithful who wished to do so.'"[7] Hence early modern authors not only used Latin translations but also were influenced by the academic tradition of the authors who referenced the Qur'ān. The great differences between the two—complete translations and quotations—demonstrate the claim of this study: Qur'ānic quotations underwent their own processes of creation and transmission and must therefore be studied independently from complete translations of the Qur'ān.

Research on the Fragmenta Alcoranica Latina (FQLat) comprises an enormous field of study, since there are numerous medieval and modern Latin authors who used Qur'ānic quotations in their works even without having produced complete translations of the Qur'ān. Most noteworthy among these authors are Ramon Martí and Riccoldo da Monte di Croce. Martí wrote the *Pugio fidei aduersus Mauros et Iudaeos* and the *Capistrum iudaeorum*, and the *Quadruplex reprobatio* has also been attributed to him. Riccoldo wrote the *Itinerarium*, or *Liber peregrinationis*, and the *Liber contra legem Sarracenorum*.[8]

The other works that we were able to consult are the following: Pedro Toledano's Latin translation of the letters of al-Kindi; the *Confutatio Hagareni* of Bartholomaeus ab Edessa; the *Liber apologeticus Martyrum* of Eulogius Cordubensis; De statu Sarracenorum by William of Tripoli; *De orbis terrae concordia* and the *Grammatica Arabica* of Guillaume Postel; the Latin translation of John Damascenus's *Liber de haeresibus*; Petrus Alfonsi's *Dialogus contra iudaeos*; Ramon Llull's *Liber de participatione Christianorum et Sarracenorum*, *Ars mystica theologiae et philosophiae*, and *Liber de gentili et tribus sapientibus*; the Santa María de Uncastillo anonymous manuscript from the thirteenth century; and the polemical works of Alfonso Buenhombre.[9]

The roster of medieval and modern authors who dealt with the Islamic religion and made use of the FQLat can be expanded to include authors appearing in anthologies. This includes the works of Peter of Poitiers, Peter the Venerable, Jacques de Vitry, Vincent of Beauvais, Guillelmus Tripolitanus, Simon Fitzsimon, and Benvenuto da Imola.[10] The study of Qur'ānic quotations provides evidence for the sources of these authors and sheds some light on the potential influence of anti-Islamic polemical texts. A new aim of the Islamolatina research project is the collection and cataloging of as many of the FQLat as possible in polemical works in order to create a database that will allow researchers to analyze the influence of Qur'ānic texts on the medieval Latin tradition.[11]

Our analysis of the FQLat in the sources we consulted allows us to draw some conclusions. First, it seems clear that it is a mistake to treat Qur'ānic fragments in Latin as texts derived exclusively from the original Arabic text or from one of the complete Latin translations of the Qur'ān. The authority traditionally granted to the authors of polemics was such that the FQLat were considered valuable in themselves, and thus later authors did not think it was necessary to go to the original Arabic text or to a direct translation of the Arabic text. The prestige of the aforementioned works by Ramon Martí and Riccoldo da Monte di Croce is a clear sign that they served as models for other authors.[12]

Examination of the FQLat also shows which passages of the Qur'ān were considered of most interest to authors of polemics. The location of the cited Qur'ānic passages seems to indicate that there was a tendency to cite the opening suras of the Qur'ān more frequently. This fact suggests that the purpose of using the FQLat was to cover not the entirety of the Qur'ānic text but only certain aspects of the Muslim creed. In this way, polemical authors seem to have satisfied their interest without the need for studying the entire text of the Qur'ān, and once the aspects of the Islamic faith that they wanted to criticize had been addressed, their interest in the text waned. The third sura attracted the most attention and was one of the most frequently cited because it includes references to Jesus and Mary that make possible a comparison between the Islamic creed and Christianity. Studies on the findings of the FQLat have also allowed for their typological classification into three groups.

1. *Original translations from Arab texts.* The following example is the same one mentioned above, Qur'ān 33:37: "Al-Kindi K. 24:13–15: When her husband Zayd will have fulfilled his commitment to her, we will give her to

you, so that this will not be difficult for the faithful in such a situation, when what is convenient to the matter and what God has ordered will be fulfilled. God's command is predestined decree."[13]

Fragments translated from the original in Arabic usually contain errors due to the difficulty of translating from a Semitic language into Latin, which are grammatically very different. These errors include graphic variations caused by mixing up phonemes, frequent confusions between short vowels, unnecessary or missing articles, misidentification of singular and plural irregular forms, and so on. Direct quotations from the Qur'ān can be found in influential works translated from Arabic to Latin, such as *Contrarietas elfolica*,[14] or in works that used Arabic to refute Islam, such as the *Dialogus* of Petrus Alfonsi[15] or Martí's *Quadruplex reprobatio*.[16] We also included in this group the independent use of Arabic sources by Godfrey of Viterbo in his *Pantheon*,[17] which has not yet been studied but shows evidence of the use of the Arabic text from the *Apologia* by al-Kindi instead of the Latin version by Peter of Toledo. It follows that he also used the Qur'ānic references from this source.

2. *Quotations from previous Latin translations.* On numerous occasions, the polemical author used the FQLat from an earlier Latin source. For example, Qur'ān 33:37 by al-Kindi was used independently by Vincent of Beauvais in his *Speculum historiale*[18] and by Jacques de Vitry in *Historia orientalis*.[19] In *Satyrica historia*, Paolino Veneto also took from this quotation: "Hic cum adamasset Çambeth filiam Gayssi, uxorem Zaidi, inducit Deum in Alchorano de ea loquentem ad se 'cum compleuerit Zaidi uir eius uotum suum in ea, ecce eam dabimus tibi.'"[20]

In the following example, note the coincidence in the translation of the Arabic genitive plural *al'alamîn*, "of the worlds," into the Latin *seculorum*.

Martí 3, 3, 7, 14[1]	**Lyra 1720**[2]
O Maria, utique Deus elegit te et purificauit te et elegit te claram super mulieres seculorum.	O Maria, Deus utique elegit te, purificauit te, elegit te claram super mulieres seculorum.

1. "Oh Mary, indeed God chose you and purified you, he chose you, bright, above the women of the world." Martí, *Pugio fidei adversus*.
2. "Oh Mary, God chose you, made you beautiful with His grace, adorned you and preferred you before all women who are mothers of any children." Buenhombre, *Disputatio Abutalib*, 65.

The term *al ʿalamîn* refers to the worlds that have been and will be; it emphasizes that God chose Mary from all other women who had existed and would ever exist. The coincidence in the translation of the term as *seculorum*, which is perfectly valid, shows, in our opinion, that one citation was derived from the other. Therefore, we can conclude that the text of Ramon Martí was the source used in the work of Nicholas of Lyra. The identification of Latin quotations is very useful for tracing sources used by polemical authors. The FQLat may undergo alteration when they are transmitted exclusively in Latin. An example of this may be found in Alfonso Buenhombre, who quotes the Lyra passage presented above in the following manner: "O Maria, Deus elegit te, et decorauit te gratia, et ornauit et preelegit super omnes mulieres omnium filiorum matres."[21]

This quotation was taken from Nicholas of Lyra, which was also Buenhombre's source for abundant information on Judaism and Islam. In this quotation, the term *al ʿalamîn* seems to have been misunderstood, since it was translated as "omnium filiorum matres." The origin of this translation can be traced to Lyra, who in turn used the translation of Martí, *mulieres seculorum*, as a source. It may very well be that the term was transmitted in an abbreviated form (*sclorum*), leading to the confusion between *s* and *f*, which would have produced the form *mulieres filiorum*. If the meaning of the genitive *filiorum* was indeed misunderstood in its context, then the author would have considered necessary to complete it as *omnium filiorum matres*.

3. *Fictitious quotations*. On some occasions, authors quoted the FQLat that did not appear in the Qurʾān. In their need to support their argument, but with no convincing excerpts at hand, some authors were not above making them up. For example, Buenhombre claims to quote a passage in which Mohammed provides his disciples with a set of principles that are very close to Christian beliefs: "Fugite uinum, amate uxores, per aquam oportet uos accipere remissionem peccatorum, nullus saluabitur qui fugerit aquam, colatis Christum, diligatis Mariam, eos blasphemantes lapidibus tundite."[22] There is evidently no such passage in the Qurʾān. In other instances, the fictitious quotations do not seem to be supporting any argument at all and appear to have been caused by errors in transmission. This is the case with the assumed presence of an evangelical verse in the Qurʾān, which according to Buenhombre is, "Item inducit in Alcorano illud uerbum euangelicum; 'Vulpes foueas habent, et uolucres coeli nidos.'"[23]

The FQLat were important to the authors because they offered justifications for their works. An interesting example of this may be found in the passage from Buenhombre cited before, about the Virgin Mary, which was collected in a later summary.[24] As noted, the origin of the passage may be traced ultimately to Ramon Martí, although there seems to have been a genuine effort to locate where the original Qur'ānic text came from. Such an effort is in evidence in folio 94v of MS 15956 from the Bayerische Staatsbibliothek in Munich. In this manuscript, the copyist left blank spaces after each Latin quotation of the Qur'ān to include the original versions in Arabic. This task would have been impossible to complete, since some of the citations were fictitious and others had undergone multiple alterations in their transmission in Latin. It soon became clear to the copyist that the task was impossible, and he gave up on his intention, leaving practically every space for the original Arabic text blank. There is one exception, which constitutes a first brave move to include the original Qur'ānic text. The result is a fragment of erratic Arabic, in which a hand with very little expertise attempted, with little success, to imitate the following Arabic text from the third sura, aleya 37:

وَإِذْ قَالَتِ الْمَلَائِكَةُ يَا مَرْيَمُ إِنَّ اللهَ اصْطَفَاكِ وَطَهَّرَكِ وَاصْطَفَاكِ عَلَى نِسَاءِ الْعَالَمِينَ[25]

Despite the inevitable failure at reconstructing the Arabic text, clearly the intention of the copyist was to provide credible evidence for the reader, which only demonstrates the great importance attached to these quotations in the context of polemical literature, which were always considered authentic.

Each of the three types of quotations is interesting for different reasons. Qur'ānic quotations translated from the original Arabic text (type 1) are important for gauging each author's knowledge of the Arabic language as well as for determining their level of access to Qur'ānic texts. Quotations taken from previous Latin translations (type 2) are useful for studying the way information was transmitted between different authors and the influence of some works on others. Finally, fictitious quotations (type 3) provide information about the authors' knowledge of Islamic culture as well as the perception of Islam created in the cultural spheres where they interacted and developed.

The recording of the FQLat in a database, whether it be the one we are developing in Islamolatina or another, becomes an important tool for researching these aspects of medieval polemical literature. Any scholarship attempting to tackle an anti-Islamic polemic that contains the FQLat should take into account the peculiarities of these quotations that we have laid out in this chapter. Failing to do so could lead scholars to treat these fragments incorrectly or, worse, to overlook valuable information.

Notes

This chapter is a result of research undertaken in conjunction with the project Islamolatina, financed by grant FFI201129696-C0202 from the Spanish DGIGPN-MIECIC and by grant 2015 SGR 53 from the Generalitat de Catalunya.

1. De la Cruz, "Trascendencia de la primera."
2. Segesvary, *L'Islam et la réforme.*
3. Formisano, "Più antica (?) traduzione italiana."
4. See the list of authors and works compiled in Thomas and Mallet, *Christian-Muslim Relations.*
5. Millet-Gérard, *Chrétiens mozarabes,* 129.
6. Franke, "Die freiwilligen Märtyrer von Cordova," 40.
7. Illam [sc. Zaynab] uero quasi ex uoce dominica in lege sua annotari praecepit: "Cumque mulier illa displicita esset in oculis Zeit et eam repudiasset, sociauit eam prophetae suo coniugium, quod ceteris in exemplum et posteris fidelibus id agere cupientibus non sit in peccatum." Cordubensis, *Liber apologeticus Martyrum 16,* 485.
8. In consulting these texts, we have used the following editions: Martí, *Pugio fidei adversus* (Leipzig, 1687); and Martí, *Quadruplex reprobatio* (Apud BNF, MS lat. 4230, fol. 152va, trans. Óscar de la Cruz). For the rest of the texts by Martí and Monte di Croce, we have used di Cesare, *Pseudo-Historical Image.*
9. We have based our study of these texts on the following editions: González Muñoz, *Exposición y refutación;* Bartholomaeus ab Edessa, *Confutatio Hagareni;* Cordubensis, *Liber apologeticus Martyrum;* Tripolitanus, *De statu Sarracenorum;* Postel, *De orbis terrae concordia;* Postel, *Grammatica Arabica;* D'Alverny, "Deux traductions latines"; Damascenus, *Liber de haeresibus;* Damascenus, *Sancti Patris Nostri;* Petrus Alfonsi, *Dialogus contra iudaeos;* Ramon Llull, *Liber de participatione;* Llull, *Ars mystica theologiae;* Llull, *Liber de gentili;* Valcárcel, "*Vita Mahometi* del códice"; and Buenhombre, *Disputatio Abutalib.*
10. For these authors, see di Cesare, *Pseudo-Historical Image.*
11. "Fragmenta Alcoranica Latina," Islamolatina, Universitat Autònoma de Barcelona, http://grupsderecerca.uab.cat/islamolatina/content/fragmenta-alcoranica-latina.
12. A clear example is the work of Petrus de Pennis, who takes Riccoldo's work as the only source for his anti-Islamic treatise. See Panella, "Ricerche su Riccoldo."

13. "Cum -inquit- compleuerit Zaidi uir eius uotum suum cum ea, tunc eam dabimus tibi, ut non sit aliquid difficile fidelibus in tali negotio, cum completum fuerit quod ad rem pertinet et quod precipit Deus. Nihil est enim prophete difficile in eo quod illi instituit. Preceptum namque Dei est predestinatio predestinata." González Muñoz, *Exposición y refutación*, 51.
14. Burman, "*Liber denudationis*," in *Religious Polemic*, 37.
15. Lacarra, *Pedro Alfonso de Huesca*.
16. Chorâo Lavajo, "Cristianismo e islamismo," 3:1031–55; Hernando, "Ramón Martí."
17. Cerulli, *Libro della scala*, 417–27.
18. Vincent of Beauvais, *Bibliotheca mundi*. This source was reprinted as *Speculum historiale* (Graz: Akademische Druck-Verlagsanstalt, 1965), xxiii, 44.
19. Vitry, *Iacobi de Vitriaco*, 9.
20. Di Cesare, "New Sources," 14.
21. "Oh Mary, God chose you, made you beautiful with His grace, adorned you and preferred you before all women who are mothers of any children." Buenhombre, *Disputatio Abutalib*, 65.
22. Buenhombre, 135–37.
23. Buenhombre, *Aduentu Messiae*, col. 335–68.
24. For some interpretations of Buenhombre, see Biosca i Bas, "Anti-Muslim Discourse."
25. An image of these annotations in the manuscript can be viewed in Biosca i Bas, 99.

3

THE MUDEJAR POLEMIC *TAʾYĪD AL-MILLA* AND CONVERSION BETWEEN ISLAM AND JUDAISM IN THE CHRISTIAN TERRITORIES OF THE IBERIAN PENINSULA

Mònica Colominas Aparicio

Introduction

The fact that there are more anti-Jewish religious polemics than anti-Christian ones written or copied by Muslims in the Christian territories of the late medieval Iberian Peninsula—where one would imagine that Christianity was the bigger threat to the Muslim minority (Mudejars) dwelling there—has not been analyzed in depth. Mudejars appear to have considered the refutation of Judaism and condemnation of Jews to be very important and produced several anti-Jewish treatises—such as the *Taʾyīd al-Milla* (The fortification of the faith, or community) and the *Kitāb al-Mujādala ma ʿa al-Yahūd wa-l-Naṣārā* (The book called disputation with the Jews and the Christians)—and narratives containing questions that Jews put to Muḥammad as well as a whole literature of encounters between Islam and Judaism. The latter includes narratives such as the battles of Muḥammad, Muḥammad's genealogy in al-Bakrī's *Kitāb al-anwār* or *Libro de las luces*, and Buluqiyyā's conversion to Islam, just to name a few that present a very negative view of Jews and Judaism. Likewise, the fact that the Mudejars' interest in polemicizing with the Jews seems to have exceeded the interest of the latter in polemicizing with the former has not attracted enough scholarly attention. Jewish attacks on Islam in the Christian territories are limited to some sporadic invectives scattered throughout the works of authors such as Ibn Daud, Joseph ben Shalom Ashkenazi, and Abraham bar Hiyya, or Ibn Adret's treatise[1] against Ibn Ḥazm. We know of no other Jewish polemical work.[2] There are several questions that arise from these facts: What do the Mudejars' polemics against Jews and Judaism tell us about the permeability between Muslim and Jewish communities under Christian rule? Could conversion between the minority religions have been a matter of concern to the Mudejars and an explanation for their polemics against Jews and Judaism? Was the intensification of anti-Judaism in Christian mainstream society a contributing factor to the Mudejars' anti-Jewish attitudes? What was the role of converts in this context?

In this chapter, I would like to look at the role of converts in the production and consumption of the treatise *Ta'yīd al-Milla* as a way of inquiring into the boundaries between Judaism and Islam in the Christian territories of the Iberian Peninsula. Specifically, the chapter attempts to discover whether the *Ta'yīd* served to clarify Islamic doctrine or whether it was an attempt at rapprochement between Islam and Judaism in order to facilitate both the assimilation of Jewish converts into the Mudejar *aljamas* and the return of Muslim apostates. First, I will provide the reader with some general information about this polemic. Then I will look at conversion between Islam and Judaism in the Christian territories. I will argue that converts from Judaism could have adapted the *Ta'yīd* into *aljamiado* (Romance written in Arabic characters) and that the audiences of these adaptations could have been made up of individuals with an intimate knowledge of Judaism, either Jewish converts to Islam or Muslim converts to Judaism. I will discuss the ways in which these groups are addressed in this treatise. Finally, I will draw some tentative conclusions about the attitudes of the Mudejars toward converts and about the permeability of the boundaries between the two communities.

The *Ta'yīd al-Milla*

The *Ta'yīd* consists of about 110 folia and is one of the lengthiest treatises against Jews and Judaism in circulation in the Iberian Peninsula, as well as one of the most widespread among the late medieval and early modern Muslim communities in Christian Iberia. The paleographical, codicological, and textual evidence from the four Arabic[3] and five *aljamiado* manuscripts of the *Ta'yīd* that are extant in European and North African libraries reveals the direct involvement of the Mudejars and the Moriscos in the transmission and adaptation of the *Ta'yīd* from the fourteenth until as late as the seventeenth century. The earliest Arabic original of the *Ta'yīd* is from Huesca from 762 H/1361 CE, and the fourteenth century appears as the *terminus post quem* for this work. The early twentieth-century scholar Miguel Asín Palacios was the first to analyze the *Ta'yīd*, and in 1969, Jacob Leon Kassin published an edition and translation of the text, to which I will refer in what follows when quoting this polemic.[4] There is still some uncertainty about the identification of the author of the *Ta'yīd*. According to Asín Palacios, he was a Morisco from Huesca,[5] but Kassin claims that he was a Jewish convert to Islam. The analysis of the contents of the *Ta'yīd* and the codicological characteristics of the Arabic and *aljamiado* manuscripts call into question the assertion that the author was of Jewish origin and make it likely that we are dealing with a Mudejar author.[6]

In the introduction, the author explains some of his reasons for writing his polemical treatise against Jews and Judaism. He refers to the attacks by groups of Jews on Islam "in the meeting-places and dwellings" in "the land of polytheism," most probably referring to the Christian territories in the Iberian Peninsula. Here, the Jews "deny his [i.e., Muḥammad's] religious law and prophetic office; and they assert that Allah . . . had not revealed a religious law or scripture to any of the nations, save to them; and they assert that Hagar, the mother of Ishmael . . . had not been Abraham's wife . . . ; she was merely his concubine."[7] The Jews claim, too, that God bequeathed the land of Canaan to their people. The archival records about the Mudejar communities in Aragon—where the oldest copy of the *Ta'yīd* was produced and where most of the *aljamiado* manuscripts of this polemic have been found—suggest that the relationship between the two religious minorities was sometimes tense. Mudejars and Jews in Fraga in 1387 and in Huesca in 1392 clashed over which group should go first in public processions organized by the Christians.[8] A document dated three years prior to the composition of the *Ta'yīd* (1358) reports attacks against the Jewish *aljama* of Borja by Christians and Mudejars, who "seek to injure them, severally and singly, confiscating their property and committing other injustices" and who "despise the Jews of the [city's] aljama."[9] Unfortunately, we do not know the contents of these verbal attacks, so it remains an open question whether they might be related to the Jewish claims against Muslims and Islam quoted by the author of the *Ta'yīd* to be later refuted one by one. That is to say, we do not know whether the Jews could have been responding to previous affronts to their communities by the Mudejars. The attacks by Jews against Muslims in public spaces described in the *Ta'yīd* bear resemblance to the attacks by Christians and Muslims on Jews mentioned in the introduction of a contemporary Jewish polemical treatise, the *Commentary on Avot*, by Rabbi Joseph ben Shoshan of Toledo (ca. 1310–80). Here, the rabbi complains about the attacks in Castilian cities by young Christians and Muslims against the Torah and the extent to which "the reins were loosened" within his own community.[10] We do not know whether the events referred to by Ben Shoshan or by the author of *Ta'yīd* ever really occurred or were merely literary topoi, but there is no question that the author of *Ta'yīd* is willing to provide a resounding and comprehensive refutation of Judaism and condemnation of Jews. In order to do so, he claims to have examined the Jewish sources (i.e., the Torah, the Psalms, and the Books of the Prophets) and uses them in the *Ta'yīd*.

The extensive quotations from the Torah are the most prominent characteristic of this treatise and provide the basis for the author's teleological account of Islam and of Muḥammad's prophecy. It is precisely the proper reading of the Jewish sources and not their categorical rejection that, in the author's view, exposes the falsehood of the Jewish accusations against Muslims, the truth of Islam, and its privileged place in God's plan throughout the history of mankind. He divides his arguments against Jews and Judaism into five sections.[11] In the first section, the author deals with the evidence found in the Torah that Ismāʿīl (Ishmael) was the legitimate son of Ibrāhīm (Abraham) and the father of the Muslims: they and not Jews are God's true chosen people. Then he addresses the possibility of abrogation of the Jewish Law by Islam, which is followed by a third section in which he argues that the coming of Muḥammad is foretold in the Torah. In the fourth section, the author provides an account of the miracles of Muḥammad. He ends his treatise with an exhaustive list of God's punishments of Israel because of the stubbornness of its people and their disobedience to his divine command. The Jews, he claims, have no choice but to acknowledge their sins before God and to take the path of Islam, in which Muḥammad is the Seal of Prophets.[12]

The willingness of the author of the *Ta'yīd* to provide an alternative and hermeneutical reading of the Torah, which is sensu stricto a source alien to the Islamic tradition, is a polemical strategy found among some Oriental

Muslim authors.[13] Yet such an approach is doubly remarkable in the case of the *Ta'yīd*, not only because we do not find it in the Muslim anti-Jewish polemical literature in the nearby regions of al-Andalus and the Maghreb, but also because it coexists with the author's profound revulsion toward the Jews and toward the idea of becoming a Jew. On this last point, it should be recalled that living among Jews seems to have been particularly disturbing for the Mudejars, who sometimes asked for physical segregation from their Jewish and Christian neighbors.[14] The members of their communities might have felt socially and economically disadvantaged in comparison to the Jews, since "unlike mudejar society," as Brian Catlos notes, "Jewish communities in the Iberian kingdoms included narrow, highly educated, and financially engaged elites whose wealth rivaled that of all but the highest strata of Christian aristocracy."[15] Moreover, the Mudejars could have seen with dismay how the Muslim provisions on the relationships between the two communities established by the pact of the *dhimma* were reversed under Christian rule and how Jews were placed in positions of power over the Muslim communities. A good example here is the Jewish bailiff in charge of collecting taxes from the Mudejars in the town of Morverdre, who "was a former Valencian *dhimmī*."[16] The demand made by the author of the *Ta'yīd* that Muslims be given precedence over Jews should be read against this background. This demand is supported by his claim that Jews are cursed by God and therefore should occupy the bottom rung of society. This idea is well illustrated in the following passage from the *Ta'yīd*: "And He dispersed you in the cities, and destroyed the Temple, and removed you therefrom, and cut off your kings and your leadership and your offerings and your fasts and your leading position and your sacrifices and your laws and your purifications and your frankincenses. And He made your names an oath for others, since people will say, 'And may Allāh not render me a Jew!'"[17]

The overt hostility toward the Jews reflected in these words shows that the attitude of the author of the *Ta'yīd* straddles the line between rapprochement with the Jewish sources and rejection of the real flesh-and-blood Jews. More importantly, the author's vehement expression ("And may Allāh not render me a Jew!") reveals the importance of conversion in his discourse and places it at the center of his polemic with the Jews. The analysis that follows will show that becoming a Jew was a concern for the Mudejars, as was the assimilation of converts from Judaism within the *aljamas*. We will see that the later copyists and adapters of the various manuscripts in Arabic and *aljamiado* of the *Ta'yīd* might have exhibited an ambivalence toward these groups that echoes the author's approach to the Torah and his attitude toward the Jews.

Conversion between Islam and Judaism in the Christian Territories

The author of the *Ta'yīd* had good reasons for warning his coreligionists against conversion and for doing his utmost to instruct them in Islam. The various extant records of conversion between the two minorities in the Christian territories provide evidence of the permeability of the boundaries between Islam and Judaism in the Iberian Peninsula. In the same way that some Jews in Muslim al-Andalus converted to Islam in order to rise in the social hierarchy and to occupy positions of power that were prohibited to non-Muslims,[18] Mudejars may have regarded conversion to Judaism (as well as conversion to Christianity) as a way to improve their economic and social position. Examples of conversion from Islam to Judaism include the case of a certain María in 1356 in Lleida,[19] Lopello de Serrah Mahomet in 1361 in Barcelona,[20] and a Muslim woman in 1451 in Talavera (Castile).[21] John Boswell argues that Muslim conversion to Judaism might have been particularly frequent in the mid-fourteenth century, since royal provisions were introduced in Aragon and Catalonia as the result of the complaints lodged by Mudejar *aljamas* about the conversions to Judaism of their members.[22] In Aragon, these conversions seem to have coincided with the depopulation of *aljamas* due to factors such as war between the Christian kings[23] and the Black Death. Under these circumstances, conversion meant not only the loss of Muslim believers but also a decrease in the *aljamas'* already reduced labor force, thus impacting the economic wealth of the communities. This could have been an additional reason for the Mudejar religious leaders to write polemical treatises against the other two communities—in particular, against the Jews—like the *Ta'yīd*.

While it seems that Muslim conversions to Judaism might have occurred fairly regularly in the Christian territories and, more particularly, in Aragon, where the *Ta'yīd* circulated, conversions from Judaism to Islam were also probably frequent. Mercedes García-Arenal notes that in the Council of Tarragona in 1234–35, King James I instituted capital punishment for conversion from Judaism to Islam and, based on the studies by David Romano, she cites the death sentences of some converts from Judaism in Aragon at the end of the thirteenth century.[24] We know of the conversion of three Jews to Islam in Zaragoza in 1280 and of a Jewess from Xàtiva in 1284.[25] Later Jewish conversions to Islam are less documented in Christian records than conversions from Islam to Judaism but are not totally absent. From a letter by the physician Astruch Rimoch (fl. 1391) in Fraga, who later converted to Christianity and took the name Francesc de Sant Jordi, we learn of the conversion of a Jewish man to Islam and the plight of his wife, who remained a Jewess.[26] Mention should be made, too, of the conversion of the former Jewess Marién in 1394 and, as late as 1489, of another woman with the same name in Soria.[27] More importantly, Nirenberg notes that as we approach the early modern period, escalating anti-Judaism among the Christians could have led Jews to conclude that by embracing Islam, they would be choosing the lesser of two evils.[28]

The fact remains, however, that historical evidence eludes us when it comes to establishing the frequency of conversion and its change over time between Mudejars and Jews in the Christian territories. This is not just because of the scarcity of records that have been preserved but also because of their nature. Nirenberg notes in his study of the relations among communities in the Christian territories that the Christians' legal provisions affecting the Mudejar and Jewish minorities were determined not only by the relationships between these groups but also by the theological concerns of Christian society. He claims that from 1400 onward, Muslims in the Christian territories were more successful in imposing corporal and financial penalties on the members of their communities for conversion to Judaism but that this was due not to an increase in the number of such cases but to the hardening of Christian attitudes toward the Jews.[29] From this, it can be argued that the written evidence available to us does not necessarily provide a complete picture of Jewish conversions to Islam from the thirteenth century onward, since these cases might have remained an internal affair of the Mudejar *aljamas*. Moreover, the views of Daniel J. Lasker in this same publication, on the possible connection between Christian anti-Jewish polemics and the mass conversion of Jews to Christianity, are instructive in this regard. He argues that "the lack of a *necessary* connection between a Christian threat and Jewish polemical output does not imply that such a connection *never* existed."[30] Converts from Judaism in the Christian territories could have destabilized the internal cohesion of the Muslim communities, since they may have encountered fewer obstacles to compete socially with Mudejars than Jewish converts would have encountered in al-Andalus and the Maghreb, where assimilation was often prevented by the Muslim majority. Moreover, Mudejar religious scholars, who were charged with the responsibility of keeping the Islamic faith alive, may have regarded the mores and traditions of the converted Jews (from al-Andalus, the Maghreb, or from the Christian territories) with suspicion. This may be true particularly if Jewish converts were highly educated because, in such a case, they could easily convey their outsider's understandings of the Islamic faith and, more disturbingly, they could corrupt Islam with Jewish thought. The innovative elements that, as we will see below, were introduced in the *aljamiado* manuscripts of the *Ta'yīd* suggest that the Mudejars not only attempted to impede the conversion to Judaism of other Mudejars but also might have adapted their discourses to meet the challenges posed by converts of Jewish origin.

The Audiences of the *Ta'yīd*

Before addressing the question of the work's audience, we first need to consider the very possibility that Jewish converts to Islam and Muslim converts to Judaism were among the audiences of the *Ta'yīd*. As stated above, the author's secondary audience is made up of Jews who, according to his own experience, condemn Muslims and Islam, but it is likely that he also has in mind the Mudejar communities. This becomes clear when he complains about "the changing times and the corruption of the people and the disappearance of learning, on account of the absence of its bearers."[31] The author seems to be deeply concerned about the impact of a climate of hostility and moral decay on the beliefs of his coreligionists living in a minority situation, and he is probably moved by the need to give the Mudejars (his intended audiences) tools to defeat the Jewish public that may also be taking notice of his text in "preparation of debates and disputations."[32]

If we now take a closer look at the Muslim audiences of the *Ta'yīd*, we note that they are diverse in both their geographical origins and their levels of literacy. The colophons of various Arabic and *aljamiado* manuscripts provide evidence that this polemic could have circulated in several places in the Christian territories. Muslims in Aragon could have been among its intended

Muslim audiences,[33] but there are good reasons to believe that the Arabic versions of the *Ta'yīd* circulated among Muslims under Christian rule in other regions as well. MS Borgiano Arabo 163, Vatican Library, dated 786/1384, has been identified by Pieter Sjoerd van Koningsveld and Gerard Wiegers as one of the Arabic manuscripts found in the Morisco village of Pastrana (Castile) after the demolition of a house in 1623.[34] As far as the audiences' levels of literacy are concerned, we can safely assume that learned Muslims belonging to the elite were in charge of reading, copying, and disseminating the *Ta'yīd* within the Mudejar communities. An example here is the scribe al-Raqilī, who in the colophon of the Arabic manuscript MS ÖNB AF 58 warns the reader that he is working with a corrupt text.[35] This points to the fact that he had no access to the original of the *Ta'yīd* and, more importantly, that he had enough knowledge of Arabic to recognize the inaccuracies in the text before him. However, this does not necessarily apply to the audiences of the *Ta'yīd* as a whole, and it seems very likely that the knowledge of Arabic among the general population of the *aljamas* was inferior to that of their religious leaders.

Evidence that there could have been various levels of literacy within the Mudejar *aljamas* is of two kinds. On the one hand, there are a few summaries of the *Ta'yīd* that have survived to present times, both in Arabic and in *aljamiado*.[36] The manuscripts are silent about the reasons for the composition of such abridgements, but I would like to suggest the possibility that they reflect learned Muslims' desire to make the main arguments against Jews and Judaism in the *Ta'yīd* accessible to the largest possible number of their coreligionists. Inasmuch as the *Ta'yīd* is a lengthy treatise, an abridgment would have entailed much less effort and cost to copy, would have made the work easier to carry, and would have been more accessible to readers with varying levels of literacy. This would undoubtedly have facilitated its dissemination among various social classes in the Mudejar and Morisco communities and perhaps, too, outside the Christian territories. Moreover, studies by Van Koningsveld and Wiegers show that the Arabic and *aljamiado* manuscripts of the *Ta'yīd* could have circulated concomitantly. The *faqīh* 'Alī al-Gharīb (or *gharībo*, a synonym of Mudejar)[37] is mentioned in a number of *aljamiado* manuscripts of the *Ta'yīd*, and according to these two scholars, al-Gharīb adapted the Arabic anti-Christian polemic by al-Qaysī, *Kitāb Miftāḥ ad-Dīn* (The key of religion).[38] On the basis of the internal references in *Kitāb Miftāḥ ad-Dīn*,[39] Van Koningsveld and Wiegers date the Arabic original of this treatise to the first half of the fourteenth century and argue that the adaptations of it by al-Gharīb were made shortly after.[40] The popularity that the *aljamiado* adaptations of *Kitāb Miftāḥ ad-Dīn* seem to have enjoyed among Mudejars and Moriscos suggests the possibility that al-Gharīb also adapted the *Ta'yīd*. At the beginning of the *aljamiado* MS BNE 4944, we find his name ("[di]senos ʿalī al-gharīb, sepas que hājar madre de ismāʿīl"; fol. 1v, lower margin). In the event that he adapted the *Ta'yīd*, the Arabic original would have been composed no later than the first half of the fourteenth century and would have been contemporaneous with some of its *aljamiado* copies. This provides evidence for a contemporaneous and more-diverse readership that included not only educated Muslims who knew Arabic but also readers who could read little or no Arabic but who had an interest in the Muslim tradition of written disputes with the Jews. Converts from Judaism could have been part of the latter group, and we should not discount the possibility that among the audiences of the Arabic and the *aljamiado* manuscripts of the *Ta'yīd* were Muslim converts to Judaism as well.

Polemical Discourse and Community Boundaries between Islam and Judaism in the *Ta'yīd*

Working from the assumption that the author of the *Ta'yīd* had as his intended audience not only Muslims but also converts, I would like to expand upon my previous findings on the *aljamiado* manuscripts of this polemic. These manuscripts are not simply translations from the Arabic but adaptations—that is, they introduce alterations in the Arabic original that point to changes in the discourses of Muslims in the Christian territories. Ryan Szpiech observes that changes in the boundaries between the Muslim, Jewish, and Christian communities in the Iberian Peninsula not only affected the internal composition of these groups but also brought forth changes in discourse. He notes that the introduction of biographies of conversion as a source of textual authority (or *auctoritas*) in the literature of polemics can be explained against the background of the large number of conversions (mainly of Jews) in the Christian territories. There was a change, too, in the Christians' polemical discourse toward Jews and Muslims as a result of the conversions to Christianity from the twelfth to the fourteenth centuries, which is reflected in the use of the figure that Szpiech refers to as the "rhetorical Muslim" as a "witness" of the truth of Christianity before the Jews.[41] Nirenberg argues in the same direction when he notes that the changes in the power relations between the Christian majority and the two minority communities could have influenced the attitudes and, by extension, the polemical discourses of the Mudejars and the Jews against each other.[42] The increasing rejection of the Jews by Christian society could have exacerbated the Mudejars' hostility toward the members of the other religious minority in the Christian territories. Some of the *aljamiado* manuscripts of the *Ta'yīd* certainly do manifest greater hostility toward Jews, but since we have no way to establish a chronological sequence for the different manuscripts of the work, it is impossible to definitively attribute this phenomenon to an increase in anti-Judaism among Christians. It would seem that more engagement with and concern about Christianity does not necessarily entail the adoption of the Christians' discourses and, moreover, that changes in the Mudejars' and Moriscos' polemical discourses cannot be explained only by an increasing adoption of Christian attitudes toward Jews and Judaism. It is thus necessary to look at the role of conversion in the changes in Mudejar discourse and its relationship to their interest in polemicizing against Judaism long after the expulsion of the Jews from the Iberian Peninsula. Insofar as conversion could have affected the internal composition of the Mudejar *aljamas*, language and language use in the manuscripts of the *Ta'yīd* can provide solid evidence of the role of converts in the transmission of this polemical treatise and the ways in which Mudejar religious leaders addressed converts from Judaism and Muslim apostates.

Examination of the *aljamiado* manuscripts reveals that Jewish converts could have been involved in the adaptation or the copying of the *Ta'yīd*. This seems to be the case in MS BNE 4944, in which the *Ta'yīd* precedes a copy of the adaptation by al-Gharīb of *Kitāb Miftāḥ ad-Dīn*. Here, there are some elements that are lacking in the *Ta'yīd*'s Arabic original and seem to a certain extent to "Judaize" its contents. For example, we find nouns and verbs of Hebrew origin such as *goím* right after the end of the *Ta'yīd* (fol. 36r). Also a passage from the Hebrew Torah is rendered in Arabic script, and we find the words *berajá* (fol. 8r) and *atemar* (fol. 7v), whose use seems to have been characteristic of the Sephardic communities.[43] There are various possible explanations for the use of verses from the Hebrew Bible transliterated into Arabic in MS BNE 4944. As I have argued elsewhere, it is possible that a copyist or al-Gharīb, as adapter, was interested in showing that he had direct access to the original sources he wanted to refute and not only to their Arabic translations. He might have been interested in making these sources accessible to his own community or, as Ramon Martí does in his *Pugio fidei*, he could have wanted to provide an "Islamic perspective" of the Jewish authorities.[44] It is also possible that he actually had access to a Hebrew version in Arabic characters of the Pentateuch such as MS Borg. Ar. 129, which appears to have circulated among the Mudejars and the Moriscos.[45] The latter is highly probable if it is, indeed, the case that we are dealing with a convert from Judaism.

Even more important for the issue that concerns us here is that this evidence—in the form of changes made to the text of MS BNE 4944—also points to Jewish converts to Islam and Muslim converts to Judaism as being among the audiences of the *Ta'yīd*. This would explain the presence in the text of the elements just discussed that "Judaize" it and that seem not to have been introduced at random. The use of *berajá*, or "blessing," is telling in this respect. *Berajá* is key to one of the main arguments of the *Ta'yīd*—namely, the contention that Sarah gave Hagar to Ibrāhīm for a wife and that this marriage was as legitimate as his marriage with Sarah because Sarah and Ibrāhīm were married without any blessing. It is, moreover, a term whose meaning makes sense to an audience acquainted with Jewish thought or to converts from and to Judaism. Likewise, the verb *atemar*, or "to finish," as Luis Girón-Negrón and Laura Minervini note, was used repeatedly in Romance translations of the Bible in the later Middle Ages and is found almost exclusively in Judeo-Spanish sources.[46] Lastly, the two biblical verses rendered into Hebrew *aljamiado* deal with the subject of ritual purity, which is of major importance in the polemics between Muslims and Jews and in the negotiation of the boundaries between the two communities. Jews and Muslims have many views in common with regard to ritual purity, and both communities understand it as part of God's commandments. It is probably no coincidence that, for example, the ablutions prescribed after a discharge of semen have a central place for the Isawiyya, a Jewish sect midway between Judaism and Islam. Founded by Abū ʿĪsā al-Iṣfahānī, the sect acknowledged both Jesus's and Muḥammad's prophecies and is one of few known instances of this kind of syncretism.[47] These ablutions are the subject of one of the two Hebrew *aljamiado* biblical verses in MS BNE 4944, which makes the argument that Jews have broken God's law and have abandoned their rituals.[48]

These elements point to various dynamics between converts and Mudejar religious leaders. On the one hand, we observe a rapprochement with those individuals whose identities were between Judaism and Islam. In this way, the quotation of Hebrew verses in Arabic script gives authenticity to the argument and increases its authority. Moreover, the "Judaization" of this verse and of other parts of the *Taʾyīd* may have helped neophytes and those who had been misled by a Jewish reading of the scriptures to gain a proper understanding of its message. Together with the Mudejars' engagement with the Torah that characterizes the *Taʾyīd,* the discourses brought forth in this polemic can be understood as a means of facilitating the integration of Jewish converts within the Muslim *aljamas* and their education in Islam and also as a call to Muslim apostates to return to the fold. We know from cases such as the one mentioned above of a Muslim woman from Talavera who became a Jewess in 1451 and then returned to Islam that this kind of return to one's original community sometimes occurred. The dynamics among the Mudejars thus seem to correspond to the "creative symbiosis" between Jews and Muslims that Steven Wasserstrom discussed in depth in his influential book.[49]

Although Mudejar religious leaders were concerned about teaching Islam to converts, they were equally concerned about the religious education of their own community and specifically about imparting a knowledge of Judaism. Religious polemics could have had an important role in this regard. An example here would be MS FDHCA L536 (Fondo Documental Histórico de las Cortes de Aragón, Zaragoza), copied in 1481. MS FDHCA L536 contains an abridged version of the Arabic original that retains the original chapter divisions but has been transformed to include a polemic against Christianity: the sources have changed with respect to the earliest Arabic version of the *Taʾyīd* known to us, and now they mention books of philosophy and logic in addition to the books of the Prophets and the Gospels, and the fourth chapter on the miracles of Muḥammad has disappeared and been replaced by four new chapters of anti-Christian polemic. This adaptation shows no signs of Jewish influence; rather, the concern here is with Christians and Christianity.[50] What is significant for the issue at hand is that this manuscript of the *Taʾyīd* is part of a miscellaneous manuscript (MS FDHCA L536) composed largely of texts on Judaism and of quotations of Jewish sources that might be considered a sort of manual against Judaism.[51] It follows that Mudejar religious leaders could have been well disposed toward

Jewish conversion to Islam, and they could have regarded a source like the Torah as a means of constructing the Muslim identity of these new converts and of the Mudejars as a whole—that is to say, as a bearer of the interpretations of Islam. The adapters of the *Ta'yīd* also could have been attempting to loosen the requirements for Jews to convert to Islam and to bridge the gap with Judaism so as to make it easier to remain in the Islamic faith. But the boundaries between the two communities were clear to the religious leaders of the *aljamas*, and they took upon themselves the task of maintaining these boundaries. In their eyes, there was no room for ambiguity or doubt: Muslims should always strive to defeat Jews and Judaism. So if these leaders were the ones who produced this manuscript, it could have been motivated by their wish to present an orthodox interpretation of Islam through Jewish sources in order to help their coreligionists guard against the possible spread of heterodox views and attempts at proselytism by Jewish converts. In short, Muslims could have found the insider knowledge of Judaism useful for addressing the Jews, for preventing and reversing conversion, and for reaffirming the faith of the members of their communities.

Conclusions

Let me conclude by returning to the main question of this article regarding the permeability between Judaism and Islam in the Christian territories. Some tentative answers can be drawn from the discussion of the *Ta'yīd* thus far. On the whole, the Arabic and *aljamiado* manuscripts of this anti-Jewish polemic indicate that conversion between Islam and Judaism occurred and that converts could have been involved in the adaptation and the copy of this treatise. However, further research is needed to establish beyond doubt whether the fourteenth-century adapter of the *Ta'yīd*, the *faqīh* al-Gharīb, was a converted Jew.

I also have provided evidence that converts from Judaism to Islam and converts from Islam to Judaism could have been among the addressees of the *Ta'yīd* and that their presence within or close to the Mudejar communities could have furthered the composition of this and other narratives against Jews and Judaism. I have contended that converts from Judaism could have been a matter of concern to Mudejar religious leaders both because neophytes were in need of instruction in correct Islamic doctrine and strengthening their faith in their new religion and also because the views on Islam and the Jewish backgrounds of these converts could have compromised orthodoxy more generally within the *aljamas*. I have also argued that Mudejar religious leaders could have found in the *Ta'yīd* an appropriate tool to call Muslim apostates to Judaism back to Islam and a means to prevent conversion within the *aljamas*.

A most interesting finding of the inquiry into language and language use in the *aljamiado* adaptations of the *Ta'yīd* concerns the attitudes of Mudejar religious leaders toward conversion between Islam and Judaism. I have argued that these attitudes could have been ambivalent. The *Ta'yīd*'s extensive use of the Torah to affirm the truth of Islam is in line with part of the production of polemics in majority Muslim countries, and it is not necessarily connected to anti-Jewish Christian discourse. However, its use as a source of authority among Muslims in the Christian territories could have been partly activated by the presence of Jews up to a certain date and, moreover, by conversion between Islam and Judaism in the Christian territories. In this way, the incorporation of Jewish knowledge into the polemical repertoire of the Mudejars can be understood as a conscious attempt by their religious leaders to strive for reconciliation between Islam and Judaism, a reconciliation that created space for converts and offered the possibility of return to those who had been misguided into Judaism. The discussion of the *aljamiado* adaptation in MS BNE 4944 points in the same direction, and we can argue that al-Gharīb, or a later copyist of this manuscript, seems to have aimed at bridging Judaism and Islam in order to facilitate comprehension of the contents of the *Ta'yīd* among converts.

At the same time, Mudejar religious leaders could have seen the presence of Jewish converts and the conversion to Judaism of their coreligionists as a threat to their communities that would weaken not only their spiritual and social cohesion but also their economic well-being. The Mudejars were, as the author of the *Ta'yīd* puts it, "in the land of polytheism . . . cut off from the adherents of our religion and destitute of learning,"[52] and thus, the religious beliefs of the Mudejars were exposed to contamination from Christianity and from Judaism, which could lead to apostasy. Such a threat could have been to them reason enough to disown converts and cut them off from their communities, to tighten community boundaries separating them from the Jews, to harshly attack them, and to teach other Muslims about Judaism and Jewish sources. In this way, I have noted that not only the *Ta'yīd* but also other

Muslim narratives concerned with Judaism in circulation in the Christian territories engage with the sources of their opponents—which is not the same as saying that they engaged with the Jews themselves. Such a distinction fits well into a discourse on anti-Judaism as described by Nirenberg, wherein the rhetoric against the Jews becomes increasingly disentangled from real-life Jews.[53] This might have been particularly the case after the expulsion, once real Jews were no longer part of the Christian society.

As a general conclusion, the discussion of the *Ta'yīd* in relationship to conversion between Islam and Judaism supports the overall claim that rhetorical hostility can be a disintegrative force from the opponent's perspective, but it can have a uniting effect within a community. The popularity of this polemic throughout the centuries adds to the existing evidence of interpenetration between the members of the two religious minorities in the Christian territories. It points to the Mudejars' need to regulate the transfer of individuals into and out of their *aljamas* and, moreover, to cope with the very idea that Judaism could permeate Islam.

Notes

The research leading to this chapter was funded by the European Research Council under the European Union's Seventh Framework Programme (FP7/2007–13) / ERC Grant Agreement number 323316, project CORPI, "Conversion, Overlapping Religiosities, Polemics, Interaction: Early Modern Iberia and Beyond." This chapter develops the main arguments in chapters 3 and 5 of my recent monograph *The Religious Polemics*, which is based on my dissertation completed at the University of Amsterdam under the supervision of Gerard Wiegers, Richard van Leeuwen, and Mercedes García-Arenal.

1. Some authors, such as Elena Lourie, argue that this treatise against Islam might actually be an attack on Christianity. Lourie, "Anatomy of Ambivalence," 56n175.
2. What is more, there might have been fairly little knowledge of and/or interest in Islam among Iberian Jews. This seems to be true, according to Esperanza Alfonso, for the anti-Christian polemic that includes a discussion of "the relationship between the three religions" most probably written in Christian Iberia by Mattityahu ben Moshe, *Sefer Aḥiṭub we Ṣalmon* (The book of Ahitub and Salmon). Alfonso, *Islamic Culture*, 31n115. Alfonso draws on the critical edition of the text by Lara Olmo, "Edición crítica." An interesting aspect is that the Muslim Salmon sides with the Jews in their attack against the Christians and finally becomes a Jew. See for this narrative Szpiech, "Converting the Queen."
3. The Arabic manuscripts of the *Ta'yīd* are MS Gy. XXXI (collection Gayangos 31), Real Academia de la Historia, Madrid (RAH); MS Borgiano Arabo 163, Biblioteca Apostólica Vaticana, Vatican City; MS ÖNB AF 58, Österreichische Nationalbibliothek, Vienna; and MS Bibliothèque Nationale d'Argélie 721,

National Library of Algeria, Algiers. The *aljamiado* manuscripts of the *Ta'yīd* are MS FDHCA L536, Fondo Documental Histórico de las Cortes de Aragón, Zaragoza; MS BNE 4944, Biblioteca Nacional de España, Madrid; MS BTNT J8 and MS BTNT J9, Biblioteca Tomás Navarro Tomás, CSIC, Madrid; and MS RAH XXXII (11/9416; *Olim.* V7). This last copy only contains the end of "la desputación con los judíos" (fol. 1v).

4. Kassin, "Fourteenth-Century Polemical Treatise."
5. Asín Palacios, "Tratado morisco," 343–66.
6. For this discussion, see Colominas Aparicio, "Religious Polemics," 152–98.
7. Kassin, "Fourteenth-Century Polemical Treatise," 1:105.
8. Nirenberg, "Muslim-Jewish Relations," 266–67.
9. Boswell, *Royal Treasure*, 375.
10. Ilan, "Between an Oral Sermon," 189.
11. Asín Palacios gives an overview of the contents of these sections in his article. See Asín Palacios, "Tratado morisco," 347–57.
12. Kassin, "Fourteenth-Century Polemical Treatise," 1:243, 2:404 (fol. 102).
13. Colominas Aparicio, "Religious Polemics," 176–79.
14. Boswell notes with regard to the case of Aragon, "They themselves [i.e., the Mudejars] did not wish Christians or Jews to live among them." Boswell, *Royal Treasure*, 375, 368 (request number 15 by the *aljamas* of Castro and Alfandequiella in 1365).
15. Catlos, *Muslims of Medieval Latin*, 409, referring to the scholarship on the subject in n. 217.
16. Meyerson, *Jews in an Iberian Frontier*, 27.
17. Kassin, "Fourteenth-Century Polemical Treatise," 1:270–71, 2:428 (fol. 126).
18. Such as the case noted by Mercedes García-Arenal of the conversions of Abū-l-Faḍl Ḥasdai ibn Ḥasdai, Abū Bakr ibn Sadray, and Ibn al-Qarawī-l-Islāmī. García-Arenal, "Jewish Converts to Islam," 233. This was only one of the reasons for converting, and Esperanza Alfonso discusses at length some Jewish responses about the status of apostates in al-Andalus after having been forced to convert to Islam during the Almohad period. Alfonso, *Islamic Culture*, 105–9.
19. Boswell, *Royal Treasure*, 351–52.
20. Nirenberg, *Communities of Violence*, 188.
21. The case has been recently discussed by Echevarría Arsuaga, "Better Muslim or Jew?," and it is mentioned in Nirenberg, *Communities of Violence*, 191–95; and Nirenberg, *Neighboring Faiths*, 143–44, 149–51.
22. Boswell, *Royal Treasure*, 379–80. See also the case of a Muslim woman who converted to Judaism in Huesca at the end of the thirteenth century discussed in Nirenberg, *Neighboring Faiths*, 139.
23. For the consequences of the war with Castile on the *aljamas* in the Crown of Aragon, see Boswell, *Royal Treasure*, 385. For an in-depth discussion of the population in the Crown of Aragon in the fifteenth century, see Ferrer i Mallol, "Comunidades mudéjares," 1:27–154.
24. García-Arenal, "Rapports entre les groupes," 98nn57–58.
25. Nirenberg, *Communities of Violence*, 188–89, following the studies by Romano, "Conversión de judíos," 337. However, Nirenberg notes on page 189 that he did not find any other cases of conversion from Judaism to Islam.
26. Fuente Pérez, *Identidad y convivencia*, 130–31 quoting on n. 37. Lascorz Arcas, *Aljama judía de Monzón*, 118. For Astruch Rimoch, see Kressel, "Rimoch, Astruc."
27. Fuente Pérez, *Identidad y convivencia*, 129n29; following García Herrero, "La voz de Marién antes llamada Dueña," in *Nacer y el vivir*, 232–33; and on the same page, n. 30 referring to Archivo General de Simancas, Registro General del Sello, 148911, 146.
28. See the arguments by Oldradus de Ponte (d. 1337?) that "the Saracen sect is not as bad as that of the Jews"—which, as Nirenberg notes, underpinned the notion that "Jewish conversion to Islam was not apostasy"—and the discussion at Talavera about the "relative merits of the two minority religions" in Nirenberg,

Communities of Violence, 190–93; and Nirenberg, "Between Muslim and Jew," 142, 149–51.
29. Nirenberg, *Neighboring Faiths*.
30. See Lasker, chapter 5 in this volume, emphasis in the original. This author shows that the presence of some innovations in Jewish anti-Christian polemics strongly suggests that there was a connection with the conversions of Jews to Christianity.
31. MS Gy. XXXI, RAH, fols. 1v–2r. I have slightly adapted Kassin's translation in "Fourteenth-Century Polemical Treatise," 1:105.
32. Kassin, "Fourteenth-Century Polemical Treatise," 1:282.
33. MS Gy. XXXI, RAH, finished in 762/1361 by an anonymous Mudejar in Huesca; and MS ÖNB AF 58, Österreichische Nationalbibliothek, Vienna, finished by the *imām* Abū Zakariyyā Yaḥyā ibn Ibrāhīm Muḥammad al-Raqilī in the Aragonese town of Pedrola in 808/1405.
34. See Van Koningsveld and Wiegers, chapter 9 in this volume, n. 11.
35. MS ÖNB AF 58, fol. 30v. هذا الكتاب كثر معوج للحن الكتاب المتسخ منه.
36. Such as the Arabic one in MS BN Alg. 721, on which Samir Kaddouri is working. He is preparing, moreover, a critical edition of the extant Arabic manuscripts of *Ta'yīd*.
37. Van Koningsveld and Wiegers, "Polemical Works," 192n104. For an additional suggestion, see Colominas Aparicio, "Disputa con los cristanos," 43. The great popularity among Iberian Muslims of al-Gharīb's adaptation of the *Kitāb Miftāḥ ad-Dīn* can be seen in the numerous manuscripts that have been preserved: MS BNE 4944 (which seems to date from the end of the fifteenth century), MS BNE 5302, MS RAH 11/9409 (*Olim.* T12), MS RAH XXXII (11/9416, box 7), and MS RAH XXXI (11/9416, box 6; *Olim.* V6), also in Madrid, in the Real Academia de la Historia. Wiegers, *Islamic Literature*, 186–88, cf. 178. To this we should add the unknown *aljamiado* adaptation of *Kitāb Miftāḥ ad-Dīn* that I have recently been able to identify in the Colegio Escuelas Pías of Zaragoza, MS CEPZ D (est. p. tab. v, no. 26), fols. 389v–396v.
38. Van Koningsveld and Wiegers, "Polemical Works," 192.
39. In particular, those referring to the expulsion of the Templars in Christian Spain and France in 1307–12 CE. Wiegers, "Biographical Elements," 512; Van Koningsveld and Wiegers, "Polemical Works," 192.
40. Van Koningsveld and Wiegers, "Polemical Works," 186–88.
41. Szpiech, "Rhetorical Muslims." See also Szpiech, *Conversion and Narrative*.
42. Nirenberg, "Muslim-Jewish Relations."
43. Hispanicized Hebrew terms for "blessing" and for "coming to an end." See Schmid, "Lengua sefardí"; and Girón-Negrón and Minervini, *Coplas de Yosef*, 56.
44. See these arguments in Colominas Aparicio, "Disputes about Purity," 132–33.
45. Van Koningsveld, "Andalusian-Arabic Manuscripts," 99–100.
46. Girón-Negrón and Minervini, *Coplas de Yosef*, 109–10, 287.
47. Wasserstrom, *Between Muslim and Jew*, 85–86. See also Pines, "al-ʿĪsāwiyya."
48. MS BNE 4944, fol. 34r, l. 5–11.
49. Wasserstrom, *Between Muslim and Jew*.
50. Colominas Aparicio, "Religious Polemics," 87–88.
51. Colominas Aparicio, ch. 3. I plan to deal in more detail with this miscellaneous manuscript in a future research project.
52. MS Gy. XXXI, RAH, fols. 1v–2r; Kassin, "Fourteenth-Century Polemical Treatise," 1:105.
53. My own summary of the views expressed in Nirenberg, "History of Anti-Judaism."

4

"SERMO AD CONVERSOS, CHRISTIANOS ET SARRACENOS"

Polemical and Rhetorical Strategies in the Sermons of Vincent Ferrer to Mixed Audiences of Christians and Muslims

Linda G. Jones

With few exceptions,[1] specialists on the conversionary preaching of the famous Dominican friar St. Vincent Ferrer (d. 1419) have focused almost exclusively upon his sermons[2] and writings concerning the Jews.[3] Whenever scholars have discussed Ferrer's proselytism of Jews and Muslims, they have tended to treat the religious minorities as a single unit, invariably placing greater emphasis on his discourses about Jews and Judaism. It is undeniable that the figure of the Jew and anti-Jewish polemic are far more prevalent in Ferrer's preaching campaigns, which had tangible repercussions in the royal legislation in Castile and Aragon discriminating against this community. Nevertheless, there are a sufficient number of sermons in which the charismatic Dominican preacher directly addressed Muslims or discussed the conversion of Muslims to Christianity to warrant a separate detailed examination of this subject.

In a recent study on the history of Dominicans in the Crown of Aragon, Robin Vose forcefully argued that "conversionary preaching does not seem to have occurred," since he found "no examples of actual preaching" to Muslims even in areas of the Crown with very large Muslim populations, such as Xàtiva and Zaragoza.[4] Vose believed that the surviving evidence did not support the long-held view that the Dominicans systematically targeted Jews and Muslims for proselytization. Yet Vose did not cite or analyze any Dominican sermons or eyewitness accounts of preaching among his primary sources. Thomas E. Burman has reached a similar conclusion regarding the Dominicans' disengagement with Islam and Muslims. In his contribution to the present volume, Burman identifies a distinct modus operandi of influential early Dominicans, such as the eponymous founder St. Dominic and Ramon Martí, of "gesturing toward and turning away from Islam" in order to devote their attention fully to the Jews.[5] In other words, Burman concedes that the Dominicans targeted the Jews for polemics and proselytization but renounced attempting to missionize Muslims.

Surviving records of Dominican sermons preached in regions of the Iberian Peninsula populated by Mudejar communities offer some intriguing exceptions to the conclusions of these studies. Manuel A. Sánchez Sánchez edited an anonymous collection of sixty-three Dominican model sermons from Castile.[6] Most of the sermons followed the liturgical calendar, but he demonstrated that thirteen miscellaneous sermons on diverse topics, "Sermones de diversis," were composed for mixed audiences of Christians, Jews, and Muslims. As model sermons, they were intended to be adapted and used by other mendicant preachers. Although we cannot prove that any of these sermons were actually delivered before mixed congregations of Castilian Christians and Muslims, their existence furnishes further evidence that at least some Dominicans envisaged using their sermons to missionize and convert these religious communities.

Likewise, in his study on preaching in medieval Catalonia, Oriol Catalán calls attention to the importance of distinguishing between preaching *about* the Jews and preaching *to* Jewish communities. He has documented the names of the Christian preachers who were assigned to preach to the Jews of Cervera, noting that many of them were Jewish converts, and considers this to be "a clear indication of the insistence and the importance accorded to this kind of preaching."[7] I do not deny that the Dominicans generally prioritized the salvation of Christian souls. Rather, I suggest that the swinging of the historiographic pendulum from the claim that the Friars Preachers dedicated themselves *primarily* to converting heretics, Jews, and Muslims to the opposing assertion that there is virtually no evidence of Dominican missionary preaching to convert non-Christians needs to be nuanced. Examining the transcriptions (*reportationes*) of sermons and other notices about preaching before live audiences as well as the model sermons intended to be delivered in areas with sizeable populations of Muslims and Jews will allow us to gauge how the Dominicans broached the topics of anti-Muslim and anti-Jewish polemics and the conversion of "infidels" before diverse audiences.

The most prominent medieval Dominican in this regard is Vincent Ferrer, whose sermons demonstrate that he specifically targeted Jews and/or Muslims for proselytization and not merely for religious polemics. The distinction is important because whereas polemical statements about Jews or Muslims may appear in sermons delivered to all-Christian or to mixed audiences, by definition, missionary preaching entails targeting non-Christians for proselytization. For instance, allusions to Muslims, Islam, and Muḥammad are found scattered throughout the sermon collections that have been edited by Josep Sanchís Sivera, Adolfo Robles Sierra, Pedro Cátedra, and others.[8] In some of the sermons, the Dominican preacher addressed himself directly to the Christians and then to the Muslims in his audience. In others, he spoke at length about the conversion of Muslims to Christianity or narrated conversion stories featuring and intended for Mudejars. In still others, he polemicized against Islam and its "false prophet," repeating the topoi of anti-Islamic discourses promulgated by his Dominican predecessors. While Vincent Ferrer may have been exceptional in the attention he accorded to proselytizing Muslims and Jews, nevertheless, these sermons merit analysis in their own right.

The aim of this chapter is to study the characteristic features and techniques of persuasion Vincent Ferrer used in his preaching to and about Muslims. It will analyze the themes, the motifs and the narrative, rhetorical, and theological strategies he deployed toward this end and evaluate how he handled his anti-Muslim polemical rhetoric in the sermons targeting mixed audiences of Christians and Muslims. In light of Robles Sierra's observation that Ferrer may have read something of the Qur'ān,[9] I will also consider how much Ferrer might have known about Islam, to what extent he was aware of or relied upon the translations of Islamic texts into Latin that were in circulation at that time, and how his rhetoric and polemics concerning Muslims and Islam compare with that of other Dominicans, such as Ramon Martí (d. after 1284). Finally, since Ferrer also addressed the Jews in some of these sermons to mixed audiences, I will examine how the Dominican preacher adapted his preaching strategies according to which religious minority he was targeting.

The primary sources for this study are a selection of edited sermons from Vincent Ferrer's preaching campaigns throughout the Kingdom of

Castile and the Crown of Aragon between the years 1411 and 1414.[10] For evidence of the impact of these campaigns, including the supposed conversion of Muslims or Jews, I have consulted Ferrer's own sermons, since during the course of preaching in one place, the Dominican preacher often referred to the reception or impact of his previous sermons elsewhere. Additionally, accounts of Ferrer's missionary work are preserved in historical documents, such as the *Chronicon* by the Dominican friar Pere d'Arenys (d. 1419) and the anonymous *Crónica de Juan II de Castilla*.[11] Other evidence includes an eyewitness report[12] of Ferrer's preaching in Toledo sent to the regent of Castile Ferdinand of Antequera in 1411[13] as well as royal and municipal correspondence, ordinances, and other official records.

Vincent Ferrer: A Short Biography

Although Vincent Ferrer has been the subject of numerous studies,[14] a brief word is in order concerning his life, his preaching, and his missionary activities. He was born in Valencia in 1350. In 1368, he began studying logic in the Dominican provincial chapter in Barcelona. He continued his studies of logic, the Bible, biblical exegesis, natural philosophy, and theology in Valencia, Lleida, Toulouse, and Paris, and by the year 1389, he obtained the title of master of theology.[15] Ferrer excelled in biblical exegesis and was fluent in Hebrew, which he learned at the *Studium haebraicum* in Barcelona. De Garganta and Forcada emphasize that Ferrer's fluency in Hebrew would prepare him for missionizing and polemicizing against the Jews.[16] Yet there is no mention of Ferrer's having studied Arabic, the Qur'ān, the Hadith, or other Islamic texts, either in Arabic or in one of the available Latin translations, needed for his preaching to Muslim audiences.[17] Nor have I found direct evidence of his having read any of the famous polemical anti-Islamic works authored by his fellow Dominicans, such as Thomas Aquinas's *Summa contra gentiles* or Ramon Martí's works, *Explanatio Simboli Apostolorum*, *De secta Mahometi*, and *Pugio fidei*. The lack of information about Ferrer's knowledge of Arabic and about Islam is perplexing given Valencia's large Mudejar population, whose Muslim quarter (*morería*) had been located inside the capital city walls since 1356.[18]

A turning point in Ferrer's career occurred in October 1398. While Vincent was in the service of the schismatic Pope Benedict XIII at the palace at Avignon, he became gravely ill. He reportedly recovered following the miraculous intervention of Jesus Christ, St. Dominic, and St. Francis, who entrusted him with the mission of evangelizing the world. This mystical experience convinced Ferrer that he was divinely chosen to act as a legate of Christ (*a latere Christi*) announcing the coming of the Antichrist and the apocalypse. In November 1399, he left Avignon on a peripatetic mission of reform and conversionary preaching throughout France, Italy, Switzerland, and the Iberian Christian kingdoms.

Scholars such as Philip Daileader, Pedro Cátedra, and Tomàs Martínez Romeros have observed that Ferrer's apocalyptic mission involved a dual strategy of, on the one hand, striving to homogenize and purify Christianity by preaching repentance and ethical reforms and exhorting the segregation of Christians from whoever threatened the integrity of the mystical and social body of Christ—heretics, diviners, blasphemers, usurers, gamblers, prostitutes, and infidels—in preparation for the coming of the Antichrist and the final judgment.[19] On the other hand, Ferrer's apocalyptic outlook convinced him that the gospel had to be preached to the entire world before the imminent arrival of the Antichrist. Hence Jews and Muslims had to be targeted for proselytization as well for the apocalyptic prophecies to be fulfilled.[20] Yet it is important to emphasize that Ferrer did not seek to convert all Jews and Muslims. As he explained in a letter to Benedict XIII, it sufficed that "a small number of believers from each nation" should survive after the Antichrist's death to help convert the last remnants of humanity.[21]

Assessing the Evidence of Vincent Ferrer's Preaching to and about the Muslims

What follows is a summary of the sermons I have located to date in which Ferrer directly addresses or mentions Muslims. In the subsequent section, I analyze three of the sermons in detail as examples of Ferrer's diverse polemical strategies. First of all, there are three sermons whose titles mention Muslims explicitly: (1) "Sermo ad conversos, christianos et sarracenos." This was one of the sermons Ferrer gave during his final evangelical campaign, in which he traveled from Valencia to Barcelona between May and August of 1413.[22] (2) "Sermón sobre cómo debemos los cristianos, los judíos y los sarracenos santificar a Cristo." This sermon, which was preached in Toledo in 1414, is sermon number 101 (CI) of the *Sermonario de san Vicente Ferrer* of the Real Colegio del Corpus Christi in Valencia.[23] (3) At the end of the index of this same collection is the "Sermón sobre las tres leyes, de cristianos, judíos y sarracenos." However, neither the date nor place where it was preached is indicated.

I have also located seven sermons with incipits specifying that Ferrer was addressing Christians as well as Muslims and Jews. Ferrer delivered these sermons in various cities and towns of Castile during his preaching campaign from 1411 to 1412.[24] (1) On April 22, 1411, in the village of Hellín in Albacete, Ferrer preached on the biblical theme "Noli est incredulus, sed fidelis" (John 20:27). He began by saying, "Ista nostra presens predicato erit quedam doctrina generalis pro christianis ad confirmandum in fide catolica et pro sarracenis et judeis ad illuminandum eos in eadem ut videant et intelligant veritatem et errorem in quo sunt positi," meaning that he was going to preach "some general doctrines to confirm the faith of the Christians and to illuminate the Saracens and the Jews so that they too would understand the truth and see the errors of their ways."[25] (2) On Friday, July 17, 1411, he preached in Toledo on the biblical theme "Dedit illi scilicet homini, Deus legem vite" (Eccles. 17:9).[26] The incipit states that the goal of this sermon was to explain "by which law man can be led to salvation," and Ferrer added that he hoped "et erit magna et bona materia pro illuminando judeos et sarracenos et instaurendo et firmando christianos in fide catolica" (that it would be good material for illuminating the Jews and Muslims and for strengthening the Christians in the Catholic faith).[27] (3) On Saturday, July 18, 1411, Ferrer preached in Toledo on the biblical theme "Dominum [autem] Christum sanctificate in cordibus vestris" (1 Pet. 3:15). In the incipit, Ferrer stated that he hoped to provide "bona instructione christianorum et illuminacionem et conversionem judeorum et sarracenorum" (some good lessons for the Christians and for the illumination and conversion of the Jews and Saracens).[28]

Some of the incipits lack this distinction between the goals of reaffirming the faith of the Christians and illuminating or converting Muslims and Jews and purport to offer the same message to all. For instance, (4) on Wednesday, August 5, 1411, Ferrer preached in Ocaña on the biblical theme "Vos estis sal terrae" (Matt. 5:13). In the incipit, Ferrer stated that since this day was the feast of St. Dominic, that "si place Deo erit bona materia pro omnibus et christianis et judeis et sarracenis" (God willing, he was going to preach some material that would be good for everyone, Christians, Jews, and Saracens).[29] (5) On Thursday, December 17, 1411, during Advent, Ferrer preached in the village of Illescas on the biblical theme "Quid existis videre? Profetam? Eciam dico vobis plusquam profetam" (Matt. 11:8). In the incipit, he declared, "Intendo predicare, sint in bonam instruccionem et reformacionem et iluminacionem omnium et christianorum et judeorum et sarracenorum" (I intended to preach in order to provide good teachings, to reform, and illuminate everyone, Christians, Jews, and Saracens).[30]

(6) On Tuesday, January 5, 1412 (the eve of Epiphany), in Illescas he preached on the biblical theme "Heredes simus secundum spem vite eterne" (Titus 3:7). In the incipit, he stated that he sought to provide "bona edificacione, alumbramiento e consolación de ómnibus christianis et judeis et sarracenis" (good edification, enlightenment, and consolation to all, Christians, Jews, and Saracens).[31] (7) Finally, on January 22, 1412, he preached in Medina del Campo on the biblical theme "Beatus vir qui in sapientia morabitur" (Eccles. 14, 22). In the incipit, he reverted to distinct messages aimed at Christians and non-Christians, stating he would provide "poterimus recipere bonas doctrinas morales pro nobis et habebimus aliqua secreta por judios et moros" (some good moral doctrines for us [i.e., Christians] and we have some secrets for the Jews and Muslims).[32]

The objective of the above mixed-audience sermons, as Ferrer repeatedly states, was to "illuminate and convert the Jews and Saracens." In addition to these sermons, there are others that mention Muslims or the Prophet Muḥammad tangentially. One example is a sermon Ferrer preached for the festival of Saints Peter and Paul on the biblical theme "Blessed art thou, Simon Bar-Jona" (Matt. 16:17). The sermon is addressed to Christians, but there is a single phrase in which Ferrer extols Peter's prompt response to Jesus's invitation to leave everything and follow him as an example for Christians, Jews, and Muslims to emulate: "See the prompt obedience of Peter. It is said here against the defect of this world. For all are called by Christ, namely Christians, Jews, Muslims, and we refuse to go. He calls us by enlightening our hearts, giving recognition of sins, and immediately we ought to follow him, but it happens to us as it did to Samuel, who was called by God and he went to Eli."[33]

The tenor of this passage accords with the inclusive messages in the above-mentioned sermons that Ferrer addressed to mixed audiences. The gist of Ferrer's allusion to Samuel and Eli (1 Sam. 3:5–7) is that God calls upon Jews, Christians, and Muslims alike, but all fail to recognize his message. Yet the majority of the tangential allusions to Muslims have some polemical aim. These polemical references may be classified into various subcategories. For instance, in some, Ferrer deploys narratives featuring Muslims in exempla that teach a moral lesson to his Christian audience. The exempla often purport to represent real events that his audience would presumably recall and serve to contrast the moral deficiencies of the Muslims with the exemplary virtuous conduct of idealized Christians.[34] Another subcategory consists of sermons that feature rhetorical or hermeneutical Muslims, wherein Ferrer uses the figure of the Muslim as a foil to teach a lesson intended for "evil Christians" or to polemicize against the Jews.[35]

Several sermons depict Muslims posing some sort of threat to Christians or Christian society. An interesting feature of the motif of the menacing Muslim is that it sometimes reflected the contemporary historical context—for instance, when Ferrer compared God's punishment for tolerating the presence of diviners within Christian society to infidels who capture a Castilian city and hand it over to the king of Granada[36] or when he mentioned the perils facing Christians imprisoned by Muslims.[37]

Other passing references to Muslims provide glimpses of the problems of Christian-Muslim *convivencia* and reveal Ferrer's role in advocating the social segregation of Christians from unbelievers. For instance, in a sermon for Lent preached in Valencia, Ferrer warned his Christian audience that being a true disciple of Christ meant staying away from infidels, not having them as companions or residing with them, a message directed particularly at merchants.[38] On another occasion when Ferrer was preaching in Valladolid, he responded to a written query regarding whether it was permissible for Christians to live alongside Jews or Muslims. The Dominican preacher famously replied that Christians should avoid residing with Jews and Muslims in this life, lest they reside with them in hell.[39] In another sermon Ferrer preached on the third Sunday of Lent, he explained the story of a disputation between Christ and the Samaritan woman at the well (John 4:7–9). Although I have not been able to determine the exact date or place of this sermon, it was probably delivered before a mixed audience of Christians and Muslim converts or somewhere near a Mudejar community. I base this on Ferrer's comment that when the Samaritan woman encountered Christ at the well, "she did not greet him, recognizing that he was a Jew by his clothing, for Jews were not talking to Samaritans." Instead of remarking that Christians do not speak to Jews, Ferrer observed, "Just as we Christians do not talk with unbelieving Saracens."[40]

Finally, a number of sermons include blatantly anti-Islamic polemical comments. A familiar trope in Ferrer's preaching on the Antichrist was to argue that Jews and Muslims have a greater affinity with the Antichrist or a diminished capacity to resist his influence.[41] Robles Sierra cites several examples in his survey of the Latin sermons compiled by the Dominican friar Thomas Rocabertí in which Vincent Ferrer polemicized against Muslims in particular or against Muslims and Jews. For instance, Ferrer affirmed that only those who believe in the Trinity would be saved, and he explicitly excluded Saracens and Jews, whom he labeled "idol worshippers since they do not worship the true God who is Father, Son, and Holy Spirit."[42] In another sermon, Ferrer preached that the Saracens could not attain salvation because they denied the Trinity, even though they believed in some of the articles of the Christian faith.[43] A sermon Ferrer pronounced on the biblical theme "Manifestavit gloriam suam" (John 2:11) declares that God manifests his glory in accordance with some peoples' circumstances, but not so to everyone, "not to Jews, nor to Hagarenes [i.e., Arabs or Muslims], nor to any infidels" (*et non aliis manifestatur, nec judeis, nec agarenis, aut aliis infidelibus*).[44] Other sermons polemicize against the Muslim fast,[45] accuse Muslims of worshipping idols[46] and of blasphemy,[47] and condemn the practice of polygamy.[48]

Admittedly, the sermons mentioned above amount to a fraction of the orations attributed to Vincent Ferrer. It suffices to note that Josep Perarnau i Espelt recorded 909 *reportationes* of sermons in his massive inventory of the Dominican friar's preaching. A closer study of the incipits and the main body of the sermons listed in Perarnau i Espelt's inventory might reveal additional references to Muslims.[49]

The foregoing survey of the sermons Vincent Ferrer preached to or about Muslims reveals a diversity of themes associated with this community as well as ambivalent and even contradictory attitudes toward Muslims. On the basis of the above, I hope to demonstrate that Vincent Ferrer deployed two distinct discourses in his preaching about Muslims. On the one hand, he used an exclusionary discourse when he sought to polemicize against Muslims. As we have seen, these polemical discourses exposing the theological errors and moral failings of Islam were either intended for internal Christian consumption or sought to achieve or reinforce the segregation of Christians from Muslims. On the other hand, he employed more inclusive discourse when preaching before mixed audiences of Christians and Muslims or in locations with a significant Mudejar population, in which cases his stated goal was to "illuminate" the Muslims as the first step toward convincing them to convert and become incorporated into the Christian community. Yet it would be inaccurate to characterize all of Ferrer's negative rhetoric about Islam as exclusionary or to assume that there were no polemical elements in his inclusionary discourse. We shall see that in some passages featuring Muslims as exempla and rhetorical Muslims, Ferrer's ultimate objective seems to have been to create a social, discursive, or theological space for Muslims within Christian society. In other words, I am suggesting that whereas polemics typically justify the social exclusion and oppression of religious others, sometimes it can be deployed in the service of religious tolerance and coexistence. This hypothesis builds upon the findings of T. L. Hettema and A. van der Kooij, who have called for "further investigations into the internal and external effects" of polemic, and of M. Dascal, who has identified three distinct types of polemic that seek to establish the truth, defeat the adversary, or persuade the adversary to accept one's own position.[50] The following section will illustrate the varied uses and strategies of polemic in Ferrer's homiletic discourses concerning the Muslims.

Three Case Studies of Polemics and Inclusive Discourse

Baptism and Conversion Narratives in Vincent Ferrer's Sermons on/to Muslims

Conversionary preaching best exemplifies how polemics can be deployed to transcend the boundaries between religious communities, since the ultimate goal is to convince the religious other to embrace Christianity. Predictably, Ferrer preached many of these sermons during the Lenten season, in keeping with the ancient tradition of celebrating the sacraments of initiation—that is, the baptism of the catechumen during the Easter Vigil Liturgy on Holy Saturday. One such sermon featuring the baptism or conversion of Muslims is found in the cycle of Lenten sermons Vincent Ferrer pronounced in the city of Valencia in March and April of 1413.[51] The sermon is dated April 6, 1413, corresponding to the fifth Thursday of Lent, and the biblical theme was "Deus visitavit plebum suam" (God has visited his people; Luke 7:16), the words that the people of the town of Nain spoke after Jesus resurrected a dead man. Ferrer explained that the Gospels mention three persons whom Christ resuscitated: a young girl whom he revived in secret (Matt. 9:18–26), the young man whose funeral was taking place in the town of Nain (Luke 7:11–16), and Lazarus of Bethany (John 11:1–46), each of whom symbolized a type of mortal sinner. As usual, the Dominican friar first directed his attention to the Christians when he interpreted the symbolism of the first two persons whom Jesus resurrected, comparing the girl's secret resurrection to those Christians whose sins are grave but only affect themselves, while the public resurrection of the young man from Nain provided a lesson for those Christians whose sins affected others.[52]

Ferrer considered the story of Lazarus's resurrection to be a model for the worst kind of sinner, "the man whose sins are . . . deep-rooted, entrenched, and hardened" because Lazarus was "an old man of thirty years" and because when Christ found him, he had already been buried several days and was "putrid and covered with worms." Such a person could only be saved through preaching and intense prayers.[53] Up until this point in the sermon, Ferrer's exegesis accorded with the traditions of the Church Fathers. Augustine of Hippo compared Lazarus with the habitual sinner who is "dead, weighed down by the load of his sinful habits," and "buried as it were, like Lazarus."[54] Indeed, in other sermons preached on the Gospel's story of Lazarus of Bethany, Ferrer restricted his commentaries to the moral and spiritual reform of Christians.[55] Yet in the sermon under consideration here, Ferrer replaced the usual parallelism between Lazarus's death and the inveterate Christian sinner with an infidel Muslim, using the same macabre imagery of putrefaction and decomposition: "A Moor who had lived for forty years in unbelief, oh, he was already putrefied and decomposed from his sins. How shall he convert? Through many sermons and with prayers and with tears. This is how one *faqīh* (jurist) converted in these past few days. Now you recommend another *faqīh*; pray to our Lord God Jesus Christ that He will want to resuscitate him through prayers and tears: *Convertimini fletu et lagrimis* (Joel 2)."[56]

In the above exemplum, Ferrer did not mention the name of the Muslim *faqīh*. Yet scholars agree that the story referred to Azmet (Aḥmad)

Hannaxa, the *faqīh* of Alfandech, who had been baptized the week before, on March 29, in the Cathedral of Valencia "in the presence of a multitude of people."[57] Azmet Hannaxa's conversion was deemed a remarkable missionary triumph. The surviving records indicate that he was the region's most prominent *faqīh* and was greatly esteemed among his coreligionists for his profound knowledge of "the laws of Muḥammad."[58] Hannaxa's conversion generated a flurry of correspondence involving the court of Ferdinand I in Valencia, Pope Benedict XIII, and Vincent Ferrer. For instance, in a letter dated March 29, 1413, Valencian jurists notified Ferdinand's court of the baptism of "the greatest and most erudite *faqīh* in all the royal feudal domains," who converted "due to the preaching of the most reverend maestro Vincent Ferrer." The letter remarked that as a sign of Hannaxa's gratitude toward Ferrer "for opening his eyes to the true faith," he chose for his baptismal name Vincent Ferrer. Furthermore, Azmet Hannaxa was not the only one baptized that day—so too were his wife, children, and "many other Moors."[59]

The existence of a Muslim quarter (*morería*) in the city of Valencia, in which Mudejars as well as Christians resided,[60] together with the legislation compelling Mudejars to attend Ferrer's sermons,[61] make it likely that this sermon as well as some of Ferrer's other Lenten sermons were preached before mixed congregations of Christians, Muslims, Jews, and converts from Judaism or Islam. Hannaxa probably attended this sermon, since Ferrer seems to address him directly, saying, "Now you recommend another *faqīh*; pray to our Lord God Jesus Christ that He will want to resuscitate him through prayers and tears."[62] Thus Ferrer wanted Hannaxa to use his influence and authority as a former *faqīh* to persuade his peers to convert other Muslims to Christianity. Studies on the internal organization of Mudejar communities in the Crown of Aragon indicate that sometimes the chief *faqīh* also fulfilled the positions of preacher and/or prayer leader of the congregation.[63] This may have been the case with Hannaxa, since Ferrer personally intervened on Hannaxa's behalf to obtain a license from Pope Benedict XIII for him to proselytize the Muslims of Valencia as well as a pension for him and his family.[64]

Interestingly, in this regard, Ferrer anticipates the approach of Hieronymite friar and archbishop of Granada Hernando de Talavera (d. 1507) and the Valencian theologian Martín de Figuerola, who deliberately targeted the *faqīhs* of Granada and Valencia, respectively. Dominicans, Jesuits,

Mercedarians, and other Christian preachers operating in early modern Spain believed that the conversion of the *faqīhs*, who under Christian rule assumed the roles of communal leaders as well as religious experts, was pivotal in encouraging other Muslims to follow suit.[65] Conversely, these *faqīhs* could use their authority to thwart Christian missionary attempts, as Mercedes García-Arenal demonstrates in her discussion of Figuerola's aggressive proselytizing tactics.[66]

To return to Ferrer's sermon, despite the polemical identification of the Muslim *faqīh* with putrefaction, symbolizing the worst of sinners, the Lazarus story operates within the logic of Vincent Ferrer's inclusive discourse on the Muslims. Ferrer used the analogy of Christ's resurrection of the long-dead Lazarus to demonstrate to his audience that the conversion of the Mudejars was possible. Such an interpretation makes sense before an audience composed of Christians and Muslims or in a region such as Valencia, which had a large Muslim population.[67]

Vincent Ferrer's preaching campaign in Caspe, Zaragoza, in the year 1412 afforded him another opportunity to deploy polemic in an inclusive sermon seeking the conversion of Muslims. The Dominican friar had been summoned to Zaragoza in April to arbitrate in the dispute over the successor of Martin I of Aragon (r. 1396–1410). The deliberations ended on June 28 with the proclamation of Ferdinand of Antequera as king of Aragon. Naturally, Ferrer's sermons addressed these political issues. Yet the town of Caspe still had a sizeable Mudejar population in the early fifteenth century,[68] and Ferrer targeted them for proselytization. He preached a conversion sermon on Thursday of the octave of the Ascension. The biblical theme was taken from Mark 16:16, "Qui crediderit et babtizatus fuerit, salvus erit" (Whoever believes and is baptized shall be saved), which are the very words the resurrected Jesus spoke to the remaining eleven apostles immediately after commissioning them to "preach the Gospel to the whole of creation" (Mark 16:15). As usual, Ferrer privileged the salvation of Christians by focusing on the first part of the sermon on Jesus's words—"Whoever believes"—to warn the Christians against becoming complacent about their religion and believing that having faith and being baptized alone would guarantee their salvation.[69]

Ferrer went on to reinterpret the second part of Mark 16:16, "But whoever does not believe will be condemned," with dual messages directed at

Christians and Muslims.[70] During the course of explaining the "true" meaning of baptism via "spiritual grace" for the Muslims, the preacher narrated two tales of Muslim conversion. In the interest of space, I will only discuss the first story, which runs as follows:

> We read in the life of St. Martin that while he was preaching he converted an infidel (*infel*), who came up to him to be baptized. Now you should know that in the olden days baptism wasn't done so easily; someone who wanted to be baptized would have to learn the minor *Credo* in the vernacular or in Latin and then, in front of the people, he would climb up on a high place and say, "Bona gent, aquesta çuna o secta que jo tenia de primer, jo conech que-m porta a dampnació (Good people, this sunna or sect that I used to follow, I now know that it will only lead me to damnation), and that is why I want to abandon it and I want to live and die in the Christian faith." He would recite the entire *Credo* and then say, "Good people, I want to live and die in this holy Catholic faith." Only after this would he be baptized.[71]

According to Ferrer, the infidel died suddenly before he could be baptized while St. Martin was away. When St. Martin returned and found out about the would-be convert's death, "he began to pray and weep with such fervor that our Lord God resuscitated him." St. Martin said to him, "So, what happened to you?" And he replied, "When my soul left my body, the angels were going to take hold of me and carry me to a tenebrous place."[72] Ferrer added that the "tenebrous place" was in fact Purgatory and that the man had been saved by his "great necessity and the contrition of his sins."[73] In other words, the man's conversion was validated, since he had not been damned to hell as an infidel, despite not having received baptism.

A comparison of Ferrer's version of this narrative with the account preserved in Jacobo de Voragine's *The Golden Legend*[74] shows that Ferrer used what Alberto Ferreiro identified as "homiletic license" or "great creativity" in filling in the gaps of his hagiographic sources[75] in order to adapt his message to the circumstances—in this case, to a mixed audience of Christians and Muslims. It bears recalling that St. Martin of Tours (d. 397) was a Roman soldier who converted to Christianity, abandoned the military, and became celebrated for his preaching campaigns to convert the Arians and pagans to Catholicism.[76] Among the miracles attributed to St. Martin was the resuscitation of a catechumen who had died before he could be baptized. Although St. Martin lived in the fourth century, Ferrer has the convert in his version use the anachronistic Arab-Islamic term *sunna*, meaning "the prescriptive norms of Islam based upon the practices of the Prophet Muḥammad." Ferrer's insertion of the word *sunna* was deliberate, since he used this word to qualify the more generic term, *sect*. This presupposes an audience that would have been familiar with the Arabic term, an audience composed at least in part of Muslims. Furthermore, the dramatic monologue in which the convert declares, "This *sunna* or sect that I used to follow, I now know that it will only lead me to damnation," is missing altogether from *The Golden Legend*.

Ferrer's homiletic license with De Voragine's narrative fulfils a dual polemical function. On the one hand, it reflects and confirms certain stock Dominican anti-Islamic accusations that Muḥammad led his people into error.[77] On the other, the deviation from De Voragine's account concerning the fate of the would-be convert seems intended to offer a response or alternative to Muslim eschatology that would appeal to Muslims in the audience. According to De Voragine, the resuscitated catechumen explained that when he died and was going to be "carried away to a tenebrous place," two angels intervened and informed the Judge (i.e., God) that St. Martin was praying for him. God told the angels that he would "restore [the catechumen] to life." Ferrer's account suppresses the reference to the Judge and the last judgment, hinting that baptism spares the infidel from the final judgment.[78] Such a denouement is entirely at odds with the theology of Ferrer's penitential and apocalyptic sermons before Christian congregations. At times, Ferrer beguiled his audience with promises of the miraculous intervention of Mary or the saints on behalf of repentant Christian sinners at the last judgment. Occasionally, he could threaten them with the saint's refusal to grant his or her intercession,[79] but he never implied that the final reckoning could be avoided altogether.[80] One possible explanation for the omission here is that it would resonate with popular Islamic discourse promising the faithful entry into paradise without a final reckoning, provided they performed certain pious acts. It bears mentioning that normative Islamic eschatological literature, beginning with the Qur'ān and the canonical hadiths, places great emphasis on the last judgment and meticulously calibrates the acts that will bring the individual closer to heaven or the eternal hellfire.[81] Nevertheless, alongside these traditions, one finds others claiming that certain acts liberate the pious Muslim from the ordeal of divine judgment. Such examples are found in a collection of Muslim sermons from late thirteenth-century Christian Aragon. The anonymous Mudejar preacher promised his audience, "There is no Muslim who was afflicted with a misfortune and patiently endured it, and who prayed for the grace of God by saying, 'We belong to God and to him we shall return' (Q 2:156), whose heart God has not filled with resolve, whose despair he has not decreased, whose heavenly reward he has not magnified *and whom he has not led into Paradise without a reckoning*" (emphasis added).[82] While it is impossible to gauge Ferrer's knowledge of Muslim eschatology, it bears noting that such traditions circulated among some Mudejar communities in the Crown of Aragon.

Finally, one more glaring discrepancy between Ferrer's and De Voragine's versions warrants mention: In order to highlight St. Martin's saintliness and willingness to suffer in imitation of Christ, De Voragine reveled in describing the tribulations the saint faced when preaching to the pagans: "They persecuted him, flinging themselves upon him, insulted him, publicly humiliated him, beat him, and expelled him from the city."[83] Ferrer omits all references to the resistance and violence of the pagans, obviously to avoid the specter of Muslim violence against the Christians.

"Sermones ad iluminacionem Sarracenis" (Sermons to enlighten the Muslims)

The following example belongs to the category of sermons in which Ferrer sought to "illuminate" the Muslims about the errors of their faith as a prelude to their eventual conversion. It is taken from the sermon titled "Sermón sobre cómo debemos los cristianos, los judíos y los sarracenos santificar a Cristo." St. Vincent preached this sermon in Toledo in 1414 before a mixed audience of Christians, Jews, and Muslims.[84] After reciting the biblical theme "Dominum Christum sanctificate in cordibus vestris" (1 Pet. 3:15), Ferrer announced in the incipit, "Para buena instrucción de los cristianos e iluminación y conversion de judíos y sarracenos, recurramos a la Virgen María diciendo así: 'Ave María'" (For the good instruction of the Christians and the illumination and conversion of Jews and Saracens, let us appeal to the Virgin Mary, saying, "Hail Mary").[85]

Ferrer divided his sermon into three unequal parts addressed to the Christians, Jews, and Muslims, respectively. In the first and lengthiest part, he explained that the best way for Christians to sanctify Christ in their hearts was through penitence, feeling contrition and pain for their sins. The sections devoted to the Jews and the Muslims are of equal length but shorter than that addressed to the Christians. The message for the Jews polemicizes against them regarding the coming of the Messiah. Ferrer argued that since the Jews do not believe that the Messiah has already come, when the Antichrist arrives, they will mistake him for the Messiah. Interestingly, he criticized the Jewish men for instructing their wives not to become baptized but rather to wait for their Messiah, the Antichrist. The implication is that Ferrer believed that Jewish women were more susceptible to conversion than men. Following a brief figurative exegesis of the Bible, referencing Daniel 2 and Genesis 48, to show that the Messiah had already come, he exhorted the Jews to "sanctify Christ as God by receiving baptism."[86] Thus Ferrer polemicized with the Jews in order to promote their conversion.

As for Ferrer's "particular words for the Saracens," he began by addressing the issue that divides Christians from Muslims—"the law of Muḥammad," which he enjoined them to renounce, "que no tiene razón" (since it is irrational), before turning to the issue that unites them: their shared belief that "Jesus never sinned, that he was holy." According to this logic, Muslims should accept the "law of Jesus and not prefer that of Muḥammad the sinner." He then quoted Psalms 17:45–46 in Latin and Castilian to show how the Muslims "claudicaverunt a semitis suis / se apartaron de sus caminos" (have strayed away from their paths).[87] It is unclear whether Ferrer deliberately sought to evoke the Qur'ānic term for the straight path, but he underscored that the word *caminos* (*semitis*) is plural because the Muslims say one thing that is true, which is that Christ is holy, but they also say something false, which is that Jesus is not God, and while they do well to believe in one God, they err by not believing in the Trinity. He acknowledged that they believed in baptism by water, perhaps alluding to the Muslim ritual ablutions, but that they erred in the form, since they do not use the baptismal formula. The Muslims were right in believing that Jesus took up the cross but wrong in asserting that he was not crucified and did not die. After refuting these stock arguments of the Muslim polemic against Christianity, Ferrer inserted a comparison with the Jews, indicating that unlike the Muslims, "los judíos se equivocan completamente, no creyendo en nada" (the Jews were completely in error, since they believed in nothing at all).[88]

There is nothing novel in Ferrer's arguments against the Jews or the Muslims. The Jews' refusal to believe that the Messiah had come was a common theme in Christian anti-Jewish polemic both in the numerous treatises composed by Dominicans and others and in the public disputations, including the infamous Disputation of Tortosa, held between 1413 and 1414, in which Ferrer participated.[89] Equally, Ferrer's assertion that Muslim beliefs about God are partially true and partially erroneous echoes the anti-Muslim polemical writings of earlier Christians, such as the Cluniac monk Peter the Venerable (d. 1156) and the Dominican friars Riccoldo da Monte di Croce and Ramon Martí, who considered Islam to be a Christian heterodoxy or heresy.[90] The main point is that in preaching before mixed audiences of Christians, Jews, and Muslims, polemic fulfils a dual internal function of reaffirming the religious identity and beliefs of the Christians and an external function of simultaneously striving to "illuminate" Jews or Muslims about the truths concerning God. That Ferrer's ultimate goal was to entice Jews and Muslims to conversion is suggested by his concluding repetition of the biblical verse "Sanctify Christ as Lord" as an exhortation to the entire audience. Taken together, the above case studies support Dascal's reflections on how polemic can serve to persuade a religious opponent to accept one's own position.[91]

Ambivalent Polemics: Dynamics of Exclusion and Inclusion

The final case study highlights the ambivalence of Ferrer's anti-Muslim polemics. Various scholars, among them Ana Echevarría Arsuaga, John Tolan, and Rita G. Tvrtković, have drawn attention to the ambivalent attitudes that Christian theologians and preachers portrayed toward Islam and Muslims.[92] Was Islam a Christian heresy or a form of pagan infidelity? Could Muslims be persuaded to accept Christianity with rational arguments? Was it legitimate to resort to "indirect coercion" or violence to force them to convert?[93] If conversion proved to be impossible, should Christians focus their polemics on advocating the segregation, destruction, or expulsion of the Mudejars?

Unlike the previous examples in which Ferrer used polemics to encourage the conversion of Muslims and Jews, the present example adopts an exclusionist, aggressive tone of reprobation and mockery. I return to the Lenten sermons Ferrer delivered in Valencia in the year 1413. The sermon is dated April 5, the Wednesday after the fourth Sunday of Lent, and took place six days after the conversion of Azmet Hannaxa, the aforementioned *faqīh* of Alfandech. The biblical theme was "Procidens adoravit eum" (Then he worshipped Him; John 9:38).[94] In the incipit, Ferrer informed his audience that the Gospel for that day concerned the miracle in which Jesus healed an old man who was born without eyes, and yet Christ "illuminated him."[95] For Ferrer, *illumination* means recognizing that Jesus is God.

In this sermon, Ferrer did not specify in the incipit that he was addressing both Christians and non-Christians, as he did in the other sermons delivered in Valencia discussed above. Yet he may have been preaching before a mixed audience of Christians and Mudejars because he spoke at length about Muslims at the end of the sermon. The lack of any allusion to the Jews or the familiar trope of Jewish spiritual blindness further suggests that the sermon may have been delivered in a region of Valencia with a sizeable Muslim population.

Ferrer develops his sermon around three themes: (1) spiritual illumination (i.e., recognition of one's sins) through penitence and acts of contrition, (2) the rigorous examination of one's faith and deeds, and (3) the final determination by which the illuminated blind man becomes a disciple of Christ. This "final determination" could be interpreted as the act of conversion, and as such, it comes as no surprise that Ferrer mentions the Muslims here within the context of his moral instruction on what it means to be a disciple of Christ.

In the beginning of this chapter, I illustrated how Ferrer used the motif of illumination in reference to non-Christians in the sense of enlightening them about the errors of their beliefs as a prelude to their eventual conversion to Christianity. Furthermore, we have just seen in the previous discussion of the sermon on the biblical theme "Sanctify Christ as Lord" that Ferrer established an explicit relation between illumination and conversion. Moreover, he implied in his final comparison between Jews and Muslims that the illumination of the latter would be easier, since they shared certain beliefs with the Christians. Yet in the present sermon, the motifs of illumination and the partial belief of the Muslims are cast in a negative, polemical light: Muslim confusion and error are portrayed as the cause of their damnation and as an instrument of the exculpation or exoneration of Christians from their sins. Moreover, whereas the previous sermon ended on an inclusive note with the invitation of the entire audience to sanctify Jesus as Lord, the denouement of this sermon is ambivalent.

Ferrer set the tone by affirming from the outset that being a disciple of Christ means necessarily separating oneself from infidels. He singled out merchants as the prototypical Christians who resist this message and exhorted them to "stay clear of the infidels and keep company with Christians, away from infidels."[96] Subsequently, he posed a hypothetical question regarding why Jesus does not despise the Muslims and instead allows them to control the Holy Land. He went on to respond that God's plan was to cause "great confusion" to the "evil Moors" who deny Christ's divinity and to provide a "justificatory excuse (*excusació*) for the Christians."[97] First of all, he interpreted Muslim possession of the Holy Land as a divinely inspired foil for the Muslims, who deny the proofs of Christ's divinity and yet bear witness to them through their residence in the very place where Christian sacred history unfolded. Ferrer achieves this by conjuring up a negative image of the Muslims as local pilgrimage guides who eagerly show Christian pilgrims the sites associated with Jesus's life, miracles, death, and resurrection, despite their unbelief. He mockingly observed that "they do not believe that Jesus died on the cross, but the monument where he was resuscitated, that they will show you. To their own confusion they show it."[98]

The second reason Ferrer offered to explain why Jesus allows the Muslims to possess the Holy Land is so that they may serve as a divine instrument of the *excusació*, meaning an exoneration or exculpation of Christian sin. According to Ferrer, the sins of the Muslims, which are magnified by virtue of their unbelief and their presence in sacred space, divert God's attention away from the Christians. I reproduce the passage in its entirety due to the convoluted nature of his argument:

> The other reason [God has allowed the Muslims to possess the Holy Land] is the exculpation of the Christians (*excusació dels cristians*). "*Non est homo iustus* (No man is just)" (Eccles. 7:21). Christians sin and Muslims sin (*Cristians pequen e moros pequen*). But Jesus Christ did not want Christians to commit sins in the Holy Land. In the chamber of the king there will be dogs (*cans*) and they piss and defecate (*e pixaran e faran femta*) and the dog will lie down with the pup. Now [imagine] if the son of the king were to enter the chamber

> and commit these same acts in the king's chamber: he would not tolerate it. So he tolerates this from his dogs but not from his sons. Likewise, to the dogs, that is, to the Moors, he (Jesus) tolerated this, but not from his sons, that is, from the Christians, our Lord God redeemer Jesus.[99]

The discursive violence of this passage is undeniable. To be sure, Ferrer does not deny that Christians sin, for as he acknowledges, "Christians sin and Muslims sin." Yet he affirms that the sins of "the evil Muslims" are far worse than the Christians by comparing them in a derogatory fashion to "dogs." The presence of the Muslim infidel "dogs" who sin ("piss and shit") in the Holy Land guarantees that they, rather than the Christians, will bear the brunt of God's wrath at the end of times. In short, Ferrer's polemic consists of depicting the Muslims as scapegoats who deflect God's punishment and wrath away from the Christians.

And yet a second interpretation is operative due to the polyvalence of the dog as a negative and a positive symbol.[100] One suspects that Ferrer is aware of the Muslim cultural aversion to dogs as impure and filthy, hence his comparison of the two. Yet in Christian culture, and especially among the Dominicans, famously nicknamed the *Domini canes* (the dogs of God), the dog is esteemed for the loyalty, companionship, and protection it provides—so much so that, as Ferrer observes, dog owners would tolerate behavior in these animals that they would not in humans. This positive symbolism of the dog, combined with Ferrer's argument that Muslim sin provides a safety valve for Christians, creates a space for Muslims in the economy of Christian salvation history. In a way reminiscent of the role of the Jews as "living letters of the law,"[101] Ferrer's Muslims play a necessary role in the construction and affirmation of Christian identity by serving as scapegoats and instruments for the exculpation of Christian sin. Thus Christians should not despise Muslims because they are essential to God's plan for Christians and because they will eventually convert, even if this occurs at the end of time. The implication here is that even the most deprecating polemical arguments against Muslims can be reframed to make a case for tolerating the presence of Muslims living qua Muslims (and not only as potential converts) within Christian society and Christian salvation history.

Conclusions

Vincent Ferrer's polemical encounters with the Muslims took shape during the sermons he delivered in towns and cities in Castile and the Crown of Aragon that had sizeable populations of Mudejars. The presence of real Muslims in the audience or town, as opposed to merely "hermeneutical" or "rhetorical" Muslims, conditioned how Ferrer framed his sermons and deployed his polemical arguments. The above analysis of Ferrer's preaching to or about Muslims before mixed audiences of Christians, Muslims, and Jews corroborates the observations of Hettema, van der Kooij, and Dascal concerning diverse types, functions, and effects of polemical discourse. Polemic against religious others intended for the internal consumption of Christians tends to be the most vituperative, since the polemicist's ultimate goal is to reaffirm the truths of Christianity and strengthen the unity of the Christian community through the discursive destruction of the enemies of Christ and their social isolation from Christian society. The sermon collections compiled or edited by Rocabertí, Cátedra, Sanchís Sivera, and others illustrate that an absolutist rhetoric certifying the damnation of Muslims and Jews and reassuring the salvation of Christians characterized some of the sermons Ferrer preached before audiences composed entirely of Christians or in the presence of Christian regents. I have called such polemical preaching exclusionary because it sought to justify the segregation and social exclusion of religious minorities. The anti-Islamic rhetoric of these sermons resembles the polemical works of fellow Dominicans such as Thomas Aquinas, Ramon Martí, and Raymond of Penyafort as well as that of earlier preachers such as Bishop Pedro Pascual (d. 1330), whose polemical treatises, apologetic writings, and sermons essentially targeted their fellow Christian friars, clergy, and laity.[102]

By contrast, the sermons Ferrer delivered before mixed audiences of Christians and non-Christians offer clear examples of polemical messages constructed for the external consumption of Muslims and Jews as well as Christians. Their function is inclusive insofar as Ferrer sought to persuade Muslims and Jews to convert to Christianity and to incorporate themselves into the Christian community. Toward this end, we have seen how the Dominican preacher marshaled various rhetorical techniques, narrative strategies, and polemical arguments in his attempts to persuade Muslims and

Jews while simultaneously reinforcing the superiority of Christianity and the priority of the salvation of Christian souls.

The most compelling rhetorical strategies of inclusiveness Ferrer employed were his explicit articulations in the introduction and/or incipit of a sermon that his message was intended for the edification, instruction, reform, or illumination of Christians, Saracens, and/or Jews alike, together with his recognition that all were sinners. He effectively used the techniques of *ad status* preaching, singling out particular messages for Christians, Jews, and Muslims. It suffices to recall Ferrer's many declarations of intent in his incipits to present "some general doctrines to confirm the faith of the Christians and to illuminate the Saracens and the Jews so that they too would understand the truth and see the errors of their ways." He used second-person speech to identify the community he was addressing: "Moro, ¿no veus?" (Moor, don't you see?) or "Catad, vosotros, judíos" (Beware, you Jews).[103] He also deployed more sophisticated rhetorical devices such as "double directionality" in his scriptural commentary,[104] introducing distinct theological and moral arguments, interpretations, and lessons depending on whether he was targeting Christians, Muslims, or Jews. Using "homiletic license," Ferrer creatively adapted De Voragine's hagiographic tales about St. Martin of Tours to the present circumstances of an audience composed of Christians and Muslims by inserting the Arabic term *sunna* into the narrative and omitting the controversial references to pagan violence against Christians.

Obviously the choice of homiletic theme also distinguishes Ferrer's inclusive preaching to mixed audiences of Christians, Muslims, and Jews from his sermons before all-Christian audiences as well as from the writings of other Dominican polemicists such as Aquinas, Peñafort, and Martí. When preaching to and about Muslims before mixed audiences, Ferrer spoke primarily on the themes of the conversion, baptism, and the "illumination" of the Saracens (and the Jews)[105]—topics that were consistent with his apocalyptic mission to proselytize and convert non-Christians. The polemical intent and function are unmistakable insofar as his efforts to persuade Muslims of the truth claims of Christianity and entice their conversion necessarily entailed Muslim acknowledgement of the "errors" of Islam and the falseness of their prophet. Yet he developed these themes by using techniques of persuasion that were intended to be inviting rather than alienating. He employed narrative (e.g., the exemplum of Ahmed Hannaxa's conversion) and miracle tales (e.g., the posthumous baptism of the would-be convert). He emphasized the common ground between Christians and Muslims, admitting, for instance, that "Christians sin and Muslims sin." He validated certain Muslim beliefs and practices, and he attributed the inability to convert more Muslims not to Muslim intransigence (as he often asserted regarding the Jews) but rather to Christian indolence and failure to set a good example in their own conduct.

The inclusive discourse in these sermons contrasts with the exclusionary messages of Ferrer's sermons before all-Christian audiences, wherein we encounter the standard denigration of Muḥammad as a false prophet, stock accusations of Muslim "blasphemy" and "idolatry," and stern warnings that Muslims will not attain salvation because of their negation of the triune God or his criticism or mockery of certain Muslim beliefs and practices such as polygamy. Nevertheless, even at his worst, Ferrer's anti-Muslim rhetoric and messages fall short of the verbal terror tactics used by some later preachers, such as Martín de Figuerola.[106] Indeed, even in the last sermon considered here, in which Ferrer ridiculed Muslim "confusion" and inconsistencies in accepting certain aspects of Christian dogma while rejecting others and vilified the Saracens as sinful "dogs," the Dominican friar was able to create a space for Muslims in the Christian economy of salvation, albeit as an instrument to exculpate Christian sinners.

Finally, and admittedly, the foregoing analysis of Vincent Ferrer's homiletic polemical encounters with the Muslims and Islam still leaves certain questions unanswered concerning the extent of his knowledge about Islam. There is no doubt that he delivered some of his sermons before mixed audiences of Muslims and Christians (and Jews), and the fact that he was born and lived much of his life in Valencia would suggest that he had some familiarity with Muslims and Islam. Yet apart from his use of the Arabic term *sunna* in one of his sermons, there is little direct evidence that Ferrer was acquainted with the Qur'ān, the Hadith, the Arabic language, or Islamic beliefs and practices. He framed his appeals to edify, illuminate, and convert Muslims as well as his polemical assertions about Islam within his discussions about Christian salvation history—for example, comparing the conversion of Muslims to the dramatic stories of Jesus's resurrection of Lazarus and his cure of the man who was born blind and without eyes. Naturally, it is plausible that Ferrer had access to the anti-Muslim polemical works of Dominican authors such as Ramon Martí and Alfonso Buenhombre, which circulated widely among the Dominican provinces of Aragon and Catalonia in the early fifteenth century.[107] Yet in the absence of direct citations, it is difficult to identify which specific texts might have inspired Ferrer's dual inclusionary and exclusionary discourses about the Muslims. Further research is also needed to determine exactly how his apocalyptic thinking informed his preaching and polemics targeting Muslims.

Notes

This chapter developed out of a paper titled "The Preaching of St. Vincent Ferrer to the Muslim Communities of Castile and Aragon: A Lacuna in the Historiography of Vicentine Sermon Studies?," which I presented in a seminar hosted by Mercedes García-Arenal of the CCHS-CSIC of Madrid. I wish to thank Mercedes García-Arenal, Gerard Wiegers, and the anonymous reviewers for their comments and suggestions. Research for this chapter was financed by the Ramón y Cajal subprogram of the Spanish Ministerio de Economía y Competitividad. It also forms part of my investigations as the principal investigator of the research project "RETROGENMED" (FFI2015-63659-C2-2-P MINECO/FEDER, UE).

1. Robles Sierra, "San Vicente Ferrer"; Martín de la Hoz, "Conversión en la predicación." See also Ferrer i Mallol, "Frontera, convivencia y proselitismo," 2:1593. I am excluding those works by Dominican authors who uncritically accept the stories about Ferrer's miraculous conversions of Muslims—namely, Pradei, *St. Vincent Ferrer*, which devotes a chapter to Ferrer's "apostolic success . . . among the followers of Muḥammad."
2. See, for instance, Vendrell, "Actividad proselitista"; Beltrán de Heredia, "San Vicente Ferrer"; Robles Sierra, *Obras y escritos*; Viera, "Treatment of the Jews"; and Losada, "Powerful Words."
3. See Robles Sierra, *Obras y escritos*, 459–577.
4. Vose, *Dominicans, Muslims and Jews*, 161.
5. See Burman, chapter 1 in this volume.
6. Sánchez Sánchez, *Sermonario castellano*.
7. Catalán, "Predicació a la Catalunya," 396, 148, 232–33.
8. Sanchís Sivera, *Quaresma de Sant Vicent*; Ferrer, *Sermons de Quaresma*; Ferrer, *Colección de sermones*; Cátedra, *Sermón, sociedad y literatura*; and Gimeno Blay and Mandingorra Llavata, *Sermonario de san Vicente*. For a list of the editions of Ferrer's sermons, see Perarnau i Espelt, "Cent anys d'estudis."
9. Robles Sierra, "San Vicente Ferrer," 153.
10. See the sources cited in note 8.
11. Medieval Iberian chronicles that mention Ferrer's preaching include Martín de Alpartil's *Cronica actitatorum*; d'Arenys, *Chronicon*; and Mata Carriazo, *Crónica de Juan II de Castilla*.
12. This is the anonymous text that Pedro M. Cátedra has baptized as the *Relación a Fernando de Antequera*, which provides an account of Ferrer's three-day preaching campaign in Toledo in 1411. For a detailed description of this manuscript and its contents, see Cátedra, "Predicación castellana," 266–67; and Cátedra, *Sermón, sociedad y literatura*, 665–72.

13. Regent of Castile since 1406 and future king Ferdinand I of Aragon (beginning in June 1412). On the famous "Compromise of Casp," see Soldevila, *Compromís de Casp*; and Mestre Godes, *Compromís de Casp*. For Vincent Ferrer's involvement, see Gimeno Blay, *Compromiso de Caspe*; and Gimeno Blay, "Sermón 'Fiet ouile.'"
14. The most recent comprehensive biographical study of Vincent Ferrer is by Daileader, *Saint Vincent Ferrer*. Other biographical works include de Garganta and Forcada Comíns, *Biografía y escritos*; Fages, *Historia de San Vicente*; Maciá Serrano, *San Vicente Ferrer*; and Mira, *San Vicente Ferrer*. See also the introductory study on Ferrer's life and preaching by Cátedra in his *Sermón, sociedad y literatura*.
15. Daileader, *Saint Vincent Ferrer*, 11–12.
16. Garganta and Forcada, *Biografía y escritos*, 23–24. On the *Studium haebraicum* in Barcelona, see Cortabarría Beitia, "*Studia Linguarum*." Vose cautions that the Dominicans had other motives for studying Hebrew and Arabic beyond the proselytization of Jews and Muslims—for instance, to read philosophical or medical texts. Moreover, knowledge of Hebrew would have been necessary to dispute matters concerning the Bible or the Talmud with the Jews, but not to preach to them, since they were conversant in the vernacular languages. See Vose, *Dominicans, Muslims and Jews*, 104–8, 111.
17. On the *Studium arabicum*, see Cortabarría Beitia, "*Studia Linguarum*," 264–69; Monteret de Villard, *Studio dell'Islam*.
18. Daileder, *Saint Vincent Ferrer*.
19. On apocalyptic imagery in Vincent Ferrer's sermons, see Delarruelle, *Piété populaire*, 329–54; Fuster Perelló, *Timete Deum*; and Esponera Cerdán, "Focos de la presentación."
20. On the possible influence of Joachim de Fiore's ideas on Vincent Ferrer and other mendicant preachers, see Reeves, *Influence of Prophecy*, 171–75.
21. "The third preaching of the Gospel throughout the world will take place after the death of Antichrist by certain faithful ones of each nation, who will have been wonderfully preserved by God for the conversion of the rest; and then will come the last consummation of the world." See Vincent Ferrer, "Letter to Benedict XIII concerning the End of the World," cited in S. M. C., *Angel of the Judgment*, 118–32.
22. MS 477, Biblioteca de Catalunya, Barcelona, fol. 125. See Perarnau i Espelt, "Aportació a un inventari," 480.
23. Ferrer preached this sermon while passing through Morella, where King Ferdinand and Pope Benedict XIII were meeting to discuss the schism in the Church, "quando estavan en ella el rey don Hernando y Benedicto trezeno tratando de la unión de la iglesia y de la extirpación de la scisma." Gimeno Blay and Mandingorra Llavata, *Sermonario de san Vicente*, sermon no. 101, pp. 382–84.
24. The sermons are listed in Cátedra's inventory of Vicentine sermons in the manuscript at the Colegio del Corpus Christi (henceforth, MS CC) in Valladolid. See Cátedra, *Sermón, sociedad y literatura*, 37–73.
25. Cátedra, *Sermón, sociedad y literatura*, 45–46; MS CC 41, fols. 31r–v; cf. *Opera omnia* II–I, 103–7.
26. The Latin Vulgate text reads, "Addidit illis disciplinam, et legem vitae haereditavit illos."
27. Cátedra, *Sermón, sociedad y literatura*, 57; MS CC 97, fol. 76r.
28. Cátedra, *Sermón, sociedad y literatura*, 57; MS CC 98, fols. 76r–v; cf. *Opera omnia* II–2, 68–70.
29. Cátedra, *Sermón, sociedad y literatura*, 61; MS CC 118, fols. 91r–92r; cf. *Opera omnia* III, 370–78.
30. Cátedra, *Sermón, sociedad y literatura*, 66, MS CC 144, fols. 118r–199r; cf. *Opera omnia* I–1, 141–44.
31. Cátedra, *Sermón, sociedad y literatura*, 70; MS CC 163, fols. 149r–150v.
32. Cátedra, *Sermón, sociedad y literatura*, 73; MS CC 180, fols. 172r–173r; cf. *Opera omnia* III, 135–46.
33. See "De beato Petro apostolo," in Ferrer, *Beati Vincentii*, 176.

34. An example is the Lenten sermon Ferrer delivered in Valencia in 1413, in which he narrated an exemplum about some ambassadors from "Barbary" who came to visit the king and contrasts the gluttony and materialism of the Muslims with the exemplary temperance of the Christians. See Sanchís Sivera, *Quaresma de Sant Vicent*, 3–4.
35. An example is the sermon Ferrer preached on Wednesday, December 30, in Illescas on the theme "Misit Deus spiritum Fili sui in corda vestra" (Gal. 4:6). In the incipit, Ferrer mentioned that he would speak about Christian men whose hearts are afflicted with "malignant spirits" and would respond to a rhetorical question that "many Jews and others" ask: "Why are there more diabolically possessed among the Christians than among Jews, Saracens, and infidels?" (quare magis et multi inveniuntur de christianis indemoniati et non de judeis et sarracenis et infidelibus). See Cátedra, *Sermón, sociedad y literatura*, 69; MS CC 157, fols. 139v–140v; cf. *Opera omnia* I–1, 194–99. For further examples of "hermeneutical Muslims" being deployed against the Jews or to correct Christian conduct, see Szpiech, "Rhetorical Muslims."
36. "Ca, si en una çibdat viniesen infieles par la tomar para el rrey de moros e la tomassen e la diesen al rrey de Granada, ¿e qué faría el rey de Castilla? Con razón toda la destroyría. Assí es de la çibdat de la christiandat, que tienen a los enemigos del rey. Los enemigos son los adevinos; el rey es nuestro Señor Jhesú Christo." Cátedra, *Sermón, sociedad y literatura*, 551.
37. Cited in Robles Sierra, "San Vicente Ferrer," 153.
38. Ferrer i Mallol, "Frontera, convivencia y proselitismo," 1593, citing Ferrer, *Sermons de Quaresma*, 64–65.
39. Cátedra, *Sermón, sociedad y literatura*, 247; MS CC 139, fol. 113.
40. See Ferrer's "Sermon for the Third Sunday of Lent, the Samaritan Woman at the Well (John 4:5–42)," cited in Ferrer, *Beati Vincentii*, sermon no. A561, http://www.svfsermons.org/A561_Lent3%20Samaritan%20Woman.htm.
41. For instance, in a sermon delivered in Toledo in July 1411 on the "coming of the Antichrist and the other things that should come at the end of the world," Ferrer declared, "And the Jews and Moors, because the Antichrist will harmonize with them (*concordará con ellos*) in many things and vanities, very soon shall they be with him because they tend toward carnal pleasures (*porque van a carnalidades*). But Christians shall have more resistance than they shall have against him, due to their virtues." Cátedra, *Sermón, sociedad y literatura*, 535–45. See also Guadalajara Medina, "Edad del Anticristo"; and Guadalajara Medina, "Venida del Anticristo."
42. "Item, qui habet falsam credentiam de Deo, facit, et adorat idola; et ideo Judaei et Sarraceni, qui non credunt Deum unum esse Patrem, et Filium, et Spiritum Sanctum, faciunt sibi idola, et deum novum, qui non est pater, neque Filius, neque Spiritus Sanctus. Et non est talis Deus in mundo, quia verus Deus unus, Pater et Filius, et Spiritus Sanctus est. Et ideo adorant idola, faciendo sibi novum deum, qui non sit Pater, etc." See Robles Sierra, "San Vicent Ferrer," 151–52, citing Rocabertí, *Sancti Vincentii Ferrarii*, 1–2, 483; cf. Cátedra, *Sermón, sociedad y literatura*, 245–46.
43. Robles Sierra, "San Vicent Ferrer," 152; Rocabertí, *Sancti Vincentii Ferrarii*, 2–1, 50–51.
44. See Ferrer's *Feria quarta* (dated 1404), MS 610, Fribourg, Cordeliers, fol. 279, cited in Perarnau i Espelt, "Aportació a un inventari," 659.
45. Robles Sierra, "San Vicent Ferrer," 154; Rocabertí, *Sancti Vincentii Ferrarii*, 1–2, 419.
46. Robles Sierra, "San Vicent Ferrer," 154; Rocabertí, *Sancti Vincentii Ferrarii*, 3, 127.
47. Robles Sierra, "San Vicent Ferrer," 154; Rocabertí, *Sancti Vincentii Ferrarii*, 2–1, 195.

48. Robles Sierra, "San Vicent Ferrer," 154; Rocabertí, *Sancti Vincentii Ferrarii*, 2–1, 106.
49. Perarnau i Espelt, "Aportació a un inventari."
50. Hettema and van der Kooij, *Religious Polemics*, xiv–xv. See in the same volume, Dascal, "Uses of Argumentative Reason," 6.
51. Ferrer, *Sermons de Quaresma*, 2:66–71.
52. Ferrer, 2:67–68.
53. Ferrer, 2:68.
54. Augustine of Hippo, *Sermons on the New Testament*, cited in Siebald, "Lazarus of Bethany," 438.
55. See especially Ferrer's "Sermon on the raising of Lazarus," in Ferrer, *Beati Vincentii*, http://www.svfsermons.org/A612_Lent5%20Lazarus.htm; and his "Sermón de cómo lloró Ihesú Christo çinco vezes en aqueste mundo," in Cátedra, *Sermón, sociedad y literatura*, 470.
56. Ferrer, *Sermons de Quaresma*, 2:68.
57. See Sanchís Sivera, *Quaresma de Sant Vicent*, xv, 199n80.
58. Sanchís Sivera, xiv. This *faqīh* became so famous that a mountain pass was named after him, "El Pas de l'Alfaquí Azmet." See García Oliver, *Sis mesquites*, 17.
59. See Sanchís Sivera, *Quaresma de Sant Vicent*, xv.
60. Barceló Torres, "Morería de Valencia"; Ferrer i Mallol, "Comunidades mudéjares"; and Ferrer i Mallol, "Sarraïns del regne de Murcia," 173–83.
61. Sanchís Guarner, "Estudi preliminari," in Ferrer, *Sermons de Quaresma*, 17; Riera i Sans, "Llicènces reials."
62. "Axí·s convertí hun alfaquí en aquests dies passats. Ara vos recoman hun altre alfaquí." Sanchís Sivera, *Quaresma de Sant Vicent*, 199.
63. On the activities of Mudejar *faqīhs*, see Hinojosa Montalvo, "Mudéjares de Aragón y Cataluña"; Albarracín Navarro, "Actividades de un *faqīh* mudéjar"; and Miller, *Guardians of Islam*, 135–36.
64. Sanchís Sivera, *Quaresma de Sant Vicent*, xiv–xv. In note 1 of page xv, Sanchís Sivera reproduces the letter Ferrer sent to the pope dated October 12, 1413.
65. See Franco Llopis, chapter 8 in this volume.
66. See García-Arenal, chapter 7 in this volume.
67. By way of comparison, one of the anonymous sermons preached to the Jewish community of Cervera on the Biblical theme "Credidi quia tu est Christus filii Dei" relates Jesus's resurrection of Lazarus of Bethany to his subsequent preaching before the Jews as a way of arguing in favor of preaching to the present Jewish audience. See Catalán, "Predicació a la Catalunya," 145, citing MS 478, Biblioteca de Catalunya, fol. 10r.
68. Álvarez Gracia, "Islam y los judíos."
69. Ferrer, *Sermons de Quaresma*, 1:99.
70. Ferrer, 1:101.
71. Ferrer, 1:103–4.
72. Ferrer, 1:104.
73. Ferrer, 1:104.
74. See de la Vorágine, *Legenda dorada*, 2:720. According to Alberto Ferreiro, Ferrer relied upon the version by Jacobo de Voragine due to the greater familiarity of this work among general public. Ferreiro, "St. Vicent Ferrer's Catalan Sermon," 545.
75. See Ferreiro, "St. Vicent Ferrer's Catalan Sermon," 545.
76. On the life and cult of this saint, see Farmer, *Communities of Saint Martin*.
77. See Martí's *Explanatio simboli apostolorum*, cited in Tolan, *Saracens*, 240: "For [Muḥammad] led the wise Saracen men into error."
78. De la Vorágine, *Legenda dorada*, 720.
79. An example of this refusal is seen in an exemplum in which the Virgin Mary states that she used to intervene at the last judgment on behalf of sinners, "but now [she has] taken up the task of being [her] Son's advocate and co-judge (*mas ara he pres offici de esser advocada del meu fill, e conjutge seu*)." Cited in Catalán, "San Vicente Ferrer: ¿paradigma o excepción?" (personal communication).
80. A spectacular example is found in a sermon Ferrer preached in Toledo in 1411 on the power of the "Hail Mary" prayer,

based upon the biblical theme "Behold, we are going up to Jerusalem" (Matt. 20:18). The final exemplum is a miracle tale of the resuscitation of a "very sinful man who committed as many sins as a man may commit and never did any good thing in his life other than say one Hail Mary with devotion every day." Although the man died without having confessed his sins, Mary intervened to convince Jesus to revive him. Afterward, the man "confessed and did much penitence for which he was saved and went to Paradise." Cátedra, *Sermón, sociedad y literatura*, 376–77.

81. On Muslim eschatology and eschatological literature, see Rustomji, *Garden and the Fire*.
82. In another sermon, he makes a similar promise, citing the Qur'ān: "Those who are steadfast [in adversity] shall receive in full their heavenly reward without a reckoning (Q 39:10)." MS RESC 100/3, Biblioteca Tomás Navarro Tomás, fols. 6 and 13, respectively. Another sermon (fol. 3) promises the same reward for steadfastness in performing the five daily canonical prayers. The preacher states that "whoever perseveres in prayer will be granted five qualities," including "protection from the anguish of life and the torture of the grave" and "he shall be led into Paradise *without a reckoning*."
83. De la Vorágine, *Legenda dorada*, 720.
84. Gimeno Blay and Mandingorra Llavata, *Sermonario de san Vicente*, sermon no. 101, pp. 382–84.
85. Gimeno Blay and Mandingorra Llavata, sermon no. 101, p. 382.
86. Gimeno Blay and Mandingorra Llavata, sermon no. 101, p. 383.
87. Gimeno Blay and Mandingorra Llavata, sermon no. 1, pp. 383–84.
88. Gimeno Blay and Mandingorra Llavata, sermon no. 1, p. 384.
89. Roca Traver, "San Vicente Ferrer"; Santoja Hernández, "Disputa de Tortosa."
90. Peter the Venerable develops these arguments in two treatises, *Summa Totius heresis Saracenorum* (*A Summary of the Entire Heresy of the Saracens*) and the *Liber contra sectam sive heresim Saracenorum* (The refutation of the sect or heresy of the Saracens).
91. Hettema and van der Kooij, *Religious Polemics*, xiv–xv; Dascal, "Uses of Argumentative Reason," 6.
92. Echevarría Arsuaga, *Fortress of Faith*; Tolan, *Saracens*; and George-Tvrtković, "Ambivalence of Interreligious Experience."
93. On this concept, see García-Arenal, chapter 7 in this volume.
94. Ferrer, *Sermons de Quaresma*, 2:58, 65.
95. Ferrer, 2:58.
96. Ferrer, 2:64: "Ací han doctrina los mercaders, que es deuen llunyar dels infels en companyes, e fer company de cristians ab infels."
97. Ferrer, 2:64.
98. Ferrer, 2:64.
99. Ferrer, 2:64–65.
100. For other examples of the polyvalent symbolism of dogs in medieval Christian thought, see Ferreiro, "Simon Magnus."
101. A reference to the book by Cohen, *Living Letters*.
102. For a brief account of the anti-Islamic writings of Aquinas, Penyafort, Martí, et al., see Kedar, *Crusade and Mission*; and Tolan, *Saracens*, 233–55.
103. In this, Ferrer was not unusual; second-person direct address is a common feature of *ad status* preaching both prior to and after Ferrer's time. For examples of the latter, see the sermons of Pérez de Chinchon, *Libro llamado Alcoran*. I thank Gerard Wiegers for bringing this source to my attention.
104. Pedro Cátedra used the expression *doble direccionalidad* to refer to Ferrer's use of double theological, exegetical, and pastoral arguments and dual interpretations of the biblical verses that formed the basis of his sermon, quoting the Hebrew version of the Bible when addressing the Jews and the Vulgate Bible when speaking to Christians. Cátedra did not indicate which version of the Hebrew Bible Ferrer might

have used. See Cátedra, *Sermón, sociedad y literatura*, 244–45.

105. See, for instance, Cátedra, *Sermón, sociedad y literatura*, 57; MS CC 98, fols. 76r; and Gimeno Blay and Mandingorra Llavata, *Sermonario de san Vicente*, sermon no. 1, p. 385.

106. See García-Arenal, chapter 7 in this volume.

107. On this, see Biosca i Bas, "Anti-Muslim Discourse." At the time of this writing, the doctoral student Sergi Gómez Ortínez was conducting research on the uses and dissemination of these texts among the Dominican provincial houses of Catalonia and Aragon under the supervision of Antoni Biosca i Bas and Cándida Ferrero Hernández.

II

AROUND THE FORCED CONVERSIONS

5

JEWISH ANTI-CHRISTIAN POLEMICS IN LIGHT OF MASS CONVERSION TO CHRISTIANITY

Daniel J. Lasker

The final one hundred years of Jewish life on the Iberian Peninsula, beginning with anti-Jewish rioting and murders in 1391 and concluding with the expulsion of 1492, was a period of intense interreligious conflict and tension. During this century, Christians made exceptional efforts at converting Jews, using a variety of tactics, including threats of murder, roving missionaries, public disputations, and literary persuasion. Indeed, many Jews did convert to Christianity at this time, either willingly or under duress. In the wake of the edict of expulsion, large numbers of Jews chose conversion over exile from their Iberian homes.[1]

This century was marked as well by the composition of numerous Jewish anti-Christian polemical treatises. Even before 1391, a number of Jewish polemicists had written against Christianity, but after 1391, the pace of such production increased greatly. The Jewish authors of these treatises were addressing not only Jews, who were still loyal to Judaism, but also *conversos*, since they were still considered Jews, whether their sin of conversion was voluntary or not.[2] Since the relative abundance of these polemical compositions was remarkable, it makes sense to examine the relation between these Jewish anti-Christian polemical treatises and the phenomenon of mass conversion to Christianity in an attempt to determine what impact the historical setting may have had on this literature.

First, we should enumerate which treatises will be examined. The pre-1391 authors are as follows:

1. Moses ha-Kohen of Tordesillas. This late fourteenth-century writer wrote two anti-Christian polemics between 1375 and 1379: *'Ezer ha-'emunah* (Aid to Faith), written in Hebrew, and *'Ezer ha-dat* (Aid to Religion), originally written in the vernacular, surviving only in Hebrew translation.[3]
2. Shem Tov ibn Shaprut. Ibn Shaprut (ca. 1340–after 1405), a native of Tudela, began writing *'Even boḥan* (Touchstone) in 1385 but augmented it a great deal after 1391, including responses to the apostate Abner of Burgos / Alfonso de Valladolid and a Hebrew translation of Matthew. The book was intended as an updated version of one of the most prominent medieval Jewish polemical treatises, Jacob ben Reuben's *Milḥamot ha-shem* (Wars of the Lord), written in 1170.[4]

The following authors wrote after 1391:

3. Profiat Duran (Isaac ben Moses ha-Levi; Christian name, Honoratus de Bonafide). Duran, mid-fourteenth century to early fifteenth century, wrote two anti-Christian treatises, despite having converted to Christianity in the wake of the 1391 riots and living outwardly as a Christian for more than two decades. One of these compositions, *'Iggeret al tehi ka-'avotekha* (Epistle Be Not like Your Fathers, ca. 1393), was specifically triggered by his conversion and that of the addressee of the epistle, his erstwhile friend David Bonjorn. It is a satirical letter, ostensibly praising his friend for not being "like his fathers," since in contrast to his ancestors, he had adopted the rationally impossible beliefs of Christianity. The other one, *Kelimmat ha-goyim* (The Disgrace of the Gentiles, ca. 1397), demonstrates great erudition in Christianity, made possible perhaps by the access Duran would have had—as a nominal Christian—to Christian theological literature. Duran employs his knowledge of Christianity to argue that Jesus had no intention of founding a new religion and that present-day Christianity is a distortion of the New Testament.[5]

4. Hasdai ben Judah Crescas. Crescas (1340–1410/11), an innovative anti-Aristotelian and anti-Maimonidean philosopher, wrote two polemical treatises in the vernacular (probably Catalan), the originals of which are no longer extant. The philosophical polemic, *Biṭṭul ʿiqqarei ha-noṣerim* (The Refutation of the Christian Principles, ca. 1398), was translated into Hebrew by Joseph ben Shem Tov in 1451, but the latter did not bother rendering the second work into Hebrew, since it was based on biblical proof texts, and Joseph felt that a sufficient number of this type of polemic already existed in Hebrew. Crescas's book consists of an analysis of ten Christian doctrines, first explaining and then refuting the assumptions that lay behind them.[6]
5. Joshua Lorki. Lorki, mid-fourteenth century to early fifteenth century, wrote a polemical epistle to his former teacher, Solomon Halevi, after the latter had converted to Christianity and had taken upon himself the name Pablo de Santa Maria. Lorki attempts to understand why a learned Jew like Pablo would be convinced by Christianity, refuting what he considers to be the arguments that led to Pablo's conversion. Eventually Lorki himself converted to Christianity, became Gerónimo de Santa Fe, and initiated the Disputation of Tortosa.[7]
6. Joseph Albo. A participant in the Disputation of Tortosa, Albo (late fourteenth to mid-fifteenth centuries) wrote a philosophical/theological work, *Sefer ha-ʿIqqarim* (*The Book of Principles*), which includes subtle criticism of Christianity. Albo argues that only Judaism, and not Christianity, fulfills the definition of a divine religion. A specifically anti-Christian section is found in book 3, chapter 25.[8]
7. Simeon ben Zemah Duran. Duran (1361–1444), who emigrated from Iberia to Algeria after the 1391 riots, included anti-Christian (and anti-Muslim) passages in his *Magen ʾAvot* (The Shield of the Patriarchs), a commentary on Pirkei Avot. These were published separately under the title *Keshet u-magen* (*Bow and Shield*). His son, Solomon ben Simeon Duran (ca. 1400–1467), was born in Algeria, but he also wrote an anti-Christian polemic, *Milḥemet Miṣvah* (Obligatory War), against Joshua Lorki.[9]
8. Hayyim Ibn Musa. This Iberian physician (ca. 1380–ca. 1460) wrote *Magen va-romaḥ* (Shield and Sword) partly in response to the

arguments of Nicholas of Lyra (d. 1349) and partly in order to supply his fellow Jews with answers to the arguments of apostates.[10]

9. Joseph ben Shem Tov. In addition to his translation of Crescas's *Refutation*, this Iberian author (ca. 1400–ca. 1480) wrote a long introduction and commentary on Profiat Duran's *Epistle*, combatting what he claimed was the Christian misunderstanding that this work was written to promote Christianity.[11] He also wrote a short treatise entitled *Sefeiqot* (Doubts) concerning the story of Jesus.[12]
10. Isaac Abarbanel. Abarbanel (1437–1508) was born in Portugal, fled to Castile after the death of his royal patron, and was exiled to Italy after the expulsion from Spain. In Italy, he wrote a "messianic trilogy" of treatises, which attacked various aspects of Christian beliefs, the most directly polemical of which was *Yeshu'ot meshiḥo* (The Salvations of His Messiah), a refutation of the Christological interpretations of rabbinic passages adduced by Gerónimo at the Disputation of Tortosa.[13]
11. Other authors and literary works. A number of other Jewish writers included anti-Christian passages in their nonpolemical works, such as Abraham Bibago in *Derekh 'emunah* (*The Path of Faith*).[14] The poet Solomon Bonafed wrote a short letter to the *converso* Francesc de Sant Jordi, encouraging him to return to Judaism.[15] It is possible that *Hoda'at ba'al din* (The Litigator's Admission), attributed to David ha-Nasi, is also Iberian in origin.[16] In addition, there are two short Jewish accounts of the Disputation of Tortosa (1413–14) in Hebrew in addition to the official Latin protocol of this public disputation. Tortosa was particularly traumatic for the Jewish community, since its leadership was forced to spend more than a year and a half at the disputation while missionaries were given free rein to proselytize among the Jews.[17]

These works are remarkable not only for their quantity but also for some of their ostensibly innovative features. These innovations—including the use of satirical poems (Duran's *Epistle* and Bonafed), close analyses of Christian doctrines (Crescas and Duran's *Disgrace*), use of the vernacular (Crescas), and the like—indicate that Iberian Jewish authors invested heavily in the polemical enterprise during this period, both in their examination of

Christianity and in their attempts to bring original approaches to their argumentation. It would seem, therefore, that the evidence of these treatises calls into question two major conclusions I have come to in my research on polemical literature. My first conclusion is the questioning of the accepted narrative that Jewish criticism of Christianity is a function merely of Christian missionary threats in their various manifestations, whether literary, physical, or economic. I have argued that the explanation for the existence of the Jewish anti-Christian polemical genre as solely a Jewish defensive measure is in need of revision and that this explanation has its own apologetical motives.[18] My second conclusion has been that Jewish-Christian polemics have changed little in the nearly two thousand years of the debate.[19] In the following, I discuss whether the multiple Jewish anti-Christian polemical treatises produced during the final century of Jewish Iberia, with their new formats and contents, should prompt a rethinking of these two conclusions.

Let me discuss first the relationship between the Christian missionary threat and the production of Jewish anti-Christian writings. Since many Jews have been accustomed to think—or at least to state—that if members of other religions left Jews alone, then Jews would leave them alone, it follows that if Jews attacked Christian doctrines openly, it must have been in reaction to Christian provocation.[20] Nevertheless, we have many examples of Jewish anti-Christian polemic in the absence of a missionary threat, a prominent example of which comes from the Islamic world. If non-Muslims (*dhimmis*) were dissatisfied with their own religion, their only legal option was to convert to Islam; they could not change to a different *dhimmi* religion. Although we have many examples of exceptions to this rule,[21] there was certainly no place under Islam for an organized Christian mission to the Jews in which Christians attempted to persuade Jews, in one way or another, to become Christians. Yet the absence of such a Christian threat did not stop Jews from writing anti-Christian treatises. It was in the ninth century in Islamic countries when Jews first began to compose such works, most notably those by the first medieval Jewish philosopher, Dāwūd al-Muqammaṣ,[22] and the anonymous treatise that eventually was translated into Hebrew as *The Book of Nestor the Priest*.[23] In the tenth century, Saadia Gaon, whose literary production covered almost all fields of Jewish knowledge, included much anti-Christian material in his philosophical work *Kitāb al-ʾamānāt wal-ʾiʿtiqādāt* (*The Book of Beliefs and Opinions*) and in other works.[24] Anti-Christian polemic was a standard feature of the Jewish sectarian Karaite works written in Judaeo-Arabic in the tenth and eleventh centuries. As noted, these authors criticized Christianity even though there was no missionary pressure upon their communities.[25] Many centuries later, seventeenth- and eighteenth-century Italian Jews wrote at least fifty-six anti-Christian treatises in Hebrew. Although at this time and place, Jews were ghettoized, they hardly constituted a major focus of intensive Christian missionary activity throughout all those territories that are part of modern-day Italy. Such a large number of anti-Christian treatises cannot be explained as merely a Jewish response to the Christian mission.[26] We see, therefore, that there is no necessary correlation between a perceived Christian threat and Jewish attacks on Christianity, and hence it is difficult to regard all Jewish attacks on Christianity as purely defensive.

The question arises: How can one reconcile the view that the Jewish critique of Christianity is not necessarily connected to Christian missionary pressure with the proliferation of such critiques in post-1391 Iberia? If I am correct that Jews engaged in the criticism of Christianity even without outside stimuli—such as the threat of mass conversion, economic competition, or perhaps trying to win favor with non-Christian rulers—how do I explain what looks like a strong correlation between the historical situation in Iberia and the production of polemical treatises? And the answer is thus: the lack of a *necessary* connection between a Christian threat and Jewish polemical output does not imply that such a connection *never* existed. In the thirteenth century, another period of intense Christian anti-Jewish activity (e.g., the public disputations of Paris, 1240, and Barcelona, 1263), Jews turned to literary critiques of Christianity and introduced the genre of the written polemic into the Northern European repertoire. The almost simultaneous appearance of the account of the Disputation of Paris, Joseph ben Nathan Official's *Sefer Yosef ha-meqanne* (The Book of Joseph the Zealous), the anonymous *Niṣṣaḥon yashan* (The Old Book of Polemic), and a few other related texts in areas that hitherto had not produced written polemics is certainly not coincidental. It would seem that, indeed, Jews were responding to Christian pressure.[27] The case in late fourteenth- and fifteenth-century Iberia would appear to be similar: greater pressure brought about more literary activity. Thus although the medieval Jewish critique of Christianity is not necessarily tied to Christian pressure, it certainly can be. The examples of thirteenth-century

Northern Europe and fifteenth-century Iberia, when juxtaposed to ninth- and tenth-century Iraq and seventeenth- and eighteenth-century Italy, merely reinforce my contention that the motives for the production of Jewish polemical literature were complex and cannot be explained by one comprehensive theory. Sometimes Jewish attacks on Christianity were defensive, but often they reflected developments in Jewish theology and the need to define the differences between Judaism and Christianity.[28]

We should also look at the tone of the polemical works being discussed. A corollary of the theory that Jewish anti-Christian polemics are always a response to a Christian threat is the assertion that the greater the threat, the greater the acerbity of these works. The use of coarse language or vulgar argumentation against Christians has often been seen as a response to a serious provocation; presumably, otherwise Jewish authors would not have adopted such offensive language.[29] Yet this generalization does not hold, as an examination of the enumerated treatises demonstrates. If there were anyone who might have been expected to express anger at Christians in the wake of the 1391 riots, it would have been Hasdai Crescas, whose only son was murdered in those riots. But his work, *The Refutation*, is dry and technical, with hardly an emotion in sight (perhaps one of the reasons that some theorize that it was written with a Christian audience in mind). But Crescas is certainly not the only polemicist to be careful in his language. Shem Tov ibn Shaprut in his *Touchstone* attempted to rewrite Jacob ben Reuben's 1170 composition *Wars of the Lord*. By Shem Tov's time, this book was out of date not only because it ignored rabbinic literature but also because of the sharpness of its language, which, Shem Tov wrote, was inappropriate in his own day.[30] In contrast, Jewish vulgarity concerning Christianity has a long history, probably going back almost to the origins of Christianity. Thus the Jewish parody of the New Testament, *Toledot Yeshu* (The Life Story of Jesus), of uncertain date and provenance but elements of which go back to the early Christian centuries, assumes Jesus's illegitimate origins and mocks his life and death.[31] The aforementioned anonymous ninth-century Judaeo-Arabic composition and its Hebrew translation, *Nestor the Priest*, are particularly vulgar in their descriptions of female anatomy and the indignities of gestation, birth, and infancy, and they were written independently of any direct Christian missionary threat. In contrast, the Ashkenazi *Old Book of Polemic*, written at a time of Christian pressure on Jews, is very nasty, but this style may simply reflect the way Ashkenazi Jews wrote and not be connected to the context of its composition.[32] The cutting irony of Duran's works in the 1390s may represent his personal frustrations with life as a secret Jew; however, his style may simply be a function of what rhetoric Duran's audience would have appreciated. In short, neither the existence of a Jewish critique of Christianity nor the style in which it is presented is sufficient to determine by itself the existence or the nature of a perceived Christian threat to Judaism.[33] Evidence from the final one hundred years of Jewish presence in Iberia does not alter this conclusion.

The second conclusion that I would like to reconsider is that the contents of the Jewish-Christian debate have been constant for nearly two thousand years. Ever since the New Testament portrayed Jews as denying the possibility that Jesus was the Messiah (e.g., Matt. 27:42: "He saved others, but he cannot save himself"), even before one could talk of Judaism and Christianity as separate religions, the basic division between Judaism and Christianity, and the contents of the debate, have been unchanging: Was Jesus of Nazareth the Messiah predicted by the prophets or was he not? The rest is commentary.

Yet if we look at the Jewish polemical works from the period under discussion, there seem to be quite a few innovations. In fact, in Joseph ben Shem Tov's taxonomy of polemical treatises, in the introduction to his commentary to Duran's *Epistle*, he cites six different Jewish tactics of argumentation (*darekhei ha-vikuaḥ*) against Christianity: (1) biblical exegesis, (2) rabbinic exegesis, (3) attacks on Christian doctrines, (4) analysis of the contradictions between the New Testament and contemporary Christian doctrines, (5) attacks on Christian principles, and (6) comparison between Christianity and the principles of philosophy. In his discussion of these categories, Joseph writes that the first two types are represented by well-known classical polemical compositions, such as Jacob ben Reuben's *Wars of the Lord*, as an example of argumentation on the basis of biblical exegesis, and Nahmanides's account of the Disputation of Barcelona, as an example of the use of rabbinic exegesis. Exegetical arguments are those that concentrate on the correct interpretation of sacred texts, and most Jewish polemical works are based upon them. In contrast, Joseph's last four methods were apparently all new and were exemplified by more-modern works: Joshua Lorki's *Epistle*, as an attack on Christian doctrines; Duran's *Disgrace of the Gentiles*, which points out contradictions between the New Testament and Christian doctrines; Crescas's *Refutation*, which discusses the principles of Christianity; and Duran's *Epistle*, dedicated to philosophical principles.[34] It would seem, then, that not only did Iberian Jews respond to the renewed Christian threat in the wake of 1391; they also innovated new polemical tactics.

I would argue, however, that these innovations in Jewish polemical works written in response to the mass conversions after 1391 are a matter of form and not content. Just as Christians began using new tactics in the twelfth and thirteenth centuries, such as public debates and references to rabbinic literature, to persuade Jews that Christianity had superseded Judaism,[35] Jews in late medieval Iberia looked for new tactics to argue against the Christian position. Twelfth-century Christians started defending their religion with the use of rational arguments, and thirteenth-century Christians discovered the Talmud and forced Jews to participate in public debates; late fourteenth- and fifteenth-century Jews attempted to undermine the Christian arguments with learned analyses of Christian beliefs, references to Christian theological literature, use of the vernacular, and even bitter sarcasm. The strategic goals of the two sides remained the same even as these new tactics were deployed.

Looking deeper, however, we see that even those tactics that looked like Jewish innovations—from the attacks on Christian doctrines and discussion of theological and philosophical principles to the use of the vernacular and bitter sarcasm—were not so new. As noted, Duran's *Disgrace of the Gentiles* demonstrates extensive knowledge of Christian sources, and he uses these sources to argue that Christianity as he knew it was an invention not originally present in the New Testament. This argument had been used more than five hundred years earlier by Dāwūd al-Muqammaṣ, who also had lived part of his life as a Christian. Echoing what may have been the arguments of Jewish-Christians who had survived into the Islamic period, al-Muqammaṣ claimed that Christianity was the invention of Paul and not of Jesus.[36] Maimonides makes a similar observation in his *Epistle to Yemen*.[37] Thus Duran's distinction between *ṭoʿim*, "the mistaken ones" (namely, Jesus and his immediate followers), and the *maṭʿim*, "the deceivers" (namely, Paul and later Christians), has deep roots in Jewish anti-Christian polemics, even if Duran did not know the work of al-Muqammaṣ directly.

Hasdai Crescas wrote his polemics in the vernacular, and as mentioned, some scholars see this as an indication that he wrote for a Christian audience with the intention of explaining to them why Jews did not convert. The fact that he refers to "princes and nobles" who had requested that he write the book reinforces this theory. I have argued that there are many reasons why the *Refutation* was intended for Jews and that the princes and nobles were Jews and not Christians. For instance, Crescas wrote that his work was intended as a form of worship of God, hardly appropriate for an academic treatise designed for a Christian readership. Also, in addition to the *Refutation*, he wrote one other anti-Christian treatise in the vernacular that did not survive, since no one translated it into Hebrew. If his intended audience was Christians rather than Jews, and his motivation was explanatory and not polemical, why was one treatise not sufficient for a Christian readership?[38] Even the use of the vernacular is no indication of an intended Christian audience. Crescas's immediate predecessor in this tactic was Moses ha-Kohen of Tordesillas, who wrote two polemics, one in Hebrew and one in the vernacular. Moses noted explicitly that he was writing in the vernacular because there were Jews who were incapable of understanding his arguments in Hebrew. It is very possible that one of the reasons for the mass conversions in Iberia was the cultural assimilation that preceded them, in which Jews had become more comfortable with the vernacular than with Hebrew.

If we consider more closely the use of language in Jewish polemics, it would seem that, just as authors chose the type of argumentation and the tone according to the needs of the intended readership, so too was the choice of language a function of making their ideas accessible to potential readers. In Arabic-speaking countries, Jews wrote their polemics in Arabic; in the early modern period, when many Jews were more comfortable with the various vernaculars than with Hebrew, the polemicists wrote in the vernacular (Spanish, Portuguese, Italian, Yiddish, and others).[39] In English-speaking countries today, Jewish polemicists write in English and, as might be expected, are careful not to offend the sensitivities of their Jewish readers who would not be amenable to vulgar attacks on Christianity.[40] The debate continues even now, especially on the internet, as a perusal of the websites of Jews for Jesus and Jews for Judaism demonstrates. In the world of polemics, therefore, the medium is definitely not the message.

Another putative innovation was the ideology of the philosophical polemicists who wrote in the shadow of late medieval Averroism. Recognizing Averroes's criticism of religion as incapable of being substantiated by philosophical reasoning, these Jewish polemicists had to offer more than just a collection of rational arguments; they had to place those arguments into a framework that was not vulnerable to this criticism. Their solution was to distinguish between possibly true divine religions—which may be based on *natural* impossibilities, such as the parting of the Red Sea, the plagues in Egypt, the manna, and the like—and patently false candidates for the status of divine religion, which are based on *logical* impossibilities, such as the existence of a divine trinity in which God is both three and one or incarnation in which an incorporeal God can take on flesh and become human. In this argument, unsurprisingly, Judaism is said to be a legitimate candidate for a divine religion, but Christianity is not. This is the framework in which rational arguments were used by Crescas, the two Durans, Albo, and others.[41] Here again, this can be seen as a case of fine-tuning argumentation to take into account the latest developments in philosophy and the sensitivities of a philosophically trained readership rather than a complete innovation. This change is similar to the Jewish transition from discussions of the Trinity in terms of the attribute theories of the Muslim followers of the Kalam to those based on Aristotelian views of the same subject. Christian theologians and polemicists also had to revise their views in light of philosophical developments, such as Scholastic defenses of transubstantiation employing Aristotelian terms like *substance* and *accident*. For Jewish polemicists, philosophical arguments are one more arrow in their quiver for fighting the wars of the Lord by trying to persuade their fellow Jews that Jesus was not the anticipated Messiah and that Christianity is a false religion.[42]

If one looks, therefore, at Jewish anti-Christian polemics in light of mass conversion to Christianity, it appears that Jewish thinkers in late medieval Iberia were motivated to write their compositions by a perceived Christian threat, a threat that had, indeed, succeeded in transferring Jewish loyalty from the Torah of Moses to the Gospel of Jesus. This threat led them to search for innovative arguments and tactics to provide a convincing critique of Christianity to their coreligionists. But just as some of their innovations had precedents in earlier Jewish polemical literature, so too was their message the same as that of other Jewish polemicists who did not face a Christian threat—namely, Christianity is false and Jesus was not the Messiah. If these Iberian polemicists were writing in order to prevent apostasy, then judging by how widespread conversion was in the fifteenth century, especially among Jews who eventually chose Christianity over exile in 1492, they had limited success.

Notes

This research was supported by the I-CORE Program of the Planning and Budgeting Committee and the Israel Science Foundation (1754/12).

1. For a review of this period in Jewish history, see Baer, *History of the Jews*. An account of fifteenth-century Christian missionary literature, mostly from Iberia; anti-Jewish legislation and papal decrees; and the Jewish response is found in Schreckenberg, *Die christlichen Adversus*, 419–571. It should be noted that although it is clear that many Jews converted to Christianity, exact figures are lacking. In addition, it is well-nigh impossible to know how many of these conversions were the result of Christian violence (i.e., threats of murder and the impending expulsion) and how many were the result of true conviction on the side of the converts. A number of these sincere Jewish converts became part of the Christian mission to the Jews—see, for example, Sadik, "Between Ashkenaz and Sefarad." Although there was Christian pressure on Iberian Muslims during this century, and eventually they too were expelled, their situation will not be considered here.
2. There are a number of ways to refer to Iberian Jewish converts to Christianity; *converso* is meant to be a neutral designation. If the polemics were addressed to *conversos* with the hope of undermining their acceptance of their new religion, they were written despite the knowledge that return to Judaism would not be possible on Iberian soil.
3. The Hebrew texts are available in Shamir, *Rabbi Moses Ha-Kohen*.
4. There is no full edition of Ibn Shaprut's work, but it can be consulted in part in Frimer, "Critical Edition of *Eben Bohan*"; and in Frimer and Schwartz, *Hagut be-Ṣeil ha-ʾEimah*; Garshowitz, "Shem tov ben Isaac"; and Niclós Albarracín, *Šem Ṭob Ibn Šapruṭ*. An edition of Jacob ben Reuben's book is available, edited by Judah Rosenthal. See Jacob ben Reuben, *Milḥamot ha-shem*.
5. These two works have been edited by Talmage, *Polemical Writings*. On Duran, see Kozodoy, *Secret Faith*. A partial English translation of the epistle is found in Kobler, *Letters of Jews*, 276–82. Duran may also have been the author of another short anti-Christian treatise, *Teshuvot be-ʾanshei ʾaven* (*Answers to Evil People*); see Niclós Albarracín, *Profiat Durán*. Kozodoy writes that this attribution is "unlikely" (*Secret Faith*, 215).
6. Lasker, *Biṭṭul ʿiqqarei ha-noṣerim*; translation: Lasker, *Hasdai Crescas' Refutation*.
7. Landau, *Apologetische Schreiben*.
8. Albo, *Sefer ha-ʿikkarim*, 3:217–45.
9. The two works were published together, first in Livorno in 1762–63 and then in Jerusalem by Makor in 1969–70. Another edition of *Keshet u-magen* is available in Murciano, "Simon ben Zemah Duran"; and the anti-Islam section was edited by Moritz Steinschneider and republished in Berlin in 1880–81.
10. Hayyim ibn Musa, *Magen va-Romaḥ*, MS Heb. 8° 787, National Library of Israel,

Jerusalem, copied by Adolf Posnanski and published in Jerusalem 1969–70.

11. Duran, *Iggeret ʾAl Tehi Ka-ʾAvotekha*, MS Heb. 8° 757, National Library of Israel, Jerusalem, copied by Adolf Posnanski and published in Jerusalem 1969–70.
12. Regev, "*Sefeiqot*."
13. Abarbanel, *Yeshuʿot meshiḥo*. On these compositions, see Lawee, *Isaac Abarbanel's Stance*; Lawee, "Messianism of Isaac Abarbanel."
14. Bibago, *Derekh ʾemunah*.
15. Talmage, "Francesc de Sant Jordi-Solomon."
16. Nasi, *Hodaʿat Baʿal Din*. My colleague Harvey J. Hames translates it thus: "Admission of Guilt," and it is he who believes the treatise was written in Iberia and not in Crete, where the author places the account. See Hames, "On This Rock." Another probable fifteenth-century Iberian Jewish polemic is *Sefer Aḥituv ve-Ṣalmon*, attributed to Mattathias ben Moses ha-Yitzhari, who was a participant in the Disputation of Tortosa. See Lara Olmo, "Edición crítica." It is unclear if the attribution is correct and when exactly this work was written.
17. The Latin protocol was published by Pacios López, *Disputa de Tortosa*. For Hebrew accounts of Tortosa, see ibn Verga, *Shevet Yehudah*, 94–107; Halberstam, "Vikkuaḥ Tortosa." A Hebrew refutation of Gerónimo's accusations against the Talmud is still in manuscript, but the part that includes the accusations was published by Valle Rodríguez, "Atalaya del judaísmo hispano." I would like to thank Yosi Yisraeli for discussing this text with me.
18. See Lasker, "Jewish Critique of Christianity."
19. See, for example, the following articles I have written over the course of a number of years: Lasker, "Jewish-Christian Polemics"; Lasker, "Impact of the Crusades"; and Lasker, "Jewish Anti-Christian Polemics."
20. See the sources adduced in my article, Lasker, "Jewish Critique of Christianity."
21. The database being developed by the Center for the Study of Conversion and Interreligious Relations at Ben-Gurion University has been documenting examples of conversions to and from all three religions in the Islamic world.
22. See Stroumsa, *Dāwūd Ibn Marwān*.
23. Lasker and Stroumsa, *Polemic of Nestor the Priest*.
24. Saadia Gaon, *Kitāb al-ʾamānāt*. See Lasker, "Saadya Gaon on Christianity."
25. On Jewish polemics against Christianity in Islamic countries, see Lasker, "Jewish Critique of Christianity."
26. Jews were forced to hear Christian missionizing sermons in Rome from the late sixteenth until the eighteenth century, and there were some Italian Jewish converts. See, for example, Mazur, *Conversion to Catholicism*. The question remains as to whether there is a correlation between specific areas of anti-Jewish missionary activity and the Jewish polemical output. I thank Emily Michelson for discussing this issue with me. An enumeration of Hebrew anti-Christian polemics written by Italian Jews in the seventeenth and eighteenth centuries is contained in a research project conducted by Károly Dániel Dobos and Gerhard Langer, who were kind enough to share this list of polemical treatises with me. See also Lasker, "Jewish Anti-Christian Polemics."
27. See Lasker, "Joseph ben Nathan." The text of *Sefer Yosef ha-meqanne* is available in Judah Rosenthal's edition. The Hebrew text and an English translation of *Niṣṣaḥon yashan* are available in Berger, *Jewish-Christian Debate*.
28. See Lasker, "Jewish Critique of Christianity," for a discussion of some of the nondefensive motivations behind Jewish anti-Christian polemics.
29. An attempt to correlate the tone of the polemics with the level of missionary

pressure on Jews is offered by Trautner-Kromann, *Shield and Sword.*

30. Niclós Albarracín, *Šem Ṭob Ibn Šapruṭ*, 7.
31. Meerson and Schäfer, *Toledot Yeshu.* Some of this mockery is reflected in certain rabbinic passages and in references contained in early Christian literature.
32. Lasker, "Joseph ben Nathan."
33. See Lasker, "Popular Polemics and Philosophical Truth"; Lasker, "Jewish Critique of Christianity."
34. Duran, *Iggeret*, 22–26.
35. Chazan, *Daggers of Faith.*
36. This is reported by the tenth-century Karaite Yaʿqūb al-Qirqisānī; see Chiesa and Lockwood, *Yaʿqūb al-Qirqisānī*, 137. For a possible Jewish-Christian connection, see Pines, "Jewish Christians."
37. See also Lerner, *Maimonides' Empires of Light*, 104.
38. As noted previously, the second treatise was not translated. See Crescas, *Refutation*, 8–10, 84; Lasker, "R. Hasdai Crescas' Polemical Activity."
39. The last major Jewish anti-Christian polemic is *Ḥizzuq 'Emunah* (Faith Strengthened), by the Karaite Isaac Abraham of Troki, completed around 1594. Subsequently, it was translated into Dutch, Ladino, Yiddish, German, English (by Jews), and Latin (by Christians who wished to refute it). See Walfish with Kizilov, *Bibliographia Karaitica*, 560–63.
40. A good example is Berger and Wyschogrod, *Jews and Jewish Christianity.*
41. See Lasker, "Averroistic Trends."
42. On the Jewish use of philosophy in anti-Christian polemics, see Lasker, *Jewish Philosophical Polemics.*

6

THEOLOGY OF THE LAWS AND ANTI-JUDAIZING POLEMICS IN HERNANDO DE TALAVERA'S *CATÓLICA IMPUGNACIÓN*

Davide Scotto

Paulina:
It is required
You do awake your faith. Then all stand still;
Or those that think it is unlawful business
I am about, let them depart.
—Shakespeare, *The Winter's Tale*

Introduction

Sometime after the death of the Hieronymite monk Hernando de Talavera (1428–1507)—the confessor of Queen Isabel—Jerónimo de Madrid, one of his disciples and a canon of the Granada Cathedral, wrote the first Castilian hagiography of Talavera, which established the general outline of how he would subsequently be portrayed and continues to shape biographies on him even today.[1] Chapter 11 of this work, "Santa vida de Fray Hernando de Talavera," is devoted to Talavera's ardent faith. Making reference to Paul, Jerónimo points to the Christian interpretation of the Jewish Law as a matter of primary relevance for Talavera's preaching activity, which was rooted in the persistent use of the Bible. Although his preaching was addressed to both Jewish and Muslim converts, former Jews are labeled "hardened" (*endurecidos*) and thus regarded as the main target audience for his sermons:

> He never preached sermons that did not touch on marvelous matters of faith, knowing well what he did. Though many new converts of both Jewish and Islamic origin listened to him, his preaching was especially needful for the Jewish converts. He made them clearly understand that their law was a figure and a shadow of the Catholic faith, proving this argument through the Scriptures, which he always carried in his hands, so insistently that even if they were hardened, he succeeded in softening them. This is true to the point that I doubt that there are still Christians belonging to this nation in the whole kingdom.[2]

As far as I know, this passage from Jerónimo's hagiography has never been discussed by scholars. Yet it reflects a supremely important aspect of Talavera's theological thinking and his long-term project of evangelization, which was conceived for both Jewish and Muslim converts. Talavera, the first archbishop of Granada following the Reconquest, has been of interest to scholars mainly for his manifold writings in moral theology[3] or his much-debated role among the Muslims in late fifteenth-century Granada.[4] Much less attention has been paid, however, to his sustained reflection on Jewish converts, which lasted at least from his appointment as prior of the monastery of Nuestra Señora de Prado in Valladolid (1470) to his polemical work against the "Judaizing heresy,"[5] the *Católica impugnación*, written sometime after 1478 and published in Salamanca in 1487.

For some reason, this treatise all but disappeared from hagiographic accounts down to the twentieth century. Only the punctilious historian José de Sigüenza mentioned it briefly in his renowned history of the Hieronymite order from 1605,[6] and a few decades later, the Sevillian bibliographer Nicolás Antonio roughly summarized its main argument in his *Bibliotheca hispana nova*.[7] The less-than-favorable reception of Talavera's work goes back to the decades immediately following his death. As far as our evidence allows us to say, the circulation of the *Católica impugnación* was rather small and met with opposition from the ecclesiastical authorities. Among Talavera's works, it was the only one to be condemned by the Inquisition—it was listed in the Valdés index of prohibited books in 1559,[8] which might explain why it survives today only in the 1487 Salamanca edition.[9] This oblivion notwithstanding, the work's importance in terms of creative theological thinking can hardly be overstated. Talavera dealt with the fine points of conversion from Islam in a few letters to the Catholic Monarchs and two brief memorandums about the education of the New Christians in Granada,[10] but the *Católica impugnación* is the only work that contains a theological discussion of his much-contested view on non-Christians, providing an apology of Christian faith and practices in the face of the threat of a Judaizing heterodoxy.

Following the rediscovery of this treatise at Rome's Biblioteca Vallicelliana in the 1930s,[11] three scholars published studies on specific aspects of it—namely, the nature of the Judaizing threat to which Talavera reacted (Francisco Márquez Villanueva), the related debate on the Inquisition in Castile (Stefania Pastore), and the use of images for evangelization (Felipe Pereda).[12] These narrowly defined studies are essential for establishing the relevance of Talavera's polemics to the growing scholarly debate on heterodoxy, Christianization, and conversion in late medieval Castile. Nonetheless, scholarship of a broader scope devoted to Talavera's biography and works has largely disregarded the *Católica impugnación* and has thus neglected to deal with its recurring, underlying theme: the thorny doctrinal discussion of Jewish Law and religious practices in light of Paul's epistles. This exegetical reflection, however, turns out to be pivotal not only to outline Talavera's harsh polemics against a Judaizing interpretation of Christian faith and practices but also to understand his attitude toward Muslims during his thirty-year pastoral activity and ecclesiastical career.

In view of the purpose of this book, I will examine the *Católica impugnación* with a special focus on the polemical arguments against a Judaizing interpretation of the "old" and the "new" Law, held by Talavera to be perniciously heretical. To do so, in the first part of this chapter, I will trace the *converso*-Christian tensions in Seville in 1478, outlining the events that led to Talavera's involvement as a preacher and, later on, to the writing of his refutation. An examination of these events must also entail an open question regarding the possible relation between the *Católica impugnación* and Talavera's previous homiletic activity as prior of the monastery of Prado. In the second part, I will shed light upon the nature of the Judaizing pamphlet and discuss the aim, method, and dating of Talavera's polemic. In the third part, I will examine the relationship between the "old" and the "new" Law by looking at the dedication, the prologue, and the first thirty-three chapters of the *Católica impugnación*, highlighting a series of exegetical arguments that have thus far gone unnoticed by scholars. Talavera applies the theology laid out in Paul's epistles in response to a concrete instance of Judaizing, thus embracing a way of arguing that can be defined as a coherent "theology of the Laws." In the fourth and last part, I will correlate Talavera's reflection on the two Laws to his heresiological thinking by tracing the subtle difference he suggests among Judaizers, Jewish converts, and biblical and contemporary Jews. The resurfacing of heresiology in late medieval Castile raises intriguing questions about the risk of syncretism, different views of evangelization, and the capacity of Christian theology to confront crucial challenges emerging from shifting interreligious circumstances. In the conclusion, I will tackle the ultimate nature of Talavera's polemic.

Seville, 1478: Christian Preaching against Judaizing Practices

The activity of Hernando de Talavera as a preacher in Seville and the subsequent polemics behind the *Católica impugnación* can be traced to a series of riots that occurred in the city between 1478 and 1480, while he was a participant in several political meetings as an influential advisor at the royal court. From July 8 to August 1, 1478, as representative of the Catholic Monarchs, he took part in the Council of Seville, an episcopal assembly summoned to address issues of ecclesiastical politics and Church reform.[13] In 1479, he played an important role in the diplomatic mediation resulting in peace treaties between Castile and Portugal. In 1480, he participated in the Cortes of Toledo, where he negotiated the reduction of annuities paid out of royal revenues to the nobility, which had been illegitimately established during the reign of Henry IV.[14]

During the Catholic Monarchs' stay in Seville from July 1477 to October 1478,[15] a serious riot broke out among the Christian population against a group of Jewish converts (*conversos*). As in previous instances of unrest in Toledo (1449–67) and Cordoba (1473), *conversos* were accused of illegally observing Jewish ceremonies, food habits, prayers, and rites rather than following Christian practices.[16] In the dedicatory letter to the Catholic Monarchs at the beginning of the *Católica impugnación*, Talavera claims that in 1478, a group of Jewish converts (*los nuevamente convertidos*) had disgraced Seville and its surroundings by weakening the Catholic faith and obstinately practicing

Jewish rituals and ceremonies. These events are recounted in more detail in contemporaneous Castilian chronicles. It is within the political circumstances they describe that Talavera performed his pastoral activities in Seville.[17]

Apart from scattered remarks in the chronicle of the Catholic Monarchs' reign written by Fernando del Pulgar,[18] the most detailed account of the confrontation referred to by Talavera can be found in an early sixteenth-century chronicle by Andrés Bernáldez, parish priest of Los Palacios and chaplain of the archbishop of Seville, the Dominican friar Diego de Deza.[19] Despite its harsh language and deeply anti-Jewish stance,[20] Bernáldez's account is valuable as a summary of the urgent issues the Church and the Crown had to face, both locally and more broadly, throughout their realms. Besides a series of derogatory remarks on Jewish dietary practices, the practice of Sabbath, and the rite of baptism, Bernáldez's account is unique in that he is the only chronicler who comments on the actions taken by the local church against the Judaizing threat.

According to this account, the Dominican friar Alonso de Ojeda, "un sancto y católico hombre," prior of the convent of San Pablo in Seville, was among the ecclesiastics who appealed to the Catholic Monarchs to intervene in the turmoil in Seville. For a long time, he had been preaching aggressively against the Judaizers and eventually, together with other unnamed churchmen, informed the monarchs about the ongoing riots, pressuring them to take a position on the spread of heresy. Hence Bernáldez accounts for the establishment of the Inquisition in Castile by claiming that in 1481, the monarchs appointed Alonso the first inquisitor of Seville as a reward for his commitment to their pastoral campaign.[21] The chronicler also feels the need to stress that this radical measure was taken after a two-year campaign of preaching against the observance of the "old" Law that had not achieved the desired result.[22] Whether this claim can be regarded as a proof of the failure of Talavera's preaching activity is hard to prove. It is worthwhile to note, however, that a similar correlation between the ineffective pastoral campaigns of unnamed churchmen (*estos religiosos*) sent by the monarchs to preach against Judaizers (*estos que judaizaban*) and the establishment of the Inquisition by papal bull is recorded in Fernando del Pulgar's chronicle. Here too the obduracy, blindness, and ignorance (*pertinaçia, ceguedat, ynorançia*) of the members of a pernicious heresy (*herética pravedat*) are seen as the main reasons behind the political shift announced by the Crown.[23]

Regardless of whatever concrete effects it may have produced in terms of persuading remiss Jewish converts, the preaching period from 1478 to 1480 is closely connected to the origins of the *Católica impugnación*. Informed about the unrest, in 1478 the monarchs requested two renowned ecclesiastics to curtail the Judaizing bent by preaching on Jewish Law and Christian religious practices. The first was the archbishop of Seville, Cardinal Pedro González de Mendoza, whom Pope Innocent VIII later appointed commissioner-general of the Bull of the Crusade in Spain; his mission also included a mandate for the bishop of Cádiz, Pedro Fernández Solís, to preach as well. The second was Hernando de Talavera, who was in charge of leading the pastoral activities.[24] From the perspective of the Catholic Monarchs, who chose two zealous churchmen well educated in theology to lead the campaign, the heretical threat raised by the presence of a group of militant Judaizers had to be countered, at least initially, by means of moral persuasion, legal warnings, and spiritual exhortation.

Among contemporary sources, only the *Católica impugnación* describes the concrete actions taken against the Judaizers following the monarchs' decision. As a first measure, Cardinal Mendoza issued an injunction on religious practices that Talavera helped draft and that was in agreement with both the Seville Cathedral chapter and the bishop of Cádiz. As Stefania Pastore has emphasized, this decision was part of a broader strategy by a group of distinguished Spanish churchmen—both "old" and "new" Christians—to prevent the establishment of the Inquisition in Castile, a much-debated measure that in 1478 was close to being enacted.[25] There are no known extant copies of this injunction, but its contents can be inferred to some extent by examining chapter 53 of the *Católica impugnación*. Here, Talavera claims to cite the injunction word for word, bearing witness to one of the core issues of the pastoral agenda promoted by the Crown. He makes clear that it imposed on all Christians, including *conversos*, the obligation to keep painted images of the crucifix, the Virgin Mary, and Christian saints in their houses in order to rouse (*provocar*) or awake (*despertar*) their faith.[26]

In the dedicatory letter to the Catholic Monarchs, Talavera elaborates on the origins of his refutation. He states that he wrote his polemic as a reaction to a pamphlet—today presumed lost—written by an anonymous Judaizer to contest the prohibition against New Christians practicing Jewish rites and ceremonies. It was Queen Isabel who made Talavera aware of this pamphlet during one of her visits to the Nuestra Señora del Prado monastery in Valladolid, hence his dedication to the Catholic Monarchs. He also claims that the pamphlet was written not just in response to the injunction on religious practices but also "against the sermons I preached in Seville in the year 1478 to extol and corroborate our very holy Catholic faith." These sermons were aimed at demonstrating the superiority of the Gospels to the "old" Law, a "dead law" whose commandments, ceremonies, opinions, and precepts—Talavera often highlights these four aspects together—had ceased to be valid after the coming of Christ.[27] This common argument, which was first expressed in Talavera's sermons, was later developed in a literary form in the *Católica impugnación*. The Catholic Monarchs' decision to send trusted preachers to Seville to confront the Judaizing threat is closely related to the doctrinal contents of Talavera's preaching on the cessation of the "old" Law. The effectiveness of this program inevitably depended on Talavera's expertise and reputation as not only a political advisor but also an expert in theology and a persuasive speaker on spiritual matters. Interestingly, Talavera's preaching activity of 1478 is recalled again in chapter 18 of his polemic in connection to the doctrinal arguments developed in this and other chapters. Here he clarifies that in Seville, he had preached "openly" and "many times" about the supersession of Jewish Law.

At this point, an obvious question arises: To what extent it is possible to infer the contents of Talavera's sermons? One source that might provide evidence for their contents is the collection of sermons preserved in MS 332 of the Biblioteca Lázaro Galdiano, Madrid. This little-known precious manuscript preserves the only extant sermons written by Talavera—namely, the *Colación muy provechosa*—together with his completely overlooked exegetical treatise on John the Evangelist, the *Tratado de loores de San Juan Evangelista*, both of them addressed to Queen Isabel.[28] The date of the sermons in the *Colación* was previously unknown, making it possible to hypothesize that these were the 1478 sermons. However, Carmen Parrilla recently ascertained beyond doubt that the *Colación* consists of a series of sermons related to Talavera's preaching at the Prado monastery the first Sunday after Advent 1475—that is, December 3, 1475.[29] A short time afterward, Isabel invited Talavera to put these sermons into writing, as she did for his treatise on John the Evangelist, also composed at the Prado monastery. As their respective prefatory chapters suggest, sometime in 1476, Talavera reworked the drafts of both these texts and soon after sent the finalized versions to Isabel.[30]

Both the *Colación* and the *Tratado* contain scattered remarks on the relation between the "old" and "new" Law, thus providing insight into Talavera's early thinking about non-Christians. In the *Colación,* he employs the classical image of the Church as a body, in which Christ is the head and the body is made of a plurality of arms, an organicist concept that Paul derived from Greek political philosophy and that was widely adopted in Christian theology from Augustine on.[31] Inspired by chapter 2 of Paul's letter to the Ephesians, this image introduces a second, less obvious metaphor: the temple or the Church as a building whose two main walls represent, respectively, two peoples who have been long opposed to one another—namely, the Christians and the Jews.[32] Moreover, in chapter 1 of the second part of the *Tratado*, wherein Christians are warned to rely not on external influences but rather on inner faith in God, Talavera turns to chapter 6 of Paul's epistle to the Galatians, in which he claims that circumcision and prepuce have no value in Christ. Accordingly, being a Jew or a pagan neither hinders nor helps becoming a good believer, a spiritual transformation that is brought about only by the new cohabitation (*nueva conversación*) with the living person of Christ.[33] Dating from two years before the riots of Seville, Talavera's homiletic and exegetical writings from 1476 provide valuable background for the theological reflection on the Laws he would later develop to confront the Judaizers. It is even possible that these early works were influential enough to have convinced Isabel to send her confessor to preach in Seville. As such, the *Colación* and the *Tratado* would represent the immediate precedents for the pastoral strategies that Talavera would employ toward the apologists of the "old" Law two years later.

Framing the *Católica impugnación*: Polemical Aims and Strategies

We know that the preaching activities of 1478, together with the injunction on religious practices, was the reason behind the spread in Seville of a "heretical, wicked, and excommunicated pamphlet" brought to Talavera's attention by Queen Isabel.[34] Since the pamphlet is thought to have been lost, one cannot reconstruct its contents in their entirety. In fact, we cannot even be certain that the pamphlet existed, given the widespread use of fictitious interlocutors in medieval interfaith polemics, literary dialogues, and epistolary treatises.[35] It is entirely possible that the Judaizing author mentioned by Talavera never existed and was, instead, a purely imaginary interlocutor. However, considering the elaborate series of focused allusions Talavera made to the pamphlet's contents, there is no compelling reason to doubt its existence. Despite the absence of literal quotations from the pamphlet, there is a remarkable amount of detail in the summaries of the Judaizing claims. In the *Católica impugnación*, various arguments from the pamphlet are presented in detail and then rejected, though it is clear that they are arranged in a way that supports Talavera's rhetorical strategy rather than respecting the order they were originally presented in the pamphlet.[36]

Over the course of the seventy-seven chapters of the *Católica impugnación*, Talavera develops a coherent response to the pamphlet's contents using the Scholastic method of dialectical reasoning—that is, argument, counterargument, and conclusive thesis. Thematically, the seventy-seven chapters can be roughly divided into three parts: in the first part, chapters 1 to 26 and 31 to 33, coherently following the same method, Talavera reacts to the Judaizer's invective at a purely doctrinal level, engaging the relation between the "old" and the "new" Law through persistent exegetical reasoning; the second and most extensive part, chapters 27 to 70 (excepting 31 to 33), is devoted to diverse Jewish or Judaizing religious practices outlined in general or for Seville in particular; in the third and last part, chapters 71 to 77, the author develops in a more systematic way his ideas about the function of the Bible scattered throughout the previous chapters, focusing on the Judaizing interpretation of the prophetic books and the Gospels.[37]

This Scholastic method allows us to infer the pamphlet's argumentative structure and assert that, like other Jewish, Christian, and Islamic writings belonging to the same genre, it had two theological purposes—namely, an apologetic and a polemical one.[38] Through apology, the anonymous author asserted that it was necessary to fully preserve the validity of the Jewish Law to seek Christian perfection and salvation. In support of this assertion, he defended an ethnic interpretation of Christ as a Jew and relied on a strictly literal reading of the Bible that safeguarded it from what he criticized as the widespread Christian habit of "syllogizing"—that is, speculating on scripture through symbolic or allegorical interpretations that distanced the text from its alleged original meaning. On the other hand, he aimed to confront "old Christians," including Talavera himself—whom he criticized personally for his preaching in Seville—on Christian doctrine (the Trinity, idolatry, etc.), religious practices (burial, slaughter, the use of images, ways of praying), and the habits of churchmen, which he harshly condemned for their immoral behavior.[39] At the same time, presenting himself as an authentic Christian in contrast to corrupted or heterodox Christians, he presumed to teach Christians about true Christian doctrine: "This insolent fool claims that he wants to teach us what the law of Christ and Christian doctrine actually are."[40]

Regardless of his real religious identity—a Jewish convert following a syncretic religion or a Jew, as Talavera seems to believe[41]—there can be little doubt that the author of the pamphlet was a real figure and, hence, that Talavera examined and refuted an existing writing. At the same time, throughout his refutation, he casts his adversary in conventional literary and theological terms. Brandishing long-established authorities, he provides a theologically meaningful characterization of his adversary and summarizes the doctrinal charges against him. He addresses him in the first person and labels him "old man" (*hombre viejo*), grown old through sin (*en pecados envejecido*), for he was not renewed by the acquaintance with Christ that according to Paul leads to the birth of "new men" through redemption. Moreover, referring to the new revelation contained in the Gospels, he claims that the Judaizer's eyes were veiled—an allusion to the widespread medieval anti-Jewish topos of *cecitas*, "blindness"[42]—for he could neither see nor comprehend what had been made open and clear.[43] Reacting to the pamphlet's incitement, he intends to show his readers the reasons behind what he considers a clear doctrinal deviation (*muy manifiesta herejía*). By his own admission, the Judaizer misunderstood the Gospels, as he read them "without affection" (*sin afección*), while he understood the First Testament commandments recalled in the Gospel of Matthew in merely legal terms rather than seeing them properly in moral terms.[44]

It is not surprising that more than once, Talavera implicitly grants the validity of the pamphlet's charges against reprehensible churchmen and the corruption of the Church in his day, reflecting his deep commitment to the reform of the Church, which stretched back to long before his pastoral experience in Granada.[45] Except for that, his reaction to the pamphlet's attack on Christian doctrine and religious practices is extremely polemical, which is reflected in both the contents and the language of his refutation. In the prologue of the *Católica impugnación*, St. Jerome's battle against ancient heresies is taken as a model to demonstrate the potential influence of the heterodox pamphlet on both doctrinal and practical levels. The doctrinal level provides the hermeneutic pattern through which the whole refutation is legitimized, including a series of subpolemics on diverse aspects of daily interfaith coexistence—for example, the use of images, religious feasts, dietary habits, and burial practices.[46]

In the prologue, Talavera explains also the counterargumentative method he employs in refuting (*impugnar*) the Judaizing claims. He intends not to transcribe the "cursed pamphlet" word for word but rather to examine a selection of its arguments to show through his refutation that they amount to "insanities, foolishness, heretical claims and idle talk." This choice of method is not due to the complexity of the pamphlet's statements or any theological difficulty in refuting its claims. Through this clarification Talavera instead attempts to reassure his readers and possible ecclesiastical censors about his intentions: if he will, on rare occasions, have to mention any of the pamphlet's arguments verbatim, it will be with the sole aim of disproving and destroying them completely. As he emphasizes, the decision to omit literal quotations from the Judaizing pamphlet follows a well-established Christian practice regarding heresy, consisting of not spreading heretical doctrine but rather summarizing it solely to the extent that it can be finally refuted and hence annihilated. Those readers who wish to learn more about the contents of the pamphlet must not engage extensively with its vain, inconsequential arguments, which he characterizes, moreover, as aimless and incoherent.[47]

There might be a further, less obvious reason for Talavera exercising caution, lest he inadvertently spread Judaizing ideas. This has a bearing on the question of the exact dating of the *Católica impugnación*. Francisco Márquez Villanueva and Stefania Pastore have wavered between 1480 and 1481 for the year when the work was written, which would mean Talavera was working on it either right before or right after the Inquisition was established and began operating in Castile.[48] This difficulty in dating Talavera's work and, in fact, the absence in its seventy-seven chapters of an explicit anti-Inquisition polemic, should warn one about relating in a one-directional way its origin to the political issues behind the establishment of the Inquisition in Castile, as if that was its predominant concern. As a full examination of its arguments shows, its main concern was instead with the persistence of a set of religious practices regarded as "Judaizing" and their profound consequences for both salvation history (i.e., conversion) and Christianization (i.e., assimilation).

In the light of more recent research and given the information provided in the work's detailed *titulus*—which states that Talavera is already bishop of Avila, an appointment he obtained only in 1485—I tend to believe that the suggested dating is too early and that the year 1487 is not just the publication date of the editio princeps but, in fact, also the most suitable date for the work's final drafting. As such, that year might also correspond to the beginning of the work's circulation beyond Talavera's circle, after having had preliminary readings by Queen Isabel and Talavera's closest colleagues. Moreover, this dating would also relate to a key episode in the late fifteenth-century *converso*-Christian controversy. On April 7, 1486, the Hieronymite order launched internal inquiries led by two monks and an additional clergyman or layman in order to identify and drive out possible "Judaizing" monks. In 1485, there had been a dangerous precedent in the case of the Hieronymite monk Diego de Marchena, a resident of the monastery of Santa María de Guadalupe. Allegedly the son of *conversos*, he was accused of living there as a Jew and in the end confessed, under torture, to having been circumcised.[49] Within this debate, the *Católica impugnación*, besides providing a focused polemic against one pamphlet in particular, could have been seen by its author as a way to defend the orthodoxy of the Hieronymite order against these insinuations.

The Gospels as *Carta de Pago*: Exegetical Arguments in the Footsteps of Paul

The *Católica impugnación* provides a vivid example of how Paul's polemical view of the "newness" and "oldness" of the Law was implemented in the context of a particular controversy. The work's extensive length, complex organization, and intellectual depth make it one of the most sophisticated medieval works specifically centering on a "theology of the Laws." In addition to Talavera's refutation, other important fifteenth-century works that dealt with Jewish-Christian polemics in Iberia were Alonso de Cartagena's *Defensorium unitatis christianae*, Juan de Torquemada's *Tractatus contra Madianitas et Ismaelitas*, and Alonso de Oropesa's *Lumen ad revelationem gentium et gloriam plebis tuae Israel*,[50] three works that also engage with Paul's ideas on the role of the Jews in Christian salvation history. Although they are marked by different theological sensitivities, all four works provide apologetic arguments in favor of *converso* communities under attack after the Toledo riots of 1449, in opposition to exclusivist views such as those expressed in Alonso de Espina's *Fortalitium fidei*.[51] Although Talavera's attitude toward the Jewish Law and the ultimate aim of his refutation are different from the main objectives of these other contemporary works, his exegetical arguments are, like theirs, indebted to Paul's view of the two Laws as outlined especially in the epistles to the Romans and the Galatians. Moreover, the prominence given to Paul's theology in the *Católica impugnación* closely resembles Juan Andrés's use of the apostle's letters as exemplary sources about conversion strategies in his anti-Islamic treatise from 1515.[52]

Talavera sees Paul as the most authoritative source for the debate on conversion and for its spiritual implications not just in the *Católica impugnación* but also in some of his other works. Evidence of Paul's influence in shaping his theological thinking before 1478 can be found in the most exacting of his moral writings, the *Breve forma de confesar*.[53] Warning bishops about the need to scrutinize the morality and religious education of their subordinates, Talavera points here to the three conditions outlined by Paul in the first epistle to Timothy: bishops must demonstrate impeccable moral behavior (one marriage only, sobriety, self-respect, no violence or quarrels, no addiction to wine or avarice, etc.), they must take care of their families and children in order to likewise take care of the Church, and they must not be neophytes, lest they fall into arrogance like the devil did (3:1–7).

Proof of Talavera's acquaintance with Paul's ideas can also be found in the homiletic writings that he composed less than two years before the Seville riots (i.e., the *Colación muy provechosa* and the *Tratado de loores de San Juan Evangelista*). In the *Colación*, he recalls Paul's allusion to original sin and interprets the metaphor of the double-walled Church in reference to the relationship between Jews and Christians.[54] Moreover, he provides a portrait of the apostle Paul as an exemplary leader who surpasses all his First Testament predecessors. This passionate description is placed at the end of a list of biblical figures, going from Abraham to Job to Samuel, evoked to urge Christian believers to behave sincerely and liberally toward their fellow beings. Relying on the metaphor of the eagle that he found in a copy of Bartholomeus Anglicus's *Liber de proprietatibus rebus* presented to him by Queen Isabel,[55] Talavera portrays Paul as a moral leader who embodies all virtues: "A good eagle, good churchman, good captain and governor, St. Paul provided himself and his fellows with that which was necessary by working with his own hands and, at night, keeping watch."[56]

In the *Tratado*, Talavera turns once again to Paul in a theologically brilliant way, comparing him to John the Evangelist, whose spiritual features he enumerates over the course of this treatise. He claims that John has been endowed with the eight beatitudes mentioned in the Gospel of Matthew (5:3–10, from the Sermon on the Mount) as well as all twelve fruits of the Spirit and nine graces (*gratis data*) described in Galatians 5:22 and 1 Corinthians 12, respectively.[57] As a powerful mirror, Paul's authoritative figure is brought into sharp focus to legitimize by analogy the exceptionality of John the Evangelist in the eyes of the readers.

In the *Católica impugnación*, Paul is again appealed to as a leading doctrinal authority, but here references to his epistles are both more numerous and more creative in their application to contemporary Christian society in that they explicitly question the value and validity of the "old" Law. In the footsteps of Paul, Talavera lays out the key argument of his anti-Judaizing polemic by closely intertwining doctrinal statements with matters of daily religious practices in Seville. This intermingling of doctrine and practice clearly emerges at the very beginning of the *Católica impugnación*, in the dedicatory letter addressed to Ferdinand and Isabel. Here it is stated that the Gospels, insomuch as they represent the "law of grace" and the "law of truth," are superior to the "old" Law, which is defined as a "law of the letter, shadow, and allegory," given by Moses to the Jewish people. This definition echoes Thomas Aquinas's *Summa theologiae* (I–II, q. 107, a. 2 co), where the Jewish Law is labeled *lex umbrae, lex figurae*, as opposed to *lex veritatis*—namely, the Christian Law. Relying on this doctrinal definition inspired by the Patristic and Scholastic debate on Paul's view of the "old" Law, Talavera aims to reiterate that First Testament commandments, rituals, precepts, and opinions ceased to be legally valid with the advent of Christ and the writing of the Gospels. As can be seen clearly in this dedication, the ultimate objective in evoking Paul's warnings is to show that there is no theological justification for continuing to observe the Jewish Law and various related practices, neither during Christ's time nor in Talavera's day.[58]

In the prologue following the dedication, he refers again to Paul's teachings, drawing from the book of Acts, which says that the "old" Law is like a master or a tutor charged with educating the Jewish people until the Messiah would come. To stress the provisional validity of the Jewish Law, Talavera employs a brilliant metaphor drawing on the economic language that often characterizes salvation history.[59] He suggests that the Gospels are like a letter of credit (*carta de pago*) whose main purpose is to remind one that all previous agreements have been fulfilled. Since contracts need not be preserved after both the promises and the obligations they stipulated have been met, there is no need to preserve either the "old" Law or its prophecies. After the notary's seal has been torn, sometimes the contract (*contrato*, i.e., the Jewish Law) is kept together with the letter of credit (i.e., the Gospels). However, even when the contract is preserved, this is done not out of obligation—for the terms have been fulfilled—but rather out of remembrance (*para memoria*). On a theological level, this implies that paradoxically, when the "old" Law survives, it does so only to remind one that it has been fulfilled. The function of memory assigned to the practice of retaining the "old" Law reflects the inclusivist approach to the Jews in salvation history, a well-established tradition stretching from Augustine to Gilbert Crispin and beyond.[60] Descending from the symbolic to the more literal level, Talavera explains that the notary's seal, which has been torn by Christ's coming into the world, stands for circumcision as well as for all Jewish ceremonies, precepts, and opinions, which thus are to be retained as abolished.[61]

In the prologue, he further develops his exegetical reasoning by referring to the pragmatic argument the apostle Peter formulated against the preservation of the "old" Law at the so-called Council of Jerusalem (ca. 50 CE), recalling also the figure of James, son of Alpheus, and again Paul in his letters to the Galatians and the Colossians. These three precedents from early Christian times provide support for the main counterargument of his refutation, which he brandishes against the most dangerous claim of the anonymous pamphlet—namely, the Judaizing pretension of maintaining the simultaneous validity and practice of both the "old" and the "new" Law. In the late medieval debate on religious laws furthered by authors such as Bonaventure and William of Auvergne, Christian faith was broadly seen as a religion based on a "law" (*lex Christi*) that was singular, exclusivist, and opposed to other, nonsalvific "laws" (*lex naturae, lex Moysis, lex Mahumeti*). Thus from Talavera's viewpoint, which echoes this debate, the pamphlet's aim implied a swerve into syncretism: "It is apparent that one cannot simultaneously observe the law of Moses and the Holy Gospels, for the Holy

Gospels, which contain the whole doctrine of the New Testament, by forbidding them, commands that the law of Moses as well as its ceremonies, precepts and opinions shall no longer be observed."[62] This firm statement perfectly summarizes Talavera's most urgent concern about the pamphlet's call for the simultaneous preservation of the "old" and the "new" Law. It is no coincidence that later on in the prologue, he polemicizes again against the simultaneous observation (*guardar juntamente*) of two Laws, referring by analogy to the Ebionite heretics, who in early Christian times sought to keep Jewish practices though they had entered Christian life: "Therefore, it is said above with good reason that he who believes and claims that it is right to simultaneously observe the old law and the Holy Gospels, is blind and much more than blind, he is an Ebionite and of weak mind."[63]

Biting arguments on the relationship between the "new" and the "old" Law are scattered throughout the seventy-seven chapters of Talavera's refutation. A full examination of them falls outside the scope of this study; however, it is possible to trace the central point of Talavera's demonstration in chapters 12 and 13, where his exegetical reasoning reaches its climax. Explicitly aimed at showing that Christ has renewed the "old" Law, chapter 12 turns out to be the most extensive and theologically intricate. It even includes a substantial appendix, where the author, after counterattacking the Judaizer's invective against him, outlines six ways in which Christ has renewed the Jewish Law. Chapter 13, considerably shorter, brings this argument to a close by showing that the "old" Law has been abrogated, having been replaced by the establishment of new Christian practices.[64]

In both chapters, Paul's teachings predominate among quotes from the four Evangelists and a smaller number from the First Testament. As for the interpretation of the "old" Law, Talavera refers to a conspicuous series of philosophical and theological authorities, from "los santos Doctores antiguos" such as Augustine to "los modernos" such as Peter Lombard, Thomas Aquinas, and Alexander of Hales, making explicit the fact that his reading of Paul is deeply indebted to a long-standing exegetical tradition going back to the Church Fathers and the later Scholastic debate.[65] Expressions such as *law of shadow*, which is certainly inspired by Paul's letters (Hebrews 10:1), though not literally excerpted from them, suggests the author's familiarity with the radically dualistic hermeneutics developed by a number of Church Fathers in their commentaries on the epistles to the Romans and the Corinthians[66] and broadly recognized by medieval writers who polemicized against the Jewish Law.[67]

However, the abrogation of the "old" Law does not imply a moral void for Christian believers. In his pamphlet, the Judaizer stated that Christ neither renewed nor invalidated the "old" Law; on the contrary, its validity for Christian believers had been preserved. Talavera responds to this claim by scrupulously examining the Ten Commandments of the First Testament. Christ, he affirms, has entirely renewed the Decalogue not just by abolishing its commandments but also by implementing a series of new compelling practices binding all believers, from innovative prayers such as the Paternoster to the replacement of Shabbat with Sunday as the day of rest.[68] This insistence on the replacement of religious practices is not without substantial soteriological consequences. Whereas the Gospels have pointed to the path leading to salvation, the Jewish Law entailed no hope for salvation, being ultimately a law that kills.[69]

The need to replace obsolete precepts is also at the core of Talavera's reception of Greek political philosophy in chapter 12. Here, he cites Aristotle's *Politics* five times as it relates to the long-standing debate about the best form of society and the way to rule it. Discussing the proper application of new laws, the different categories and age groups of citizens as well as the common good of society are the main concerns emerging from Talavera's reading of Aristotle.[70] Aristotle's insistence on the necessity of carefully distinguishing different components in society is the golden thread running through all five quotations. Relying on a philosophical authority acknowledged at that time not only at the medieval university but also in humanist circles and royal courts, Talavera intends to stress the urgency of adapting previous laws to a series of cultural and social challenges arising from the universalist assimilation policy promoted by the Catholic Monarchs. Though not explicitly evoked in this chapter of the *Católica impugnación*, the challenges he alludes to were in fact those affecting newly Christianized cities in Castile, whereas his mention of earlier laws to be replaced refers implicitly to the Jewish Law and related practices.[71] Talavera's use of Aristotle in his anti-Judaizing polemic is analogous to his use of Paul, being both ancient authors marshaled in support of his hermeneutic purposes. The Greek philosopher provides the theoretical framework in which the law and the context of its enactment can be analyzed in the abstract, while the Christian apostle points to the theological ground on which the "new" Law has to be implemented and its doctrinal values carefully clarified to believers.

The discussion of the relationship between the two Laws is taken up again in chapter 18, resulting in a subtle interpretation of the destruction of the "old" Law through the issue of a new revelation. Recalling his preaching in Seville on the "old" Law, Talavera claims that Christians received a "new testament" (*otro testamento nuevo*), whose existence implied that the previous testament had grown "old" and "greyed" and finally perished.[72] However, Christians did not destroy the Law, even if they claimed that it was an old, rotten house, and a rock.[73] According to chapter 3 of Paul's letter to the Romans, which states that the "old" Law no longer entails obligation, Christians did not in fact destroy the Law nor diminish it; on the contrary, they disclosed its true essence (*su verdadero ser*).[74] To bolster this statement, Talavera employs a metaphor inspired by a typological reading of chapters 26–27 of the book of Exodus. The "old" Law is as the tabernacle sent by God into exile, filled with his glory and often used by him to convey messages to his people. The tabernacle lost its sacral function when King Solomon built a more magnificent temple in Jerusalem, and yet, though in exile, it was not destroyed or diminished but rather understood newly, according to its ultimate meaning.[75] This hermeneutic strategy aims to show the danger behind a mistake in interpreting the ultimate essence of the "old" Law as living and still valid: "Instead, if we said and stated that its obligation would continue to take precedence afterward, we would destroy it, because to do so would be to affirm what is not and to say that it is what it is not, and accordingly your great maliciousness, presumption and foolishness destroy it, when you thought to have kept and saved it."[76] Paradoxically, it is suggested that only the Christian understanding of the "old" Law as a pure memory device is able to avoid its destruction and hence to save it. This is a recurring medieval idea that Gilbert Crispin and Nicholas of Lyra had already expressed when they wrote about the need to preserve the existence of the Jew as a fossil from a time passed.[77] According to Talavera, the guilt for the destruction of the Jewish Law falls entirely upon the anonymous author who attempted to preserve it in spite of the evidence of its true meaning disclosed by the new revelation.

So far, Talavera has limited its target to Judaizing. At this point, however, he takes a clearly anti-Jewish stance. He claims that the argument that the "old" Law was not a good law (*ley no buena*) even prior to the coming of

Christ—the time when it was most valid—should not be regarded as wrong. Turning to the First Testament, he states that the prophet Ezekiel corroborated this interpretation by warning the Jews about the wrong commandments deliberately sent to them by God, who acted against his people by deceiving them as a form of punishment. Here, Talavera evidently adopts the strategy of using First Testament prophets against the Jews that was prevalent in medieval anti-Jewish polemics—for example, Peter the Venerable's *Adversus Iudaeorum inveteratam duritiem*.[78] According to Talavera, the Jewish Law, which in the present day has been abrogated, was not reliable even in its own time. Moreover, in chapter 15, he draws a stark contrast between the Jewish Law (*ley mosaica*) and the Law of the Father (*ley del Padre*). He shows that when the Judaizer in his pamphlet defines the Jewish Law as "the law of the Father," he is wicked and wrong, for he relies on a definition that Talavera never heard of or read about. The Law of the Father, in Talavera's opinion, coincides entirely with the Father's will, which in turn coincides with the coming of Christ into the world; therefore, this expression can be meaningfully used and accepted only by understanding it in this way. The polemical objective is to deny that the Jewish Law can be considered a divine Law and thus to affirm that only the Father's will through Christ had salvific value for mankind. One might conclude from this that Talavera was concerned not just about the risk of syncretism, the heterodox combination of the "old" and the "new" Law, but also about the contents of the Jewish Law in its own right. This negative view of Jewish precepts and behaviors, especially the remark about God's deception of his people, which Talavera himself admits is difficult to understand (*lo cual no es ligero de entender*), leads us to an examination of the distinction he makes between Judaizers, Jewish converts, biblical, and contemporary Jews in light of his conception of heresy.[79]

Enacting Medieval Heresiology in a Fifteenth-Century Interfaith Polemic

The *Católica impugnación* provides eloquent proof of the hermeneutic pliability of medieval heresiology, showing its capacity for adapting over time to shifting interconfessional or interreligious circumstances.[80] The terminology and theological discourse employed in the *Católica impugnación* are typical of heresiology and therefore make clear the connection between this polemic and Talavera's role as a preacher committed to staunching the Judaizing heresy. It is no coincidence that heresy is evoked first in the full *titulus* of his refutation[81] and later discussed in the dedication to the Catholic Monarchs, where he calls it the most urgent challenge of his time. To underline its importance, Talavera refers to a triad of holy Christian authorities engaged in refuting heretics: first, the apostles Peter and Paul, who had provided Christians with well-grounded theological arguments to correct heresy; second, the Virgin Mary, who is recalled as a soteriological mediator and solitary fighter against all heresies in the ecumene according to the antiphon "Cunctas haereses sola interemisti," which dates back to before the eighth century and was incorporated into Pius V's *Breviarum romanum* after the Council of Trent;[82] and third, St. Jerome, the spiritual father of the Hieronymite order, who is referred to as the "hammer of heretics" (*martillo de los herejes*) and regarded as an exemplary model of a polemicist who continued to fight heretics even after his death by means of his intercessory power as a saint.

Talavera's polemics make use of the doctrinal distinction between apostasy and heresy in order to distinguish a gradation between biblical Jews, contemporary Jews, Jewish converts, and Judaizers in the specific context of late medieval Iberia. Writing after 1478, he was aware that he was making an accusation of heresy against a group of Jewish converts in Seville soon after a thorny debate about the establishment of the Inquisition in Castile had arisen. To avoid external pressure from the Crown in ruling on heretics, he felt the need to underline that according to canon law, the identification and persecution of heretics fell exclusively within ecclesiastical jurisdiction. A series of scattered references to civil and canon law, in addition to a number of theological authorities, is marshaled against Judaizing. Characterized by panegyric language,[83] Talavera's letter to the monarchs lays bare the potential consequences, both political and legal, of a serious theological inquiry (*inquisición*), thus seeking to meet the expectations of the work's recepients.[84]

Yet Talavera's attitude toward heresy was not purely destructive. According to Paul (1 Cor. 11:19) and Augustine (*De civitate Dei*, I, viii), even though heretics have the potential to deceive others into error, they are necessary within God's plan because they serve to define by contrast what it means to be a true believer.[85] What is more, heresy ought to be distinguished from apostasy, an offense that Talavera defines in general terms but does not ultimately ascribe to his adversary. Judaizers are to be labeled apostates only "if they completely abandon the holy law of the Gospels and resolutely believe in, follow, and observe the Law of Moses or the Muslim sect."[86] This, at first glance, does not seem to have been the case of the Sevillian author, who claimed to be a baptized Christian and to follow the Gospels in addition to the "old" Law. Though the Judaizer must have stressed his Christian beliefs several times in the pamphlet, Talavera harbors serious doubts about his religious identity,[87] focusing upon the consequences of his heterodox practices. If, theoretically, apostasy represents a worse offense than heresy ("for it would have been better not to believe and not to learn about salvation than to leave it completely as apostates do"[88]), the charge of heresy carried harsher consequences for the accused. As Talavera states in chapter 8 on a doctrinal level and again in chapter 59 in reference to burial practices, heresy may even potentially lead to the death penalty: "It is true that in some cases, these people have to die as both canon and civil law stipulate. . . . For I heard a very authoritative person say that in order to condemn all of them as heretics, nothing more was needed but to check how they were buried in those places."[89]

Besides recalling the related penalties, Talavera warns about the present controversy on burial and other practices as well as its thorny correlation with doctrinal condemnation, for this might easily lead to harsh polemics and profound divisions between "old" and "new" Christians.[90] Conceivably, reckless accusations of heresy could be turned against Christians too, as is seen in the Judaizer's complaint about the accusation of heresy that "old Christians" had indistinctly made against "all New Christians." Rejecting this claim, Talavera argues that the accusation of heresy should be limited to cases where there is an undeniable persistence of Jewish religious practices among those who have been baptized. Aware of the late fifteenth-century debate about the role of Jewish converts among Christians, Talavera was as committed to defending sincere *conversos* as he was to eliminating Judaizers: "Nor today have all new converts been labelled heretics as this wicked heretic claims. On the contrary, this label is given to wicked unbelievers like him who, though they are baptized and have adopted Christian names and even some works and signs, they are still found to keep Jewish or Muslim ceremonies and rites."[91]

The discussion of heretical pertinacity in the *Católica impugnación* leads to a precise definition of the "Judaizing heresy," a heresiological subtype whose origins are tellingly traced in Andrés Bernáldez's chronicle. Bernáldez dates the beginning of the Jewish deviance (*heregía musaica*) back to the massacre of 1390–91, at the time of Henry III of Castile and Vincent Ferrer's preaching, implicitly suggesting that it had been spreading for more than a century at the moment he was writing in the 1520s.[92] Talavera clearly derives his definition of Judaizing (*judaizar*) from Castile's long experience with this "Jewish deviance" and the ways in which it had been portrayed by chroniclers and polemicists throughout the fifteenth century.[93] He claims that, similar to those heretics who deviate from true faith after having known its salvific value, Judaizers deviate from true faith, which they have known through baptism, by observing only partially (*en algo*) the precepts entailed by the Gospels.[94] Among them was the anonymous author of the pamphlet, whom Talavera in fact charged with spreading a syncretic practice of the two Laws in Castile that threatened Christianization.

A long list of epithets directed at the anonymous author illustrates the harsh language of Talavera's polemic. More than once, as in chapter 44, Talavera labels him an Ebionite (*ebionita*) or another Ebion (*otro Ebion*), equating his doctrine with the heresy of the Pharisees (*herejía de los fariseos*) and all those who combined Jewish and Christian practices in early Christian times: "According to what has been told already in the prologue, he is a much-mistaken heretic, as the Nazarenes and the Ebionites were."[95] Interestingly, here as well as in a few other passages, the Moors (*moros*) and the Muslim sect (*secta mahometica*) are recalled beside the Jewish Law, as if in terms of legal obligation, Muslims were equal to those who followed the Law of Moses (*ley mosaica*). Elsewhere, the anonymous author is denounced as a traitor (*traidor*), referring to his betrayal of Christianity after having experienced the rite of baptism, or in general moral terms, as foolish (*necio*), wicked (*malvado*), braying (*buznarro*, likely a neologism created by Talavera), a spiteful fox (*raposo malicioso*), a simpleton (*sandío*), and also, as already mentioned, as an old man (*hombre viejo*), an expression inspired by Paul's idea of Christians as "new men."[96]

This impressive variety of derogatory labels does not leave any doubt as to Talavera's opinion about the Sevillian author and the reasons behind his polemic. At the same time, his polemical discourse is more intricate than a mere condemnation and raises a broader question about his theological view of the Jews—both biblical and contemporary—and the Jewish Law in its own right. I have already shown that chapter 18 of the *Católica impugnación* records a sudden shift from doctrinal refutation of Judaizing attitudes to a denigration of the value of Jewish Law in biblical times. At the end of the prologue, moreover, Talavera steps back from meticulous arguments against Judaizing and claims that his adversary is neither an "old" nor a "new" Christian but ultimately a Jew (*judío*), "obstinate" and "wicked," as his heretical pamphlet clearly shows.[97] What kind of Jew did Talavera have in mind?

Chapters 31 and 33 are emblematic of his apparently ambivalent thinking. As its title suggests,[98] chapter 31 has three parallel aims: to explain what the term *people of Israel* means today and who belongs to this people, to demonstrate that Jews do not belong to the people of Israel, and to rebuke those who despise both good New Christians (*los buenos cristianos nuevamente convertidos*) and old Christians (*los viejos*). The whole chapter is drawn up in accordance with a persisting typological interpretation of the concept of the people of Israel, relying on the dualistic opposition between "flesh" and "spirit" approached through the episode of Jacob wrestling with the angel as well as Paul's letters, especially the epistle to the Galatians.[99] Talavera devotes chapter 33 to providing a brief gallery of ancient people and religions in order to show the nonexceptional, ordinary character of the Jewish people with respect to other ancient civilizations. Though he admits that in biblical times, the Jewish people were wise and astute, as they knew God and lived according to the divine precepts disclosed by Moses in the book of Deuteronomy, he rejects the notion of a "chosen people" who surpasses other "nations," thus situating the Jewish people even a step lower than the others: "That people was not wiser, nor keener, nor more ingenious than any other people, nor are their descendants, rather they were perhaps less wise, as it is shown by other people and nations of that time." Offered as proof of this assertion is a litany of praise for the Chaldeans, the Greeks, and even the Arabs regarding creativity and knowledge of the sciences.[100] In addition, chapter 31 connects the discussion of the people of Israel to the Jews living in Talavera's day. Relying upon Paul's letter to the Romans (11:17), he states that Jews, after the coming of Christ, are no longer to be considered as belonging to the people of Israel, whose former members have been replaced by "good" Christians of both "old" and "new" lineage. This supersessionist implication, typical of authoritative medieval commentators belonging to the Franciscan and Dominican orders, clearly resurfaces in the final definition of the people of Israel provided later on in chapter 31: "And if he uses the label 'people of

Israel' for Jewish people today, this wicked man is mistaken also in doing so, as today they are not 'people of Israel' nor true Jews, but they are the synagogue and Satan's council. . . . As the Apostle claims, they are dried branches with no benefit, cut from the good trunk wherein instead of them, all good Christians are grafted though they descend from evil trunks."[101]

Yet physical Jews were not, either in biblical times or in the present, to be despised in their own right. At the end of chapter 31, Talavera acknowledges that those who today are known as Jews could be retained as part of the people of Israel. This apparently contradictory statement aimed to protect communities of living Jews from violent attack, since the conception of love behind the Gospels did not permit any form of violence or compulsion toward the Jews. Moreover, since the times of Augustine, these "hermeneutical Jews" served a purpose in Christian salvation history. However, Jewish converts whose conversions were not in earnest as well as potential converts to Judaism needed to be warned against seeking to be saved by the "old" Law. Toward living Jews, Talavera writes, Christians have behaved morally and shall continue to do so, loving them almost as their neighbors, even though they live segregated from the rest of society, are marked so as to be identified as Jews, and are not allowed to hold public office, since allowing them to do so would be sinful.[102] Talavera rebukes Christians who show hatred toward this people, abusing both the Jews and their carnal descendants—namely, the *conversos*. In doing evil to them, they commit such a serious sin that they can no longer be called Christians.[103]

On the Nature of a Late Medieval Controversy

To the eyes of modern readers, Talavera's vacillating definition of people of Israel—which he applied to present Jews and sincere converts to Christianity but not to biblical Jews and Judaizers—might appear ambivalent or contradictory. Still, in the *Católica impugnación*, this seemingly illogical distinction makes sense when understood from the point of view of Paul's universalist thinking, in that it helps identify potential Christians from amid people of Jewish origins, thus fostering further conversions. Talavera's view spanned the biblical past and the Iberian present and used a theological rather than a chronological or ethnic criterion to make the necessary distinctions. To his way of seeing, the sincerity of conversion and the subsequent accomplishment of the teachings handed down by the Gospels came before scholarship, humanism, and politics.

Further proof that Talavera was committed to protecting converts who were true Christians is his recognition that there was a linguistic facet to stigmatization; thus he firmly rejected the widespread terms *marranos* or *marrandíes* for Jewish converts,[104] arguing that Christians and *conversos* must behave as a united body; the worst that could happen in their daily interactions would be for their growing community to be divided from within.[105] The charge of "schismatic" directed at the author of the pamphlet, which echoes Dante's interpretation of Muḥammad as a sinner and a schismatic in the *Divine Comedy* (*Inferno*, 28:22–33),[106] reflects Talavera's concerns about the spiritual and political consequences of a potential struggle within Christendom.[107]

During the same years that Talavera was engaged in pastoral activities, European humanists were becoming increasingly attracted to the subjects of the Hebrew language and the Jewish tradition. Interest in the Kabbalah and the Talmud among learned churchmen was flourishing in Italy, Spain, France, and Germany. The linguistic and theological works of Pico della Mirandola, Egidio da Viterbo, Arias Montano, Guillaume Postel, and Johann Reuchlin provide paradigmatic examples of this intellectual trajectory. Though deeply acquainted with humanism and the study of languages, as is shown by his translation of Petrarch's invective against a physician or the Castilian translation of Francesc Eiximenis's *Vita Christi* he promoted and personally emended,[108] Talavera approached the Jewish tradition as a militant churchman rather than a humanist. He was concerned not with linguistic and genealogical debates related to Jewish history but with a concrete scenario wherein intellectual (i.e., theological) and practical (i.e., interreligious policies) matters intersected to such a degree as to become indistinguishable. As a trusted advisor of the Catholic Monarchs sent to Seville to preach against the persistence of the "old" Law, he provided through the *Católica impugnación* a firm refutation of all forms of syncretism, according to which the Gospels were not fully embraced as the new, uniquely valid, salvific religious law, to the point of considering the death penalty for Judaizers. Equally, as a monk truly convinced of the universalist apostolic message emblematically recorded in Paul's epistles, his purpose was to protect the Jews still living in Spain before 1492 as well as all "good *conversos*" (*los buenos cristianos nuevamente convertidos*)[109] from both political and legal threats coming from those Christians who, by persecuting them, sinfully betrayed the spirit of the Gospels. While he condemned biblical Jews and possible converts to Judaism according to Paul's rejection of the "law of death," he wanted to "love" and protect the living Jews of his time in the spirit of the Gospels, even though he agreed that they ought to be segregated from Christians.

This view of "historical" or "hermeneutical" Jews, present Jews, or Jewish converts clearly shows that the understanding of doctrinal arguments as marginal with respect to the social and political issues raised by the presence of "Judaizers" is not consistent with Talavera's spiritual view of education, daily life, and power.[110] It is indeed the preponderance of the religious view on a variety of topics pertaining to private and community life that led, at the dawn of twentieth century, to Talavera's literary production being classified as no less than "mystical."[111] And it is not only in the case of Talavera that scholarship focusing on interfaith relations in medieval and early modern Europe has chosen to deny the religious dimensions of polemic. The case of the Spanish theologian Juan de Segovia (1393–1458), the promoter of the first trilingual edition of the Qur'ān, provides another significant example of modernizing historiographic projections.[112] In their study with a broader chronological and religious scope, on the contrary, Mercedes García-Arenal and Béatrice Leroy showed that for four centuries, the Christian confrontation with both Jewish and the Muslim converts in Iberia was primarily of a religious nature.[113]

Distinguishing between theology and religious policies when discussing interfaith polemics results in a dualistic view that, divorcing religion from politics and social implications, does not reflect the unique combination of concerns of a late medieval churchman who was not only a royal advisor and confessor but also a prolific religious writer and a spiritual man.[114] For a Hieronymite monk who perceived his earthly mission primarily in religious terms, doctrinal claims would not have been matters of secondary relevance.[115] On the contrary, they served as the authoritative basis for education and reform, two aims that were considered central to the universalist program promoted by the Catholic Monarchs and implemented by the members of their entourage.[116]

In Talavera's project of evangelization, theology was the primary tool to enact the Gospels in politically defined contexts. The mindful, rational elucidation of doctrine intersected with the social and political issues that he and other preachers or advisors of the Catholic Monarchs sought constructive ways to address. Pointing explicitly to theological argumentation as essential to confronting the Judaizing heresy, one of the opening statements of the *Católica impugnación* speaks in this regard for itself: heresy has to be eradicated by means of Catholic and theological reasons (*católicas y teologales razones*) besides due punishments and lashes (*castigos y azotes*). Evidently, this argument challenged the conversion strategies the Church had to enact in Iberia and beyond, but it did not necessarily imply a claim against the recourse to coercion in the matter of conversion. It has been often observed that according to the *Católica impugnación*, any strategy using violence or force to compel conversion would not allow new believers to effectively embrace the Christian faith and ought to be avoided. This argument, certainly the most cited by scholars, is regularly quoted out of context as proof of the centrality of love and nonviolence in Talavera's attitude toward Jewish converts and even toward Muslims with whom he coped years later in Granada. This is misleading, since Talavera systematically expresses strong opposition to the Jewish Law in this passage as much as anywhere else in his polemic.[117] Even if he discourages Christians from persecuting the Jews, he theologically contrasts the Law of Christ to the Law of Moses, which he argues, following the Gospel of John, is based on fear (*temor*)[118] and does not allow one to reach heavenly bliss (*bienandanza*) unless it is abandoned through conversion.[119] Ultimately, the *Católica impugnación* provides further evidence of a Christian yearning deeply rooted in the medieval theology of salvation—namely, to convert Jews or reluctant converts not just in terms of external signs and sacraments but also and primarily in terms of faith. Only by considering this spiritual objective in its own right, rather than seeing it as a mere rhetorical tool in the service of religious politics or social demands, can we truly understand the harsh stance taken by Talavera in this polemic.

Notes

This research was conducted at the Spanish National Research Council (CSIC), Madrid, as part of the project "Conversion, Overlapping Religiosities, Polemics, Interaction: Early Modern Iberia and Beyond" (CORPI), funded by the European Research Council under the European Union's Seventh Framework Programme (FP7/2007–13) / ERC Grant Agreement number 323316. I extend my heartfelt gratitude to Mercedes García-Arenal, Yonatan Glazer-Eytan, and Gerard Wiegers. This research is part of a book project tentatively entitled *Hernando de Talavera and*

His Interreligious Legacy in the Premodern Mediterranean, funded by the German Federal Ministry of Education and Research (BMBF), research group "Rationalität und Vernunft im Leben und Denken der Muslime im globalen und pluralen Kontext. Konzeptionen islamischer Theologie," Centre for Islamic Theology (ZITh), University of Tübingen, 2013–17.

1. On this and other sixteenth-century hagiographies, see Scotto, "Resplandeciente y terso espejo," 438–40, 448–51.
2. *Santa vida de Fray Hernando de Talavera que compiló y ordenó el licenciado Jerónimo de Madrid*, transcribed from MS 2042, BNE, fols. 9–57, in Martínez Medina and Biersack, *Fray Hernando de Talavera*, 376: "Nunca predicó sermón que no tocase cosas maravillosas de la fe y sabía bien lo que hacía, que como le oían sienpre muchos nuevamente convertidos de moros y judíos era así necesario especialmente para los convertidos de judíos a los que les daba a entender muy claramente que su ley era figura y sonbra de la Santa fe católica provándoselo por la sagrada Escritura que él tenía tan 'pre manibus' que aunque ellos estuviesen endurecidos los ablandaba y es así la verdad que dudo haber tales cristianos de esta nación en todo el reino."
3. Resines, *Hernando de Talavera*.
4. This period in Granada deserves further research based on contemporary sources that can balance the overwhelming influence exercised on scholarship by the hagiographic tradition. See remarks on diverse aspects of Talavera's pastoral activities in Vega García-Ferrer, *Fray Hernando de Talavera*; Harris, *Muslim to Christian Granada*, 8–27, 88–107; Iannuzzi, "Educar a los cristianos"; García-Arenal and Rodríguez Mediano, *Orient in Spain*, 35–43; and Scotto, "Resplandeciente y terso espejo," 445–53.
5. According to the polemical character of this refutation, I will use "Judaizer" or "Judaizing" (arguments, claim, interpretation, etc.) to point to the anonymous author of the pamphlet confronted by Hernando, setting aside for the conclusion a discussion on Talavera's understanding of the Jewish tradition. See López Martínez, *Judaizantes castellanos*, which includes an edition of the anonymous anti-Judaizing booklet known as *Alboraique* (Llerena, 1488). Márquez Villanueva, "Sobre el concepto de judaizante"; Amran, *Judíos y conversos*, 88–90.
6. Pastore, *Un'eresia spagnola*, 36, 36n115.
7. Antonio, *Bibliotheca hispana nova*, 1:390. Márquez Villanueva noticed that Nicolás Antonio could have come to know about the *Católica impugnación* without consulting a copy of it, as the absence of specific publication date in his description would suggest. See Márquez Villanueva, "Estudio preliminar," 7n2.
8. Fernando de Valdés, *Cathalogus librorum*, 49.
9. See Pastore, "Presentación," xxi. This later edition reproduces the text of the 1961 edition, adding only the new "Presentation" and a reprinted article by Márquez Villanueva in the appendix. Since the 1961 edition is more familiar to scholars, I will refer throughout to that edition.
10. See, respectively, Iannuzzi, *Poder de la palabra*, appendix, 511–14; Azcona, *Isabel la Católica*, 761–63; Martínez Medina and Biersack, *Fray Hernando de Talavera*, appendix, 352–57.
11. Accurti, *Editiones saeculi XV*, 32–33.
12. For the first two topics, see Villanueva and Pastore's contributions mentioned above, note 7, 8 and 10. On the use of images, see Pereda, *Imágenes de la discordia*, 62–73, 254–87.
13. The acts of the 1478 council state that Talavera sat in the town hall (*cabildo*) in *Corral de los olmos* from the very beginning of the assembly, on Wednesday July 8, and that he was, at that time, confessor of Queen Isabel. See the opening section addressed to the Catholic Monarchs (*Actas* XVII):

Miércoles, ocho de Jullio, á terçia, año del Señor de mill é quatroçientos é setenta é ocho años, en la casa del cabildo de los Señores de la iglesia desta mui noble çibdad de Sevilla ques en el corral de los olmos; estando ayuntados el Reverendísimo Señor cardenal despaña, é el Reverendo Señor don Fadrique obispo de Mondonedo, é el Reverendo Señor don pedro de Solís obispo de Cadis, é el Reverendo Señor don a.° obispo de Córdoba, con los otros procuradores de los perlados é iglesias destos reynos, capitularmente ayuntados, entre sí tratando é comunicando de las causas de su venida é congregaçión,–por parte de los Señores Reyes, vinieron á la dicha congregaçión los venerables padres é señores el prior de prado de la horden de Sant Gerónimo, confesor de los Señores Reyes.

Right below, Talavera is mentioned as "devoto padre el prior de santa María de Prado" and again later on, with respect to July 22, in the account of the Monarchs' response to the cathedral chapter (*Actas* XVI). See Fita, "Concilios españoles inéditos," 220–21.

14. See Pulgar, *Crónica de los Reyes*, 1:415.
15. Isabel was in Seville from July 25, 1477, to October 2, 1478, with several short-time absences. As is well known, she gave birth to her only son—John, Prince of Asturias—in Seville on June 30. Fernando was with her from August 25, 1477, to February 10, 1478, and again from April 13 to October 2, 1478, not counting several long absences. See Rumeu de Armas, *Itinerario de los Reyes*. Right before the monarchs entered the city, the German traveler, Hieronymus Münzer, witnessed the expectations of the local community about their visit and the restoration of the Alcázar. See Pfandl, "Itinerarium hispanicum Hieronymi Monetarii"; Spanish translation in Münzer, "Relación del viaje por España y Portugal," 1:375: "Cuando nosotros nos encontrábamos en la ciudad, los sevillanos estaban esperando la llegada del rey, y por esta causa haciánse obras de enlosado en el alcázar." A recent introductory essay is provided by Zuili, "L'Itinerarium . . . de Jérôme Münzer."
16. For an insight into the exegetical-theological issues involved in *converso*-Christian polemics, see Orfali Levi, "Jews and Conversos." A repertory of the written works related to the Toledo riots is provided by González Rolán and Saquero Suárez-Somonte, *Sentencia-estatuto de Pero Sarmiento.*
17. On the previous Muslim and Christian regimes in Seville and the consequences for the minorities living under these regimes, including the 1391 massacre of the Jews fomented by the Crown and Christian preachers, see Deimann, *Christen, Juden und Muslime.*
18. Pulgar, *Crónica de los Reyes*, 334–35. On *conversos*, Pulgar also wrote important letters, including the one to the archbishop of Seville, Pedro González de Mendoza, wherein he harshly attacked the Judaizers in Seville. See Cantera Burgos, "Fernando del Pulgar y los conversos," 306; Roth, "Anti-converso Riots."
19. Bernáldez, *Memorias del reinado*. On the ideological attitude behind this chronicle, especially on Bernáldez's autobiographical remarks, see the introduction by the editors. For the work's relation with the origins of the Inquisition, see Gerli, "Social Crisis and Conversion."
20. On Bernáldez's general attitude toward *conversos*, see Netanyahu, *Origins of the Inquisition*, 1137–40, where the chronicler is labeled "racist" according to the militant language employed by the author throughout the whole book.
21. Francisco Ramírez de Solórzano, *Historia del real convento*, MS APB (Archivo Provincia Bética), Seville, bk. 1, ch. 9, brought to light by Larios Ramos, "Dominicos y la Inquisición," 86n5.
22. Bernáldez, *Memorias del reinado*, 96, 99.
23. Pulgar, *Crónica de los Reyes*, 335. The chronicler had already pointed out the

risk of respecting neither the "old" nor the "new" Law in his description of unspecified episodes that took place in the private houses of *conversos* in Toledo: "Algunos onbre e mugeres que escondidamente fazían ritos judaycos, los quales con grand ynorancia e peligro de sus ánimas, ni guardavan una ni otra ley" (210).

24. Márquez Villanueva, "Ideas de la *Católica impugnación*," (A)iv.
25. Pastore, *Un'eresia spagnola*, 30–31.
26. Talavera, *Católica impugnación*, 186. The author mentions the *ordenanza* also in chapter 57: "De lo cual todo, se sigue que la ordenanza puesta arriba, que este necio malicioso reprehende y tache, no fue mal hecha, ni mal ordenada, ni debe ser derogada como él dice, antes muy bien guardada" (199). The controversial use of images for Christian devotion is treated at length in the *Católica impugnación*, chs. 27–29, 53–54, 56–58, on which see Pereda, *Imágenes de la discordia*, 62–73.
27. Pereda, *Imágenes de la discordia*, 68–69.
28. The existence of these works was highlighted by Juan Antonio Yeves in his 1996 catalog and more recently by Pereda in his monograph on images in fifteenth-century Castile. See Yeves, *Manuscritos españoles*, vol. 1, no. 17, pp. 86–87, where a first description of the manuscript is provided; and Pereda, *Imágenes de la discordia*, 259. Finally, in 2014, Carmen Parrilla provided a scrupulous critical edition of both these texts. Parrilla, *Hernando de Talavera*. For the codicological description of the manuscript, see pp. 87–96.
29. Parrilla, *Hernando de Talavera*, 46–47.
30. Talavera, *Colación*, 103–5; Talavera, *Tratado*, 138–39.
31. This reflection is developed all along Augustine's *Exposition on the Psalms*. Among his many remarks, see the comments on Psalm 35: 19; 38: 5, 6, 15, 21, 26; 40: 5, 25; 44: 10; 56: 8, which reflect also the coeval heresiological debate. The image of the Church as a body is related to the role of the Jews in Christianity as early as Paul, who first used this metaphor: see Stow, *Popes, Church and Jews*, 7. For an overview of Augustine's use of Paul, see Canty, "Saint Paul in Augustine," 136–37. In medieval political thought, this image has also been discussed with respect to the legitimization and the development of corporatism within the Church (cathedral chapters, religious orders, brotherhoods). See Ladner, *Images and Ideas*, 2:444–50.
32. Talavera, *Colación*, 117–18.
33. Talavera, *Tratado*, 165: "Y el apóstol: 'En Ihesuchristo no vale nada la circuncisión ni el preputio, mas la nueva creatura' [see Gal. 6:15]. Como si dixiesse más claramente: 'para que alguno sea salvo y a Ihesuchristo, nuestra muy sancta cabeça encorporado, ni le estorva ni le ayuda aver seído judío o pagano, mas la nueva conversatión conforme a la de esse messmo Salvador.' Y en otro lugar dize que ni daña ni aprovecha ser judío o griego; libre o siervo; macho o henbra [see Gal. 3:28], mas ser baptizado y vestir y seguir las costunbres de Ihesuchristo, nuestra muy sancta cabeça."
34. Talavera, *Católica impugnación*, 68.
35. See Novikoff, "Dialogue and Disputation"; Glei, "Religious Dialogues."
36. For a reconstruction of the pamphlet's arguments, see Márquez Villanueva, "Estudio preliminar," 30–34; Lobera Serrano, "Los conversos sevillanos."
37. Talavera, *Católica impugnación*, "Tablas de los capítulos," 59–68.
38. For a theoretical proposal, see Valkenberg, "Polemics, Apologetics, and Dialogue." See also interesting theological suggestions in Valkenberg, *Sharing Lights on the Way*, 93–98.
39. Talavera, *Católica impugnación*, 47, 49, 51, 69.
40. Talavera, 83: "Dice este necio presuntuoso que nos quiere enseñar qué es verdaderamente ley de Cristo y doctrina evangélica."
41. See the section "Enacting Medieval Heresiology in a Fifteenth-Century Interfaith Polemic" for a detailed discussion of this point.

42. Evidence for this can be found in Petrus Alfonsi's *Dialogus contra Iudaeos*, written in 1108–10, especially *titulus* IV. See Alfonsi, *Dialogue against the Jews*, 139–45. As is well known, Petrus Alfonsi's polemic is one of the main sources of the scathing treatise written by Peter the Venerable in Cluny between 1144 and 1147, *Adversus Iudaeorum inveteratam duritiem*. Besides arguing against the Talmud, Peter devotes entire sections of his polemic to showing that Jews are guiltily ignorant about their own scriptures, hence their denial of Christ's advent due to blindness and deafness (Peter the Venerable, *Adversus iudeorum inveteratam duritiem*, ch. I., l. 227, p. 10: "Aperite tandem oculos, reserate aures et soli caeci in mundo apparere, soli surdi inter mortals remanere erubescite"). See Peter the Venerable, *Against the Inveterate Obduracy*, 60: "Open your eyes at last, open your ears, and be ashamed that you are clearly the only blind people in the world, the only deaf people to remain." In the mid-fourteenth century, Ramon Martí took up this polemical line in his *Pugio fidei* to argue against the persistence of Jewish religious practices. For an overview, see Cohen, *Living Letters*, 317–89. According to Hartley Lachter's recent debatable proposal, a radically distinct narrative is found in contemporary reflections on the role of the Jews by Christian cabalists from late thirteenth- and early fourteenth-century Spain: Lachter, *Kabbalistic Revolution*, 100–129.
43. Talavera, *Católica impugnación*, 87: "No pudiste hallar, ni ver, lo que está tan abierto, tan manifiesto y tan claro de conocer."
44. Talavera, 87: "Mas no es maravilla que no lo entendieses, pues tú mesmo confiesas que lo leíste sin afección. . . . Ca, como en el prólogo fué tocado y como parece largamente en los capítulos quinto y sexto y séptimo de San Mateo, innovó Jesucristo los mandamientos morales, que tú, herético ebionita, llamas neciamente legales."
45. Márquez Villanueva has detected in Talavera's radical call for moral reform in the Church and his universalist missionary view the possible motive for his trial by the Inquisition in 1505–6. See "Estudio preliminar," 19, 28. On the depiction of Talavera as a reformist both before and after his death (1507), see Azcona, "Tipo ideal de obispo"; Iannuzzi, "Biografía del reformista fray Hernando"; Scotto, "Resplandeciente y terso espejo," 453–64.
46. I have presented my initial findings on this topic at the international workshop "Shifting Cultures in the Medieval Mediterranean," organized by Clara Almagro Vidal and Jessica Tearney-Pearce on July 18–20, 2016, at the Kulturwissenschaftliches Kolleg-Institute for Advanced Study, Bischofsvilla, Konstanz. I hope to expand the research in this chapter for my monograph on Hernando de Talavera.
47. Talavera, *Católica impugnación*, 72–73.
48. See Márquez Villanueva, "Estudio preliminar," 7, 21–22, 29–30. Márquez Villanueva has also alleged that the year 1487 is too late for the publication of the *editio princeps* (7n2). See Márquez Villanueva, "Ideas de la *Católica impugnación*," (A)vii–viii, where the author provides a contradictory argument about the dating of the *Católica impugnación*. On (A)vii, he claims that this work "no refleja todavía el impacto de las primeras actuaciones del Santo Oficio," whereas on the next page, (A) viii, he states, "Escritas, por tanto, con posterioridad a la puesta en marcha del aparato represor [of the Inquisition] a principios de 1481, las páginas de Talavera consideran sus actuaciones andaluzas como un castigo merecido y, aún peor, torpemente buscado." As for Pastore, see *Un'eresia spagnola*, 31; and her "Presentación," xxvi.
49. On the accusations against the Hieronymite order, see Roth, *Conversos, Inquisition*, 231–36; Starr-LeBeau, *Shadow of the Virgin*, 217; Santonja Hernández,

"Sobre judíos y judeoconversos," 202. On the case of Diego de Marchena, see Sicroff, "Caso del judaizante jerónimo."

50. See Avalle-Arce's review of *Católica impugnación*, in Avalle-Arce, "Review of Hernando," 384. Márquez Villanueva noted that these works share the conception of "inquisición" as an inquiry into heresy and apostasy with the consequent forms of punishment. See Márquez Villanueva, "Estudio preliminar," 19–29. For an overview, see Netanyahu, *Origins of the Inquisition*, 351–583, 855–96. For Cartagena and Torquemada, see Rosenstock, *New Men*, 22–52, 53–68. For Oropesa, see the introduction to Alonso de Oropesa, *Luz para el conocimiento*, 7–48. Alonso de Oropesa's treatise has to be further investigated as an influential precedent for Talavera's spiritual outlook and exegetical approach, as suggested by Pastore, *Un'eresia spagnola*, 9–26, 32–33. See also interesting remarks in Berger, *Persecution, Polemic*. For a series of case studies from the twelfth to the sixteenth centuries, see the essays collected in McMichael and Myers, *Friars and Jews*.
51. See Vidal Doval, *Misera Hispania*. On Paul's importance in this treatise, see Soyer, "All One in Christ Jesus."
52. Szpiech, "Preaching Paul."
53. Hernando de Talavera, *Breve forma de confesar*, in Mir y Noguera, *Escritores místicos españoles*, 3–35, esp. 16. See Pastore, *Un'eresia spagnola*, 98n111.
54. Talavera, *Colación*, 130 and 117–18, respectively.
55. Parrilla, *Hernando de Talavera*, 47–49.
56. Talavera, *Colación*, 110: "Buen águila, buen religioso, buen capitán y governador sant Pablo, que aun por sus manos trabajando y, de noche, velando, ganava lo que a sí y a sus compañeros era necessario." Stressing the value of working with one's own hands, Hernando clearly alludes to 1 Thess. 4:11: "Also, make it your goal to live quietly, to mind your own business, and to work with your own hands, as we instructed you."
57. In his letter to the Galatians, Paul lists only nine gifts of the Holy Spirit in contrast with the nine works of the flesh. Medieval writers, from Augustine to Thomas Aquinas, later commented on them, and a substantial debate of this topic developed. In traditional homiletics based on the Vulgate, there are twelve fruits of the Holy Spirit. See Talavera, *Tratado*, 192–93.
58. See Talavera, *Católica impugnación*, 68–69.
59. For theoretical insights into the use of economic metaphors, see Ruel, "Christians as Believers." A close reading of Paul's language and conception of salvation in his letters to Timothy and Titus has been made by Wieland, *Significance of Salvation*. This language has often entailed anti-Jewish readings of Christian salvation history down to nineteenth century. See McReynolds, *Redemption and the Merchant God*.
60. See Cohen, "Slay Them Not"; Cohen, *Living Letters*; Fredriksen, *Augustine and the Jews*.
61. Talavera, *Católica impugnación*, 71–72.
62. Talavera, 72: "Así que parece claramente que no se puede guardar la ley de Moisén y el Santo Evangelio juntamente, como el Santo Evangelio, que es toda la doctrina del nuevo testamento, mande y viede que la dicha ley y sus ceremonias, observancias y juicios no se guarden más."
63. Talavera, 72: "Pues con razón es dicho arriba, que es ciego y más que ciego ebionita y menguado de todo entendimiento el que piensa y afirma que se pueden guardar juntamente la ley vieja y el Santo Evangelio."
64. Further remarks related to this topic can be found in Talavera, ch. 16 (again on the interpretation of the "old" Law); ch. 37 (a comparison of the debate on the two Laws with the rules of St. Francis, St. Dominic, and St. Benedict, and with the *Siete Partidas*); ch. 73 (remarks on the Gospels); ch. 49, esp. pp. 179–80 (against the conception of the "old" Law as the "Law of

the Father"); and ch. 76 (on the mystical and literal sense of the Bible).

65. Talavera, *Católica impugnación*, 86.
66. See Origen, *Commentary on the Epistle*; St. Jerome, *Commentary of Galatians*; Chrysostom, *Homilies on the Epistles*; Chrysostom, *Discourses against Judaizing Christians*. Augustine's remarks on Jews and the Jewish Law are scattered throughout several of his works, including the *Confessiones* and *De Doctrina Christiana*. For a survey of his inclusivist view, see at least Fredriksen, "Divine Justice and Human Freedom"; Unterseher, *Mark of Cain and the Jews*; Szpiech, *Conversion and Narrative*, 30–58; and see Talavera, *Católica impugnación*, chs. 16, 37, 73, 49, 76.
67. An introduction to Paul's reception in the Middle Ages is provided in Cartwright, *Companion to St. Paul*. On Abelard and Nicholas of Lyra's readings of Paul, both involving polemical views of the Jewish Law, see Campbell, Hawkins, and Schildgen, *Medieval Readings of Romans*, 70–97, 167–81.
68. See Talavera, *Católica impugnación*, 87–93.
69. Talavera, 87: "La cual esperanza no mandaba ni daba la ley mosaica . . . con el velo, como dice el Apóstol de la letra de Moisén, la cual, come él dice mata."
70. The passages he cites from the *Politics* are from 5.2, 4.14, 6.1, 3.6, and 3.5. For insight into the variety of medieval uses of Aristotle, see Bianchi, *Christian Readings of Aristotle*.
71. Talavera's politics, which were based on an original combination of Aristotle and the Gospels, deserve further research. A preliminary approach to this topic can be found in Martínez Medina and Biersack, *Fray Hernando de Talavera*, 161–66.
72. Talavera, *Católica impugnación*, 118: "Ca diciendo nuestro Señor que daría otro testamento nuevo, dió a entender claramente que aquel era viejo; y es claro que lo que se antigua y ennegrece, que está cerca de la muerte y que finalmente perece."
73. Talavera, 119: "Pues, así, no destruímos la ley de Moisén, diciendo que es vieja y podrida casa y roca: come sea así verdad."
74. Talavera, 118: "Todo esto dice el santo Apóstol y diciéndolo él y nos también, no destruímos ni amenguamos la ley, como ese santo Apóstol dice: antes la estatuímos y afirmamos, declarando su verdadero ser, oficio y condición, como no destruyen la primera materia, ni la amenguan, los que dicen que la crió nuestro Señor *proper nihil*."
75. Talavera, 118.
76. Talavera, 119: "Antes la destruiríamos, si dijésemos y afimásemos que duraba después acá como primera su obligación, porque afirmaríamos lo que no es y diríamos que es la que no es: según que la destruye tu gran malicia, presunción y necedad, pensando la conservar y salvar."
77. See Klepper, *Insight of Unbelievers*. See also note 67 above.
78. See note 51 above.
79. Talavera, *Católica impugnación*, 119: "Y aún si alguno presumiese de se más adelantar y quisiese decir que la ley de Moisén fué ley no buena, aún en aquel tiempo en que más valió, y que cuanto a la guarda y ejercicio de aquellas ceremonias y juicios tuvo más fuerza: si estos quisiese decir, per ventura no erraría mucho en ello. Hablando de lo que mandaba obrar y no de lo que figuraba, diciendo nuestro Señor, por el profeta Ezquiel, que dió a aquel pueblo mandamientos no buenos, y tales, que no vivieses en ellos. Lo cual no es ligero de entender."
80. A recent attempt to address heresiology in the three Abrahamic religions is provided by Ames, *Medieval Heresies*, 263–322. See comparative outcomes in Bade and Freudenberg, *Von Sarazenen und Juden*. As for the times of Hernando, there are some hints in Iannuzzi, *Poder de la palabra*, 337–41. For the shifting definition of heresy between the late Middle Ages and early modern times, see Asad, *Genealogies of Religion*, 39n21; Asad, "Medieval Heresy." On Aquinas's

influence on later medieval debates, especially on the doctrinal classification of non-Christian practices, see Martínez Gázquez, "Vtrum ritus infidelium." A promising, innovative interpretation of fifteenth-century heresiology based on the case study of Alonso de Espina is provided by Cavallero, "Temporalidad del lenguaje."

81. Talavera, *Católica impugnación*, 59: "Católica impugnación del herético libelo maldito y descomulgado."
82. Talavera, 68: "Cunctas haereses sola interemit in universo mundo." See "Cunctas haereses sola interemisti," now part of the "Office of the Blessed Virgin Mary," *Breviarium Romanum*, Comm. Fest. B: M. V. in 3 Noct. ant. 7. See Tinti, *Maria debellatrice*; Emmen, "Cunctas haereses sola intermisti"; Barré, "Antienne et reponse de la Vierge."
83. Evidence of Talavera's interaction with Queen Isabel, as it relates to his knowledge of the anonymous pamphlet and his subsequent polemic, is found in the *Católica impugnación*, 69:

> Y aun porque, como buen siervo vuestro, Reina cristianísima y muy esclarecida, vos tornase yo el dicho libelo con usuras como el santo Evangelio quiere que lo haga todo buen siervo; que vuestra real mano fue la primera, que me lo comunicó dentro de este vuestro y nuestro monasterio en que sirvo sin provecho. Pues suplico a vuestras altezas y a vuestra reverendísima señoría, a quien tanto o más incumbe aquesto, lo quieran recebir con aquella sinceridad con que se presenta, y lo manden examinar y, lo que tal no pareciere, corregir y enmendar. Ca yo todo lo que digo y a mí con ello, someto a la corrección y determinación de la santa madre Iglesia y vuestra.

84. See Contreras, Pulido, and Benítez, *Judíos y moriscos*. As for legal implications, especially those related to the Inquisiton's activities at the beginning of sixteenth century, see Dedieu, "Herejía y limpieza de sangre"; Alcalá Galve, "Herejía y jerarquía."
85. See Talavera, *Católica impugnación*, chap. 3, 77.
86. Talavera, 180: "Si dejan del todo la santa ley evangélica y determinadamente creen siguen y guardan la ley mosaica o la secta mahomética."
87. See note 104.
88. Talavera, *Católica impugnación*, 181: "Porque era mejor no creer ni conocer la vida de salvación que dejarla del todo, como la deja el apostata."
89. Talavera, 83: "Y estos tales, es verdad, que en algunos casos deben morir como largamente lo dispone el derecho canónico y también el derecho civil." See also 203–4: "Ca yo oí decir a persona de gran autoridad que no era más menester para los condenar a todos por herejes, sino ver cómo en tales lugares se usaban enterrar."
90. Talavera, 204: "Así que, por quitar esta calumnia y opinión, y la división y diferencia, que se sigue de ella entre cristianos nuevos y viejos. Y dije y amonesté, y digo amonesto, y siempre diré y amonestaré, que los tales enterramientos y sepulturas deben cesar y deben ser prohibidos y vedadas a los semejantes."
91. Talavera, 83: "Ni agora fué puesto a todos los nuevamente convertidos nombre de herejes, como se queja este malvado hereje, mas es puesto a los malvados descreídos tales como él; que seyendo bautizados y teniendo nombre y aún algunas obras o muestras de cristianos, se halla que guardan cerimonias y ritos de moros o de judíos."
92. Bernáldez, *Memorias del reinado*, 94:

> La herética prabedad musaica reinó gran tienpo escondida y andando por los rincones, no se osando manifestar, y fué disimulada y dado lugar por mengua de los prelados, arçobispos e obispos de España, que nunca la acusaron ni la denunciaron a los reyes ni a los papas, según devían e

eran obligados. Ovo su comienço esta eregía musaica en el año de Nuestro Redenptor de mill e trecientos e noventa años, en el comienço del reinado en Castilla del rey don Enrrique, tercero de este nonbre, que fué el robo de la judería por la predicación de fray Vicente, un santo e católico varón docto, de la Orden de Santo Domingo, que quisiera en aquel tienpo, por predicaciones e pruebas de la Santa Ley e Escriptura, convertir a todos los judíos de España e dar cabo a la inveterada e hedionda sinagoga.

93. Rosa Vidal Doval has traced the origins of this conception to the Fourth Lateran Coucil while studying the case of the Toledo rebellion of 1449. See Vidal Doval, "Matriz medieval," 13–28.
94. Talavera, *Católica impugnación*, 181: "Y como desvía el que, guardando el Evangelio en algo, judaiza."
95. Talavera, 171: "Es hereje muy errado, como lo fueron los cristianos nazarenos y hebionitas, según que en el prólogo ya fue dicho." And in the next line Talavera reiterates: "y como lo era y mostraba ser este malvado, que compuso este libelo."
96. Talavera, prologue, chs. 7, 12, 59, 64.
97. Talavera, 75: "Aunque este malvado se finge y dice aquí cristiano viejo, pero yo más creo que no fuese cristiano viejo, ni nuevo, sino obstinado y malicioso judío como parecerá adelante en muchos lugares de este maldido libelo."
98. The title is "Declara brevemente y muy bien quién se debe hoy llamar pueblo de israel; y cómo no lo son los judíos; y cómo yerra gravemente el que a los buenos cristianos nuevamente convertidos tiene malquerencia y aún el que la tiene a los viejos."
99. Talavera, 147: "También los cristianos, que descienden de la gentilidad, so un pueblo de Israel verdadero, a que llama el santo Apóstol, Israel según el espíritu."
100. Talavera, 150–51: "El pueblo judiego no fué más sabio, ni de más sotil ingenio que las otras naciones naturalmente hablando, ni lo son los que de ellos descienden." See also 151: "No fué aquel pueblo más sabio, más sotil, ni más ingenioso que otro, ni lo son los que descienden de él, antes por ventura menos, como parece claramente por otras gentes y naciones de aquellos tiempos."
101. Talavera, 148: "E si llama pueblo de Israel el que hoy es pueblo judiego, también yerra este malvado en ello, porque éstos no soy hoy pueblo de Israel, ni judíos verdaderos, mas son sinagoga y ayuntamiento de Satanás. . . . Ramos secos son y sin provecho, como dice el santo Apóstol, cortados de aquel buen tronco, en el cual buen tronco son insiertos en lugar de ellos todos los buenos cristianos aunque desciendan de troncos malos."
102. Talavera, 148: "Y aunque los que hoy se llaman judíos se pudiesen llamar pueblo de Israel, aun no es verdad que [el] pueblo cristiano les tiene enemiga, antes los trata humanamente y cuasi como próximos, no obstante que quiere que vivan apartados y anden señalados y que no usen de algunos oficios por evitar muchos pecados."
103. Talavera, 147–48, about the Jewish converts: "Ni los cristianos verdaderos tienen enemiga ninguna a los cristianos convertidos del judaismo, ca si la toviesen pecarían muy gravemente en ello y no serían verdaderos cristianos, que quiere decir discípulos de Jesucristo, el cual quiso que en esto fuésemos conocidos por sus discípulos: en que nos amásemos unos a otros, como Él nos amó a todos." Further about the Jews at page 148: "Verdad es que algunos cristianos los denuestan y maltratan y les tienen odio y malquerencia, sin les dar a ello nueva causa y no solamente a los judíos, más aún a los cristianos que descienden de ellos, como poco antes decíamos."
104. Talavera, 82–83. The expression *marrandíes* has raised interesting etymological speculations, thus far

unresolved. See Asensio, "Erasmismo y las corrientes," 58.

105. On Talavera's conception of the Church's unity, some remarks were recently made by Salomons, "Church United in Itself," 651. Though the fifteenth-century debate on the conception of the Church (ecclesiology) in relation with non-Christians might be of great relevance to scholarship (especially in light of conciliarist ideas), this contribution fails to provide any suggestion or proposal in this regard, merely reiterating other scholars' claim on Talavera's opposition to the Inquisition and providing banal observations on his obvious confidence in the ecclesiastical jurisdiction and his self-evident obedience to the Church's authority. See, for example, "The authority of the Church was everything to Talavera, and that, more than any tolerant leanings, affected his attitudes towards conversion and minorities" (p. 659) or "This leaves us with a man who was the product of his education and experience. The Church was Talavera's life, and from an early age we see its importance to him, and his absolute belief in its authority" (p. 662).

106. Dante Alighieri, *Comedia, Inf.*, 28:22–33: "Già veggia, per mezzul perdere o lulla, / com' io vidi un, così non si pertugia, / rotto dal mento infin dove si trulla. // Tra le gambe pendevan le minugia; / la corata pareva e 'l tristo sacco / che merda fa di quel che si trangugia. // Mentre che tutto in lui veder m'attacco, / guardommi e con le man s'aperse il petto, / dicendo: 'Or vedi com' io mi dilacco! // vedi come storpiato è Mäometto! / Dinanzi a me sen va piangendo Alì, / fesso nel volto dal mento al ciuffetto.'"

107. See Talavera, *Católica impugnación*, 189–91, 222–25.

108. See, respectively, Martínez Medina and Biersack, *Fray Hernando de Talavera*, 155–61; and Robinson, *Imagining the Passion*, 10–22.

109. Talavera, *Católica impugnación*, 147.

110. See Márquez Villanueva, "Problema de los conversos," 61: "The problem of the new Christians was in no way racial, but rather social and, secondarily, religious." Márquez Villanueva expressed the same opinion earlier in his "Converso Problem." In 2009, moreover, Isabella Iannuzzi published a biography of Talavera where the lens of "power" systematically prevails over religious and theological aspects, both seen as subordinate to politics. See Iannuzzi, *Poder de la palabra*, esp. pt. 3, where the "instrumentalización de elementos religiosos para finalidades socio-políticas" is made explicit in a chapter title (353).

111. Mir y Noguera, *Escritores místicos españoles*.

112. An influential overview of his attitude toward Islam was provided by Southern in his well-known book *Western Views of Islam*. Based on a progressive history of ideas, this overview embraces a static concept of knowledge as the key to appraising Western understandings of Islam. Modern concerns continuously merge with medieval concerns—for example, at one point, the author emblematically claims that Segovia's ideas represent "words which will strike a chord in modern breasts" (91–92). On the influence of the Cold War context on Southern's approach, see Skottki, "Medieval Western Perceptions," 114.

113. See García-Arenal and Leroy, *Moros y judíos en Navarra*, 13.

114. See Márquez Villanueva, "Ideas de la *Católica impugnación*," (A)xiv: "Es lo que justifica que su impugnación haya puesto de hecho más ahínco en los signos visible de la apostasía que no en lo puramente teológico o doctrinal." And later on along this line, "El libelista no hace teología, sino política religiosa, y Talavera ha de responderle, acorde en este mismo plano." Interestingly enough, Villanueva himself warns readers about the complexity of the human implications and religious attitudes involved in this controversy—at least on the side of the *conversos*: "No debemos cerrar el estudio de la *Católica impugnación* sin que nos

detengamos a meditar brevemente, pero con serenidad, acerca de las perspectivas espirituales que a través de ella hemos contemplado y que son tan complejas, tan rebosantes de dolores humanos y de angustias del alma, que todos nuestros esfuerzos por comprenderlas serán siempre pocos." True to his approach, however, soon afterward, he recalls again the social and cultural relevance of the "*Judeoconverso* problem." Márquez Villanueva, "Estudio preliminar," 43. See also where the author relies on concepts such as "lucha de clases" and "odio político-social" (44), an interpretation according to which religious aspects are clearly instrumental to political confrontation. On Márquez Villanueva's contribution to the study of Talavera, see Barrios Aguilera, *Suerte de los vencidos*, 333–47.

115. For a first insight into the relation between Talavera and the Hieronymite order, see Martínez Medina and Biersack, *Fray Hernando de Talavera*, 20–29, 194–96.

116. Suárez Fernández, *Política internacional*; Rumeu de Armas, *Política indigenista*; Pérez Collados, *Indias en el pensamiento político*; Alonso Acero, *Cisneros y la conquista española*.

117. I linger on this controversial debate in a forthcoming article: Scotto, "Neither by Habits."

118. See Talavera, *Católica impugnación*, 106:

> Debió nuestro Redentor Jesús dar nueva ley y nuevos mandamientos mayores y más difíciles en sí mesmos al pueblo cristiano, que le tiene caridad y amor, que los que dió primero al pueblo judiego que le tuvo temor; y por esta razón parece que los mandamientos, que tenía el pueblo judiego, ni debían, ni podían ser perpetuos como lo son y deben y pueden ser los mandamientos del santo evangelio, porque lo que se hace por miedo y como por fuerza más que por voluntad, no puede mucho durar, como dura y es perpetuo lo que se hace por amor y por caridad.

119. Talavera, 243.

7

THE DOUBLE POLEMIC OF MARTÍN DE FIGUEROLA'S *LUMBRE DE FE CONTRA EL ALCORÁN*

Mercedes García-Arenal

In June 1521, in Valencia, Mossen Johan Martín de Figuerola finished writing a work that he had begun two years earlier, on November 1, 1519, entitled *Lumbre de fe contra el Alcorán* (1519). He dedicated it to His Majesty King and Emperor Charles V, and in it he exhorted the king to consider the spiritual dangers for his Christians vassals represented by Muslims living in the Crown of Aragon and implored him to decree their conversion to Catholicism or, if they would not convert, their expulsion.[1] According to Figuerola, for Muslims to practice their religion in Aragon was blasphemous, and it was urgent to put an end to it. This was the ultimate goal of all his actions and of all his writing. There is scant information about who Martín de Figuerola was, and most of what we know is to be found in his work: he was from Valencia, a master in *sacra theologia*, who referred to himself as chaplain of the pope, probably because of his contact with Adriaan of Utrecht, as will be said later, though also as a simple priest (*beneficiatus*) in the cathedral church of Valencia. He died in about 1532.[2]

In this chapter, I analyze Figuerola's polemical strategy through an examination of his *Lumbre de fe* and his campaign to convert the Muslims of Aragon as described by himself. This included combative and aggressive measures such as entering mosques, interrupting sermons, and challenging Muslim preachers in the presence of their followers and within their sacred spaces, mainly in the Zaragoza mosque. What Figuerola did was unprecedented. It differed from previous evangelizing campaigns and from the actions taken by the group of preachers in Granada who, like him, had been influenced by Martín García, bishop of Barcelona. Figuerola's dramatic turn toward an aggressive polemical strategy offers a unique case study, especially since we have, in his writings, an account both of his tactics and of the reactions they elicited. Should Figuerola be understood as an exception or as reflecting a broader pattern? In what follows, I will make the argument that Figuerola's polemical strategy reflected a broader change in the development and adoption of the doctrine of "indirect coercion." Moreover, Figuerola's polemic was directed not solely at Muslims but also at Aragonese nobles who, as part of a seigneurial power structure, protected them. Figuerola was writing at a moment when this power was being fiercely contested and when the new king and emperor, Charles V, recently arrived in Spain, was also being challenged. It was a time, therefore, in which the balance of power was shifting.

Lumbre de fe contra el Alcorán

Lumbre de fe, a most extraordinary work, remains unpublished, a fact that has obscured the importance of its very combative and influential author, about whom we know little more than what he himself says or can be gleaned from his work. The work is preserved in a manuscript at the Biblioteca de la Real Academia de la Historia in Madrid.[3] This manuscript appears to have been prepared with the intention of having it printed, since the writing is extremely clear and it includes elaborate pen-drawing illustrations of Aragonese Muslims, their customs, their beliefs, and the stories of the prophets of which they were so fond. The illustrations are part of the polemic and one of the book's means of persuasion. The fact that *Lumbre de fe* includes a great deal of Arabic text is one reason why it may not have been printed, since there was no Arabic type in Spain at the time. Another reason, as will be seen in this chapter, is because historic events conspired to change the terms of the debate about Muslims, making Figuerola's work irrelevant before it could ever be published.[4]

Lumbre de fe is divided into two parts. The first contains disputations against Islam based mainly on the Qur'ān and on works of *tafsīr* or Qur'ānic exegesis. In this first part, Figuerola is very clear about the need to dispute with Muslims using their own scripture and especially the *glosadores*—that is, the authors of works of *tafsīr*.[5] His text includes more than 185 Qur'ānic quotations, each of which is written in three versions: Arabic in Arabic script, Arabic transcribed in "inverse *aljamía*" (viz. phonological Arabic transcription in the Latin alphabet), and Romance vernacular. The quotations are also often glossed and explained according to Muslim *tafsīr* authorities. It is a rich and fascinating text, almost unique considering that the Qur'ānic texts written in Spanish in the sixteenth century that have come down to us are extremely rare.[6]

The polemical disputes in the first part of the book are complemented in the second part by a first-person and highly vivid narrative of Figuerola's campaigns during the years 1517 and 1518. He undertook the campaigns to proselytize Mudejars at the request of the aforementioned bishop of Barcelona, Don Martín García, who at that point was too old (in fact, he died in 1521) to continue the task he had been assigned by the Catholic Monarchs, Ferdinand and Isabel—namely, to preach a sermon to Aragonese Muslims four times a year.[7] Martín García, archdeacon of Daroca before becoming bishop of Barcelona, and Figuerola had already been preaching together in Aragon in the late fifteenth century, not only to Muslims but also to converts from Judaism as shown in Inquisition documents.[8] Figuerola writes that he accepted the new assignment because he had some knowledge of Arabic and the Qur'ān.[9] He began by delivering the four sermons but soon discovered that it was a waste of time because afterward, the *alfaquíes*[10] would take the Muslims back to their mosques and contradict everything they had heard from Figuerola. He decided therefore to employ a different strategy: he would go into the mosques in Zaragoza and other towns on Fridays and challenge the *alfaquíes* there with his own copy of the Qur'ān in hand. He would, he tells us, target the sermon the *alfaquí* had just preached, often interrupting him, in the presence of the whole congregation.

During his campaigns in the *morerías*, Figuerola was accompanied by the person from whom he says he had learned what Arabic he knew and who had provided him with Arabic books and explained numerous Islamic concepts to him. This was Maestre Juan Gabriel, the former *alfaquí* of Teruel who had converted to Christianity and who was, as Katarzyna K. Starczewska and I have argued elsewhere, none other than Ioanes Gabrielis Terrolensis, the man who provided Cardinal Egidio da Viterbo (1469–1532), papal nuncio (legate) in Spain, with a copy of the Qur'ān in Arabic, written in his own hand and accompanied by a Latin translation.[11]

Lumbre de fe is also interesting because it contains what we could call anthropological or ethnographic information about the Muslims of Aragon—the way they practiced their religion as well as what they ate and wore, what their houses contained, and so on. Figuerola came by this information from his experience working in the small rural *morerías* in Aragon. The shepherds and peasants of these communities were profoundly despised by Figuerola, who saw them as uncouth and ignorant. They could neither read nor write, and they did not know Arabic.[12] Despite his attitude toward these rural Muslims, and despite the fact that they were ignorant both of Arabic and, according to him, of the Qur'ān—which raises the question of why he included Arabic texts accompanied by phonological transcription, which I will address later on—he provides us with remarkable descriptions of local religiosity, dietary traditions, magical and medicinal practices, burials, and so on that deserve a whole study of their own and cannot be addressed here. But all his descriptions of the customs he observed among the Muslims—from their fondness for sweets, to the starkness of their houses and mosques, to the simplicity of their attire—only serve as proof that their religion is false. The only thing he considers worthy of respect and imitation by Christians is the fact that Muslims separate women from men in the mosques at prayer time and that women there are protected from the eyes of men.

The text of *Lumbre de fe* also includes a detailed account of the actions taken by Figuerola in connection with civil and religious Christian authorities in his effort to promote the compulsory conversion of Muslims in Aragon, as had already happened in the territories under the Crown of Castile, where conversion to Catholicism had been decreed in 1502. Martín de Figuerola's project was, as I will show, a double polemic—a dispute not only with Muslims but also with Aragonese nobles, who very much depended on Muslim labor to work their vast estates and who were thus outspoken advocates for patience and appeasement toward Muslims and for maintaining the status quo.

Johan Martín de Figuerola

Johan Martín de Figuerola was, as I have said, connected to the bishop and inquisitor Martín García. As a churchman close to the Catholic Monarchs, Martín García participated from 1500 onward in the evangelization of the

Muslim population in recently conquered Granada and later of the Mudejars in Valencia and other kingdoms of Aragon.[13] Martín García gathered a circle of men to help him in his proselytizing campaign in Granada, and he had a profound influence on this group of individuals.[14] Several men in this circle published important works of disputation and polemics. These authors—notably Lope de Obregón and Juan Andrés[15]—were all involved, like Martín García himself, in preaching activities in Granada and later in the evangelization of Aragonese Mudejars between 1500 and 1520. Their works were constructed according to the same principles that were characteristic of Martín de Figuerola, using direct dialogues that rhetorically address Muslims ("próximo mío de Moro") and referring solely to Muslim sources. Their attempts at proselytizing using the Qur'ān were intended to challenge the Muslims' confidence in the tenets of their faith by pointing out the supposed inconsistencies and paradoxes in their sacred text, the aspects that defied "natural reason." The campaign was aimed at sowing doubt and confusion in the Muslim population rather than at instruction in the tenets of Catholicism as well as showing that the Christian way of life—and here again, Figuerola contrasts the finely appointed houses of the Christians, the richness and beauty of their churches, their dietary and other cultural practices to the Muslim way of life—was proof of the superiority of the Christian religion. The exegetical and historical deconstruction of the Qur'ān introduced by Martín García and his followers was fleshed out by Figuerola's empirical observations of the flaws in Muslims' lifestyle and ethics. Figuerola's belief that the Muslims' sacred text and way of life were a sham led him to dismiss them as true polemical adversaries and to an intellectual intolerance that, we will see, is manifest in his treatise.

The campaigns conducted by Martín García and his followers had been conceived for Arabophone Moriscos (in Granada), who by 1502 had already been forcibly converted to Catholicism by royal decree. The Mudejars in Valencia—who were more familiar to Martín de Figuerola, himself a Valencian—were also Arabophone and still legally Muslim. Muslims elsewhere in Aragon no longer spoke Arabic, though many still memorized portions of the Qur'ān, even if they did not employ Arabic as a spoken language, and would have held in high regard both the authority conferred by the text and the language itself. Thus Figuerola's use of Arabic made his audience more receptive to his polemical discourse. But his treatise clearly shows that he was not addressing *moros* in general but specifically *alfaquíes*: they were the target of his disputations. He exhibited his knowledge of the Qur'ān as a source of his own authority, over both the Muslims and the Christian elites and authorities who disapproved of his aggressive methods.[16] At the end of his *Lumbre de fe*, Figuerola includes instructions for others who might want to dispute with Muslims and try to convert them. He advises against discussing intricate matters of faith and dogma because Aragonese Muslims are too ignorant to understand these debates. He insists that only the Qur'ān should be used, because when other Muslim authorities are quoted, the Moors say the Christians do not understand them properly. And even with the Qur'ān, he suggests that it is best to merely point out contradictions and paradoxes. The Old Testament can be used and also the stories of the prophets recognized by Muslims as prophets. This is the strategy that he himself followed.

Figuerola wants to confuse and sow doubts in the Muslims, to convert the *alfaquíes* in the conviction that, if they convert, the whole community will follow. But he is also impatient and full of urgency: he argues that the conversion of Muslims must be decreed or that they must be expelled from the land, as was done with the Jews. He considers it an outrage that the Inquisition persecutes converts from Judaism as *judaizantes* while Muslims are allowed to continue to live as they please. He argues again and again that it is preferable to force them to be Christians rather than allow them to continue to blaspheme in Christian territory.

Having been influenced by the tactics used by Martín García, Figuerola was a staunch believer in religious conversion by "indirect compulsion" and advocated compelling the Muslims to convert by citing the usual religious authorities, in particular Duns Scotus. In his *Lumbre de fe*, Figuerola refers repeatedly to the necessity of exerting "indirect compulsion" (*coerción indirecta*) should the decree of forced conversion be postponed. I will return later on to this idea of "indirect compulsion."

In addition to his criticism of Inquisition policies (regarding the different attitudes toward Jews and Muslims) and his advocacy for "indirect compulsion," Figuerola also urged the king to support the goal of conquering Jerusalem, at the time considered a distinct possibility. As readers, we can see that Figuerola was possessed of messianic zeal and longed to hasten the day when there would be only one Law, only one king for all humanity.

He maintains, as in the Gospel of John 10:16 ("et fiet unum ovile et unus pastor"), that "at the End there will be only one shepherd, Jesus Christ, and one fold, the Roman Catholic Church,"[17] and "one god, one law, one king and no other."[18] In these passages and arguments, we hear echoes of the sermons given by Martín García, who had tried to convince King Ferdinand of the need to conquer North Africa and thereafter Jerusalem (reaching the sacred city by way of previously conquered ports on the southern shores of the Mediterranean, such as Oran and Tripoli), thereby stamping out Islam before the approaching End of Times.[19] Figuerola also insists on the goal of conquering Jerusalem, but his most persistent obsession is expressed by his saying, "Que la tierra quede limpia" (May the land be cleansed).[20] In his insistence on "indirect compulsion," together with his millenarian ideas, we see clear evidence of Figuerola's Franciscan ideology, an ideology that had been dominant in Valencia and Catalonia since the Middle Ages.

Toward Forced Conversion: Figuerola's Campaign

In addition to his calls for conversion and crusade, Martín de Figuerola gives, as I have said, a detailed account of his attempts to convince the authorities to decree forced conversion. Firstly, as he recounts, he traveled to Valladolid to implore King Charles I (later Holy Roman Emperor Charles V), who had just arrived in Spain for the first time, and his regent, Cardinal Adriaan of Utrecht, to compel the Muslims to convert.[21] In this attempt to petition the new king, he was not successful, since he was not even received by the king. He presented a request (*súplica*) to the Royal Council and to Adriaan of Utrecht. On his way back to Valencia, he went to Roa to visit Cardinal Cisneros, who had been the main promoter in the conversion of the Muslims of Granada and who promised to broach the subject with the king. He did not have the opportunity to do so, since he died in November 1517.[22] On May 9, 1518, the king arrived in Zaragoza with his entire retinue to be recognized as king of Aragon. Figuerola once again went to see him—and again did not succeed in getting access to the king—but he sent another request.[23] This document was illustrated with a crucifix that was being attacked by Muslims with stones, on each of which was written an article of the Catholic faith that Muslims rejected. This document, which was hand-delivered to Adriaan of Utrecht so that he might present it to the Royal Council for consideration, succeeded only in eliciting some appeasing words, and nothing was done. The document proves the importance of images and illustrations for Figuerola and shows how he tried to use them for persuasion. Figuerola seized the occasion of the king's visit to Zaragoza to deliver a famous sermon in that city's cathedral, and Muslims were required to be present. The Muslim authorities had entreated the king not to oblige them to attend, but the Inquisition intervened, and they were compelled to go. The sermon was calculated to instill fear in the Muslims and was followed by protests. Figuerola was asked to stop his proselytizing. At that time, Figuerola also hosted a banquet at his house in Zaragoza and invited the entire royal court. When some noblemen, hoping to prevent or at least delay an edict of conversion, claimed that the measure Figuerola proposed could not be taken by the king alone and had to be ordered by Rome, Figuerola insisted repeatedly on his access to Cardinal Adriaan, or Adriano, who had recently been appointed cardinal of Tortosa (August 1516). Figuerola claimed that he had spoken with Adriaan many times and that the latter was very much in favor of mandatory conversion. Figuerola is adamant in his book that the pope should order the king to convert the Muslims living in his lands, and he tries to influence the cardinal to help ensure that this happens.[24] He tells us that he had previously stressed the urgency of this conversion during his many visits to Archbishop Alfonso de Aragón, the illegitimate son of King Ferdinand, and the inquisitor Toribio de Saldaña, both members of the Aragonese high clergy who, however, remained doubtful about the project and elusive about their commitment to it. In fact, they asked him to suspend his preaching to the Muslims until the situation calmed down because the Mudejars were starting to abandon their lands, and the nobility—furious about the potential loss of their work force—was pressuring the king. Due to this pressure, Alfonso de Aragón ordered a punishment of one hundred lashes (*azotes*) for anyone who said in public that the Muslims were going to be expelled.

Figuerola then approached the Inquisition Council in Madrid. He writes that he went to speak to its members to ask for support and permission to continue preaching, but he found them lukewarm, "without ardor and with little faith and there was nothing they were prepared to do to help [him]," and so he returned to Zaragoza.[25]

Though he was not successful in his petitions to the king and high clergy, Figuerola had many opportunities to try to convince them. It may strike us as surprising that Figuerola, a minor religious figure, possibly a friar, found it so easy to gain access to important personalities and councils. At the end of his work, we learn that his family connections may have helped in this regard. He complains that, just as he is finishing writing the *Lumbre de fe*, he has lost whatever influence he may have had because his uncle, the bishop of Pati, died in May 1518.[26] Indeed, other sources confirm that this bishop was Miguel de Figuerola, "vicario general del arzobispo don Alfonso de Aragón," and therefore very close to Cardinal Adriaan of Utrecht.[27] In January 1522, Adriaan was elected pope. Through his uncle, then, Figuerola had been able to plead his case before important members of the clergy and the royal administration.

Even so, Archbishop Alfonso de Aragón repeatedly criticized Figuerola for taking too aggressive an approach with Muslims, going further than Martín García had ever gone in Granada and Aragon. As I have said, one very interesting feature of his treatise is that it allows us to see the different tactics that Figuerola used, because he describes not only his own actions but also the reactions of those around him. For example, Figuerola tells us that Archbishop Alfonso asked him to show compassion and benevolence.[28] Although Figuerola describes his actions toward the Muslims, he never speaks of his threats—only of his disputations—nor of the reasons why the cardinal would have urged him to be more compassionate. However, when Alfonso de Aragón reproves him, we learn that the Muslim authorities have complained of Figuerola's harassment while pursuing his particular understanding of "indirect compulsion," and his threats included his intention to convince the Aragonese authorities to close down mosques and take Muslim children away from their families. By reading such sources between the lines or "against the grain," we also learn that the *alfaquíes* contacted Charles I's Burgundian entourage, that they presented gifts to the courtiers and other noblemen, and that they routinely sent poultry, fruit, and mutton to Archbishop Alfonso de Aragón. Figuerola rebukes the archbishop for accepting and consuming meat that has been slaughtered according to Muslim specifications—in other words, meat that is *halāl*.

Figuerola also indirectly reveals the polemical strategies that the noblemen employed against him when he narrates his responses—for example, when Figuerola tells the reader about his response to the count of Ribagorza, who was sent by the nobility on a mission to Charles I in Flanders to ask him to honor the word of his grandparents that the Muslims were not going to be expelled or forced to convert. Figuerola reserves the full force of his invective for noblemen like Ribagorza, accusing them of caring more for their honor and material interests than for God. He threatens them with rotting in hell if, at the next Consejo de Aragón, they vote against the forced conversion of Muslims. He is clearly capable of vicious verbal abuse of the nobility. In Figuerola's depiction of the exchange, another nobleman, the count of Aranda, says, "It is you who will rot, we will live one hundred years!" Later Figuerola adds the colorful epithet that the count applies to him ("Cojones el bastardo, catalán y sin barba").[29] The noblemen complain to the king that the Mudejars are selling their things and starting to leave. For this, Figuerola tells the reader, he is "very much hated." It seems to me that he pronounces this "soy tenido en mucho odio" with a certain self-righteous satisfaction, as proof to his readers of his superior morality and love of God, his disdain for material goods, and the fervor of his messianic faith.

Compelle Intrare (Indirect Compulsion)

Before focusing on Figuerola's campaigns in the *morerías*, it is necessary to explain his ideology, his insistence on "blasphemy" and "indirect compulsion" in the context of the discussion about the forced conversions that were taking place at the time elsewhere in Iberia.

The Franciscan theologian Duns Scotus had been very influential in Spain during the reign of the Catholic Monarchs and would continue to be so under Charles I.[30] At the beginning of the fourteenth century, the Subtil Scotus—as he was known at the time—had stated that the Christian Prince was alone authorized to order the conversion of the children of Jews and other infidels and that, moreover, it was for him a pious duty to force non-Christian adults to convert "by threats and fear" (*minis et terroribus*). He maintained that baptism carried out by force or coercion was acceptable on both theological and political grounds. By imposing high taxes on communities of other religions, mainly Jews, and by curtailing their rights and social status, royal power could and should induce conversion. He referred to all these measures as "indirect coercion" (*coerción indirecta*).[31] Although the opinion of Thomas Aquinas, who was opposed to forced conversions, was dominant among theologians of the time (Thomas Aquinas's statement that pagans and Jews should not be forced to accept Christianity "because faith is a voluntary act" was very clear),[32] the Scotist line was promoted by other Franciscan authors like Francesc Eiximenis in his treatise *Lo Cristià* (The Christian), a *summa theologica* written around 1385 and published in Catalan in 1484, and Alonso de Espina, whose *Fortalitium Fidei* (Fortress of the faith) was written around 1460 and published in 1470.[33] Figuerola quotes Eiximenis repeatedly.[34] It was the Scotist doctrine, followed by Cardinal Cisneros, that had provided the necessary legitimization for the forced conversion of Muslims in Granada, a conversion decreed by Queen Isabel and negotiated previously with Granada's Muslim elites.[35] Of course, there were serious doubts about its effectiveness in achieving a complete and sincere conversion on the part of the New Christians; every contemporary observer agreed that Muslims forced to convert in this way would not truly abandon their own religion. But it was believed that coercion would succeed in the long run, particularly among the children and their descendants in later generations. To promote this process, children should be separated from their parents and their corrupting influence. That is what Scotus claimed and what the supporters of forced baptism understood. In about three generations, the descendants of forcibly converted infidels would become good, sincere Christians.[36]

As Isabelle Poutrin has shown, Duns Scotus cites the precedent of the Visigothic king Sisebut, who in the seventh century had decreed the forced conversion of Jews living in Visigothic Iberia. Duns Scotus also uses the *Decretales* of the Council of Toledo, which had expressed its support for the forced conversion of the Jews. The Fourth Council of Toledo had left an instrument for this, the canon *Iudeorum filios*, later inserted in the *Decree* (2 C.28 q.1 c.11). This canon ordered children to be removed from their Jewish parents to avoid the transmission of apostasy when the children were baptized. Figuerola was versed in this juridical literature and quotes the *Decretales* frequently.[37] These precedents gave force to Figuerola's threats to remove Muslim children from their parents. The noblemen, however, insisted that the Council of Toledo was invalid because the pope had neither attended nor sanctioned its sessions.

What was at stake in this controversy was the power of the Christian prince to dictate the conscience of his subjects. Thomas Aquinas had been against forced conversion but had also pointed to cases in which infidels should be separated from Christians so that they would not corrupt the latter's faith through blasphemy: "Ut fidem non impediant vel blasphemiis, vel malis persuasionibus, vel etiam apertis persecutionibus."[38] The Dominican Francisco de Vitoria (d. 1546), in his commentary on the *Secunda Secundae*, poses the question of whether it is legitimate to prohibit the blasphemies of infidels and in particular the Qur'ān. He distinguishes between written blasphemy that is not disseminated and oral, public blasphemy. The prince might know that the Qur'ān contains some blasphemous material against Christ and Christians, but that does not make it legitimate to burn Qur'āns, because as long as this blasphemy is not publicized, it can do no harm to Christians. Moreover, burning Qur'āns would constitute a grave outrage for infidels. But if infidels blaspheme in public, which is an offense to Christians and an obstacle for those who do want to convert, then they must be punished.[39] This scholastic approach was based on the difference between potential and actual blasphemy. Figuerola, as someone who was not a detached scholar but who encountered Muslims in his campaigns, insisted on actual blasphemy: he tirelessly argued that the mere presence of infidels was an insult to Christians and blasphemous, since they were publicly worshipping a false god.

Figuerola was responding not to Francisco de Vitoria, who wrote after his time, or the circle of theologians in Salamanca to which Vitoria belonged but rather to the milieu and events in contemporary Valencia. This is what shaped and framed his text. It is important to recall that he finished writing his work in Valencia in November 1519. At the beginning of that very year, just a few months after Charles I left Spain to be crowned emperor in Germany, the Revolt of the Brotherhoods (*rebelión de las Germanías*) began in Valencia, led by the city's craft and merchant guilds. During that year, the city of Valencia was the scene of violent riots. The rebels would defeat the royal troops in Gandía on July 25, 1521, and go on to control a large part of the territory south of Valencia, Orihuela, and Xàtiva. During the summer of 1521, thousands of Muslims were led to baptism by the *Agermanados*, as the members of the *Germanías* were known, in some cases under mortal threat, in other cases as the result of panic or indirect pressure applied by local authorities who sought in this way to preempt an attack by the rebels.

In 1519, as Figuerola himself tells us, he was in Cocentaina, south of Valencia, near Alicante.[40] He must have written a good part of his book there because he mentions being in Cocentaina several times at the beginning and end of the book. There he had the opportunity to debate with an old *alfaquí*. He says that he was a fugitive from the "deaths" and massacres in the city of Valencia. He does not specify what those *muertes* meant, nor is he very clear about whether he or the *alfaquí* was the fugitive. The words of the old *alfaquí* seem to refer to justice in the afterlife and are connected to these *muertes*.[41] In another passage, Figuerola again refers to the *muertes* of 1519, and there it is clear that he is the fugitive, because he explains that he was speaking with the *alfaquí* at the latter's house.[42] He does not provide any further explanation nor does he voice any opinions about the rebels or current events: he was probably in Cocentaina to escape the disturbances created by the *Germanías* in Valencia, but there is no doubt that he shared certain aspects of the *Agermanados'* ideology, such as their antisegneurial and anti-Muslim sentiments and their millenarianism.

The *Agermanados'* motives in attacking the Muslim communities were a mixture of economic and social grievances against the landlords combined with millenarian ideas aimed at achieving the conversion of the "infidels."[43] These millenarian ideas were inspired by Francesc Eiximenis, Ramon Llull, Arnau de Vilanova[44] (all of them often quoted by Figuerola), and most especially, Joan Alamany's work predicting the arrival of the Antichrist and the need to convert all Muslims, published in Catalan in 1480 and reprinted in 1520.[45] Alamany made use of medieval prophetic-eschatological cycles that had been introduced by the Franciscans in Catalonia, where Arnau de Vilanova was the first to use the messianic prophecies about the conquest of Jerusalem and universal royalty in support of the Catalan-Aragonese dynasty. These prophecies, which had originated in the thirteenth century among Byzantine and Muslim inhabitants of the Holy Land terrorized by a crusading king from France and the Hohenstaufen emperor, were now applied to a completely different context—against the Habsburg emperor—giving them renewed vigor. Of a clearly messianic cast and deeply imbued with Franciscan ideology, those prophecies had played an important role in the conquest and evangelization of the Americas.[46] In the context of sixteenth-century Spain, these ancient prophetic and apocalyptic motifs formed part of an ideology of exclusion, of absolute eradication of all who did not belong to the group that was to triumph at the Final Hour and especially Muslims, the Jews having already been expelled. As formulated by Alamany and deployed by the *Agermanados*, these prophecies assumed a clearly anti-Islamic dimension, making the Mudejars the principle targets of the rebels.

After the defeat of the *Germanías* in 1522, the conversion of Muslims that had taken place under the rebels' illegal uprising against their king was challenged by influential sectors of Valencian society, especially the nobility. Many converts returned to their previous religion, and the Inquisition intervened and put together a detailed report on the "apostasy" of the baptized Muslims. Under pressure from the grand inquisitor, Emperor Charles V called a meeting of prelates, theologians, and lawyers of his councils, known as the Congregation of Madrid. The assembly studied the results of the inquiry submitted by the Inquisition and came to the conclusion, in March 1525, that the baptisms performed during the *rebelión de las Germanías* were valid. The compulsory conversion of Aragonese Muslims was decreed a few months later. In November 1525, the emperor wrote to the captain general of Catalonia that the decree of expulsion applied to all Muslims and was, as on previous occasions (Jews in 1492, Castilian Muslims in 1502), to be commuted only by conversion. Muslims were given a choice: convert or be expelled. Following the Scotist line, Charles V wrote that "it would be good to tell them, in the sermons, that if they are obstinate and hardened in their sect and resolve to go out of these realms, they have to leave their children to become Christians, because this will have a great weight in converting the parents."[47]

Eschatological Predictions

Lumbre de fe, "the fire of faith," is what runs through Figuerola's text and his unflinching campaign against both Muslims and Christian authorities, a twofold crusade to overturn the status quo in Aragon. He is writing, as we have seen, at a moment when the balance of power is tipping.

In addition to clashes with the nobility, Figuerola's campaign in support of conversion caused very real disruptions and anxieties for the Muslim population. They were so distressed—*alborotados* and *alterados* are the words used in the text—by this militant preacher and his campaign that many fled from Aragon to Valencia, crossing over to North Africa in such numbers as to alarm the nobility. The atmosphere in Valencia prior to the *Germanías* revolt must have instilled fear, and with good cause, in the Aragonese communities. And Figuerola's aggressive campaign played an important part in this. The authorities of the Muslim communities had tried to negotiate with Figuerola to hold his debates someplace other than in their mosques and to convince him that there was no need to call for the Inquisition, but they were unable to get any respite—he would make no truce.

Figuerola's visits to the Aragonese mosques and his disputes with *alfaquíes* were part of a premeditated strategy of pressure and intimidation that became an important factor in the waves of emigration that were so vexing to the nobility. To elucidate the reasons why Figuerola was able to strike such a chord with Muslims, I will first describe his campaign and then I will explain how it was well tailored to exploit the eschatological fears and anxieties of Aragonese Mudejars and threaten their sense of community and their sacred history.

As he tells it, Figuerola first went to the mosque of what appears to be Zaragoza in January 1517. He sat there to listen to the *alfaquí* and tried to contradict him. He was thrown out of the mosque along with those who accompanied him. His next visit took place on February 6, 1517, when he repeated this course of action in the same mosque. In Figuerola's narration, the *alfaquí* begs him to desist because the congregation is horrified and outraged by his flagrant disrespect and violation of their privacy. As an alternative, the *alfaquí* offers to receive Figuerola afterward in his own house. Figuerola accepts because he thinks that if he manages to convert the *alfaquí*, the whole community will follow.

Sunday, February 8, 1517, finds him at the house of the *alfaquí*, with all the prominent members of the *aljama* as well as the elders of a number of small villages nearby. Figuerola brings his books and his Qur'āns and proposes a discussion of the sura on the angels Arot and Marot. Another similar debate is held a few days later, but the *alfaquíes* object to discussing their Law because in doing so, they endanger themselves, since they live in Christian lands, where engaging in debate exposes them to accusations of attacking Christianity or blasphemy. They argue that both the king and the Justicia de Aragón would forbid them from disputing. The *alfaquí* of Muel leaves, dejected and dismayed.

But Figuerola, of course, is not satisfied, and so the *alfaquíes* and *adelantados* of the *aljamas* decide to nominate two persons, Muḥammad Galip and Yuza de Bedmar, to debate with him. However, they also maintain that he cannot force them to hold a debate, for only the king has authority over them. They ask him to confine his preaching to the churches, promise that they will go and listen to him, and ask him never to return to their mosques. The following week, still in February 1517, Figuerola goes to the *alfaquí*'s house, but he has gone away and in his stead left his son, who claims to know nothing other than how to direct prayers. The son says he has no religious knowledge that would enable him to engage in debate. On September 11, Figuerola goes to the mosque again and finds the *alfaquí* preaching in the *mimbar*. Figuerola and his retinue of men ("letrados y no letrados") sit there and listen to the *alfaquí* with the Qur'ān in hand. The *alfaquí* starts to mumble, loses his thread, and becomes disconcerted.

This continues every Friday for months. Figuerola's description of his tactics shows that they become increasingly threatening. He enters the mosques with ever-larger groups of Christians. And since the *alfaquí* of Zaragoza would normally go twice a year to visit the small *morerías* in other Aragonese localities, Figuerola decides to follow him, to everyone's consternation. Finally, after nearly a year of this campaign of disruption and intimidation, the Muslims get fed up and tell Figuerola that if he continues with his campaign, they will leave for Africa.[48] To this, Figuerola basically responds, "Good riddance: they should leave so that the land will be cleansed."

Finally, on February 14, 1518, Figuerola suspends his campaign. It had been going on for more than a year, despite the interference we have mentioned by Archbishop Alfonso de Aragón and by the nobility. Figuerola's crusade ceased with the death of his uncle, the bishop of Pati, and his subsequent loss of important supporters. But in the meantime, we can perceive very clearly an escalation of the pressure, the harassment, the threats, and the number of persons involved.

Occasions Chosen by Figuerola to Intervene in Sermons

Space forbids me to offer a more detailed description of this process of intimidation as told by Figuerola himself, but I would like to devote some attention to how Figuerola planned his campaigns and, in particular, the occasions chosen by him to visit the mosque, because it illuminates his polemical strategy. He chose these occasions, I believe, with great care, which implies a good knowledge of local Islam and the meaning accorded by Aragonese Muslims to their calendar—to certain days but also to the stories told on those days. This can be seen through a parallel reading of the Morisco literature both in Arabic and in *aljamiado*—vernacular Spanish written in the Arabic alphabet, produced mostly in Aragon—alongside Figuerola's text. *Aljamiado* narratives are in many cases extensive elaborations on specific Qur'ānic suras and were written and collected to help *alfaquíes* prepare their sermons. As Vincent Barletta has remarked, one of the striking characteristics of *aljamiado* narratives is their tendency to take verses and even whole stories from the Qur'ān and recontextualize them in other settings, not unlike Christian "thematic preaching," which became widespread in the later Middle Ages.[49] Muslim preachers in Aragon, as in other regions, developed rhetorical techniques along with the recitation of scripture, Hadith, and other authoritative texts not only to invoke the key symbols and myths of origin associated with the time of the Prophet or the eschatological future but also, above all, to apply these mythic discourses to their own communities and for their own purposes.[50] They were important for the creation of a sense of community. There is no doubt that Figuerola or rather his advisers (notably Juan Gabriel but probably also other persons from Martín García's entourage, such as Juan Andrés, who is quoted by Figuerola) were familiar with those narratives and therefore with the sermons that were being preached.

The first day Figuerola goes to the mosque in January 1517 is *'Id al-aḍha*, or the Feast of Sacrifice ("Pascua del degüello," as he calls it), one of the most important festivities in the Islamic calendar. It is a festivity that commemorates the sacrifice of Ismail, son of Abraham. Of course, Figuerola interrupts the sermon and claims that Isaac was the one who was sacrificed (a recurrent theme in anti-Muslim polemics), aggressively defending his version, including quoting the Qur'ānic suras containing the episode.

To understand the sermon that Figuerola would have interrupted on that day in January 1517, and thus how the audience might have perceived his outburst, we can turn to the *aljamiado* literature that I have already mentioned. For example, the *Alhadith del xakrifixio de Ismael*, of which several copies are extant, gives us a good idea of what the *alfaquí*'s sermon might have included.[51] One of these versions begins with a combined reference to the sermon's audience as well as to its temporal setting, the *'Id al-aḍha*: "Servants of God, God has purified this your day, and has made it a Holy Day and an obligation for Muslims and a path to your religion. It is a day in which you give alms and a day in which all of your good works are multiplied and your sins lessened" (Junta 25-124-125). The sacrifice of Ismail as presented in the *aljamiado* narratives situates the text and its performance in a time linked to the traditional past through the events in the story and to a potential future through the themes of redemption and divine providence.

The second time Figuerola goes to the mosque to dispute with the *alfaquí*, the latter is preaching a sermon about Jonas, or Yunus. Again, the occasion is well chosen for furthering Figuerola's agenda. The story of Yunus, which is also contained in different *aljamiado* versions, was a popular and compelling narrative about a man being swallowed by a whale, living inside the dark interior of the beast, and being saved by invoking God.[52] Once again, the narrative behind the sermon on the second day that Figuerola visits the mosque perfectly fits Christology and Christian ideas of redemption. This suggests that Figuerola may have organized his alleged direct experience according to his theological views: he is constructing a narrative, a polemical narrative.

The story of Yunus is also one of penitence, redemption, and divine providence. Yunus has an eschatological function. He doubts divine omniscience and his own prophetic mission, experiences a *metanoia* (a conversion of his soul) inside the whale, and endures a second birth when he is delivered on a beach by the whale, weak as a newborn baby. The so-called people of Yunus have a place in mystical thought. According to Ibn al-ʿArabī, they persisted to his day, and he even claims to have found them among the "Andalusi," the people of al-Andalus or Muslim Iberia, a chosen people for the End of Times. According to Ibn al-ʿArabī, "The blessings of Yunus arise in his people because Allah had attached them to himself."[53] In *aljamiado* literature, the people of Yunus share certain similarities with the *ghurabāʿ* or the *algaribos* of *aljamiado* texts, the "strangers" who will be chosen at the End of Times.[54]

The term *algaribos* is interesting. It means "strangers," but it also can be read as "people from the West." A famous *fatwā*, known as the *fatwā* of the mufti of Oran—which was addressed to Moriscos and allowed them to conceal their religion under duress without losing their identity as Muslims—is, according to the *aljamiado* version that circulated in Aragon, addressed to the *algaribos* or, in the Arabic version, *ghurabāʿ*.[55] This term *al-ghurabāʿ* and the way that it was used in the *aljamiado* literature that the Aragonese *alfaquí* would have been familiar with are essential to my argument about the eschatological concerns of the *alfaquí*'s flock, anxieties that Figuerola had figured out how to exploit, probably because they intersected with his own millenarian and eschatological interpretations. But he surely knew through his master, Martín García, about the Muslim belief that the End of Time was nigh, and he was doing what Martín García himself had done: acknowledge as real the Muslims' eschatological predictions and beliefs but give them a meaning opposite to the Islamic interpretation.[56] The eschatological use of the term *algaribo*, as Maribel Fierro has shown,[57] is taken from the Hadith that says "Islam began as a stranger and shall return to being a stranger just as it began. Thus blessed be the strangers!"[58] This Hadith was widely known in Islamic Spain: true Islam will return to being *gharib* at the End of Time—indeed, the time of the *ghuraba*—at which stage the *mahdī*, the Islamic messiah, will appear. The last Muslims in Iberia saw themselves as a chosen people, to whom the Prophet would entrust the task of restoring Islam to its origins; they saw themselves as the repositories of this heritage of absolute purity. Figuerola, by disrupting the sermon of Yunus, disrupted an important affirmation of the Muslim communities' salvation.

On a later occasion, Figuerola goes to the mosque because it is *Mawlid*, the day commemorating the birth of Muḥammad, the most solemn celebration, he says, in the Muslim calendar.[59] Figuerola claims to know many of the stories about Muḥammad because Juan Gabriel, the translator and interpreter I mentioned at the beginning of this chapter, has instructed him. He is well informed regarding not only the story of Muḥammad but also the ways Muslims celebrate his life and the meaning this celebration has for them. Figuerola starts speaking aloud during the sermon and comparing the stories the *alfaquí* is relating about Muḥammad with the life of Christ,[60] asserting Jesus's superiority based on the fact that he performed miracles while Muḥammad did not and referring also to the well-known story of Zaynab to further comparison between a lustful Muḥammad and a chaste Jesus. He also rebukes the Muslims for not celebrating the birth of Jesus Christ when they celebrate *Mawlid* and also the birth of John the Baptist, the son of Zechariah and Jesus's precursor. Reading his description of these events, we get a clear sense of how completely he disrupted the festivity.

Figuerola also attended a sermon concerning Job, or Ayyub, which explored the misfortunes suffered by the just, the virtues of patience and resilience (*aljamiado* legend in MS 5305 23–41), and the final reward of redemption.[61] Figuerola points to aspects that are extant only in the *aljamiado* legend about the different temptations suffered by Job at the hands of Iblis in the form of a wise man, or a physician; the mistreatment of his wife, Ramah, at the hands of Jews; and so forth.[62] Comparing this version of the Job story with the Old Testament, Figuerola attempts to show that what the Muslims say of Ayyub merely reiterates the Law of Moses, that it is a corruption of the story that the Christians believe.[63] By using both *aljamiado* and Old Testament texts, Figuerola makes a very disturbing argument indeed.

In sum, Figuerola chooses to go to the mosque on precisely those days when the sermons deal with prophets whose stories have been developed by Aragonese Muslims, as shown by the *aljamiado* literature, into narratives of redemption and salvation, with messianic, eschatological implications. Figuerola seizes on stories that bring hope for the future but also speak of "redemption" in this life. Conversion—which for Figuerola is the subtext of these stories—is always possible. Figuerola went to the mosques on certain dates and for particular sermons that he handpicked as the ones that most served his purpose of demoralizing the Mudejars. In fact, the sermons and subjects are so well suited to his agenda that we cannot but wonder if they really reflect his experience or if what we have in the *Lumbre de fe* is a polemical narrative of his own creation. The question has no real importance for my argument, which concerns Figuerola's use of eschatology and redemption as the axis of his polemics against Muslims. He was also aware—like his predecessor Martín García, as we know from García's sermons—about the predictions that circulated among Aragonese Muslims, based on Abū Maʿshar's calculations and indications of planetary conjunctions, that the world would end in the year 1524.[64] I suggest that Figuerola was sensitive to the eschatological meaning of the sermons delivered on the particular days he chose to visit the mosques because he himself subscribed to a Christian messianic ideology and was of an eschatological frame of mind. The dispute he was interested in was not only about blasphemy but about who would prevail at the End of Times. Millenarianism was an important part of Figuerola's polemical strategy and, together with the strategy of "indirect compulsion," was the product of Franciscan theology, which was very influential at the time and place in which he lived.

As we know from his own depictions of the resistance and censure he faced from the high clergy and nobility, Martín de Figuerola was not immediately successful in convincing the king or the government of Aragon or even Pope Adriaan (whose tenure lasted only one year due to his untimely death) to decree the forced conversion of Muslims. The decree would nevertheless come just a few years later, in 1526, and the ultimate reason was the rebellion in Valencia against the nobility and the king. By that time, the Mudejars had become a pawn in the nobility's confrontation with a popular movement, and as scholars have long insisted, their relative freedom to practice their religion was a casualty of that conflict. Figuerola's incensed and combative text was no longer relevant in this context. His strategies also show, as is my argument in this chapter, the confrontation of two millenarianisms—of two parallel eschatological expectations that differed in the religion that would prevail at the End of Time.[65] One eschatology in conflict with another is what transpires throughout Figuerola's text.

Notes

The research presented in this chapter was funded by the European Research Council under the European Union's Seventh Framework Programme (FP7/2007–13) / ERC Grant Agreement number 323316, project CORPI, "Conversion, Overlapping Religiosities, Polemics, Interaction: Early Modern Iberia and Beyond."

1. See Johan Martín de Figuerola, *Lumbre de fe contra la secta mahometana y el alcorán* (1521), MS Gayangos 1922/36, Biblioteca de la Real Academia de la Historia, Madrid, fol. 253. Partially edited by Guillén Robles, *Leyendas de José*. See Ruiz García, "Joan Martí Figuerola." Elisa Ruiz García and Luis F. Bernabé Pons are currently preparing an edition.
2. In his own words, "Empieza este tratado que se dize *Lumbre de fe contra la secta macométicha*, dictado por mossén Johan Martín Figuerola, maestro en sacra Theología, acólito y capellán de su Sanctedat, simple beneficiado en la Yglesia Mayor de la insigne ciudat de Valencia" (fol. 1r). Information included in Antonio, *Bibliotheca hispana nova*, 1:738–39.
3. Guillén Robles, *Leyendas de José*; Ruiz García, "Joan Martí Figuerola."
4. Antonio, *Bibliotheca hispana nova*, 1:738–39: "Ineditus hactenus ob difficultatem Arabici sermonis, quo passim utitur, typis repraesentandi." Antonio also says that the papal legate, the nuncio Camillo Massimo, had another copy that he took with him to Rome, copied by the Maronite Nicola Naironi. I have not been able to find this copy in the Biblioteca Apostolica Vaticana.
5. Figuerola, *Lumbre de fe*, fol. 253:

   Porque el alfaquí después de yo haver predicado juntava toda la gente en la mezquita, según yo fui informado que les dezía, que todo lo que a dixo Mossen Figuerola no a dicho verdad ni le creáis y ellos como simples e ignorantes que no saben leer ni entender el Alcorán ni saben algarabía que todos son aljamiados darán fe al alfaquí y yo siendo certificado uve de tenelles otra arte y les dixe en una prédica todo lo que el alfaquí azía y por tanto yo determinaría de hir cada viernes que ellos tienen aljama y allí en la mezquita delante de todos con el Alcorán los mostraría ser verdad todo lo que yo les predicaba y assi empeçé de azer los infrascriptos disputas en su mezquita a las quales mucha gente azi letrados como no letrados concorrían.

And he recommends to priests and preachers, "Usa el Alcorán, tómales tú la mano con los doctores suyos que an glosado el Alcorán."

6. García-Arenal and Starczewska, "Law of Abraham."
7. Figuerola, *Lumbre de fe*, fol. 253r. A biography of Martín García with hagiographical overtones was written in 1700 by Hebrera, *Vida prodigiosa*; Sánchez López, "Martín García Puyazuelo."
8. As an example, Juan Rodríguez, who was denounced to the Inquisition because he left the church after a sermon by "maestre Figuerola." Marín Padilla, *Relación judeoconversa*, 93. In several passages in his work, Figuerola mentions having read polemical works against Judaism in the library of the Valencia Cathedral (fol. 207).
9. Figuerola, *Lumbre de fe*, fol. 253.
10. The term *alfaquí* is a Romance loanword derived from the Arabic *faqīh*, which means "an expert in Islamic jurisprudence." However, in the context of early sixteenth-century Spain, the term is used in a much wider sense to refer to the leader of a Muslim *aljama*, or community—someone who is knowledgeable about Islam and performs the functions of the *imām* in the mosque, as is described in Martín de Figuerola's text. About the role of *alfaquíes* in late medieval Spain, see Miller, *Guardians of Islam*.
11. García-Arenal and Starczewska, "Abraham the Catholic"; Starczewska, "Latin Translation."
12. Figuerola, *Lumbre de fe*, fol. 253r: "Simples e ignorantes que no saben leer ni entender al Alcorán ni saben algarabía que todos son aljamiados"—that is, Romance speakers—and afterward, addressing Muslims: "Que no sabeys lo que haveys de guardar y seguir, cosa es confusa tener y seguir una scriptura que nadie puede entender." We should recall that translations of the Bible into the vernacular were forbidden in Spain.
13. García Puyazuelo, *Sermones eminentissimi totiusque Barchinonensis.*
14. See Ruiz García, "Estudio preliminar," in Andrés, *Confusión o confutación.*
15. Andrés, *Confusión o confutación*; Obregón, *Confutación del alcorán.* See also Szpiech, "Witness of Their Own"; Starczewska, "Apologetic Glosses."
16. Soto González and Starczewska, "Authority, Philology and Conversion."
17. "Que a la fin no a de haver sino hun pastor, Christo, y un corral, la Yglesia Christiana romana." Figuerola, *Lumbre de fe*, fol. 9.
18. "Un dios, una ley, un rey y no más." Figuerola, fol. 265.
19. Cirac Estopañán, *Sermones de Don Martín*, sermon no. 40, p. 73.
20. "Hay que trabajar por cobrar Jerusalem." Figuerola, *Lumbre de fe*, fol. 37r.
21. Figuerola, fol. 260.
22. Figuerola, fol. 264r.
23. Figuerola, fol. 265r–v.
24. Figuerola, fol. 37v.
25. He says he went to speak to the Inquisition Council (Consejo de la Suprema Inquisición) to ask for support and permission to continue preaching, but "el negocio fue con tan poca fe ni ardor de aquella que cosa ninguna quisieron hacer, en que yo me bolbí a la ciudad de Zaragoza." Figuerola, fol. 264v–r.
26. Figuerola, fol. 264r.
27. Fernández Serrano, "Órdenes sagradas en Zaragoza," 163–66.

28. "Aver dicho que los pueden quitar los hijos, que pueden ser compellidos en la fe de Cristo ellos no queriendo, más en lo que los aveys tribulado en decir que les quitasen las mezquitas, alfaquíes, dos cosas muy recias de modo que están tan alvorotados que se van muchos—acordaos deveys de que el arzobispo de Barcelona a predicado muchas veces a los moros y no los a dicho esto que vos." Figuerola, *Lumbre de fe*, fol. 260v.
29. Figuerola, fol. 261v.
30. According to Poutrin, *Convertir les musulmans.*
31. Quoted from Poutrin, "Jewish Precedent," 77.
32. "Et tales nullo modo sunt ad fidem compellendi, ut ipsi credant, quia credere voluntatis est." Aquinas, *Summa Theologica*, IIe–II^{ae}, q. 10, a. 8 co.
33. Eixemenis, *Dotzè llibre del Crestià*, 371; Espina, *Fortalitium fidei*, bk. 3; Echevarría Arsuaga, *Fortress of Faith.*
34. See, for example, Figuerola, *Lumbre de fe*, fols. 49r, 183v.
35. García-Arenal, "Granada as a New Jerusalem."
36. Pérez García and Fernández Chaves, "Infancia morisca."
37. For a detailed view of Figuerola's use of this canonical literature, see Ruiz García, "'Criptobiblioteca' de un polemista," 244.
38. "Respondeo dicendum, quod infidelium quidam sunt qui nunquam susceperunt fidem, sicut gentiles et Judaei; et tales nullo modo sunt ad fidem compellendi ut ipsi credant, quia credere voluntatis est; sunt tamen compellendi a fidelibus, si facultas adsit, ut fidem non impediant vel blasphemiis, vel malis persuasionibus, vel etiam apertis persecutionibus." Aquinas, *Summa Theologica*, IIe–II^{ae}, q. 10, a. 8 co.
39. Vitoria, *Comentarios a la Secunda Secundae*, 1:195–96:

    12. Circa secundam conclusionem est dubium: an liceat prohibere blasphemias infidelium. Dico quod aliud est de blasphemiis scriptis quae non divulgantur, et aliud de his quae palam proferuntur. Nam licet principi constet quod in libris sarracenorum vocato Alcoran sint aliquae blasphemiae contra Christianos et contra Christum, non tamen licet ei comburere illum, quia fieret gravis injuria paganis, et illud non est in detrimentum christianis, cum non publicetur. Sed si infideles publice blasphement christianos aut Christum sic ut vergat in detrimentum christianitatis, sicut ob suas blasphemias impedirent ne aliqui converterentur ad fidem Christi qui prius volebant converti, potest princeps prohibere blasphemias eorum et punire eos licite, quia magna fit injuria christianitatis.

    I am grateful to Isabelle Poutrin for giving me this reference.
40. "Estando yo en Cocentaina por las muertes." Figuerola, *Lumbre de fe*, fol. 187r.
41. "Me dijo un alfaquí viejo en la villa de Cocentayna en el anyo de mil y quinientos y diecinueve, estando fuydo de Valencia por las muertes, hablando desta materia dixo que si una piedra cahe y topa con otra, aquella que recibió el golpe se quexará el día del juicio a dios de la otra." Figuerola, fol. 18r.
42. Figuerola, fol. 49r.
43. Vallés Borrás, *Germanía*, 15–23.
44. Vallés Borrás, 14.
45. Alamany, *Obra de fray Joan Alamany*; Durán Grau, "Refutació valenciana de l'Islam"; Durán Grau, "Mil·lenarisme al servi."
46. Milhou, *Colón y su mentalidad*; Phelan, *Millennial Kingdom.*
47. "Será bien que en las predicaciones se les declara que en casso que ellos estuviessen pertinaces y endurecidos en su secta y determinassen irse fuera de nuestros reynos, han de dexar sus hijos para que sean christianos, porque esto será mucha parte para convertir los padres" (Charles V to the captain general of Catalonia,

November 10, 1525), quoted in Redondo, *Antonio de Guevara*, 249.

48. During the dispute with the *alfaquí*, "su hijo dizo diziendo que si en esto avían de estar cada viernes que por allá se pasaría a África, en que le dixe que mucho enhorabuena que lo hiziesse." Figuerola, *Lumbre de fe*, fol. 259r.
49. Barletta, *Covert Gestures*, 111.
50. Jones, *Power of Oratory*, 111.
51. Barletta, *Covert Gestures*, 111–12.
52. Vespertino Rodríguez, *Leyendas aljamiadas*; Viguera Molins, "Glosa aljamiada"; Hermosilla, "Versión aljamiada."
53. Ibn al-ʿArabī, *Bezels of Wisdom*.
54. García-Arenal, "'Réconfort pour ceux.'"
55. Stewart, "Identity of the *Muftī* of Oran"; Stewart, "Dissimulation in Sunni Islam."
56. García-Arenal, "'Réconfort pour ceux.'"
57. Fierro, "Spiritual Alienation."
58. Wensinck, *Concordance et indices*, 4:473.
59. García-Arenal, "Shurafa."
60. "En algunas disputas que tuve con ellos maldecían al alfaquí que me había enseñado tantas cosas." Figuerola, *Lumbre de fe*, fol. 33v.
61. Hermosilla, "Versión aljamiada," 211–14.
62. "Y vosotros próximos míos de moros hos quereis inmiscuir como escarabajo en borra que no se puede valer: no podeis llevar la carga de vuestra secta y querey hos poner a cuestas la Ley de Moysen. Dejad ya todo esto y venid a Nuestra Ley Christiana." Figuerola, *Lumbre de fe*, fol. 189.
63. Barletta, *Covert Gestures*, 18–20.
64. Cirac Estopañán, *Sermones de Don Martín*, 20–21:

    Porque esta secta en breve debe acabar: pues dice Abulmazar en el Libro de las grandes conjunciones, diferencia séptima: "que el tiempo de la duración de la secta mahometana era de 875 años." Y como yo lo oí de los sabios de aquella secta, no había de durar mil años y esto dicen las historias del propio Mahoma. Y dijéronme algunos de los doctos moros, que según la ley, por las declaraciones de los doctores, la perdición de la secta debía empezar por la perdición del reino de Occidente, como se llama en árabe, más en nuestra lengua se llama reino de Granada. . . . Y así es evidente que la perdición de esta secta empezó entonces (con la conquista Cristiana de Granada) y esperamos que debe acabar del todo en el año del Señor de 1524.

65. Wiegers, "Jean de Roquetaillade's Prophecies."

8

ART OF CONVERSION?

The Visual Policies of the Jesuits, Dominicans, and Mercedarians in Valencia

Borja Franco Llopis

Introduction

At the beginning of the seventeenth century, Gaspar Escolano pointed out in his work *Decadas* that Valencia was full of preachers spreading the word of God among both Moriscos and Old Christians.[1] During that period, three orders were very active in this regard: Jesuits, Dominicans, and Mercedarians (the Franciscans had forfeited their leadership in this field in the early modern period). This chapter deals with these orders' visual policies with respect to the Moriscos (Spanish Muslims forced to convert to Christianity in the sixteenth century). These policies grew out of internal debates within these communities regarding the question of Moriscos' assimilation or expulsion. As Paolo Broggio has argued,[2] the attitudes espoused by these communities depended on individual ideologies. Religious orders were not a monolithic army controlled by the papacy but heterogeneous entities characterized by an extraordinary ability to adapt in order to address specific problems. Each individual member had to reconcile his own interests with the rules of the order, while the community as a whole adapted to the political ideology of local elites.

It should be mentioned that the main problem when researching this topic is that several visual policies were the result of individual initiatives rather than of real consensus among all the members of the order, and thus it is difficult to generalize about the attitudes toward the Muslims who were the targets of these orders' proselytizing campaigns. Another important problem is the varying number of sources that have been preserved that relate to these policies. The Jesuits preserved a considerable number of letters and annals that mention works of art being sent from Rome to indoctrinate the people in Valencia and the iconographies that were used to promote genuine conversion among Moriscos. However, this is not the case with the Dominicans.[3] Despite the large number of books and manuscripts about their history or the construction of new monasteries, the number of documents about art and its uses is negligible. There are only some tangential references to this topic, most of them highly subjective: they are expressions of a particular individual's thoughts rather than reflections of an organized plan to indoctrinate or condemn crypto-Muslims. There is a similar issue with documentation on the Mercedarians, although in their case, there are several extant Valencian and Iberian treatises that deal with images and their use, and thus it is possible to reconstruct the visual policies of this order.

The Jesuit Indoctrination Plan

In previous studies,[4] I have analyzed Jesuit attitudes toward crypto-Muslims and the creation of a visual program to indoctrinate them. I demonstrated that from the foundation of the order by St. Ignatius,[5] but mainly under Borgia's generalship, the Jesuits were committed to converting not only Moriscos in Valencia but also in the "Indias."[6] Borgia created a school for Moriscos in Gandía and supplied it with the best-prepared priests, a large number of bilingual books and Bibles, many crosses, and several copies of the image of *Maria Salus Populi Romani*, either on canvas or engraved. In fact, Borgia used this image not only as part of his Morisco indoctrination plan but also as a diplomatic gift to kings and princes[7] around Europe in order to encourage their devotion to the Mother of God.

It is a matter of debate whether he commissioned the first copy of this image,[8] located in Santa Maria Maggiore in Rome. Regardless, Borgia's association with this image had an influence on his own iconography: he appears in several representations holding this picture in one hand and with the crowned skull of Empress Isabel of Portugal. Borgia presented these images as gifts to Moriscos and Old Christians in the Valencia region to teach them how to be devoted believers. In doing so, he followed the assimilation program that Hernando de Talavera had used in Granada,[9] in which Moriscos were presented with representations of Mary, whose iconography was venerated by them as an example of a good mother (although not the Mother of God). This indoctrination plan also included several prints with crosses, which the Moriscos found to be much more objectionable.

Another strategy of Talavera's was also adopted in Valencia—namely, converting the *alfaquíes* first, which, it was believed, would have a beneficial effect on those who were instructed by them. There are numerous extant letters written by Jesuits that claim that *alfaquíes* (and therefore the entire community in their care) were truly being converted by the preachers' efforts and describe how Valencia was becoming "de-Islamicized."[10] This highly positive view of the acculturation process has little in common with the version of events given in other contemporary sources.

Modern research by scholars such as the Jesuit Francisco de Borja de Medina, who takes as his source of information a report written in 1579,[11] offers a somewhat tangential examination of the use of different visual representations in the campaigns undertaken by the Society of Jesus.[12] The report suggested that the preachers had a positive impression of the way they were received among the people who witnessed their sermons, pointing out that the people even requested metal images (the iconography was not specified), which was proof that they were good and pious Christians. I believe that this material requires a more nuanced approach. I do not wish to pronounce on whether the impressions given in these documents reflect the reality of the evangelizing campaigns or simply an attempt by the Jesuits in Valencia to secure more support from Rome by contradicting those who claimed that these campaigns were a failure. But I am of the opinion that the request for images could be explained as a pretense on the part of the Moriscos, a strategy for avoiding condemnation. We should take note of the curious fact that these metal pieces were not very common in dowries or inventories of the estates of deceased Christians in Valencia,[13] but they are made of the same material as *herces*, a kind of property that was common among Moriscos. These *herces* were artifacts made of precious metal that contained fragments of the Qur'ān. We might ask whether Moriscos used the "metal badges" that are referred to in the source cited above to preserve their tradition by means of a new iconography that allowed them to avoid being arrested and tried by the Holy Office.[14]

Moreover, an analysis of the epistolary literature and the annals of the order preserved in the Archivum Romanum Societatis Iesu indicates that this order used images in similar ways in its evangelizing efforts in the "interior Indies,"[15] which would include Valencia, and the "foreign or exterior Indies."[16] The systematic distribution of pieces of popular devotion, principally images of the Virgin Mary,[17] or of Bibles in different languages was an integral part of the Jesuits' approach, as was attention to the language of evangelization; in other words, the Jesuits were sensitive to the need to make themselves understood.[18] Nevertheless, my use of the word *similar* is very deliberate, since it is important to keep in mind the fact that Francis Borgia, before becoming superior general of the Society of Jesus, was duke of Gandía, so his interest in converting the Moriscos was not only religious but also political. As (ex)governor of a territory teeming with new converts, he was aware of their potentially destabilizing effect. That is why, with the support of families such as the counts of Oliva, the Centelles, he concentrated his efforts on converting Moriscos in Valencia by sending images from Rome that were intended to indoctrinate. Obviously, any attempt at conversion and indoctrination has a political objective, and the case of the American colonies is no exception. But Borgia's interest in this regard in Valencia was also personal, as has been pointed out by scholars such as Santiago La Parra,[19] and that is why he used all means at his disposal (his contacts both with the Spanish Crown and with the papacy) to achieve his ends.

To all of this must be added the support that the order received from important figures such as the archbishops of Valencia Francisco de Navarra[20] and especially Juan de Ribera, who provided economic assistance to the campaigns carried out during their pontificates.[21] Thanks to this financial support, important friars like Ignacio de las Casas (1550–1608) preached in this area. This Jesuit father also controlled the use of images by friars and preachers, censored some ambiguous representations with hidden Islamic messages, and negotiated with political and religious leaders to continue the work of the Jesuits to convert crypto-Muslims.[22] But Ignacio de las Casas was not the only Jesuit who controlled and censored the use of images with ambiguous content or dangerous iconography; there were other members of this order who collaborated with the Inquisition in this task, despite the fact that their knowledge of Islamic theology was not as thorough as that of De las Casas. Their assessments where art censorship was concerned were therefore more likely to be based on whether a particular work violated the rules of decorum established by the Church rather than on a detection of forbidden Islamic messages.[23]

Another interesting point about the Jesuits' use of images that is linked to its approach to Islam is that, unlike the other two orders, as we will see, it wasn't until many years after the expulsion that the Jesuits produced any visual representations of the Christian victory over Islam. All their efforts had been focused on devising a plan for converting the infidels, and they were aware that an attack on the Morisco minority would be counterproductive to this end. It was therefore not their policy to use the image for polemical purposes. However, years after the Morisco expulsion, the Society of Jesus would forget its peaceful attitude in Valencia and would begin to ridicule Muslims after the latter had disappeared from the kingdom of Valencia. Thus for the celebration of the four-hundredth anniversary of the conquest of Valencia (1238–1638), the Jesuits erected a large altar in front of the Colegio de San Pablo, where they displayed emblems showing the triumph of Catholicism over the infidel. This was the most hostile and intellectual of any of the iconographic programs against the Muslims that were produced in Valencia for the celebration.[24]

What happened after the expulsion of the Moriscos did not develop ex nihilo. From the very beginning of the Jesuit order, there was an internal debate about "purity of blood," about the participation of Jesuit converts in the efforts to evangelize Moriscos, and even about the validity of the campaigns that they carried out.[25] This debate—which was intimately related to the situation in Valencia—was silenced because of the urgent need for people who knew Arabic to convert Moriscos, a fact that worried both Diego Laínez (second superior general of the order) and Francis Borgia. Therefore, the latter, who counted among his friends humanists such as Juan Bautista Agnesio (1480–1553) and was familiar with the relative success of Hernando de Talavera's campaigns in Granada, made sure that these internal conflicts did not affect the strategies for assimilating the infidel. But once the Moriscos had been expelled from the Iberian Peninsula and Francis Borgia had died, the ideology that had been silenced years earlier resurfaced.

From Acceptance to Belligerence: The Dominican Attitude toward the Other

Researching the Dominicans' artistic approach to Muslims is not easy. There is no precedent for this kind of analysis, either for Valencia or Iberia in general in the early modern period, and as has been mentioned, the extant sources are scarce. First of all, we must remember that this order was created to convert infidels and combat heresy by building convents in Muslim or Jewish areas.[26] The Dominicans participated in the first indoctrination plan for Valencia in 1525 (the year of the forced conversion of Muslims in Valencia), employing the same methods they had used throughout the medieval period,[27] which emphasized the errors of the infidel (for the benefit of the faithful) rather than instructing Muslims in the tenets of the Catholic faith. The Dominicans had pioneered the creation of schools of Arabic for training friars to go out and preach, something that the Jesuits would take up centuries later in their campaigns.[28] They also defended the creation of a school for Moriscos in Valencia, known as the Colegio del Emperador because Charles V supported its founding.

But little by little, several hostile voices inside the Dominican congregation proclaiming the impossibility of converting the Moriscos forced the order to change its strategy. As Callado Estela[29] has suggested, the failure of its first campaigns, the context of increasing aggression on the part of the Ottoman Empire and Barbary pirates, and fierce internal debates occasioned a redefinition of Dominican ideology, which began to entertain support for expulsion. This attitude was sometimes advocated by Patriarch Ribera, who at times was strongly influenced by Father Vitoria and St. Luis Beltrán and reversed his opinion about the Morisco question,[30] drifting away from the Jesuit position and instead lending economic support to the Dominicans, for example, for the construction of new monasteries between 1569 and 1611,[31] as we will see below.

This about-face in Dominican policy created a rift between them and the Jesuits. The Dominicans viewed the growing power of the newly created Jesuit order with suspicion, seeing the latter's policy of evangelization and control of Inquisitorial trials as two strategies for gaining ascendancy.[32] Dominicans such as Jaime Bleda, Damián Fonseca, Jerónimo Javierre, Diego de Mardones, and Luis Aliaga were extremely critical of Jesuit policies and attempted to discredit their campaigns to convert Muslims by writing several

FIG. 8.1. Miguel del Prado, *Saint Vincent Ferrer Preaching in Valencia* (ca. 1520), altarpiece detail, oil on panel, 494.5 × 387.0 cm. Museo de Bellas Artes, Valencia.

pamphlets about the need to expel the Moriscos. They also wrote several letters to Patriarch Ribera expressing their view that the time and money spent indoctrinating the Moriscos (i.e., the support for the Jesuits) were bad investments, since they were not going to convert.[33]

But not all Dominicans endorsed the same agenda. Some friars, like Juan Micó, defended the possibility of genuine conversion. Micó was prior of St. Onofre in Museros and, years later, of the new Dominican friary in Llombai, founded by Francis Borgia as part of his political and religious plan to create spaces of control and conversion for crypto-Muslims. We should recall that this city was part of the duchy of Gandía, which was governed by his family, which is why Borgia bequeathed a significant sum to facilitate the evangelization of the Moriscos.[34] With this money as well as royal economic support, Juan Micó organized an indoctrination plan with the help of Antonio Ramírez de Haro, bishop of Calahorra, and Francisco de Navarra, bishop of Ciudad Rodrigo.[35] For these men, Vincent Ferrer (d. 1419) exemplified what could be accomplished by a commitment to converting Muslims and people of other religions. It is therefore easy to understand why the Valencian artist

Miguel del Prado created a large altarpiece (dating from around 1520 and currently held at the Museo de Bellas Artes in Valencia) for the Dominican friary in Museros—where Micó was, years later, prior—showing Vincent Ferrer preaching to the Muslims and performing miracles to convert them. The message of the painting is clear: it links the Muslims whom Ferrer converted with his sermons to those who were the concern of the Dominicans in Valencia. This painting was an exemplum not for the faithful but rather for the fathers who were being trained in the art of preaching.

This idea of presenting Ferrer as a model of teaching and conversion was taken up, almost fifty years later, by Juan de Ribera, archbishop of Valencia. In fact, during one of the periods when he favored the conversion of Moriscos, he decided to use an image of Ferrer in his design for the decoration of the Corpus Christi School, presenting him as a model for preachers who were studying there. In the church at this school, Bartolomé de Matarana painted images of Ferrer on three walls of the transept, the middle one depicting the Perpignan sermon, in which Ferrer converted a large number of Jews and Muslims, which was the very mission that the new generation of preachers studying at the school was tasked with. Archbishop Ribera understood the murals in this church to be like a sermon in images.[36] Ferrer was also important because he had defended images as necessary for the understanding of the Christian faith.[37] According to all the biographical texts written about him in the sixteenth and seventeenth centuries, he thought that the cross was the most important tool for spreading the truth.[38] Other friars, such as Luis Beltrán, following the example of Ferrer, made several crosses to aid in preaching. However, it is important to stress that Beltrán considered these artifacts to be a weapon against Protestant iconoclasm and not a tool for teaching Muslims, whom he considered incapable of conversion. He spoke of this in the sermons he delivered before leaving for America in Vinalesa, Montcada, Lliria, Bunyol, Albuixec, and Borriana, all of which are in the Valencia region.[39] Moreover, these crosses later became part of his iconography, and there are many accounts of miracles being performed through them.[40]

Beltrán's refusal to try to convert Muslims perfectly reflects the internal tensions among the Dominicans that were mentioned above. It was not only apologists like Bleda or Fonseca, whose polemical works on Islam have come down to us, who were opposed to the evangelization of Moriscos.

Beltrán—who is considered an heir to Vincent Ferrer because of his skill and training and should have been his natural successor in the campaign to convert Moriscos and who, moreover, thought art to be of great importance in the evangelizing process—was more concerned with the arduous task of battling Protestantism and with the situation in the "exterior Indies" than with his Morisco neighbors.[41] His letters contain harsh judgments against the newly converted, to whom he would even deny baptism:

> They are heretics, and even apostates, which is worse, and they openly display the dislike they feel toward Christians and they observe their Mahometan ceremonies to the extent that they are able . . . therefore baptism should not be administered to the children if they are to live in the home of their parents, because there is moral evidence that they will become apostates like them, and it is better for them to be Moors than heretics or apostates. It is as intrinsically bad to baptize these children, if their lives are not in imminent danger, given everything said above, as it would be for a Christian to baptize Moorish children in Barbary and leave them there with their infidel parents, even if the latter agreed, in order to gain respect, to the baptism of their children, with the understanding that later they would pervert them.[42]

Furthermore, returning to properly artistic matters, it is interesting that in the documents about the new monasteries built in the Valencia region, including the restoration of the "Casa Profesa" in the capital, there are detailed descriptions of liturgical decorations and paintings but none about images intended to indoctrinate. The sources describe the beauty of the artworks or their models,[43] how the Dominicans used images to shield themselves from misfortune before a journey,[44] but never their evangelizing function, not even in the case of the Llombai friary, founded by Borgia to indoctrinate Moriscos in the area.[45] Until very recent times, scholars[46] have focused on the large number of representations commissioned by the Dominican order in the early modern period and their function in private devotion, ignoring their possible use in the indoctrination of the population (whether Old or New Christians). As we noted before, most of the Dominicans didn't want to proselytize Moriscos, since they took for granted that their expulsion was imminent and because they assumed Muslims didn't really want to be converted to Christianity. Following Luis Beltrán—who used crosses strictly to counteract the destruction of images by Protestants and turned a blind eye to Morisco iconoclasm altogether—other friars stopped commissioning works of art to aid in preaching. However, we know they reused images to spread the word of God. As Saborit stated in his biography of Beltrán,

> In his sermons he would frequently commend the Holy Rosary, to which he was always extremely devoted, and he charged his listeners to pray for the souls in Purgatory and for those who were in deadly sin, and particularly for the state of the Holy Roman Church, our mother. He would also present examples or miracles from the Holy Virgin or the Saints, in imitation of the reverend Father Master Micon; and in this way he bore much fruit in these kingdoms, this being also the custom of Pope St. Gregory, as we can see in many of his homilies.[47]

So why do the sources speak only of the decoration of convents or the superstitious use of images and not about how Dominicans employed them to evangelize the Muslim population? Maybe because it was assumed in Dominican theology that all images had a dual function: to pray and to teach. In that case, it would not have been necessary to remark on the evangelizing function of art.[48] Or maybe it was because they were not actively creating new images for the express purpose of evangelizing—as were the Jesuits, a recently established order—but were using ones they already owned. This was typical in the medieval and modern periods and demonstrates the capacity to adapt to new problems in the indoctrination of the people. In any case, after consulting all the extant manuscripts, I cannot support the idea that the Dominicans created a true campaign for converting Moriscos in Valencia using visual representations.

Nonetheless, we can find references to art and Moriscos in the texts by supporters of the expulsion, such as Bleda and Fonseca. They speak of crosses, representations of the Virgin Mary, and other icons, mainly describing how Moriscos were destroying or desecrating them, an important reason—they argued—for this minority to be expelled.[49] Fonseca, for example, remarked how the inquisitors, assisted by Dominican fathers, found a number of broken or desecrated images in Morisco homes. According to

Fonseca, Moriscos followed the Christian laws of keeping Christian images in their homes but did not show them proper respect.[50]

These claims can be compared against several Inquisition trials, where we find the same accusations against Moriscos.[51] These accounts contributed to the creation of a "stereotypical" conception of the "other."[52] It is my contention that the apologists were mainly concerned with art as a symbol of their faith, a symbol that should be protected from the infidels' desecration.

A further factor that distinguishes the Dominicans from the Jesuits is that the former commissioned apologetic art against Moriscos before their expulsion. There are two examples of this: the famous Santiago Matamoros altarpiece (1603–6, Francisco Ribalta) in Algemesí and another unknown piece—now disappeared—dedicated to Raymond of Penyafort. We know that during the Middle Ages, several representations of Muslims were painted in various places in Castile, as has been studied by Inés Monteira Arias,[53] among others, but this was not the case in Valencia, where "defamatory paintings" were more likely to depict the Jewish minority rather than Muslims.[54]

Several scholars have argued that the Ribalta altarpiece was painted in Algemesí because it was inspired by Jaime Bleda (who was born in this city).[55] According to their contention, the painting reflects Bleda's—and the Dominicans'—intransigent ideology. These scholars base their argument on the fact that there is an image in the center of the altarpiece showing Santiago on a white horse that is trampling Muslims, an image that is very similar to what Bleda describes in his text. They take this coincidence, together with the fact that Bleda was from this city, to corroborate the connection between them. This argument, which at first glance seems convincing, is questionable for three reasons. The first and most obvious of these reasons is chronological: Bleda's works are later than the canvas. Maybe Ribalta had access to Bleda's manuscripts, but we do not currently have any evidence for this. The second reason, which I have addressed in previous studies,[56] is related to Bleda's personality. In his writings, Bleda never referred to his work in relation to the altarpiece, though he mentioned that a painter was either working on it at that time or had completed it. As is well known, Bleda was proud of his work, and in his texts, he always remarked on his tireless efforts in the fight against Muslims or Moriscos. If he had played a part in conceiving this altarpiece, he doubtless would have stressed it in his writings. In fact, the similarity between Ribalta's painting and the description of Santiago in

Bleda's work[57] is probably due to the Dominican having been inspired by the powerful icon depicted by the artist. And lastly, the third reason to question the argument that Bleda inspired the altarpiece is related to issues of form: it is well known that the iconography of Santiago in Clavijo was codified many centuries earlier, and it was traditional for the saint to be depicted on a white steed. Thus the depiction of Santiago in the altarpiece should not be seen, as some have wanted to do, as dependent on Bleda's ideas, but rather as dependent on the history of Santiago's iconography.[58] Even so, and notwithstanding my interpretation, which is that there is no direct link between the altarpiece and the Valencian friar, I have decided to include the former in the section about the Dominicans because the historiography on this painting does take a link for granted. Thus I leave the question open to the possible discovery of some document that can settle it one way or the other.

However, as I mentioned before, this is not the only example of artwork depicting Muslims that was commissioned by the Dominicans before the expulsion. An altarpiece showing Raymond of Penyafort in the sacristy of the Church of Dominicans in Valencia, now lost and until now ignored by scholars, was painted at the end of the sixteenth century or the beginning of the seventeenth.[59] In the eighteenth century, Francisco Sala provided a complete description: the saint appeared with an unsheathed sword in one hand, helping James I of Aragon in the conquest of Valencia, while on his other side was an image of the Dominican friary in Valencia; completing the scene were several defeated Muslims. This description was followed by a short biography of the saint, remarking how he fought against the infidels in Mallorca and Valencia and even making several references to Muslim chronicles in which Raymond of Penyafort appears as a Christian warrior. In fact, he was one of the most important Dominican friars in the history of the order, and his writings were also known, as Francisco Diago has noted,[60] to defend the use of images in preaching. Devotion to the cross was criticized by Muslims, but Penyafort attempted to show how venerating a cross was not idolatry but a commendable Christian tradition that evoked the sacrifice of Christ. The iconography in the painting of Penyafort is reminiscent of the attitude toward Moriscos among Dominicans in Valencia and is not typical of other representations of the saint, who is usually portrayed with several books (to signify that he was a theologian), a key (to mark his fidelity to the papacy), and a miter on the floor (representing his rejection of a bishopric).[61]

In sum, these altarpieces represent the order's visual policy in Valencia regarding the Morisco population, which was very different from the Jesuits' strategy. While the order of St. Ignatius developed a coherent visual program for new converts, the Dominican strategy is considerably more complicated to describe. The existence of two opposing factions and the scarcity of sources make it difficult to arrive at definitive conclusions about the Dominican strategy. However, on the basis of the parallels between the few extant visual manifestations, the apologetic texts, and the commentaries of Luis Beltrán, we cannot assert that there was a specific policy of using visual representations for converting Moriscos. Rather, the Dominican policy focused on defending Christian icons from the Moriscos' continuous iconoclastic attacks and on creating certain images in which Muslims were depicted as vanquished by a Christian army. Although these kinds of images were common in the kingdom of Castile, especially in the borderland areas, they were not at all common in Valencia, and thus it is necessary to note the anomaly and reflect on it.

The Mercedarian Friars and the Creation of a Critical Image of Islam in Seventeenth-Century Valencia

The third order I am going to analyze is the Mercedarian order, whose position on the Moriscos was very similar to that of the Dominicans.[62] As is well known, this congregation was created mainly to rescue Christian captives in Muslim territory, with conversion of infidels as a secondary goal.[63] In the Middle Ages and at the beginning of the early modern period, the Mercedarians used art for the conventional purposes—that is, as visual documentation of the history of their own order, as an educational tool, and as an emblem of the Christian victory over the infidel. Mercedarian art includes numerous references to Santa María del Puig, a miraculous image of the Virgin Mary that was said to have appeared on a hill near Valencia in 1247 and is credited with aiding James I in his conquest of the city and in the defense of the Valencia coast from Berber and Ottoman pirates.[64] (According to legend, the Virgin had also appeared to James I in about 1218, asking him to help found a new order dedicated to rescuing Christian captives, giving rise to the Mercedarians.)

The Mercedarians understood art as an important component of their order's identity and wrote several treatises about how it should be used to positively influence New and Old Christians alike. Tirso de Molina explicated several artworks and their uses in his book about the history of the order, highlighting the long tradition of Mercedarian iconography and, particularly, this triumphalist use of art against Muslims.[65] But more significant is the treatise by Friar Felipe Guimerán, *Breue historia de la Orden de Nuestra Señora de la Merced de Redempción de cautiuos christianos*, written in 1591, which contains a long chapter on images.[66] Following John Damascenus, Eusebius of Caesarea, and the Patriarch Nikephoros, among others, he defended the representation of God and Christ against iconoclasm, remarking on the educational value of such images for explaining the Christian faith and distinguishing veneration from adoration.[67]

Guimerán also discussed Santa María del Puig and her role in the conquest of Valencia as a powerful weapon against the enemy. He described several miracles involving Moriscos and their conversion or annihilation as a result of the appearance of her image. In fact, he used similar sources and a style identical to Bleda's in his text about the miracles of the cross.[68] Guimerán repeatedly condemns acts of iconoclasm and recounts supernatural incidents associated with images. He does not provide a detailed description of their shape, color, or how they were made. Rather, he is concerned with demonstrating the power of these icons, particularly those linked to the Mercedarian order.

Guimerán's ideology of pitting Christians against infidels and advocating the cult of images can also be linked with an earlier Mercedarian friar, St. Pedro Pascual (d. 1300),[69] and his work *Sobre la Se[c]ta Mahometana* (c. 1296).[70] This work argues for the importance of art as an emblem of faith and, following the *Antialcorano* tradition,[71] criticizes Islamic and Jewish ideology by setting these against Christian theology.

The theories of Guimerán and Pedro Pascual, among other post-Tridentine treatises, were taken up centuries later by another Mercedarian, Interián de Ayala, author of one of the most important treatises on religion written in Spain, entitled *El pintor christiano y erudito ó Tratado de los errores que suelen cometerse freqüentemente en pintar y esculpir imágenes sagradas*.[72] In this text, he analyzed the most common mistakes made by artists in their use of iconography and their conception of art for spreading the faith, criticizing important painters such as Michelangelo because of the nudes in the Sistine Chapel. He deplored how, in the eighteenth century, these issues had still not been resolved; criticized various works such as the Sistine Chapel, pointing out doctrinal errors; and explained the uses of works of art in Mercedarian theology and their value in the battle against infidels and in the final victory of Catholicism over other religions.

However, despite the importance of the treatises by Guimerán, Pedro Pascual, and Interián de Ayala and the fact that Mercedarian images were a great indoctrination tool and had enormous value for constructing the order's identity through depictions of iconic figures such as Santa María del Puig or the order's most-celebrated members, there are no documents or letters describing the order's official policy regarding the use of art in evangelizing. Thus it is impossible to compare theory and practice. I studied the inventories of churches and monasteries, some unpublished sources in the Biblioteca Nacional de España,[73] as well as several chronicles of the order,[74] but I could find no evidence of images created with the express intent to evangelize. However, we know the Mercedarians collaborated with Jesuits like Francis Borgia in the indoctrination task.[75] We might conclude that this lack of evidence is due to the order's economic difficulties and the multiple administrative crises that undermined its stability during the fifteenth and sixteenth centuries. However, another explanation might be found in the fact that, unlike the Dominicans, the Mercedarians did not have a medieval tradition of using imagery for evangelization purposes. As Taylor pointed out,[76] the Mercedarians received significant monetary support from the political authorities, and besides, Mercedarian altars had always been replete with images. It therefore seems reasonable to insist that if the order did not produce images to be used for evangelizing purposes during either the medieval or the modern period, it was because a visual campaign was just not part of their agenda. They focused their energies on other activities: they preferred to avail themselves of the power of words or, above all, to hand their bodies over to redeem captives rather than work toward a true assimilation of non-Christians, as other orders had done, such as the Dominicans in the medieval period or the Jesuits in the modern period. The Mercedarians' work was therefore distinctive, and we should understand the numerous post-Tridentine treatises on art produced by this order as theoretical meditations on the value of imagery as a visual aspect of religiosity in general, rather than a reflection of an official policy regarding the use of art in evangelization.

On the other hand, although I did not find evidence of a visual campaign to evangelize Moriscos, I can confirm that the Mercedarians made an apologetic

FIG. 8.2. José Orient, *San Pedro Pascual* (ca. 1670), oil on canvas, 270 × 179 cm. Universitat de València.

use of images. We should not forget that the image of Santa María del Puig appeared to James of Aragon during the conquest of Valencia, something that all Mercedarian chronicles boast of. But that is not all: in the seventeenth century, other triumphalist icons were created, once the Moriscos had been expelled, depicting the victory of Christianity over the infidel. To illustrate this point, I will focus on the representations of St. Pedro Pascual from Valencia, and specifically the one painted by José Orient, circa 1670, now in the main building of the University of Valencia.[77] This large oil on canvas, discovered only recently in 1988, represents the Mercedarian friar praying to the mystical apparition of the Immaculate Conception while trampling a man with several Islamic books. The image represents, on the one hand, Pedro Pascual's devotion to the Mother of God (an important article of faith defended in his texts)[78] and, on the other, the victory over the Moriscos, which he had discussed in his work. He died in the battle to defeat Islam, and this painting glorifies his efforts.

I want to focus on this image for a few different reasons. The first is its originality. If we review the Mercedarians' visual tradition in Valencia up to this point, we will not find any other triumphalist representations of Islam. While it is true that there are images of the redemption of captives, famous saints, the Virgin Mary, and some Navis Christi, in them the infidel is not trodden underfoot like in the work that concerns us here.[79] Thus it is interesting to note that, at the precise moment when the Mercedarians were trying to get their most saintly members canonized (which did not happen until the seventeenth century), this warlike image of Pedro Pascual was created in Valencia. The only other artwork with similar iconography is also from Valencia, painted by José Vergara for the monastery of Santa María del Puig, and other engraving by the Mercedarian friar Salazar, dated slightly later, from 1672.[80]

Interián de Ayala recommended depicting St. Pedro Pascual using "canonical" iconography—that is, as an old man with the symbols of the office of bishop, his neck pierced by a sword, surrounded by some books to indicate his work as a theologian.[81] Interián did not make any reference to Islamic themes, nor did he recommend using the saint to symbolize victory over the infidels. Maybe these noncanonical representations were intended to show the importance of this saint and why he ought to be canonized.[82] Or possibly they were used as part of the discourse to justify the expulsion of the Moriscos. This rhetoric of obligatory exile developed during the reigns of Philip III and Philip IV, as Antonio Feros has pointed out.[83] The Spanish Crown, as well as the orders that were most opposed to the assimilation of new converts, the Mercedarians prominent among them, used this kind of imagery to represent the victory over the Muslims, the existence of a Hispania free of heretics and apostates. To all of this, it is necessary to add, as has been pointed out, that no Mercedarians had been canonized before the seventeenth century. Thus the Mercedarians were now eager to depict Muslims in their artwork in order to remind the viewer that Mercedarians had always supported the expulsion of Moriscos and—in presenting the expulsion as a validation of their policy, a recognition of the order's long-standing defense of the orthodoxy of the faith—to make an argument for the canonization of members of their order.

Another interesting question to ask is why these representations were created mainly in Valencia. Zurbaran's depiction of St. Pedro Pascual (Museo de Bellas Artes, Seville), painted in 1631, shows him as a venerable theologian but does not include any criticism of Muslims other than the representation of his book *Contra la secta de Mahoma*. This suggests that the body of works painted in Valencia glorifying Pedro Pascual has an importance that must be interpreted in the light of this region's particular social situation, complicated not only by the cohabitation of Moriscos and Old Christians but also the possibility of attack by the Ottoman Empire or pirates abetted by rebel Moriscos. As was mentioned, the Mercedarians were closely associated with the conquest of the city, and Santa María del Puig was an icon of the final victory of the Christians. The Mercedarians did not usually participate in the active work of proselytizing the Islamic population. They remained working in territories with Muslims and criticizing the political attitude of assimilation developed by the Crown. So when the Mercedarian communities in Valencia—and mainly, the Santa María del Puig monastery—needed to create the holy representation of one of the most important friars in their territory, they used a powerful image of Pedro Pascual, another icon. This metaphoric medieval image concept of the victory against the infidels[84] gradually assumed a more specific meaning visualized in these violent representations showing the real conception of the "other" that the order had after the Reconquest, but they could not be disseminated because of the ("pacific") indoctrination plan developed by several archbishops in Valencia. The expulsion of Moriscos, but mainly the Habsburg necessity to justify their exile, was the spark to light the fire.

Conclusions

In sum, the three religious orders discussed here followed different policies in their artistic depictions of Moriscos in Valencia during the sixteenth and seventeenth centuries. These differences are reflected in both the artworks and the writings produced by the different orders. We began this study with the Jesuits, who conceived a visual policy for the assimilation of Moriscos and did not abandon that policy until the latter's expulsion. Only then did they reveal any signs of hostility toward the Moriscos, through hieroglyphs commemorating the conquest of Valencia that were hung from an altar at the Colegio de San Pablo in 1638. Secondly, we looked at the Dominicans, and this part of the study entailed some difficulties. The Dominicans traditionally used imagery for indoctrination purposes, so one would expect that they would have continued to do so. However, this cannot be confirmed by the sources. The internal crises that developed in most Dominican monasteries over what stance to take toward the Moriscos make it impossible to identify a single, consistent policy adopted by the order as a whole. It seems likely, however, that Dominican policy was more centered on Old Christians and on dealing with the challenge posed by Protestantism. When they did make use of images, they tended to reuse those that they already possessed—which were perhaps not ideal for evangelizing purposes—rather than create new ones. However, some friars, even one so clearly cut out for missionizing as Beltrán, simply refused to confront the Morisco population and chose to perform their ministry by "exiling themselves" to the "exterior Indies." On the other hand, the Dominican order did create images with strong apologetic content, which arose from these internal conflicts and the differences of opinion regarding the complicated situation in Valencia (the cohabitation of Morisco and Old Christian communities and the threat of Ottoman or pirate attacks mentioned above). Lastly, the Mercedarians' writings show a theoretical interest in using art as a tool of indoctrination, but there is no evidence that they ever put this into practice. Apart from the treatises written by individuals belonging to the enlightened faction of the order, such as Guimerán, Pedro Pascual, and Interián de Ayala, the Mercedarians did not produce any inventories of or commentaries on actual works of art that suggest an official policy with regard to Moriscos or even Old Christians; the Mercedarians' labors seem to have been focused on redeeming captives and face-to-face confrontation with their enemies. Not until after the expulsion of the Moriscos did they demonstrate—in visual terms—their true conception of the other, taking up Philip IV's policy of justifying the Morisco exile, which dovetailed with their campaigns to have some of their illustrious members canonized. This differentiation is what led to the selection of the orders that have been studied in this work: three attitudes that are clearly divergent yet coexisted in the same land.

In essence, all three of them defended the educational use of art in theory, but in the end, they each used art in different ways. These differences are a reflection of the artistic richness and multiplicity that characterized Valencia during this period. It bears asking whether we should think about the existence of an art of conversion or rather speak of the creation of policies that required visual representations to be emblems of Christianity, examples of virtue, or aspects to defend from the attacks (real or not) of a religious minority, which was quite common in sixteenth-century Europe. On the other hand, the creation of an iconography in which Muslims are depicted as vanquished is nothing new in the early modern world, although it is true that in the Valencian baroque, this iconography was informed by a variety of contemporary texts. Jesuits, Dominicans, and Mercedarians responded in diverse ways to the political and religious stimuli that surrounded them, and they constructed a discourse in images steeped in controversy and nuance, as I have shown here.

Notes

This work is part of the I+D Research Project HAR2016-80354-P, "Antes del orientalismo: Las imágenes del musulmán en la Península Ibérica (siglos XV–XVII) y sus conexiones mediterráneas." Principal investigator: Dr. Borja Franco. I would like to thank professors Felipe Pereda, Mercedes García-Arenal, and Gerard Wiegers for their helpful suggestions on previous versions of this chapter.

1. Escolano, *Décadas de la Insigne*, 1037.
2. Broggio, "Órdenes religiosas," 153.
3. Broggio stated that it was difficult to research this order because of the Napoleonic Wars and other problems: "Se trata, en primer lugar, de una dificultad de índole documental, pues en la mayoría de los casos las fuentes conservadas en los archivos centrales de las diferentes órdenes religiosas no permiten de hecho proceder a una reconstrucción suficientemente articulada y convincente sobre la actitud que prevalecía en los centros de gobierno de una determinada orden religiosa. . . . Por lo que respecta a dominicos y franciscanos, desafortunadamente, la mayor parte de la correspondencia entre las provincias españolas y la curia general se perdió, sobre todo en el momento de la invasión napoleónica." Broggio, 151.
4. Franco Llopis, "Espiritualidad, reformas y arte"; Franco Llopis, "Propaganda, misión y oración"; and Franco Llopis, "Arte y misión."
5. O'Malley, "Sant'Ignazio," 29–30.
6. On early attempts to convert Moriscos in Iberia and how the strategy evolved in the seventeenth century, see Colombo, "Jesuitas y musulmanes."
7. We have documentation showing that Borja sent this image to various illustrious personages in Europe. As for copies in Spain, we do know that he sent a copy to Madrid that ended up at El Escorial, but after consultation with Almudena Pérez de Tudela, the national patrimony delegate for this historic site, we have not as yet been able to locate it. In other cases, such as the copy sent to Catherine of Braganza, we know that Borja entreated her to place the image in her private oratory as a means of increasing her devotion to the sacred image. See *Monumenta Borgia*, 5:112–13.
8. See D'Elia, "Prima diffusione."
9. See Pereda, *Imágenes de la discordia*; and Iannuzzi, *Poder de la palabra*.
10. "Tienen mucho amor á los de la Conpañía, porque les favorecemos en lo que podemos, y convertidos 20 ó 30 alfaquís que puede aver todos los demás se convertirán, y si oviese quien los solicitase, presto con el fabor divino sería hecho, porque ya ay dos alfaquís convertidos, y el uno nos tienen tanto amor, que dize que daría su sangre por nosotros. Esto confiesa muchas veces." "Letter from Cristophorus Rodríguez to Ignatius of Loyola, Gandía, 27th April, 1556," in *Epistolae Mixtae ex variis Europae Locis*, 5:296. See also "Letter from Cristophorus Rodríguez to Ignatius of Loyola, Gandía, 30th December, 1555," in *Litterae Quadrimestres*, 3:444–45.
11. "Información de algunas cosas que se me ofrecen acerca delos Christianos

nuevos deste Reyno de Valencia delo que toca a su conversión después de aver vivido entre ellos y tratadolos algun tiempo," in *Archivum historicum Societatis Iesu* (ARSI), Epist. Hisp. 127, *Epistolae Hispaniae* 1579.

12. Borja de Medina, "Compañía de Jesús," 37.
13. I looked at these dowries in my paper for the conference Domestic Devotions in the Early Modern World (Cambridge, University of Cambridge–St. Catherine's College, July 2015) titled "The Moriscos' (Artistic) Domestic Devotion(s) Viewed through Christian Eyes in Early Modern Iberia."
14. This practice can be linked to *taqiyya*, a well-known form of dissimulation employed by Muslims living under Christian rule. On this, see the monographic issue, García-Arenal, "*Taqiyya*."
15. Arranz Roa, "Indias de aquí"; and Broggio, *Evangelizzare il mondo*.
16. See García-Arenal, "Moriscos e indios"; Gonzalbo Aizpuru, *Educación popular*; O'Malley, *First Jesuits*, 156–57; Zubillaga, "Métodos misionales"; and El Alaoui, *Jésuites, morisques et indiens*.
17. On the Virgin Mary and Jesuit piety, see Guibert, *Spiritualità della Compagnia*, 302; O'Malley, *First Jesuits*, 270; and Martínez Naranjo, "Congregaciones marianas."
18. See "Letter from Jerónimo Doménech to Diego Laínez, 14th April, 1562," in ARSI, Epist. Hisp. 99, *Epistolae Hispaniae* 1562, n.d. See also El Alaoui, "Ignacio de las Casas"; Vincent, *Minorías y marginados*, 105; Lea, *Moriscos of Spain*, 214; and Rodríguez Paniagua, "Recursos sintácticos."
19. La Parra López, "1609 en el Ducado de Gandía"; and La Parra López, "Moriscos y moriscas."
20. *Monumenta Borgia*, 3:616–17.
21. ARSI, Arag. 37. Juan B. Bosquete, *Historia y primer centenar de la Casa Professa del Espíritu Santo y Compañía de Jesús de Valencia (1579–1631)*, vol. 1, fol. 5; Benítez Sánchez-Blanco, *Heroicas decisiones*, 353–54; Escrivá, *Vida del Venerable Siervo*, 72; and El Alaoui, *Jésuites, morisques et indiens*.
22. See Franco Llopis, "Ignacio de las Casas."
23. Astrain, *Historia de la Compañía*, 2:545.
24. See Antonio Ortí, *Siglo quarto*, 67–88.
25. See Medina Rojas, "Ignacio de Loyola"; Sicroff, *Controverses des statuts*.
26. Burns, *Moros, cristians i jueus*; Tolan, *Sarracenos*; and Vose, *Dominicans, Muslims and Jews*.
27. I have used the following sources to analyze the first indoctrination plan and the use of images for this purpose: Biblioteca Histórica de la Universitat de València (BUV) MS 933, José Teixidor, *Necrologio de este real convento de Predicadores de Valencia. Devidas memorias a sus hijos nativos, con extensión en los más ilustres, recogidas de monumentos authénticos i seguros*, vol. 2, fols. 293–315; Escolano, *Década* primera, 1743–80; and BUV MS 801, *Memoria puesta a su Magestad el rey Felipe II por el padre Provincial*, fol. 578. Most of these manuscripts are cataloged in Robles Sierra, "Manuscritos del Archivo," 385. For further information, see Seguí Cantos, "Presencia de la Orden."
28. Diago, *Historia de la Provincia*, 4; and Delgado Criado, *Historia de la educación*, 489.
29. Callado Estela, "Dominicos y moriscos." See also Robles Sierra, "Reforma entre los dominicos"; and Galmés Mas, "Cuestión de los moriscos."
30. Alabrús Iglesias, "San Juan de Ribera"; Callado Estela and Alfonso Esponera, "San Luis Beltrán"; and Robles Sierra, "Correspondencia de San Luis," 347–48.
31. Between 1578 and 1595, seven new Dominican convents were founded in Morisco areas (Ayodar, l'Olleria, Castellón de la Plana, Alicante, Almenara, Castellón de la Ribera, and Algemesí, these last two dedicated to Vincent Ferrer). See Esponera Cerdán, "Ne nos fratres praedicatores"; Collell Costa, "Ayer de la Provincia," 241; Garganta, "San Juan de Ribera"; and Robles Sierra, "Reforma entre los dominicos."
32. On Dominicans and the Inquisition, see *Praedicatores Inquisitores*.

33. This issue is explored in Esponera Cerdán, "Ne nos fratres praedicatores"; and Callado Estela and Esponera Cerdán, "1239–1835."
34. See "Codicilo de Francisco de Borja ante Melchor Monroig, Gandía, 17 de Junio, 1547," in *Monumenta Borgia*, vol. 6.
35. Callado Estela, "Dominicos y moriscos."
36. Benito Goerlich, "Parets que ensenyen."
37. Recently, scholars such as Cynthia Robinson have studied the Vincent Ferrer sermons and his differences with other medieval thinkers like Eiximenis. See the first chapter of Robinson, *Imagining the Passion*. These ideas can be compared to similar ones focused on the history of Valencia in Robles Sierra, "San Vicente Ferrer." See also Jones, chapter 4 in this volume.
38. There are a few sixteenth-century biographies of Ferrer, but I will mention only the most important ones: Antist, *Vida e historia*; and Diago, *Historia de la vida*.
39. More information about the use of images of Luis Beltrán for evangelizing purposes can be found in Saborit, *Historia de la vida*, 96, 97, 230.
40. See Puig Sanchís and Franco Llopis, "Juan de Sariñena."
41. See Corbín Ferrer, "San Luis Beltrán."
42. Robles Sierra, "Correspondencia de San Luis," 347–48:

    Son herejes, y aún apóstatas que es peor, y claramente muestran la ojeriza que tienen con los cristianos y guardan las ceremonias de Mahoma en cuanto pueden [. . .] por ello no se administre el bautismo a los niños hijos si han de vivir en casa de sus padres, porque hay evidencia moral que serán apóstatas como ellos, y más vale que sean moros que herejes o apóstatas. Es tan intrínsecamente malo dar fuera del peligro de muerte el bautismo a estos niños, presupuesto todo lo sobre dicho, como si un cristiano bautizase los niños hijos de los moros que están en Berbería dejándolos allá entre padres infieles, aunque ellos consistiesen por algún respeto en el bautismo de sus hijos, entendiendo que después los habían de pervertir.

43. BUV MS 529, *Libro de memorias de algunas cosas pertenecientes al Convento de Predicadores de Valencia que an sucedido desde el año 1603 hasta el 1628, observadas i escritas de mano i industria del R. P. Fr. Geronymo Pradas hijo de dicho convento.*
44. BUV MSS 162–63, Francisco Sala, *Historia de la Fundación y cosas memorables del Real Convento de Predicadores de Valencia* (Valencia, 1719), fol. 16.
45. See Archivo Histórico Nacional (AHN), Osuna, CP. 49. D. 3, *Original del Testamento y Codicilos del Santo Francisco de Borxa 40 Duque de Gandía, firmados de su propia mano a saber: El Testamento en 26 de Agosto de 1550, y los codicilos en el 28 del mismo mes y año ante Onofre Pérez de Culla*; and AHN, Osuna, CP. 48. D. 24, *Original del último Codicilo del Santo Francisco de Borxa Duque de Gandía y Marqués de Llombay, firmado de su mano en Gandía á 17 de Junio de 1547, ante Melchor Monroig Notario Publico à quien se le entrego según consta del numero 2757.*
46. Pérez Ruiz, *La fe, la historia*, 46. We can find more information in Benito Goerlich, "L'herència artística"; and Blaya Estrada, "Imatge de l'orde."
47. "Encomendava mucho en sus sermones el santo rosario, del qual siempre fue devotíssimo, y encargava a los oyentes, que rogasen por las almas del purgatorio, y por los que están en pecado mortal, y muy en particular por el estado de la Santa Iglesia Romana madre nuestra. Procurava también de traer algún exemplo o milagro de nuestra Señora o de los Santos, imitando al Venerable Padre Maestro Micon, que desta manera hizo grande fruto en estos reinos, la qual costumbre también fue de San Gregorio Papa, como se ve en muchas de sus Homilías." Saborit, *Historia de la vida*, 230.
48. Robinson reflects on the problematic uses of images in multiconfessional

societies. See Robinson, *Imagining the Passion.*

49. Bleda also wrote other treatises about the cross and Eucharistic adoration, defending them from Muslims and protestants. See Bleda, *Libro de la Archicofradía*; and Bleda, *Qvatrocientos milagros.*
50. "Las imágenes de los santos que con particular mandato de los visitadores tenían en sus casas siempre las veíamos mal puestas, unas veces de lado otras cabeza abajo, llenas de suciedad y telarañas y rasgadas y escupidas, dávanles nombre de oprobio y las hazían otras semejantes afrentas, por las cuales fueron muchas veces castigados." Fonseca, *Iusta expulsión*, 128.
51. I have addressed this in Franco Llopis, "Consideraciones sobre el uso."
52. See Perceval, *Todos son uno*, 183.
53. Monteira Arias, *Enemigo imaginado.*
54. See Franco Llopis, "Identidades reales, identidades creadas."
55. Checa Cremades, *Carlos V y la imagen*, 417; Fontcuberta Famadas, *Imatges d'atac*; Gomis Corell, *L'obra pictòrica*; and Olivares Torres, "Nuevas lecturas."
56. I have developed this topic more thoroughly in Franco Llopis, "Nuevas tendencias historiográficas."
57. "Y viendo en la vanguardia al Apóstol de Iesu Christo sobre el cavallo blanco, y un estandarte blanco, y en él una cruz colorada, como lo avía prometido, se animaron tanto que hizieron tanta matança en los Moros, apellidando a grandes vozes: Santiago, Santiago." Bleda, *Coronica de los moros*, 250–51.
58. See Cabrillana Ciézar, *Santiago Matamoros*; Maíz Eleizegui, *Devoción al Apóstol Santiago*; García Páramo, "Iconografía de Santiago"; and, more recently, Linares, "Saints matamores."
59. "Se pinta teniendo en la mano izquierda el Convento de Valencia y en la derecha una espada desembainada, como se ve en un lienzo grande pintado con otros santos en la Sacristía de este convento." In the margin of this document, there is a note saying that he was represented with several emblems of the order. BUV MSS 162–63, Sala, *Historia de la Fundación*, fol. 41.
60. Talking about the work of Penyafort, Diago stressed, "En los captivos christianos y en los moros, los quales por la mayor parte estavan entonces en una grande ignorancia condemnandos a los Católicos por Idólatras (como agora hazen los Luteranos) por la veneración y reverencia que hazemos a la Cruz del Señor y a las imágines. Del qual infernal engaño los sacaron los religiosos." Diago, *Historia de la Provincia*, 124.
61. Sometimes he also appears with chains in an allusion to the foundation of the Mercedarian order. See Carmona Muela, *Iconografía de los santos*, 389–90; and Piquer Jover, *Vida i els miracles.*
62. I studied this topic deeply in Borja Franco, "Mercédaires, musulmans et morisques."
63. See Brodman, *L'orde de la Mercé*; Brodman, "Community, Identity and Redemption."
64. See Biblioteca Nacional de España (BNE), MSS 8294, *Fragmentos históricos tocantes a la Orden de la Merced de la Provincia de Valencia y Varios*, fol. 38. It was common to attribute to the Virgin this power to repel attacks and to convert non-Christians, and these types of claims are not unique to the Mercedarian order. See O'Callaghan, *Reconquest and Crusade*, 190–93; Christian, "Santos a María," 61; and Robinson, "Preaching to the Converted."
65. Téllez (Tirso de Molina), *Historia General*, 1:46, 161, 271–73, 335, 400.
66. Guimerán, *Breue historia.*
67. Guimerán, 118. A primary approach to these ideas in Guimerán's treatise can be found in Zuriaga Senent, *Imagen devocional*, and in the concise work of Falomir Faus, "Patriarca Ribera y la pintura."
68. Bleda, *Qvatrocientos milagros.*
69. There is debate about whether this saint actually existed. See Riera i Sans, "Invenció literària."

70. We used the 2011 edition of Pascual, *Se[c]ta mahometana*, edited by Fernando González Muñoz.
71. For further information about the purpose and style of the *Antialcorano* tradition, see Bunes Ibarra, "Enfrentamiento con el Islam."
72. Interián de Ayala, *Pintor christiano y erudito*. See also Argelich Gutiérrez, "Pintor cristiano y erudito."
73. BNE MSS 8294, *Fragmentos históricos*.
74. In addition to Tirso of Molina's work, I have looked at BNE MSS 4159, Felipe Colombo, *Historia general de la real y militar Orden de Nuestra Señora de la Merced Redención de cautivos, desde su milagrosa fundación hasta nuestros tiempos* (this was written in the second half of the sixteenth century, but the copy I consulted is from the eighteenth century); San Cecilio, *Annales de la Orden de Descalzos*; Torres, *Regula et constitutiones*; and Zumel, *Regula et constitutiones*.
75. Tirso de Molina explained how several Mercedarian friars were students of Jesuits schools and even how they had interesting discussions with Borgia about the conversion of Moriscos. See Téllez, *Historia General*, 471. Some of these relationships were studied in Taylor, *Structures of Reform*, 240.
76. Taylor, *Structures of Reform*, 362–69.
77. For a stylistic and formalist analysis, see Benito Goerlich, "Pintura recuperada"; and Benito Goerlich, "Visión de San Pedro Pascual," 2:130–31.
78. Callado Estela, "*Tota Pulchra es amica mea*."
79. For a complete analysis of Mercedarian iconography, see Zuriaga, *Imagen devocional*.
80. García Gutiérrez, *Iconografía mercedaria*, 78–79.
81. Interián de Ayala, *Pintor christiano y erudito*, 439. For further information about other representations of this saint, see Mateu Ibars, "San Pedro Pascual."
82. Burke, "How to Become a Counter-Reformation Saint," in Burke, *Historical Anthropology*.
83. Feros Carrasco, "Retóricas de la Expulsión."
84. Here I am following Ringbom's ideas about the materialization of mental images and concepts in works of art in the medieval world. See Ringbom, "Devotional Images"; and Ringbom, *Images des dévotion*.

9

MARCOS DOBELIO'S POLEMICS AGAINST THE AUTHENTICITY OF THE GRANADAN LEAD BOOKS IN LIGHT OF THE ORIGINAL ARABIC SOURCES

Pieter Sjoerd van Koningsveld and Gerard Wiegers

Introduction

The Granadan Lead Books affair presents us with an excellent case study of a polemical debate about the relations between Islam and Christianity in Europe and North Africa. This interesting episode began in 1588 when, during the demolition of a tower located in the center of Granada, relics and a parchment were discovered. The Parchment contained prophetical texts in Arabic, Spanish, and Latin, the contents of which proved to be controversial. The tower in which these materials were found was allegedly of Roman origin and had been the minaret of the Grand Mosque in Muslim times. Beginning in 1595, the so-called Lead Books were discovered on the slopes of the Valparaiso hillock, which is known today as Sacromonte. The Parchment and Lead Books, which contain Arabic texts, describe the life and religious ideas of a group of Arabic-speaking Christians, who, in the company of the apostle St. James himself, lived in Granada in the first century CE and were martyred by the Romans. The Parchment describes a Granadan bishop, Cecilio, who committed to writing a prophecy of St. John about the end of time. This prophecy had allegedly been written by St. John in Hebrew and was translated into Greek and, for later generations, into Spanish, the language used in the Parchment, which also includes a commentary in Arabic that paraphrases the Spanish prophecy. The commentary states that its esoteric meaning would be explained by a servant of God at the end of time, "when the City of the Sea will be possessed by the Oriental."[1] The document was to be hidden from the infidels—that is, the Moors (*mauri*). The twenty-one Lead Books, which were discovered on the slopes of the Sacromonte between 1595 and 1599, refer back to the Parchment and the tower (the Lead Books refer to it as the Turpiana Tower) and present a collection of pseudo-Christian writings written by two Arabian brothers, one of them the aforementioned Cecilio. The brothers, who allegedly were miraculously cured by Jesus, present themselves as reliable witnesses of Jesus's life.

The Lead Books became the object of veneration, giving rise to pilgrimages and religious festivals, but opponents very soon claimed that they were Muslim forgeries and accused the Moriscos of concocting them. After a prolonged debate, they were sent to the Vatican in 1642 and examined there by committees of Arabists and theologians. In 1682, Pope Innocent XI condemned them for containing Muslim heresies. The Lead Books remained in the Vatican until they were returned by Pope John Paul II to Granada in 2000. The affair of the Parchment and the Lead Books has puzzled students of Spanish history and Muslim-Christian relations ever since they were discovered. In recent decades, the topic has generated a lot of scholarly interest, and numerous studies have appeared. But until relatively recently, the documents themselves were not available for research. In 2003, the Sacromonte archive allowed the present authors to study the Parchment and publish an article in the journal *Al-Qanṭara*.[2] The original Lead Books became accessible in 2010. In that year, the archbishopric of Granada gave us permission to study them also and to prepare a critical edition.

In the present chapter, we will focus on the heated polemical debates about the Parchment and the Lead Books that took place in Spain between 1595 (the year in which the first discoveries were made) and 1638 (the year in which a very important polemical text was published). As we will see, there was one central theme that dominated the discussion: whether the Parchment and Lead Books were authentic early Christian documents or not. Interestingly, some of the translators who studied the original Lead Books argued that they were authentic, while others argued, on the basis of the same texts, that they were forgeries. Anyone who studies the polemics about the Lead Books will at some stage be confronted with the question of how such widely differing interpretations were possible even though these early readers of the Lead Books had empirical, firsthand knowledge of the original texts. Very early on, the religious authorities—in particular, Pedro Vaca de Castro y Quiñones (1534–1623), archbishop of Granada and Seville, who was the Lead Books' most important advocate and a staunch defender of their interpretation as authentic Christian documents—were accused of manipulating the discussions and, in any case, of not allowing opponents to voice doubts about their authenticity. Without access to the original documents, it was very difficult to judge the nature and background of the individual contributions to the polemical and scholarly (less polemical) debates, but we can now begin to form a better idea about this and thus make some progress in solving the mystery. Of course, it is impossible to evaluate the entire debate here, nor can we pretend to do full justice to its many complexities. Needless to say, the polemical character of the debate was influenced not only by different views on the contents of the books but also by religious, political, social, and economic interests. It was closely connected, for example, to the economic interests of Granada as a pilgrimage center, to its prestige as a sacred and historical site, and to the religious authority of the Granadan church and its archbishop.[3]

We will focus here on a particular case, the work and activities of Murquṣ al-Duʿābilī al-Kurdī (ca. 1572–1654), a man who in Spain became known as Marcos Dobelio. Unlike some of the Lead Books' other early translators, Marcos Dobelio knew Arabic very well. He took part in the debates in Spain between about 1610 and 1638 in several ways.[4] García-Arenal and Rodríguez Mediano consider his assessment to be one of the most important contributions to the debate about the Lead Books in Spain. In addition, his is an outright polemical contribution and one that is a straightforward attack on the authenticity of the Lead Books.

Probably an Eastern Christian of Kurdish origin who had lived for some time in Aleppo, Marcos Dobelio was well acquainted with both Eastern Christianity and Islamic thought and practice. In about 1597, he arrived in Rome, where he stayed in the neophytes' college and also taught Arabic at the University of La Sapienza. In view of his excellent knowledge of the Qurʾān and the Islamic tradition, we think it is very likely that he was a Muslim convert to Christianity. In October 1610, Dobelio traveled from Rome to Granada, having been summoned there by a committee assembled by King Philip III in 1609, which was presided over by the cardinal of Toledo, to review the case of the Lead Books and decide how to proceed with the evaluation process.[5] In Granada, Dobelio had access to the original texts when he worked in the service of Archbishop Pedro de Castro. As mentioned before, Pedro de Castro was a staunch defender of the Parchment and Lead Books as orthodox, authentic early Christian documents. From 1595 onward, he tried to find translators who were not only capable of understanding and rendering the texts accurately but also inclined to interpret them in such a way that they confirmed his own views. The background of Dobelio's arrival in Spain seems to indicate, therefore, that it was not Castro who had requested him to come but rather circles in which there were critical voices who questioned the authenticity of these texts and advocated for the Vatican rather than the Spanish church or Castro himself to be responsible for their translation. Dobelio's work on the Lead Books soon came to an end. After having translated the first two Lead Books that had been found, he informed Castro that he considered them to be forgeries. Castro broke with him. Needing money and increasingly frustrated, Dobelio apparently departed Granada in search of work.[6] He tried to earn a living in the service of the Inquisition, teaching Arabic and studying, translating, and editing Arabic manuscripts and documents. García-Arenal and Rodríguez Mediano argue that Dobelio prepared several draft translations that he organized around the titles of some of the Lead Books he studied and commented upon in the years 1610–11.[7] As we will see, on closer study, these drafts appear to date from a much later time, 1633, and do not include translations of several Lead Books but in fact only one, the *Vita Jesu*, Lead Book 7. We will return to this below.

On July 23, 1613, Dobelio wrote a letter in Arabic from Madrid to the great classical scholar Isaac Casaubon (1559–1614), in which he informs Casaubon about his services to the papal library and to the royal committee (for which, he tells him, a fee of six hundred escudos was promised[8]) and tells him about the dramatic dénouement of his rift with Castro.[9] He was considering going to England, he writes, where Casaubon lived at the time, but was still awaiting his payment.[10] Dobelio never did end up going to England. In the following years, he apparently made a living by teaching Arabic to, among others, the Basque translator Francisco de Gurmendi, to whom we will return below.[11] Dobelio possessed an important collection of Arabic manuscripts, so impressive that the Dutch Arabist Thomas Erpenius (1584–1624) referred to it as one of the most important in Europe in his second inaugural lecture about the merits of the Arabic language, delivered in Leiden in 1621.[12] Dobelio describes his private collection in a handlist, at the end of which is a short remark that he had left other manuscripts in Seville and Rome. The list may have been drawn up for the English Arabist Thomas Bedwell, as García-Arenal and Rodríguez Mediano maintain.[13]

Dobelio's foremost contribution to the discussions about the Lead Books is the analysis he offers in his *Nuevo descubrimiento de la falsedad del metal* (The new unveiling of the falseness of metal), the introduction of which can be dated to 1638.[14] In fact, this introduction is the only part of the work that is extant today, but it is a complete treatise in itself, and we do not know whether the author ever wrote any additional chapters. Of this text, the subject of the present chapter, at least three manuscripts are extant today. We are using here the manuscript at the Biblioteca de Castilla-La Mancha, Toledo.[15]

In the following pages, we will first briefly discuss the sources of Dobelio's text, then discuss his analysis and compare his views to the original Arabic texts of the Lead Books, especially *Kitāb maḥāsin sayyidinā Yaṣūʿ wa maʿājizihi wa-ummihi Maryam al-ṣāliḥa al-ʿudhrā* (*Book of the Outstanding Qualities and Miracles of Our Lord Jesus and of His Mother the Holy Virgin Mary*), Lead Book 7, henceforward referred to us as the *Vita*. We include an edition of the Arabic with an English translation of this hitherto unpublished and inaccessible text at the end of this chapter. In the third and fourth sections, we take a look at the broader perspective of the polemical debate about the Lead Books in Spain and in the Vatican and Dobelio's contribution to them. We will finish with some conclusions.

Sources of the *Nuevo descubrimiento de la falsedad del metal*

Dobelio bases his extensive analysis of the Lead Books mainly on three books—namely, (1) *Kitāb qawāʿid al-dīn li-Tisʿūn ibn ʿAṭṭār, tilmīdh Yaʿqūb al-ḥawārī* ("Book of the Fundamentals of Religion by Tisʿūn ibn ʿAṭṭār, a *Disciple of James* the Apostle"), or, as it was called in Latin on its now-lost cover, *Liber Fundamenti Ecclesiae Salomonis characteribus escriptus* (Lead Book no. 1 of the Sacromonte Abbey in Granada);[16] (2) *Kitāb li-Tisʿūn ibn ʿAṭṭār fī al-dhāt al-karīma* ("Book by Tisʿūn ibn ʿAṭṭār about the Venerable Essence [viz. of God]"), called, in Latin, *Liber de essentia Dei* (Lead Book no. 2); and

(3) the *Vita* (Lead Book no. 7). He bases his argument primarily on a translation of this last book, since he claimed that "God had permitted me that the life of our Lord Jesus came into my possession in a translation from which I have taken everything which the 'laminaries' have always kept secret as an excuse."[17] The *Vita* may be considered one of the most important Lead Book texts. We will return to it below. The two other books we just mentioned were also the first Lead Books to be discovered, on April 22 and 25, 1595. Both books have strongly theological and dogmatic content, as their titles indicate. These were also the two Lead Books that Dobelio studied in 1610 while still in the service of Archbishop Pedro de Castro.

In his study of the Lead Books in the introduction to the *Nuevo descubrimiento de la falsedad del metal*, Marcos Dobelio presents useful drawings of some of the leaves, including their pictorial engravings.[18] He also discusses at length a translation of another Lead Book, referred to by him as the *Oraçión y nómina de Jacob el Zebedeo el Apóstol*. This is in fact Lead Book number 3, entitled *Duʿā wa-ḥirz li-Yaʿqūb ibn Shamīkh al-Zabadī al-ḥawārī* ("Invocation and Amulet by the Apostle Yaʿqūb ibn Shamīkh al-Zabadī").[19] In this case, his direct source was not his own work but a lecture about the Lead Books written by someone referred to as Morillo, who quoted a transcription made by Alonso del Castillo.[20] The Morillo in question is probably Gregorio Morillo, a chaplain in the Collegiate Church of the Sacromonte and one of the defenders of the Lead Books.[21] Alonso del Castillo (1525–1607) was one of the Granadan Morisco translators of the Lead Books and an official Arabic translator of the king.[22] From the documents preserved in the Archive of the Sacromonte Abbey, it appears that in 1611, Dobelio transcribed parts of the Arabic texts of the Parchment and made attempts to translate them.[23] We also find a sheet on which he wrote the first lines in Arabic of the *Cathechismo Maior* (Arabic title: *Kitāb nadhrat al-ḥawāriyyīn*)—namely, Lead Book number 5. In conclusion, Dobelio's work on the Lead Books and the Parchment is based partly on his own work on the original texts and partly on transcriptions and translations made by others. With regard to his most important source, the *Vita*, he had to rely on a translation only. But that was not all he had at his disposal.

Dobelio made extensive use of his wide readings in Islamic and Christian Arabic manuscripts in the Vatican Library, among them an Islamic version of the Psalms.[24] He also refers to manuscripts kept in the library of the count of Humanes, Francisco de Eraso,[25] and most important, to a collection of

Andalusian Arabic manuscripts in the possession of the Inquisition that had been discovered in about 1622, hidden in a cave in or near the Castilian village of Pastrana. Pastrana had been a well-known center of Morisco economic, intellectual, and religious activity.[26] Dobelio had probably come across the Pastrana manuscripts while he was in Madrid. He was asked by Don Pedro Pacheco of the Council of the Inquisition[27] to make a selection of the best manuscripts among them for the library of the count-duke of Olivares.[28] He refers, for example, to texts such as al-Qāḍī ʿIyāḍ's *Kitāb al-shifā fī ḥuqūq al-Muṣṭafā*, al-Bakrī's very popular *Kitāb al-anwār*, and a magical text in which Solomon/Sulaymān plays an important role, *Kitāb al-asrār fī funūn madhāhib al-shuṭṭār wa-hum al-ṭayālīq*.[29] Dobelio also cites a Spanish polemical manuscript, the *Libro de la disputa contra los judíos y cristianos* (Book of the disputation against the Jews and Christians), written by "an Arab Spaniard who was not only learned in the Holy Writ, but also in the Hebrew language."[30] His use of these manuscripts in his interpretation of the Lead Books has been discussed by García-Arenal and Rodríguez Mediano. They convincingly argue that because the collections represent such a good cross section of the Morisco written heritage, they explain why Dobelio was able to argue that the Lead Books were written by Moriscos.[31] In addition, Dobelio quotes extensively from the Qurʾān, which he often cites in Arabic and apparently knew very well.

That Dobelio bases his argument on a translation rather than on the original Arabic text of the *Vita* is due to the fact that his break with Castro occurred before he was able to study this important book. Who was the author of that Spanish translation? The translation used by Dobelio is certainly not the one by Miguel de Luna, which we traced in the Archive of the Real Chancillería de Granada, the only other contemporary translation known to us and discussed by us in the notes to the edition and translation of the *Vita* we include at the end of this chapter.[32] Rather, Dobelio used a Spanish translation made by a Maronite interpreter named Sergio probably from about 1629–30, when Sergio is known to have worked in the service of the Marquis of Estepa.[33] After Castro's death in 1623, Estepa became one of the most important defenders of the Lead Books. In 1629, he obtained permission to use the original Arabic tablets to prepare a Spanish translation. His Spanish version would serve as the basis of Miguel Hagerty's Spanish edition of the Lead Books, which has remained a standard reference work until today.[34] It presented the Lead Books as Christian texts. As we know, this translation was prepared under the supervision of Estepa by the aforesaid Sergio and a Morisco by name of Juan Bautista Centurión. That this is indeed the translation that served as the main source for Dobelio can be surmised from a manuscript preserved in the Real Academia de la Historia in Madrid.[35] This manuscript includes texts that García-Arenal and Rodríguez Mediano interpret as draft translations of various Lead Books made by Dobelio in 1610–11, when he was still in the service of Archbishop Pedro de Castro. A closer examination of the notes, however, reveals that this assessment is incorrect. The manuscript includes two texts, both related to Morisco and Mudejar themes. First of all, it includes the *Lumen fidei contra sectam Mahumeti et doctrinam Alcorani* (Light of the faith against the Muhammadan sect and the doctrine of the Qur'ān) by Johan Martín de Figuerola (1521), discussed by Mercedes García-Arenal in her contribution to the present volume. This treatise occupies folios 1–267r. The second text in the manuscript is a study by Marcos Dobelio, probably originally entitled *Discurso sobre el libro que se hallo en el monte de Valparayso y entitulado uida y milagros de Xro nuestro señor* (Discourse on the book which was found on Mount Valparaíso entitled *Life and Miracles of Christ Our Lord*).[36] It occupies folios 269r–387v, but the original order of the leaves has not been preserved. Most, if not all, the references in it to material in the Lead Books in fact appear to refer to one Lead Book only—namely, the *Vita*. The disarray into which the treatise has fallen perhaps explains why earlier researchers were unable to fully understand its title, text, and authorship.[37] Dobelio makes clear that he had come across the translation of Lead Book number 7 in March 1633, when he was inspecting Arabic manuscripts at the Escorial Library on the orders of the Spanish king.[38] That Dobelio was indeed working in the service of the king at that time is confirmed by the historian Luis Tribaldos de Toledo (1558–1636), who had been Dobelio's close friend for more than twenty-six years (i.e., since 1607). Tribaldos writes in February 1633 that Dobelio "had been [Arabic] translator to Paul V in Rome and is now working in the service of His Majesty."[39] In fact, the part in the manuscript of the Real Academia de la Historia that can be attributed to Dobelio is a draft of his later *Nuevo descubrimiento*. We may therefore surmise that Dobelio conceived of writing both his *Discurso* and the *Nuevo descubrimiento* after he had come across Sergio's translation.

In the *Nuevo descubrimiento*, Dobelio focuses on the *Vita* and far less on other books. He tells us that this decision was more or less forced by the fact that the first two books had already been claimed as the domain of sacred theology by his opponents, the "laminaries." More than once, all those involved in the debates about the Lead Books had been warned by religious authorities in Spain that Pope Clement VIII had forbidden in his *Brief* of 1595 any discussion of their theological contents.[40] It was the Vatican, they argued, that should be responsible for the evaluation of their doctrine. Offering a critique of the *Vita* implied analyzing a narrative, and not dogmatic doctrine, Dobelio argues.[41] Another, perhaps more important, reason may be that the *Vita* is a longer and richer text, which enabled Dobelio to make a much stronger case against the authenticity of the Lead Books.

Dobelio's Assessment and the Original Arabic Texts of the Lead Books

We have seen above that Dobelio's interpretation of the Lead Books, and primarily of the *Vita*, was not based on his knowledge of the entire collection. His knowledge stems rather from his analysis of some of the original texts, a few available transcripts, and the aforementioned translation, which he compared to Islamic sources such as the Qur'ān, a number of Islamic Pastrana manuscripts, a number of Arabic Christian texts from his own collection, and others. All this was sufficient, as we will see, to convince him of what he saw as the partly Islamic, partly heterodox Christian polemical intentions of the Lead Books. Since space does not allow us to deal in an exhaustive way with Dobelio's work, we will select a number of paradigmatic elements for closer analysis.

First of all, it is clear that Dobelio closely follows the narrative of Sergio's Spanish translation. Very soon, he puts his cards on the table. He considers it to be a central idea of the Lead Books that they identify Muḥammad as the savior promised in the Jewish and Christian scriptures—in other words, "the promised one" (*prometido*) is the Prophet Muḥammad, while many elements of Jesus's life and characteristics attributed to him are in fact derived from the (sources about the) life of Muḥammad.[42] This idea (which we think is correct) returns in several places in Dobelio's analysis. It is the paradigm that informs his entire interpretation of the Lead Books, which he derives from Sergio's translation; his knowledge of the other Lead Books we mentioned; as well as his readings in the aforementioned Islamic and Christian Arabic manuscripts.

We will illustrate with a few examples how Dobelio uses Sergio's translation. According to Dobelio, the text recounts that on the eighth day after his birth, Jesus was baptized,[43] an act later repeated by John the Baptist. According to Dobelio, this first baptism serves to conceal the author's true intention—namely, to introduce the Muslim (and Jewish) custom of infant circumcision.[44] This is a bizarre argument, since the New Testament mentions Jesus's circumcision explicitly (Luke 2:21). The original Arabic text of Lead Book 7 (fol. 10b) says *circumcision*, though the word has the same Arabic root as the word used for Jesus's baptism in the River Jordan.[45] Dobelio's error may be due to the fact that Sergio's version mistranslated the Arabic original and speaks of baptism instead of circumcision.[46]

The identity of the Blessed One, the promised Messiah (Ar. *al-man'ūm*), is discussed by Dobelio in reference to the translation of a passage we can find on folio 6a of Lead Book number 7. Here, Gabriel tells Mary that after Adam and Eve were expelled from Paradise, it was promised that they would be saved by the Blessed One, symbolized by the name *hīd mīd*. Dobelio quotes this passage from Sergio's translation and interprets the words *Aid Magid* to be a faulty rendering of the Hebrew *bi-meod meod*, which he translates as *vehementemente* (exceedingly). In order to understand this expression, he then turns to an anti-Christian and anti-Jewish polemical treatise found in Pastrana, in which the author identifies this name as a reference to the Prophet Muḥammad. Indeed, the words, found in Genesis 17:20, play a key role in anti-Jewish polemical texts. We find them, for example, in Samau'al al-Maghribī's well-known anti-Jewish polemic *Ifḥām al-yahūd*.[47] It is therefore very likely that the same sort of Islamic polemical argument was found in one of the Pastrana manuscripts.

On the subject of the death of Jesus, the Spanish translation that Dobelio used apparently said that when Jesus was betrayed and arrested in the Garden of Gethsemane, the disciples were dispersed with great fear and lost their faith, and that for that reason, "God admonished them and promised them the Kingdom," without going into the question whether it was in fact Jesus who was crucified.[48] According to Dobelio, the author was not very familiar with the Christian creed and the story of the passion.[49] Here and later in his narrative, the author tries to convince his readers that they should not believe the Christian narrative of Jesus's life and crucifixion. This becomes apparent in the way the author of Lead Book 7 presents Peter, who is said to have mourned and wept for seven years and three months after Jesus's death.[50] According to Dobelio, the author introduces this long period of mourning to create a temporal and doctrinal gap between Jesus's life and the early Christian community. He believes that it is the Lead Book narrative and doctrinal views about Jesus's life and death that fill this gap.[51] Thus the readers are told that the disciples based their beliefs on faulty evidence; the only true witnesses to the life of Jesus are Tisʿūn ibn ʿAṭṭār and his brother Saʾis al-Āyah, the Cecilio who later became bishop of Granada. The Lead Book narrative posits, according to Dobelio, an Islamic view about Jesus's life and death but also introduces innovations (*novedades*), such as the Solomonic symbols and the numerous references to magic practices, which Dobelio considers to be proof that the Lead Books were contemporary Morisco falsifications. Based on these insights, Dobelio asserts that the entire narrative of Jesus's birth, life, and death as presented was composed on the basis of Islamic sources about both Jesus and the prophet's lives instead of the canonical Gospels. We will now turn to the evidence of the Arabic texts—in particular, Lead Book 7.

A comparison of Dobelio's *Nuevo descubrimiento* with the original Arabic text of Lead Book 7 as preserved in the Sacromonte Abbey, published here for the first time, immediately makes clear that he was in many ways headed in the right direction. We are indeed dealing with a Gospel text in which many Islamic elements have been interwoven into a polemical narrative. These Islamic elements serve to represent Jesus as a sort of proto-Muḥammad, denying his crucifixion while suggesting that the savior was the Prophet Muḥammad himself. However, the Spanish translation that Dobelio used lacked the precision that would have allowed him to come to entirely reliable conclusions about the content of the Lead Books. One example must suffice here: the crucifixion. As we have seen above, Dobelio posited that the *Vita* casts doubt on the crucifixion, but he did not find any passages in Sergio's translation that flatly denied it. However, the original Arabic text is clear. Using a wording that is clearly inspired by sura 3:54–55, it says about Jesus that God completed his time through the angel (*tawaffāhu Allāhu waʿdahu*[52] *bi-al-malak*) when he was arrested in the Garden of Gethsemane. In the text following this passage, the possibility is left open that the person who was crucified was not Jesus but another.[53] It therefore implicitly denies the crucifixion. This, however, remained unclear to Dobelio because Sergio's translation reads differently. According to Dobelio, the discourse of the Lead Books was, in many respects, frank and open but hidden and ambiguous in others. It was hidden and ambiguous in the sense that, even though the text of the *Vita* followed the broad pattern of Jesus's life as described in the canonical Gospels, the subtext in fact often made use of elements from the life of Muḥammad as described in Muslim sources. And this is entirely correct, as our edited text shows.

On the subject of the Trinity, Dobelio argues that the Lead Books express not Trinitarian beliefs but rather a form of Christian heterodoxy that he deems to be close to Muslim ideas. The words *Lā ilāha illā Allāh* are taken by him as an expression of the rejection of the Trinity. He bases his argument on a work by al-Ghazālī on the Trinity and a lengthy discussion of the first two Lead Books. Here, he accuses the authors of being ambiguous and vague, with the goal of sowing doubt among Christians in order to prepare them to accept Muslim ideas without expressing outright any Muslim beliefs.[54] Dobelio's inclination to see the Lead Books as Islamic lore also holds true for his interpretation of the expression *Lā ilāha illā Allāh* and the accompanying letters: *mīm* and *rā'* found in Lead Books 2 and 6. Most critics (as well as Dobelio) interpret this as an abbreviated or cryptic reference to the Islamic confession of faith—*Lā ilāha illā Allāh; M[uḥammad] R[asūl] Allāh* ("There is no God but God; Muḥammad is the Envoy of God")—and Dobelio is of the opinion that the authors of the Lead Books were exploiting the fact that *mīm* and *rā'* could be read as *al-masīḥ rūḥ Allāh* (Jesus is the spirit of God) as well as Muḥammad *rasūl Allāh* in Lead Book, no 2 and in the other Lead Books, in which this combination of letters occur.[55] He thinks that the intention of the authors of the Lead Books, again, was to refer covertly to Muḥammad.[56]

Dobelio and the Broader Perspective of the Polemical Discussions about the Lead Books in Spain

The interpretation that Dobelio defends in his work, he tells us, had been thoroughly rejected by those he refers to throughout his text as the "laminaries" (*laminarios*)—that is, the defenders of the authenticity of the *láminas*, the Lead Books—and as the "theologians," a label that he applies to them because they argue that those without a theological background lack the expertise required to judge the Lead Books. Dobelio's opinions caused him great difficulties, starting with the rift with Castro, especially since the latter had spread many rumors about him.[57] The "laminaries" even went so far as to threaten their opponents, and Dobelio was not the only target. In his *Nuevo descubrimiento de la falsedad del metal*, he mentions one of the others who was persecuted by name, Ludovico de Malta.[58] It is interesting to observe, however, that in his *Discurso* of 1633, Dobelio also includes Sergio, the author of the Spanish translation, among the translators who were unable to express themselves honestly about the contents of the Lead Books. According to him, Sergio had, for financial reasons, dissimulated (Spanish: *disimular*) in his translation from the Arabic.[59] Evidently, Dobelio's Islamic, messianic, and eschatological interpretation of the contents of the Lead Books propelled him into the midst of a heated polemical exchange in the decades preceding the Lead Books' transfer to the Vatican. In that polemical exchange, matters of religious and political authority played an important role. The "laminaries" apparently accused him of lacking the appropriate theological background, but they made only two of the books (*Kitāb qawāʿid al-dīn* and *Kitāb fī ʾl-dhāt al-karīma*, Lead Books 1 and 2) available to the common people (*el vulgo*), while he himself also knew other texts, which, he added, the "theologians" had always kept secret.[60] However, with the support of the Council of the Inquisition, Dobelio was now, in this text, going to demonstrate that in order to understand the true (Islamic) nature of the Lead Books, it was not enough to be a theologian.[61] The authors of the Lead Books were, in Dobelio's opinion, Moriscos, and he mentions explicitly Miguel de Luna and Alonso del Castillo as the two authors. He repeats this allegation various times throughout his book, but remarkably, nowhere does he give any proof for it.[62]

It is clear that Dobelio's text was meant as a contribution to a debate that had already turned intensely polemical. Around 1617, translations of Lead Books 1 and 2 were circulated and made public. These translations were probably made by the Basque student of Marcos Dobelio, Francisco de Gurmendi.[63] Gurmendi served as an Arabic, Persian, and Turkish translator to King Phillip III.[64] He had close ties to other opponents of the Lead Books—in particular, the humanist Pedro de Valencia—and at some stage, he became a member of the circle that Valencia founded. Gurmendi seems to have come into the possession of a transcription of the two Lead Books after the death of his protector and employer, Don Juan de Idiáquez (1540–1614), who is said to have been the transcription's original owner. Juan de Idiáquez had been chairman of the Council of the Military Orders, a member of the Council of State, and for some time, secretary of Philip II. It was probably Phillip III who commissioned the translation from Gurmendi in the latter's capacity as the royal translator. Gurmendi's translation appeared along with the equally critical theological commentary written by the Jesuit theologian Martín Derrotarán y Mendiola. The defenders of the Lead Books, probably led by Pedro de Castro, reacted to it by publishing at least two anonymous polemical pamphlets.[65] It is in particular the first of these pamphlets that concerns us here. From this anonymous pamphlet, in which the name of the authors' opponent is also not mentioned, we can extrapolate some of the positions taken by Gurmendi in his translation. As we will see, these positions seem to have been very close to those of Dobelio. Not only are the ideas that are refuted identical to the ones expressed by Dobelio in his *Nuevo descubrimiento*; the terms are identical to those used by Dobelio and analyzed here. Let us first briefly discuss the contents. At the very start, the polemicist mentions the fact that the king had received a translation into Romance of two Lead Books by the translator of the two books, accompanied by a "comment against them." He then sets out to argue why the king should disregard that assessment right away.[66] The polemical attack is entirely directed at the Spanish translator (Spanish: *intérprete*), Gurmendi; the commentary plays no role at all. In fact, the polemicist states that the translation and commentary were written by one and the same person. According to the polemicist, this translator—his opponent (whose identity he says he does not know)—lacked the necessary expertise (and orthodoxy) to prepare such a translation, since he was not a theologian, nor did he have the philological competence to translate the books adequately. The polemicist states that the translator's interpretations of the Arabic were wrong and that he had not studied the original texts but only drafts (*borradores*).[67] They are labeled mere nonsense, *disparates* (a word, it should be noted, that was also frequently used by Castro to refer to interpretations he disagreed with).[68] The translator is even mocked: would a noble, learned, and pious person such as Archbishop Pedro de Castro spend a fortune on Islamic lore? The archbishop, he states, might as well have put a statue of the Prophet Muḥammad above the altar of the church of the Sacromonte between the ashes of the Granadan martyrs. And why, he continues, did the critic ignore Pope Clement VIII's brief prohibiting any further discussion of this sacred matter?[69] According to the translator of the two books, the authors of the Lead Books were Moriscos, and the language they were written in was the corrupt Arabic used by Moriscos.[70] But according to the author(s) of our pamphlet, Miguel de Luna and Alonso del Castillo were among those who best understood these texts, and De Luna considered them to be very ancient.[71] The translator had also asserted that the contents of the books were derived from the Qur'ān, but because of his lack of expertise, he had failed to see that Arabic Christian texts were known to have included doctrinal expressions similar to those of the Lead Books. This even held true for the Trinity, which, according to the anonymous translator, was denied in the Lead Books. Not so, according to the author of the pamphlet. The archbishop himself had used the Arabic language to pronounce the confession of faith in Arabic in the presence of Oriental Christians.

At this point, we note that a number of passages attributed to the anonymous translator are in fact entirely identical to Dobelio's arguments. We are referring especially to the discussion about the words *wa-kafā bi'llāh shahīdan 'alā dhālika, lā ilāha ilā 'llāh, mīm rā'*, which occur in both Dobelio's text and the text attributed to Gurmendi. This holds true for the quotation of the first words, the creed (interpreted as a denial of the Trinity), and the letters *mīm rā'*. The first part of the sentence refers to the preceding passages of the Lead Book ("And let it be enough that God is [my] witness on that, there is no god but God. M[uḥammad] is the M[essenger] of God" or "Jesus is the Spirit of God"). According to Dobelio, the words about God as a witness are derived from the Qur'ān, sura 12.[72] Both Dobelio's *Nuevo descubrimiento* and the translation attributed to Gurmendi see the creed as a denial of the Trinity and the letters *mīm* and *rā'* as references to the Islamic creed about "M[uḥammad] as God's Envoy (R[asūl])." Both Dobelio and Gurmendi seem to offer an extensive discussion about the meaning of the Arabic word *ṭahāra* (purity), interpreted as a reference to Islamic rituals: partial ablution (*wuḍū'*) and circumcision (*khitān*).

In conclusion, it seems clear that the labels, arguments, accusations, and terminology used in the polemic that we find in Dobelio's *Nuevo descubrimiento* of 1638 were already present in the debates between Gurmendi and the circle around Archbishop Castro in 1617, which centered on one question: Could the Parchment and Lead Books be considered authentic early Christian documents? How is this similarity to be explained? Dobelio respected Gurmendi very much. He knew Gurmendi had translated *Kitāb qawā'id al-dīn* and *Kitāb fī 'l-dhāt al-karīma* and had rejected them as Morisco fabrications. Gurmendi also refers to Dobelio as an expert in the matter.[73] We think that Gurmendi owed many of his ideas to Dobelio, who not only had a far superior knowledge of Arabic and Islam but had worked with the original materials, whereas Gurmendi only had a transcription. Long after Gurmendi published these ideas in 1617, Dobelio expressed them again in his *Discurso* of 1633 and his magnum opus, the *Nuevo descubrimiento de la falsedad del metal*, in 1638.

Dobelio and the Condemnation of the Lead Books in Rome

While it is probably true that the most influential arguments against the authenticity of the Lead Books in the debates that took place in Spain between 1595 and 1638 were made by Dobelio, especially in his 1638 treatise, his views were only partly based on firsthand knowledge of the original Arabic texts of the Lead Books. That he was able to come to argue that the books were Islamic forgeries was also the result of his access to various collections of Arabic manuscripts (in the Vatican, the Escorial, and the Pastrana collection) and the manuscripts he had collected himself. In this regard, Dobelio was one of the first Arabists who worked in a truly European context. In fact, the highly polemical discussion in which he took part in Spain was only partially based on expert and direct knowledge of the Arabic texts, access to which remained very restricted. Added to this were the papal restrictions on discussions about the contents of the Lead Books. This becomes even clearer when we now take a look at the last stage of the discussions, when, after a prolonged debate, the books were finally transferred to Rome in 1642 and were submitted to a Vatican committee for evaluation.

In the year 1666, one of the foremost experts on the Vatican committee, Ludovico Marracci (1612–1700), presented a study of 128 folia as his *votum* to the Vatican evaluation committee, entitled *Disquisitio laminarum Granatensium quinque partibus comprehensa*. Marracci was an Italian Arabist who was the chair of Arabic at La Sapienza between 1656 and 1699. He was involved in two major projects: the publishing and printing of the Sacra Biblia Arabica (1671) and the assessment of the Lead Books.[74] He was an influential figure at the Vatican, also serving as Pope Innocent XI's confessor between 1676 and 1689. Marracci was openly polemical in his intentions, as can be seen from the translation of the Qur'ān he published. His *votum* is by far the most thorough and extensive of those of the nine assessors of the evaluation committee preserved in the Vatican Archive file dedicated to the Lead Books.[75] Marracci's views were influenced by the work of Dobelio, which he must have had in front of him, although he does not mention his name. The resemblance between the language and ideas of the Qur'ān and other Islamic sources, on the one hand, and the Lead Books, on the other, was demonstrated by Dobelio with a long series of examples from the *Vita*. Marracci applied Dobelio's method to the whole collection of Lead Books and demonstrated that his views were valid for all of them. Marracci integrated the examples adduced and the Islamic sources quoted by Dobelio, adding to them a long list of additional examples from the books Dobelio had not mentioned. Dobelio discussed his points in the order in which they occur in the *Vita*. Marracci's work, on the other hand, is an analytical study based on all the Lead Books.

In the first part, Marracci demonstrates that the Lead Books are replete with Islamic words, sentences, fables, and errors.[76] He then demonstrates, in the second part, that the Lead Books contain many elements that deviate from sound (Christian) doctrine in a way that often parallels Islamic error.[77] Following up this same line of thought, he shows in the third section that the Lead Books often deviate from the holy (biblical) and ecclesiastical traditions while concurring with Islamic traditions.[78] After presenting in section four various notes that do not fit under the subject headings of one the first three parts,[79] Marracci concludes his *Disquisitio* with a masterly summary in chapter 5, dealing with the artifices of the Lead Books and the purposes of their author.[80] In this last section, he argues that the origins of the Lead Books are to be found in the Ottoman conquest of Cyprus in 1571 and its repercussions for the Moriscos in Habsburg Spain.[81] Marracci had transcribed and translated the original plates of all the Lead Books, while Dobelio appears to have been mainly directly familiar with the Arabic texts of the first two books only while having to rely upon a translation (in Spanish) of the *Vita*, which was the main text upon which he based his views. However, the conclusions of both scholars were the same, and through the work of Marracci, Dobelio's insights were to form the basis of the official condemnation of the Lead Books in 1682.

Conclusions

We have seen how Dobelio became involved in the Lead Books affair in 1610, when he was summoned to Granada by the committee headed by the cardinal of Toledo. There, he worked for some time on several Lead Books, as well as on the Parchment of the Turpiana Tower, until he told Castro that he believed they were Morisco forgeries and Castro dismissed him. From that moment onward, he no longer had access to the original texts and had to rely largely on available transcriptions and translations. In the 1610s, his ideas became known among opponents and supporters of the books, including Gurmendi. We have argued that there are close parallels between the ideas expressed by the latter and those of Dobelio, which can be explained by assuming that Gurmendi was aware of Dobelio's views. Gurmendi's translation and the anonymous refutations of it make clear that as early as 1617, the relations between critics and defenders (*laminarios*) had taken the form of a fierce polemic. Like Gurmendi, Dobelio pointed to De Luna and Castillo as the two most likely forgers. Dobelio's contribution to the debate was highly polemical, something that can be explained as an expression of his frustration about the situation in which he found himself. As we have seen, in about 1616, two "parties" seem to have emerged: the "laminaries," supported by Archbishop Pedro de Castro, and the group that argued against the authenticity of the Lead Books, among them Martín Derrotarán y Mendiola, Diego de Urrea, Pedro de Valencia, Marcos Dobelio, and Francisco de Gurmendi. That the circle around Castro chose to react anonymously to Gurmendi's translation, commissioned by the king himself, was probably due to the papal brief forbidding further discussion of the Lead Books. This debate pitted scholarly expertise against religious authority. Could the "theologians" claim expert knowledge on the sacred matter of the Lead Books, or were they out of their depth? The "laminaries," on the other hand, cast doubt on their opponents' scholarly, ethical, and religious expertise in an attempt to undermine their credibility. These are all well-known tricks of the polemical trade: to attack not only the sources but also the opponent as an individual person. Dobelio compensated the paucity of his direct acquaintance with the original Arabic texts in an original way—namely, by reading widely in Morisco literature (i.e., the manuscripts of Pastrana) and by using other Arabic manuscripts, including those in his own collection. We have shown how part of the Pastrana collection found its way to the Vatican Library. In 1633, Dobelio came across the Spanish translation of the *Vita* made by Sergio, the Maronite translator working in the service the Marquis of Estepa in 1629–30. He found out about it when he was inspecting Arabic manuscripts in the service of the Spanish king. The *Discurso*, preserved in the manuscript of the Real Academia de la Historia in Madrid, shows that around that time, he started to work on a polemical text that was eventually made public in the *Nuevo descubrimiento*. In it, he tried to convince his readers of the Islamic contents of the Lead Books and the errors of the *laminarios*. Thanks to the fact that we now have access to the Arabic texts of the Lead Books, we know that Dobelio and Marracci were right. The Lead Books should be seen as forged proto-Islamic texts whose purpose was to legitimize the presence of Arabic speakers in the Iberian Peninsula by fabricating the existence of an early Arab "Christian" community at a time when the crypto-Muslim community was under threat, and establishing a link with an alleged ancient, proto-Islamic past would have provided this community with a historical and religious genealogy that they lacked and needed to survive. Where modern scholars would differ with them is perhaps that they, and especially Marracci, considered not only the Lead Books but also the Qur'ān itself and, by extension, Islam to be cunning devices (Latin: *technas*): according to Marracci, the aim of Islam was no less than the destruction of the Gospel—that is, Christianity.[82] Another conclusion we may draw from a comparison of the actual Lead Books and the various works they spawned is that very little progress was made in elucidating their true nature while the Lead Books were still in Spain because first-hand knowledge of the plates was rare and the discussion fraught with censorship. The progress made by Dobelio in his *Nuevo descubrimiento* of 1638 was due far more to his work on the Arabic Islamic manuscripts we described above and far less to an extensive knowledge of the Lead Books themselves. He used Sergio's Spanish translation of the *Vita*, even though he was convinced that the translator had not been faithful to the original Arabic text. Only in Rome would the full scope of the Lead Books become clear to the evaluators after they had been duly studied outside the sphere of public polemics. But it would take another four hundred years before the texts would be made available for research.

BOOK OF THE OUTSTANDING QUALITIES AND MIRACLES OF OUR LORD JESUS AND OF HIS MOTHER THE HOLY VIRGIN MARY

كتب محاسين سيدنا يصوع ومعاجزه وامه مريم الصالحة العذرة

Edition and Annotated Translation of Sacromonte Lead Book Number 7
(Pieter Sjoerd van Koningsveld and Gerard Wiegers)
Lead Book 7, Sacromonte Abbey, Granada, fol. 2b

Annotated Translation
Arabic Text
List of Abbreviations

FIG. 9.1. *Book of the Outstanding Qualities and Miracles of Our Lord Jesus and of His Mother the Holy Virgin Mary*, Lead Book 7, fol. 2b, 62.69 mm diameter × 2.17 mm thick. Photograph by the authors, Granada, August 13, 2012.

[2a] Book of the Outstanding Qualities and Miracles[1] of Our Lord Jesus[2] and of His Mother the Holy[3] Virgin Mary

[2b] Book of the outstanding qualities of our lord Jesus and of his mother the Virgin Mary and of his lifetime and his miracles, from the day he was sent until his demise and his ascension to heaven, by Tisʿūn[4] ibn ʿAṭṭār, disciple of James the Apostle.[5]

My father, Ṣāliḥ ibn ʿAṭṭār, was an Arab by origin from the town of Daws[6] of Arabia Minor, of a noble stock and enjoying a great reputation. Endowed with knowledge and great wealth, he was born with a high pedigree going all the way back to Ṣāliḥ,[7] the prophet of God, to whom Prophethood and the Spirit had been granted.

1. Arabic: *maʿājīz* (plural of *muʿjiza*) in Islamic theological language usually indicating the miracles, granted by God to prophets to allow them to prove their claim to prophethood, contrary to the *karāmāt* of saints (*awliyāʾ*). *Muʿjiza*, "miraculum," is also documented in CDAA, s.v. "ʿjz," where the *Vocabulista in Arabico* (often ascribed to Ramon Martí) is the only source quoted for this meaning.
2. Always written in the original Arabic as *Yaṣūʿ*, with emphatical *ṣ*, in contradistinction to *Yasūʿ* (with *sīn*), as usually found in Christian Arabic sources, also from al-Andalus. Only in the Granada Parchment is Jesus indicated by his Qurʾānic name, *ʿĪsā*. To disguise his all-too-obvious Islamic intentions, the author decided to change his strategy concerning this name in the Lead Books, adopting its Christian Arabic form but with a pseudo-archaic spelling added to suggest that his name was more ancient and more original than the one found in more recent Christian Arabic sources. Dobelio (fol. 6a ff), comments that "our lord Jesus" is not a Christian way to designate Jesus Christ. He adds (fol. 10bf) that in the *Vita*, there is no reference to Jesus as the Son of God, while in the *Fundamentum fidei* and the *De essentia Dei*, this doctrine is only referred to between parentheses.
3. Arabic: *al-ṣaliḥa* (*al-ṣāliḥa*). *Ṣāliḥ* as the meaning of "sanctus" is documented in CDAA, s.v. "ṣlḥ," where the Leiden Mozarabic *Latin-Arabic Glossary*, s.v. "sanctus" is the only source quoted for this meaning.
4. Literally, "ninety." Old translations as well as contemporary studies have read the name as *Taṣfūn* and translated it as "Thesifon." However, the Lead Books consistently read *Tisʿūn*. Tisʿūn and two of his brothers have names ending in *ūn*, frequently to be found in al-Andalus.
5. Dobelio (fol. 18b f) points out that *al-ḥawārī* and *al-ḥawāriyyūn* are the Islamic designation for the apostles of Jesus with the denigrating meaning of *lauanderos*. According to him, Christian Arabs are using the word *al-rasūl*, *al-rusul*. However, in biblical translations from al-Andalus, the word *al-ḥawārī* is in fact used—for example, *Baulush al-Ḥawārī* in Cod. Ar. 4971 of the BNE in Madrid.
6. The Arabian Banū Daws are mentioned by Lammens, L'Arabie occidentale avant l'hégire, 115–16. Dobelio (fols. 16b–17a) says, "El autor dice que fue Árabe noble de la tierra de دوس Dus (laqual no halla en toda Arabia)"; he adds (fols. 19b–20a) that he had seen a book written in Spain by an author dealing with Islamic Law who called himself "fulano al-Dūsī, Addusio, que significa natural de Dūs. A mi parezer sera el autor de un lugar de África y vino a ser grande en España (conforme se puede congeturar)."
7. About Ṣāliḥ as an Arabian prophet in the Qurʾān and the Islamic tradition, see A. Rippin, in EI^2, s.v. "Ṣāliḥ." Dobelio (fol. 19a sq) stresses that there is no relation between this Ṣāliḥ, a descendant of Thamūd, and the biblical Saleh, great-grandson of Noah.

He had four male and three female children. The names of the males were ʿĪsūn, Saʿdūn, I, Tisʿūn, and Ibn al-Raḍī; the females were Shamsa, Yaqūta and Durriyya.

I was created blind.[8] My brother Ibn al-Raḍī was created deaf and dumb. Our father was sad about us, and when he heard news about our lord Jesus, the Trustworthy Spirit of God,[9] [and] about how he cured the blind born, the lepers, the deaf, the blind and the lame, and how he cast out the devils from people and revived the death in the Holy Land, so that [people] traveled towards him in search of his blessing, he prepared the necessary provisions and servants, and put myself and my brother Ibn al-Raḍī on two camels. He set out by night to the Land of Galilee, where he found him and his disciples in the company of seventeen men he had cured of leprosy.

At that occasion, Ṣāliḥ said to him: "My Lord, I took the roads towards you from the town of Daws, lest you cure for me these two children from blindness, dumbness and deafness. I see you are a great wonder-worker [3a]. I put my trust in you and I am confident that without any doubt no one in the world but you can cure them."

Jesus said to him: "Ṣāliḥ, your faith is strong, and I will fulfill your wish." He then took some earth in the palms of his hands, stamped it with his saliva and put it on my eyes, thereby returning to me (my) eye-sight. He ordered me to wash it off in the place for purification[10] of the prayer-hall (*al-masjid*).

---

8. Literally, "seeing," but the opposed meaning is implied here.
9. In Arabic: *Rūḥ Allāh al-Amīn*. Jesus is referred to in the Qurʾān as "a spirit from Him"—that is, of God (sura 4:171)—which, from an Islamic point of view, would allow to call him Rūḥ Allāh, as he is also occasionally referred to in the Lead Books. In the Qurʾān, the expression *trustworthy spirit* (without the explicit attribution of the Spirit to God), however, refers to Gabriel (Jibrīl), not Jesus. Cf. J. Pedersen, in EI², s.v. "Djabrāʾīl." In the Lead Books, Jesus is most frequently referred to as *Rūḥ Allāh al-Amīn* as an almost standard expression. It would seem that the epithets, in this specific form, are a fusion of Jesus's Qurʾānic qualifications and the honorific name given to Gabriel in the Qurʾān—namely, "the Trustworthy Spirit" (*al-Rūḥ al-Amīn*). This central point in the doctrine of the Lead Books will be discussed further in our introductory study to the edition of the Arabic texts and their English translation. In his translation of 1596, Miguel de Luna systematically translates this expression as "Nuestro Señor Jesus hijo de Dios verdadero," concealing its Islamic tendency.
10. De Luna, in a marginal note: "La dicción arábiga [al mahda] significa agua en fuente o en pila o de otra manera." Compare CDAA, s.v. "mḥḍ: mīḥāḍ" (latrine) from the Vocabulista in Arábigo (often ascribed to Ramon Martí). Dobelio (fol. 23a): "Mi parecer es que el autor entiende por los lavacros de los templos los lavatorios que hazen en sus templos los Mahometanos antes de entrar en sus azalas, dichos comunmente al-wuḍūʾ."

He then put his hand on the head of my brother Ibn al-Raḍī, blew into his mouth three times, cured him and filled him with knowledge, so that he (even) talked different languages. The first thing he said was: "I testify that there is no god but God and that you are the Trustworthy Spirit of God."[11]

Thereupon our Lord Jesus said to him: "You are (from now onwards) Saʾis al-Ayah."[12] Thus that name was imposed upon him by our Lord Jesus, meaning: 'preacher of the faith, making it victorious.'[13] He then looked at his disciple James the Apostle—our master—and said to him: "These two are your holy pupils in order to assist (our) faith, take them under your care and provide them with the necessary (knowledge/means) for that purpose."

At that occasion, our father Ṣāliḥ ibn ʿAṭṭār donated our Lord Jesus a hundred Arab pieces of gold, putting them into the hands of Peter[14] the Apostle by his order and asked him to buy for him a house so that he would dwell near to him. He then traveled to the town of Daws [3b] in order to bring to him his whole family, leaving us (and our) sisters in his care and in (the care of) our master James.

---

11. De Luna: "Que vos soys su hijo verdadero." Dobelio (fol. 23a ff.): "El deçir 'No hai Dios, sino Dios, Ihesus spiritu de Dios' es propriamente la negatiua de la santissima trinidad y de la Diuinidad de la 2a persona." To substantiate this view, Dobelio quotes al-Ghazālī "en el libro 1° escriuiendo de la fe, tratado 1°, parte 2ª," where al-Ghazālī explains, among other things, that the formula *lā ilāha illā 'llāh* implies a denial of the Trinity as professed by the Christians. Dobelio also quotes Abū Bakr Muḥammad ibn al-Ḥasan Al-Naqqāsh in his explanation of the word *al-tawḥīd* in sura 38 (fol. 25b). Exactly the same information is provided by Marracci (fols. 23a–b), including the sources quoted.
12. In the Arabic original, the name is written in two separate words, viz. *Saʾis al-Ayah*. If it had been intended as a mere transcription of "Cecilio," it would likely have been written as a single word. It is possible to understand the name Saʾis al-Āyah in Arabic as a pun meaning "leader of the sign." De Luna writes, "Çay Çeleyah."
13. The author is providing a (fancy) Arabic etymology for the name Cecilio, explaining its origin and meaning in the ancient, paleo-Christian Arabic only accessible to himself.
14. Here, the Arabic original reads *Badruh*, with *b*; elsewhere in the Lead Books, it is frequently written with *yāʾ*, thus *Yadruh*. A possible explanation might be that in the original the scribe/engraver was working from, Peter's name had been provided with *three* dots underneath its first letter in order to indicate the letter *P*, as was done, for instance, in the *aljamiado* alphabet and in the Ottoman-Turkish and Persian alphabets. Not understanding the meaning of these *three* dots, the scribe/engraver confined himself in those cases to *two* dots, erroneously changing Peter's name into Yadruh. In his lengthy quotations from the Lead Books, Al-Ḥajarī also consistently writes *Yadruh* in his autograph manuscript preserved in the National Library in Cairo of *Kitāb Nāṣir al-Dīn ʿalā al-Qawm al-Kāfirīn*.

At that occasion, Jesus ordered Peter to distribute that money as a charity to those turning to him. Thereupon Peter said to him: "My Lord, to which of those turning to us shall I give it as a charity, as they are many? Those who are turning to you are destitute, poor, sick and aiming at attending (your) admonition. (Moreover,) the owner of that money is alive; how shall I give it away without his permission, while he wishes to buy a house?"

Our Lord Jesus answered him: "The world is a house for those who have no house! Give that money during the life of Ṣāliḥ to whoever asks you, even if he comes on a horse and asks for it,[15] so that it will be a living work, because that which belongs to God will never perish and the reward of those who do well will never get lost.[16] Do not you know that to give charity during one's life is a living work but after death it is a work that has died? Therefore, give during life (and) before death, because the best gift is before passing away. And I say unto you that the charity that reaches God is given during life and this appeases the Lord's wrath. He who gives charity is near to God and God is with him in every place." He then [4a] gave away that money as a charity to those asking for it.

At that time my father came to him with all his family and asked him: "My Lord, did you buy for me the house?" He answered him: "Ṣāliḥ, I indeed built a house for you in Paradise,[17] so that you will live near to me in this world and in the Hereafter, because your intention is beautiful and your faith is great and it is accepted by God." He then brought him to his house, where he caught a fever and passed away after three days. Our Lord Jesus said unto him: "Blessed are you, Ṣāliḥ! You lived a blissful life (*saʿīdan*) and you died

---

15. Dobelio (fol. 60b f) refers to "un predicador Mahometano, el qual exortando la gente a dar limosna, diçe desta manera *fī faḍl al-ṣadaqa* de la exçelencia de los limosnas . . . *wa-qāla al-nabī ṣallā Allāhu ʿalaihi wa-sallama: inna al-ṣadaqa la-taqaʿu bi-yad al-Raḥmān qabla an tūḍaʿu bi-yad al-sāʾil fa-taṣaddaqū wa-law atākum ʿalā faras mulajjam masrūj*." Dobelio informs us that this quotation was taken from an acephalous manuscript dated 870 Hijra (fol. 61b). Marracci (fol. 21a) quotes the same: "*Liber Mahumethicus, cui titulus est fī faḍl al-ṣadaqa* id est de excellentia eleemosyane, cuius auctor vixit ante ducentos fere annos legimus: Dixit propheta Mahumetus: Facite eleemosynam, etiam, si ille, qui eam petit, uenerit ad uos super equum freno et ephippiis ornatum."
16. Dobelio (fol. 60b): "El Alcorán y sus doctores diçen las mesmas palabras que pone el autor." Marracci (fol. 19a) remarks that the expression "and the reward of those who do well will never get lost" is found in "sect. 6, par. 126" of the Qurʾān.
17. A more neutral translation by De Luna is "En la bienabenturanza."

as a martyr (*shahīdan*). You left your family in a blessed state." And again also after three more days my mother Rebecca,[18] his wife, passed away. After them, because of the miracles of our Lord Jesus, our brothers and sisters and our family believed in him and belonged to the holy.

We then thanked God, I, as well as my brother Ibn al-Raḍī, for having been saved from error and (having been given) the greatest of faiths. We stayed in the service of James, who favored us [4b] over all his disciples and he chose us from among them for the benefit of his affairs in the obedience of God.

Therefore, we are in need of the grace of our Lord Jesus and of my master who commanded me to write down his noble character and high descent, his life and his miracles until his death. In doing that, I write down what I eyewitnessed (myself) and other matters which I did not witness, related from him and from his mother, the Holy Virgin Mary, from Joseph, her husband, as well as from all the apostles, his disciples, until his ascension to Heaven and afterwards, including the last report necessary to chronicle the truth. All that will be for the glory of God and the admonishing of his servants, Amen.

Chapter on His Noble Character (*ḥasab*), His High Pedigree (*nasab*), His Country, and the Miracles Connected to His Being Conceived

Our Lord Jesus, the son of Virgin Mary, was a Hebrew. The house of the parents of his mother from the side of her father was from Naṣrān,[19] while the family of her mother was from Batlān, both of which were belonging to the smallest towns in the Holy Land. As a human being he was of an outstandingly noble character and of the highest pedigree among the Israelites. He was born in a row of forty-two venerable prophets who were announcing the Blessed One (*al-manʿūm*)[20] in the Tawrāt,[21] the best of the descendants of Adam,[22] sent

18. De Luna: "Rubaka."
19. The author suggests that this is the ancient Arabic name of Nazareth. Compare *Jarjalān* for "Jerusalem" and *Batlān* for "Bethlehem." All these names are repeatedly used in our text as well as in the Parchment and the other Lead Books.
20. De Luna translates this expression consistently as "Messias" (occasionally also "el Messias prometido").
21. The author uses the Qurʾānic name of the Old Testament. Here and elsewhere in the text, De Luna translates *Al-Tawrāt* as "la Sagrada Escriptura."
22. Dobelio (fol. 62b): "Y quando diçe que es el mejor de los hijos de Adam no por esto diremos que es Christo, porque Mahoma se intitula Señor de los hijos de Adam y el mejor dellos y que desciende de los prophetas de Dios." Dobelio refers here to the Hadith, "anā sayyid wuld Ādam wa-lā fakhr," which evoked the well-known Islamic epithet for Muḥammad: *khair wuld Ādam*.

(to realize) the victory announced by the Gospel,[23] God's Trustworthy Spirit and Redeemer from sin by mediation (*al-shafʿ*) and salvation (*al-falāḥ*). All of them-belonged to the descendants of the Prophet, son of Shaykh al-Raḍī, Abraham, the Friend of God,[24] who was strengthened with the Holy Spirit.

Holy Mary said that Gabriel told her: "When God created the angels in the most beautiful shape, and when they disobeyed their Lord out of jealousy because of his having been conceived, the Throne, the heavens and the earth trembled[25] so that the intimate angels became fearful." And when He had put our father Adam [5a] and our mother Eve in Paradise, they ate whatever they wished, but He forbade them (to eat from) the tree. They (lived) in everlasting bliss and were wearing jewels and tunics[26] the value of which is known to God only. They did not experience the evils of the world, but they were not thankful to God for that bliss. Thus, their pudenda became apparent to them,[27] because of their lack of thankfulness, though they were not aware of it. Then they were overcome by temptation towards sin and disobedience. That was the cause of their pleasure to (commit) the dubious[28] sin, because God is wise and just, and by that justice he decides whatever He wishes. Thus they ate the fruit of the forbidden tree. And when they had disobeyed the commandment of their Lord,[29] once again the Throne and the earth trembled a second time and the angels feared, and He expelled them from Paradise [6a], and God attached him to a place in his Creation of His choice, which none of His servants would find without His will.

They descended to the earth, where they became repentant to the extent that the color of them both blackened because of the sin. Stretched out on the earth, they cried about it. They did not interrupt their weeping until their eyeballs were consumed and the flesh of their faces lacerated, saying: "Our Lord,

---

23. Arabic: *bi-al-fatḥ al-munajjāl*. See also *mubashshirīn bi-al-fatḥ*: LP I/2. De Luna: "El que vino a el mundo a enseñar el euangelio hijo de Dios uerdadero."
24. *Khalīl Allāh*, as in the Qurʾān (Dobelio).
25. The translation used by Dobelio (fol. 63a) reads, "Que los çielos abaxaron al suelo con los ángeles, quando conçiuiò, y çercaron el estrado." To this he comments, "Esto diçen los Mahometanos de su propheta."
26. Compare CDAA, s.v. "ḥll: ḥulla" (purple tunicle; based on the Leiden Mozarabic Latin-Arabic Glossary, s.v. "clamis" and "fulua").
27. For this expression, Marracci (fol. 22b) refers to the Qurʾān: "Alcor. Sect. 6 Ahraph" and "Alcor. Sect. 19 Tah. §122."
28. This concept seems to refer to the theological issue of whether the sin of Adam was committed out of free will or because it had been preordained by God. In his translation, De Luna chooses the latter possibility, translating "El peccado contingente." This is also the position of our text, as will become clear in various passages.
29. Dobelio (fol. 63b): "Todo esto lo diçen los autores Mahometanos."

we have harmed ourselves. If you do not accept our repentance and forgive us and grant us mercy, we will be lost."[30] Then the angel Gabriel descended to them and brought them the good tiding of their salvation. [He wrote on the back of Adam: Hīd Mīd, (meaning:) he is your mediator, and the mediator of your offspring.][31] He also said: Adam, stand up, you and your wife, God has heard your prayer and accepted your repentance and forgiven you, on the condition of faith, thankfulness for blessings, as well as the atonement of (your) sins. You should (also) expect the Blessed One written [on your back].[32] From that time, the prophets announced among their people the good tiding of the Blessed One, (who would come) to intercede for [6b] men, as well as to admonish them about intercession and salvation.

When the time came for Holy Mary to conceive of him,[33] in other words: she said that when the angel Gabriel descended to her and informed her that she was going to conceive of him, while she was reading the Book,[34] he said to her: "Holy Mary, who receives the mercy (of your Lord), God is with you, you are blessed among the women." This blessing was because of her being untouched by the original sin which was not attached to her because God had chosen her for this task, while all others who came after Adam were affected by faults because of the sin, but she was not affected thereby, as she had remained unimpaired by it. This was consented upon in the Council of the Apostles as we described in the Book of the Foundations of the Faith.[35] Whosoever dissents from it, will be lost.

30. Dobelio (fol. 64a): "Todo esto lo tenemos notado con authoridades bastantes de los Mahometanos, donde hablan cosas increibles de la penitençia que hizo Adam, quedando negro él y su muger del continuó llorando hasta que Dios les perdonó y entonzes se volvieron blancos."
31. The passage between square brackets was left blank in De Luna's translation as one of the passages he claims not to have been able to understand (!). Dobelio (fol. 64a): "Diçe después el texto de las láminas que en las espaldas de Adam estaua escrito la venida del prometido con todo lo que sigue, todo sacado de los authores Mahometanos."
32. The passage between square brackets was left blank in De Luna's translation as one of the passages he claims not to have been able to understand (!).
33. De Luna: "Encarnar."
34. De Luna: "La Scriptura Sagrada."
35. Dobelio (fol. 66b):

Halló en los libros de los Mahometanos (como está notado) que a Xristo nuestro Señor y a la Virgen su Madre no les alcanzó el peccado primero en este modo. Diçen que quando nasçen los hijos de Adam; el Demonio llega y les passa la mano por enzima de la caueza, o, les da en el lado una puntada con el dedo, que por esto nasçemos llorando; y este es el peccado primero que es el Demonio, el qual fue el primero a peccar, y que quando la Virgen nasçió, los ángeles la çercaron con una cortina, y hauiendo llegado el peccado primero para tocarla con la mano o darla con la punta del dedo, dio en velo, y assí no la alcanzó.

So when she heard his words, she became afraid and lifted her head in order to seek help from God, while she was thinking about who would be (the person) who had spoken (to her).

Then Gabriel took on the shape towards her of a most beautiful human being, who was spreading a glittering light. [7a] He said to her: "Do not be afraid! God enters upon you[36] in His mercy to grant you a son in your womb who is the Spirit of the Exalted,[37] and you will call him Yaṣūʿ, of the descendants of David, who will live forever in the House of Jacob. His kingship will never perish." She asked him: "How will this happen, while no human being has touched my matter, and I do not desire this (either)?"

The angel answered her: "That is easy for God,[38] (it will occur) through His Holy Spirit upon you. [And when he will have born, he will be called Spirit of the Exalted God.]"[39]

She answered him: "Make me a sign for that!"[40]

He said to her: "Elisabeth, your friend, is (already) pregnant for six months, notwithstanding her advanced age following her sterility, but everything is easy for God."

At that point, Mary said: "I am the servant of God, obedient to Him, like (to) your truthful words."

Then the angel left her and her fear turned into joy. She thanked God with incomparably eloquent speech, as required for the obedience of God at (hearing) such elevated news, related from the prophets (concerning) the arrival of the Intercessor of mankind, about which she had been reading in the Book.

During various days she did not divulge this secret to her husband Joseph, until she visited Elisabeth. Then her fetus John manifested himself to him while (she was) kissing her, in order to greet him, saying: "Peace upon you, o Trustworthy Spirit of God!"[41] And Elisabeth said: "What a welcome event, that the mother of my Lord the Blessed One is visiting me!"

36. De Luna: "Porque Dios está con vos."
37. De Luna: "Hijo del alto."
38. In his commentary, Fakhr al-Dīn al-Rāzī explains the Qurʾānic expression *wa-mā dhālika ʿalā Allāh bi-ʿazīz* with the words *bal huwa hayyin ʿalā Allāh*, using the same words as our author.
39. The passage between square brackets left untranslated in De Luna's translation. Dobelio (fol. 68a): "San Lucas diçe *et filius altissimi vocabitur*, y el autor quiere que se diga spíritu y no hijo de Dios."
40. Dobelio (fol. 68a): "Después alterando la doctrina del Euangelio, diçe que la Virgen pidió señal al ángel para çertificarse, si era verdad lo que deçía: el Alcorán diçe lo mismo."
41. De Luna: "Saludo hijo de Dios verdadero." Dobelio (fol. 68b): "De donde se descubre que no quiere en ningun modo que se diga hijo de Dios."

Joseph felt shocked but did not talk about that shock. Thereupon the angel came to him while asleep that night, and he told him who our Lord Jesus was. So he said to the angel: "Make me a sign for that." He answered: "The sign is: in radiant light there will be written on his back: 'Jesus, the Truthful and Trustworthy Spirit of God.'"[42] He thanked God for that.

[Chapter on His Birth and the Miracles Thereof][43]

My master James told me from the Holy Virgin Mary, from the angel Gabriel that he had said to her concerning the blessings and virtues of our Lord Jesus and his that God had shown parts of the Well-Preserved Tablet[44] He saw fitting (for that purpose) [8a] to Moses on the Mountain of Al-Ṭūr.[45] Moses said to Him: "My God and my Lord, I see in the Tablet a nation[46] invoking one (punishment) for an evil deed, but ten (rewards) for a praiseworthy deed."

He answered, speaking to him: "Moses, that (nation) will be in the end of time."

He said: "My God, I see in the Tablet a nation upon whom your full mercy descends."

He answered: "Moses, that (nation) will be in the end of time."

He said: "My God and my Master, I see in the Tablet a nation reading the faults of all people, while the people (themselves) do not read their defects."

He answered: "I postponed them until the end of time, because they are my servants and I do not want to inform the people about their faults, and (also) lest their bodies remain on the earth only a few days."

---

42. De Luna: "Que sobre el con luz resplandiente ueras scrito: 'Jesús hijo de Dios uera uerdad trayda al Mundo.'"
43. The chapter title between square brackets was left blank in De Luna's translation. Miguel De Luna annotated in the margin, "Aquí queda un blanco que no sea entendido por agora. M. de L."
44. *Al-Lawḥ al-maḥfūẓ*, Islamic and Qur'ānic concept par excellence. De Luna obscures the Islamic nature of the expression and translates (here and elsewhere in our text) as "Su libro de sabiduria." Dobelio (fol. 70b) refers to "un libro muy antiguo intitulado Vida de los Prophetas [probably *Qiṣaṣ al-anbiyā'*, K-W], quando introduçe a Moysen hauiendo tales preguntas diçe desta manera: ilāhī wa-sayyidī innnī ra'aytu fī al-alwāḥ." Parallels of the ideas following in the text are probably also to be found in the Arabic *Munājāt Mūsā* literature.
45. Qur'ānic name of the Mountain of Sinai. De Luna: "La dicción arábiga [tor] es nombre de monte y puede ser el Monte Sinay llamado de los árabes [toriçinai] que quiere deçir monte Sinay. Aye de uer para esto las historias arábigas porque no se equivoque un monte con otro y se entienda de qual monte habla aquí, que hasta agora no se entiende. M. de L."
46. Arabic: *umma*, important Islamic concept.

He said: "My God and my Lord, I see in the Tablet the One Blessed by You (mentioned) in the Tawrāt. To which people in the world are You going to send him?"

He answered: "Moses, I will send him to the people mentioned (and) shown in the Tablet to you."

He said: "My God, describe to me their merit."

[8b] He answered: "Moses, his merit over you is like your merit over your nation and over all the prophets (before you)."

He said: "My God and my Lord, make me one of his family, so that I can obtain part of his superiority."

He answered: "Your wish will be fulfilled, Moses."

He said: "My God and my Lord, I ask from Your grace that you will show me that I am seeing you."

He answered: "Moses, you should know that it is preordained in My knowledge that no human being will see me in the world with outward eyes, and I only speak unto him by revelation or from behind a veil."[47]

He said: "My God and my Lord, show me part of Your Light."

At that moment God radiated on the mountain from the light of His venerable face the amount (of light) that shines through the eye of the needle of a tailor, whereupon it (=the mountain) was crushed. Moses fell down on the ground dumbfounded [and was it not for the grace granted to him before by the Tablets that God had made for him, he would have been broken by the rays of that light].[48] Thus, the angels passed him by in his bewilderment expressing their dislike of him to God and admonishing him to ask God's forgiveness for that sin.

When he had recovered from his bewilderment, he said: "My Lord, I repent to you; if you do not accept my repentance, forgive me and have mercy upon me, I will be lost."[49]

---

47. Qur'ānic.
48. The passage between square brackets left blank in the translation of De Luna.
49. At this point, Dobelio (fols. 70b–75b) draws a comparison between Exodus 33 and sura 6, concluding that the author follows the Qur'ānic version of the story of Moses in his conversation with God, especially in his assumption that Moses had sinned by asking God's permission to see Him, a view absent in the biblical story. Marracci (fol. 20a) refers here to "Alcor. Sect. 6 §19" as the source for Moses's repentance. He adds that elsewhere in this book, the same prayer is put into the mouth of others like Solomon and Peter (see fols. 6a and 21a in our Arabic text and translation).

God answered him: [9a] "Moses, I elected you through My message and my speech. Take with firmness what I have given to you, and do not neglect the invocation of God,[50] and belong to those who are grateful.[51] Admonish My servants and announce them the Blessed One (mentioned) in the Scriptures as I have commanded you to do, and take with you your brother Aaron for that cause. I will fill you with light and knowledge through the Holy Spirit."

At that moment, the heavens and the earth tremble from fear of God, and all this points to our Lord Jesus, and after him, to the Spirit by the descending of God's mercy [upon the (gathering) of the apostles].[52] Because in his conception[53] in the eastern part of the Holy Land in Naṣrān, and his cradle in Batlān, in other words: in the place where Holy Virgin Mary gave birth to him in *al-tīttrt* (=?),[54] the angel Gabriel descended upon her, while with her was her husband Joseph. And that house was filled for them by the angels with heavenly light and mercy. The Throne, the heaven and the earth trembled, the divine mercy descended on earth and she begot him as a virgin [9b], while his birth took place in the month of *al-milād.*

After he had been sent Joseph said he wanted to witness his masculinity. Thus Joseph put his left hand on his pudendum, but his [viz. Jesus's] right hand withheld Joseph (from looking) out of shame, lest he would be uncovered. So he gave up (pursuing) this purpose.[55]

---

50. In the Arabic: *dhikr*. De Luna: "El camino de mi serviçio."
51. Dobelio (fol. 74b) quotes sura 6 as the real source of the preceding sentences.
52. De Luna: "Y la venida del mismo Spirito quando uino sobre los apóstoles." De Luna adds in the margin, "Esta claúsula está obscura, es menester explicarlo mejor."
53. Marracci (fol. 100b):

    Sermo est de conceptione Christi, quam author uocat intibādh, nempe *discessum*. Nam apud *Camus* et omnes lexicographos linguae Arabicae *intabadha* est *discedere* aut *recedere*. Cur autem iste ita uocet conceptionem actiuam B. Virginis preter omnium usum, nulla potest afferi ratio, nisi quia in Alcorano sect. 19 de Maria §14 loquens Mahometus de B. Virgine, quando recessit (ut ipse fingit) a suis, et in recessu concepit Christum, utitur hoc uerbo: *intabadhat*, dicens: *Et commemora in Libro Mariam, quando recessit (intabadhat) a suis uersus locum orientale. Et misimus ad eam spiritum nostrum, qui dixit ei: Ego sum missus a Domino tuo, ut donem tibi puerum*. Et uide qua ratione Noster dicat *conceptionem Christi fuisse in parte orientali terrae sanctae* scilicet *in Nazareth*: loquitur scilicet cum Alcorano. Nam alias certum est Nazareth esse in extrema parte occidentali terrae [101a] sanctae.

54. De Luna: "En el pesebre."
55. De Luna: "Quiso considerar su hermosura y perfección corporal y que boluió los ojos mirando y le uido que con las manos por honestidad tenia cubiertas las partes occultas y estonçes se abstuuo de aquel propósito por no uerlo."

His birth took place in extreme cold and snow had fallen that night. The angel had informed the shepherds who were around that dwelling place in order to[56] witness that place. And in their presence Gabriel wrote with radiant light on his back: "There is no god but God, Jesus is the Truthful and Trustworthy Spirit of God."[57]

And it is related from Joseph that he said: "The angel Gabriel informed Holy Virgin Mary that the name of the Blessed One had been written with radiant light on the trunk of the Throne,[58] before God created heavens and earth, and it means: the Saviour of Mankind. And when he created it and the angels asked God about him, He related to some of them his mission, who were unable to endure that, which was the cause of their fall," as we described in the book.[59]

He has another name in the Well-Preserved Tablet, 'Truthful and Trustworthy Spirit of God.'[60] [10a] He has (also) a name in [the Leaves][61] of Abraham,[62] 'Hīd Mīd' Guide of Men towards (eternal) Bliss. It (also) contains another name, 'Farūq Jamīṭ' which means: the one who separates between truth and falsehood.[63] Among the prophets he is called 'Ṭabṭabā,' which means good, good. In the Tawrāt he is called the Blessed One (al-Manʿūm), which is the one who leads men out of the darkness to the light. Then also his name is Al-Māḥī, which means the one who wipes out infidelity from the world.

56. The Arabic text has "that they should not" (*allā*).
57. De Luna: "Le mostró Gabriel aquella luz referida sobre él que dezía no ay otro Dios sino Dios, Jesús hijo de Dios, uera uerdad trayda al Mundo." Dobelio (fol. 77b) refers to *Kitāb al-Anwār* by Al-Bakrī, "donde se puede ver todo lo que el autor habla de nuestro señor Ihesus, es de Mahoma encubierto debaxi del nombre de Ihesus." Dobelio stresses that the manscript used by him had been copied in 694 Hijra in Denia. Similarly, see Marracci on fol. 25a, with additional sources.
58. De Luna: "En la presencia diuinal con luz resplandante," concealing the throne and its trunk.
59. This is probably a reference to *Kitāb Qawāʿid al-Dīn* (LP 1), where the punishment of the angels is dealt with at the very beginning. However, the same subject is dealt with in other Lead Books as well—for example, in LP 9. De Luna: "Assí como tenemos referido en escritura."
60. De Luna: "Spírito de Dios uerdadero que quiere decire enuaxador de la uerdad al Mundo."
61. Left blank in the translation of De Luna.
62. Qurʾānic and Islamic concept par excellence.
63. Marracci (fol. 36b): "*Duo alia nomina* tribuit Christo author laminarum, nimirum *Fariq Jamīṭ*. Primum nomen Pharec significat *separans* et ita laminae ipsae interpretatur. Secundum relinquit sine interpretatione et quidem apparet manifeste esse praue scriptum. Debebat enim pro *Jamīṭ (Gemit)*, quod nihil significat, scribi *Jamīʿ (Gemih)* quod significat *congregator*, oppositum per antithesin priori."

In addition to this he has in the books of the prophets, apart from his name written on his back,[64] fifteen names.[65] And in the universe[66] (he has) seventy-seven names, but God knows best about His hidden world. To God belong the attributes which are innumerable. No one can count them but God (Himself).

He also said: "In that site that night in which he was born, they did neither see cold nor heath, but when anyone of them left the place, he believed to freeze to death. Yet, that (same) night dry wood thrived notwithstanding the extreme cold, and it bore fruit after seven years. And water bubbled up in its well, after ten years. Moreover, the silent angels talked in various spoken languages with beautiful voices [10b], praising God for this event. Mercy descended upon men, and the sun and the moon were shining beyond (their) limit. The trees bowed to him, [the jinns were reviled],[67] men put on cloths of purity in their hearts, while the demons were chased away. Idols were collapsing in the prayer-halls, while the stars were hitting one against the other.[68] The hearts of the misguided became fearful.[69] Herod rallied his assembly of scholars and informed them that an impostor of his law had been born in his land, and that he was confused, not knowing what to do."[70]

Let us now return to our Lord Jesus: he was circumcised on the eighth day of his birth in fulfilment of the religious precept.

Holy Virgin Mary said that the Trustworthy Gabriel informed her that God on the day He created heavens and earth had created a star the like of which he had not created among the (other) stars. He hid it (somewhere) in His cosmos until He sent our Lord Jesus. When he was sent, that star rose at the oriental horizon. Three [11a] kings from the people of Midian saw it, who were informed by way of the ancient stories of their ancestors, the signs whereof were that star. So they gathered and agreed to undertake a mission

---

64. De Luna: "Sobre el."
65. Dobelio (fols. 80a–85b) refers to parallels for these same names with reference to Muḥammad in two Islamic sources, viz. (1) "El autor del libro de la disputa contra Judíos y Xristianos prouando con authoridades del Testamento Viejo y Nueuo" (perhaps the work of Juan Alonso Aragonés, K-W) and (2) *Kitāb al-Shifā* by al-Qāḍī ʿIyāḍ.
66. De Luna: "Y los nombres occultas en la sabiduria de Dios."
67. Omitted in the translation of De Luna.
68. De Luna: "Mostraron señales nouistas."
69. For Islamic parallels of the preceding details related to Muḥammad, Dobelio (fols. 86b–89b), refers to *Kitāb al-Anwār* of Al-Bakrī as well as to the Qurʾān. Parallels to many of the preceding passages are in fact to be found in numerous works dealing with the *Sīra* of Muḥammad.
70. Dobelio (fol. 90a) points out that the same remark is found in Islamic sources but with reference to Chosroes, king of the Persians.

(following) those signs. They prepared for themselves and their people and came out of the eastern parts of the earth to look for him.

After they had traveled distance of one day, the angel Gabriel appeared to them in their dream: "Follow the star which will guide you to your purpose. Wherever it will stand still, you will fulfil your mission."

So traveled towards the West, together with the star, they entered the City of Jarjalān, in the land of which the star stood still. They asked the people: "Where is the place the lord of the rightly guided Israelites was brought to life? We saw a star in the East as a sign of his birth and we came to adore him for that matter."

At that moment the king remembered the words said in his meeting, and he ordered them once again to look into that matter.

The kings passed to Batlān, rightly guided, they entered upon him and his mother, believing in him. They gave him from their money and donated him a vessel of gold, incense and myrrh.

In that night there appeared to them [11b] in their dream a vision of the angel Gabriel: "Kings, return safely to your land through another road than the one you came by." So they did.

The angel said to Joseph: "Travel with the child and its mother to Egypt, because Herod the King is killing the children because of Jesus. He killed three hundred children (already)." So he traveled that (same) night, but Satan, his enemy, informed Herod in his dream telling him about his journey. Therefore his servants together with his council went out to pursue him.[71]

At that moment Gabriel descended in the form of a man who was guarding a field with young crops from birds near their road to the land of Egypt. They asked him: "Slave, did you see people passing by in front of us with a small child on their back?"[72]

He answered: "Yes, I saw them passing by at the time this crop was planted." And he was right, because a miracle of God made it grow at once in order to save our Lord Jesus.

71. De Luna translates here "[Y assí salio Ibrabii] su criado con mucha gente." Hagerty: "Y assi salió en su seguimiento Abrahe, su criado, con mucha gente." Hagerty annotates, "Es possible que este nombre recuerde a Abraha, el jefe abisinio que atacó la Meca en la época preislámica" (109n48).

72. The Arabic: *al-kāhil*, "upper part of the back." See CDAA, s.v. "khl" (quoting the *Vocabulista in Arábico*, often attributed to Ramon Martí). De Luna: "En brazos"; Hagerty: "En pañales."

They said: "The people passed by days after that [12a] matter; we will not be able to reach them." They thus returned from behind him by God's will whose order cannot be turned off.

Thus Joseph and Mary traveled until they land of Egypt on the [. . . ?][73] of a mountain in front of which there was a plain. Mary wept vehemently because of her exile and her need of everything, as hunger and thirst and the separation from her family exhausted her. Nevertheless she said to God: "My God and my Lord, I am patiently obeying your commandment and you know about my patience." Joseph wept similarly. Then the Trustworthy Gabriel descended to them and said to her: "Mary, do not despair; God is with you." Thereupon the mountain trembled and by the will of God the construction of a house was opened. At its door a tree grew which stilled their hunger every day. At once there descended heavenly food to nourish them with. The earth opened and a delicious well sprang up for those who wanted to drink. Jesus wore a dress of heavenly silk. He concealed with God's permission so that, with God's permission, no one could take notice of them. [12b] He reserved them (there) until a time, He would command whatever He wished.[74]

My master James told from Joseph that he had said: "By God, I never saw a more beautiful odor than the odor of Jesus, neither a figure superior to his, a nicer smile than his smile, or a more radiant light than his light and splendor than his light, or a better person than he."[75]

They remained in that cave dwelling for seven years and three months, without anyone taking notice of them. Joseph was making himself familiar with the manufacturing of ladles, while Virgin Mary assisted him, so that both of them would refrain from idleness. They paid through (those ladles) the amount they were obliged to pay[76] and it was distributed as alms among the poor. They were adoring God night and day, without neglecting of that anything, even during the twinkling of an eye. And they nourished themselves from the tree that fully provided them their provisions every day.

---

73. De Luna: "Una parte de tierra llana"; Hagerty: "Sobre la cima de un monte."
74. Dobelio (fol. 95b–96a) draws a parallel here with suras 22 and 18 and some relevant Qur'ānic commentaries.
75. Dobelio (fols. 99a–101b) refers to various Islamic sources, like *Kitāb al-Shifā*, and works by al-Ghazālī, and al-Bakrī, for parallels to these qualities of Jesus—especially his odor—in descriptions of Muḥammad.
76. Arabic: *al-madīna al-farḍiyya*, a reference to the *zakāt*. De Luna: "Y lleuáuala al pueblo de Caridiata y las daua por amor de Dios"; Hagerty: "Y venía con ellos y la ciudad de Phardiet y dábalas a pobres."

Our lord Jesus used to play on the mountain taking into his hands a poisonous snake, that did not bite him. He (also) walked on the sea[77] but did not drown in it. When his mother finished her religious exercise, he lowered his eyes, took his right leg[78] [13a] and kissed it, while laying down his body on the ground and reclining on his head, while he said to her: "My mother, I was commanded to be righteous towards God and you. My merit lies not in (my) faith, but my merit from God lies in my obedience towards Him and you." He never interrupted the holy invocation of God. When he slept, he was sleeping on his right side, and he put his right hand under his right cheek and his left hand on his left thigh.[79] His sleep was light, and Gabriel and the angels were protecting him with love by the commandment of God from everything feared to obnoxious.

When the assigned time was fulfilled, the angel Gabriel said to them: "Return to the Holy Land, because God has wiped out your enemy and your dwelling-place will be Naṣrān." At that moment Joseph lost his fear that had surrounded him (all the time).

My master James told from Holy Virgin Mary that she had said: "I took Jesus by my hand and Joseph (took) my hand by his hand. [13b] Gabriel traversed the earth and immediately we arrived at Naṣrān. We entered it, without anybody recognizing us, until we informed the people about our journey. They rejoiced, and the maternal cousins Jesus and John embraced each other, so that nothing failed them both at all after their spiritual separation and (due to) the love through God's blessing that had been awarded to them both before. But God protected him in the best land, like He preserved Jesus in order to do whatever He wished as it was preordained in His knowledge of old."

Again also my master James said from Holy Virgin Mary that she had said: "From the day he entered Naṣrān, our Lord Jesus, as a human being, did not stop invoking God,[80] because he was in reality a human being. Most often, he would eat dates, bread of barley, and honey. Apart from that, he did not touch any food. When he felt appetite, he ate, but when he had no appetite, he left it.[81] On him was the odor of bliss. [14a] That odor would remain in any place he had entered, without ever being extinguished."

77. De Luna: "Y se pasaua por las aguas del Nilo."

78. De Luna: "Su mano derecha."

79. Like Muḥammad, as Dobelio (fol. 102b) points out with reference to al-Ghazālī.

80. In Arabic: *Lam yaftur bi-al-insaniyya min dhikr Allāh.*

81. Dobelio (fol. 104a–b) refers to the Islamic sources for parallels of the simple food eaten by Muḥammad.

Chapter about His Baptism[82] in the River of the Proof[83]

John, Jesus' maternal cousin, said in a quotation from himself (Jesus) that he, having reached the age of thirty years, in other words at the age Adam was created,[84] was ordered to divulge the secret God had confided to him in order to save Adam and his offspring. He commanded him to baptize the people in His name and to bring them good tidings. He went out to the desert of the Land of the Jews,[85] behind the River of the Proof, while preaching the glad tiding that God's Grace was drawing near. He did not return to the inhabited world, but was eating locusts, honey and plants, while baptizing people flocking towards him from everywhere, who were confessing their sins. Some people asked him: "Saint, are you the one whom we are waiting for, or not?" He answered them: "I baptize you with holy water, but I say to you: the one who will come after me is higher than me in rank, and I am not worthy to carry his sandals."[86]

Then Jesus came to him, saying: [14b] "Baptize me!" He answered: "How shall I baptize you while I am obliged to be baptized by you (myself)?" He answered: "All of us are equal in that (respect) in the Law (*al-sharīʿa*)." So he baptized him with water in the holy River of the Proof.[87] Heaven opened and the earth shone with light and the Holy Spirit of God descended upon him in the shape of a dove. And lo, there was a call from near God saying to him: "You are My beloved Spirit and My delight!"[88]

When he had finished this, Satan attempted to seduce him (again) saying to him before the mountain in the shape of an aged old man: "Say: God is the creator of the heavens and the earth. There is no Lord but He!"

---

82. We read the Arabic as *ṭuhrihi*. This same word is used in the meaning of "baptism" in various other Lead Books. The single and only lexicographical source providing the meaning of "baptism" for *ṭuhūrun* and *ṭuhrun* is the Leiden Mozarabic Latin-Arabic Glossary, s.v. "Babtismum" (see also in DS, s.v. "ṭhr"; and in GAA, s.v. "ṭhr"). This indicates that the author of the Lead Books might have used ancient Mozarabic sources to coin the Arabic terms for Christian concepts and customs to be used in the Lead Books. This point will be discussed more extensively in our introduction to the Arabic text and English translation of the Lead Books.
83. *Wadī al-Burhān*, playful reference to the River Jordan (elsewhere: *Al-Wadī al-Burhānī*).
84. De Luna: "La perfecta edad de consistençia en laqual crió Dios a nuestro padre Adán."
85. An implicit reference to Judea.
86. De Luna: "De limpiar sus çapatos."
87. Here: *al-wadī al-burhānī al-muqaddās*.
88. Compare Luke 3:22: "Thou art my beloved *son*; in thee I am well pleased." Note that the word *son* was replaced by the words *Holy Spirit*. De Luna: "Uos soys mi hijo amado en quien está todo mi contento y gozo."

Our Lord Jesus answered him: "I say that (indeed), but I do not say that because you said so. Leave me alone, you cursed one!" At that moment he ascended the mountain, to adore God there. And he fasted on it for forty days and nights, without being saturated by any food.

When he had completed that fast, Satan tempted him (again) saying: "Jesus, you are now overcome by hunger and need. If you are God's Spirit,[89] then make from that [. . .] a bread."[90]

He answered him: "Man lives not by bread alone,[91] but his life is in the Word of God. Leave me alone, you cursed one!" He then parted from him.

And he attempted to seduce him [15a] two more times in various ways of seduction. But he chased him away.

Holy Virgin Mary said: "By God, had he answered the call of Satan, after him none of the holy servants of God would be saved from falling to shame. But God rescued him from that temptation."

When having finished this, he started to preach the obedience of God the Exalted and the entrance of Heaven. He went down to the coast of the Lake of Galilee at Tiberias.[92] He chose seventy believing men similar to the seventy men Moses chose to keep him close company. From them he privileged twelve, whose names were Peter, James, John his brother, Bartolomeo,[93] Filibūn, Idrīs,[94] Mateo,[95] Thomas,[96] James Alfeo, Simeon the Canaanite,[97] Tadeo,[98] Judas al-Athraṭī.[99] After that he completed (their) number (again) to seventy, while adding two more, but some of them became sinful after him. Those twelve he called apostles, similar to the twelve runners (*sawā'ī*) of the Israelites with whom Moses crossed the sea.[100] [15b] He asked them: "Will you help God?" They answered: "Yes!" He then remained with them on a mountain.

They asked him: "Our lord, tell us what we should do and (what path) should we follow?"

---

89. De Luna: "Hijo de Dios."
90. The Arabic reads *fa-'sna' min dhālika al-salām ni'ma*. One would have expected a word denoting "stone." For *ni'ma* in the meaning of "bread," see DS II, 692; this meaning is not given in CDAA.
91. We read the Arabic as follows: *Laysa bi-ni'matin ḥaḍḍan (ḥaddan, bi-al-taḥdīd) huwa ya'īsh al-insān.*
92. Arabic: *saḥīl baḥr Ghalāliya al-Tabariya.*
93. The name is given in the original Arabic as *Martulumiyuh*, but we presume there is a scribal error here. (This error may, of course, have occurred already in the author's source.)
94. Here and elsewhere in our text, *Idrīs* instead of *Andreas.*
95. The name is given in the original Arabic as *Matāyūh.*
96. Arabic: *Tumah.*
97. Arabic: *Shim'ūn al-Qanānī.*
98. Arabic: *Tadiyūh.*
99. Judas Iscarioth.
100. De Luna: "Los 12 tribus de los hijos de Ysrael."

He answered them: "Blessed are the poor who are patient, because for them is prepared the Paradise of Heaven. Blessed are the merciful because God will have mercy upon them. Blessed are the pure of hearts because they will see the face of God. Blessed are those who weep about their sins because God will give them patience. Blessed are the rightly guided[101] because they are the children of God. Blessed are those who are in need of justice (*sharʿ*), because they belong to the inhabitants of the Paradise of Heaven. Blessed are you if you have been taken prisoner and are persecuted on your flight for my sake. Rejoice, because your reward is on God in Heaven, because all that has been fulfilled by the prophets before you. You are the salt of the earth. Obey God, and He will guide you along the right way."

Chapter about His Miracles

My master James said: "Were the power of a miracle to be ascribed to him, then when his name was mentioned over a dead person, who would then be revived thereby. But God reserved him for another purpose in His preordained knowledge."[102]

We will now return to the mission he was sent for. My aforementioned master said that God sent Moses in the time of magicians, and he sent Jesus in the time of the sick,[103] in order to reveal His power and His splendor, even though the infidels detest it.[104] When the assigned time for Jesus to reveal his miracles had come, he chose from his companion apostles Peter whose name was Simeon before he (entered) the faith, our master James and his brother John the son of al-Zabadī.[105] He ascended with them the Mountain of al-Ṭūr,[106] to the place where God spoke to Moses, His Spokesman.[107] He stood between them and his light shone and his face reflected a radiant light by with the rays

101. In Matt. 5:1–12, those who will be called the children of God are the "makers of peace." In Qurʾānic language, the "rightly guided" (*al-mahdīn*) are Muslims who are following the right path by God's guidance, rather than Jews or Christians. De Luna: "Paçíficos."

102. De Luna: "Que nuestro Señor Jesus no le auía embiado Dios para manifestar la potençia que tiene sino para redemir al mundo porque si su contento fuera manifestarla con mentar solo el nombre de Jesús sobre el sepulcro de un muerto resuscitara, mas este mysterio de potençia dexole Dios reseruado para quando fuere su uoluntad como tiene determinado en su sabiduria."

103. Dobelio (fols. 111a–113b) refers to *k. Zād al-wāʿiẓ wa-rawḍ al-ḥāfiẓ* (a book of sermons) for Islamic parallels to this idea.

104. *Wa-law kariha al-kāfirūn*: Qurʾānic expression.

105. This name refers, of course, to Zebedee, but let us keep in mind that *Al-Zabadī* = "milkman."

106. This is a reference to the Qurʾānic name of the mountain climbed by Moses to talk with God.

107. Arabic: *kalīmahu*. In Islam, Moses has the epithet *Kalīm Allāh*.

of the sun eclipsed, and the earth and the garment lightened up like snow. There had appeared Moses [16b] al-Kalīm at his right and Elijah at his left side. He told them: "With which good tiding have you been sent to the world?"

They answered: "With (the message) that you are the Spirit of God (and) the Mediator of Men through the Venerable Gospel."[108] They then saw a veil in the clouds which radiated a dazzling light. The mountain trembled and an angel voiced, and lo a call from near God was saying: "This is my Spirit and my pleasure!"[109] When they heard that, they fell to the earth, dumbfounded and frightened.

He said to them: "Stand up, and fear not, because God is with you." They lifted their face and only saw our lord Jesus alone between them. Then, when they descended from the mountain, he commanded them to preserve this secret which they had seen, until after the resurrection of the Son of Man.

Peter the apostle said: [17a] "Our lord Jesus did not take any moment rest from the times of prayers. And he only performed a miracle for the reason of (providing) proof (of his mission), like on the day when he fed five thousand hungry men, without (counting) the children and women, with five loaves of barley bread and two fishes.

"Nothing was asked from him without him complying with the person's request. Whenever he was asked to administer justice, he applied the religious rules according to the essence of the Law. He never uttered a light-hearted word, but he cured the blind born, the lepers, the blind, the lame, the handicapped, the deaf and the thumb. He forgave sins, revived the death, cured and guided the poor among the descendants of Adam through the venerable Gospel. He walked on the lake without drowning, he summoned the winds and they stopped blowing.[110] The jinns obeyed him and he drove out the demons from the people. He fathomed the greatest of secrets in their hearts."

Nobody can describe his miracles [17b] their causes and their virtues, or write them down in a book. Holy Virgin Mary said about him that he told her that the number of his greater miracles were like the number of the Children of Israel whom Moses freed from oppression and with whom he split the sea to complete his goal, because the liberation of every one of them from the power of Pharaoh was a miracle which signifies his miracles to cure the hearts

108. Arabic: *bi-al-injīl al-ʿazīz*, applying to the Gospel the Islamic epithet of the Qur'ān, *al-qurʾān al-ʿazīz*. De Luna: "Que uos soys hijo de Dios el redemptor del género humano."

109. De Luna: "Este es mi hijo amado en quien está todo mi contento."

110. De Luna: "Y subía por el ayre y no se caía."

with faith, as their liberation signifies the liberation of the Children of Adam from the sea of this world to the bliss of the Hereafter, (like) the apostles signify the liberation of man from the danger of the world to the (eternal) bliss in order to fulfil the law. And after he had completed the afore-mentioned number (of miracles), he fulfilled the commandment to leave the world and ascend to heaven. The apostles passed after him, together with the multitude of the faithful, the sea of the world and the limbo and their dangers, and led them [18a] from misery to bliss, like Moses had passed the sea with the runners of the Children of Israel and his army to the land promised to them, whereby the promise was fulfilled. May God make us belong to the saints, Amen.

Chapter on His Good Qualities and His Morals, as Well as of His Mother Mary

My master James said that Holy Virgin Mary was asked about the morals of our lord Jesus. She answered: "If you want to know his morals, you should know that they are (identical to) the Gospel. If you know it, you know Jesus' morals, all of them."[111] Thus also Joseph, her husband, said about the angel Gabriel that he informed him that the children of Adam and his wife Eve were of outstanding form and the most beautiful morals, because God created them, formed them both with the hands of His might and blew into them both (His) spirit. David, the prophet of God, was similar to them, and Joseph the son of Jacob was also similar in nature and morals. (Also) Zādiḥa[112] was similar to Eve in nature and morals. [18b] Jesus and his mother Mary surpassed all of them by far as both of them were attached to all the prophets in nature and morals, and in knowledge and speech. Not (a single beautiful) young man could ever equal them.[113] His stature was straight, his backside wide, his breast high, his face round, his skin wheat-colored, his hear had the color of ripened dates. His face was beautiful, his gaze full of mercy, both in public and in the deepest of secrets. No human being would meet him without his heart being inclined towards him. He would only leave him against his own will.

111. Inspired by the Hadith: *kāna khuluquhu al-qur'ān* (with reference to Muḥammad). Muslim, *musāfirūn*, p. 139; *Abū Dāwūd, taṭawwu'*, p. 26; *Ibn Ḥanbal*, VI, pp. 54.91, 163.216. See Addas, *Quest for the Red Sulphur*, 44.

112. De Luna: "Zenobia"; Hagerty: "Raquel."

113. The following physical descriptions of Jesus find their origin (directly or indirectly) in various hadiths. See EQ, s.v. "Jesus," physical description (Robinson). Dobelio (fols. 126a, 128b–131a) refers here to many parallels in descriptions of Muḥammad in *Kitāb al-Shifā* and al-Ghazālī.

Also his mother's stature was straight, her skin wheat-colored, her face round, her breast high, her hair had the color of the hair of her son. Her excellent qualities and her morals were like those of him. Nobody would wish a meeting with her to be devoid of her presence, unless against one's own will.

Chapter of His Demise

When our lord Jesus had completed his preaching, he entered Jarjalān [19a] and said to the Apostles: "Don't you know that the announced time has come for the son of man to be crucified?"

It was the Feast of the Sheep. Thus he took dinner with them at a table. After he had divided the bread, he gave them from it, saying: "Eat, because this is my body." And after having finished eating, he took a large glass[114] and said: "Drink, this is my fresh blood shed in the [. . .][115] book."

He then said to them: "In this night the shepherd will be taken away and his sheep will be dispersed."

Peter asked: "Who is the shepherd?"

He answered: "That is me."

Peter said: "I will (only) leave you in death."

He answered him: "In this same night you will deny me three times, before the crowing of the cock."

In that time the ruler in Rome was Tiberius Caesar and his governor in Jarjalān was Pilate. The Pharisees looked for Jesus to crucify him by false witnesses. [19b] When they entered the garden, viz. the place where he used to invoke his Lord, the Apostles dispersed and lost all their confidence. But God completed his time through the angel.[116]

The one who sold him for a fixed price of silver, Judas, said to them: "Take the one kissed as the person sold." So they took the one kissed who was exemplified in the Tawrāt and they carried him to the governor, but he found

114. Arabic: *qumṣāl*; see CDAA, s.v. "qmṣl."

115. At this place, there is a hole in the original, allowing for (no more than) two letters. De Luna: "Eso es mi sangre del nuevo testamento."

116. We read "Wa-lakīn [*wa-lākin*] tawaffahu [*tawaffāhu*] Allāh wʿdh [*wa ʿdahu*, which in fact = *waqtahu*] bi-al-malak" (God completed for him [Jesus] his time through the angel). This is clearly inspired by the Qurʾān (cf. i.a. 3:54–55). Most commentaries usually assume that these verses refer to the Jews' plot against Jesus's life and God's counterplot to rescue him by having them crucify a look-alike substitute. There are more parallels and details in EQ, s.v. "Jesus" (Robinson). De Luna: "Mas ya le auiía Dios explicado su determinada uoluntad por medio del ángel." Hagerty: "Mas hízole haber pavor Dios y confortole por medio de un ángel." The translation used by Dobelio (fol.

no cause against him. However, the Jews demanded him to be whipped, and Pilate chastised him, putting a turban of thorns on his head.

He told him: "Don't you know that I can crucify you if I wish, and set you free if I wish?"

He answered him: "You have no power over me, apart from the (might) given to you by Him who dwells in Heaven."

So, because of the obstinate Jews, he sent him to be crucified, and he was crucified between two thieves, as [20a] was their customary penalty. They opened his breast with a stick and gave him myrrh and vinegar to drink.[117] Before his time (had come), he said: "My God, my God, why hast thou [forsaken] me?" And he said: "It is fulfilled." At that moment the earth trembled enormously, the sun sank, darkness spread and the new moon appeared. The stars were hitting each other and the veil of the prayer-hall tore down, while the dead were revived from their graves. But the people feared and were bewildered, saying: "Undoubtedly, this was no one else than the Spirit of God, but we have done great injustice to ourselves."[118]

After this, his family took him by permission and laid him in the grave. They informed about him after three days but did not find him. Then our lord Jesus appeared to the Apostles saying: "Did I not say to you when I was living among you that whoever will see me after my demise will have seen me truly?" They answered: "Yes." He answered: "I am your teacher, teach the Gospel[119] to all men in the world. Whosoever repents, believes, is baptized with water and performs good deeds, will be saved. But whosoever does not do that, will perish."

Holy Virgin Mary said: "The first he visited was she." After that, during forty days he visited her every night,[120] and other people God wished (to be visited by him) after her. When that period had been completed, he ascended to heaven.

135a) reads "Por esto Dios los castigò y les prometio el Reyno." Marracci (fols. 104[a]–107[a]) recognized the Qur'ānic meaning of *tawaffāhu* and presents a long discussion about the implications of this passage for the understanding of the story of Jesus's passion as presented in these Lead Tablets. He suggests, among other things, that the systematic absence of any reference to the name of Jesus in the passion story as presented here casts doubt about the true identity of the person crucified, in accordance with the Islamic doctrine.

117. Dobelio (fol. 142a): "Después, quando San Marcos diçe que el vino era mezclado con myrra; el autor diçe que era vinagre; pienso que lo haría por euitar el escándolo que causaría, si dixera vino por ser vedado en su ley, por este pone vinagre en lugar de vino."

118. De Luna: "Sin duda ninguna este es hijo de Dios."

119. Marginal annotation by De Luna: "En el original de este libro en este lugar ay una parte escrita en quatro letras, no se entienden ni leen porque no son arábigas parecen hebreas. Miguel de Luna." In fact, after the word *al-injīl*, a space was left open in the original of about one word. De Luna's remark is a mystification.

120. In accordance with Islamic mourning customs.

(And it was transmitted) from Idrīs the Apostle that he had said: "When Peter realized his sin of denying (him), while Jesus during his life had told him: 'You are a stone and on this stone I will found my Holy House,[121] I give you the vicariate (*al-khilāfa*) on earth to loosen and to bind, as well as the keys of heaven. Whomsoever you will justly bind will be bound in heaven, and whomsoever you will loosen, will be loosened',—he was overcome by repentance and he wept so profoundly over his sin, that his eyes dried out, while the flesh [21a] of his face stuck to his bones by fasting. His prayer was: 'My God and Lord, I repent to you, and if you don't accept my repentance and forgive me and have mercy upon me I will be lost.' And after seven years and three months he was praying in the cave while the night was coming, lo and behold a voice from the side of God was saying to him: 'Peter, stop your action, I have forgiven you!'"

Holy Mary said: "Our father Adam, God's Prophet David and his son Solomon were profoundly weeping over their sins.[122] Both of them were forgiven, but the vicar (*al-khalīfa*) Peter surpassed them both in weeping, while he was the first to weep over his sins after the demise of our lord Jesus, but God's grace for him was great."

Below all these events there are marvelous mysteries and a great enigma only known and grasped by God and those of His servants He wishes. First of all, I wished to be brief [21b] and to omit long-windedness. I described a part of (those matters) that God granted me, whereas my goal was to describe the life of our lord Jesus, his miracles until his demise, while omitting the secrets below all that to whomever God will grant a higher degree and (a greater) portion than me. If I have missed anything in this book, I did not omit it (out of negligence) but I hid it because of a necessity which God will make known through the Apostles and their reports to the servants he wishes. God be praised for everything. He is the first and the last, all knowledge is with Him. He who preserved me to finish this book, though the writing of it was completed by myself as well as by my brother and assistant Sa'is al-Āyah, during the illness that befell me, may God grant him and all his holy servants a garden in Paradise, Amen!

To God belongs the Unity!

There is no god but God; Jesus is the Spirit of God![123]

---

121. De Luna: "Mi yglesia cathólica."

122. Dobelio (fols. 148b–154b) provides a long discussion of the Islamic stories on Solomon, including his weeping, as an additional argument for his theory of the Islamic background and intention of the work and its author.

123. De Luna: "No ay otro Dios sino Dios; Jesús hijo de Dios."

[2و] كتب محاسين سيدنا يصوع ومعاجزه
وامه مريم الصالحة العذرة[124]

[2ظ] كتب محاسين سيدنا يصوع والعذرة مريم امه وعموره[125] ومعاجزه من يوماً بعيث الى وفاته وطلوعه للسما لتسعون ابن عطار تلميذ يعقوب الحوري،

كان ابي صلح ابن عطار اعربي اصلا من بلد دوس الاعربية السغرة من حسباً ونسباً ومجداً كبيراً واهباته[126] علمًا وملا كثراً قد نتج علي نسبا عليا من نبي الله صلح المويد بالنبوة والروح،

وكان له اربعة اولاد ذكوراً[127] وثلاثة انثا، فاسم الذكورة[128] منهم كان عيسون[129] وسعدون وانا تسعون وابن الرضى، والاناث شمسة ويقتة [ودرية،

وقد خـ]ـلقت انا بصراً واخي ابن الرضى خلق بكماً وعماً[130]، [وكان ابـ]نا محزنا علينا، ولما سميع خبراً بسيدنا يصوع روح الله الامين كيف كان يشفي الاكمها والابرصا [والصما] والعميا والفلجا ويخرج الشياطين من الناس [ويحي] الموتى بالارض المقداس فاتوا[131] للصفار[132] اليه استبركاً، ولذاك يعوال[133] نفسه بالزاد والخدام والقا ليا ولاخي ابن الرضى على بعران، واسرى على الطريق الى ارض غلاليا، فاصبه وتلاميذه على سبع[134] عشرة رجلا قد اشفهم من الجذام،

فعند ذلك قال له صلح يا سيدي اني قصدت اليك طرقا من بلد دوس لتشفي لي هؤلا الابنان من العما والبكما والصما، اني رايتك محسنا [3و] عظما وانا امنت بك ويقنت ان لم يشفهما في الاجود غيرك احد بلا شك،

فقال له يصوع: يا صلح انت قوي اليقين وانا اقضي[135] حجتك، فعند ذلك اخذ ترباً في كفيه وضربه برقه والقاه على عينيا فارتد عليا البصار وامراني بغسله في محصة المسجد والقى يده على راس اخي ابن الرضى ونفخ في فه ثلاثة مراة فشفه وملا علما وتكلام بانواع الالسان واول قوله قال شهدة ان لا اله الا الله وانك روحه الامين،

فقال له يصوع سيدنا: انت هو سيس الايه فاستوجب ذلك الاسم من يصوع سيدنا يعني به خطب الدين مستفتحه، فعند ذلك نذرا لتلمذه يعقوب الحوري—شيخنا—وقال له: هتي تلامذك الصلحين الى نصر الدين، اكفلهم بالواجب اليه،

---

124. Words and passages of the text between square brackets have been provided from the available contemporary transcriptions of the Lead Books, especially MS A1 of the Sacromonte Archive in Granada, as well as from the transcriptions made by the Vatican Commission made in Rome in the sixties of the seventeenth century. Most of these passages have become partly or completely illegible in the original lead disks during the course of time, presumably by wear and tear. There are also some disks that have been severely damaged with the loss of smaller or larger parts of the lead, as is the case in the second disk of the present text (compare our photograph of f 2b).

125. LG: *fī ʿumrihi.*

126. Read perhaps *wa-ahabahu Allāh.*

127. LG: *dh.kr.nan.*

128. LG: *fa-asmāʾ al-dh.k.ra.*

129. LG: *ʿĪṣūn* (with *ṣād*).

130. LG: *wa-ṣamman.*

131. LG: *fa-nawū.*

132. LG: *al-ṣafār.*

133. LG: *taʿawwāla.*

134. LG: *sawāʿ.*

135. LG: *wa-anā qaḍī.*

فعند ذلك ابنا صلح ابن عطر اهب لسيدنا يصوع ماية ذهاباً اعربية وجعلها في يد[136] بدره[137] الحوري[بامره[138]] ورغبه يشتري له داراً [ليسكن[139]] جواره[140]، ورحال الى بلد [دوس] [3ظ] ليتي اليه باهله اجمعين وتركنا[141] الاخوات في كفلته وشيخنا يعقوب،

فعند ذلك سيدنا يصوع امر لبدروه[142] بتصدق[143] ذلك المال للقصدين اليه، فقال له: يا سيدي لاي قصدين اصدقه وهم كثيرة، القصدين اليك مسكين وفقار[144] ومرضا وعمدين النذرة وذلك المال صحبه حيًا وكيف اعطه بغير سحه[145] وهو يبغي به يشترا[146] الدار؟

فقال سيدنا: الدنيا داراً لمن لا دار له! اعط ذلك المال في حياة[147] صلح لمن يسئلك ولو جا على فراس ، وعليه سئله [ليكون] عملا حيا لانه[148] كان لله لم يفنا ولا يضيع اجر المحسنين ابداً، اوما علمت ان التصديق في الحياة هو عملا حيا وبعد المامات هو عملا ماة[149]؟ فاعطي في الحيا قبل المامات لان خير الاعطاء[150] قبل الوافات، واقل لك انَ الصدقة البلغة لله هي في الحيا وهي تطفي غضاب[151] الرب، والمتصدق[152] قريب من الله والله معه في كل مكان ، فعند [4و] ذلك تصدق ذلك المال للطلبين،

فاتاه عند ذلك ابي باهله اجمعين فقال له أسيدي، اشتريت لي الدار؟ فقال له: اصلح اني بنيت لك دارا في الجنة لتسكون جواري في الدنيا والاخرة لان نيتك جميلة ويقنك كبير وهو مقبول عند الله، فعند ذلك حمله الى داره فاتته الحمة[153] وتوف[154] بعد ثلاثة ايام، فقال له سيدنا يصوع: طبى لك اصلح! عشت سعيداً ومت شهيداً واسعدت اهلك من بعديك، ايضا كذلك بعده بثلاثة ايام اخرى توافت امي ربك زوجته، وبعدهم من اجل معاجيز سيدنا يصوع آمنوا به اخواننا[155] واهلنا فكانوا من الصلحين،

فعند ذلك شكرنا الله، انا واخي ابن الرضى، على النجة من الضلال والايمان الاكبار، وبقينا في خدمة يعقوب ففضلنا [4ظ] تفضلا على جميع تلامذه فاخترنا بينهم لصلاح اموره في طعة الله،

فعند ذلك اجب علينا رضوان سيدنا يصوع وشيخي الذي امراني بكتب حسبه ونسبه وعيشه ومعاجزه الى وفته، وانا افعال ذلك فما رايته بعين البيان وما دون ذلك الذي لم رايته اسطره مروين عنه وعن الصلحة مريم العذرة امه وعن يسوف زوجها وعن سائر الحواريون تلامذه حتى الى طلوعه للسما وبعده الى اخير الحديث الضرور لتوريخ الحق، ذلك كله يكون لمرضية الله ونذرة عباده، امين،

---

136. LG: *yaday*.
137. Here, the original reads *Badruh*, with *b*; elsewhere in the Lead Books, it is usually *Yadruh*, with *y*. As a rule, we are following the spelling of the original Lead Books. But wherever one or both diacritical dots are lacking, we are writing *Badruh* or *Badrūh*. LG: *Yadruh* (!).
138. LG reads *bi-amrihi*, but we corrected this to *tilmidhihi*.
139. LG: *li-yaskūna*.
140. LG: *jawarahu*.
141. LG: *wa-tarakānā*.
142. LG: *li-Yadruh*.
143. LG: *yataṣaddīqa*.
144. LG: *wa-faqīr*.
145. Sic! Read *samāḥihi*. LG: *samaḥihi*.
146. LG: *ashtarī*.
147. LG: *ḥayyat*.
148. LG: *li-an mā*.
149. LG: *māyit* (with *tā' marbūṭa*).
150. LG: *li-anna khayr al-ʿaṭā*.
151. LG: *ghaḍab*.
152. LG: *wa-al-mutaṣaddīq*.
153. LG: *al-ḥamā*.
154. LG: *wa-tuwuffiya*.
155. LG: *akhawātunā*.

باب[156] في حسبه ونسبه وارضه ومعاجيز حمله

كان سيدنا يصوع ابن مريم العذرة البتلة عبرني وكان دار اباء امه [5و] من جانب ابها من نصران، وآل امها من بتلان من اسغار المدون بالارض المقداسة، وكان في الانسنية من اشرف حسبا واعلى نسبا في بني اسرائيل قد نتج على نسلة اثناني واربعين نبيا من الانبياء الكرام المباشرين بالمنعوم في التورة، خير ولد ادام المبعث بالفتح المناجل، روح الله الامين ونقيض من الذنب بالشفع والفلاح، وكلهم من آل النبي ابن شيخ الرضى خليل الله ابرهم المواید بالروح المقدَاس،

وقالت الصالحة مريم عن جبريل انه قال لها: لما خلق الله الملئكة في احسن تقوم ولم عصوا ربهم من اجل الغيل على حمله[157] اهتد العرش والسماوات والارض حتى خفت الملائكة المقرابين، ولما القا ابنا ادام [5ظ] وزوجته حوة في الجنان ياكلوا ايها[158] شأوانهما عن الشجرة، كان[159] في نعيم دائم وكان عليهم الحلي والحلال لا يعلم قيمته الا الله، وكان لم جرَبان أفات الدنيا وكان غير شكران لله في ذلك النعيم، [فـ]بدأت لهما سوأتهما من قلة الشكر وهما لا يشعرون بها، فنحست عليهما الوسوسة للذنب والعصيان، وكان ذلك سباب الارضا للذنب المشكـ[وك] لان الله هو حكيم عديل وبذلك العدل هو يقضي ما يشاء، فاكلان فكهة الشجرة المنهى عنها، فلما عصان امر ربهما ايضا كذلك اهتدَ العرش والسموات والارض ثني مرة وخفا[ت] الملئكة واخرجهم[160] من الجنان [6و] ولحقه[161] الله اي موضع شاء في كونه لم يطلاع عليه احد[162] من عباديه الا من يشاء،

وهبطان الى الارض ودركتهما الندمة بقدر ان اسودَ لونهما من اجل الذنب وبكه مطرحان على الارض ولم يفتروا من البكا حتى سالت مقلتهما وتمزقت لحوم وجههما قيلان: ربنا ظلمنا لنفسنا وان لم تتب علينا وتغفر لنا وترحمنا لكونا خصران، فنزل عليهما الملك جبريل وبشرهما بالفلاح وكتاب[163] في ظهر ادام: هيد ميد هو شفعك وشفيع ذريتك، وقال: يا آدام قوم انت وزوجتك انَ الله سماع دعاكما وقبل ندمتك[164] وغفار لك بشروط الايمان وشكور النعام[165] والتكفر المعاصي[166]، وانتذار المنعوم المكتب في ظهرك، ومن ذلك الوقت بشاروا الانبياء في قومهم بذلك المنعم لشفع[167] [6ظ] العباد ولينذرهم للشفع والفلاح،

فاذا وصل الوعد لانتباذه[168] الصلحة مريم اي قالت لما نزل عليها الامين جبريل وأخبرها بانتباذها به وهي تلية في الكتب، وقال لها يا صلحة مريم يا مرحمة، الله معك، مبركة انت في النساء وذلك البركة هي من اجل تطهرها من الذنب الاول، لم يلحقها[169] لان الله اخترها لذلك الامر لان ما دونها من بعد آدم دركهم الخطاة[170] من اجل الذنب ولم دركها من اجل التطهر منه، وذلك مجمع عليه في جمع الحواريين كما وصفنا في كتب قواعيد الدين ومن خلافه كان خصيراً، فلما سميعت كلمه خفات ورفعت رسها مستعيذة بالله مفكرة من ذلك المتكليم،

فتمثال[171] لها جبريل في احسان سرة بشرية يتلال نوراً شعشعنيا [7و] وقال لها: لا تخف ان الله دخالاك[172] في رحمته[173] لاهب لك في رحمك ابناً روح الاعلا وتسمه يصوع من آل داود وسكين[174] في دار يعقوب الى الاباد، وملكه لم يفنا ابداً، فقالت له كيف يكون ذلك واني لم يمسا شأني[175] بشاراً ولم ابغ ذلك؟

---

156. LG: *bābī*.
157. LG: *min ajli al-ʿiṣyān ʿalā khalqihi*.
158. Sic! Read *ayyamā*. LG: *sāʾū* (or *shāʾū*) *ayyahā shāʾa*.
159. Read probably *kānā*.
160. LG: *wa-akhrajahumā*.
161. LG: *wa-akhafahu*.
162. LG: *lam yuṭliʿ ʿalaihi aḥadan*.
163. LG: *wa-kanāt*.
164. LG: *minka*.
165. LG: *wa-al-dhikr al-muṣallīn*.
166. LG omits *wa-al-takaffur al-maʿāṣī*.
167. LG: *li-shifāʾ*.
168. LG: *li-intibādh*.
169. LG: *lam yudrikhā*.
170. LG: *al-khaṭaʾ*.
171. LG: *fa-imtathāla*.
172. LG: *nafakhā lāk*.
173. LG: *wa-raḥmatuhu* (instead of *fī raḥmatihi*).
174. LG: *wa-yaskūnu*.
175. LG: *wa-lam yamsusnī basharun* (instead of *wa-lam yammussā shaʾnī bashāran*).

فاجبها الملك: ذلك هين على الله بروحه المقداس عليك، فاذا امتحضا يسما روح الله الاعلى،

وقالت له: اجعال لي آية لذلك!

فقال لها: الاشبة صحبتك حملة في ستة اشهور في كبار عمورها بعد عقمها وكل شي هين على الله،

فعند ذلك قالت مريم: انا عبدة الله طيعة اليه مثل[176] قولك الصديق،

فذهب عنها الملك وخوفها ارتدا عليها تمرحباً وهي شكرة لله بالسان[177] طلق وفرداً طليب[178] على ذلك الخبار العلي لطعة الله المرو عن الانبياء القدوم [7ظ] لشفع الانسان الذي كنت تليتيه في الكتب،

فبقت ايماً لم تنجي بذلك السير لزوجها يسف حتى زرت الاشبة فتجلّ جننها يحنا اليه عند تقبلها ليسلم عليه، وهو قيل: سلام عليك يا روح الله الامين! وقالت الاشبة: مرحباً بك لتزراني ام سيدي المنعم!

وتصداع يسف[179] في نفسه ولم ينطق بذلك السداع[180]، فاته الملك في النوم تلك[181] الليلة وقال له من كان يصوع سيدنا، فقال للملك: أجعال[182] آية لذلك، فقال ايته[183] بالنور السطيع في ظهره يكون[184] مكتب: يصوع روح الله الصديق[185] الامين، فعند ذلك شكر[186] الله على ذلك،

باب[187] انتبذه والمعاجز فيه

قال شيخي يع[188] عن الصلحة مريم العذرة عن جبريل الملك انه قال لها عن انعم[189] سيدنا يصوع وفضئله ان الله اعرضا[190] ما يلق من من[191] الاوح[192] المحفوظ على[193] [8و] موسى[194] كلمه في جبال الطور، وقال له موسى: الاهي وسيدي انَي ارا في الاوح[195] امة تدعا السية بوحدة[196] والحسنة بعشر،

فقال له يكلمه: يا موسى هي في اخير الزمان،

فقال له: الاهي وسيدي اني ارا في الاوح[197] امَة تنزيل عليهم رحمتك التمة،

فقال[198]: يا موسى هي في اخر الزمان،

قال: الاهي ومولاي اني ارا في الاوح[199] امَة يقرأ عيوب الناس كلهم الناس[200] لم يقرا عيباهم[201]،

قال: يا موسى اخترتهم[202] الى اخير الزمان لانهم عبادي ولم اريد اطليع الناس على عيوبهم وليمكثوا اجسدهم في الارض ايماً قليلة،

قال: الاهي وسيدي اني ارا في الاوح[203] المنعوم[204] عليك في التورة، لاي قوم تبعثه في الاجود؟

---

176. LG: *umaththilu.*
177. LG: *bi-lāsān.*
178. LG: *ṭābat* (?).
179. LG: *Yusūf.*
180. LG: *al-tasdī*ʿ.
181. LG: *dhālika.*
182. LG: *ij*ʿ*ālnī.*
183. LG: *āyatuka.*
184. LG: *yakun.*
185. LG omits *al-ṣiddīq.*
186. LG: *shakāra.*
187. LG: *Bābī.*
188. LG: *Ya*ʿ*qūb* (no abbreviation).
189. LG: *an*ʿ*ām.*
190. LG: *a*ʿ*raḍa.*
191. Sic! LG omits the second *min.*
192. LG: *al-lawḥ.*
193. LG: *ilā.*
194. LG adds *lamma.*
195. LG: *al-lawḥ.*
196. LG: *bi-waḥīda.*
197. LG: *al-lawḥ.*
198. LG: *qāla lahu.*
199. LG: *al-lawḥ.*
200. Read *wa-al-nās.*
201. LG: ʿ*uyūbahum.*
202. Read probably *akhkhartuhum.* LG: *akhtartuhum.*
203. LG: *al-lawḥ.*
204. LG: *al-man*ʿ*um.*

قال: يا موسى انا ابعثوه[205] للقوم تبعثه للقوم[206] المدركين[207] المعرضين[208] في الاوح[209] اليك،

قال: الاهي وسيدي، أصف لي فضله،

[8ظ] قال: يا موسى، فضله عليك كافضلك على امتك وعلى الانبياء كلهم،

قال: الاهي وسيدي، اجعلني من اهله لأنال من فضله،

قال: لك ذلك، يا موسى،

قال: الاهي وسيدي انَي اطلب من فضلك ان تراني انذير[210] اليك،

قال: يا يا[211] موسى، متقول[212] انَي سباق[213] في علمي ان لم يراني في الاوجود[214] بشراً بعين الظهر ولم اكلمه الا وحيا او من ورا حجاباً[215]،

قال: الاهي وسيدي فأريني من نورك شياً،

فعند ذلك تجلّ الله الجبال من نور وجهه الكريم ما يلج على سم الخياط[216] فتدكدك،

وخرَ موسى سعيقاً ولولا رحمة سبقت عليه بالالواح الذي جعلهم الله عليه لاختراق بشعاع ذلك النور فجزات عليه في سعقيه الملكة[217] رغبين لله عنه ونهين[218] اليه بالاستغفار لله من ذلك الخطا،

فلما اتنها[219] من سعقيه قال: ربي تبت اليك وان لم تبت عليا وتغفر لي وترحمني اكون خصراً،

وقال له الله: [9و] يا موسى انَي اسطفيتك برسلتي[220] وكلامي فخذ[221] ما اتيتك بقوة ولا تغفال عن الذكر وكون[222] من الشكرين، انذير عبادي وبشرهم بالمنعم في الكتب كما امرتك وخذ اخك هرون معك لذلك الامر، وانا املكما نوراً وعلماً بالروح المقداس،

وعند[223] ذلك اهتدات السموات والارض من خشية الله خوفا منه وذلك كله يعني عن المنعوم[224] سيدنا يصع[225] ومن[226] بعده من[227] الروح لشفع العباد بنزول الرحمة [للملايه الحورية][228] لان في انتبذه في مشرقية الارض المقداسة في نصراً[229] ومحضه في بتلان اي موضيع اصبها الانتباذ به الصلحة مريم العذرة في التيترت[230] نزال عليها الملك جبريل وكان معها زوجها يسف[231] وامتل ذلك البيت عليهم من الملئكة بالنور والريحة السموية[232]، واهتز العرش والسموات والارض ونزلة الرحمة الربنية في الارض وتنفسته بكراً [9 ظ]، كما انتبيتده[233] في شهر الملد،

---

205. LG: *ab'athuhu.*
206. Sic! LG omits the second *tab'athuhu li-al-qawm.*
207. LG: *al-muwāyadīn.* Read probably *al-madhkurīn.*
208. LG: *al-mu'radīn* (with *dāl*).
209. LG: *al-lawḥ.*
210. LG: *andhūr.*
211. Sic! LG omits the second *yā.*
212. LG: *mā taqūlu.*
213. LG: *sabaqa.*
214. LG: *al-ujūd.*
215. LG: *aw min warā'l ḥijaban.*
216. LG: *al-kh.y.ṭ.*
217. LG: *al-mala'ika.*
218. LG reads also *nahīn.* Read probably *nabihīn* (?).
219. LG: *atanabbahā.*
220. LG: *bi-risālatī.*
221. LG: *fa-'khudh* (with preceding *alif*).
222. LG: *wa-kun.*
223. LG: *fa-'inda.*
224. LG: *al-man'um.*
225. LG: *Yaṣū'.*
226. LG: *wa-mā.*
227. Probably read *'an.*
228. The reading between square brackets also found in LG.
229. LG: *Naṣran.*
230. LG: *al-t.y.th.r.t.*
231. LG: *Yusūf.*
232. LG: *al-samawāya.*
233. Sic! LG: *intabadhāt bihi.*

فقال يسف[234] لم بعث:[235] ارد يشهد[236] ذكرنه[237] فجعال يسف يده[238] اليسرى على عورته واليمنا منع يد يسف[239] استحيًا[240] لم يكشف عليه، فتركه عن ذلك القزد، وكان نفسه في شدة البرد وكان نزل[241] الثلج تلك اليلة واخبار[242] الملك المرعين الذي كانوا حول المنزيل الا[243] يشهدوا ذلك المقام وفي حضرتهم كتب في ظهره جبريل بالنور السطيع: لا الاه الا الله، يصوع روح الله الصدق[244] الامين،

وعن يس[245]: روي انه قال: اخبار[246] جبريل للصلحة مريم العذرة: ان اسم المنعم[247] كان مكتبا[248] في ساق العرش بالنور السطيع قبلا[249] خلق الله السموات والارض، وهو يعني النقيض للعباد، واذا خلقها والملئكة سئلوا عنه لله، فروي لبعضهم بعثه ولم يحمله بصبر، وكان سباب وقعهم كما وصفنا في الكتب،

وله اسم آخر في اللوح المحفظ[250]: روح الله الصدق[251] الامين ،[10و] وله اسماً في صحوف ابرهم[252]: هيد ميد[253] هدى الناس للنعيم، وفيه اسم اخار[254]: فروق جميط[255]، يعني يفراق بين الخلق[256] والبطيل، وعند الانبيا يسما طبطبا[257] يعني: طيبا طيبا[258]، في التورة يسمى المنعم يعني خريج الناس من الظلمات[259] الى النور، ايضا كذلك اسمه الماحي يعني يمحي الكفر من الاجود، له ما دون ذلك في كتب الانبيا من[260] دون اسمه المكتب في ظهره خمسة عشار اسمً، وفي الكانات[261] سبع وسبعين اسم والله اعلم بغيبه ولله الصفات[262] ليس لها عدداً ولا يحصهم[263] الا الله،

وقال ايضا كذلك: ان في ذلك المنزل[264] تلك الليلة الذي اولد فيها لم يروا برداً ولا حراً، فاذا فراغ احدهم منه مة[265] بالبرد، فذلك[266] الليلة افلح العد اليبس في شدة البرد واثمر[267] بعد سبعة سنين وتبلع[268] الماء في البر بعد عشرة اعوام، وتكلام الملئك السكة[269] بانواع لغات الكلام باصوتاً[270] [10ظ] حسان شكرين لله على ذلك الامر، ونزلة الرحمة على العباد واشراق الشمس والقمار فوق الحد، وخضاع

234. LG: *Yusūf.*
235. LG: *buʿītha.*
236. LG: *yashhadā.*
237. LG: *dhakrānahu.*
238. LG: *fa-aḍaʿa yadahu* (omitting Joseph).
239. LG: *manaʿat li-Yusūf.*
240. LG: *istiḥyaʾan.*
241. LG: *nuzūl.*
242. LG: *wa-akhbara.*
243. One would have expected *an* rather than *allā*. LG: *li-yashhadū.*
244. LG: *al-ṣiddīq.*
245. LG: *Yusuf.*
246. LG: *akhbara.*
247. LG: *al-manʿūm.*
248. LG: *maktub.*
249. LG: *qablan* (with *tanwīn* = *qabla an*).
250. LG: *al-maḥfūẓ.*
251. LG: *al-ṣiddīq.*
252. LG: *Ibrāhim.*
253. LG adds *yaʿnī.*
254. LG: *ākhar.*
255. Marracci proposes to read as *al-jamīʿ* (*al-jāmiʿ*). See our translation and the corresponding note.
256. Read probably *al-ḥaqq*. LG: *mufarrīq bayna al-ḥaqq.*
257. LG: *Ṭabṭaban* (with *tanwīn*).
258. LG: *ṭayyiban ṭayyiban* (with *tanwīn*).
259. LG: *al-ẓulūmāt.*
260. LG: *mā.*
261. LG: *al-kāʾināt.*
262. LG: *wa-al-muḍafāt* (without *li-ʾllāhi*).
263. LG: *wa-lā yaḥsāhum.*
264. LG: *al-manzīl.*
265. In LG with *tāʾ*.
266. LG: *wa-dhālika.*
267. LG: *wa-athmāra.*
268. LG: *wa-nabaʿa.*
269. LG (with corrections): *al-malaʾu al-samāwī*; originally written as *al-malak al-sakit* (with *tāʾ marbūṭa*).
270. Read *wa-takallāmu al-malaʾika al-sakita bi-anwāʿ lughāt al-kalām bi-aṣwātin ḥisān.* LG: *bi-aṣwat* (with *tāʾ marbūṭa*).

الشجر[271] اليه، وتعيار الجين[272] ولبسات[273] العباد ثوب النقا[274] في قلوبهم وانهزماة[275] الشيطين[276] ووقعات الاصنام في المساجيد[277] وضربات الكوكب[278] لجلجا[279] عكساً بعكس، وخفات قلوب الضلين وشعه[280] ردس لتجمعاته[281] بالعلماء وأخبرته ان في الارض قد بعث متمريق دنه[282] وكان بارضه وكان حيراً لم يدري ما يفعال[283]،

ورجعنا لسيدنا يصوع انه طهير في اليوم الثامن[284] من بعثه ليكمال الدين الشريعي،

والصلحة مريم العذرة انهى[285] قالت ان الامن[286] جبريل اخبرها ان الله يوما خلق السموات والارض خلاق[287] نجما لم يخلق مثله في النجوم واخفه في كونه حتى ابعث[288] سيدنا يصوع، فلما بعيث[289] طلاع ذلك النجم على الافق المشراق[290]، فراوه ثلاثة [11و] ملوك من اهل مديان وكانوا عالمين بمتراق[291] السير عن ابائهم وكانت[292] علاماته ذك[293] النجم فتجمعوا واجمعوا ببعثهم[294] على ذلك العلاماة، فاعولو[295] انفسهم واهلهم وخراجوا من مشاريق الارض في فشته[296]،

فلما رحلوا مرحلة اعيض[297] عليهم في النوم بالملك جبريل: اتبعوا النجم يهدكم لقزدكم، فاى موضع يمكث عليه تقضا حجاتكم،

فطراقوا[298] للمغرب[299] والنجم معهم ودخلوا[300] الى مدينة جرجلان وقف[301] النجم بارضها، وكانوا[302] سيلين: ايها الناس اي موضع هو للمبعث[303] مولا بني اسرايل المهدين؟ راينا نجما في المشرق[304] علامة[305] لبعثه وجين لنعبده في ذلك الامر،

فعند ذلك تذكار[306] الملك لقول ملائه وامرهم[307] بالنذرة مرة اخر[308] لذلك الامر،

والملوك جزوا لبتلان مهدين ودخلوا عليه وامه ومعه[309] مومنين به، واعطوه[310] من اموهلم وهده[311] اناية[312] ذهاب ولوبان ومو[313]،

---

271. LG: *al-shajār.*
272. LG: *wa-taghayyara al-ḥīn.*
273. LG: *wa-labisat.*
274. LG: *al-tuqā.*
275. LG: *wa-inhazāmāt.*
276. LG: *al-shayāṭīn.*
277. LG: *fī al-māsjīd.*
278. LG: *al-kawākib.*
279. LG: *liḥājan.*
280. Read *wa-sha'aba.* LG: *wa-sha'ata.*
281. LG: *tajamuʿāt.*
282. LG: *dīnihi.*
283. LG: *yaʿmāl.*
284. LG: *al-thāmīn.*
285. = *innahā.*
286. LG: *al-amīn.*
287. LG: *khalaqa.*
288. LG: *baʿatha.*
289. LG: *buʿitha.*
290. LG: *al-mashrāqī.*
291. LG: *bi-mitrāf* (?).
292. LG: *wa-kanāt.*
293. LG: *dhālika.*
294. LG: *bi-baḥthihim.*
295. LG: *fa-ʿawwalū.*
296. = *fatshihi.*
297. LG: *ū ʿīḍa.*
298. LG: *fa-ṭaraqū.*
299. LG: *li-al-maghrīb.*
300. LG: *fa-dakhalū.*
301. LG: *fa-waqafa.*
302. LG: *wa-kanū.*
303. LG: *al-mab ʿuth.*
304. LG: *al-mashrīq.*
305. LG: *ʿalamatan.*
306. LG: *tadhakkara.*
307. LG: *wa-amarāhum.*
308. LG: *ukhrā.*
309. LG: *maʿahu* (without prefixed *wa-*), which is the correct reading.
310. LG: *wa-aʿṭāwhu.*
311. LG: *wa-hadūhu.*
312. LG: *āniyat.*
313. LG: *mūr* (which is the correct reading).

فذلك الليلة اعيض عليهم [11ظ] في النوم رويته جبريل الملك: ايها الملك[314] ايها الملوك[315] ارجعوا الى ارضكم امنين على طرق[316] غير الطرق[317] الذي اطيمه[318] ففعلوا ذلك،

وقال الملك ليسف[319]: ارحال بالطفل وامه للميسر لان ردوس الملك يقتل الاطفال من اجل يصوع، وكتال ثلث ماية طفلا، فرحال ذلك اليلة والشيطان عدوه اخبار[320] في النوم لرديس قيلا له عن ارتحله، فخراج في اتبعه ابراح في اتبعه[321] خدمه[322] بملائه،

فعند ذلك نزال جبريل في سورة بشار يحرز فدان الزرعي[323] المسبل من الطير جوار طارهم[324] الى ارض الميسر فسئلوه: ايها ايها[325] العبد أرايت نسا جزوا قدمنا بطفلا سغيرًا في الكهل؟

قال: نعم اني رايتهم جزوا بوقة نبات هذا الزرع، وكان على حق لان معجزة الله اسبلته في الحين لنجة سيدنا يصوع،

فقلوا[326] القوم جزات ايمًا بعد ذلك [12و] الامر ولم دركه[327]، فارتدوا من وره باذن الله[328] الذي لا مستردًا لامره،

فطرقان يسف[329] ومريم حتى الى ارض الميسرر[330] على شوع[331] (؟) جبال قدمه الارض المبسطة فبكت الصلحة مريم العذرة بكاً[332] شديدا على غربتها واحتياجها من كل شياً لان احرقها الجوع والعطش والغربة من اهلها ولكين قولها لله: الاهي وسيدي انا صبرة[333] لامرك وانت علم[334] بذلك الصبر، وبكا بكاها[335] يسف[336] زوجها فنزال عليهما الامين جبريل وقال لها: يا مريم لا تقنط، الله معك فاهتد الجبال وانفتاح باذن الله سنيع بيت[337] ونبتة[338] على بابه شجرة تطعم جعهم كل يوم وانزال في الحين الطعام الكوني ليتزودان به، وانفتحات[339] الارض ونبعات عيناً لذيذاً[340] للشربين ، والباس ليصوع ثوبا من السندوس الكوني، وحجبهم باذن الله لم يطلاع[341] عليهم احداً [12 ظ] باذن الله[342]، ووخرهم لوكت[343] يمير فيه ما يشا،

وقال شيخي يع[344] عن يسف[345] انه قال: والله لم رايت ابداع ريحة من ريحة يصوع ولا افضل سورة من سورته ولا اخف بشنة من بششته ولا اسطاع[346] نوراً وبهاءً من نوره وبهائه ولا اطيب نفساً منه،

---

314. LG: *al-mulūk.*
315. Sic!
316. LG: *ṭarīq.*
317. LG: *al-ṭarīq.*
318. = *ataytumūhu.* LG: *aṭaytumuhu.*
319. LG: *li-Yusūf.*
320. LG: *akhbara.*
321. Sic! Most probably a corrupted dittography of *fa-kharāja fī ittibāʿihi.*
322. LG: *fa-kharaja fī ittibaʿihi ʿbrāḥ* (the second *fī ittibāʿihi* crossed out) *wa-khadamahu.* De Luna thus maintained *ʿbrāḥ*, not identifying it as a corrupted remnant of a dittography of *fa-kharāj.*
323. LG: *al-zarʿ.*
324. Read probably *ṭarīqihim.*
325. Sic! LG omits the second *ayyuhā.*
326. LG: *fa-qalū.*
327. LG: *adrakahu.*
328. LG adds: *taʿālā.*
329. LG: *Yusūf.*
330. Sic! LG: *al-Maysīr.*
331. LG: *shawāʿ.*
332. LG: *bakaʾan.*
333. LG: *ṣabīra.*
334. LG: *ʿalīm.*
335. LG: *li-bakahā.*
336. LG: *Yusūf.*
337. LG: *baytan.*
338. LG: *wa-nabatat* (with *tāʾ*).
339. LG: *wa-infataḥat.*
340. LG: *l.ddatan.*
341. LG: *yaṭlaʿ.*
342. LG crossed out this second *bi-idhn Allāh.*
343. LG: *li-waqt.*
344. LG: *Yaʿqūb* (no abbreviation).
345. LG: *Yusūf.*
346. LG: *asṭāʿ.*

ومكثوا[347] في ذلك البيت الكهفي سبعة اعوام وثلاثة[348] شهور لم يطلاع[349] عليهم بشراً، وكان يسف[350] يعتراف[351] نفسه في سنع المغريف والصلحة مريم العذرة تعونه ليهربان المراح، وكان يتي[352] بهم المدينة[353] الفرضية ويتصدق على الماساكين، وكان يعبدان الله ليلًا ونهاراً لم يغفلان طرافة عين[354] من ذلك شيا، ويتزودوا[355] من ذلك الشجرة التي كنات تشبع رزقاهم[356] في كل يوم[357]،

وكان سيدنا يصوع يلتعيب في الجبال ويخذ الحياة[358] المسممة[359] بيديه ولم يلسعه، وكان يطا اليم[360] ولم يغرق فيه، واذا فرغات[361] امه من العبدة كان يغض[362] عينييه ويخذ رجلها[363] اليمنا و[13و] يتقبله ، ويطرح[364] جسمه[365] في الارض ويلقه على راسه قيلا لها: يا امي اني امرت بالبر لله واليك لان لم استوجب بالايمان ولكين استوجابي[366] على الله بالطعة اليه واليك، وكان لم يفتر من الذكر الصلح ابداً، واذا نام نام على عضديه اليمنا وجعل يده اليمنا تحت خده اليمنا واليسرى على فخضه اليسرى، وكان نومه نوما خفيفا، وكان جبريل والملئكة يحرصنه[367] بالود بامر الله من كل شي يخاف ضره،

فاذا كمال الوعد والموصف قال لهما الملك جبريل: ارجعوا الى الارض المقداسة، لانَ الله هلك عدواكم ويكون[368] سكنكم في بلد نصران، هذا ما وعدكم الله على[369]، فعند ذلك ذهب عن يسف[370] الخوف المحيط به،

وقال شيخي يع[371] عن الصلحة مريم العذرة انها قالت: اخذت بيدي يصوع[372] ويسف بيداه[373] [13ظ] في يدي واطوا جبريل الارض واتينا في الحين قبل نصران فدخلنا اليها، لم يميزنا احداً حتى اخبرنا القوم بسعينا[374] ففرحوا[375] بنا فتعشقان البناة خلة يصوع ويحنا[376] لم ينقصهما نقيصا[377] بعد الفراق الروحاني والحب في نعمة الله السبعة[378] عليهما، ولكين احصنه الله في اجود[379] الارض مثل حراص[380] ليصوع ليفعال ما يشا كما سباق[381] في سابق[382] علمه،

ايضا كذلك قال شيخي يعقوب[383] عن الصلحة مريم العذرة انها قالت: كان سيدنا يصوع من يوم[384] دخال[385] لنصران لم يفتر بالانسنية من ذكر الله لان كان في الحقيقة انسان وكان اكثر اكله التمر

---

347. LG: *fa-makathū.*
348. LG: *wa-thalāth.*
349. LG: *yaṭla'.*
350. LG: *Yusūf.*
351. LG: *yaḥtarifu.*
352. LG: *ya'tī.*
353. LG: *li-al-madīna.*
354. LG: *ṭarafat 'ainan.*
355. LG: *wa-yatazawwādū.*
356. LG: *rizqahum.*
357. LG had written *yawma,* but we corrected this into *yawm.*
358. LG: *al-ḥayyāt* (with *tā'*).
359. LG: *al-musamma.*
360. LG: *al-yām.*
361. LG: *faraghat.*
362. Read probably *yaghmuḍu.* LG: *y. 'ḍ.*
363. LG: *yadahā al-yumnā.*
364. LG: *wa-yaṭrāḥu.*
365. LG: *jasadahu.*
366. LG: *istawjabī* (with short *a*).
367. LG adds *ma'an.*
368. LG: *wa-yakun.*
369. LG: *'alayya.*
370. LG: *Yusūf.*
371. LG: *Ya'qūb* (no abbreviation).
372. LG: *akhadhtu Yaṣū' bi-yadī.*
373. LG: *bi-yadihi.*
374. LG: *bi-sha'yinā.*
375. LG: *fa-farīḥū.*
376. LG: *wa-Yūḥannā.*
377. LG: *naqḍan.*
378. Read *al-sabiqa* (?). LG: *al-sabigha.*
379. LG: *luḥūd.*
380. LG: *ḥaraṣ.*
381. LG: *sabaqa.*
382. LG: *sabiq.*
383. LG: *Ya'* (abbreviated form).
384. LG wrote originally *yawman,* but we corrected this into *yawmin.*
385. LG: *dakhala.*

وخبز الشعير والعسل ولم يلم[386] طعمًا ما دون ذلك، فلما اشتهه اكله وان لم يشتهه تركه[387]، وكانت عليه ريحة النعيم [14و] اذا دخل في موضيع سكنات[388] فيه ذلك الريحة لم تفنا منه ابداً،

باب[389] طهره في ودي البرهان

قال يحنا ابن خلة سيدنا يصوع عنه انه اذا بلاغ ثلاثين سنة اي كان على وقة[390] خلق الله لآدام[391] امير بفصح[392] السير الذي اوداع الله عنده ليفلح آدم[393] وذريته وامراه بتطهير العباد على اسمه وتبشيريه فخراج الى فلاء ارض اليهود خلف ودي البرهان وهو خطب بشرة[394] بقرب رضون[395] الله، وكان لم يرجع لمعمور ويكل الجريد[396] والعسل والعشاب[397] ويطهار[398] الناس من كل موضع[399] القصدين اليه مستقيرين[400] ذنوبهم فسيله اقوماً: ايها السعيد، انت هو الذي نحن منتذرين اليه ام لا؟ فقال لهم: اني اطهركم بالما المقداس واقل لكم ان الذي ياتي من بعدي هو اعظم مني درجة ولم انا مستهيل حمل نعليه،

فااتاه[401] سيدنا يصع فقال [14ظ] له: طهراني[402]! فقال له كيف اطهرك وانا يجب عليا ان تطهراني؟ فقال له: نحن اجمعين بذلك نعدلون في الشريعة، فتطهره بالماء في الودي البرهاني المقداس، وانفتاح السماء واشرقات الارض بالنور وهبط عليه روح الله المقداس شبهه[403] حممة واذا بالنداء من قبال[404] الله ايلا له[405]: انت هو روحي المحبوب وافتراحي!

واذا فراغ[406] من ذلك داسه[407] الشيطان قيلًا له قبل[408] الجبال في شبهة شيخا كابراً[409] ايصوع: قل الله فطير السموات والارض لا رباً غيره،

قال له سيدنا يصوع: اني اقلها، ليس اقلها لقولك، اليك عني يا لعين، فعند ذلك طلع[410] الجبال ليعبد فيه الله، وصم فيه اربعين يوما بليلها لم يتشبع[411] طعمًا،

فاذا قضى ذلك الصوم دسه الشيطان قيلاً: ايصوع دركتك المحمصة والاحتياج، ان كنت روح الله اسنع من ذلك السلام نعمة،

فقال له: ليس بنعمة حضاً هو يعيش الانسان لكين عيشه في كلام الله، اليك عني يا لعين، فبعد عنه، ودسه[412] [15و] مراتان[413] اخرى بانواع التدسيس وهو مهربه،

فقالت الصلحة مريم العذرة: بالله[414] لو اجب قول الشيطان[415] لم يسلم بعده من الاستحية عبداً من عباد الله الصلحين، ولكين الله نجيهم من ذلك الفتنة،

---

386. LG: *yalūm.*
387. LG: *tarākahu.*
388. LG: *sakanat.*
389. LG: *bābī.*
390. LG: *waqt.*
391. LG: *li-Adam.*
392. LG: *bi-faḍḥ.*
393. LG: *Âdām.*
394. LG: *bashīra.*
395. LG: *riḍwān.*
396. LG: *al-jarād.*
397. LG: *w-al-ʿashab.*
398. LG: *wa-yuṭahhīr.*
399. LG: *mawḍīʿ.*
400. LG: *mustaqarirīn* (two separate *rā's*).
401. LG: *fa-atahu.*
402. LG: *tahhirnī.*
403. LG: *fī shibhat.*
404. LG: *qibal.*
405. Read *qāʾilan lahu.* These words omitted in LG.
406. LG: *faragha.*
407. LG: *dassahu.*
408. LG: *qubāla.*
409. LG: *kabīran.*
410. LG: *ṭalāʿa.*
411. LG: *lam yash.q.h.*
412. LG: *fa-dāssahu.*
413. LG: *marratan.*
414. LG: *wa-ʾllāhi.*
415. LG adds *Yaṣūʿ.*

فلما فراغ[416] من ذلك بدا النذرة لطعة الله[417] الاعلى ودخول[418] السماء، وهبط لسحيل بحر غلالية التبرية واختار[419] سبعين رجلا مؤمنين على تمثل السبعين رجلًا الذي اختر موسى لمقتربه[420]، منهم[421] فضل اثنان عشار واسميهم[422] كنوا[423] بدره[424]، ويعقوب، ويحنا اخه، ومرتلميوه، وفلبون، وادريس، ومتايوه، وتمه[425]، ويعقوب الفي، وشمعون القناني، وتديوه، ويداش الاثرطي[426]، وكمال بعد ذلك عداد[427] السبعين وازداد[428] اثنين ولكين بعضهم فسقين من بعده، وذلك الاثنان[429] عشار سماهم حواريون على تمثل سواعي[430] باني اسرايل الذي شق موسى [15ظ] بهم البحر وقال لهم: أتنصدوا[431] الله؟ قالوا: نعم! فمكث بهم على جبال،

فقالوا له: أسيدنا أخبرنا بما نحن عملين ونسجين[432] اليه،

فقال لهم: طبى للفقراء الصبرين لان اعدات[433] لهم جنة السماء، وطبى للرحمين لان الله يرحمهم، طبى للخلصين قلوبهم لان هؤلاء يراو[434] وجه الله، وطبى للبكين[435] ذنبهم[436] لان يتهم[437] الله الصبر، وطبى للمهدين لان هؤلاء هم اولد الله، وطبى للفقرين من الشرع لانهم من اهل جنة السماء، وطبى لكم اذا سبيتم[438] واتبعتم مهزبين[439] من أجلي: أفرحوا[440] لان اجركم على الله في السماء لان ذلك كله قضا الانبيا من قبلكم، انتم ملح الارض، اطيعوا الله يهدكم طريق الراشاد[441]،

[16و] باب[442] في معجزه[443]

قال شيخي يعقوب: كن لسيدنا يصوع لونسبات قدرة[444] اية اليه[445] اذا ذكير اسمه على ماٍةٍ[446] لاستحيا به، لكين[447] الله وخاره[448] لقزدًا غير ذلك سبق في علمه، ورجعنا الى الامر الذي بعث اليه، قال شيخي المذكور ان الله بعث موسى في زمان السحرة وبعث يصوع في زمان المرضا ليشهر قدرته ونوره ولو كره[449] الكفرين، فلم وصل ذلك الوعد ليشهر سيدنا يصوع معاجزه اختر من صاحبه[450] الحوارين[451] يدره الذي كان اسمه[452] شمعون قبل ايمنه[453] [ولشيخي يعقوب واخه يحنّا اباني (؟) الزبدي وطلاع بهم جبال الطور اي موضع كلام الله لموسى كلمه فوقف بينهم واشرح نوره ووجهه يتلال نوراً شعششعنياً قد خسف نور الشمس شعاعه واشرقات الارض والثوب مثل الثلج وقد امتثلان

416. LG: *faragha.*
417. LG omits *Allāh.*
418. LG: *dukhul.*
419. LG: *wa-akhtara.*
420. LG: *li-m.q.t rabbihi* (two words).
421. LG: *wa-minhum.*
422. LG: *wa-asmāʾihim.*
423. LG: *kānū.*
424. LG: *Yadruh.*
425. LG: *wa-T.mma* (with *tashdīd* and *fatḥa*).
426. LG: *al-Aqraṭī.*
427. LG: *al-ʿadad.*
428. LG: *wa-ʿzdada.*
429. LG: *al-ithnain.*
430. LG: *sawāʿ.*
431. Read probably *tanṣurū.* LG: *a-tanṣurū.*
432. LG: *nasiḥīn.*
433. LG: *iʿtadāt,* omitting *li-an.*
434. LG: *yarāʾu.*
435. LG: *li-al-bākīna.*
436. LG: *dhunūbahum.*
437. LG: *yatāhum.*
438. LG: *usbītum.*
439. Read probably *muharrabīn.* LG: *muhazzabīn.*
440. LG: *afrīḥū.*
441. LG: *al-rashād.*
442. LG: *bābī.*
443. LG: *maʿājizihi.*
444. LG: *q.d.r.hu.*
445. LG: *ayat Allāh.*
446. = *mayyit.* LG: *mayyitan.*
447. LG: *wa-lakin.*
448. LG: *wakhkharahu.*
449. LG: *wa-law karihā.*
450. LG: *ṣaḥābihi.*
451. LG: *al-ḥawāriyūn.*
452. LG: *yusammā.*
453. LG: *īmānihi.*
454. Between square brackets inserted from LG.

موسى الكليم ليمنه واليس لشماله وقال لهما بما ذا ارسلتم موبشرين في الاجود؟ قلان: بانك روح الله شفيع للعباد بالانجيل العزيز فعند ذلك رءآ][454] حجاب[455] في الصحاب يتلال نوراً خطفاً للابصار فهد الجبال وهتاف الملك واذا بالندا من قبل الله قيلا: هذا هو روحي وافتراحي، فاذا سمعوا ذلك[456] ساجدوا[457] في حضرته سعقين مرعبين،

فقال لهم: أقموا ولا تخفاو ان الله معكم فرفعوا رسهم ولم يراو[458] الا سيدنا يصوع وحده بينهم، فاذا هبطوا من الجبال امرهم ليبحوا[459] بذلك السير الذي راهم حتى لبعد بعث ابن الانسان،

وقال بدره[460] الحوري[461] [17و]: ان سيدنا يصوع لم امرح[462] من اوقات العبادة[463] طرفة عيناً ولم عمال معجزة الا بسباب البرهان مثل يوم اطعام خمسة الف رجلاً في مخمستهم[464] دون الاطفال والنساء بخمسة عليف[465] شعير وحتان،

ولم سئل حجة الا وقد قضها للطالب، ولم طلب بشريعة الا وتكمال الشرع في حقيقة الدين ولم يطلق الاندية[466] فاشفا الاكمها والابرص[467] والعميا والفلجى والمباطيل والصمه[468] والبكما، وغفار[469] الذنوب ويحيا[470] الموتِ[471] واشفا[472] ووهدى[473] الفقارا[474] من ذرية ادم بالانجيل، ويطىء[475] البحر ولم يغرق ويلح في الرياح[476] ولم يهو[477]، وطعته الجنون واخراج الشيطين من الناس وكان حيطواً[478] مكشفاً على الاسرار العمظة[479] في الصدور،

ومعاجزه و[17ظ] اسبابها[480] وفضلها[481] لم يقدار يصفها وصف[482] ولا يسطرها كتب،

وقالت الصلحة مريم العذرة عنه انه قال لها ان عداد[483] معاجزه الكبار كانت عداد[484] باني اسرايل الذين اخراج موسى من الضيق وشاق[485] بهم البحر لكمال القزد لان خروج كل وحد منهم من قهر فرعون كان معجزة يمثل[486] لمعاجزه[487] ليشفي الصدور بالايمان لان كان خرجهم[488] يمثل لخروج باني ادام من بحر الدنية[489] الى نعيم الاخرة، كان[490] الممثل بالحوارين لخروج الانسان من غرار الدنية[491] الى النعيم لكمال الدين، فلم كمال العداد[492] المذكور وهي[493] الامر في خروجه من الدنية[494] وطلعته[495]

---

455. LG: *ḥijāban.*
456. LG: *dhālika al-nidā.*
457. LG: *kharrū.*
458. LG: *yarawna.*
459. LG: *lam yubiḥū.*
460. LG: *Yadruh.*
461. MS A1: "No esta esta linea en el original."
462. LG wrote, as it seems, first *amraḥ*, then corrected this to *afraḥ*.
463. LG: *al-ʿamāl.*
464. LG: *fī mujammaʿātihim.*
465. LG: *raghāʾif.*
466. LG: *wa-lam yanṭuq illā bi-ḥikma.*
467. LG: *wa-al-abrāṣ.*
468. LG: *wa-al-ṣammā.*
469. LG: *wa-kafāra.*
470. LG: *wa-aḥyā.*
471. LG: *al-mawtā.*
472. LG: *wa-ʾstasqā or istasfā.*
473. Sic! LG: *wa-hadā.*
474. LG: *al-fuqarā* (with *alif maqṣra*).
475. LG: *wa-aṭā* (with *alif maqṣra*).
476. LG: *al-rīḥ.*
477. LG: *yahwī.*
478. LG: *ḥ.ṭ.wān.*
479. LG: *al-ghamīḍa.*
480. LG: *asbabuhā.*
481. LG: *wa-faḍaʾiluhā.*
482. LG: *waṣīf.*
483. LG: *ʿadad.*
484. LG: *ʿadad.*
485. LG: *wa-shaqqa.*
486. LG: *mumāthil.*
487. LG: *li-māʿajizihi.*
488. LG: *khurūjuhum.*
489. LG: *al-dunyā.*
490. LG: *wa-kāna.*
491. LG: *al-dunyā.*
492. LG: *al-ʿadad.*
493. LG: *qaḍā.*
494. LG: *al-dunyā.*
495. LG: *wa-ṭulūʿihi.*

للسما، وجزو الحواريون بعده بجسد[496] المومنين على بحر الدنية والمطبق[497] وغرارها[498] واخرجاهم من [18و] من[499] العار[500] للنعيم مثل جز موسى البحر بسواعي[501] باني اسرايل وجيسه الى الارض المنعمة اليهم وبذلك كمال الودي[502]، جعلنا الله من الصلحين، امين،

باب[503] في محاسنه وخلوقه وامه مريم

قال شيخي يعقوب ان سئل الصلحة مريم العذرة عن خلوق سيدنا يصوع فقالت: اما تريد[504] تعراف[505] خلوقه اعلام[506] انها الانجيل فاذا عرفته عرفت خلوق يصوع كلها،

وايضا كذلك قل يسف[507] زوجها عن الملك جبريل انه اخبره[508] ان ابنا ادام وزوجته حوة كانا حسان سدراً[509] واجمال خلوقا ان خلق[510] الله لان سورهما بيدي قدرته[511] ونفاخ فهما الروح ونبآ[512] بالله[513] داود[514] شبه بهم[515]، ويسف[516] ابن يعقوب شبيه[517] ايضا كذلك في الخلق والخلوق، وزادحة[518] شبهة لحوة في الخلق والخلوق، [18ظ] ويصوع سيدنا وامه الصالحة مريم جزان الجمع فوق الحد لان لاحقان[519] الانبياء كلهم بالخلق[520] والخلوق وفي العلم والكلم[521]، لم يلحقهما احداً من الشابين[522]، فكان معتقل[523] القيمة، وسيع الارداف، علي الصدر، مدوار الوجه، قمحي اللون، وشعره لون الرطبة المنتهية، حسين الوجه، ونذرته مرحمة بالاعلان والسير الغميض[524]، لم يلتقه عبدا[525] الا واما ل قلبه اليه لم يبغى تركه الا كرها على نفسه،

وايضا كذلك امه كانت[526] معتدلة[527] القيمة، قمحية الاون[528]، مدورة الوجه، علية الصدر، وشعرها لون شعر ابنيها[529] ومحاسنها مثل محاسنه وخلوقها مثل خلوقه، لم يشتهي مجلسها يفراغ[530] من حضرتها الا كرهاً على نفسه،

باب الوفات[531]

لما كمال سيدنا يصوع النذرة دخل لجرجلان [19و] وقال للحوارين: اوما علمتم ان وصال الوعد الذي هو يصلب فيه ابن الانسان؟

---

496. LG: *bi-jaysh.*
497. Read: *wa-al-maḍīq* (?).
498. LG: *wa-m.ḥ.r.r.hā* (?).
499. Sic (*ditt.*). The first use of the word can be interpreted as a "catchword" placed at the end of the page and corresponding with the identical first word of the next page. LG omits the second *min.*
500. LG: *al-ʿāʾi.*
501. LG: *bi-sawāʿī.*
502. LG: *al-dīn.* Sic (read *al-waʿd*).
503. LG: *babī.*
504. LG: *a-turīdu*, instead of *ammā turīdu.*
505. LG: *taʿrifu* (without *alif*).
506. LG: *iʿlam.*
507. LG: *qālu Yusūf.*
508. LG: *akhbarahā.*
509. LG: *aḥsan ṣuwaran.*
510. LG: *an khalāqa.*
511. LG: *qudrānihi.*
512. LG: *wa-nabāʾi.*
513. Read *wa-nabiyyu Allāh.* LG: *Allāh.*
514. LG: *Dawud.*
515. LG: *shabihan li-Adām.*
516. LG: *wa-Yusūf.*
517. LG: *shabihuhu.*
518. LG: *Zāʾiḥa* (?).
519. LG: *m.ʿān*, or *m.qān?*
520. LG: *fī al-khuluq.*
521. LG: *wa-al-karām.*
522. The reading is uncertain. LG: *al-s.l.b.īn* (?). (The *lām* is connected to the following letter but is loose from the preceding *sīn*).
523. Read *muʿtadil.* LG: *maʿdūl.*
524. LG: *al-ʿāmīṣ.*
525. LG adds *'mh* as a separate word (?).
526. LG: *kānat ummuhu.*
527. LG: *maʿdulat.*
528. LG: *al-lawn.*
529. LG: *ibnihā.*
530. LG: *yafraghu.*
531. LG: *bābī al-wafat.*

وكان عيد الجمال فتعشى على المئدة معهم، ولما قسم النعمة اعطهم منها وقال: كلوا لان هذا جسدي[532]، فاذا فراغ[533] من الاكل أخذ[534] قمصال وقال: اشروبوا، هذا هو دمي في الكتب الـ[. . .][535] الطارى المهرق[536]،

ثم قال اليهم: في ذلك اليلة يهرام الرعي وتتفرق نعجه[537]،

قال بدره[538]: من هو الرعي؟

قال له: انا،

قال بدره[539]: اني لم افرقك بالموت[540]،

فاجبه: في ذات اليلة تنكرني ثلث مرات قبل صراح[541] الديك،

كان[542] عند ذلك الوقت امير في رمة تبريه سجار[543] وحكمه بلطه في جرجلان وكانوا يفتاشون[544] لسيدنا يصوع الفرس لصلبه[545] بشواهد[546] الزور، [19ظ] فلما دخلوا في الجنان ا[547] موضيع كان يدع[548] ربه تفرقوا الحاورين ولم يبقى لهم شيا من اليقين، ولكين[549] توفه الله وعده[550] بالملك،

وقال[551] اليهم: بيعه يداش بلثمان المعدد من الورق[552]، هتي المبيع بالاقبال، فاخذوا المقبول[553] الممثل في التورية[554] وحماله[555] الى الشرع فلم يجد عليه عضراً[556]، ولكين يدعو له[557] اليهد[558] جلده[559] وخداده[560] بلطه والق على راسه عمامة[561] الشوك،

وقل [لـ]ه: اوما علمت اني ان شيت اصلبك وان لم شيت اطالقك[562]؟

فقال له: ليس لك عليا قهراً ما دون الذي اعطك من سكن[563] السماء فمن اجل اليهود المتعندين[564] ارسله للصلب فصلبه بين السرقان كما [20و] استعودوا الامتحان، وفتحوا صدره بالعصة واسقوه المور[565] والخال، وقبل وقته قال: الاهي الاهي لما[566] ا[. . .]تني؟ وقال: قضى الامر،

---

532. *Hadhā jasadī* between square brackets in LG.
533. LG: *faragha.*
534. LG: *aḥ/kh.ḍa.*
535. LG has left a blank space here for one word.
536. LG: *al-ṭarī al-muftarīq.* In LG, the passage *Hadhā huwa* until *muftarīq* is given within square brackets.
537. LG: *ni ʿājuhu.*
538. LG provides no points for deciding between *Badruh* or *Yadruh.*
539. LG: without points.
540. LG provides the same text. Read perhaps *illā bi-al-maut.*
541. LG: *ṣarākh.*
542. LG: *wa-kāna.*
543. LG: *sājir.*
544. LG: *yafshaw.*
545. LG: *li-yuṣallibahu.*
546. LG: *bi-shawāhīd.*
547. LG: *ay.*
548. LG: *yad ʿī.*
549. LG: *wa-lakin.*
550. LG: *wa-ʿahadahu.*
551. LG: *fa-qāla.*
552. LG: *fa-qāla ilaihim bayi ʿuhu Yudāsh di-al-iqbāl Allāhu ʿajaba minhu: hatī . . .*
553. LG: *al-maftūn.*
554. LG: *al-tawrāt.*
555. LG: *wa-ḥamālnāhu.*
556. LG: *ʿ.t.ban.*
557. LG: *yad ʿūhu.*
558. LG: *al-yahūd.*
559. LG: *jalādahu.*
560. LG: *wa-ḥaddadahu.*
561. LG: *ʿamamat.*
562. LG: *uṭliquka.*
563. LG: *sakīn.*
564. LG: *al-muta ʿannīn.*
565. LG: *al-mur.*
566. LG: *l.mm afr . . . ānī* (not clear; apparently DL could not read it).

فعند ذلك اهتد[567] التراب[568] هداً وخسفة الشمس واتاة الظلمة والقمر اتاته اهله[569]، والكوكب[570] لطمات بعضاً ببعض وانفتاح حجاب المسجيد وانبعثوا الموت[571] من القبور ولكين خفوا القوم حائرين قائلين: لا شكاً ان هذا الا روح الله فالقوم حائرين[572] ولكين ضلمنا انفسنا ظلمًا[573] كبيراً به،

بعد ذلك اخذوه اهله بالصمح[574] والقاه في الاحد، استخبروه بعد ثلث ايام ولم يصبه، فتجل سيدنا يصوع للحوارين قيلاً: ما اقلو لكم في الحيا بينكم انا من راني بعد الوافة[575] فقد [20ظ] راني حقفا[576]؟ قل[577]: نعم، قال: وانا هو موادبكم فانذروا[578] في الاجود لكل اناس بالانجيل[579] فمن تاب وامنا[580] وتطهار[581] بالما وعمال صلحاً يفلاح، ومن لم يفعال ذلك كان خصراً،

وقالت الصلحة مريم: ان اول[582] من زار بعد وقته[583] زرها وبعده[584] في اربعين يوم كان يزرها كل ليلة ولمن شا الله بعدها من العباد، فلما كمال ذلك الوعد طلع للسما،

وعن ادريس الحوري انه قال: لما را يدره خطه للنكران[585] لكين[586] يصوع في حياته قيلًا له: انت حجراً وعلى ذلك الحجر اقعيد بيتي المقداس واعطيك الخلفة في الارض بالحال[587] والربط ومفاتيح[588] السماء فمن ربطته بالعدل كان في السماء مربطاً ومن حللته[589] كان محالًا[590]، دركته النديمة وبك[591] ذنبه بكاً[592] شديداً حتى سلت عينيه[593] وتمزقات لحوم [21و] لحوم[594] وجهه والتصق خاده[595] لعظمه بالصوم[596]، وكان دعائه: الاهي وسيدي تبت اليك وان لم تبت علييا وتغفر عني[597] وترحمني اكون[598] خصرا، ومن بعد سبعة[599] اعوام وثلثة[600] شهور الذي[601] كان يدع[602] في الكهف ويجي اليل فاذا الندا من قبال الله قيلاً له: أبدره[603] استنف العمال فقد غفرتك[604]،

---

567. LG: *ihtaddā.*
568. LG: *al-arḍ.*
569. LG: *wa-al-qamar aḍāʾat,* instead of *wa-al-qamar atāahu ahilluhu.*
570. LG: *wa-al-kawākib.*
571. LG: *al-mawtā.*
572. Sic! The expression *al-qawm ḥāʾirīn* seems to be an erroneous repetition (dittography) of the same words as appearing in the immediately preceding sentence.
573. LG: *fasan* or *fassan.*
574. LG: *bi-al-samaḥ.*
575. LG: *al-wafāt.*
576. LG: *ḥaqqan* (with *tashdīd*).
577. LG: *qālū.*
578. LG: *andharū* (without preceding *fa-*). After this word, a space was left open in the original of about two words. The same in LG.
579. After this word, a space was left open in the original of about one word.
580. LG: *wa-amāna.*
581. LG: *wa-taṭahhara.*
582. LG: *awwālu.*
583. LG: *wafatihi.*
584. LG: *wa-baʿdahā.*
585. LG: *bi-al-nikrān.*
586. LG: *wa-lakīn.*
587. LG: *li-al-ḥāll.*
588. LG: *wa-mafātiḥ.*
589. LG: *ḥalāltahu.*
590. LG: *muḥallalan.*
591. LG: *wa-bakā.*
592. LG: *bakaʾan.*
593. LG: *muqlat ʿaynaihi.*
594. Sic (*ditt.*). It is possible that the first appearance of the word is used as a "catchword" placed at the end of the page and corresponds to the first word of the following page. LG omits the second *luḥūm.*
595. LG: *jilduhu.*
596. LG: *bi-al-ṣawm li-ʿiẓamihi.*
597. LG: *lī.*
598. LG: *akun.*
599. LG: *tisʿat.*
600. LG: *wa-thalāth.*
601. LG: *an.*
602. LG: *yadʿī.*
603. LG: *a-Yadruh.*
604. LG: *Qad ghufira laka.*

فقالت الصلحة مريم: ان ابنا ادام ونبي[605] الله داود[606] وابنه سليمان كان[607] ذنبهما بكاً[608] شديداً، وغفير[609] لهما ولكين الخلفة يدره جزاهما[610] في البكاء وكان اول من بك ذنبه بعد وفات سيدنا يصوع، ولكين فضله كبراً[611] عند الله،

وتحت ذلك الموف[612] كله اسراراً عجبة[613] ولغزاً كبيراً لم يعلمها ولم يعصها[614] الا الله ومن يشا من عباده، واول احببته الاختصار [21 ظ] وترك التطول اوصفت منها حظاً[615] اهب لي الله ولكين قزدي وصف[616] عمر سيدنا يصوع وماعجزه[617] الى الوفات و ترك ما تحت ذلك كله من سير لمن اته[618] الله اعلى درجة وحضاً مني، فان فرطت شياً في ذلك الكتب لم سميت عنه[619] ولكين اخفيتها[620] لضرورة يشهرها الله على يدي الحواريون وما رويهم لمن يشا من عباده، والشكر لله على كل شياً، هو الاول والاخر وعنده العلم كله، الذي اخراني[621] لكمال الكتب، ولكين كمال كتبه على يدي ويدي اخي سيس الايه ومعوني[622] في المراض الذي احاط[623] بي، رزقه الله جنانا[624] في الجنة ولجميع عباده الصالحين، امين،

التوحيد[625] لله،

لا اله الا الله، يصوع روح الله

List of Abbreviations Used in the Edition of the Text

CDAA = Corriente, *Dictionary of Andalusi Arabic.*

De Luna = *Libro de las excelençias de nuestro Señor Jesús, y sus milagros, y de su madre María la bendita uirgen.* Annotated translation by Miguel de Luna. Dated March 11, 1596. Archivo de la Real Chancillería, Granada, N° 2432–14, fols. 146r–160v.

Dobelio = Marcos Dobelio, *Nuevo descubrimiento de la falsedad del metal.* Biblioteca de Castilla-La Mancha, Toledo, MS 285.

DS = Dozy, *Supplément aux Dictionnaires Arabes.*

EI² = Bearman et al., *Encyclopaedia of Islam.*

EQ = Dammen McAuliffe, Gilliot, and Graham, *Encyclopaedia of the Qurʾān.*

Hagerty = Hagerty, *Libros Plúmbeos.*

---

605. LG: *wa-nabāʾu.*
606. LG: *Dawud.*
607. LG: *bakāni.*
608. LG: *bakaʾan.*
609. LG: *fa-ghufira.*
610. LG: *jazahumā.*
611. LG: *kabīran.*
612. LG: *al-mawṣuf.*
613. LG: *ʿaẓima.*
614. Thus also in LG. Read perhaps *yuḥṣihā.*
615. LG: *ḥaḍḍan mā.*
616. LG: *fī waṣf,* instead of *qazdī waṣf.*
617. LG: *maʿājizihi.*
618. LG: *wa-rakā ḥattā Dhaka kullihi min sāʾir (corr.).*
619. LG: *lam sahaytu ʿanhu.*
620. LG: *akhfaytuhu.*
621. LG: *akhtarānī.*
622. LG: *muʿawinī* (without *wa-*).
623. LG: *aḥaṭa.*
624. LG: *ḥaḍḍan.*
625. LG: *al-tawḥid.*

Leiden Mozarabic Glossary = *Glossarium latino-arabicum.*

LG = Museo Lázaro Galdiano (Madrid), MS 147.

Marracci = Ludovicus Marracci, *Disquisitio Laminarum Granatensium Quinque partibus comprehensa.* Archivio della Congregazione per la Dottrina della Fede, Vatican City Rome (ACDF), 17e, fol. 14–140.

Vocabulista = Schiaparelli, *Vocabulista in Arabico.*

Notes

The authors are very grateful to Professor Pat Harvey (Wellington) for his valuable remarks on the edition and English translation of the Lead Book included in the present contribution and to Teresa Soto (CSIC, Madrid) for helping us, in the early stages of our research, obtain copies of parts of the Dobelio manuscript in the Real Academia de la Historia in Madrid. The research of Gerard Wiegers received funding from the HERA project Encounters with the Orient in Early Modern Scholarship (EOS) and the European Research Council under the European Union's Seventh Framework Programme (FP7/2007–13) / ERC Grant Agreement number 323316, project CORPI: "Conversion, Overlapping Religiosities, Polemics, Interaction: Early Modern Iberia and Beyond."

1. Parchment of the Torre Turpiana, Archive of the Sacromonte Abbey.
2. Van Koningsveld and Wiegers, "Parchment of the 'Torre Turpiana'" (includes photos of the parchment).
3. For the historical aspects, see the recent study by Olds, *Forging the Past.*
4. Important studies about Dobelio are, in chronological order, Levi della Vida, *Ricerche sulla formazione,* 280–87; Morocho Gayo, "Estudio introductorio a *El discurso sobre el pergamino y las láminas de Granada,*" especially "Primera etapa de Marcos Dobelio (1610–1630)," in Morocho Gayo, *Pedro de Valencia,* 4:307–14; and in particular García-Arenal and Rodríguez Mediano, *Oriente español,* 251–307. In the present chapter, we refer to the original Spanish edition while sometimes referring also to the English translation, *The Orient in Spain.*
5. We owe the information that he traveled to Spain at the request of this committee to his *Discourse* of 1633, preserved in a manuscript kept in the Real Academia de la Historia (RAH) in Madrid, MS 19-2-2 36, to which we will return below. In fol. 363v, he mentions "hauiendo sido llamado por orden de la junta que mandó hacer el rey Phelipe 30," and a few lines later, he mentions the name of its president, the cardinal of Toledo, Bernardo de Rojas y Sandoval, leaving no doubt that it was this committee.
6. García-Arenal and Rodríguez Mediano, *Oriente español;* Archivo General de Simancas, Legajo 2645.
7. Their source is MS Gayangos 19-2-2 36, RAH. See García-Arenal and Rodríguez Mediano, *Orient in Spain,* 251–52. Among these drafts, they state, there is a draft translation entitled the *Vida y milagros de Cristo, Nuestro Señor* (*Life and Miracles of Christ, Our Lord*)—that is, a translation of Lead Book number 7, our edition and translation of which are included at the end of this chapter.
8. But see Harvey and Wiegers, "Translation from Arabic," 65: "Marco Dobelio, que fue intérprete de Paulo Quinto en Roma, y lo hoy es de su Magestad . . . que aviéndole llamado el Arçobispo a Sevilla y viendo luego lo que dellos le mostró, al punto le desengañó, diziéndole cómo todo era

invención Morisca, y cosa indigna de apoyarse por buena, y el Arçobispo le dijo que no avía llamado por eso, y así le dio cien escudos y le despidió." Here, the fee is said to have consisted of no more than one hundred escudos.

9. Levi della Vida, *Ricerche*, 282–83.
10. García-Arenal and Rodríguez Mediano, *Oriente español*, 236.
11. Medina Conde, MS 1271, BNE, fol. 34v; García-Arenal and Rodríguez Mediano, *Oriente español*, 237.
12. Erpenius, *Orationes tres*, 39–96. See the translation in Jones, "Thomas Erpenius." Erpenius refers to the existence of public collections of Arabic manuscripts in Europe—which the students may use to learn the language—in Leiden, Heidelberg, and Spain (El Escorial, PSvK, and GW). He also mentions private ones—namely, his own collection in the Low Countries and the library of "Marcos Dobelo."
13. García-Arenal and Rodríguez Mediano, *Oriente español*, 260 (referring to Ussher MS 27610, Bodleian Library, Oxford). The shelfmark of the manuscript is MS Add C. 296, fols. 174–81 (the note is on fol. 176r), a collection of papers once belonging to Archbishop Ussher. Here, we base our analysis on the manuscript.
14. The title refers to the Lead Books but perhaps also in an indirect way to counterfeit copper coins that were circulating in Spain.
15. The text is extant in three manuscripts: St R7-C, Archivio della Congregazione per la Dottrina della Fede, Vatican City Rome (ACDF), fols. 7–176; MS 285, Biblioteca de Castilla-La Mancha, Toledo; and Archivo de la Abadía del Sacromonte (no shelfmark known), García-Arenal and Rodríguez Mediano, *Oriente español*, 275. MS 285 seems to represent a more advanced stage of the text compared to the Vatican manuscript. For example, fol. 27r of the Toledo manuscript shows an image of fol. 3v of *Kitāb fī 'l-dhāt al-karīma*. This image is absent from the Vatican manuscript.
16. We emend the Arabic and Latin to their classical orthography. Note, however, that the documents contained idiosyncratic linguistic elements. For the language used by the authors, see Van Koningsveld, "Parchemin et les livres."
17. "Pues ha permitido que la vida de nuestro señor Jesucristo . . . llegase a mis manos traduçido de donde he sacado todo el sobredicho y lo que sigue el qual lo tuvieron [viz. the 'laminaries'] secreto siempre con escusa." MS 285, fol. 127v; and see fol. 5r, where he notes that in this book, Jesus is never called Christ ("Demás de lo susodicho no he podido topar con el nombre de xpo en todo el libro traducido de las láminas").
18. Dobelio also quotes from the parchment of the Turpiana Tower (MS 285, Toledo, fol. 47r).
19. The original of this book is lost—that is, it is not found among the Lead Books that were returned to the archive of the Sacromonte Abbey by the Vatican. Transcriptions are extant in MS A 1, Archivo del Sacromonte de Granada, and documents about the evaluation process preserved in the Vatican archives.
20. MS 285, Toledo, fol. 50r. Dobelio criticizes Alonso del Castillo, saying that his Arabic transcription is more extensive than the original text of the Lead Book, accusing him implicitly of not being faithful to the Arabic text. Moreover, Castillo's text lacks the translation.
21. Harris, *From Christian to Muslim*, 161n2.
22. On him, see García-Arenal and Rodríguez Mediano, *Oriente español*, 107–27 and the sources referred to by them.
23. See Archivo del Sacromonte de Granada, Leg VI, s.n.; also mentioned by García-Arenal and Rodríguez Mediano, *Oriente español*, 270. They refer to Isabel Boyano Guerra's ongoing research on the Lead Books.
24. MS 285, Toledo fol. 169v. For the Islamic Psalms, see Sadan, "Some Literary Problems."
25. MS 285, Toledo, fol. 37v.
26. On Pastrana, see García-Arenal and Rodríguez Mediano, *Oriente español*, 275–302; al-Ḥajarī, *Kitāb Nāṣir al-Dīn*, 35, 47–48. Some of these manuscripts

later found their way into the Vatican Library and are still to be found there. See Levi della Vida, "Manoscritti arabi de origine spagnola" (= Studi e Testi 220). We have been able to trace five Pastrana manuscripts mentioned by Dobelio in the Vatican Borgia Arab. Manuscripts described by Levi della Vida: (1) Borg. Arab. 125: Al-Bakrī, *Kitāb al-anwār*, dated 694/1295, pp. 153–55 (pp. 20–23); (2) Borg. Arab. 130: *Zād al-wāʿiẓ wa-rawḍ al-ḥāfiẓ*, dated 803/1401, pp. 157–58 (pp. 24–25); (3) Borg. Arab. 163: *Mujādala maʿa al-yahūd*, dated 786/1384, pp. 165–66 (pp. 32–33); (4) Borg. Arab.171: "Letter of Bū Jumʿa from Fez (et alia)," pp. 169–71 (pp. 37–38); (5) Borg. Arab 129: "Pentateuch in the Arabic translation of Saʿadyah Gaon," pp. 173–75 (pp. 39–42).

27. MS 285, Toledo, fol. 36v.
28. MS 285, fol. 73r.
29. MS 285, fol. 31v. On this text, see Albarracín Navarro and Martínez Ruiz, *Medicina, farmacopea y magia.*
30. "Un árabe español docto no solo en la sagrada escritura, pero también de la lengua hebrea." MS 285, Toledo, fols. 80r–81r. García-Arenal and Rodríguez Mediano identify this as a reference to a polemical work written by the Morisco Muhamad Alguazir in about 1611 (*Oriente español*, 297). It is also possible, however, that it refers to the polemic written by the converted priest Juan Alonso Aragonés. See Wiegers, "Muhammad as the Messiah."
31. See García-Arenal and Rodríguez Mediano, "Libros de los Moriscos."
32. Miguel de Luna, "Libro de las exçelencias de nuestro Señor Jesús y sus milagros, y de su madre María la bendita virgen." Annotated translation by Miguel de Luna, dated March 11, 1596, Leg. 2432–14, Archivo de la Real Chancillería, Granada, fols. 146r–60r.
33. A manuscript version of the translation of the *Vita* that came into being under the supervision of Estepa is found in BNE MS 10503, fol. 16r fols. This manuscript includes the complete translation of the Lead Books.
34. Hagerty, *Libros Plumbeos del Sacromonte.*
35. MS 19, 2–2 36, RAH. We will discuss the manuscript below. On Sergio, see Alonso, *Apócrifos del Sacromonte*, 244–45, 265. Alonso notes that not much is known about him. Sergio came from Rome to Madrid and then from Madrid to Granada in 1622, when he started working on the Lead Books there. Castro was not impressed by his knowledge of Arabic. Dobelio mentions Sergio briefly in an autobiographical passage in MS 19, 2–2 36, RAH, fol. 323r. It is interesting that Dobelio does not mention Sergio in his *Nuevo descubrimiento.*
36. This title is found on fol. 298r.
37. It also explains why some earlier authors posited that the manuscript included a third text, a Spanish translation of the *fatwā* by the Moroccan mufti Ibn Bu Jumʿa (found on fol. 343r ff), but in fact, the translation of the *fatwā* was done by Dobelio as part of his *Discurso*. An Arabic manuscript containing it was found in the Pastrana collection, and from his remarks, it seems clear that he is indeed referring to that particular manuscript. This same manuscript was among those that were later transferred to the Vatican Library, as we have seen. Dobelio interpreted the existence of such a *fatwā* and its circulation among the Moriscos as evidence for the Morisco authorship of the Lead Books. This translation was analyzed by Rosa-Rodríguez, "Simulation and Dissimulation," 143–80. The author of this article did not identify the role of Dobelio. Dobelio mentions the *fatwā* in the *Nuevo descubrimiento* as well (MS 285, Toledo, fol. 36v).
38. MS 19-2-2 36, RAH.
39. Harvey and Wiegers, "Translation from Arabic," 65.
40. Floristán, "Francisco de Gurmendi," 366.
41. MS 285, Toledo, fol. 4r. The anonymous and titleless pamphlet against Gurmendi's translations of the Lead Books is found in a convolute, BNE MS 1271, fol. A 2r. The same fear of accusations of heresy in matters of faith is expressed by other opponents.

42. This is an important difference with the *Gospel of Barnabas*, in which the story of Jesus's life is based on a Gospel harmony.
43. MS 285, Toledo, fol. 91r–v.
44. MS 285, fol. 91v.
45. The Arabic text of the Lead Book reads *ṭuhhīra*—that is, *ṭuhhira*; in the second example, it uses the *maṣdar* form *taṭhīr*. In the first case, it means "circumcision"; in the second case, "purification" (viz., by baptizing).
46. MS 285, Toledo, fol. 91v: "Después de lo susodicho, el autor dice, que nuestro Señor Jesús fue bautizado en el 8° día de su venida para cumplir con la ley legal." The translation by Miguel de Luna says *circumcision*.
47. See the references in Lazarus-Yafeh, *Intertwined Worlds*, 107.
48. MS 285, Toledo, fol. 135r: "Partiéronse todos con grande temor, y no quedó en ellos ninguna fe, por esto Dios los castigó y les prometió el Reyno." Apparently, the translator read in Arabic *wacada* (instead of *wa-cadda*) and *mulk* (instead of *malak*). De Luna reads, "Mas ya le auía Dios explicado su determinada uoluntad por medio del ángel."
49. MS 285, Toledo, fol. 135v: "El autor no supo el credo donde diçe passus sub Pontio Pilato, a que lo haze para introduçir novedades en la fe."
50. Lead Book 7, fol. 21a.
51. MS 285, Toledo, fol. 146r–147r.
52. For *waqtahu*, as occurs in other places in the Lead Books as well.
53. As rightly observed by Bernabé Pons, "Mecanismos de una resistencia," 488.
54. MS 285, Toledo, fol. 161r ff.
55. See, for example, MS 285, fol. 30r.
56. Not all books read "Lā ilāha illā Allāh" with the accompanying letters *mīm* and *rā'*. We do indeed find it in the Arabic text of Lead Book 2, *Kitāb fī 'l-dhāt al-karīma*, fol. 3v and in Lead Book 6. It should be noted that Miguel de Luna's Spanish translation of Lead Book 2, dated May 20, 1595 (Archivo de la Real Chancillería, Granada, leg. 2432–20, fol. 437r), renders the same passage in the Arabic text of Lead Book 2 as follows: "No hay Dios sino Dios—," adding the following personal comment: "Luego tras esto se siguen quatro letras singulares litera proparte, que por agora no se entienden—." These words refer to the four dots that are found around the *mīm* and *rā'*. However, in a copy in Arabic script of Lead Book 2 prepared by the same Miguel de Luna and dated October 1, 1596, preserved in the Museo Lázaro Galdiano in Madrid, this passage reads, "Lā ilāha illā Allāh; Ṣ. R. Allāh" (There is no God but God; Ṣ is the R of God), probably to be read as "Yaṣū' Rūḥ Allāh" (Jesus is the Spirit of God; Museo Lázaro Galdiano, MS 147). In order to understand the background of this variation, it is important to look at parallel passages in other Lead Books. This leads us to the following. At the end of Lead Book 6, *Bukā Bidruh al-Ḥawārī al-Khalīfa* (*Llanto de San Pedro*), the same passage appears: "Lā ilāha illā Allāh; M. R. Allāh," again emended by De Luna in his translation of this Lead Book in the same manner as before—both in his Arabic transcription and in his translation. However, these appear to be the only two (!) passages in the Lead Books where this textual phenomenon appears. The phrase "Yaṣū' Rūḥ Allāh" (Jesus is the Spirit of God), on the contrary, appears no fewer than twenty-four times in the Lead Books: seventeen times in the body of the Lead Book, five times as a marker at the end of a book, and once as a marker at the beginning. In addition, the expression "Rūḥ Allāh," not preceded by "Yaṣū'" but nonetheless referring to Jesus, appears another twenty-nine times in the Lead Books. Therefore, it can be stated that, in fact, the idea that "Jesus is the Spirit of God" is a more central doctrine of the Lead Books than the (ambivalent) doctrine included in "mīm-rā'." In this light, we must perhaps *reconsider* the significance of the words "Lā ilāha illā Allāh; M. R. Allāh" as found in Lead Books 2 and 6. Are these the genuine, authentic readings belonging to the original text or corruptions of the

text due to a copyist, like so many others we were able to indicate in the notes to our forthcoming diplomatic edition? Or should we perhaps consider them to be as a concept that was later on replaced by another (less conspicuously Islamic) symbol?

57. MS 19-2-2 36, RAH, fol. 364r.
58. MS 285, Toledo, fol. 165r; MS St R7-C, Archivio della Congregazione per la Dottrina della Fede, Vatican City Rome (ACDF), fol. 170v.
59. MS 19-2-2 36, RAH, fol. 323r.
60. MS 285, Toledo, fol. 127v.
61. MS 285, fol. 128r.
62. MS 285, fol. 56r.
63. As mentioned explicitly by one of the defenders of the Lead Books, Cristobal Medina Conde, in his *Informe*, MS 1271, BNE, fol. 34v. See also Magnier, "Pedro de Valencia," 205n21. According to Morocho Gayo, *Pedro de Valencia*, 327n592, the original treatise, dated 1617, is extant in the Vatican process documents (shelfmark MS R7i) and in the Archive of the Sacromonte, Leg 6, parte 2, fols. 1137r–1142v. This treatise would later serve as an important source in the request by theologians and cardinals to the pope to condemn the Lead Books. The text deserves a separate study and cannot be dealt with here. We do not think, however, that the manuscript kept in the Sacromonte is the original treatise. See, for general information on the period, Alonso, *Apócrifos del Sacromonte*, 201, esp. 210, on the translation that Gurmendi made with *scholios* by Mendiola, documents that were sent to the Concejo Real and the Inquisition in 1616. On Gurmendi, who died on March 31, 1621, see Kendrick, *St. James in Spain*, 104, who describes Gurmendi as a "rogue." According to Kendrick, some transcriptions of the Lead Books in the possession of Juan Idiáquez had been stolen by Gurmendi, his staff member, who in turn provided the enemies of the books with information about their contents. Kendrick does not mention his source. For Gurmendi, see also Magnier, "Pedro de Valencia"; García-Arenal and Rodríguez Mediano, *Oriente español*, 246–49; Morocho Gayo, *Pedro de Valencia*, 324–32; and Floristán, "Francisco de Gurmendi."
64. According to Medina Conde, in his aforesaid *Informe* (MS 1271, BNE, fol. 34v), Gurmendi succeeded Miguel de Luna as royal translator after the latter died in 1615. However, Floristán, "Francisco de Gurmendi," 359, posits that this date is not correct and that Gurmendi was active as a translator as early as 1604. Perhaps we have to distinguish between various offices and tasks. Further research is needed here. It was Dobelio himself who introduced Gurmendi to the Arabic language. He writes in his *Discurso* (MS 19-2-2 36, RAH, fol. 364r), "Y hauiendo entroducido [*sic*] a Francisco de Gurmendi en la lengua."
65. This pamphlet is extant in MS 1271, BNE, fols. 1–11r; in MS 6437, BNE, fols. 24–37r; and in the Archivo de la Real Chancillería in Granada. Here, we base ourselves on BNE MS 1271, a convolute of various handwritten documents and printed texts, and follow the foliation of the pamphlet itself.
66. MS 1271, BNE fol. A r.
67. MS 1271, fol. A v, B r.
68. MS 1271, fol. A 2v.
69. MS 1271, fol. A 2r.
70. MS 1271, fol. B r.
71. MS 1271, fol. B v. The author is very likely referring here to De Luna's remarkable lecture held in Granada in 1595 in which he defended the authenticity of the Lead Books. See Van Koningsveld and Wiegers, "Five Documents," 239.
72. MS 1271, BNE, fol. C v; and MS 285, Toledo, fols. 28r–v, with a reproduction of the original lead plate leaf on 27v (Lead Book 2). The words are indeed Qurʾānic. See, for example, sūra 4:166 and other places, where it is said that God suffices as a witness. The words *ʿalā dhālika* are not part of one of any of these Qurʾānic passages and refer to the preceding

passage in the Lead Book. The expression is not found in sūra 12.

73. Dobelio describes him as "vn hombre inteligente en la lengua árabe y traduxo las láminas, que se hallaron en el Monte Valparaíso, que la vna se intitula: Libro de la los fundamentos y reglas de la ley y la otra De Essentia Dei. Que parece inuención de moriscos." Magnier, "Pedro de Valencia," 210, 211n45.

74. On Ludovico Marracci, see Bevilacqua, "Qur'ān Translations"; and the recent study by Glei and Tottoli, *Ludovico Marracci at Work*.

75. Archive of the Congregazione per la Dottrina della Fede, documents related to the Lead Books of Granada, no. 17e, 315 fols. (papal bull of 1682 and "votos" of the evaluators of the assessment committee).

76. "Pars prima: Laminas Granatenses Mahumetanicis verbis, sententiis, fabulis, erroribus respersas esse."

77. "Pars secunda: Laminas Granatenses multa sanae doctrinae dissona, quorum pleraque Mahumetanicis erroribus consonant, continere."

78. "Pars tertia: Laminas Granatenses a sacris et ecclesiasticis historiis saepe dissentire, cum Machumetanicis conuenire."

79. "Pars quarta: Alia quaedam a laminis Granatensibus confusim adnotata."

80. "Pars quinta: Laminarum Granatensium techna et earundem authoris scopus," fol. 122r.

81. "Pars quinta, Laminarum Granatensium techna," fol. 126v.

82. Marracci, *Disquisitio*, "Pars quinta," fol. 122r.

III

MEDITERRANEAN AND EUROPEAN TRANSFERS

10

PRISONS AND POLEMICS

Captivity, Confinement, and Medieval Interreligious Encounter

Ryan Szpiech

Introduction

In the spring of 1307, the Catalan polymath Ramon Llull, at the age of seventy-four, made the second of three missionary trips to North Africa that he would undertake in his lifetime. His biographical *Vita coetanea* (*Contemporary Life*; 1311) describes this scene upon arrival in the North African port of Béjaïa (Bougie), ruled at the time by the Ḥafsid dynasty: "From there, Ramon . . . sailed to a certain Saracen land called Bougie. In the main square of the city, Ramon, standing up and shouting in a loud voice, burst out with the following words: 'The Christian religion is true, holy and acceptable to God; The Saracen religion, however, is false and full of error, and this I am prepared to prove.'"[1] Ramon was nearly stoned to death by hostile crowds, and then he was imprisoned for six months. In jail, he discussed his faith and his argument for proving the truth of Christianity with various local intellectuals before being expelled from the city.[2]

The *Vita* was written in 1311 (some four years after the events), allegedly dictated by Llull to "certain monks who were friends of his," probably the Carthusian monks of Vauvert in Paris.[3] Ramon had already described the same scene of his imprisonment and disputation in a contemporary work written in Pisa in 1308 just after his return from Tunis. Llull allegedly began this work in prison, writing it in Arabic and sending a copy to the local Muslim "bishop," prompting his expulsion from the city.[4] However, during his return trip from North Africa, this Arabic original was lost in a shipwreck, and thus Ramon wrote the work again in Latin, finishing a second version, entitled *Disputatio Raimundi christiani et Homeri saraceni* (Disputation of Raymond the Christian and ʿUmar the Saracen), while staying in the monastery of San Donnino in Pisa. In this surviving Latin version, he describes his prison encounter in terms similar to those used in the *Vita* a few years later. The account in the *Disputatio* offers more details than that in the *Vita*, including the name of Llull's principal Muslim interlocutor:

> Ramon went to a certain city of the Saracens named Béjaïa in which, while preaching and praising the holy Catholic faith, he was captured in a street of the Saracens, beaten, and put in jail. While Ramon was in jail, a certain learned Saracen named ʿUmar came regularly with other Saracens to dispute with him about faith at the order of a Saracen bishop, who was said to be very learned, in order, with his arguments, to lead Ramon to the faith of Muḥammad. As the two disputed for a long time . . . Ramon said that each should make a book of disputation.[5]

Ramon and ʿUmar debated the nature of God and the Trinity according to the terms that seem to be taken from Ibn Sīnā, and Llull claims that his adroit argumentation won him an upgrade to a better prison.[6] Llull's imprisonment offered an opportunity that his public preaching alone did not, creating the circumstances in which he was able to debate with a Muslim about the merits of each faith and giving him the impetus to compose his polemical work against Islam.

Just two years after Ramon Llull began the account of his polemical disputation with ʿUmar while in a North African prison, a North African author from the Ḥafsid city of Tunis contemplated his own religion while in captivity in the Catalan city of Lleida. In 1309, Muḥammad al-Qaysī wrote the anti-Christian treatise *Miftāh al-dīn wa-l-mujādala bayna l-naṣārā wa-l-muslimīn* (The key of religion and the conflict between Christians and Muslims), which now survives in Arabic in manuscript 1554 of the Bibliothèque Nationale d'Algérie and also a subsequent *aljamiado* version preserved in at least four other manuscripts.[7] After a detailed presentation of what he claims are scriptural references taken directly from the Hebrew Bible and New Testament (although his quotes are taken from corrupt references in other sources) as well as the Qur'ān, al-Qaysī summarizes a lengthy debate he had with a local Christian priest while in captivity: "I was cast among the 'band of Satan' in the land of unbelief and oppression. I served the sinful Christians, as well as the priests and the monks in disputation and shame."[8] Al-Qaysī gives his name in the Arabic text, and further details about the author's identity and situation are given in the *aljamiado* version of the text, which claims that al-Qaysī was "a learned scholar from the al-Zaytuna mosque" in Tunis and "was a captive in Lleida in the kingdom of Aragon."[9] Moreover, the author says he drew his material from an otherwise unknown anti-Christian polemic by an earlier author, one *ʿAbdallāh al-Asīr bi-Ifranjah*, or as it is rendered in the later *aljamiado* version, "Abdullahi . . . kativo en Francia," a name that translates as "ʿAbdallāh the (war) prisoner/captive in France."[10] Al-Qaysī relates that ʿAbdallāh's polemic against Christianity was the product of his experience of being compelled to debate with a local monk about Jesus and the Incarnation. Al-Qaysī also suggests that he suffered from some degree of limited eyesight and also was more used to speaking the local Romance vernacular than his native tongue, requiring him to find an assistant to help him write his text in Arabic.[11] The *Key of Religion* thus presents us with not one but two stories of captivity, both telling of Muslim captives made to debate theology with their Christian captors and both leading to the production of written polemical material.

The parallels between al-Qaysī's and Llull's stories are striking: both Llull and al-Qaysī wrote in a single span of a few years (1308–10); both wrote of Christian-Muslim polemical encounters, presenting arguments defending the truth and superiority of their own religion and the false premises of their rivals; both describe not only theoretical or general polemical arguments but also a real-world debate they undertook with a member of the local religious intelligentsia; each figure gained some proficiency in the language of their captors (Llull learning Arabic from his Muslim captive, al-Qaysī learning Romance from his captors and those he encountered in Lleida); both texts were written in Arabic and also circulated in later versions in other languages; both works were disseminated from the time of composition in the fourteenth century into the early sixteenth century; and most important, both men began writing their texts while facing captivity or imprisonment, and the experience of each seems to mirror that of the other (Llull, a native speaker of Catalan from Mallorca, writing in prison in North Africa; al-Qaysī, a native speaker of Arabic from North Africa, writing in captivity in Catalonia).[12] Van Koningsveld and Wiegers have even suggested the possibility (albeit remote) of a direct encounter between ʿAbdallāh al-Asīr or al-Qaysī and Llull himself, given their overlapping chronologies and Llull's itinerary of travels in Spain and France in the same years.[13]

Yet at the same time, the depiction of confinement in their respective texts is not at all the same. Al-Qaysī presents captivity as a trial by God for the purpose of using the author as a tool to argue against the Christians and expose their erroneous beliefs. Llull, on the other hand, depicts his imprisonment as evidence of his own pious devotion to his cause and as evidence of the authenticity of his knowledge and arguments. While al-Qaysī laments his fate and even at one point despairs and hopes for death, Llull seeks his fate out and seems to relish his trials as following in the footsteps of earlier Christian martyrs.[14] How can we understand this difference, given the many other similarities between the two cases? Asking this question leads to other, more general ones: What is the role of captivity in late medieval polemical writing, and how does that role differ, if at all, in works from different religious traditions? Why does captivity seem so important in Christian sources in particular?

In this chapter, I will offer preliminary answers to a few of these questions by considering the connection between captivity and medieval Christian polemical writing, focusing on the western Mediterranean in the twelfth century and after. Using the different reactions by Llull and al-Qaysī as a starting point, I note first that captivity and imprisonment served as a real and recurrent circumstance of concrete knowledge transfer that in fact may have facilitated and encouraged interreligious attacks and polemics. Secondly, I propose that in Christian writing, authors make reference to captivity, confinement, and imprisonment in metaphorical terms at least as often as they refer to these as real circumstances that stimulated and facilitated their writing. In fact, the mention of imprisonment in Christian polemical writing seems to be calculated as a strategic move by the authors, helping them express an essential logic of the polemical argument itself—that of polemical exegesis as a sort of capture or conquest of a rival scripture. Thirdly, by way of conclusion, I will consider what might account for the particular character of Christian images of captivity. I propose tentatively that Christian notions of captivity can be explained as a direct effect of Christian notions of sin and redemption, which are quite different from those found in Islam and other religious traditions.

Captivity and Contact in the Later Middle Ages

Before turning to the metaphorical uses of captivity in Christian writing, it is necessary to establish more clearly the extent of real captivity before the sixteenth century. I am approaching the question without strictly distinguishing between terms for confinement—*slavery* and *captivity*—although some historians attempt to quantify and study these independently. My approach is justified for a number of reasons. Most importantly, medieval Latin and Romance sources that mention people in confinement, whether in physical or metaphorical terms, speak most often of "captives" (*captivus, cautivo, cavtivo, catiu*, etc.). The term for "slave" (*sclavus*), derived from the Byzantine Greek *sklavos* ("Slav," which in Arabic was rendered *ṣiqlabī* to denote captives of Eastern European origin), is less common. Moreover, there is not abundant evidence that a firm conceptual distinction between "ransom captives" and "labor slaves" existed in the medieval Mediterranean, and the term for "slave" becomes widespread only in the sixteenth century, when "slavery" comes to be consistently differentiated from "captivity."[15]

Efforts to quantify Mediterranean captivity and enslavement have largely focused on the early modern period. Robert Davis has estimated, based on lists of ships taken captive, contemporary estimates of captives in various cities, and other sundry anecdotal sources, that "between 1530 and 1780 there were almost certainly a million and quite possibly as many as a million and a quarter white, European Christians enslaved by the Muslims of the Barbary Coast."[16] Salvatore Bono has by contrast estimated that "from the sixteenth to the nineteenth century at least two million slaves from the Muslim Mediterranean world entered European countries, while a million European slaves and at least double that number of black slaves crossed over (directly or indirectly) into the Islamic world—giving a total of five million."[17] Nabil Matar has questioned the size of such figures, although there is no easy way to confirm or deny them.[18] If one assumes even half those amounts to be credible, that would constitute more than a million people, Muslims and Christians, who were taken captive in the early modern Mediterranean region between 1500 and 1700. Such numbers would imply that before 1700, Mediterranean captive trade was a larger enterprise than the contemporary Atlantic slave trade. In any case, as Daniel Hershenzon has established in detail, captivity was an important feature of the early modern Mediterranean economy, and historians have partially documented and analyzed its importance in sixteenth- and seventeenth-century political and cultural history.[19]

Although the early modern captive economy was many times larger and more complex than that of the late medieval period, captive-taking and ransoming activities were persistent features of life around the Mediterranean in the later Middle Ages as well. Based on demographic guesswork, one might propose that captives of different types could have constituted perhaps 1 to 3 percent of medieval Mediterranean society.[20] Captivity was prevalent in the western half in the thirteenth and fourteenth centuries due to Christian advances into Muslim territories in southern Iberia. As William Phillips has noted, slavery was a permanent feature of life in Iberia from the beginning of recorded history, from before the time of Carthaginian colonization through the period of Roman settlement and all the way to the eighteenth century.[21] The first Christian redemption orders, the Mercedarians and the Trinitarians, were founded in the thirteenth century (in Iberia and France, respectively), although their period of greatest activity seems to have been the sixteenth century. Jarbel Rodríguez has pointed out that references to redemption activities appear in Aragonese archival sources from the twelfth-century period of conquest and settlement, including both royal documents and regional charters.[22] Whatever the exact numbers, there is no doubt that captivity and slave trade were quotidian aspects of Iberian societies in the thirteenth and fourteenth centuries, and the majority of slaves and captives in Europe were, at least until the period of the Black Plague, of Muslim North African or Iberian origin (rather than sub-Saharan African, Greek, Slavic, or Tartar). Only in the latter half of the fifteenth century did this captive and slave trade begin to involve a significant number of black Africans, as Spanish and Portuguese explorers worked their way farther down the west coast of Africa.[23]

Reports about medieval captives abound in Christian and Muslim sources, especially along the military frontiers between Islamic and Christian lands. Among the many stories of captivity surrounding the Crusades, for example, perhaps the most famous figure is that of Reynald, an infamously aggressive aristocratic French crusader who fought against Saladin and who faced sixteen years of imprisonment in Aleppo.[24] Similarly, the thirteenth-century Armenian historian Kirakos Gandzaketsi, in recounting conflicts in the Caucasus involving Georgians, Armenians, Persians, and eventually Mongols, tells the story of Grigor, an Armenian nobleman captured in a local squabble and sold to the Persians, who executed him for blaspheming Islam.[25] It is possible to collect anecdotes of captivity from medieval writing from across the Mediterranean, elaborating the themes found in more abundant but more telegraphic archival sources and affirming the importance of captivity in the economic and religious activities of the region. Even narrowing the focus to the Iberian frontier, examples are numerous, including in polemical and apologetic texts, and it is not surprising that polemics such as those of al-Qaysī, ʿAbdallāh al-Asīr, and Ramon Llull grew out of the experience of captivity. Such examples show how captivity could function as a vehicle of intercultural contact between Islamic and Christian worlds of the Mediterranean, providing a shared circumstance that forced people from different groups to confront each other and often providing both parties in such a confrontation with knowledge and linguistic skills. Captivity was, to use Robert Burns's words about medieval Mediterranean piracy, "an interface between Islamic and Christian societies—a point of regular contact for all classes."[26]

A vivid portrayal from Iberian literature of the possible role of captivity in setting the stage for interfaith debate is found in the *Cantigas de Santa María* of Castilian king Alfonso X (reg. 1252–84), a collection of more than four hundred lyric songs in Galician Portuguese that portray miracles of the Virgin Mary in music and with abundant images. Among the eight or so songs to mention captivity at the hands of Muslims, two offer a depiction of cultural transfer resulting from the encounter.[27] Cantiga 265 tells the story of St. John Damascenus, Syrian monk and doctor in the Greek Church (d. ca. 754), who, according to hagiographic legend, was the son of a high-ranking official in the court of Caliph ʿAbd al-Malik in Damascus. Alfonso's version of the saint's legend, which alters some of the key details from the Greek versions, claims that John was captured by Muslim soldiers and sold as a captive "in Persia." Because of his devotion to Mary, however, "she caused him to be loved by his master so that he allowed him to enter at will into his house and to teach his son to read and write as he wrote, and they could scarcely recognize nor distinguish which of them wrote the better."[28] When John was returned to "Rome" (i.e., the Byzantine Empire), the son became envious and forged letters implicating John in treason against the emperor, who then had one of John's hands cut off, only to have it miraculously restored by Mary.[29] While the core of Alfonso's version of the story deals with Mary's miracle after John's unjust punishment by the emperor, the background and pretext of the miracle present a scene of captivity as cultural transfer: Forced into the house of a Muslim in Persia, John taught the Muslim's son to read and write in his own language. Although the Muslims are presented in a negative light, just as they are in most other Cantigas where they are mentioned, the trials of captivity are nevertheless depicted favorably as a vehicle for cultural transfer.

The contact and intellectual transfer resulting from captivity leads to theological disputation in one other song of Alfonso, Cantiga 192, which tells of a Muslim captive who belonged to a Christian.[30] The Christian loved Mary and "argued persistently for her sake every day, as I heard tell, with a Moor of Almería, who said that her power was worth nothing. This moor belonged to that man and was his captive and a confirmed disbeliever."[31] The man locked his slave in a cave—a kind of double confinement—where he wrestled with the Devil, biting one of his fingers off. The Virgin appeared and encouraged him to convert to Christianity, and he was baptized after being released from the cave—a kind of double liberation. In this case, captivity provides the grounds for interreligious disputation and debate, as is depicted in the initial panel illustrating this encounter in the El Escorial "Códice Rico" manuscript of the *Cantigas*, in which Christian and Muslim face each other with an index finger raised, indicating that each is attempting to make a point to the other.[32] Captivity also serves as the motive of the Muslim's conversion and liberation at the end of the poem.

Written only a few decades after the *Cantigas*, Ramon Llull's biography provides further evidence of this role of captivity as a vehicle of transfer. Decades before his own missionary trips to North Africa, Llull learned Arabic by purchasing a Muslim slave and studying with him for nine years. This example is significant for various reasons, including the fact that it portrays a transmission of knowledge from captive to master rather than master to captive, as we find in the *Cantigas*. In the *Vita coetanea* (*Contemporary*

FIG. 10.1. The "Códice rico" of the *Cantigas de Santa María*, El Escorial, MS T-I-1, fol. 252v.

Life), Llull emphasizes how essential this was to his mission by telling of his visions and lamenting that he "had none of the knowledge necessary for his undertaking" because he was "totally ignorant of the Arabic language."[33] Llull's language resonates with details from al-Qaysī's text, in which the author claims that he debated with a monk who had some knowledge of Islamic texts and traditions. This monk's knowledge was striking enough to prompt al-Qaysī to ask where he learned such things, but he then warns the Christian not to proceed with the debate because it would require knowledge of Arabic, which he did not yet have. Al-Qaysī also mentions his own knowledge of the local vernacular (probably Catalan), attesting to the two-way effects of captivity.[34] In the *Cantigas*, which offer a relatively accurate portrayal of medieval social classes and divisions, captivity is sometimes a circumstance that allows for people of different communities to come into direct contact with each other and a conduit that allows each side to learn the languages and cultural habits of the other. As Van Koningsveld has argued, "There is reason to suppose that Muslim prisoners who were thoroughly grounded in theology were forced to play, as teachers, a very important part in the earliest study of Arabic and Islam in Christian Western Europe during the late Middle Ages."[35]

This understanding of captivity as a fortuitous circumstance that allowed for the transfer or discovery of knowledge as well as the opportunity for language learning is, however, only part of the significance of imprisonment in the history of polemical literature. While the exchanges facilitated by captivity allowed for the transfer of knowledge in both directions between captive and captor, this was, for the latter, always also a situation of violence and bondage imposed on him against his will. Thus beyond the questions of circumstance and the transfer of knowledge, captivity was often a source of anger and ill will, a bitter or difficult experience that could precipitate the polemical encounter itself. Llull's nine years of Arabic study with his slave in fact ended with a polemical "encounter" of a very concrete nature. When his Muslim captive one day "blasphemed the name of Christ," Llull, "impelled by a great zeal for the faith, hit the Saracen on the mouth, on the forehead, and on the face. As a result, the Saracen became extremely embittered, and began plotting the death of this master."[36] One might imagine that if the slave had had the opportunity and education, he could have channeled his blasphemy into a carefully worded polemical treatise against Christianity resembling the work of al-Qaysī.

Llull was forced by this conflict to confront the tension inherent in his employment of a captive for the augmentation of his own learning and edification. On the one hand, he was committed to disproving any possible arguments in favor of Islam, while on the other, the knowledge and ability to undertake this project—as he readily admitted—relied on his material support of and peaceful engagement with his Muslim slave. When the slave attacked Llull, he was torn between punishing and pardoning him: "For it seemed harsh to kill the person by whose teaching he now knew the language he had so wanted to learn, that is, Arabic; on the other hand, he was afraid to set him free or to keep him longer, knowing that from then on he would not cease plotting his death." When he found the slave "hanged himself with the rope with which he had been bound"—a description that might be taken as a figurative metaphor for the Muslim's defeat in theological debate—Llull "joyfully gave thanks to God not only for keeping his hands innocent of the death of this Saracen, but also for freeing him from that terrible perplexity concerning which he had just recently so anxiously asked Him for guidance."[37] It was the unwanted altercation with his own slave that led Llull to retreat to nearby Mount Randa, where God granted him his first vision of the *Art*, his system for argumentation and conversion that he would later work to implement in his missionary work in North Africa. In a double sense, Llull's entire polemical project is the product of captivity, for it gave him knowledge of languages and also created the circumstances that led to the development of his polemical method.

This scene is not the only example in Llull's work of real flesh-and-blood captivity leading to polemical attack and even physical violence and crusade. In Llull's story *Blaquerna* (*Blanquerna*), the title character, after he becomes a bishop, addresses his canons on the subject of lamentation. He tells them the story of a woman, whose husband was in captivity, who went begging and weeping in public, together with four small children, to raise the money for his ransom. While this passage has been used by historians to highlight the economic realities of captives, it is told in Llull's text as an allegorical lament over the fact that "in captivity are the places where he—the Lord—was conceived and where he was born and imprisoned, crucified and died, because they are in the power of the Muslims."[38] Llull's writing contains numerous similar references to captivity in both a real and a metaphorical sense. In his examples, we see the wide variety of meanings and functions that writers could assign to captivity in late medieval Iberia, using it as a vehicle of cultural transfer as well as a provocation to polemical disputation.

Llull was not the only one to cast the Crusades to recapture the Holy Land as a task like the redemption of captives. The outrage provoked by witnessing captivity, rather than simple curiosity or a real need to missionize or debate, might be seen as one of the primary motives provoking polemical encounters. In his letters on the Fall of Acre in 1291, Llull's contemporary, the Dominican Riccoldo da Monte di Croce (d. 1320), bemoaned the successes of Islam, which he contrasted with the pleasures of Baghdad. He begins his first letter by stating, "So it came to pass that I was in Baghdad, 'among the captives by the river of Chebar' [Ezekiel 1:1], the Tigris. This garden of delights in which I found myself enthralled me. . . . Yet I was saddened by the massacre and capture of the Christian people. I wept over the loss of Acre, seeing the Saracens joyous and prospering, the Christians squalid and consternated: little children, young girls, old people, whimpering, threatened to be led as captives and slaves into the remotest countries of the East."[39] Riccoldo's experience shows how his indignant response to the captivity of fellow Christians replaced his ambivalence over the splendors of the Islamic caliphate in Baghdad, pushing him into a career of polemical debate and attack. Riccoldo thus allegedly debated theology with Muslims during his subsequent years in Baghdad in the 1290s, and by 1300, he was back in Florence, where he finished his polemical attack against Islam, *Contra legem Sarracenorum* (Against the law of the Saracens). Not surprisingly, the polemical treatise begins with a direct reference to servitude, a quotation from Psalm 118: "How many are the days of your servant?"[40] A concrete experience witnessing the captivity of fellow Christians seems to have stoked his zeal and became a theme he would repeatedly evoke in his polemical argumentations.

While we can attribute Riccoldo's polemical motivation at least in part to his confrontation with the captivity of others, we find more polemics like Llull's and al-Qaysī's in which the personal experience of being a captive is named explicitly as the reason for writing. This association is common enough that it was even falsified or embellished. One of the polemics attributed to the name "Pedro Pascual" is a good example of the invention of a story of captivity as a framing device. Although the figure of Pedro Pascual was long considered to be that of a real Valencian bishop—a figure who, after being taken captive, wrote various works of theology and polemic and was beheaded as a martyr in Granada around 1300—recent research has cast his existence into doubt. According to the pioneering study by Jaume Riera i Sans, the name "Pedro Pascual" (or Petrus Paschasius) was falsely attributed by friars of the Mercedarian order in the seventeenth century to a real bishop of Jaen who died in Granada around 1300, to whom a host of anonymous works from the fifteenth century were also falsely attributed. Such falsifications were made beginning in 1629 in preparations for a campaign of canonization that culminated in 1670, when Pope Clement X declared Pedro a saint. After this moment, Pedro's life was embellished in a hagiographic biography, and the various works now attributed to him were published under his name.[41] Not surprisingly, given his alleged association with the Mercedarian order, which was dedicated to the redemption of captives, the *Disputa del Bispe de Jaen contra los jueus* (Dispute of the bishop of Jaen against the Jews) begins with an evocation of the circumstances of captivity allegedly suffered by the author. The first-person voice attributed to Pedro says,

> Since I was taken prisoner by the power of the king of Granada, I saw many Christians as captives, not knowing letters and unfamiliar with the faith of the Christians, every day one and another turning to the evil sect of the Moors. Seeing this, and with faith in God's help, I began to search the books of the Bible and all the Prophets that speak of the Incarnation and the Birth . . . and other things having to do with Jesus Christ. . . . Showing this to the Christians who were captives here, many Jews who were here came every day to urge and enjoin them to believe in the false sect of the Moors. When I criticized those who did and said this, that is, who did what the Jews did to the Christians (who believed them on these matters [about Islam]), a few tricky Jews, especially two [known] as rabbi Moses and rabbi Jacob Moses, knowing that I argued against the league of the Jews and Moors to maintain the Catholic faith, were moved by great ill will and malice to write works that they sent to me. In these, they made many different demands, not least that they wanted to dispute with me.[42]

While the content of the polemic that follows is unremarkable in its arguments or use of sources—formulaic anti-Jewish material based on standard biblical *testimonia*—this opening frame makes a unique and surprising claim: arguing with Jews about theology was motivated by the threat that they posed in leading innocent Christians to convert *to Islam*. The Jews are seen as being "in league" with the Muslims, who present a grave threat as captors. While such a scenario certainly strains credulity, it is not surprising to find it in a text made as a post hoc hagiography to shore up the legend of Pedro Pascual.[43] Because Jews themselves were never captors, and yet the figure of Pedro Pascual was associated with missionary work and martyrdom in Islamic Granada, the topos of captivity is adapted in a unique way to fit an anti-Jewish rather than an anti-Muslim argument.

Captivity as a Claim to Authority and Authenticity

Captivity as a vehicle of knowledge transfer and a provocation to polemical engagement can be seen in both Christian and Muslim texts, as the two examples of Llull and al-Qaysī show. At the same time, the mention of captivity seems to have signified different things in texts from the two traditions. In Christian texts like Llull's, captivity served as a guarantee of the authenticity of one's polemical arguments. Llull's claim to have been imprisoned for his polemical activity and to have debated theology while in prison is meant as more than an explanation of the circumstances under which his text was developed. It also serves as proof that his arguments had been tested in the real trenches of interreligious disputation, a fact that is highlighted in the later reception of the text in the sixteenth century, when the title page of the first printed edition of 1510 was decorated with a woodcut depicting Llull debating with his Muslim captors from behind bars. In this context, captivity is not merely a circumstance but also evidence of the authenticity of Llull's arguments.

A few decades after Llull wrote, this appeal to captivity as a sort of badge of knowledge or a proof of the authenticity of one's claims is even more apparent in the polemical treatises of the Dominican Alfonso Buenhombre (d. ca. 1353). What little is known of his life has been pieced together from a few surviving shreds of evidence including a document written by Pope Clement VI, dated January 5, 1344 (*nonis ianuarii*), in which Buenhombre was appointed "Bishop of Morocco."[44] Buenhombre was the author of various polemical texts, and he states specifically that they were the products of his imprisonment in North African jails. In the prologue to his *Historia Ioseph* (History of Joseph), he claims to have written the text while in jail in Cairo:

> When I, your servant, brother Alfonso Buenhombre was sold by the Sultan of Babylon [i.e., Cairo], I was thoroughly deprived of human aid, stripped of books and many things. . . . When I was in the beginning of the aforesaid desolation, I asked the head jailer to lend me some little book or other, and God granted that I found favor in the man's eyes, and he brought me the *History of Joseph*, which coincides [in its details] with many of our calamities and miseries, above all the fact that we as explorers were captives and afflicted with the

FIG. 10.2. Ramon Llull, *Disputatio Raimundi christiani et Homeri saraceni* (1510), book cover. Biblioteca Nacional de España, Madrid, MS R/3108.

> fear of death, just like the brothers of Joseph, who sought food for their families [in Egypt], not to spy out the country. When I had read through this story, I translated it from Arabic to Latin.[45]

Curiously, although the author invokes a certain parallelism between his situation and that of Joseph, he identifies in his captivity not with Joseph himself but with Joseph's brothers, who had plotted to kill him and whom Joseph himself imprisons on accusations of spying when they come to Egypt seeking grain. In this detail, one wonders if the reasons for Buenhombre's real imprisonment were actually related to charges of espionage.

If this story of an Arabic book discovered in captivity and translated into Latin were to have appeared only here and in no other text, readers may not have called its credibility into question. However, Buenhombre's initial account is parallel to another tale of captivity that he tells in the prologue to another work, a captivity allegedly endured by the author a second time a few years after the first. Miraculously, this captivity, through a similar experience of receiving books from his jailer, leads the author to discover an Arabic polemic against Judaism and Islam, which he also alleges to have subsequently translated into Latin. In the opening to his *Disputatio Abu Talib* (Disputation of Abu Talib), a text made up of letters between a Muslim and a Jew who come to affirm, through friendly dialogue, the truths of the Christian faith, Buenhombre affirms, "I am brother Alfonso the Spaniard and this most ancient little book came by chance into my hands when I was in captivity of the Saracens in Morocco. It was formerly hidden for a long time by a Jew, and I now pass on a new translation made by me from Arabic into Latin."[46] He uses very similar language, mentioning a "very old text" coming "by chance" into his hands when introducing yet a third text, the *Epistola Rabbi Samualis* (Letter of Rabbi Samuel). The *Epistola*—which took the form of a letter written by a rabbi known as "Samuel the Moroccan" to another rabbi, "Isaac of Sijilmasa"—is certainly his best-known work, surviving in more than 250 manuscripts, translations into at least six languages, and abundant early printed copies, easily making it one the most popular and widely copied anti-Jewish polemics of the later Middle Ages in the Latin West.[47] The prologue states, "I send to you as a small gift this very old little book, which by chance came into my hands, having been previously hidden for a long time, in a new translation done by me from Arabic into Latin."[48]

Although, as Antoni Biosca i Bas and others have shown, Buenhombre's reliance on contemporary Latin authors such as Jiménez de Rada and Nicholas of Lyra belies Buenhombre's claims to have used an old Arabic text (as does his repeated use of the same account of a miraculous discovery), Buenhombre's corpus is most striking in its use of captivity as an authenticating device.[49] Like Llull and pseudo–Pedro Pascual, the story of captivity endows the polemic that follows with the authority Buenhombre allegedly gained from the hard experience of being a captive. As in Llull's texts, captivity is, as it were, worn like a badge of honor and a seal of proof. Unlike earlier models, however, Buenhombre's text also uses captivity to give the text a greater authenticity. By claiming his books were lost and hidden and came to him only in the hidden recesses of the captor's jail, Buenhombre suggests that the texts themselves, and not just their author, were in a kind of "captivity" in a foreign land. By emphasizing the antiquity of the texts, he implies that they had languished "in captivity" for some time. By claiming that both texts were originally written in Arabic, he further suggests that this metaphorical captivity was not only physical but also linguistic. By presenting himself as the text's discoverer and translator rather than simply its author, Buenhombre casts himself as both captive and redeemer, at once discovering the text through his own captivity and also freeing the text from its own "captivity" to its old and foreign state by copying and translating it into a "new" and familiar Latin.[50]

The Christian Topos of Captivity

The evidence of forging—or at least fudging—stories of captivity, as we see in the texts of pseudo–Pedro Pascual and Alfonso Buenhombre, underscores the power of captivity as a justification for writing, a symbolic power that derived from the fact that captivity was a traditional and long-running metaphor of Christian polemical writing—in particular, of Christian anti-Jewish polemic. Captives appear in many biblical narratives, from Abraham's freeing of Lot (Gen. 13–14), to Joseph's captivity in Egypt (Gen. 37–47), to Daniel's captivity in Babylon (Dan. 1, etc.), to the captivity of the Israelites themselves (Exod. 1–13; 2 Kings 25), whom the Lord repeatedly brings out of captivity (*sheboot*) and exile (*galut*) as part of his covenant with them. These biblical stories, on the one hand, provided a motif for Jewish writers to evoke their longing for liberation from the burden of diaspora—consider the frequent mention of captivity in figurative terms by Iberian Jewish poets[51]—but they also served as models for medieval Christian writers, who found in the history of redemption from captivity a metaphor for the liberation from sin and freedom from the "old Law" of the Jews.

The story of Abraham's freeing of Lot was of particular significance for medieval Christians, beginning in the patristic period. In Genesis 14, Abram's nephew Lot is taken captive by a local chieftain, Chedorlaomer, in a conflict between local kingdoms, and Abraham leads a raid to redeem him and his family. Not only is this the first story involving both war and captivity in the Bible; it is also the first act of redemption, literal or metaphorical.

Early Christian exegetes interpreted Abraham's freeing of Lot allegorically as the freeing of the soul from the captivity of sin and doubt. In the fourth century, Ambrose of Milan read this story as a tale of sin and salvation in which the local kings are like the five senses and Lot is the soul itself. He explains, "And so the various lords wish to hold us in slavery. The devil presses on, his servants work their wickedness, the passions and movements of the body stir restlessly like internal enemies within the house."[52] Ambrose's younger Iberian contemporary, Prudentius, saw fit to begin his *Psychomachia* with a meditation on Abraham's act of redemption: "It chanced that insolent kings overcame Lot and took him captive when he was dwelling in the wicked cities of Sodom and Gomorrah." This provides him with a rich paradigm for an allegorical meditation on the battle waged by the soul against sin: "This picture has been drawn beforehand to be a model for our life to trace out again with true measure, showing that we must watch in the armour of faithful hearts, and that every part of our body which is in captivity and enslaved to foul desire must be set free by gathering our forces at home."[53] Here, the tension between virtue and sin is expressed in terms of foreignness and domesticity. Being taken captive is likened to being carried off to the foreign land of sin, while redemption is seen as a defense against invasion "at home."

The Christian model of captivity included the images of Abraham as faithful redeemer from sin and Paul of Tarsus as one who suffered captivity for the faith. Already in the New Testament itself, captivity appears in a double guise as a metaphor for both sin and faith. Paul wrote of himself as a "prisoner" (Phil. 1:1)—various Pauline epistles, including Philippians and Philemon, were actually penned in captivity—as well as a "slave" or "servant" (*doulos*) of Jesus (Rom. 1:1), who redeemed him from being a "captive to the law of sin" (Rom. 7:23). Paul uses captivity to highlight the power of faith to triumph over sin, boasting, "We take every thought captive to obey Christ" (2 Cor. 10:4). In this way, captivity was represented through a set of two distinct metaphors: on the one hand, as the trammels of sin, and on the other, as the righteous suffering and martyrdom that one must endure to be redeemed from such sin. Such double metaphors—which all give voice to the inherent love of cosmic irony and the paradoxical inversion of order in the Christian message (the last are first, the weak are strong, the captive are free, the dead are risen)—allowed captivity to function in medieval Christian polemics alternatively as a characterization for infidelity as well as faith. Like the Israelites enduring the captivities of Babylon and Egypt, suffering captivity—whether real captivity at the hands of infidels or metaphorical captivity to sin and carnality—was proof of Christian fidelity.

At the same time, the long-standing medieval image of the hermeneutical Jew, who serves to testify to Christian truth by virtue of his own blindness and infidelity, was built on the language of captivity and redemption. Misreading is itself a kind of captivity to error, as Augustine insists in *De Doctrina Christiana*: "It is, then, a miserable kind of spiritual slavery to interpret signs as things, and to be incapable of raising the mind's eye above the physical creation so as to absorb the eternal light."[54] The Jews, as the prime example of "corporeal" readers too tied to the flesh and not able to lift their eyes to the spirit, are captives to their blindness. As keepers of the divine text of the Hebrew Bible, who are at the same time unable to understand its deeper meaning, the Jews are *capsarii nostri*, "our book-carrying servants"—that is, they are like "servants when they carry books of their lords to class and then wait outside for them."[55] There are many hundreds of references to *Iudaeorum captivitas* (the captivity of the Jews) in medieval Latin literature. Bernard of Clairvaux's famous statement about Jews as "letters" of the Law also reiterates the theme of their hermeneutical captivity: "The Jews are indeed for us the living letters of scripture, constantly representing the Lord's passion . . . dispersed and subjugated they are; under Christian princes they endure a harsh captivity."[56]

The motif of captivity is thus at the center of the medieval Christian doctrine of supersessionism. The "captivity of the Jews" is part of a divine process of salvation history that prefigures the liberation of the Christians. Augustine states, "We also must know first our captivity, then our liberation: we must know Babylon, in which we are captives, and Jerusalem, whither we long to return."[57] The hagiographic praise of the early saints' own real martyrial imprisonment was easily inverted into anti-Jewish condemnation of the Jews' captivity to sin and blindness, and medieval polemics against Jews alternate between these opposed readings. In the twelfth-century *Dialogue against the Jews* of Petrus Alfonsi, the Christian voice of Peter can assert paradoxically to his Jewish interlocutor and former self, Moses, that "Christ's death is the cause of your captivity."[58] He then adds, "This long captivity has occurred on account of the death of and malevolence toward Christ . . . you will not escape it until you correct the sin of your fathers, that is, until

FIG. 10.3. Alonso de Espina, *Fortalitium fidei*, copied by García de San Esteban de Gormaz (1464), parchment, 365 × 276 mm. El Burgo de Osma, Biblioteca y archivo capitular, MS 154.

you believe what they did not believe."[59] Abner of Burgos, known as Alfonso of Valladolid after his conversion around 1320, starts his Hebrew-language anti-Jewish polemic with a reference to the captivity of the Jews as the initial cause of his despair and conversion: "I saw the burden of the Jews, my people from whom I am descended, who are, in this long captivity, oppressed and broken and burdened heavily by taxes." But this appeal to a Jewish notion of captivity in the Diaspora, in the land of Edom, quickly morphs into a Christian polemical assault, in which "the Jews have been in this captivity for such a long time because of their folly and stupidity and for lack of a teacher of righteousness through whom they may know the truth."[60] Abner/Alfonso goes even further, not only attributing the captivity of the Jews to their sin in rejecting Jesus, but also claiming that God spares the Jews excessive suffering as a way to keep them in that captivity for the remainder of history: "The curse and everlasting captivity that was cast upon you is that you have tribulations with gentleness and without a great harshness. For if you had captivity with great harshness in such a way that you could not endure or that you were wiped out with one blow, in this way your dishonor, which was to be ongoing, would be ended."[61] A telling depiction of the ongoing figurative captivity of the Jews appears in oldest manuscript copy of the *Fortalitium fidei* (*Fortress of Faith*), of fifteenth-century polemicist Alonso de Espina (d. 1491).[62] The detailed image on the opening folio (1r) shows a towering castle being besieged from all sides by various enemies—Jews, Muslims, heretics, and devils—and depicts the Jews as clustered in a group, blindfolded and bound in the chains of captivity.[63]

The image of Jewish captivity to blindness and sin thus equates sight and insight—belief with freedom from the bondage of misunderstanding. Liberation is synonymous with exegesis itself, making Christian *allegoresis* a kind of liberation from literal reading, a freeing of the text from its historicism and its "carnality." The link between reading and liberation in Christian thought—which has been preserved in modern Western philosophies of interpretive reading, even to the present day[64]—is made in both a military and a sexual sense. On the one hand, reading as liberation from captivity appeals to an ancient metaphor for language translation as cultural conquest and *translatio imperii*, an image that persisted through the Middle Ages.[65] In exegetical terms, the link between liberation and reading is evident in the perennial image of Christian reading of pagan authors and the Old Testament as "gold carried out of Egypt" upon liberation from bondage. Augustine favored this metaphor over the more overtly sexual and militaristic connotations of the inverse image of exegesis as a taking captive of another. The reading-as-capture motif appears in image of the "fair captive" taken in battle, another metaphor for Christian reading of classical texts, which likened the text to a female war captive who, following Deuteronomy 21:11–13, must be shaved and cleaned before being taken as a wife.[66] This conflation of sexual conquest and cultural transfer is built on Horace's classical construction that compares the Roman imitation of the Greeks to a captor being seduced by his captive concubine: "Greece, the captive, made her savage victor captive, and brought the arts into rustic Latium."[67]

The combination of sexual and exegetical images to represent cultural contact and conquest is evident in the legend of La Romía, the name given to the fifteenth-century Christian girl from Castile, Isabel de Solís. She was taken captive in raids on the border with Granada and eventually ended up as concubine of the sultan, Mulay Hasan, who called her Zoraya and married her (making her stepmother of Boabdil, the "last Moor" of Nasrid Granada). Given her young age upon being taken captive, it is hard to say accurately if she converted to Islam or simply was raised in the faith from the age of reason, but later Christian chroniclers such as Hernando de Baeza (fl. late fifteenth century) depict her Islamic identity as a conversion and link it with what is perceived as her sexual treason. When, in 1492, she allegedly returned to a Christian life under the name Isabel de Solís, her "reversion" of faith is similarly linked to the just Christian reconquest of Nasrid Granada.[68]

While there are abundant examples of the real-world intersection of captivity and sexual conquest in archival references to interfaith concubinage, the explicit characterization of captivity in sexual terms is evident in various literary examples as well.[69] The best-known early modern example is certainly Cervantes's "Captive's Tale," inserted as a frame story within the narrative of *Don Quijote* (I.39–41), in which the captive's escape accompanies the conversion and marriage of Zoraida, against the dictates of her culture and the heartfelt pleas of her father.[70] This tale has numerous medieval parallels and precedents in stories of captives falling in love across the divisions of religious identity. The Old French *chantefable* of *Aucassin et Nicolette*, for example, tells of the Saracen girl Nicolette, a "captive maid . . . from far country" and "a little child when men sold her into captivity," who became the love fancy and wife of the noble knight Aucassin.[71] A similar text is *Floris and Blancheflor*, a twelfth-century tale surviving in numerous versions (*Floire et Blancheflor* in the French version; *Flores y Blancaflor* in the Castilian, among others) and telling the story of two children, the Muslim boy Floris born to the "Queen of al-Andalus" and the Christian girl Blancheflor, born to her captive lady-in-waiting. As they grow up, they fall in love, and Floris eventually converts to Christianity after they marry (against the wishes of the Muslim king). After the king's death, they rule al-Andalus as Christians, leading their subjects to conversion as well.[72] In such widely circulating narratives, captivity is a gateway to conversion and sexual conquest. Similar Romance examples abound, from the *Roman de la Rose* (*Romance of the Rose*) in the thirteenth century, to Juan Ruiz's *Libro de buen amor* (*Book of Good Love*) in the fourteenth, to Diego de San Pedro's *Cárcel de amor* (*Prison of Love*) in the fifteenth, among numerous others. These sources underscore the importance of considering the metaphor of captivity in gendered as well as religious terms. The opening words to the *Libro* most explicitly combine the parallel topoi of sexual desire as prison and Jewish perfidy as captivity: "Lord God, who once delivered from their long captivity / In Pharaoh's power, the Jews, a nation cursed by destiny, / and from the pit in Babylon, delivered Daniel free / Now from this evil prison deliver wretched me."[73]

The double representation of exegesis as both a liberation from captivity and a taking of captives reflects the double meaning of captivity itself in medieval Christian thought as both sin and salvation. Captivity appeared as a common topos in Christian polemical writing in part because it played this multivalent role at once as a physical circumstance that facilitated interreligious encounter, as a proof of struggle in such circumstance that legitimated the works that it generated, and as an operative metaphor of both sin and salvation that served to express the very essence of Christian polemical argumentation—a "taking captive" of Hebrew scripture, an arrogation of prophecy through a supersessionist *translatio scripturarum*. As Paul writes in Galatians (4:22, 4:31), "Abraham had two sons, one by a slave woman and the other by a free woman . . . brothers, we are children, not of the captive but of the free woman."

Conclusion: Metaphors of Captivity in Christian Sources

For Ramon Llull in the early fourteenth century, captivity was determined in every way by the themes identified here: Llull's polemics against Islam were facilitated by the knowledge he gained by purchasing a captive Muslim slave, and his arguments were tested, honed, and proven during his direct engagement with Muslim audiences while in captivity in North Africa. Llull, like many Christian authors, invokes captivity in two almost diametrically opposed ways. By invoking the symbolism of religious conversion, which implies both a turn from sin and a turn to truth, Llull implies that captivity symbolizes both the sin from which one must turn and also the commitment of fidelity that motivated and sustained that reforming turn.

The notions of captivity expressed by Llull's direct contemporary, the Muslim al-Qaysī, are notably different, despite shared circumstances and experiences. Although the common Mediterranean context of physical captivity did in fact serve as a real and recurrent circumstance of concrete knowledge transfer that often provoked interreligious encounters and facilitated language learning and cultural comparison between Muslims and Christians, the *meaning* of captivity for Christians was often determined—indeed, was "overdetermined"—by theological metaphors in a way it was not for Muslim writers. Thus while al-Qaysī makes explicit reference to his captivity as the circumstance, ordained by God, that led him to know Christian culture and language and provoked him to write against Christian belief, he does not represent that captivity as a symbol of either his sin or his spiritual redemption. Rather, he depicts it as an opportunity for reflection on God's mercy in providing relief from the misfortunes of life: "I longed for my death and that of my family. I wished that he would make us their ransom. Then I pondered over God's saying, 'And certainly We shall try you, till We know those among you who strive hard [. . .]' The lives of the Muslims are certainly a salutary gift to him who looks at them and a satisfactory lesson to him who meditates about them. So let him who will read this book of mine or to whom it will be read know that the bounties of God are a gift to him."[74] Polemical sources like al-Qaysī's are not unique. Van Koningsveld, who has explored other examples of Muslim polemics by captives in medieval Iberia such as al-Khazrajī (b. 1125) and Muḥammad al-Anṣārī al-Andalusī (fl. fifteenth century), remarks that "the example of the learned slave of Raymundus Lullus does not stand alone."[75] Nabil Matar has surveyed accounts of Muslim captives in the late sixteenth to early eighteenth centuries and offers the same assessment.[76]

Yet at the same time, as Matar notes about sources from the Maghreb, not only were Muslim captivity accounts sometimes more terse and less dramatic than Christian accounts; Muslim writers often

> did not have, like their European Christian counterparts, the theological imagery (and vast iconography) of a suffering Christ whose pain the captive was willing to emulate—and to describe to others. They did not have a theological legacy where torture, humiliation, and defeat/crucifixion were part of the victory over the wicked. Captivity was not a matter in and by itself, revealing personal tribulation leading to salvation and 'redemption' . . . but part of the larger narrative of the Muslim in his submission to Allah. Captivity was God's will, and every Muslim had to accept it and not make too much of it. It was an episode in Allah's mysterious destiny for His followers, and His followers had to submit without trying to turn themselves into heroes.[77]

According to Matar's characterization, captivity for Muslims was meaningful as an individual experience but was not described to prove the theological superiority of Muslim belief or the abrogation of Christian and Jewish Law in the revelation of the Qur'ān. While not all historians agree with Matar's differentiation of the "terseness" of Muslim and Christian representations of captivity, it is certain that captivity carried a notably different theological value in each tradition.[78]

While limitations of space and scope do not allow a lengthy consideration of medieval Muslim notions of captivity and redemption—such a project remains a major scholarly desideratum—this distinction between theological traditions might allow for a few tentative observations. Where al-Qaysī seems only to reflect on captivity in theological terms as a reflection of God's will, Christian accounts of captivity like Llull's—and one can say the same for contemporary conversion stories as well—cast individual experience as exemplary of larger trends in Christian experience and thus dramatize in miniature the narrative arc of Christian salvation history writ large. Christian notions of sin—like those evident in Llull's account—lead Christian writers to characterize imprisonment as a prefiguration and foreshadowing of future redemption, thus allowing captivity stories to express a core narrative of Christian salvation history. The particular characterization of captivity in such accounts is determined above all by particularly Christian notions of sin, salvation, and sacred history. Although the history of Muslim captivity remains to be studied in greater detail, the picture of the Christian side given here can provide a preliminary framework for comparison. Given the particularity of the Christian representation of captivity in physical as well as figurative terms, historians should not approach captivity as a transhistorical reality comparable across historical periods and vast ideological boundaries. Rather, they must treat it, along with other related theological phenomena, as a culturally determined metaphor whose meaning varied considerably according to context and period.

Notes

This research was undertaken as part of the project "Legado de Sefarad. La producción material e intelectual del judaísmo sefardí bajomedieval. 2ª parte" (principal investigator: Javier del Barco, FFI2015-63700-P), supported by the "Proyecto excelencia I+D convocatoria 2015 del Ministerio de Economía y Competitividad del Gobierno de España." Earlier versions of this chapter were delivered at the Polemical Encounters conference in Madrid (2014), the University of Chicago (2014), and the University of Minnesota (2016). I am grateful to those who offered me helpful feedback at these presentations, especially to Nabil Matar for his questions and to Daniel Hershenzon for his comments on an earlier draft.

1. "Hinc Raimundus . . . transfretauit ad quandam terram saracenorum, quae uocatur Bugia. In cuius ciuitatis sollemni platea stans Raimundus, clamabat alta uoce, prorumpens in haec uerba: 'Lex christianorum est uera, sancta et Deo accepta; lex autem Saracenorum falsa et erronea. Et hoc sum paratus probare.'" Llull, *Opera Latina VIII*, 297. Translation in Llull, *Doctor Illuminatus*, 35.
2. "Cui episcopus dixit: 'Si ergo credis legem Christi esse ueram, legem uero Machometi falsam consideras, rationem necessariam, hoc probantem, adducas.' Erat enim episcopus ille famosus in philosophia." Llull, *Opera Latina VIII*, 297; Llull, *Doctor Illuminatus*, 35.
3. "Raimundus, quorundam suorum amicorum religiosorum deuictus instantia, narrauit scribique permisit ista." Llull, *Opera Latina VIII*, 272; Llull, *Doctor Illuminatus*, 24, and see also 10 for remarks on the identity of the monks.
4. "Raimundus christianus posuit in arabico praedictas rationes. Et facto libro misit ipsum ad episcopum Bugiae, rogando quod ipse et sui sapientes hunc librum uiderent et ei responderent. Sed post paucos dies episcopus praeccepit, quod praedictus christianus fuisset eiectus a terra Bugiae." Llull, *Opera Latina XXII*, 261. "The Christian Ramon put the aforesaid arguments down in Arabic. And the book being made, he sent it to the bishop of Bíjaïa, asking that he and his wise men look through this book and respond to him. But after a few days the bishop ordered that the aforesaid Christian [Ramon] be thrown out of the land of Bíjaïa" (translation mine). For an overview of these events and how they are reflected in the *Vita* and *Liber disputations Raimundi christiani et Homeri saraceni*, see Fidora and Rubio, *Raimundus Lullus*, 101–4.
5. "Raimundus iuit ad quandam cuitatem Saracenorum, cuius nomen est Bugia, in qua ipse praedicando et laudando sanctam fidem catholicam, in platea Saracenorum fuit captus, percussus, et in carcerem positus. Raimundo sic in carcere existente, ad eum quidam Saracenus litteratus, qui uocatur Homer, cum aliis Saracenis frequenter ueniebat, ad disputandum cum eo de fide ex parte praecepti episcopi Saracenorum, qui dicitur esse magnus litteratus, ipsis opinantibus Raimundum deducere ad fidem Mahometi. Dum sic diu disputauerunt inter se . . . Raimundus dixit, quod ambo facerent unum Librum de disputatione." Llull, *Opera Latina XXII*, 173.
6. The later reference to the experience in the *Vita* claims that the Muslim recommended not putting Llull on trial before other Muslims because "he will bring up arguments against our religion that we will find difficult or impossible to answer . . . they therefore changed him to a less severe prison," where he allegedly stayed for six months until he was expelled from the kingdom. On the resemblance of the arguments to those of Ibn Sīnā, see Daiber, "Raimundus Lullus," 157.
7. Algiers, Bibliothèque nationale d'Algérie (BNA), MS 1557, fols. 49–90. The most important *aljamiado* manuscript is Madrid, Biblioteca Nacional de España (BNE), MS 4944. For an overview and discussion of the *aljamiado* manuscripts, see Van Koningsveld and Wiegers, "Polemical Works," 186–88; Cardaillac, "Polémique anti-chrétienne"; García-Arenal, *Moriscos y cristianos*, 149–50; Thomas, "Al-Qaysī," 732–36; and Colominas Aparicio, "Disputa con los cristanos," 43–48. See also Colominas

Aparicio, "Religious Polemics," 78–79, 131–32.

8. "Wa-ramānī bayna ḥizb al-shayṭān fī dār al-kufr wa-l-ṭughyān akhdimu al-naṣārā al-isyān wa-l-qiṣṣīṣīn wa-l-ruhbān fī l-mujādalati wa-l-hawān." BNA, MS 1557, fol. 81. Van Koningsveld and Wiegers, "Polemical Works," 178n61 (my translation).
9. "Era sabidor de la meçkida de Azeytuna de Tūneç i fu.e kativo en lerida del reyno de aragon katalunia." BNE, MS 4994 fol. 59r–v, reproduced in Cardaillac, "Polémique anti-chrétienne," vol. 1. Al-Qaysī identifies himself by name twice in the Arabic manuscript, including at the end of a Zajal poem about the Aragonese siege of Naṣrid Algeciras and Almería in 1309–10. BNA, MS 1557, fol. 79. The poem was published and translated by Lévi-Provençal, "'Zaǧal' hispanique," with al-Qaysī's name on p. 392. For reference to the second mention of his name, see Van Koningsveld and Wiegers, "Polemical Works," 183.
10. BNA, MS 1557, fol. 87. See also BNE, MS 4944, fol. 59v, which speaks of "Abdulllahi el kativo," who was a "kativo en Francia."
11. Van Koningsveld and Wiegers suggest that this assistant may have been the same person who made the subsequent *aljamiado* version, a mysterious figure referred to as one "'Alī al-Gharīb," a name that likewise suggests a Muslim living in Christian lands "in the ghurba, viz. outside Dār al-Islām." Van Koningsveld and Wiegers, "Polemical Works," 192n104. The authors also suggest that 'Alī al-Gharīb may possibly have been the same person who assisted al-Qaysī in writing down his Arabic text (179). See also Colominas Aparicio, chapter 3 in this volume.
12. Al-Qaysī's text survives in one Arabic text and in various *aljamiado* copies, including one estimated to be from the early fourteenth century and others as late as the sixteenth, bringing the text to bear on the Christian conflicts with both Mudejares and Moriscos; Llull's work now survives in some eighteen manuscripts or fragments from the fourteenth to the seventeenth centuries as well as an early printed edition from 1510 (of which more than a dozen copies are extant). The 1510 edition was printed in Valencia, a center of Morisco-Christian encounters in the early sixteenth century, by Juan Jofre, who would print only five years later the anti-Morisco polemic of the ostensibly real convert Juan Andrés, *Confusión o confutación*.
13. Llull was in Montpellier and Lyon various times in 1305 and possibly in 1306. He was in Montpellier in May 1308 and again from October 1308 to April 1309 and in Paris by fall 1309. On Llull's itinerary of travels, see Llull, *Selected Works*, 1:45n167. Bonner's overview is reprinted in condensed form in Llull, *Doctor Illuminatus*, 1–44.
14. On al-Qaysī's characterization of his captivity, see his words in BNA, MS 1557, fols. 81–82; and Van Koningsveld and Wiegers, "Polemical Works," 177–78. On Llull's image of captivity, consider the scene when he is warned by the Muslim "bishop" that blaspheming Islam in public is grounds for death, and he replies, "Verus Christi seruus expertus fidei catholicae ueritatem mortis corporalis pericula timere non debet, ubi uitae spiritualis gratiam potest animabus infidelium adipisci." Llull, *Opera Latina XXII*, 297. See the translation in Llull, *Doctor Illuminatus*, 35: "The true servant of Christ who has experienced the truth of the Catholic faith should not fear the danger of physical death when he can gain the grace of spiritual life for the souls of unbelievers."
15. Pace the claim of Jarbel Rodríguez that "the two terms meant different things, even if the difference was a subtle one." See Rodríguez, *Captives and Their Saviors*, 38. For the classic historiographical distinction between the terms, see Verlinden, *L'esclavage dans l'Europe médiévale*, 2:999–1010. On the subsequent debate over the

terminology, see Fontenay, "Esclaves et/ou captifs," 15–24; Rotman, "Captif ou esclave?," 25–46; Meillassoux, "Esclaves, vénacles, captifs et serfs," 367–73; and the introduction to Ferrer Abárzuza, *Captius i senyors*, which cites these sources and provides data for the predominant use of the word *captive* before 1500. I also leave aside the question of hostageship, the exchange of prisoners as surety, on which see Kosto, *Hostages*, especially the discussion of terminology on 11–18.

16. Davis, "Counting European Slaves," 118. See also Davis, *Christian Slaves, Muslim Masters.*
17. Bono, "Slave Histories and Memories," 105. See also his longer studies, Bono, *Schiavi musulmani*; and Bono, *Schiavi.* See also Rotman, "Forms of Slavery," 263–78. For an overview of this scholarship, see Hershenzon, "Para que me saque," 11, 31n3.
18. Matar, *British Captives*, 9–14. I am grateful to Professor Matar for his comments to me on this question and on the general topic of this paper.
19. See Hershenzon, "Para que me saque"; and Hershenzon, "Political Economy of Ransom."
20. If one accepts the demographic estimates of Josiah C. Russell (which are, admittedly, no more than informed guesswork), the population of the regions bordering the Mediterranean around 1340 (before the Black Death) may be estimated to between 35 and 50 million people, of which a total captive population of 1.0–1.5 million would represent about 3 percent. See Russell, *Late Ancient and Medieval*, 148. Such a guess, although not precise or verifiable, is not out of sync with Braudel's estimate that the population of the Mediterranean region around 1600 was "60 or 70 million." See Braudel, *Mediterranean World*, 1:394–95.
21. Phillips, *Slavery in Medieval*, 15–17. González Jiménez, "Esclavos andaluces."
22. Rodríguez, *Captives and Their Saviors*, xv–xvi. See also Phillips, *Slavery in Medieval*, 19–20. On Mercedarians, see Brodman, *Ransoming Captives.*
23. See Austen, "Mediterranean Slave Trade."
24. On his captivity and release, see Hillenbrand, "Imprisonment of Reynald." On Christian captives in the context of the Crusades, see Friedman, *Encounter between Enemies.*
25. See the bibliography provided by Cowe, "Kirakos Ganjakec," 438–42.
26. Burns, "Piracy as an Islamic-Christian Interface."
27. Cantigas mentioning captivity include 83, 95, 158, 176, 192, 227, 265, 325, and 359.
28. "Pois cativou / de mouros, e levado foi en prijon . . . / a Perssia; e un mouro rico deu por el seu aver, e ficou servo sseu / . . . E ela o fez a seu sennor amar, / assi que o leixou entrar a baldon . . . / En ssa casa e amostrar a ller / a seu fill' e outrossi a escrever / com' el escrevia, que sol connocer / non podian nen fazer estremaçon . . . / Qual deles escrevia mais nin mellor." Alfonso X, *Cantigas de Santa María*, 3:19–20. Translation in Kulp-Hill, *Songs of Holy Mary*, 321.
29. The traditional legend tells the story differently. John's father, according to this legend, purchased a captive Christian from Italy named Cosmas to educate John. John later fell out of favor after criticizing Byzantine emperor Leo III (the Isaurian) for his iconoclasm, prompting the emperor to have a letter forged in John's hand criticizing the caliph. When the caliph subsequently had John's right hand cut off in punishment for the false crime, the Virgin Mary, in response to John's faith, had his hand restored and made sound again. For an overview of the legend of John and his restored hand, see Louth, *St. John Damascene*, 17–18.
30. On captives in the *Cantigas*, see Bagby, "Moslem in the Cantigas"; and O'Callaghan, *Alfonso X*, 91–93. On Cantiga 192 in particular, see Bagby, "Moslem in the Cantigas," 184–86.
31. "Muy gran porfia / por ela prendia / sempre cada dia / com oý dezir / con un d'Almaria / un mouro que dezia / que ren

non valia / o seu poder. / Aqueste mour' era / daquel om' e seu / cativo, e fera- / ment' era encreu; / e ja o quisera / de grad' e fezera / chrischão e dera- / lle de seu aver." Alfonso X, *Cantigas de Santa María*, 2:219. Translation in Kulp-Hill, *Songs of Holy Mary*, 229.

32. See El Escorial MS T-I-1, fol. 252v. Here the finger indicates the freedom to debate, denied the devil when he lost his finger but maintained by the man in the cave.
33. Llull, *Doctor Illuminatus*, 12–13. "Ad tantum negotium nullam se habere scientiam . . . cum ipse linguam arabicam, quae Saracenorum est propria, penitus ignoraret." Llull, *Opera Latina VIII*, 275.
34. Van Koningsveld and Wiegers, "Polemical Works," 180.
35. Van Koningsveld, "Muslims Slaves and Captives," 12. Hershenzon has similarly provided numerous examples of Christian captives learning Arabic from their Muslim masters.
36. Llull, *Doctor Illuminatus*, 16–17. "Saraenus ille . . . nomen Christi blasphemaret. Quod um reuersus cognouit Raimundus ab his, qui blasphemiam adiuerant, nimio fidei zelo motus percussit illum Saracenum in ore, fronte ac facie." Llull, *Opera Latina XXII*, 279.
37. Llull, *Doctor Illuminatus*, 17. "Severum namque uisum sibi fuit illum perimere quo docente sibi linguam multum optatam, scilicet arabicam, iam sciebat. Dimittere uero illum uel tenere diutius netuebat, sciens, quod ipse non cessaret ex tunc in mortem ipsius machinari." Llull, *Opera Latina XXII*, 279. "Invenit quod ipse fune quo ligatus fuit iugulauerat semet ipsu. Reddidit ergo Raimundus gratias Deo laetus, qui et a nece praedicti Saraceni seruauerat manus eius innoxias, et eum a perplexitate illa graui, pro qua paulo ante ipsum anxius exorauerat, liberauerat" (280). Llull's phrasing is similar to the common trope of "slaying you with your own sword," evident in Gregory of Tours and Petrus Alfonsi, among others. See Szpiech, *Conversion and Narrative*, 92.
38. "Qui es qui faça son poder en honrar son creador, recreador, benfactor, senyor de quant es? Aquest senyor es pus amable que no es lo marit de la dona; en catiu es lo loch on fo conçebut e nat a crucificat, cor sserrayns lo tenen en poder." Llull, *Blaquerna*, 318. For use of this passage to discuss the economics of captivity, see Rodríguez, *Captives and Their Saviors*, 149.
39. "Et factum est cum essem in Baldacto in medio captivoru iuxta fluvium Chobar (Ezek. I, 1) Tigris, et me ex una parte delectaret amenitas iridarii, in quo eram . . . et ex alia parte me urgeret ad tristiciam strages et captura populi christiani atque deiectio post flebilem captionem Accon, cum viderem Sarracenos letissimos atque florentes, christianos vero squalidos atque mente consternatos, cum puelle eorum et parvuli et sense cum rumoribus ad partes remotissimas orientis inter barbaras nations captive et sclavi minabantur gementes." See Röhricht, "Lettres de Ricoldo," 264; text corrected by Panella, "Presentatione." On the letters, see Shagrir, "Fall of Acre."
40. "Quot sunt dies serui tui?" Mérigoux, "L'ouvrage d'un frère," 60. For the most recent study of Riccoldo with full bibliography, see George-Tvrtković, *Christian Pilgrim*.
41. See Riera i Sans, "Invenció literària"; and the critical introduction by González Muñoz in Pseudo Pedro Pascual, *Sobre la se[c]ta mahometana*, 63–70. While we know from papal correspondence of Boniface VIII that Jaen did have a bishop named Pedro between 1296 and 1300 and that this figure was in fact taken captive by Muslims in Granada during pastoral work in Jaen in 1297 or 1298 and ransomed along with other Christians for the sum of five thousand gold doblas, as González Muñoz argues, this could not be the same author of the text itself, which seems datable to the latter half of the fourteenth century. On the forgeries in support of a wave of petitions for canonizations of

Mercedarian figures in the seventeenth century, see Taylor, *Structures of Reform*, 407–11. See also Franco Llopis, chapter 8 in this volume.

42. Barcelona, Universitat de Barcelona BU, MS 75, fols. 2r–v:

    > Com yo religios, e bisbe per la gracia de deu de la ciutat de Jaen del Regne de Castella . . . com per mia ventura fos pres en poder del Rey de Granada, e vehent molts dels Christians esser catius, no sabents letres ne be dela ffe dels christians, tot die qui un qui altre se tornaven a la mala secta dels moros; e vehent yo aço, fiantme en al aiuda de Deu, misme a incercar los libres dela biblia, e de tots los profetes, qui parlat havian dela encarnacio e del naximent . . . e dela adoracio e de les altres coses de Iesu Christ. . . . Mostrant ho yo als christians, qui aqui eran presos, los quals per molts iuheus, que aqui eran, tot dia venian per ells amonestar e enclinar a creura la falsa secta dels moros. E yo reptant aquells de ço que fahian e dehian, ço es los iuheus als christians, qui daço los crehien, alguns suptils iuheus, specialment dos assi anomanats, primerament Moxi rabbi e Jacobi Moxi rabbi, saben que yo contradehia ala lig dels iuheus e dels moros, e aço per mantenir la fe christiana catholica, moguts de gran fellonia e malicia, feren scrits, e aquells trameteren a mi; en los quals scrits havia moltes e diverses demandes, e no res menys a mi e devant mi volgueran disputer.

    See also the faulty printed edition in Pascual, *Obras de S. Pedro*, 2:1.

43. About missionaries in Tunis, Vose says, "These missionary pastors were interested above all in ministering to the needs of Christian captives, mercenaries and merchants. Conversion of Muslims was evidently less of a concern." See Vose, *Dominicans, Muslims and Jews*, 208.

44. For the text, see Archivo Segreto Vaticano, Clementis VI Registra, #157, ep. 171 (fol. 37); and Registra Avenionensia 74, fols. 507v–508, which has been printed in López, *Memoria histórica*, 57–58; and again in Beltrán de Heredia, *Bulario de la universidad*, 1:354–55. See also Eubel, *Hierarchia Catholica*, 1:327; and Meerseeman, "Chronologie des voyages," 77, 96n58.

45. "Cum ego, seruus uester frater Alfonsus Bonihominis, Hispanus, essem per Soldanum Babylonie occasionibus quas scitis carceri mancipatus, satis humano auxilio destitutus, libris exspoliatus et rebus multis . . . supplicaui preposito carceris quod michi de libello aliquo mutuo prouideret, deditque michi Deus gratiam in conspectu eius, michique portauit historiam Ioseph, que in multis calamitati nostre et miserie congruebat, illud maxime quod nos tanquam exploratores fuimus capti et timore mortis afflicti, sicut fratres Ioseph, qui alimenta pro suis querebant, non patriam explorare. Hanc ergo historiam cum perlegissem, de Arabico transtuli in Latinum." Alphonsus Bonihominis, *Opera Omnia*, prologue to *Historia Ioseph*. I am very grateful to Professor Biosca for providing me with an advance copy of his edition.

46. "Ego frater Alfonsus, Hispanus, libellum hunc antiquissimum qui nuper casu deuenit ad manus meas cum essem apud Marrochium in captiuitate Sarracenorum, et fuerat prius multis temporibus ocultatus a Iudeis, noua translatione de Arabico in Latinum per me interpretatum uobis transmitto, legentibus maxime qui Arabicarum peritiam habetis litterarum, quia in eis ipsi Arabi Iudeis et Christianis sibi notis scribunt confidenter secreta sua que ab aliis uolunt occultari." Alphonsus Bonihominis, *Opera Omnia*, prologue to *Disputatio*.

47. On the manuscripts of the work, see the introduction by Biosca i Bas to his edition of the *Opera Omnia*. See also Robles, *Escritores dominicos*, 120–35; and Kaeppeli, *Scriptores Ordinis Praedicatorum*, 1:48–55,

4:22. On the popularity of the work, see also Limor, "Epistle of Rabbi Samuel," 184–85.

48. "Hunc libellum antiquissimum qui nuper casu deuenit ad manus meas, et fuerat in antea tot temporibus occultatus, noua translatione de Arabico in Latinum per me interpretatum paruum excennium transmitto uobis." Alphonsus Bonihominis, *Opera Omnia*, prologue to *Epistola*.

49. On Buenhombre's sources, see Biosca i Bas, "Anti-Muslim Discourse."

50. There are surviving accounts of Muslim rulers "rescuing" Arabic books held in Christian lands. See, for example, Van Koningsveld, "Andalusian-Arabic Manuscripts," 78–79.

51. Judah Ha-Levi's best-known poem provides a good example: "Libi be-mizraḥ ve-anokhi ve-sof maʿarav. / Eikh eṭʿamah et asher okhal ve-eikh yeʿerav / . . . be-ʿod / Ṣion be-ḥevel edom ve-ani be-khevel ʿarav?" (My heart is in the East and I am at the edge of the West. / How can I taste what I eat and how enjoy it / . . . while / Zion is in the realm of Edom and I am in Arabia's chains?). See Ḥaim Shirman, *Ha-Shirah*, 1:489 (#208.2). Also, Moses Ibn Ezra: "Eshmeʿah naʾakat ṣeviyah teyelil / miklu'ei edom u-maʾsar ʿaravim" (I hear the sigh and wail of the gazelle / from Edom's prison and jail of the Arabs). Shirman, *Ha-Shirah*, 1:405 (#163.2). For a study of the concept of exile in medieval Sephardic literature, see Alfonso, *Islamic Culture*, 52–82. For a more general study of *galut* in Jewish thought, see Baer, *Galut*.

52. "Diuersi ergo domini in seruitute nos uolunt tenere: incessit diabolus, infestant angeli eius, passions motusque corporis velut domestici atque intestine hostes inquietant." Ambrose of Milan, *Hexameron, De paradio*, 616. On this reading, see Smith, *Prudentius' Psychomachia*, 226.

53. "Loth inmorantem criminosis urbibus / Sodomae et Gomorrae, quas fouebat aduena/ pollens honore patruelis gloriae. / (l. 16–18) . . . haec ad figuram praenotata est linea, / quam nostra recto uita resculpat pede: / uigilandum in armis pectorum fidelium, / omnemque nostri portionem corporis, / quae capta foedae seruiat libidini, / domi coactis liberandam uiribus (l. 50–55)." Prudentius, *Aurelii Prudentii Clementis Carmina*, 167–69. Translation in the preface to Prudentius, *Daily Round*, 275–79.

54. "Ea demum est miserabilis animae servitus, signa pro rebus accipere et supra creaturam corpoream oculum mentis ad hauriendum aeternum lumen levare non posse." See Augustine of Hippo, *Doctrina Christiana*, 140–41.

55. "Nobis seruiunt iudaei, tamquam capsarii nostri sunt, studentibus nobis codices portant." (The Jews serve us as if they were our book-carrying servants, they carry books for us students.) *Enarrationes in Psalmos* 40:14 in Augustine of Hippo, *Enarrationes in Psalmos I–L*, 459. Also, "Quomodo serui, quando eunt in auditorium domini ipsorum, portant post illos codices et foris sedent, sic factus est filius maior filio minori." (Like servants, in the classroom of their lords, carry books behind them and then sit outside, thus an older child does for a younger). See Sermo 5.5 in Augustine of Hippo, *Sancti Aurelii Augustini*, 56. Both texts are translated in Cohen, *Living Letters*, 36n32. On Christian supersessionist typology, see Biddick, *Typological Imaginary*.

56. "Vivi quidam apices nobis sunt, repraesentantes iugiter Dominicam passionem . . . ita factum est dispersi sunt, depositi sunt; duram sustinent captivitatem sub principibus christianis." Epistola 363 in Bernard of Clairvaux, *Opera*, 8:316–17; quoted in Cohen, *Living Letters*, 238.

57. "Debemus et nos nosse prius captiuitatem nostram, deinde liberationem nostram; debemus nosse babyloniam, in qua captiui sumus, et ierusalem, ad cuius reditum suspiramus." See 64:1 in Augustine of Hippo, *Enarrationes in Psalmos I–L*, 823.

58. "Mors Christi captivitatis vobis causa exstitit." Pedro Alfonso, *Diálogo contra los judíos*, 59. Pedro Alfonso, *Dialogue against the Jews*, 107.
59. "Probatum indubitanter arbitror esse, tam longevam hanc captivitatem ob Christi mortem et malevolentiam evenisse. Concluso autem quod propter Christum sit captivitas facta, consequitur quod et vos de ea non exibitis, donec patrum vestrorum in vobis peccatum emendabitis, id est, quod non crediderunt, credetis." Pedro Alfonso, *Diálogo contra los judíos*, 69. Pedro Alfonso, *Dialogue against the Jews*, 119.
60. "Caté la premia de los judíos, el mi pueblo donde yo era, que sson en esta luenga captividad quexados e quebrantados e angustiados en ffecho de los pechos . . . los judíos están desde tan grand tienpo en esta captividad por su locura e por su nesçedad e por mengua de 'Mostrador de Justicia' donde conoscan la verdad." See Paris BNF, MS Esp. 43, fol. 12r, in Abner of Burgos / Alfonso of Valladolid, *Mostrador de Justicia*, 1:13.
61. "Esto es de la maldicion e captiuidad perdurable que ffue sse[n]tenciada ssobre uos en que ayades las tribulaciones con manssedunbre e ssin grand graueza. Ca ssi la ouiessedes con grand graueza, en guisa qu las non pudiessedes sofrir o que ffuessedes astragados en vna uegada, seria la uuestra desonrra otrossi acabada, que auie a ser perdurable." See Paris BNF, MS Esp. 43, fol. 336v, in Abner of Burgos / Alfonso of Valladolid, *Mostrador de Justicia*, 2:434.
62. MS Burgo de Osma 154.
63. For a discussion and reproduction of the Burgo de Osma image, see Rodríguez Barral, *Imagen del judío*, 53 (and cover). A color reproduction can be found in Alfonso et al., *Biblias de Sefarad*, 312–14.
64. In the "Task of the Translator," Walter Benjamin likens translation as a redemption and a liberation: "It is the task of the translator to release in his own language that pure language which is exiled among alien tongues, to liberate the language imprisoned in a work in his re-creation of that work." See Benjamin, *Illuminations*, 80. In "Ulysses Grammaphone," Jacques Derrida speaks of being "captive in a network of language, writing, knowledge, and *even narration*." See Derrida, *Acts of Literature*, 281. Fredric Jameson fittingly describes Derrida's discourse as itself "imprisoned": "His philosophic language feels its way gropingly along the walls of its own conceptual prison." See Jameson, *Prison-House of Language*, 186.
65. For example, early twelfth-century abbot Baudri de Bourgeuil writes, "Hostili preda ditetur lingua Latina, / graecus et hebreus serviat edomitus" (Let the Latin tongue be enriched by enemy booty. / Let the vanquished Greek and Hebrew serve). On this passage, see Szpiech, "Latin as a Language," 67.
66. For Augustine's comments on the "Gold out of Egypt" motif, see *On Christian Doctrine*, bk. 2, pt. 40, pp. 124–25. On the motif of the "beautiful captive," see Lubac, *Exégèse médiévale*, 1:290–304.
67. "Graecia capta ferum victorem cepit et artes / intulit agresti Latio" (Epistles, bk. 2, epistle 1, lines 156–57). See Horace, *Satires. Epistles*, 408–9. On this passage in the context of exegetical ideas, see Szpiech, "Latin as a Language," 69.
68. On Baeza and the sources and legend relating to Isabel de Solís, see López de Coca, "Making of Isabel de Solís," 225–41; and Szpiech, "Conversion as a Historiographical Problem," 24–38.
69. On sources in the Cairo Genizah mentioning converted captive concubines, see Perry, "Slave Women"; and see also Friedman, "Captivity and Ransom," 121–39; and Friedman, *Encounter between Enemies*, 162–86. On captive concubines in Iberia, see Barton, *Conquerors, Brides, and Concubines*, 99–108; and Nirenberg, *Communities of Violence*, 185–87.
70. Among the many studies of the captive's tale, see Garcés, "Zoraida's Veil."

71. See Kahf, *Western Representations.*
72. See Grieve, *Floire and Blancheflor,* 196–98.
73. "Señor Dios, que a los jodíos, pueblo de perdiçión, / sacaste de cabtivo, de poder de Far[aón], / a Danïel sacaste del poço de Babilón / saca a mí, coitado, d'esta mala presión." Edition and translation in Ruiz, *Book of True Love,* 20–21.
74. BNA, MS 1557, fols. 71–72, translated in Van Koningsveld and Wiegers, "Polemical Works," 175–76.
75. Van Koningsveld, "Muslims Slaves and Captives," 12.
76. Matar, *Europe through Christian Eyes,* 27. Matar surveys this material on pp. 27–71 and translates his sources in part 2 of his study. Matar also refers to numerous accounts of Ottomans held captive abroad. See the sources listed on p. 256n59 and selected essays in Dávid and Fodor, *Ransom Slavery.*
77. Matar, *Europe through Christian Eyes,* 40–41.
78. See Hershenzon, "Plaintes et menaces," 441–60. Hershenzon offers numerous examples of detailed and dramatic accounts of captivity by Muslims. He notes, "Cette séparation en deux objets distincts a pour conséquence l'occultation dommageable d'un grand nombre de liens que les réalités de la captivité tissaient entre le Maghreb et l'empire des Habsbourg" (442).

11

THE *LIBRE DE BONS AMONESTAMENTS* BY ʿABD ALLĀH AL-TARJUMĀN

A Guidebook for Old and New Christians

John Dagenais

Inquisition documents in Madrid from 1582 contain a report from the tribunal in Mallorca in the case of "censures of the little book in Catalan entitled 'Fray Anselmo Turmeda,' also known as ʿAbd Allāh."[1] The "little book" in question was a copy of the pamphlet known familiarly through the contraction of its title as the *Franselm* (or, in its Castilian translation, *Fransel*), familiar to generations of people in Catalonia, Valencia, and the Balearic Islands. Although it included a varying set of prayers and devotional items, its central piece was the text known today as the *Libre de bons amonestaments* (Book of good counsel), written by the Mallorcan apostate Franciscan friar Anselm Turmeda in 1398, when he was already living in Tunis as a Muslim, having converted and taken the name ʿAbd Allāh.[2]

The report of the Mallorcan deliberations of 1582 was sent "to the most illustrious Lords of his Council Major of the Holy General Inquisition," together with the Catalan text and a Castilian translation of it.[3] Among other things, the inquisitor Ebía de Oviedo is concerned because "many people on this Island, as evidenced in a variety of depositions found in the books of this Holy Office, stated and affirmed that in order to escape the gallows it was licit to swear a false oath, citing in evidence what it says in stanza 58 [of the poem by ʿAbd Allāh al-Tarjumān included there] that, in a case of necessity, one is permitted to lie."[4]

The Mallorcan Tribunal determines that the use of the title "Reverendo Padre" in the work's prologue should be expunged, as they find it inappropriate for an apostate.[5] The Tribunal also censures several of the more anticlerical stanzas of the book, including lines best known today through their adaptation to music by Raimon in the 1960s—namely, those dealing with the power of money and the particular attraction it holds for members of the religious establishment, including the pope.[6] But the Tribunal's strongest, and most unequivocal, condemnation is reserved for the lines in which the authority of ʿAbd Allāh al-Tarjumān undermines the very foundations of the Inquisition itself: people believe it is licit to swear a false oath to inquisitors because "Brother Anselm Turmeda, also known as ʿAbd Allāh," says it is permissible to do so. The inquisitors state quite simply, "This phrase is erroneous and heretical."[7]

All in all, these seem to be a rather implausible set of circumstances. Word is abroad among a significant group of individuals living on the island of Mallorca ("muchas personas en esta Isla") at the end of the sixteenth century that, on the authority of "Fray Anselmo Turmeda" (book and author), it is permissible to lie to the Inquisition if it will save one from execution. Not only this, but they have mentioned this "escape clause" in depositions before the Tribunal itself—that is to say, nearly two hundred years after its composition, ʿAbd Allāh's book is not only known (rather well-known, it seems) but treated as an authority significant enough to cite in standing up to one of the most powerful Iberian institutions of the day (one might even say thumbing one's nose at it in rather blatant fashion). Nor do the inquisitors themselves treat this matter as a trifle. They too recognize its threat to their procedures and censure portions (but not all) of it, sending a report of the proceedings on to their superiors in Madrid. Who were these *personas* and how did an apostate friar writing nearly two centuries before gain such renown among them and such authority? More importantly, what are the elements of this text that might make it particularly attractive to these *personas*? Can a closer reading of the text itself help us answer these questions? These are the issues that will be explored in the present chapter.

The writer ʿAbd Allāh ben ʿAbd Allāh al-Tarjumān (ʿAbd Allāh, son of ʿAbd Allāh, the Translator) is known to European literary history as Anselm Turmeda.[8] Archival evidence suggests that he was born in Mallorca around the year 1350 and was a member of the Franciscan order by the year 1375.[9]

Most of the rest of what we know about his life comes from his literary works and, most important, from the autobiography that opens his *Tuḥfat al-adīb fī al-radd ʿala ahl al-ṣalīb* (Gift of the lettered man, which contains the refutation of the followers of the cross; 1420).[10] According to this autobiography, Turmeda pursued university studies in Lleida in mainland Catalunya and in Bologna. In Bologna, it was revealed to him by an admired professor cleric that the Paraclete of the Gospel of John (cf. 14:15–27; 15:25–26; 16:7–8) was, in fact, Muḥammad and that Islam was the true faith. Around age thirty-five, then, Turmeda traveled to Tunisia and, after some months living in Tunis, made a public proclamation of his conversion to Islam. From this moment forward, he served the Hafsid sultans in various administrative positions—most importantly, as a translator for the sultan's customs office in the Port of Tunis. Hence the name by which he is known down to today in the Muslim world: ʿAbd Allāh al-Tarjumān (ʿAbd Allāh the Translator).[11] We do not know the precise date of his death, but it was sometime after 1423, when a letter was addressed to him by King Alphonse the Magnanimous of Aragon.[12]

One of the great puzzlements of ʿAbd Allāh's story is that, despite his very publically announced conversion before a group of Catalan merchants, he continued to write texts in his native Catalan on ostensibly Christian topics for a presumably Christian audience.[13] ʿAbd Allāh's *Libre de bons amonestaments,* included in the "little book" that caused such trouble for the Mallorcan inquisitors, is one of these texts. Following on this rather successful period of writings for Christian lands in his native Catalan, and toward the end of his life, ʿAbd Allāh wrote his first-known Arabic-language book, the *Tuḥfa.* This book recounts ʿAbd Allāh's conversion and argues forcefully against the very same Christian beliefs ʿAbd Allāh had seemed to promote in his Catalan works. This book remains, down to today, one of the most important reference texts for Muslims engaged in disputes with Christians regarding their respective faiths.[14]

The dual projection of Anselm / ʿAbd Allāh in Christian Aragon and Muslim North Africa has raised a number of quandaries for scholars: How do we explain the fact that ʿAbd Allāh writes works in the Catalan vernacular that seem to promote the most essential tenets of the Catholic faith even as he has publically rejected that faith and is living in Tunisia as a Muslim, with Muslim wives and a son named Mohammed?[15] How should we understand the role in the formation of the Catalan culture and identity of a Catalan writer, of unsurpassed popularity across four or five centuries, whose Arabic work declares, in the most in-your-face manner, that he was virulently opposed to Christianity?

I argue here that the binary rhetoric that dominated discourse in Anselm / ʿAbd Allāh's Mediterranean world must be understood as the very tool that allowed ʿAbd Allāh, and entire populations, to function in a much more complex world of continuous shuttling between those binaries. The debates over the *man* Anselm / ʿAbd Allāh's supposed duality and, for some, duplicity—especially the idea that his works must be either of the purest Christian inspiration or cynical manipulations—have had the unfortunate side effect of depriving ʿAbd Allāh's *work* of the most basic close readings that might situate them, and his person, more concretely in his world. In closer reading, in tandem with the apparently simple—even childish—surface of his texts, we discover a complex imagined (and, if the Inquisition document cited above is to be believed, real) set of readers. This group of readers cycled between, and sought to function beyond, the binaries that were the rhetorical—though not always the social—structure of the world they lived in. I propose to begin such a reading here using ʿAbd Allāh's *Bon amonestaments*, the core of the "little book" submitted to the inquisitorial authorities in 1582, as our primary text.

The *Bons amonestaments* was written by ʿAbd Allāh al-Tarjumān in Tunis 1398, more than a decade after his conversion to Islam. It is a book of ostensibly Christian teachings written in a highly memorable verse form.[16] In addition to religious instruction, the book is full of practical advice about money, women, the value of chastity, the love of one's home, and how to get along in a complex world. The nucleus of the poem is a translation of a thirteenth-century Italian text, the *Dottrina dello schiavo di Bari*, which chiefly offers practical rather than religious proverbs. It seems quite possible that ʿAbd Allāh encountered this text during his time as a student in Italy, and it is certainly possible that he began his Catalan version there before his journey to Tunis and his conversion to Islam.[17] But ʿAbd Allāh adapted the Italian text in significant ways, adding to it a satirical element and bits of religious teaching not present in the Italian original.

Paradoxically, perhaps, it came to form the heart of one of the most-published and most-read medieval pamphlet books in any vernacular language in the history of Western European letters. This book, fondly known as the *Franselm* or *Fransel*, was printed dozens of times, in both Catalan and Castilian, over the course of five hundred years. The conservative bishop Josep Torras i Bages famously said in 1892 that the *Franselm* "for centuries was like the fifth Evangelist of the Catalan people."[18] It is hard to think of any other medieval vernacular text that has such uninterrupted popularity or has had so great an influence at the most intimate levels of a culture—in this case, Catalan, Valencian, and Balearic cultures—over such a long period of time.

Nine fifteenth- and sixteenth-century manuscripts have survived, and it is found already in an inventory of *printed* books purchased by Gaspar Mir and Antoni Vernet in Barcelona on March 28, 1498.[19] The most interesting datum in the inventory, beyond the fact that it shows that ʿAbd Allāh's text was published as an incunable, is that it shows that by 1498, the book already bears the title by which it will be known to Catalan and Valencian schoolchildren for the next half millennium: *Franselm.* We cannot begin to understand why individuals knew and cited ʿAbd Allāh's *Bons amonestaments* to the Mallorcan Tribunal until we understand the phenomenon of the *Franselm.*

The *Franselm* is a pamphlet book generally containing the text of Anselm / ʿAbd Allāh's *Bons amonestaments*, together with a series of prayers to St. Michael, to the guardian angel, and to Saints Roque and Sebastian and often including the prophecy of the Sybil and a morning prayer. Henceforth, I use *Franselm* to refer to this printed pamphlet collection popularly attributed in its entirety to "Fray Anselm Turmeda also known as ʿAbd Allāh."[20] I use *Bons amonestaments* to refer to the original Catalan poem, written by ʿAbd Allāh in 1398, which forms the core of the *Franselm* collection.

Martí de Riquer offers a good starting point for appreciating the importance of the *Franselm* in Catalan culture across four centuries: "Strange as it may seem, the *Libre de bons amonestaments* was, until the beginning of the nineteenth century, the basic primer that was placed into the hands of Catalan children right after the catechism and copies [of the *Franselm*] are still being found in forgotten corners of farmhouses. . . . The fact that at least twelve generations of Catalans, principally in the countryside, learned to read and to think using such a disconcerting text is a phenomenon which might be of interest to sociologists."[21] Riquer is not the only literary historian to find this simple, extraordinarily popular school text "disconcerting," of course, and his suggestion that it "might be of interest to sociologists" is perhaps his way of saying that it is of scant interest as literature.

But we can go beyond Riquer in demonstrating the significance of the *Franselm* in many of the former lands of the Crown of Aragon right up until the beginning of the past century—that is, well beyond the "beginning of the nineteenth century" that Riquer takes as the limit of its influence. It would, in fact, be difficult to overestimate the importance of ʿAbd Allāh's book in the fifteenth through the end of the nineteenth centuries in Catalonia and Valencia. It seems likely that nearly everyone exposed to the most rudimentary education knew what a *Franselm* was: it was probably among the very first books they had read (or had read to them). We can probably go beyond this to say that in sixteenth- through eighteenth-century Catalonia and Valencia, if a person was able to read at all, he or she had probably read the poem by the apostate Franciscan friar found in the *Franselm.*[22] Even if this person were unable to read, he or she may well have learned and remembered some of its maxims orally.[23]

Until the very close of the nineteenth century, the cachet of the *Franselm* was being used by authors of new books to promote their own ideas. The galloping verse form of the *Bons amonestaments* was so embedded in the minds of Catalan readers and writers that just about any ideology or topic could be set to it with great effect, as in Jaume Collell's the *Nou Fra Anselm, llibre de bons consels, compost per un estudiant de theologia* (The new *Franselm*, a book of good advice, written by a student of theology; 1870) and, the next year, and by the same author, Jaume Collell, the *Novíssim Fra Anselm, católic monárquich; Llibret de bonas máximas compost per un hermitá* (The even newer *Franselm,* Catholic monarchic; A little book of good maxims, written by a hermit).[24] In Collell's versions, we find an ultraconservative defense of the monarchy and the Catholic Church on the eve of the founding of the First Spanish Republic. Still later, in a thoroughly (truly, exclusively) scatological pamphlet entitled *Colecció de Sentències y Concells per Anselm Ximenis* (Collection of proverbs and advice by Anselm Eiximenis) published in "Manresa" in 1899, we read in the author's prologue that the work will be "following the didactic and sententious *Franselmista* style, that commends itself to the memory so well, and using the clear and Catalan language used by Fra Francesc Eiximenis."[25] In other words, the title *Franselm* and the language and style of ʿAbd Allāh's *Bons amonestaments* are expected to be familiar to readers of Catalan living just over half a millennium after the latter's original composition in Tunis in 1398.

The dual identity of the author as both Brother Anselm and a Tunisian Muslim named ʿAbd Allāh was in no way a secret through all these generations (although the fact that Brother Anselm and ʿAbd Allāh al-Tarjumān, author of the anti-Christian *Tuḥfat*, were the same person was unrecognized until the early twentieth century). The double identity was announced, without any apparent sense of contradiction, in the prologues to the thousands of printed copies of the *Franselm*, beginning with the oldest manuscripts known: "In the name of God and of the glorious and humble Virgin Mary. A book composed in Tunis by the Reverend Father Brother Anselm Turmeda, also named ʿAbd Allāh, containing some good teachings, although he himself followed them poorly. However, thinking to earn some merit in providing them to the public, and so that God might let him end well, as his heart, with great hope, desires. Amen."[26]

For Riquer and other scholars, the problem boils down to this: How can Catalan culture—rural Catalan culture, especially—be considered "pure" when it bears this taint of Islam and this rather blatant stain of ʿAbd Allāh's apostasy and hypocrisy?[27] The persistence and cultural penetration of the *Franselm* to all levels and facets of Catalan society is our answer to the question of why individuals knew and cited ʿAbd Allāh's *Bons amonestaments* to the Mallorcan Tribunal.

The double acceptance of Anselm / ʿAbd Allāh in his own day, and in the five centuries following, stands in stark contrast to the efforts of modern literary scholars. A common reaction has been to defend the Christian orthodoxy of this text, despite its author's own rejection of the Christian faith and reference to himself as ʿAbd Allāh—literally, the slave of Allah. In 1959, the Catalan literary historian Manuel de Montoliu states, "Whatever else, the content of the *Book of Good Counsel* is of the most solid Christian morality."[28] More recently, Albert Hauf agrees with this assessment, calling ʿAbd Allāh's program in the text "essentially Christian" (*essencialment cristià*) even in some of its more questionable assertions, the most problematic of which is that it is permissible to lie "in cases of necessity."[29] Hauf goes on to say, "We can go on then, with perfect logic, to deduce that, if through several centuries in which everything passed through the rigid scrutiny of Inquisitorial censorship, one still chose precisely this little collection by the Mallorcan ex-Franciscan for the extraordinarily important task of moral and intellectual guidance, it was because those responsible for education, that is, the Church and civil authorities, agreed in accepting its doctrinal, religious, ethical, and pragmatic underpinnings, which they considered essential for an obedient acceptance of the established order."[30]

But Hauf's confidence in this circumstantial evidence seems misplaced, in this instance, and Riquer's discomfort fully justified by the difficulties that emerge in quite dramatic fashion in 'Abd Allāh's native Mallorca in 1582. The Inquisition document from 1582 allows us to begin to imagine a more nuanced approach to these issues. This evidence of additional readings that were neither "essentially Christian" nor "essentially un-Christian" but were what we might call today "oppositional" is highly suggestive, and it is the basis for the remainder of this study.

The incidents in Mallorca in 1582 suggest that at least some of those who felt empowered to lie to the Inquisition by 'Abd Allāh's text were in a situation similar to 'Abd Allāh's own: they were living between two religions. It is clear also that in 'Abd Allāh's book, they found materials that helped them negotiate this difficult situation. Over the centuries, the individuals who read the *Bons amonestaments* in this way in the Iberian Peninsula may have been numerous. Indeed, even if we agree with Hauf that the *Bons amonestaments* was *essencialment cristià*, this does not rule out the possibility that, in those centuries when the *Franselm* was at the height of its popularity, many of its *readers* were not. Rather, they were Catalans, Valencians, and Mallorcans—whether "Old Christians" or converts—who were trying to negotiate that very difficult world in which their "Christian essence" was under continual scrutiny by their neighbors and by the Inquisition. The Inquisition document I have cited is a rare but incontrovertible piece of evidence for just such a reading. And it is this document that has led me to return to the *Bons amonestaments*, often tossed off by literary scholars as a piece of youthful drivel—and a largely plagiarized one, to boot—to read it through a new lens and to investigate to what extent the text itself, not just the circumstances of its reading, justify such an interpretation.

We are dealing with two moments, then. The later moment is the 1582 report of the Mallorcan Inquisition that serves to establish the existence of this "oppositional" *readership* of the *Bons amonestaments*. We can be confident that this was, indeed, a genuine issue in Mallorca in the late sixteenth century: Inquisition records show that between 1579 and 1582, no fewer than eight individuals—mostly Muslim slaves, but one of them a *christiana nueva*—were "reconciled" after being accused as "Muslim apostates." More severe penalties were reserved for Jayme Torrello, a Turk and a freed slave, who was *relajado* (that is to say, executed) on June 4, 1582, "for being a Mohammedan apostate" (*por apóstata Mahometano*). Josep Gener, "native and resident of the island of Menorca" (*natural y Vecino de la Isla de Menorca*), was also accused as an *apóstata Mahometano* but had to be *relajado en estatua* (executed in effigy), presumably because he had fled, on November 26, 1584.[31]

Perhaps the individuals mentioned in the 1582 report had found in the book by the Mallorcan ex-friar materials that they hoped might help them find their way through a difficult, even life-threatening, situation. And this also suggests, given the wide distribution of the *Franselm* in both Catalan and Castilian across more than four hundred years, that this particular use of the *Bons amonestaments* by ʿAbd Allāh was not limited to a small group of troublesome Mallorcans at the end of the sixteenth century. Further archival research may find additional instances in which this type of reading came to the attention of authorities in the centuries of the *Franselm*'s popularity. For now, I want to focus on the earlier moment—the moment of the original composition of the text by ʿAbd Allāh al-Tarjumān. Was such a reading also a part of the *authorial* intention for his text?

We should remember, first of all, that ʿAbd Allāh wrote his book of advice in 1398, just a few years after the explosion of violence against religious minorities, especially Jews, that took place throughout the Iberian Peninsula, including Mallorca, in 1391. This violence, with its subsequent forced conversions, created a rather complex situation in which the binary opposition between Christian and Jew or Christian and Muslim lost its precision. The new situation meant that there were many individuals who were, like ʿAbd Allāh himself, perhaps, in varying proportions and, according to this binary rhetoric, not only Christians but also Muslims or not only Christians but also Jews.

That the difficult situation of those who had been baptized by force is a genuine concern to ʿAbd Allāh is demonstrated in the prophecies he wrote in Catalan around 1405–7, prophecies that seem to have circulated widely in Christian Iberia. The first is known as "Les prometences" (The vows). This prophecy was written slightly more than a decade after the events of 1391 and seven to nine years after the composition of ʿAbd Allāh's *Bons amonestaments*.

ʿAbd Allāh prophesies, "The Moorish people, following that day, will be forced to undergo baptism, from which a great schism will certainly be born."[32] And Anselm / ʿAbd Allāh also foretells a solution to the problem: "Following such a spectacle [that of forced baptisms], a Friar Minor will go on an embassy to the great Holy Father on account of the outrage committed on the Moorish people because of baptism given by force, and once the just case is stated, without hesitation, there will be the response that, by the imposition of such a sophism such baptisms are without legitimacy."[33] It is certainly possible that ʿAbd Allāh was proposing himself, despite his conversion to Islam, as the "Friar Minor" who would undertake this mission to the Christian pope. But more importantly, these lines suggest, despite their pose as prophesying future events, a quite explicit protest by the Muslim apostate friar ʿAbd Allāh against recent events of forced baptism in his native lands. They show us an ʿAbd Allāh deeply engaged, from his North African port, in the plight of his coreligionists in these lands who had undergone the trauma of forced conversion and the scrutiny of the Aragonese inquisitorial authorities.[34] The ʿAbd Allāh who emerges is far more sympathetic than the cynical trickster that Riquer and others have constructed.[35]

When we turn to examine the *Bons amonestaments* carefully, we find that there are several stanzas that invite just such an interpretation. These stanzas remain subject, quite naturally, to an "essentially Christian" reading but also open up to another sort of reading, one with a particular message for recent forced converts (and, indeed, to any Christian brought before authorities and questioned about his or her faith). I limit my comments to those stanzas of the *Bons amonestaments* that we can be reasonably certain were original with ʿAbd Allāh himself rather than translations from his source text in the *Dottrina dello schiavo di Bari*. I start with two stanzas appearing toward the middle of the text that, for me, suggest a clearly inquisitorial (in the general sense) context for the poem, a context that seems to go well beyond that of a series of quasi-catechistic questions posed by a teacher to a schoolboy.

In stanza 63, the same stanza that caused such problems for the Inquisition in Mallorca (in their copy, it was stanza 58), the statement that it is permissible to lie "in case of necessity" has quite naturally been the focus of scholarly (and, as we have seen, inquisitorial) inquiry. But it is extremely important to note the context in which this statement is made. The specific context, in fact, seems already to anticipate a situation in which one will have to decide between lying and telling the truth, not in a general way, but in the specific context of a response to a question: "Always tell the truth *about what you are asked* [de ço que seràs demanat], but in case of necessity, you can tell a falsehood."[36] We find ʿAbd Allāh's escape clause being used in precisely such an inquisitional context in 1582.

Near the end of the poem, at stanza 102, ʿAbd Allāh makes quite explicit his reasons for having written the book: "I have written this book so that, if you are asked about some deed/fact, you will be informed concerning what you should answer."[37] This echoes strongly the same inquisitorial situation found in stanza 63, suggesting a context that goes beyond that of various bits of practical and religious advice being offered to one in which one must know how to respond to specific questions. In ʿAbd Allāh's adaptation of the *Dottrina dello schiavo di Bari*, the text is no longer simply a collection of proverbs and advice in the style of the *Disticha Catonis*, for example—or rather, it is not such a collection exclusively—it is a book for people who will be asked about their acts, their lives, and above all, their beliefs. Brother Anselm's book will teach them how to answer.

When we return to look closely at the beginning of ʿAbd Allāh's book, we see that there are really two beginnings, both of them starting with the phrase *en nom de Déu*. The second occurrence of this phrase (stz. 6) clearly belongs to ʿAbd Allāh's translation of the Italian text. But the first occurrence constitutes a new "prologue," five stanzas in length (stzs. 1–5), that ʿAbd Allāh has added at some point to the beginning of his source text. I list these five new stanzas in their original Catalan, together with the earliest stanza that is based on the *Dottrina*, each followed by its English translation:

1. *En nom de Deu omnipotent*
 vull començar mon parlament.
 Qui apendre vol bon nodriment
 Aquest seguesca.

(In the name of omnipotent God, I wish to begin my discourse. The person who wishes to learn good advice should follow it.)

2. *Primer, pus sies batejat,*
 creuràs que en la divinitat,

és ésser en trinitat
de les persones.

(First, after you are baptized, you will believe that in the Divinity is a being in a trinity of persons.)

3. *e que Jesús, fill de Déu viu,*
és Déu e fill de Daviu;
aço és ver, e així ho diu
la Santa Escriptura.

(And that Jesus, Son of God, lives. He is God and son of David. This is true, so says the Holy Scripture.)

4. *Dels altres articles, fill meu,*
creuràs ço que la Esgleia creu;
e si no hi basta lo seny teu,
la fe t'hi basta.

(Regarding the other Articles [of Faith], my son, you will believe what the Church believes. And if your good sense is not enough [to understand it], faith is sufficient.)

5. *Tu, legidor, qui llegiràs*
lo meu llibre, si hi veuràs
algun bon dit, aquest pendràs,
e l'altre lleixa.

(You, reader who reads this book of mine: if you see a good saying there, take it, and leave the rest.)

6. *En nom de Déu deus començar*
totes les obres que vols far.
Entre les gents, lo poc parlar
és saviesa.

(You should begin all the things you wish to do in the name of God. In public, speaking little is wisdom.)[38]

The first five stanzas have no parallel in ʿAbd Allāh's Italian source text, and so they are of particular interest in understanding his own goals for his text. Their purpose, coming as they do at the very beginning, is to change the direction and the sense of ʿAbd Allāh's source text.

Among these stanzas, the second one is especially interesting: What is the sense of "creuràs que en la divinitat, / és ésser en trinitat / de les persones" (after you are baptized, you will believe that in the Divinity is a being in a trinity of persons)? It is, first of all, clear that ʿAbd Allāh is not referring to typical cases of the infant baptism here. This is a situation in which someone has been baptized after reaching the age of reason, baptized as a person who is capable of holding beliefs. In this stanza, ʿAbd Allāh clearly marks the change of belief that must occur at the moment of baptism (something that does not occur, I would argue, in the case of infant baptisms) and the necessity to believe immediately in the most central—and most difficult—of the Catholic Articles of Faith: the Holy Trinity.

But there is an even more telling way to understand the phrase "pus sies batejat" if we think of it as applicable to *conversos* of ʿAbd Allāh's native Mallorca. It could mean, quite simply, "After you have become a convert." This is, in fact, the only meaning for the word *batejat* as noun given in the *Diccionari català-valencià-balear*: "Saracen or Jew converted to Catholicism" (*Sarraí o jueu convers al catolicisme*).[39] Thus ʿAbd Allāh may be referring to the situation of converts far more directly than at first appears.

Still more interesting is the following stanza (number 3), which advances an apparently simple—but not, perhaps, very helpful—solution to the other Articles of Catholic faith: "Regarding the other Articles, my son, you will believe what the Church believes" (*Dels altres articles, fill meu, creuràs ço que la Esgleia creu*). This appears at first to be a rather superficial cop-out, an easy way for ʿAbd Allāh to get on with his poem without having to go through the whole list of the Articles of Faith. But these lines take on new depth when read in conjunction with Bernard Gui's *Practica Inquisitionis Heretice Pravitatis*, written earlier in ʿAbd Allāh's own century. Gui provides a sort of "mock interview" as a guide for other inquisitors who must deal with the clever evasions of Christian heretics—in this case, a "Waldensian." He begins, "It should be noted however that the Waldensians are very difficult to examine and question and in getting the truth out of them regarding their errors on account of the lies and verbal duplicities that they concoct so that they are not caught out."[40] Gui then shows how the heretic will answer certain questions in his attempts to deceive inquisitors: "Asked about the faith that he holds and believes, he will answer, 'I believe everything that a good Christian ought to believe.' . . . Asked who he thinks should be considered a good Christian, he will answer, 'The person who believes as the Holy Church teaches us to believe and hold to.'"[41] Beneath the apparent declaration of a simple and mechanical belief in whatever the Catholic Church teaches that ʿAbd Allāh advises, "creuràs ço que la Esgleia creu," then, we can read another text in which answers to the thorny questions of the Articles of Catholic faith can be supplied to those who might ask: "I believe exactly what the Church believes." ʿAbd Allāh's text supplies an answer to the question "What faith do you hold?" that might help someone escape the scrutiny of an inquisitor or at least one that might be advanced in such an attempt. Gui's text suggests a sort of "coaching" that may have gone on among heretical sects, and it is entirely possible that ʿAbd Allāh's *Bons amonestaments* was intended, in part, to serve as such coaching. That Bernard Gui had already anticipated this strategy does not rule out the possibility that those under scrutiny would try it—or that an inquisitor less adept than Gui might fall for it. And we should remember that all of this is set forth under ʿAbd Allāh's proviso that it is perfectly fine to lie "in cases of necessity."[42]

Several antimonastic stanzas precede and follow this one, stanzas also condemned two centuries later by the Mallorcan Inquisition. The general idea is that Church officials themselves—in their behavior, at least—are not reliable models for how a Christian is to behave. Simple imitation may get one into trouble.[43] Such stanzas were among those that most preoccupied the Mallorcan Tribunal of 1582. It feared that they might cause "scandal" and that believers would be less inclined to trust as they should in the clerical establishment.[44]

There is also one intriguing stanza in which language that will become an integral part of the language of the later Inquisition is found:

79. *De amic reconciliat,*
de vent que entre per forat,
e cell qui va simple con a gat:
d'aquests te garda.

(Beware of a reconciled friend, of a wind that blows in through a hole,
and of the person who goes around acting simple like a cat.)[45]

This could mean, simply, that you should not fully trust a friend with whom you have had an argument, even if you have reconciled your differences. But more specific meanings are possible. Though it may be that the word *reconciled* did not yet possess the precise meaning it was given in later Inquisition procedures, it is certain that the understanding of this word (*reconciliat*) as referring specifically to the "reconciliation" of errant Christians to Catholicism was alive in ʿAbd Allāh's day. The *DCVB* finds the following meaning already in Bernat Muntaner's *Chronicle* (1325–28): "To restore to the bosom of the Church" (*Restituir al gremi de l'Església*). We can read this stanza, then, as warning: "Beware of a friend who has been through the hands of authorities and been 'reconciled.'" This friend may not be trustworthy; in fact, he may be dangerous. The remaining advice in this stanza could be interpreted in similar ways: Who is listening through that hole in the wall where the wind comes in? That person who seems too simple and too transparent to be true probably is not.[46]

We have seen that stanza 63, on the permissibility of lying in cases of necessity, posed grave problems for the sixteenth-century Inquisition in Mallorca. This stanza is perhaps the one most clearly problematic from an orthodox Catholic perspective. But we should not forget, as Albert Hauf has argued, that similar ideas are expressed even in orthodox Christian texts.[47] My point is not that any of the passages I have mentioned are inherently, or "essentially," un-Christian; it is that they can be read in a variety of contexts and, often, used for purposes at odds with those of the Church and, especially, of the Inquisition—as we know this stanza, in fact, was nearly two hundred years later.

And finally, it is worthwhile to point out that the *Bons amonestaments* was not written primarily as a book for children, although it was certainly used by children, as well as adults, for many centuries. The frequent address to "mon fill" derives chiefly from the language of the *Dottrina*, ʿAbd Allāh's primary source. ʿAbd Allāh tells us very clearly who his anticipated audience is at the end of the book: "And I didn't write it in Latin [i.e., I wrote it in the vernacular], / So that the old man, the youth, / The foreigner and the cousin / Can understand it."[48] It is for the old *and* the young, the foreign and the familiar. And I think that both "foreigner" (*estranger*) and "cousin" (*cosí*) are potential objects of attention for the type of reading I am suggesting.

The cumulative evidence presented here suggests that beneath the apparently simple, even childish, surface of the text—good advice for good

Christian Catalan kids—there is another text that addresses itself to a group who needed the same advice on the practicalities of life in this world but who also needed special help with negotiating a dangerous, suspicious, and persecuting society. I am not arguing that the *Bons amonestaments* is monolithically a sort of crypto-guide for *judaizantes* or *moriscos,* though it is clear that it was used that way, probably by many readers (and not only by the group found in Mallorca at the end of the sixteenth century). There is significant reason to believe, I think, that the *Bons amonestaments* was written by a Muslim who had great sympathy for his coreligionists and others back in Iberia who were trapped by forced baptism into a world with new rules and constant suspicion. The *Bons amonestaments* is a messy text for messy times, times when even the most devout could find their beliefs questioned. It is broad advice for the world of late medieval Iberia—much of it traditional advice on how to get along in society that has nothing to do with religion per se, some of it delightful satire (and yet also a warning) against the clerical establishment.[49]

The idea that issues of crime and punishment back in Mallorca were on ʿAbd Allāh's mind at the time is supported by his own expressed fears of returning to Mallorca, found in another work written in the same year as the *Bons amonestaments* (1398): the *Cobles de la divisió del regne de Mallorca* (Verses on the divisions in the Kingdom of Mallorca). In that text, in response to an imagined invitation from an allegorical Queen Mallorca for "Frare Anselm" to return to his native island to help resolve the rampant social divisions there, ʿAbd Allāh declines the invitation based on two episodes he has witnessed "next to the moat at the Porta Plegadissa [Gate of the Drawbridge] beside a hedge I saw my companion burned; I saw another scorched alive that same year in Ibiza."[50] There is no clear indication that it was the specific crime of Muslim apostasy or of practicing Islam in secret for which ʿAbd Allāh's "companions" were punished, but whatever their crime may have been, it is clear that ʿAbd Allāh, a former Franciscan friar, fears he could be found guilty of a similar capital crime.[51]

Finally, it is extremely important to remember, in connection with the reading I am proposing, that this uncertain religious status is at the very heart of ʿAbd Allāh's own conversion to Islam. As he tells it in his *Tuḥfa,* it is under the influence of a Christian cleric and professor in Bologna—who is, it turns out, a crypto-Muslim—that ʿAbd Allāh makes his own decision to convert. This professor passes as a great Christian authority and confesses to the young Franciscan friar that he is afraid to come out publically as a Muslim: the Christians would kill him if they caught him; even if he managed to escape, he would lose all the wealth and privileges he enjoys as a famous Christian theologian; and at his advanced age, he would still be a stranger in a strange land even if he managed to make to Islamic territories. He concludes, "And so I remain in the religion of Jesus and in what he revealed."[52] This rather muddy message, not a flash of clear revelation, is at the origin of ʿAbd Allāh's own conversion to Islam, even as he tells it in his anti-Christian treatise. The importance of secretly practicing one religion while manifesting another is, in many senses, the foundational idea of Anselm Turmeda's new world as ʿAbd Allāh.

ʿAbd Allāh appears to transgress most of the boundaries modern readers of his life and works would set for him, and yet, in the world in which he lived, such boundaries, although they clearly existed, also seem to have been remarkably easy to cross. ʿAbd Allāh lived in a world that represented itself through a binary rhetoric: Christian-Muslim. And certainly, Anselm / ʿAbd Allāh lived his own life taking full advantage of this rhetoric. But we must not be taken in by this rhetoric in our efforts to understand ʿAbd Allāh. Such binary interpretations can only lead to the necessity to interpret ʿAbd Allāh's Catalan works either as expressions of a sincere Christian faith that this Muslim had to hide in his North African residence or as texts written by an author who was a hypocrite, a trickster, or a cynic.

Behind this apparently simple text lies a complex set of ideas and a very complex readership—a readership of good Christians, to be sure, but also another readership composed of individuals who found themselves living at various distances from Christianity, individuals who needed to learn the basics of Christianity very quickly and needed to learn how to survive as Christians in a hostile environment. In the end, it seems quite logical that a book like ʿAbd Allāh's might exist and that it would have been written by someone like ʿAbd Allāh. In fact, it is difficult to understand the existence of a book like this, written by a Muslim, without this explanation. This reading of the *Bons amonestaments* as a guide for New Christians, as well as old ones, solves many problems with our understanding of ʿAbd Allāh's so-called Christian works—their seeming simplicity in stating and restating basic doctrines of Christianity, their apparent contradictions such as advice about lying, their frequent anticlerical asides, and perhaps especially, their apparent contradiction with ʿAbd Allāh's new Muslim faith. I think we can come much closer to understanding ʿAbd Allāh and his Catalan works, all of them written when he had already been a Muslim for many years, when we realize that there were never just two terms: ʿAbd Allāh's world was composed of individuals and, indeed, an entire society for whom these binaries, however loudly they were proclaimed, disguised the much more complex situation of a population caught between them.

Notes

Research for this study was supported, in part, by funding from the UCLA Academic Senate Committee on Research and from the University of California Mediterranean Studies Multicampus Research Project. I wish to express my deepest gratitude to Sharon Kinoshita and Mercedes García-Arenal for their careful readings of earlier versions of this text and for their many helpful suggestions for its improvement. I would also like to thank Sergio La Porta, Chris Chism, and other participants in the UC Mediterranean Seminar meeting held at UC San Diego in April 2015 for their helpful comments as well as Roser Salicrú for her kind invitation to present an earlier version of this material at the Institució Milà i Fontanals in Barcelona in June 2014.

1. "Censuras del librillo en Catalán titulado, 'Fray Anselmo Turmeda'—y por otro nombre 'Abdalá'" (Madrid, Archivo Histórico Nacional [AHN], Inquisición, leg. 4436, no. 24, cover page). This document was first studied by Samsó Moya, "Turmediana," 82–84. He notes that it was discovered by Louis Cardaillac and was known to Mikel de Epalza (82n27). I wish to thank Bretton Rodríguez for his assistance in obtaining a copy of this document.
2. On ʿAbd Allāh in general, the most important monographic study remains that of Epalza, *Fray Anselm Turmeda.* See also Agustín Calvet's foundational study, *Fray Anselmo Turmeda.* Both Martí de Riquer's *Literatura catalana,* 2:265–308, and two new general histories of Catalan literature devote sections to ʿAbd Allāh. See Hauf, *Panorama crític,* 354–89; and Pedretti, "Anselm Turmeda." For an important reading of ʿAbd Allāh's oeuvre and useful general information on scholarship on him, see Pedretti, "Letture politiche." The title *Libre de bons amonestaments* is a modern one. See Pedretti, "Letture politiche," 26n1. See also, on ʿAbd Allāh in general and his prophecies in particular, Ryan, "Byzantium, Islam," 223–38.
3. "A los muy Ilustres Señores del Consejo Magor en la Santa General Inquisición." AHN, leg. 4436, no. 24, back cover leaf.
4. AHN, leg. 4436, no. 24, p. 1: "Que muchas personas en esta Isla segun consta por diversas depositiones que hay en los libros deste Santo officio dezian & affirmauan que para quitar a vno de la horca se podia hazer vn Juramento falço allegando lo que dize en la copla 58, que en caso de necessidad se puede dezir mentira." In citing this document, I add punctuation and expand abbreviations without indications.
5. AHN, leg. 4436, no. 24, p. 2. For a version of the text of this prologue, see below at n. 26.

6. Unless otherwise noted, I cited the text of the *Bons amonestaments* from ʿAbd Allāh al-Tarjumān, "Libre de bons amonestaments," in Olivar, *Bernat Metge*, 144–59. The stanzas on money criticized by the Tribunal are 67–68 (p. 154, ll. 5–12), 70 (p. 154, ll. 17–20), and 72 (p. 154, ll. 25–28). Raimon and Anselm Turmeda, "Elogi dels diners" (In praise of money), on *Clàssics i no*, track 9 (Picap, 2003).
7. "Sententia hec erronea est et heretica." AHN, leg. 4436, no. 24, p. 3.
8. I cite the version of the author's name found in the *Tuḥfa* (see following paragraph) as edited by Epalza, *Fray Anselmo Tumeda*, 192–93. So far as I know, ʿAbd Allāh does not himself use the *nisba al-mayurqi* that is found in some renderings of his name. Other descriptive titles that sometimes accompany his name (e.g., *al-Muhtadi*, "the well-directed," referring to his conversion to Islam) are later attributions (Mikel de Epalza, "Introducció," in Epalza and Riera i Gassiot, *Anselm Turmeda*, 8–9). In three of his Catalan works, he refers to himself as "Abdala" or "Abdela," among other spelling variants: *Libre de bons amonestaments* (prologue), the prophecies "Les prometences" (introduction), and "No crec pas" (final stanza). The name "ʿAbd Allāh" or "al-Qaid ʿAbd Allāh" appears frequently in documentary sources. See below, n. 27.
9. I follow the dating proposed by Epalza, *Fray Anselm Turmeda*, 11–13. Epalza favors 1350 as the date of birth but says it could be as late as 1354 or 1355.
10. On ʿAbd Allāh's conversion story and its relation to religious polemic, see García-Arenal, "Dreams and Reason" (translation of a portion of the autobiography, pp. 111–15); Szpiech, "Original Is Unfaithful"; and Szpiech, *Conversion and Narrative*, 231–45.
11. I refer to this author simply as "ʿAbd Allāh" or "ʿAbd Allāh al-Tarjumān." The practice of European literary scholars has, naturally, been to refer to him by his original Christian name or to use some compromise form such as Anselm / ʿAbd Allāh to reference his supposed dual authorial personality. But I think it is worthwhile, in referring to him, to recall—not dogmatically, but experimentally—that all of his known literary works, whether in Catalan or in Arabic, were written while he was living in Tunisia, as a Muslim, under the name "ʿAbd Allāh." "Frare Anselm Turmeda" (Brother Anselm) becomes a sort of the pseudo-autobiographical author/protagonist in his Catalan works, a sort of alter or quondam ego. See the aforementioned list of Catalan works in which he uses this name. "Brother Anselm" seems also to have been one of the identities he performed in the course of his duties for the Hafsid sultans, at least in their relations with the Crown of Aragon and its citizens. See below for some royal and other documents addressed to ʿAbd Allah that use both Christian and Arabic names. To complicate matters further, there are good documentary, grammatical, phonetical, and paleographic reasons to think that ʿAbd Allāh's given name may actually have been "Telm," the name that emerges in English as "Saint Elmo" (Epalza, "Introducció," 7). The Catalan definite article that proceeds this name in almost all of the Latin and Catalan documents pertaining to ʿAbd Allāh's life is *en*, yielding "En Telm." Epalza suggests that ʿAbd Allāh took on the more prestigious name "Anselm" as part of his religious persona, though it is unclear when he might have started using this name (I suggest it might be the name he adopted on becoming a Franciscan friar). ʿAbd Allāh's penchant for fluid personal names may have begun well before his conversion to Islam.
12. See n. 27 below.
13. His surviving Catalan works are *Libre de bons amonestaments*, 1398 (Catalan verse); *Cobles de la divisió del regne de Mallorques*, 1398 (Catalan verse); a series of prophecies (Catalan verse)—

"Les prometences," 1405–7;"En nom de l'essència," 1417–18; "Oh Babilònia, tu Barcelona" (date uncertain); "No crec pas" (date uncertain)—and *Disputation de l'asne*, 1417–18 (presumably chiefly in Catalan prose; the earliest textual evidence is found only in sixteenth- and seventeenth-century French translations—only fragments of the medieval Catalan version survive).

14. From the many, many sources one might use to demonstrate the continued popularity in the Muslim world, one in particular is quite telling it its own way: ʿAbd Allāh the Translator's story is deemed important enough for his life story, as told in the *Tuḥfa*, to be made into a rather interesting made-for-TV movie in Turkish in the early 90s: https://vimeo.com/16858533. One can also hear his life story told in English by Brother Abdur Raheem Green on Youtube: https://www.youtube.com/watch?v=lW1owzBmXjU.
15. For the plurality of wives, see the document cited in n. 27. For his son, see the *Tuḥfa* (Epalza, *Fray Anselm Turmeda*, 228–29).
16. See the 107 four-line stanzas in ʿAbd ʿAllāh al-Tarjumān, "Libre de bons amonestaments," in Olivar, *Bernat Metge*. The rhyme scheme is a a a b, c c c d, and so on, with the metric structure 08 08 08 04. The short final verse of each stanza allows for an epigrammatic, or ironic, punch while moving the reader quickly on to the next.
17. Calvet provides a side-by-side comparison of the *Bons amonestaments* (as edited by Aguiló i Fuster, *Cançoner de les obretes*) with the text published by Romagnoli, *Dottrina dello schiavo*. So far as I know, there is no modern critical edition of the *Dottrina*. The closest we have is Babudri, *Figura del rimatore*; but see Folena's review in "Duecento," 104–5. Babudri's study and tentative edition suggest that we might learn much about ʿAbd Allāh al-Tarjumān by investigating more closely the textual tradition of the specific version of the *Dottrina* that ʿAbd Allāh used as the basis for his translation, whether or not, as both Romagnoli and Babduri assert, the variants are scribal additions. In Babudri's "proposta d'un testo critico" (*Figura del rimatore*, pp. 163–80), it is clear from the variants he lists that ʿAbd Allāh uses a version quite similar to that found in Florence, Biblioteca Medicea Laurenziana, Plut. 43.27 (S. XV?), fols. 89v–91v, rather than the version Babudri edits as his critical text. A fuller investigation of the Laurenzian manuscript's provenance and of the textual tradition of the version of the *Dottrina* it contains might serve to shed more light on ʿAbd Allāh's years in Italy (or his time in Sicily or Tunisia, for that matter). Where and how could he have gained access to this specific version as opposed to other circulating versions of this text?
18. "Per sigles fou com lo cinquè evangelista de la catalana gent." Torras i Bages, *Tradició catalana*, 240. At the time Bishop Torras made this comment, we should note, it was not known that Anselm Turmeda had also authored an anti-Christian text under the name ʿAbd Allāh al-Tarjumān.
19. Madurell Marimón and Rubió y Balaguer, *Documentos para la historia*, 271–76 (#151, item 8). For the manuscripts and some printed editions, see Faulhaber, *PhiloBiblon*; in Avenoza, Soriano, and Beltran, *BITECA*, see texid 1960; and in Faulhaber, Gómez Moreno, and Salvador Miguel, *BETA*, see texid 4269.
20. See the full prologue, cited in n. 26 below.
21. Riquer, *Literatura catalana*, 2:280.
22. The Valencian Enlightenment figure Gregorio Mayáns y Siscar puts the *Franselm* on a par with Aesop's *Fables* in its importance to Spanish culture: "En efeto las Fabulas de Isopo se hicieron tan comunes en Grecia, que passò a ser proverbio aplicado a los necios, *que ni aun a Isopo avian leido:* como si digeramos en España: *No ha leido a Frai Anselmo de Turmeda.*" Mayáns y Siscar, "A

los letores [*sic*] de las Fabulas de Isopo," in *Aesopi Fabulae Latiné*, front matter. Later in that same century, Francisco Pérez Bayer describes with affection the use to which the *Franselm* was put by young students in his native Valencia: "Opusculum aliud metricum ab auctore nomine *Franselms* Valentinis vernaculè appellatum, saepiusque Valentiae editum: quo nostrates pueri postquam litteras nôrunt easque in syllabas iungere incipient, uti consuevêre." Antonio and Pérez Bayer, *Bibliotheca Hispana Vetus*, "Addendi," 2:363.

23. Aguiló i Fuster, in *Cançoner de les obretes*, comments on the oral knowledge of the *Franselm* at the end of the nineteenth century among rural folk: "Catalans y valencians durant mes de quatre segles, passades les 'Abeceroles,' aprenien de llegir en est moral poemet, que molts dels nostres pagesos encara saben de cor y tot hom alguns de sos adagis" (n.p.).
24. Published in Collell, *Nou Fra Anselm*; and Collell, *Novíssim Fra Anselm*. On Collell, see Requesens i Piquer, "Poesía política."
25. "Seguint el didáctic y sentenciós istil *franselmista*, que tan be s'encomana a la memoria, y usant un llenguatge clar i catalá còm ho feu en son temps Fra Francèsc Eiximènis." Eixemenis, *Colecció de sentencies*, v–vi. I offer one mild example of the tenor of this text: "Parlar clar, no es inmoral: / Tot ho anomèno còm cal: / Orinal, al l'orinal: / Mèrda a la mèrda" (2).
26. "En nom de deu sia: e dela gloriosa e humil verge Maria libre compost en Tuniç per lo Reuerent pare frare Encelm Turmeda: en altra manera Anomenat Abdalla de alguns bons ensenyamens: jatsia que ell mal los haja seguits Empero pensen hauer algun merit de diuulgar los ala gent. E per que deu lo deixe ben finar axi com lo seu cor ab gran esperança desija. Amen." From the many versions of this prologue, most with slight, though some with significant, variants, I use the version from the 1527 Barcelona edition as transcribed for *PhiloBiblon*, *BITECA*, manid 2347. It is similar to the one cited in the Inquisition document. This prologue, with its multiple ironies, appears already in the earliest manuscripts and is, it seems likely, by 'Abd Allāh himself.
27. Anselm / 'Abd Allāh's dual identity seems not to have troubled Christian authorities of his day in the least, any more than it seems to have caused major issues for most of those who published, taught, and learned to read through the *Bons amonestaments*. In documents relating to 'Abd Allāh during his lifetime, the name of "Brother Anselm Turmeda, also known as 'Abd Allāh," was an accepted part of his identity. Roger de Montcada, viceroy of Mallorca, mentions both names in the safe-conduct he issues to Anselm / 'Abd Allāh in 1402: "Guidamus et assecuramus vos fratrem Encelm Turmeda ordinis Sancti Francisci confessoris, oriundum jamdicti regni qui fidem sanctam catholicam instructu diabolico, immemor salutis eterne abnegastis, sectam pravam machometi assumendo, eamque, cum nomine abdella, approbando." Arxiu Històric del Regne de Mallorca, Lletres comunes, vol. 1442, no foliation; cited in Sans i Roselló, "Fra Anselm Turmeda," 405–6. In a letter of 1414, Ferdinand of Antequera, king of Aragon, refers to 'Abd Allāh's apostasy in a letter: "Brother Anselm Turmeda, a renegade, living in Tunis" (Fra Encelm renegado stant en Tuniz). Rubió i Balaguer, *Literatura catalana*, 1:358; Arxiu de la Corona d'Aragó [ACA], C, reg. 2407, fol. 33v. On December 8, 1421, Alphonse the Magnanimous, king of Aragon, drafts a letter to the "Firstborn Son of the King of Tunis." He has an additional copy sent to "Brother En Telm Turmeda, also known as al-Qaid Abdalla" (Frare entelm turmeda en altra manera apellat alcayt abdalla). Calvet, *Fray Anselmo*, facs. facing p. 152; ACA, R. 2672, fol. 110r. Two years later, the same king writes directly to "you, our beloved Bronther Entelm

Turmeda, alias al-Qaid ʿAbd Allāh" (vos dilectum nostrum ffratrem Entelmum Turmeda alias alcaydum Abd Alla). Calvet, *Fray Anselmo*, 41–43 and facs. facing p. 216; ACA, R. 2681, fol. 138v. The king invites ʿAbd Allāh to return "with your wives, sons and daughters, manservants and maidservants, Saracens and Christians" (cum uxoribus, filiis et filiabus, servitoribus et servitricibus serracenis et xpianis). Calvet, *Fray Anselmo*, 41.

28. Montoliu, *Eiximenis, Turmeda*, 83.
29. Hauf, *L'home que riu*, 50.
30. Hauf, 37.
31. Cortés i Cortés, Forteza Pinya, *Inquisición de Mallorca*, 150–51, 267.
32. "La gent morischa / pres tal jornada / sera forçada / prendra babtisme, / de que gran cisme / cert s'engenra." Al-Tarjumān, *Libre de bons amonestaments*, p. 100, ll. 650–55.
33. "Apres tal dança / un menor fraire / al gran sant paire / sera misatge / pel gran ultratge / fet al morisma, / ço per la crisma / per força dada, / e riçitada / la vera causa, / sense fer pausa, / haura resposta / que per l'amposta / de tal sofisme / lo dit babtisme / valor no aje." Al-Tarjumān, p. 101, ll. 690–705. The issue of the validity of such forced baptisms is crucial for it is having undergone the sacrament of baptism, which allows an individual to come under the jurisdiction of the Inquisition. If this baptism is ruled invalid, the individual is no longer a Christian and therefore, in theory, not subject to Inquisitorial investigation as an apostate or secret practitioner of Judaism or Islam. Samsó Moya's arguments and conclusions regarding this prophecy are similar to mine: "Creo que puede concluirse que esta profecía acerca de la conversión forzosa de los mudéjares de una ciudad de la Corona de Aragón puede muy bien estar inspirada en un acontecimiento real más o menos semejante: sabemos que hubo asaltos a varias morerías del reino de Valencia; la relación de fuerzas sociales que intervienen en la profecía, a favor o en contra del elemento musulmán, es perfectamente correcta" ("Turmediana," 71). Samsó Moya's study of this prophecy is quite valuable in providing context for the argument I am making here (67–71). Samsó Moya feels, however, that this prophecy is "el único caso en que Turmeda muestra, en su obra catalana, una manifiesta simpatía por los musulmanes" (67). In the present study, I seek to extend his conclusions about this prophecy to another work by ʿAbd Allāh, the *Bons amonestaments*, a case in which, I believe, the sympathy is there, though it may not be "manifest." For a full and recent study of this and other prophecies by ʿAbd Allāh, see Ryan, "Byzantium, Islam," 223–38, esp. 235–36.
34. The medieval Inquisition in the Crown of Aragon was, in general, a far less well-organized and consistent institution than the later Spanish Inquisition. It was also far less centralized, even within the Crown of Aragon. It developed out of the Inquisition established by Pope Gregory IX in 1231 and continued well into the fifteenth century. The Inquisition in Aragon functioned as did other European Inquisitions of the medieval period: "Dominicos y franciscanos, en calidad de legados pontificios, actúan de acuerdo con los príncipes, ateniéndose a una legislación conciliar universalmente establecida y a unas prácticas codificadas hasta en sus más mínimos detalles." "Inquisición," in Aldea Vaquero et al., *Diccionario de Historia Eclesiástica*, 2:1194–95. See also Lea, *History of the Inquisition*, 2:162–80; Vincke, *Zur Vorgeschichte*; and Fort i Cogul, *Catalunya i la inquisició*. See also now Vose, *Dominicans, Muslims and Jews*, 85–88, 165–91; and Tartakoff, *Between Christian and Jew*, 16–22. The level of activity of the inquisitions of the Crown varied widely, often according to the degree of zeal of the current inquisitor general. During significant stretches of ʿAbd Allāh's early life, that inquisitor was the hyperzealous

Nicholas Eymerich, whose *Directorium inquisitorum* became the manual for inquisitors for centuries to come (and who was deposed by two kings of Aragón precisely for his excessive zeal). On Eymerich, see Heimann, *Nicolaus Eymerich*; and Sullivan, *Inner Lives*, 169–96.

35. Riquer, *Literatura catalana*, 2:304–8.
36. "Vulles totstemps dir veritat / de ço que seràs demanat; / mas en cas de necessitat / pots dir falsia." Al-Tarjumān, "Libre de bons amonestaments," stz. 63, p. 153, ll. 17–20, emphasis added.
37. "Aquest llibret io t'he dictat, / per ço que, si est demanat / d'algun fet, sies informat /de la resposta." Al-Tarjumān, stz. 102, p. 159, ll. 5–8.
38. Al-Tarjumān, stzs. 1–6, p. 144, ll. 21–24, p. 145, ll. 1–16.
39. Alcover, Moll, *Diccionari* (hereafter cited as *DCVB*).
40. "Notandum est autem quod Valdenses sunt valde difficiles ad examinandum et inquirendum et ad habendum veritatem ab eis erroribus suis propter fallacias et dupplicitates verborum quibus se conlegant in responsionibus suis ne deprehendantur; et ideo de eorum dupplicitatibus et fallaciis aliqua perstringenda sunt in hoc loco." Gui, *Practica Inquisitionis*, 252–53. See now the discussion by Sullivan, *Inner Lives*, 124–45, esp. 131–37.
41. "Interrogatus de fide quam tenet et credit respondet, 'Omnia credo que debet credere bonus christianus.' . . . Examinatus vero quem reputat bonum christianum respondet, 'Illum qui credit sicut sancta Ecclesia docet credere et tenere.'" Gui, *Practica Inquisitionis*, 253.
42. Looking further into ʿAbd Allāh's text, we find what may be instructions on behavior in church, especially what is a familiar situation for anyone attending an unfamiliar religious service: the need to know when to stand, when to sit, and when to kneel: "A la esgleia vulles anar / per Déu e los sants aorar, / e si oges preïcar / tantost t'asenta" (If you hear preaching, sit down immediately). Al-Tarjumān, "Libre de bons amonestaments," stz. 36, p. 149, ll. 21–24.
43. See, for example, "No et fius massa de vestiment / qui burell sia" (Don't be too trusting of the habit / Made of sackcloth; Al-Tarjumān, stz. 35, p. 149, ll. 17–20) or "Ço que oïràs dir faràs, / e ço que ells fan esquivaràs: / d'aicells ho dic qui lo cap ras, / porten, e barba" (Do what they *tell* you to do / And avoid doing what they actually *do*: / I am talking about the people who have their head shaved / And wear a beard; stz. 37, p. 149, ll. 25–28).
44. AHN, leg. 4436, no. 24, pp. 2–3.
45. Al-Tarjumān, "Libre de bons amonestaments," stz. 79, p. 155, ll. 25–28.
46. ʿAbd Allāh seems to present the opposite advice here: "Qui en est món va simplement, / certes va fiançosament. / Déus ha l'hom en avorriment, / de dues cares" (The person who goes simply in this word goes surely; God hates the man with two faces; Al-Tarjumān, stz. 56, p. 152, ll. 21–24). This stanza serves Riquer as his parting shot at what he believes to be ʿAbd Allāh's cynicism (Riquer, *Literatura catalana*, 2:308). But perhaps other readings of this stanza are possible.
47. Hauf, *L'home que riu*, 48–50. ʿAbd Allāh's license to lie is sometimes seen as a reflection of the Muslim principle of *taqiyya* (dissimulation), under which it was considered permissible to lie, especially when facing forced conversion. On *taqiyya* in later periods, see García-Arenal's introduction to the monographic section on "*Taqiyya*"; and Rubio, "*Taqiyya* en las fuentes cristianas." It could be argued that those citing ʿAbd Allāh's text in Mallorca in 1582 are, in fact, understanding and using it as a sort of *fatwā*. For attitudes toward usefulness of lying by inquisitors themselves, see Sullivan, *Inner Lives*, 172–80, concerning the fourteenth-century Aragonese inquisitor Nicholas Eymerich (and his late sixteenth-century editor Francisco Peña).

48. "E no l'he dictat en llatí, / per ço que el vell e lo fadrí, / lo estranger e lo cosí / entendre el puixen." Al-Tarjumān, "Libre de bons amonestaments," stz. 103; p. 159, ll. 9–12.
49. The final stanza of 'Abd Allāh's prologue (Al-Tarjumān, stz. 5, p. 145, ll. 9–12; see above) is another that we might skip over as a common topic of the exordium, and it was certainly that. But it also describes very nicely the type of patchwork reading I have been discussing here, in which some readers will find certain meaning and other readers will focus on very different ones. 'Abd Allāh is not the only medieval writer to make sardonic use of this topos, of course: we need look no further than his near contemporary Juan Ruiz, archpriest of Hita, in the sermon prologue to the *Libro de buen amor* and in its opening and closing *cuaderna vía* stanzas (11–19, 44–70, and 1626–34).
50. "Aprés lo vall, / a la porta plegadissa, / al costat d'una bardissa / viu mon companyó cremar; / un altre en viu socarrar / dins aquell any en Evissa." Al-Tarjumān, "Cobles de la divisó," in Olivar, *Bernat Metge*, stz. 91, p. 132, ll. 17–22. The Porta Plegadissa of Palma de Mallorca was a common site for public executions in the Middle Ages. In the late fifteenth century and after, it was the place in which those condemned by the Spanish Inquisition were executed.
51. If *aquell any* means "that same year," we might be able to learn something further about 'Abd Allāh's chronology and just who he considered to be his "companions" by seeking such overlaps in the historical record: a year when there were public punishments of the types described in both Mallorca and Ibiza. Riquer believes that this passage refers to "dos framenors condemnats per acusacions d'heretgia . . . el suplici dels quals degué presenciar Turmeda quan encara era cristià i frare i degué influir poderosament en la seva apostasia" (Riquer, *Literatura catalana*, 2:285). Riquer is thus suggesting that 'Abd Allāh was a "companion" of Spiritual Franciscans. Although most European scholars who have dealt with this issue have looked for Christian "companions" for 'Abd Allāh at this time in his life, it seems to me that one answer to the question of who he considered to be his "companions" might be "other Muslims"—that is, "companions" in his Islamic faith rather than necessarily companions in some form of Christianity. Annual notations taken by the notary Mateo Salcet and others list a few such public punishments, slightly after the date of the *Bons amonestaments*. On February 4, 1407, "se publicó una sentencia del Vicario General y del Inquisidor de las Heregías, en el lugar llamado el Padró, cerca de la Seo, condenando á un converso llamado Juan Galiana, por haber apostatado dos veces de la fé cristiana: fué relajado al brazo secular; . . . y el Bayle con los Prohombres condenó al converso á ser quemado publicamente." Campaner y Fuertes, *Cronicon mayoricense*, 147. This may be the case of a convert from Judaism who has returned to his original faith, but several cases of Muslim slaves who have committed blasphemies and other crimes are noted by Salcet. For example, on November 17, 1413, a "cautivo cristiano" described as "de nación berberisco" is burned for child molestation "en las afueras de la Puerta Plegadissa" (152). Historical sources may exist, then, that will allow us to pin down the date at which 'Abd Allāh says he witnessed these executions in Mallorca, combining them with an event "in that same year" in Ibiza. Jaume Riera has suggested recently that 'Abd Allāh's *companyó* was a "sodomite" and that therefore, by extension, so was 'Abd Allāh: "No s'hi val a fingir que l'expressió 'mon companyó' és genèrica, i que s'ignora que, a final del segle XIV, a Mallorca, fora la porta Plegadissa, hi eren cremats els sodomites." Riera i Sans, *Sodomites catalans*, 594. Riera's

suggestion is certainly worthy of further investigation. In a case that could have been witnessed by ʿAbd Allāh, in Mallorca in 1378, a couple was burned for "heresy" for having used a presumably magical "perfume" on the wife of a Christian: "Un esclavo y una esclava de Ramón Oliver sufrieron la muerte de hoguera, por haber administrado ciertos perfumes á la esposa de su amo. Leyóse la sentencia en el lugar llamado lo *padró*, declarando herege al sarraceno." Campaner i Fuertes, *Cronicon mayoricense*, 73. Another case from Mallorca, in 1416, describes the type of punishment ʿAbd Allāh is probably referring to as having taken place in Ibiza "that year," using the verb *socarrar*:

> Un moro apellat Issa, catiu den Johan Tanyo, mercader, lo qual moro estant devant lo cor de la Iglesia de Sta. Eulalia de la ciutat de Mallorques, havia ditas paraulas deshonestas e malvadas contra lo precios cos de Jesu-Crist Salvador nostre, e havia ab gests de sa persona ab gran deshonestidat fetas viltas de boca, e per las parts insans de son cors devant la custodia de dita iglesia, per la qual rahó fou sentenciat que corregués la ciutat ab azots ab lengua clavada, e fos passat per los lochs hon comunament se apleguen los moros, e aprés lo dit moro fos amanat en la plassa de las Cols devant la dita iglesia, e aqui per forsa fos assegut sobre una pella fogatfant [*sic*] e ben vermella, sens bragues, en manera que las anques en las parts insanas fossen ben *soquerradas*. (152, emphasis added)

52. Epalza, *Fray Anselmo Turmeda*, 218–21. The identity of the crypto-Muslim professor, who may have been named Nicolas Fratello or Nicolas Myrtle (depending on how one reads the Arabic text in manuscripts), has been a subject of much investigation and several specific suggestions. We cannot go into these here. Nevertheless, it is important to remember that this text, autobiographical in form, may have nonautobiographical, even literary, models and sources. In this regard, the suggestion by García-Arenal ("Dreams and Reason," 100–101) of a possible Arabic source text (early fourteenth century) for this figure in a crypto-Muslim Knight Templar is especially important.

12

POETICS AND POLEMICS

Ibrahim Taybili's Anti-Christian Polemical Treatise in Verse

Teresa Soto

Introduction

Studies of Morisco polemics have largely overlooked Ibrahim Taybili's *Contradictión de los catorce artículos de la fe Cristiana* (1628),[1] a versification of Mohammad Alguazir's polemical anti-Christian treatise.[2] In 1628, already exiled in Tunisia, Taybili composed his treatise at the behest of the Ottoman authority Yusuf Dey, with the main aim of providing Moriscos with doctrinal material.[3] The scarce scholarly attention to the *Contradictión* may have to do with the idea that it is subordinate to Alguazir's work—a mere rendering in verse. How the polemics are embedded within the poetics seems, however, to be a very relevant question in anti-Christian Morisco polemical discourses, where theological disputations involve layers of discursive dependencies. This chapter brings to light a second, previously unidentified source—namely, a book of religious poetry by José de Valdivielso. My comparison of Taybili's book with Valdivielso's reveals that Taybili clearly used this work of Christian poetry as a pattern for the meter of his Islamic text and, more importantly, as a textual source throughout the book. I will argue that his use of verse and mimesis is not a simple matter of ornamentation but an active part of his rhetorical tactics.

Taybili's use of Valdivielso is apparent already in the very first canto, also called "Invocación del Autor" (fols. 18r–19v). Taybili thanks God for saving him from heresy and then compares himself to the prophet Daniel, who was saved by God from the fire. After the comparison to Daniel, a series of biblical tales ensue: the trials of Ahasuerus, Mordechai, Moses, Absalom, and Judith are presented as examples of the working of God's will. These stories of changing fortunes and adversity seem to be a prelude to what is going to be narrated afterward, which is the fate of the Moriscos, expelled by Philip III from Spain in 1609–14 and dispersed to different cities in *dar al-Islam*. Philip is represented here as a ruler who, though convinced he is making this decision through his own strength, is really no more than an instrument used by God to grant the Moriscos a path to freedom from Christianity. The canto adopts a more dynamic rhythm as we witness the expelled Moriscos *happily* leaving their houses and belongings behind to set out on a journey that will lead them along paths where abundant provisions come to them before finally sailing away to Barbary, delivered from heresy. A conclusive passage praising God might be expected here, and indeed, it does come, in the final verses, hand-in-hand with a declaration about the unity of God and a refutation of the false faith of pagans.

Thus the text comes full circle: the canto ends as it starts, giving a sense of completeness, underlined by other textual mechanisms such as the uniformity of the rhyme, the repetition of words, and the title. What we see gives us the impression of a structure that functions as a whole despite the inconsistency of some of its parts, almost like a visual trick, a trompe l'oeil. First of all, the choice of this particular episode about the prophet Daniel is an unusual model in this context, since it is not included in the Qur'ān or in most compilations of *Qiṣaṣ al-anbiyā'*.[4] Secondly, the choice of biblical figures—who, except for Moses, are not part of the Islamic tradition—is unexpected. Finally, there is the tone in which the story of the expulsion of the Moriscos is told, in messianic terms, and their happy acceptance of their fate.

The construction of this canto could very well represent the text as a whole, where similar mechanisms persist (a sense of completeness despite elements that do not quite fit). Most of Taybili's additions (foreword, prologue, epilogue, "Canto Primero," and opening and closing stanzas) are interlaced with verses and stanzas that come from a work by José de Valdivielso (ca. 1560–1638, chaplain of the Mozarabic rite in Toledo) entitled *Vida, excelencias y muerte del Gloriosissimo patriarca y esposo de nuestra Señora S. Joseph*. Valdivielso's book was an account in verse of the life of St. Joseph and was a very popular text first printed in Toledo in 1604 and from then on regularly republished, with thirty-nine reprints in the seventeenth century, the last one in Cádiz in 1696.[5] The rhyme scheme of Taybili's work also follows the versification of the *Vida de José*. The meter used in both is characteristic of the Spanish epic poetry's *octava real*, or *rima octava*.[6] The aforementioned biblical accounts that precede the narration of the expulsion of the Moriscos are extracted from Valdivielso's work verbatim, while the subsequent stanza is an adaptation. Oddly enough, it appears that these cultural references that come from a Christian context do not undercut the author's Islamic authority, since the final message of the text is abundantly clear (i.e., Islam is the one true religion). Furthermore, we might note that these passages have not presented a problem for modern critics, who have not misread Taybili's work as a Christian text or identified any conflictive sources in it.

However, the insertion of very well-known Christian religious poetry in a text such as the *Contradictión*, whose nature is mainly to contest Christianity, remains problematic, as is the fact that some parts are modified, whereas others are left as is, even when in apparent conflict with the message of the text (e.g., the biblical characters). What does this imitation mean and how does it fit into the construction of the polemical text? More generally, I hope to answer the question of how this may be connected to the process of imitation in Golden Age Spanish literature. First, I propose that the *imitatio* carried out by Taybili can be better understood in connection with the literary phenomenon of the *contrafactum*, or *a lo divino*, where profane poetry was recast in religious terms. The transference from *Vida de José* to the *Contradictión* in the preliminary texts (foreword, prologue, and "Canto Primero") will be analyzed here with this connection in mind. Secondly, I will examine the way in which Taybili goes about adapting Alguazir, for which purpose I will analyze the chapter on the Mass as a close reading. Here, I will argue that Taybili opts to actively make use of his own Christian background as a textual strategy, representing in detail both the Mass and the community's memory of it in order to create both proximity with a shared past and distance from the object his book endeavors to contradict. Finally, by way of conclusion, I will propose that the *Contradictión* constitutes a sort of poetic construction where imitation, *contrafactum*, and other poetic strategies contribute to the creation of a polemical discourse whose decidedly anti-Christian message is not at odds with the author's extensive use of Christian material and is arguably a typically baroque creation.

Juan Pérez / Ibrahim Taybili: From Toledo to Testur

Other than the biographical facts that he himself provides, we know very little about Ibrahim Taybili (Toledo, ca. 1562–?; Christian name: Juan Pérez). His self-representation is that of a studious author who is very much opposed to spending time on social gatherings and devoted to his quill pen and books.[7] Nearly all his time, then, is dedicated to studying and copying books. In fact, his extensive involvement in the North African Spanish production that has come down to the present is quite remarkable. From this extant corpus of Morisco manuscripts from Tunisia, the following five works are the result of Taybili's activity: MS RAH S2 (*Tratado de los dos caminos*), MS BNE 9653, MS BNE 9654, MS Vatican 14007, and the *ʿibādāt* treatise based on the Ḥanafī school contained in manuscript 40 of the University Library of Uppsala.[8] Louis Cardaillac, in his foundational 1977 study *Morisques et chrétiens. Un affrontament polémique (1492–1640)*, first proposed a common authorship for three of these books[9] based on compelling evidence to this effect.[10] Since then, the hypothesis of Taybili being more than a mere copyist has been always considered.[11]

At the outset of my research, I began by looking closely at the Tunisian context, and specifically at Testur,[12] but ultimately was drawn back to Toledo. Despite having written all his books in Testur, there is very little testimony on Tunisia to be found in *Contradictión*. Toledo, on the contrary, comes up often. In MS BNE 9654, there is a very interesting aside about the Inquisition of Toledo that could shed light on several connections to the author before the expulsion and ultimately lead to a hypothesis about his identity. According to this account, a Morisco from Toledo was imprisoned in the secret prisons of the Inquisition in Toledo. While sitting in his cell, a friar nicknamed Pico de Oro arrived, who made wild gesticulations and yelled at everyone he could. In his rage, he did not even notice that another person was sitting in the back of the cell. When he finally acknowledged his presence in the cell and realized his new cellmate was a Morisco, he immediately started arguing with him about religion.[13]

The case referred to in the manuscript actually corresponds to a real one—that of Jerónimo de Rojas. Rojas was originally from the town of Hornachos but lived and worked in Toledo as a "mercader de espeçiería." He was imprisoned in 1601 at the age of forty-four, accused of heresy and practicing Islam.[14] Rojas shared his prison cell with Friar Hernando de Santiago, nicknamed "Pico de Oro" by Philip II.[15] Records of conversations on Christian-Islamic matters conducted by Rojas and Hernando de Santiago have been preserved in the trial documents, even though they differ considerably from the testimony that MS 9654 provides. Apparently, Rojas wrote several letters to be smuggled out of prison in order to try to establish communication with friends and family members. These notes, however, were intercepted and confiscated with the help of Friar Hernando himself. Among the names that appear in Rojas's notes, that of Juan Pérez comes up on more than one occasion.[16] This shows that there was a close relationship between this Juan Pérez and Rojas's family and that they most probably participated in a similar intellectual environment. He also says in a letter that most probably, Pérez had already left because he had been imprisoned by the Inquisition previously, until being released after denying his charges under torture, and would not want to repeat the experience.[17] Rojas is careful not to provide the names of any leaders or members of circles of people interested in studying or reading books about Islam. Actually, he points solely toward Ibn Tuda[18] (who is not in Spain at the time) as the main authority and person responsible for all the points he makes about religious matters.[19]

More documentation from the time—particularly a census of the Morisco population of Toledo requested by the priest of the church of San Isidoro, Luis de Vinuesa, in 1589—contains further evidence as to Juan Pérez's biography. The census proves that there was indeed a "Corral Rojas" and also a "Casa Juan Pérez" in the neighborhood of Las Covachuelas, holding four families in two houses.[20] Concerning Juan Pérez's case with the Inquisition, it has not been preserved with the Inquisition files of Toledo, but a description contained in a *Relación de causas* (Summary of cases) from 1594 provides a convincing match. It consists of a case against "Joan Pérez Mozagues morisco ortelano vecino de Toledo" (Joan Pérez Mozagues, Morisco gardener residing in Toledo).[21]

So far, the information available about Ibrahim Taybili matches up with this Juan Pérez: he was from Toledo, was more or less prosperous, knew Rojas's case, and must have frequented the circles of many Moriscos of Toledo who were interested in religious matters. Several pieces of evidence contained in the documents cited herein further point to a connection between these two characters. First, Rojas says he worked in the "huerta del Rey" and now owns a forge and that he lives in Las Covachuelas. They were more or less the same age (Pérez being slightly younger). Juan Pérez was imprisoned mainly for dealing with books related to Islam. This image is not at all far from the one we have been given by Ibrahim Taybili / Juan Pérez. The interests of the Juan Pérez of Rojas's account coincide with those of Taybili.

At the center of the literary life of the city of Toledo where Taybili lived were two authors whose verses appear often in the Tunisian corpus in which he is involved: José de Valdivielso and Lope de Vega.[22] Since I will just focus here on the *Contradictión*, the only book that Ibrahim Taybili actually signed, I will introduce the poet who is most relevant for this study. Even though today he has been largely forgotten, José de Valdivielso was a famous poet and a respected censor at the beginning of the seventeenth century, a well-known figure in Toledo's literary circles and a close friend of Lope de Vega (1562–1635)—who, in fact, wrote one of the laudatory poems that open the *Vida de José*—together with the other so-called *cisnes del Tajo* (swans of the Tagus), a group of poets associated with the Academia de Fuensalida. Here, literary debates took place among the authors about the "Romancero Nuevo," and the city of Toledo itself came to the fore as a poetic subject.[23] Lope lived in Toledo in different periods (1589 to 1590 and 1604 to 1610), so at the time the book was published, he had already taken up residence there for the second time. It is more than likely, then, that Ibrahim Taybili himself was familiar with this milieu. His "Canción del autor" in fact emphasizes his Toledo roots and engages with this literary topoi: "Take heart my pen / start writing without fear / do not show any cowardice / for your origin is the great Toledo, / the best city in Spain / whose fields the clear Tagus laps."[24]

Counterfacting Christianity into Islam

In Lope's praise poem to the *Vida de José*, he plays with the idea of how the human Joseph (José de Valdivielso) writes about the divine Joseph (St. Joseph) and, by doing so, becomes more divine himself: "Joseph sings to Joseph, human Joseph / sings to divine Joseph, and the divine / if his merits would grow together with his praise / more divine would be by his hand / thus the humane to become divine came."[25] The coincidence of the name *Joseph* therefore opens a door allowing one category (human) to pass over to its opposite (divine), suggesting that poetry is a space fit for both the sacred and the profane, where the two are just one hendecasyllabic verse apart. Lope is clearly referring first of all to the task of the poet, whose verses bring him prestige and fame, conferring on him a divine-like status. But at the same time, he is also talking about Valdivielso as an *a lo divino* poet, one who was well known for being versed in both schools of writing ("maestro en lo profano y en lo divino"). He was in fact one of the main *contrafactistas* of his time and, by adapting profane romances, helped make the Bible more popular through poetry. His book *Vida de José* was a tremendous success, as was the *Romancero espiritual* (1612), where he abundantly quoted the Song of the Songs, Revelation, David's Psalms, the epistles of St. Paul, and other biblical texts, although he based most of his compositions on earlier profane poems.[26]

The term *contrafactum* was coined by Bruce W. Wardropper in his seminal study on *a lo divino* poetry in Western Christianity (1958), in which he defined it as a religious literary text that is a reworded version of a preexisting secular text.[27] Counterfacting is a technique closely connected to the concept of mimesis, or imitation of nature. During the baroque, mimesis was a relatively vague concept and could refer to anything ranging from the direct imitation of the material world to the imitation of classical authors. For El Brocense (1523–1600), a poet who imitates nature is one who knows how to insert others' verses into his own work without it being noticeable,[28] the classic example being Garcilaso de la Vega. Thus counterfacting has to do with the controversial practice of imitating others' words. Among the treatises on poetics written during the time of Valdivielso and Ibrahim Taybili, Luis Alfonso de Carvallo's *Cisne de Apolo* (1602) is the one that deals most directly with this point. In the fourth dialogue, under the section "De la imitación, del contrahacer y hurtar ajenas poesías, y del centón," Alfonso de Carvallo (1571–1635) speculates about whether it is acceptable to imitate "verso, copla, estilo y materia juntamente" (verse, stanza, style, and topic all together).[29] His answer is yes, that this is the so-called art of "contrahazer o volver a lo divino" (counterfacting or rendering in the divine style). The verse and its *a lo divino* equivalent given by way of example differ merely in the substitution of one name for another: "Por el rastro de la sangre / que Durandarte dejaba" (By the trail of blood / that Durandarte left), which becomes, "Por el rastro de la sangre / que Jesu Cristo dejaba" (By the trail of blood / that Jesus Christ left).[30] Alfonso de Carvallo stresses the importance of this type of poetry, since "there are some letters received in the vulgar tongue about such dirty things that God and help are required to banish them from thought because they have tunes of some grace and wit. And therefore it is needful to countermake them."[31] Thus it was already suggested at the time that the *contrafactum* could serve as a form of erasure, as a way of rewriting or correcting a profane text. This is the perspective on *a lo divino* poetry that would be passed down to modern criticism, as fundamentally moralizing and strongly influenced by the Reformist trends of the Council of Trent.[32]

In any case, the process of counterfacting, so deeply rooted in the imitative processes of sixteenth- and seventeenth-century poetic discourses, is connected with the idea not just of substitution but also of transformation. There is a clear dynamic of intertextuality whereby the change in meaning comes about not just through substitution but also through the intertext's relationship of both analogy and dissent with respect to the meaning of the profane text upon which it is based.[33] As Alfonso de Carvallo puts it, what can be salvaged from profane writing is "alguna gracia y donaire" that is usually found in the "tonadas" (i.e., in the musicality).[34] *A lo divino* poetry appropriates the "grace and wit" of the source text in order to transmit the correct(ed) message, but the original should still remain there at the root, suggested. Thus *a lo divino* poetry may be understood not just as a mere transposition of a profane theme into a sacred one but rather as a process in which the human starting point remains in place and "shifts its teleology" toward the sacred. This establishes a point of contact between the thinking of the profane poem and the religious meaning of the *contrafactum*.[35]

A legitimate question here would be whether Taybili's transfer of material from Valdivielso's book over to his own is at all related to the poetic device of *a lo divino* poetry. Can we still speak of *contrafactum* when a Christian model is used for an Islamic text? Is this what is happening in the *Contradictión*? On the one hand, there is a clear rejection of Valdivielso's text, while on the other, there is a relationship of continuity and analogy that is quite suggestive, insofar as it adds to the text's complexity. Wardropper discusses the contacts between Christianity and other religions but refers mainly to paganism and not to Islam.[36] Works in which a connection between Islam and Christianity is established in lyrical *a lo divino* terms often make use of a more satirical variant of this technique, the so-called reverse *a lo divino*. An example is the "Confesión de los moriscos," a poem attributed to Quevedo and written in 1609.[37] It is a sort of polemical anticredo that parodies the Moriscos' lack of faith and knowledge of Catholic doctrine. The names of the apostles Pedro (Peter) and Pablo (Paul) are confused with Perro (dog) and Palo (stick), and other key terms such as *apóstoles* (apostles) and *penitencia* (penitence) become *apóstatas* (apostates) and *pestilencia* (pestilence).[38] Another profane credo would be the "Misa de amor," in which an abbot shaken by the sight of a beautiful lady mispronounces his prayers.[39]

In any case, none of the tendencies that are characteristic of the reverse *a lo divino* technique (toward hyperbole, the profane, or even transgression) can be found in Taybili's work, despite the fact that the polemical context might invite such an approach. Instead, what we see in his work is the gesture of erasing, correcting, and contacting. This gesture is similar to the practice of counterfacting, although the latter, as has been explained, does not exhaustively account for what is going on in the *Contradictión*. We do indeed see a process of substitution along the lines of the example given by Alfonso de Carvallo (Durandarte for Jesus Christ). Here, Philip III is substituted for Caesar, and Joseph, who is banished back to his homeland (Bethlehem), is replaced with the Moriscos. It is clear that even though the immediate objects of this transposition are not instances of religious language, both poems, when taken as a whole, are indeed of a religious nature. Valdivielso's original poem is about the tragedy of Joseph and his divine destiny, and Taybili's is about divine providence in the case of the Moriscos, who are set on the path to discovering the true faith—a profound transformation indeed. Likewise, the semantics of the Moriscos' exile are easily identifiable with the story of Joseph, making the transformation come off quite naturally. We can therefore see the dual process of analogy and of rejection or erasure; the contact between the two texts persists, even while other specific parallels are rejected. Below, I have included the stanza where this adaptation takes place [1], followed by the original version by Valdivielso [2]. Marked in bold are the variations in Taybili's poem.

[1]
Felipho, rey de España, se dispone
pensando descubrir su fortaleça,

y es que por instrumento dios le pone
de su infalible y inmortal çerteça
hordena dios que el bando se pregone
que salgan los moriscos con presteça
y biene a ser camino esta salida
para que en libertad passen la vida.[40]

[2]
Manda César que el mundo se empadrone,
pensando descubrir su fortaleza,
y es que por instrumento Dios le pone
de su infalible y inmortal certeza.
Ordena Dios que el vando se pregone,
Porque Ioseph acuda a su cabeça,
a su patria Bethlem, donde está escrito
que ha de nacer estrecho el infinito.[41]

"Qual dirá que ay berssos hurtados"

There is another sort of transposition that does not involve an entire stanza along with its rhyme scheme but rather takes up single verses. In Taybili's text, these come in the section that deals with the diversity of the world as described by Pliny in the seventh book of his *Natural History*.[42] Valdivielso writes about this diversity in his tenth canto to conjure the hardship and fear that Joseph had to face as he went into exile, unsure which way to turn. The lands that he imagines are scorched, frozen, or otherwise inhospitable. The people who inhabit them are the same ones found in Pliny: Troglodytes, Lotophagi, Scythians, Arimaspi, and Cyclopes. Taybili takes up this menacing background but uses it instead to compare these backward or monstrous peoples with the Christians. Even the Scythians, Troglodytes, and Lotophagi—"infernal" nations living in darkness—"menos herraron / que los cristianos en lo que fundaron" (erred less in what they founded than the Christians did) and did not act so boldly against God. Taybili uses some of these verses in the stanzas that lead into the second and fourth cantos [3], in which he develops Alguazir's first seven articles against Christianity [4].

[3]
Entre los arimaspos y los sçithas,
bárbaros en bibir y en su gobierno,
lothophagos, cíclopies, troglodictas,
naçiones cuya istançia es el infierno,
sin otras mill naçiones infinitas,
no conoçieron al que es Dios eterno,
y con no tener luz menos herraron
que los cristianos en lo que fundaron.[43]

Desde el profundo de la Çithia elada
*hasta los **ethiopes abrassados,***
y quanto alumbra el sol en su jornada
en abitable tierra y despoblados,
y quanto alcança de la mar salada,
los reinos conoçidos y apartados,
no ay naçión contra dios tan atrebida
que la cristiana infiel deconoçida.[44]

[4]
¿Ausentaréme de mi bella amada?
¿Iré sin alma, pues la di a mi esposa?
*¿Iré a la inhabitable **Scitia elada,***
o a la inhumana Libia ponçoñada?
*¿Iré a la **Etiopía negra y abrasada,***
o a los desiertos de África arenosa?
*¿Viviré **entre arismaspos, entre scitas,***
latophargos, cíclopes, trogloditas?[45]

While Taybili's transposition is not identical to *a lo divino*, it does manifest a clear relationship with it. The source text has a set of qualities—Alfonso de Carvallo's "grace and wit"—and in transferring over a piece of text from a poem such as *Vida de José*, a number of modifications must inevitably be made before it can fit into a work like *Contradictión*. The kinds of modifications and how they are made is sometimes not what one might expect. For example, some of the stanzas are rewritten, but others, such as the stanzas about the biblical characters, are preserved. In both cases, the text is appropriated either through rewriting or through placement in a clearly Islamic context. Of course, preserving the text about religious characters not present in the Islamic tradition still seems odd. However, these fragments are not related to the most controversial or problematic topics in the polemics between Christianity and Islam. Nevertheless, the tension remains.

Although imitation of classical authors was an established tradition, there was always the possibility of going too far and committing what was referred to as *hurto* (theft). According to *Cisne de Apolo*, while almost anything can be imitated ("versos, coplas, stilo, lenguaje, aire, conceptos y todo lo más tocante a este arte"),[46] there are certain limits to bear in mind. Alfonso de Carvallo asks, in a dialogue between himself and the Greek grammarian Zoilus (in representation of poetry's detractors), "And taking a whole stanza, or an exordium, from someone else's romance and fitting it into my works, selling it as my own, taking advantage of others' work—would that be permitted?" The answer is categorical: "By no means, because that is stealing." To which Zoilus replies, "Well it's not at all uncommon," making clear that such "theft" must not have been out of the ordinary.[47] Alfonso de Carvallo uses a series of zoological metaphors to list the types of poets who, far from being white swans, are magpies, donkeys, and monkeys who imitate men but do so in a preposterous way. This is a practice that good poets should not follow, and Alfonso de Carvallo is of the opinion that those who do should be punished as thieves of others' property and honor: "Qui enim alienis pro suis utitur fur est." Returning to his zoological imagery, he says that these authors deserve not the emblem of the white swan but rather that of the cuckoo, who steals the eggs of other birds to take advantage of them, or the crow, who—according to legend—dressed itself with feathers from all the other birds.

Ibrahim Taybili is no stranger to these debates, writing in his "Prologue to the Reader," "Qual dirá que hay berssos hurtados" (Some will say that there are stolen verses).[48] However, in the prologue itself, as well as in the foreword, he copies or imitates Valdivielso. In the first introductory text in prose, the foreword, all that Taybili changes from the original text are the reasons that led him to write the book. In the second case, the "Prologue to the Reader," he replaces a personal anecdote that Valdivielso tells about a bookstore with a bookstore-related anecdote of his own. In the passage in question, Valdivielso describes an encounter in a bookstore as a cautionary tale about the dangers of giving opinions on matters one really has not read up on. In this case, when asked about an unpublished work by Valdivielso, the man in the anecdote says that the book, which he cannot have possibly read, is not good. Taybili uses the frame of the bookstore too, but he focuses more on literary taste and *bon sense*. This is in fact one of the most famous anecdotes from Taybili's text, often quoted in studies on this author.[49] Taybili recalls how he bought six volumes, providing the titles of three of them: *Césares* by Pedro Mexía and *Reloj de Príncipes* and *Epístolas* by Guevara. While there, he met a foolish man who only read chivalric romances and was not interested in reading anything else. In recounting his conversation, Taybili names such characters as Amadís, Palmerín, Belianís de Greçia, and Don Quijote, showing that he is well aware of the literary trends of the time and using them to evoke the well-known image of the educated and studious man of letters who is quintessential of the Golden Age. Together with the use of a number of marks of Spanish cultural prestige, he carefully allows this discourse to coexist alongside an image of himself as a pious Muslim who has rediscovered his religiosity, as a sort of "new convert."[50]

These issues are difficult to resolve because of the desire to establish clear and sound dichotomies between either sacred and profane or Islam and Christianity when thinking about early modern Spain. Barbara Fuchs, in her book *Mimesis and Empire*, suggests some very useful approaches to the Moriscos' mimetic practices. For her, these practices "undo the easy oppositions between Christian and Moor, to suggest that the binary Spaniard/Morisco in fact functions as a dyad. Despite their powerless role as the internal colonized, the Moriscos crucially affect the debates over Spanish identity, primarily by blurring the neat distinctions on which such a hegemonic identity seems to depend."[51] Furthermore, the dichotomy between sacred and profane was also far from being so clearly established. Alfonso de Carvallo's *Cisne de Apolo* echoed Horace's *Ars Poetica* by saying that poetry was supposed to teach how to distinguish one from the other: "Poetry was the science that taught how to distinguish between the public and the private, the sacred and the profane, to build cities, to make laws to govern them."[52] But in reality, this strict opposition—so common in the period's literature—corresponds more to a rhetorical topos, proof of which is the constant substitution and superposition of the sacred and profane in the various arts.[53]

Mass as Vanitas

In his 1942 study on the poetry of San Juan de la Cruz, in which he argues that San Juan was directly influenced by Sebastián de Córdoba's *Garcilaso a lo divino* (Granada, 1575),[54] Dámaso Alonso is surprised to discover how profoundly the meaning of the poem "El Pastorcico" is transformed by changing just the last four verses and a handful of words throughout the body of the poem, going so far as to call it a *prodigio* (marvel), as "nadie notaría la soldadura" (no one would notice the seams).[55] Thus Alonso seems to suggest that invisibility—in the sense of the seamless splicing of the new text, whose modifications are unrecognizable, hidden, dissimulated (and, in the case of San Juan, perfected, overcoming what Alonso identifies as Córdoba's clear awkwardness)—is another of the *contrafactum*'s major achievements. However, it does not seem that the aim in *a lo divino* poetry is to hide the artifice so that it becomes invisible; rather, as we have mentioned, it is important for the original to be suggested so that it is activated in the memory of the reader or listener as both vehicle and counterexample.

I think this is also at work in Taybili's text. Taybili states that the reason he decided to write this book was that, while enjoying a peaceful, quiet life of retirement in Testour, Alguazir's book crossed his path and reminded him that his past life had been trivial, confused, misguided, and heretical. It is also through his testimony that we know that Alguazir was a native of Pastrana (Castile). He therefore set about to write a verse adaptation of Alguazir's text in order to argue against Christianity for the benefit of his fellow Moriscos. An author's stated intentions are not always to be trusted, but this past life as a New Christian in Spain does appear in a variety of ways in the text, reminding the reader of the need to overcome it in order to reach the right path, which can only be found in Islam. Thus a sort of "activation" of memories takes place in the text and becomes an important factor in the polemical strategy. This helps the author not only create two well-established, opposite paths but also establish a rapport with the reader through a wealth of details that evoke the Moriscos' previous lives in Spain in a picture-like form. I believe that this strategy is even more visible in the body of the chapters where Taybili is adapting Alguazir—more precisely, in the chapters such as those describing the Mass or the Host, where particular details about the practice of the religion are presented, as we shall see shortly.

Alguazir's work is preserved in two different manuscripts,[56] along with a Latin version.[57] Scholars agree that the polemical tone and the rhetorical apparatus of the text were aimed at Christian audiences, and this is borne out by the history of the treatise's circulation and reception.[58] In addition to circulating in North Africa, it was also known in the Netherlands, where it was translated into Latin.[59] As to its organization, the manuscript of Alguazir's work preserved in the Biblioteca Nacional de España contains several parts with sections that appear to be clearly defined: a first part including the anti-Christian treatise developed over fourteen articles organized into seven chapters (fols. 1r–67v); a second part containing the attributes of God, which corresponds to the eighth chapter (fols. 68r–113v); and a third and last part related to the attributes of God (fols. 115r–123r).[60] Taybili includes just the first and the second parts in his work, organizing them into fourteen cantos. However, the refutation proper only takes up the first eight cantos, while the remaining six focus on the attributes of God. Closing and opening codicological features mark the textual content of the manuscript as a single unit, even though the two parts are differentiated. There is a colophon at the end of the book and connecting stanzas that indicate continuation between the two portions.[61] The correspondence between these two parts is clear, as is the dialogue between them: disputation and doctrine seem to arise as a necessary unity, two actions that are interconnected and suggest a simultaneous deconstruction and construction of ideology.[62]

On folios 57v to 63r of Alguazir's work can be found the sixth chapter: "On the Contradiction of the Christian's Mass." The chapter opens with a general description of the Christian Mass as a gathering in a temple, which is explained as a place with an altar holding idols, a chalice, and the Host. Alguazir points out that this Mass must be conducted by a cleric in order for it to be valid. Here he introduces the first comparison, saying that this is different in Islam, where believers can pray alone or with a *priest*.[63] He goes on to describe the ritual itself, which consists of reading from the Gospels and epistles and "then saying some words to say that God descends to the host, and they raise it up and beat their chests, worshiping it as God."[64] The Mass is rejected for three reasons: (1) there is idolatry, as the material objects bread and wine are considered idols; (2) there are women and men mixing in church; and (3) the temple's conditions are not suitable, as it is dirty, and the congregation is allowed to talk and act as if they were out in a public square.[65]

He mentions the presence of organ music and the use of fire.[66] After providing these arguments, he spends the rest of the chapter describing how Muslims pray.[67] The entire chapter is marked by this essentially descriptive tone and by the contrasts drawn between the two religions. Many more details are given in the description of prayer in Islam than in Christianity.

Taybili's adaptation of Alguazir's chapter on the Mass is one of the best examples of the process of broadening the content through the use of almost pictorial details.[68] When comparing the two texts, one cannot help but notice that Taybili dedicates a great deal more space to the Christian Mass (both describing it and refuting it) and much less to its Muslim counterpart. He spends a mere five stanzas describing Muslim prayer and mosques, as opposed to nearly thirty describing the Mass and related Christian practices. His descriptions of Islamic rites are headed with anaphoric formulas such as "No diré por extenso" (I am not going to say too much), "No me quiero alargar" (I do not want to take too much time), and "Que no diré lo que es tan sabido" (I am not going to say what is so well known).[69] These establish the rhythm of each stanza and create a sense of familiarity that is rhetorically very different from Alguazir's work.

The sixth canto is framed by two quotations from the Qur'ān written in Arabic, one introducing the text and the other closing it. The first is taken from *sūrat yā-sīn* and the latter from *sūrat al-baqarah.* Taybili glosses the first quotation with a paraphrase of the content of the Qur'ānic text as follows: "Those who adore something other than God and do not follow God's principles, adore the *Saytan* and follow him."[70] The position of these texts and their relative subordination to the rhetorical device of the negative anaphora ("I am not going to . . .") suggest they are something extra, external, and almost unnecessary, which nevertheless takes on much more relevance in the text. A look at the content of these two ayas reveals that both insist on the idea of the separation of the two paths and the need to choose the path of truth, the path that leads to God: "O children of Adam! that you should not serve the Shaitan? Surely he is your open enemy, / And that you should serve Me; this is the right way."[71] The message, though placed in the margins as paratext, is absolutely relevant within the context of the canto.

Therefore, out of the whole book, it is in this canto that Taybili exercises the most freedom in adapting Alguazir's original text. He opens with a lyrical introduction full of descriptors that are much more weighted against

Christianity than in Alguazir's version. Indeed, Christianity is full of insolence, it is a false and barbarous law, and it is heretical. Mass is a fabrication made up of tales, amounting to nothing more than a most profane sacrifice. With this polemical tone, he covers the same three arguments against the Mass used by Alguazir but then goes a step further, criticizing the Christians' own lack of devotion. Beyond just following the wrong creed, they lack the spirit of devotion and hardly ever go to Mass, only on Sundays and Holy Days of Obligation ("Si no es domingo o fiesta no ay ninguno / que oyga missa xamás entre semana"). Anyone who does go more often is written off as sanctimonious ("Si no es entre çiento que ay alguno / que es algo santurrón en su ley bana").[72]

He further depicts this same ignorance or lack of devotion by recounting how, when asked who blessed the holy water, Christians answer that their prelate did and that Christ blessed it when John the Baptist baptized him in the River Jordan. He exemplifies what he sees as the blind faith of the majority through the tale of the coal maker on his deathbed: When asked by his confessor what he believed in, he repeated over and over that he believed in the Holy Mother Church. When the confessor pressed him to explain what this belief consisted of, he just kept repeating that he believed in the Holy Mother Church. As for the Trinity, Taybili affirms that Christians are equally ignorant on the subject and will only respond that it is a mystery and in general follow the doctrine. Lastly, Taybili adds that the Mass lacks a sound foundation and has been repeatedly corrected, modified, and revised, leaving it looking like a mended cape with a laughable array of so many colors and patches that it is hard to tell which color is the original. He even criticizes the fact that the clergy profit from saying both public and private masses, such as the Mass of All Souls on All Souls' Day, when the sacristan does not hesitate to collect all the offerings of candles, pastries, and fine wine.[73]

Apart from the details of his polemical apparatus, what is interesting about this canto is that it contains a series of descriptions both of the place of worship and of the rituals carried out there whose development and level of detail are impressive. Whereas Alguazir sums up the Mass in a single paragraph (a gathering in a temple where a Gospel and an epistle are read and people worship the Host), in Taybili we find a wealth of detail. He starts by describing the font with holy water located at the entrance to the church and the words one says when dipping in all four fingers to make the sign of the cross. Next he describes the space, with benches and pews where men and women are mixed together. The priest comes out of the sacristy and walks up steps to stand at the altar, facing the missal. There the Gospel and epistle are read before eating God and drinking his blood. After this overview of the Mass, he goes on to discuss the music that accompanies the services, which he describes as delightful and pleasant, with organs, shawms, and cornets. He provides service times, lists common elements and the different types of Mass, and so on. Each of these detailed descriptions generally leads to a repudiation of the foregoing information, or it ends with a satirical comment on what has been presented. What this amounts to is a sort of inventory of objects, places, and times that precisely situates the described reality. This inventory is accompanied by specific perceptions and observations such as the filth of the church, the smells left by the dogs that roam in and out, people's attitudes during the rituals, and the words spoken throughout the service ("This water, my Lord, which is so blessed / make it my spiritual health and life, / and my prayer accepted and granted").[74]

There is a pictorial quality to this minute level of detail. As is made clear in the first books of rhetoric in Spanish, such as Miguel de Salinas's *Rhetorica en lengua castellana* (1541), narrating is a way to paint a picture of reality. This book's twelfth chapter, "De la narración de cualquier cosa en general," talks about telling something "with the aim of emphasizing it or putting it right in front of someone's eyes so the listeners can judge it as if they were seeing it" in order to have an effect on the reader.[75] Taybili's Mass is described in such vivid, almost palpable detail that the reader experiences it from the inside. Some critics have seen in this vivid and prominent presence a hidden thread of nostalgia for this past life. However, any initial ambiguity as to what position one is to take regarding this world is challenged by such unflattering descriptions. Like the skull in a *vanitas* painting, in the representations we have seen here, there is always some element in the picture that appears to be faulty and showing its false, weak, misguided, wrong side. Taybili takes pains to represent a reality and make us participate in it just to show us its twisted, vain, and artificial side.

*

The present chapter has sought to reveal what strategies of his own Taybili employs in contesting Christianity and how his rewriting of Alguazir gives rise to a new discourse, despite being based on the same arguments. The main focus has been to examine Taybili's poetic devices—in particular, the multiple ways he models his versification on the conventions of Christian religious poetry. In this perspective, the conventional terms of religious polemics become blurred, affording a richer understanding of how Morisco writings against Christianity were constructed. Starting from the first canto of his long anti-Christian polemic poem, Taybili borrows José de Valdivielso's biblical accounts of fortunes, adversities, and above all God's will to frame the expulsion of the Moriscos from Spain. By analyzing the function of this and similar passages where Valdivielso's poetry is interlaced, I have shown that by adapting and borrowing, Taybili is participating in contemporary debates on the craft of the writer. According to contemporary author Alfonso de Carvallo, imitation or counterfacting can also be employed to rewrite a profane text, erasing any unsavory nonreligious elements, a widespread model in sixteenth-century Spain known as *a lo divino* poetry. This framework can provide interesting new insights into Taybili's process of adaptation, which he performs not just through a clear-cut substitution of terms but also through an intertextual relationship of both analogy and dissent with respect to the source text. In addition to the borrowing from *Vida de José*, in our analysis of the chapter on the Mass, we saw how Taybili is also able to draw on his own knowledge of Christian practices—including personal memories, places, and concrete examples—in order to provide a picturelike reality in support of his discourse. Likewise, based on the exciting new connections I have drawn among Taybili, the Rojas trial, and networks of knowledge exchange in preexpulsion Castile, it is altogether possible that Taybili and Alguazir participated in similar circles. Taybili's negotiation of authorship and veracity, in line with ideologies of the baroque period in Spain and Europe, can therefore broaden our perspective on Morisco polemics generally, forcing us to look beyond the content of what is said and question the form.

Notes

The research for this chapter was funded by the European Research Council under the European Union's Seventh Framework Programme (FP7/2007–13) / ERC Grant Agreement number 323316, project CORPI, "Conversion, Overlapping Religiosities, Polemics, Interaction: Early Modern Iberia and Beyond." Preliminary versions of this text were presented in Madrid at the international conference Polemical Encounters, organized by the CSIC at the Residencia de Estudiantes (2014), and in Boston at the 2016 MESA annual meeting. This work has benefitted from the comments of those in attendance at these conferences and especially from my colleagues at CORPI, ILC-CSIC and SEAR, Universidad de Oviedo.

1. Taybili's book is preserved in one manuscript held at the Biblioteca Casanatense di Roma (BCR), MS 1976, fol. 15r. I will be referring to the original manuscript here. There is an edition and preliminary study of Taybili's book, prepared by Bernabé Pons, *Cántico islámico*, which also includes an additional study by Epalza on the author, "A modo de introducción." These are the two most extensive studies on the author to date. Likewise, Balabarca wrote her PhD dissertation on the subject of the *Contradictión* (Balabarca, "Polémica cristiano-musulmana") and has informed me that she is currently working on a book based on this dissertation.
2. Several polemical works in Spanish were produced by Moriscos in seventeenth-century North Africa (in particular, Tunisia and Morocco). Among them was the work by Mohammad Alguazir, from Pastrana (Castile), which was commissioned by Muley Zaidan, sultan of Marrakesh (r. 1603–27), on which Taybili based his *Contradictión*. On Alguazir's work, see Wiegers, "Obras de polémica religiosa"; and Wiegers, "Andalusi Heritage." On Morisco polemics, see Cardaillac, *Moriscos y cristianos*.
3. It also received the protection of the Sharīf ʿAlī al-Niwālī: "Sacada y amparada por el señor Sarif Ali Alniguali Abençerraxe cahia del ylustríssimo y exçelentísismo señor Yuçuf Day, capitán general y gobernador del Reyno de Túnez, a quien va enconmendada como a su protector" (BCR MS 1976, fol. 1v). Further along in his prologue, Taybili says that he has not chosen to write this text to gain fame or monetary compensation; rather, he has a penchant for reclusion and writing. His testimony, however, allows us to infer that he did in fact receive some form of economic compensation: "No me a mobido a escribir y a gastar el tiempo y trabajar con el entendimiento *el ynterés de la Renta, que por ello se me signa*, ni el ganar fama o loa por ello."
4. For example, the famous ones by al-Thaʿlabī (d. 427/1035) and Ibn Bishr (d. 821) do not include the episode to which Taybili refers here (Dan. 3:17–30). This version is, however, widespread in the Christian tradition and often used by preachers in homilies. Tottoli, *Biblical Prophets*, 145; and Al-Taʿlabi, *Araʾis al-Majalis*, 566–75, 644. Another similar reference may be found in the book by the Morisco Mohamad Rabadán, *Canto de las Lunas*, "Daniel fue libre de fuego," in Lasarte López, *Poemas de Mohamad Rabadán*, 296. However, in the longer work written by Rabadán, *Discurso de la luz*, the references to Daniel are all about the beasts (137, 144, 145, 217) and none about the story of the fiery furnace.
5. Valdivielso, *Vida, excelencias y muerte*. I will refer exclusively to this edition, from now on abbreviated as *Vida*. Madroñal, "Primera edición." A list of the editions is included in the appendix, pp. 291–93.
6. Defined by Juan de la Cueva (1543–1612) as a meter used mainly as a vehicle for heroic narrative with a lyrical undertone: "Esta es la Rima Octava, en quien floresce / la Eroyca alteza, i Epica ecelencia, / i en dulçura a la Lirica engrandece." Cueva, *Exemplar poético*, 94–96. Valdivielso's *Vida* was the most widely read epic poem at the time according to Pierce's studies on the heroic genre in the Golden Age. Pierce, *Poesía épica*, 48.
7. BCR MS 1976, fols. 16v–17r. He even says that people welcome him when they see him on the street, thinking he has been abroad: "Mi condiçión tan cassera y amiga del recoximiento que a beçes me suelen dar el parabién de mi benida sin aber salido de mi cassa como no me ben en la plaça, en juntas ni corrillos" (fol. 17r).

8. On the first identification of the same handwriting in the *aljamiado*-morisco manuscripts, see Villaverde Amieva, "Manuscritos aljamiado-moriscos," 123, 128. For a partial edition of the manuscript from Uppsala containing the Ḥanafī *'ibādāt* treatise, see Kart Vilhem Zetterstéen, "Notice sur un rituel musulman"; and Tornberg, *Codices arabici*, 250, 269.
9. S2 RAH; BNE 9653; and BNE 9654.
10. Cardaillac, *Moriscos y cristianos*, 168–80.
11. Bernabé Pons, "Aljamía lejana," 123; and Bernabé Pons, introduction to *Cántico islámico*, 65–68.
12. There was an important community of Moriscos living in Testur at this time. References from a variety of contemporary chronicles testify to this fact, among them Ibn Abu Dinar, who talks about the prosperity and the wealth that the Moriscos brought with them. I would like to thank Carla Ramos for sharing with me the paper on the Tunisian Historian Ibn Abu Dinar that she presented at Mediterráneos International Conference of Junior Researchers in Mediterranean and Near Eastern Languages and Cultures (Madrid, CSIC, 2012). There is abundant bibliography about the community in exile, among them Epalza, *Moriscos antes y después*; Bernabé Pons, *Moriscos*; and more recently García-Arenal and Wiegers, *Moriscos.*
13. BNE MS 9654, fols. 8v–9v:

    Y al cabo de rato que se le quitó la cólera bolbió la cara y halló al morisco sentado y le preguntó quién era y le dixo era fulano pues como lo conoció de morisco le dixo el otro día leyendo un libro que deçimos contra Curán hallé en él que se contaba el milagro que diçen los moros del partirse la luna y entrar por las mangas sabeys qué tan grande es la luna fulano sabed que es tan grande como el mundo treynta beçes pues cómo siendo tan grande pudo entrar por una cosa tan chica con que enten deceys que es cosa fuera de camino. El morisco lo estubo oyendo atento y mobido su coraçón a la fe tan grande que tenía en el conoçimiento del poder de dios le dijo: senor, ¿quál es más grande: Dios o la luna? Dijo: pues ay duda en que Dios es mayor sin número que la luna. Dijo entonçes: ¿pues cómo si es mayor y cabe a entrar por el garguero que es más pequeno que las mangas no cabrá la luna que es menor por lo que es mayor que son las mangas? El diablo de Pico de oro se quedó elebado y se le acreçentó la furia de manera que comenςó a dar golpes en la puerta y bino el alcayde y les dijo lo que pasaba y que si este hombre quedaba bibo bastara para bolber moros a toda España con que fue sentençiado a quemar radia Allahu "anhu."

14. I will not go into detail about the causes and process of his case, since it is already being studied by García-Arenal and Benítez Sánchez-Blanco. I want to thank García-Arenal for sharing this material with me for the present chapter.
15. Pérez, *Fr. Hernando de Santiago*, 135.
16. He mentions him at least twice: once when Rojas asks his son-in-law Ribera to give a sum of money to Juan Pérez and again when mentioning the reading of various papers related to Arabic or prayers:

    Nota bien estas palabras en arábigo: *de chomoatza como toca fin liemurçi ley huia mile anagaquez guali huyr bealezar ene fitarrguina le haque el uhun y eszcuno fal fondarli charaboe lezer cole han yaro bo guo lamarene huny etensufi hereale bay* y esto no lo hagás bos *mine yemeze a hadazuy tensi lambre temosta biabele guatecos la lamanle ye mi yezera hada*. . . . Y si ezestes quenta con Juan Perez aquelas palabras de escritos en arabigo notada le bino con trasladarlas con vuestra mano las entendres queren dize que huna aquel que es prestamos el espada y todas y su muger y si han huydo mi lo envíes a decer que mi emporta mucho. (AHN, Inquisición, leg. 197, exp. 5, fol. 26r)

"Si os priguntaren quén entró en nuestra casa, deze que toda Toledo bien abri cullos, y entran y salen, hasta nigro. Haze quinta con Juan Pérez en cadal V M DCXCIII" (fol. 24r). "En el punto que mi prendieron abía bindido Alonso Ruyz todas las sábanas y si no está ay a Juan Pérez pidilde el dinero con que mi lo abía librado en casa de Murcia. Dios os guarde a todos. Enbiame la respuesta luego" (fol. 26v). "De vuestra merced no está declarado, no esto solo lo que declaró Juan Pérez, y enbiastemi a deçir de Villa Robledo, reýos de eso. En mi casa deçí que no estén trestes, sino que canten y valen y se vistan como suelen y, a mi yerno, no estorbe la boda de su hermano, que todo esto es por Dios; y responder a todo muy claro porque todo viene siguro" (fol. 11r).

17. AHN, Inquisición, leg. 197, exp. 5, fols. 60r–60v:

> Dijo que muchas veces en conversación ha dicho el dicho Rojas que entiende que, después de su prisión, deben haber huido de aquí un Juan Pérez, morisco, que vive en las Covachuelas y tiene tienda de herrero en la Sillería, que vino con el dicho Rojas de Sevilla la última vez que de allá vino y tenía compañía con él de unos lienzos que allí compraron, y que el dicho Juan Pérez ha estado preso en esta inquisición siete meses y salió libre y que, como escapó aquella vez por haber negado en el tormento, no querrá verse en otra y que es muy buen moro. Y que el dicho Juan Pérez, cuando aquí fue preso, era hortelano en la huerta del Rey y traspasó esta huerta a unos moriscos con quien trataba Francisco Enríquez, los cuales cree también que habrán huido y que lo habrán acertado por no verse en lo que él está, y que si entendiese de cierto que estos son idos, declararía de ellos, porque todos guardaban la secta de Mahoma como el dicho Rojas.

18. Abd al-Karim Ibn Tuda, lord of numerous lands to the north and west of Morocco, served Saadi sultan Muley Muhammad al-Mutawakkil (1573–78). The character Albacarín Ibn Tuda in Lope de Vega's play *Tragedia del Rey Don Sebastián y Bautismo del Príncipe de Marruecos* is based on this figure. In his study of this play, Oliver Asín suggests the possible Morisco origin of Ibn Tuda even though this has not been proven. For different reasons connected to the wars of succession in Morocco, Ibn Tuda spent a period in the Spain of Philip II. See Oliver Asín, *Vida de Don Felipe*; Cabanelas, "Caíd marroquí," 75–88; and García-Arenal, "Andalusíes en el ejército."
19. "Yo he dicho en mi dicho que era moro y me dejeron quén me av[ía] ensenado; deje que el alcaide Abuntute, el que estaba en Talabera y en los Caramancheles." AHN, Inquisición, leg. 197, exp. 5, fol. 123r. He also showed a great deal of caution not to accuse any of the Moriscos currently in Toledo: "Y en el papel octavo escribe ciertas palabras en arábigo y dice que avisen a ciertos moriscos se huyan. Y en el noveno papel avisa de cosas de su hacienda y dice que 'antes morirá mil muertes que traiga a nadie aquí, cuanto más a vosotros que sois la lumbre de mis ojos,' y que estén apercibidos si vieran que prenden a alguien que les toque y vieren que anda todo de malo, que se fuesen a Alicante etc." Also see García-Arenal's forthcoming study.
20. Rodríguez de Gracia, "Censo de moriscos," 523.
21. AHN, Inquisición, leg. 2105, exp. 30 (1594); and AHN, Inquisición, leg. 2105, leg. 31 (1595).
22. The MS RAH S2 includes several poems by Lope de Vega's *Rimas Sacras* (1614). This led to the groundbreaking article by Oliver Asín on the topic, "Un morisco de Túnez, admirador de Lope." López-Baralt expands on the topic in her preliminary study, included in the edition of the manuscript *Dos caminos*, 29–183.
23. Madroñal, "Entre Cervantes y Lope," 317–22.
24. "Ánimo pluma mía / començad a escribir sin ningún miedo / no mostréis cobardía /

que vuestro orijen es el gran Toledo, / çiudad mejor de España, / cuyos campo[s] el claro Tajo baña." BCR MS 1976, fol. 17v.

25. "Ioseph canta a Ioseph, Joseph humano / Canta a Joseph divino, y el divino / si crecieran sus méritos sus loores / más divino quedara de su mano, / y assí el humano a ser divino vino." Lope de Vega, "Al maestro Joseph de Validivelso," in Valdivielso, *Vida*, xxiii.
26. Aguirre, *José de Valdivielso*, 165.
27. "Una obra literaria cuyo sentido profano ha sido sustituido por otro sagrado. Se trata pues de la refundición de un texto. A veces la refundición conserva del original el metro las rimas y aun—siempre que no contradiga al propósito divinizador—el pensamiento." Wardropper, *Historia de la poesía*, 5–7.
28. "Ansí tomar a Homero sus versos y hacerlos propios, es erudición, que a pocos se comunica. Lo mismo se puede decir de nuestro Poeta (Garcilaso) que aplica y traslada los versos y sentencias de otros Poetas, tan a su propósito, y con tanta destreza, que ya no se llaman agenos, sino suyos; y más Gloria merece por esto, que no de su cabeza lo compusiera, como afirma Horacio en su Arte poética." El Brocense, "El Maestro Francisco Sánchez al Lector," in *Obras del Excelente Poeta, iii.*
29. Alfonso de Carvallo, *Cisne de Apolo*, 343–51.
30. See Alfonso de Carvallo, 345:

    —¿Sería lícito imitar verso, copla, estilo, y materia juntamente?

    —Esto es lo que llaman contrahacer, o volver, como aquel romance viejo que dice: "Por el rastro de la sangre / que Durandarte dejaba." Lo van contrahaciendo a lo divino todo, imitando la materia, verso y asonancia diciendo: "Por el rastro de la sangre / que Jesu Cristo dejaba."

31. "Porque hay algunas letras recibidas en el vulgo, de tan sucias cosas, que es menester Dios y ayuda para desterrarlas, por tener las tonadas de alguna gracia y donaire. Y así es muy necesario el contrahacerlas." Alfonso de Carvallo, 345.
32. Indeed, this phenomenon, going back to the Middle Ages, would reach its peak from the mid-sixteenth to early seventeenth century. In contrast to this moralizing vision, other critics like John Crosby have interpreted it first and foremost as a metapoetic resource without the express aim of moralizing. Crosby, *A lo divino*, 82. See also Menéndez Pelayo, "Poesía mística."
33. Sánchez Martínez, *Historia y crítica*, 24.
34. Alfonso de Carvallo, *Cisne de Apolo*, 345.
35. "La posibilidad de la creación contrafactista residiría en los posibles puntos de contacto emocionales entre el pensamiento expuesto en el poema profano y la significación religiosa del embriónico contrafactum." Aguirre, *José de Valdivielso*, 59.
36. Wardropper, *Historia de la poesía*, 43–55.
37. "Yo, picador, macho herrado, macho galopeado, me confieso a Dios barbadero y a soneta María tampoco, al bien trobado san Sánchez Batista y a los sonetos apóstatas san Perro y san Palo, y a vos, padre esperetual, daca la culpa, toma la culpa. Vuélvome a confesiar a todos estos que quedan aquí detrás, y a vos, padre esperetual, que estás en lugar de Dios, me deis pestilencia de mis pescados, y me sorbáis dellos. Amén, Jesús." Quevedo y Villegas, *Obras completas*, 101.
38. These and other negative terms are used in theory as a humorous device, an essentially linguistic mockery to imitate the malapropisms of a speaker whose native language is Arabic ("mis pescados y me sorbáis de ellos" instead of "mis pecados y me absolváis de ellos"; "yo, picador" instead of "yo pecador"), but one also inevitably sees how this confusion could constitute a form of blasphemy ("Dios barbadero" instead of "Dios verdadero"; "a Soneta María tampoco [me confieso]" instead of "a Santa María"), which ultimately creates a polemical tone ("Padre esperetual que estáis en lugar de Dios").

39. Menéndez Pidal, *Flor nueva de romances*, 206–7. This second version of profanization is related to the issue of fifteenth-century *religio amoris*, which has been studied in Lida, "Romance de la misa." See also Lida, "Hipérbole sagrada."
40. "King Phillip of Spain disposes / believing it will show his strength, / but God makes of him an instrument / of his infallible and immortal certainty / God orders that the proclamation be announced / for the Moriscos to leave quickly / and this exit becomes a path / to spend the rest of their lives in freedom." BCR MS 1976, fol. 19v.
41. "Cesar orders that the world get registered / believing it will show his strength / but God makes of him an instrument / of his infallible and immortal certainty / God orders that the proclamation be announced / For Joseph to come to the front / to his homeland Bethlehem, where it is written / that the infinite will shortly be born." Valdivielso, *Vida*, canto 12, fol. 164r.
42. Plinius Secundus, *Historia Natural*. Hernández's translation remained unpublished at the time. The first Spanish edition was the one translated by Gerónimo de Huerta, published in Madrid in 1624 by Luis Sánchez.
43. "Among the Arimaspi and Scythians, / barbarians in their way of life and their government, / Lotophagi, Cyclopes, Troglodytes, / nations whose home is in hell, / without other infinite thousands of nations, knew not he who is God eternal, / and having no light erred less / than the Christians did in what they founded." BCR MS 1976, canto 2, fol. 20r.
44. "From the depths of frozen Scythia / to the burnt Ethiopians, / and as far as the sun shines in its daily journey / on habitable and deserted lands / and as far as the salty sea reaches / the known and the remote kingdoms / there is no nation as bold against God / as the unknown infidel Christian nation." BCR MS 1976, canto 4, fol. 45r.
45. "Shall I take leave from my fair beloved? / Shall I go without my soul, for I gave it to my wife? / Shall I go to an inhabitable frozen Scythia, / or inhuman poisoned Libya? / Shall I go to black and burnt Ethiopia / or the deserts of sandy Africa? / Shall I live among Arismaspi, among Scythians, / Lotophagi, Cyclopes, Troglodytes?" Valdivielso, *Vida*, canto 10, 132r. Also, in canto 18, 242v: "En lo remoto de la Scithia elada, / dentro de un bosque pálido y sombrío, / hecho de una arboleda deshojada, / que baña un triste cenagoso río, / Ay una antigua gruta socavada, / en las entrañas de un peñasco frío, / cáense las paredes de podridas, / y las incultas piedras carcomidas."
46. Alfonso de Carvallo, *Cisne de Apolo*, 345.
47. See Alfonso de Carvallo, 350:

> —¿Y tomar una copla entera, o más, un exordio, romance ajeno y encajarlo en mis obras vendiéndolo por proprio mío, aprovechándome del trabajo ajeno, sería permitido?
> —En ninguna manera, porque eso es hurtar.
> —Pues no se suele usar poco.

48. "Ya me parece que estoy escuchando a los lectores de esta umilde obra, acabado que ayan de leer los barios pareçeres, la diferençia de gustos. Qual dirá que el bersso es inperfecto, qual dirá que es inpropio a la obra, qual dirá que es corto, qual dirá que es largo, qual dirá que ay berssos hurtados y que no pudo fulano haçellos o cómo se atrebe a haçer libro y otra ssemejança de murmuraçión que casusará mi libro." BCR MS 1976, fol. 117r.
49. This anecdote contributed to the famous debate about the date of publication of *Don Quijote de la Mancha* by Cervantes. See Oliver Asín, "*Quijote* de 1604."
50. Szpiech, *Conversion and Narrative*.
51. Fuchs, *Mimesis and Empire*. Also, Vincent Barletta analyzes how the use of *cuaderna vía* meter in early Morisco poetry represents a vehicle of legitimization by adopting a poetic form used in a prestigious Christian religious context. Barletta, *Covert Gestures*, 133–55.

52. "Que la poesía era la ciencia que enseñaba a distinguir lo público de lo particular, y lo sagrado de lo profano, y a edificar ciudades, y dar leyes para su gouierno." Alfonso de Carvallo, *Cisne de Apolo*, 168.
53. Sánchez Martínez, *Historia y crítica*, 59–60. Also the responses to these transpositions were diverse: just few *a lo divinio* texts were censored (*La caballería celestial* is one well-known example of a censored text from the genre of the chivalric romance), but some led to heated responses, such as the *Auto de Polifemo* by Juan Pérez de Montalbán, where Góngora's text is rendered in divine terms such that Ulysses becomes Jesus Christ. For Quevedo, who contested the work at length in Perinola (1632), not even a *moro buñolero* would think of doing what Pérez de Montalbán had done: "Por ir con la fábula, hace a Cristo Ulises. Ésta no es alegoría, sino algarabía; no hiciera cosa tan malsonante ni indecente un moro buñolero: porque la persona de Cristo no se ha de significar por un hombre que los propios gentiles idólatras le llamaron engañador, embustero y mentiroso" (Astrana Marín, *Vida turbulenta*, 850–51). It is not hard to imagine what Quevedo would have thought of Taybili's *Contradictión*.
54. De Córdoba, *Garcilaso a lo divino*.
55. Alonso, *Poesía de San Juan*, 257.
56. BNE 9074; and Wadham College, Oxford, MS A18.15.
57. Bodleian Library, Oxford, MS Arch. Selden B 8. See also Wiegers, "Andalusi Heritage"; and Harvey, "Second Morisco Manuscript."
58. Alguazir himself wrote in the proem that since most Christians do not know Arabic, they cannot read the content of the books that argue with them, for which reason he decided to write it in Spanish: "Por haber tan grandes sabios entre los moros que en este particular an escripto pero por abello escripto en arábigo y los cristianos no lo entienden atrevime por entender la lengua castellana por aberme criado entre los christianos y saber y entender la ley y las costumbres que guardan." BNE, MS 9074, fols. 1v–2r. All the references to this text are extracted from BNE, MS 9074. I want to thank Teresa Madrid Álvarez-Piñer for sharing with me her transcription of this manuscript.
59. Wiegers, "Moriscos and Arabic Studies," 603.
60. There is some evidence that these parts circulated separately: the Latin version (Bodleian Library, Selden B8), for example, just reproduces the first part, whereas MS 40 from the University Library of Uppsala reproduces the third one. A folio is left blank before the section starts. The opening is the traditional formula of the basmala, and the previous section ends with a closing formula as well: "Glorificado sea su nombre, amen. Al-Hamdulilah." It could also be understood as a closing chapter.
61. For example, this one that closes the eighth canto and marks the end of the polemical portion of the book: "Con esto, pluma mía, acabar puedes / de dar fin a este canto y a esta obra." BCR MS 1976, fol. 78v.
62. As he puts it,

    Mi boluntad no es más de poner mi trabajo y gastar el tiempo para solo que te entretengas y si as de passar los ojos y entretener el tiempo en alguna leyenda profana, le gastes en esta umillde obra donde hallarás deshecha y aniquilada la falssa ley cristiana y su artifiçiossa trinidad, de do la inmensa probidençia de dios te sacó y libró de sus herrores. También hallarás cómo el inmenso dios es uno en essençia y atributos y obras, que es eterno en su deidad, que es infinito, que fue antes de toda cossa será después de toda cossa. (BCR MS 1976, fol. 15v)

63. "Y al contrario de la de los moros, que cada uno dellos puede haçer su çala solo u acompañado con sacerdote o sin él." BNE MS 9074, fols. 57r–58v. Note the use of Christian religious language, *sacerdote*.

64. "Hasta dezir ziertas palabras con que dizen que dios deziende a la ostia, alçándola en alto se dan sobre los pechos adorándola por dios." BNE MS 9074, fols. 58v–59r.
65. "Porque pueden hablar y todo lo que en las plaças se haçe lo pueden haçer." BNE MS 9074, fol. 69v.
66. The use of fire leads him to compare it to hell and provide a polemic metaphor; the fire is a sign that because they celebrate the Mass, they are going to end up in hell: "Señal y prodijo del que por çelebralla an de padezer en el infierno." BNE MS 9074, fol. 60r.
67. "Y al contrario de todas estas cosas, en la ley divina de los moros pues lo primero que hacen en llegando la hora de la oración y sacriffizio se sube el que tiene cargo de llamar la gente en una torre, y en lugar de las canpanas que los christianos tienen." BNE MS 9074, fols. 60r–63v.
68. Taybili's criticism of the Mass, like Alguazir's, occupies the sixth chapter, but in Taybili, this chapter comes before the chapter on the Host, and in Alguazir, it comes after. Thus this canto follows a different order than that of the manuscripts held in the Spanish National Library, BNE (Alguazir, MS 9653).
69. BCR MS 1976, fols. 68r–68v.
70. "Que el que adora en otra cossa que dios y no sigue los preçeptos de dios adora al saytan y le sigue."

    يبني [*sic*] آدم أن لا تعبدوا الشيطان أنه لكم عدو مبين أن
    أعبدوني هذا صراط مستقيم

    BCR MS 1976, fol. 64v.
71. Qur'ān, sūrat yā-sīn (36:60–61): "[Did I not charge you,] O children of Adam! that you should not serve the Shaitan? Surely he is your open enemy, / And that you should serve Me; this is the right way." English translation by M. H. Shakir.
72. BCR MS 1976, fol. 65r.
73. "Inbentó una misa con que ensalma / sus saçerdotes y les apodera / de çera, roscas, bino y aun dinero, / a costa de la viuda y jornalero." BCR MS 1976, fol. 70r.
74. "Esta agua, señor, que es tan bendita, / me sea espiritual salud y bida, / y mi rogaria açepta y conçedida." BCR MS 1976, fol. 65r.
75. See Salinas, *Rhetórica en lengua castellana*, 43:

    Quando contamos alguna cosa como es guerra combites, amores, pestilencias, renzillas o otras cosas fuera de las personas, lugares y tiempos de que ya está dicho conviene poner las particularidades que en ella passaron, todas o aquellas que pueden favorescer al primer intento sobre que aqeullo se vino a contar. Como si contássemos alguna guerra que oviesse passado *con intento de encarescerla o ponerla delante los ojos para que los oyentes pudiessen juzgar della como si la vieran*, diríamos los fuegos que en ella uvo, los derribamientos de edificios, el ruido de lloros y gritos, el huir de los unos a los otros y encontrar con sus enemigos, y las muertes diversas: las madres muertas con los hijos en los braços, las donzellas perdidas y todas las otras particularides, poniendo algunas muertes en especial y derribamientos, o algunas de las otras cosas. Y lo mismo si hiziéssemos relación de algún combite o exequias, o de qualquier otra cosa. (emphasis added)

13

TORAH ALONE

Protestantism as Model and Target of Sephardi Religious Polemics in the Early Modern Netherlands

Carsten Wilke

The question of the effects that the schisms and internal controversies of the Western Church had on Jewish intellectual self-awareness during the early modern period is a broad and multilayered one that has been discussed frequently and from quite different angles. In one of the pioneering studies on this topic, published in 1970, Hayim Hillel Ben-Sasson noted "the relative paucity of articulated opinions found in contemporary Jewish sources," which are mostly concerned with the political fallout of the Christian schism for Jewish-Christian relations, particularly its effect on the levels of hostility or trust between communities. For Ben-Sasson, Luther's rebellion indeed fostered "Jewish hopes for an amelioration of their exiled status," but these hopes were soon to be disappointed. Whether observed with hope or frustration, the upheaval in the Christian world was interpreted in the religious view of history as a series of calamities leading up to the coming of the Messiah. As Ben-Sasson concludes, "Jewish reaction to the Reformation may here be seen as one of the factors that brought about a renewed flare-up of Messianism. At a later stage the same reaction impelled the religious and social elements of Jewish thinking towards a positive evaluation of individuality and personal freedom."[1] Jewish participation in the crucial events shaping Christianity was thus rather superficial. Remaining "an outside observer,"[2] the Jews were definitely more concerned about the political disorder caused by the schism than about the theological and intellectual issues at stake.

Ben-Sasson focused on Ashkenazi and Italian Jewish sources from the sixteenth and early seventeenth centuries.[3] More-recent research has taken the Sephardim into account and revealed a different picture. This community was not only interested in the question of whether the Reformation was good or bad for the social status of the Jews but had the intellectual desire to participate in its debates. As Yosef Kaplan writes, "The Sephardi Jews' great expertise in the subtleties of Christianity and their being a community with knowledge of many languages, especially Latin, created the infrastructure for the common discourse such as had been hitherto unknown in the relations between Jews and Christians."[4] Miriam Bodian has pointed out that certain aspects of Protestantism, especially the stress laid on the authority of the scriptures against tradition, seem to have infiltrated the religious thought and language of the Portuguese crypto-Jews as early as the mid-sixteenth century.[5]

Besides the appropriation of specific Protestant theologoumena, I will study on the following pages the intellectual insertion of the Sephardim into the overall European order of religious pluralism that emerged in the wake of the Reformation. After the publication of Jonathan Israel's seminal work *European Jewry in the Age of Mercantilism*, early modern historians began to take this research question seriously. More specifically, they started to take a closer look at the considerable impact that the internecine warfare within Christendom had on Jewish self-representation. Israel, however, formulated his explanation of the change in Jewish-Christian relations entirely on the basis of the secularization thesis. Around 1570, he argues, Christianity grew weary of confessional strife and explored the new complex of secular politico-economic thought that historians call mercantilism. An intellectual "upsurge of radical skepticism" characterized philosophy in the age of Montaigne, and according to Israel,

> During the final third of the sixteenth century, though, both Reformation and Counter-Reformation lost their former momentum and the hitherto universal Christian foundations of western culture began to crack and contract. It was now that Christianity embarked on that age-long retreat which has since become its familiar

> role in western culture—no longer the all-embracing, universal whole but what, to all appearances, had been a shrinking force compelled to compete with a host of rival outlooks and attitudes and, in particular, a rising tide of doubt, deism, and atheism.[6]

The turning point in this changeover from religious to political thought, according to Israel, was the 1570s, a decade that consequently witnessed the return of the Jews to Prague, Hamburg, London, Pisa, and other cities in the West. However, this construction of a long, drawn-out secularization process does not seem to do justice to the religious passions that marked the decade of the Battle of Lepanto, the Saint Bartholomew's Day Massacre, the Dutch Rebellion, and the mystics of Ávila and Safed. Instead of the simple de-Christianization narrative, historians have more recently applied a different model, which has become known as the confessionalization thesis. Developed by Wolfgang Reinhard and Heinz Schilling during the 1980s, with respect to Germany, this thesis considers the institutional and theological standardization of religious difference as a tool of political government and social discipline that was characteristic of the early modern period. Mercedes García-Arenal has stressed the inner ambivalence of this early modern transformation: "Confessionalization is the process of formation and definition of separate religious communities, and is in turn part of the formation process of the state."[7] The confessionalization thesis considers that in the early modern period, we are dealing not with the retreat of *religion* but rather with the expansion of *religions*, and that it is this development toward religious pluralism that had its characteristic effects even outside the areas that were immediately affected by religious differentiation. Starting with the Reformation, this process had spillover effects outside the realm of Christianity. Making the observation that "there have been no attempts to examine whether and to what extent the concept of confessionalization is relevant to the developments in early modern Islamdom," Tijana Krstić has been among the first scholars to make this point. She contends that "the Ottomans experienced analogous developments and even implemented policies leading to integration of politico-religious spheres similar to those taking place throughout the Habsburg and other contemporary European domains."[8]

After the collapse of the Catholic dominance that had characterized much of medieval Christianity, the new political and theological competition among churches also became the frame of reference for a Jewish community that had ceased to be the only religious minority and that could take steps to carve out for Judaism a place in the mosaic of confessions. To my knowledge, the first historians who thought about the confessionalization thesis in a Jewish key were Gerhard Lauer in a 2003 article "Die Konfessionalisierung des Judentums" and subsequently Dean Philip Bell in a book chapter titled "Confessionalization and Social Discipline in Early Modern Germany: A Jewish Perspective."[9] From an Iberian Jewish angle, it is most significant that the leading expert on Amsterdam Sephardi Jewry, Yosef Kaplan, has embraced this thesis in various recent publications. While his earlier work made some space for the secularization theory, according to which "sacred values were concentrated within the four walls of the religious institution,"[10] his more recent work has placed a new emphasis on the interconnectedness of religious and political change. In particular, the doctrinal and cultural confrontation with the Christian "other" became more important than ever for Jewish self-definition: "The entire raison d'être of the Diaspora was formed in confrontation and penetrating, uncompromising controversy with all the churches and sects of Christianity."[11] Kaplan clarified the relations between the two analytic concepts in a 2012 lecture titled "Confessionalization and Secularization in the Judeoconverso Diaspora."[12]

In the present chapter, I would like to contribute to this ongoing reflection by distinguishing various Sephardi positions that were formulated with respect to the process of religious differentiation in the Christian world in the sixteenth century and thereafter. What I will try to point out is how the process described by Ben-Sasson, where Jews give a meaning to the Christian Reformation by inserting it into their traditional representations of providential history, is gradually abandoned in favor of an inverse process in which Judaism as a socioreligious entity is located somewhere on the spectrum of the political, ideological, and cultural positions that determined confessional identity in post-Reformation Europe. From the time of their arrival in the North European ports, Portuguese Jews acknowledged this diversified map of religious groups and subgroups, and they intelligently occupied and defended their place among these groups by using the common discursive means of interconfessional controversy. We will see how Jewish authors, many of them laymen, developed strategies of doctrinal self-definition and polemical self-defense that helped them navigate a period of unprecedented religious pluralism while pretending to maintain the simple rabbinic opposition between Jews and idolaters.

An extremely rich source that documents this laboratory of early modern Jewish self-identity is the clandestine Sephardi literature written against the Christian religion, mostly in Amsterdam from the late sixteenth to the early eighteenth centuries in a progressively more diverse environment. Having explored this vast textual corpus for a number of years, I published in 2014 the foundational text of this polemical genre, the *Marrakesh Dialogues*, which was the anonymous work of a Portuguese New Christian that was most probably written in 1583 during the period of Calvinist rule in Antwerp.[13] Making use of this edition, as well as of my research on some later authors,[14] I am here going to investigate the question of how New Christians, after again becoming professed Jews, judged the new plurality of Christian churches.

Christian Diversity versus the Unbroken Chain of the Jewish Tradition

Jewish thinkers inherited from the medieval period a polemical attitude toward any manifestation of Christian disunion, an approach that is frequently encountered in early modern Islamic apologetics as well. Medieval Jewish authors from the time of the Great Schism, such as Profiat Duran, already pitted the alleged unanimity of the rabbinic chain of tradition against the chaotic infighting among the Christian authorities. By the time of the Reformation, this argument had become so standardized and outworn that the Portuguese humanist João de Barros depicts it in an allegorical dialogue, in which personified Understanding delivers a caricature of Jewish positions, while personified Reason presents the victorious Christian counterarguments. In one of the attacks, Understanding mocks the fragmentation of Christianity into sects, whose manifold dogmatic propositions this Jewish literary character calls a "salad bowl of withered herbs that is delicious for the fools and incomprehensible to the wise."[15]

This medieval Jewish argument is recycled from Barros by the Jewish author of the *Marrakesh Dialogues* into a real polemical context. This author—whom I identify with an Algarvian called Estêvão Dias, who was educated in Portugal during the first two decades of his life—lifted two pages from Barros, translating them from Portuguese into Spanish and adding further details about the ancient Christian sects and their specific dogmatic characteristics, which are copied out of Saint Isidore's *Etymologies* and set next to each other in order to create a comical impression of utter confusion. With the words of Barros's literary caricature, the real Jew ridicules real Christians who claim to have brought peace to the world while they have been continuously at war, not only with non-Christians, but with other Christians as well. It is ridiculous in Jewish eyes to see two armies of soldiers bearing the same cross and crossing themselves on their foreheads march against each other in battle.[16] A second polemical topos that permeates Sephardi anti-Christian writing is the relentless theological strife inside the Church. Already shortly before the Reformation, Abraham Farissol highlighted the desperate disunion among Christian scholars, and the *Marrakesh Dialogues* conclude in the same vein: "Since Christ was put to death 1583 years ago, they have never stopped besieging that rock upon which they pretend their Church is built. So many sects have existed among them and appear every day, each one trying to prove its rightful ownership."[17] In this context, the ancient heretics and the new Protestant churches are interpreted as manifestations of the same phenomenon of dogmatic uncertainty. Barros mentions in 1534 only the Lutherans, while the *Marrakesh Dialogues* in 1583 enumerate "Lutherans, free-thinkers, Calvinists, Anabaptists" (*luteranos, libertinos, calvinos, rebaptizados*). The author then throws in Barros's salad bowl quote, adding the remark that in Judaism, there are many sinners but few heretics.[18] In sum, the Jewish-Christian comparison comes to the same result for the humanist of 1534 and for the Jew of 1583 insofar as both emphasize the disunion and internal strife that reigns in the Church and contrasts with the stubborn consensus with which the Jews defend their law.

Among other ways of integrating the Reformation into a Judeocentric view of history is the interpretation of the Christian civil wars as birth pangs of the Messiah or as collective punishment of the Gentiles for their misdeeds against the Jews, an interpretation that Ben-Sasson documents most frequently among Ashkenazim.[19] These apocalyptic reactions to the Reformation can be found among the Sephardim as well: even crypto-Jews in Tavira (Algarve) interpreted the advance of Calvinism in France in 1562 as a sign that the Roman Church would lose its grip over religious life in Europe and that Portugal would soon grant religious liberty to Judaism as well.[20] The author of the *Marrakesh Dialogues* emerged from this turbulent environment, and in his work he welcomes the Flemish revolt with wild hopes for world redemption. Twelve years later, a possessor of the manuscript (who was possibly the author himself) would add a few disillusioned glosses, which I reproduce here in square brackets with an asterisk. Speaking about the idolatrous excesses of the Catholic cult of the saints, his protagonist Obadia makes the following proclamations:

Obadia: You see what a multitude of idols has grown from the initial principle of the Trinity. This did not remain a secret: England, Flanders, Germany and large parts of France, those countries that had been the first to believe it, discovered in the course of time all the fraud organized by the popes and prelates for the profit that they draw from it; they threw the yoke off their shoulders and do not obey the Roman Church any longer. And as the [*edifice of your] faith is already starting to crumble, I place my hope in our Lord that my eyes will see its final collapse, when all men will reject the devil's yoke that they now carry upon their shoulders, know God and observe His sacred Law, which His Divine Majesty be pleased to make happen in our days.

Andrew: What do you mean by that? You prefer the Lutherans over the Catholics?

Obadia: One is as good as the other [*if you want to go to hell]. True, the Lutherans [*—and even more, the Calvinists—] have already climbed a step up when they rejected the idols and started marching, and if there was someone capable of showing them the right haven, they would enter in it [*if the hatred that they all harbor against the Jews did not block the path to their understanding]. You know what they are like? They are like a ship that, anchoring in a dangerous port, suddenly recognizes the threatening damage, sets sail and escapes into the open sea. But as the ship has no captain to guide it towards a safe haven, it goes astray, tossed by the dangerous waves, [*and when the crew discovers a bay in enemy territory, they despise it, even more so when they find out that the entrance into the port would cost a fee almost equal to the value of their entire ship]. This is how they get lost as well, having no merit from their parents to be illuminated, until our Lord will decide to illuminate them, which He will do if they from their side get prepared to receive His Holy Law.[21]

As we can see from this excerpt, the Sephardi author endeavors to integrate the Reformation and especially the irruption of Calvinist iconoclasm into the traditional Jewish narrative of the coming of the Messiah. However, in contrast to the undiscriminating reactions of the Ashkenazim to the confessional turmoil, he identifies with the Calvinist position in the controversy over image worship and thereby gives the schism an additional meaning from a Jewish point of view. Jewish and Calvinist goals overlap quite a bit, with the difference being that the Calvinists do not go far enough in their return to the scriptures. After inserting the Reformation into the story line of Jewish apocalyptic expectations, Dias also locates Jewish aniconism on the doctrinal map of contemporary confessionalization. This field, however, is not a plotted plain but a stormy sea: Dias proposes an allegorical depiction of Protestantism as a ship that has to decide between one harbor that is life-threatening, another one that is safe but with exorbitant entrance duties, and a storm, for which the crew has no competent pilot. The first harbor, as you may guess, is Catholicism; the second is Judaism; and the sea is the unstable territory in between that is shared by the Protestant churches and sects, which recognize the prohibition against idolatry but are reluctant to submit to the other commandments.

The Anti-Catholic Alliance

Sympathy for the Protestant rebels against papal power can be documented in early modern Sephardi polemics right from the beginning. We find it as early as 1553 in Samuel Usque's *Consolation for the Tribulations of Israel.*[22] Among Jewish refugees from the Iberian Inquisitions, this reaction must have been natural, as they shared with the Dutch the hatred of the Inquisition and of Catholic repression in general. The arsenal of anti-Catholic stereotypes developed by Dutch Calvinists soon became a flexible cultural code that could be shared by Portuguese Jewish immigrants and their Christian hosts. The huge amount of polemical material that the new Jews inherited from their Protestant environment is particularly striking in the early clandestine texts. The *Marrakesh Dialogues* make their pro-Protestant bias explicit in multiple contexts. When the author defends the popular reading of the Bible, he claims that this practice undermined Catholic rule in Germany, England, the

Netherlands, a large part of France, and other countries.[23] In addition, the Jewish author writes in amazing detail about the corruption in the Catholic Church in order to make the absence of clerical abuses in Judaism appear as a selling argument in the latter's favor. Dias develops a series of antitheses between Christ and the pope,[24] pointing out the sharp contradictions between the message of the Gospel and the practice of the Church in the manner of a genre that since Luther was popular in Protestant religious polemics. The Church, according to our Jewish author, shows its inherent perversion by promoting image worship and simultaneously forbidding Jewish converts to keep the divine commandments included in the Mosaic Law. The author, in a way similar to Marnix's Dutch polemical satire *The Beehive of the Holy Roman Church*, denounces the prelates' economic exploitation and their love of money and power by developing in particular the subject of the seduction of women and girls by priests in the confessional.[25] One gets the impression that the Jewish polemicist simply takes a ride on the Protestant bandwagon for a long stretch of his road to religious truth, ready to jump off at the fork where reformed Christianity departs from Jewish tradition.

There is, however, a more intricate set of relations at work between the traditional Jewish-Gentile duality and the polemical Jewish self-identity newly accredited by the appropriation of Protestant polemics. This comes to the fore in the equating of Catholicism with pagan idolatry, which was common in both Jewish and Protestant self-representations.[26] The *Marrakesh Dialogues* offer a series of playful enumerations[27] in which the veneration of the Roman Catholic saints is compared to various ancient Roman cults. This time, our Jewish author plagiarizes a Spanish Erasmian author, Alonso de Valdés, who formulated an early attack against the cult of the saints in his clandestine *Diálogo de la cosas ocurridas en Roma* (Dialogue on the events that happened in Rome), which he composed in 1528. Valdés has one of his characters in the dialogue submit to an exercise in self-criticism. Catholics, he says, have given to the saints tasks just like the gods had among the polytheists. Saint James and Saint George have taken on the function of the god Mars. The pagan divinity Neptune still protects sea travelers, though he is now called Saint Elmo. Instead of Bacchus, believers venerate Saint Martin; Saint Barbara has replaced Eolus, and Saint Mary Magdalene has assumed the functions of Venus.[28]

Estêvão Dias has lifted this entire passage into his own text. However, in the vein of medieval Jewish polemicists starting with Profiat Duran,[29] he imagines a process of religious substitution taking place at some point during the emergence of Gentile Christianity: "There came the pagans, everyone bringing with him his favorite idol, and though he now called himself a Christian, he venerated it as he had done before. Saturn was renamed God the Father, Jupiter became Christ his son, and Mercury was called the Holy Spirit. Mars was renamed Saint James by some, by others Saint George. In the place of Juno they put Mary, instead of Venus they now said Mary Magdalene, and likewise for all the other gods that they [the Gentiles] brought with them."[30] We see in the comparison that here, a Protestant attack against a Church tradition has been appropriated as an element of the Jewish-Christian debate. "They only changed the names" is the punch line in various Sephardi texts. This saying, of Protestant coinage, will be quoted all through the seventeenth century as if it were an anti-Christian mantra.[31]

Indeed, the polemical historical conjectures of the *Marrakesh Dialogues* concerning the metamorphoses of gods into saints reappear in a number of clandestine works written in the Sephardi diaspora. Isaac Orobio de Castro (1617–87), for example, in his "Warnings against the Vain Idolatry of the Gentiles" (*Prevenciones contra la vana idolatría de las gentes*), writes the following about the pagan idols: "The first one is Saturn, imagined in the figure of an old man. The other one is presented as a young man and called the Son, in other words, he is Jupiter's successor, and the third one has the form of a pigeon, is called the Holy Ghost and in his messenger functions, he resembles Mercury pretty well. In addition, there are the images of a huge number of dead people, whose corpses are religiously venerated."[32]

In the 1680s, Abraham Gómez Silveyra wrote a satirical epic on the life of Jesus, which he starts with the observation that the many modern mythographers do not cover Jesus among the pagan gods. He ironically laments the great offense made to this deserving divinity, which should be honored as a real god no less than the great Jupiter: "I find it strange that they ignore this lad in such a scandalous way: are the other gods so much better fictions than him?"[33]

Gómez Silveyra launches the traditional accusation of idolatry at the Christians, but the target of his attack has now shifted from the cult of images, relics, and the host toward the dogmas on Christ and the Trinity. In this way, the appropriation of Protestant anti-Catholic motifs allows him to open a doctrinal battle against Christianity as such. Orobio and Gómez Silveyra reused elements of internal Christian polemics for an outside attack, which might confirm at first glance the age-old dual positioning of rabbinic tradition, according to which Jews alone participate in divine revelation while the Gentiles, be they pagans or Christians, are image-worshippers who do not even belong to the same category of religion.[34] However, Portuguese Jewish polemicists' abundant intertextual borrowings from Christian confessional sources show in fact the exact opposite: by using the rhetorical convention of presenting the other as a pagan on the basis of mythological and ethnographic proof, Jews had integrated a popular polemical model that lay at the foundations of early modern confessionalized Christianity.

Socinians and Skeptics

Jewish authors of the seventeenth century developed a subtle strategy of taking sides in the post-Reformation theological rivalry between Christian churches. They were well aware of the new turn in the pluralization process, which started when the Arminian, Jansenist, Spinozist, and Enlightenment controversies initiated a progressive internal diversification of the confessional camps and occasionally even blurred the boundaries between them. Each Christian denomination offered various polemical positions; Jews could fraternize with one of them while keeping their distance from the others. The Jewish doctrinal standpoint could finally be defined as a well-argued compromise between Christian theological extremisms.[35]

Rabbi Menasseh ben Israel's interest and intervention in the Arminian controversy that split the Dutch Reformed Church provides the most sophisticated expression of this strategy. Henry Méchoulan wrote that "his artistry in the role of privileged interlocutor of the non-Jews was not merely confined to the sphere of diplomatic activity or the description of the spiritual status of non-Jews. For it is in the field of theology that our rabbi shows his true worth."[36] In his theological works published between 1632 and 1642, Rabbi Menasseh ben Israel supported the cause of the Remonstrants not only because this persecuted sect was more sympathetic to Jews in Amsterdam public life but also because the Remonstrants defended freedom of will against the dogma of predestination that was espoused by staunch Calvinists. In his treatise on human weakness (*De la fragilidad humana*) of 1642, Ben

Israel argues against Pelagianism by stressing humanity's need for divine grace *ab auxiliis*, but at the same time, he defends the power that every man has to make a choice between good and evil. By discussing the Jewish answers to the problems of sin and grace, the rabbi points out that Calvinism and Pelagianism are both inadmissible according to Judaism, although the latter is closer to the Pelagian than the Calvinist position.[37]

The Latin edition of the book is dedicated to Gherbrand van Anslo, a young man from an Anabaptist family, to whom ben Israel writes the following: "People have come to believe that friendship can only exist among those souls who share the same religious faith. This opinion is all the more wrong as it contradicts the ancient masters who taught that Man is social by nature . . . I am always deeply amazed when I realize how much black poison circulates in the souls of the multitude, and how they deny the natural social instinct of humanity by refusing to join anyone who does not share their opinions."[38] Friendship, in ben Israel's view, could very well coexist with doctrinal disagreement. Distinguishing not only between a man and his creed but also among different tendencies inside a given religious community and finally among convincing and unacceptable propositions in the work of one and the same theological author, Amsterdam Jewish polemicists developed a critical and very subtle theological assessment of each and every position in the Christian world, discovering surprising affinities with Protestant scripturalism, Catholic traditionalism, Unitarian strict monotheism, and even Islamic and Masonic teachings on divine unity and universal ethics. This selective approach can be found even in Orobio, who states that in the doctrine of justification, the "papalists" are right against Calvin, even though with respect to the Bible and images, Calvin is superior to them. Orobio uses scholastic differentiation when he observes that "Calvin and many theologians, even some of ours, confuse sanctification and glorification."[39]

There are in particular many expressions of mutual acceptance in the literature of the Jews and of the Unitarians. The related theological discussion between these two radical opponents of orthodox Christianity has not yet been sufficiently studied. Daniel de Breen, a Dutch Unitarian, was one of the first Christians to try to gain access to the clandestine polemical texts of the Jews, and he was one of the first who got a hold of some of them.[40] From the 1630s, he argued with Rabbi Saul Levi Mortera, and these conversations prompted the latter around 1655 to begin his huge unfinished manuscript titled *On the Truth of the Law of Moses.*

Rabbi Mortera distributes throughout his work his agreement with and repudiation of different Christian confessions in a nuanced way. In principle, he is in favor of the theology of the Reformed Church over and against Catholic teachings. Calvin's writings help the Amsterdam rabbi in his polemic against the temporal power of the popes and the cruelty of the Inquisition as well as Catholicism's worship of images and relics.[41] However, Calvin only finished half the job. He still believed in the Trinity and in the Gospels, the books that promote the divinity of Christ as an "intellectual idolatry."[42] The reformed fell into some additional errors of their own over matters in which the Jewish position happens to have a close affinity with that of the Catholics, especially with respect to the doctrine of predestination and the Holy Spirit, which according to Calvinist theology, continuously assists the believer when he affirms his faith.[43]

In all these points of view, Socinian Christianity is indisputably on Judaism's side, and Mortera therefore salutes these dissenters as allies in the fight for strict monotheism.[44] However, the question of Christ's messiahship and the inspired character of the Gospels remains the bone of contention between these allied dissidents. As Méchoulan writes, "Brothers in suffering persecution, Jews and Socinians are not brothers in theology."[45] Mortera relates an encounter that took place around 1634 with one of the Dutch dissidents. This was, the rabbi writes, "an old man of kind manners and much learning who in discussion with me told me that there was hardly a difference between them and us. I asked him how he could affirm this, as we believe in God being a single and very pure essence, whereas the Socinians confess the Trinity."[46] The man told Mortera that he was mistaken, as they believed that there was no God but the creator. Mortera remembers how much he was surprised by this encounter, the first he had with one of the "new reformed that are vulgarly named Socinians." Mortera asked the Socinian whether he believed in Christ at all, and his interlocutor told him that he believed in him not as a divinity but as the purest and most sovereign creature that God ever formed.

The Socinians, Mortera learned, insist on the status of the Gospels as revelation in order to claim that Jesus was the Messiah. Since this is the central matter of their faith, Mortera focuses on the argument against the credibility of the Evangelists' testimony on Jesus, even if the latter is considered by the Socinians merely as the Jewish Messiah and a religious teacher and not the divinized Christ of Church orthodoxy. In the first pages of his treatise, Mortera gives a fascinatingly elaborate allegory of the religious controversies that crisscrossed the Netherlands, definitively supporting the Socinians as his favorite team in the competition. His image of denominational strife is, however, that of a naval battle, which turns the encounter among multiple religious communities into a duel between divine truth and human error—a battle that in fact every Protestant wages with Church tradition.[47] For Mortera, as a Jew, the fight against Protestantism and even Unitarianism is only the second and the third stage, respectively, in his war against Christianity. He sums up his strategy by interpreting Deuteronomy 13:7, "You shall not serve the gods of the nations that surround you, close or far," to mean that with the arguments that reveal the falseness of the gods that are near to us (such as the palpable host), we will also recognize the falsity of the gods that are far from us (such as the spiritualized ideal of Christ).[48]

It is in this context that Mortera documents the emergence of a typically skeptical argument. In the private discussions he had with Socinians, one of his interlocutors claimed that just as Mortera questioned the coherence of the Gospels and their value as a religious source (as he did in the clandestine texts he had been writing since 1631), any Christian could likewise deconstruct Mosaic Law, and both faiths would wind up without any foundation whatsoever for their religious world views, resulting in a breakdown of all authority, something that needed to be avoided at all costs.[49]

In reaction to this skeptical argument, Rabbi Mortera gives a dramatic turn to his image of the naval battle, which is clearly reminiscent of Dutch military accounts and naval paintings from the period. At the moment of defeat, a battleship threatens to set fire to its gunpowder and to blow up both ships in order to avoid being captured by the enemy. This is the gesture of the Christian skeptics, who threaten to demolish all certainty and faith when the pseudoarguments they had wished to use in defense of their dogmas have been proven powerless.[50] Mortera, then, has to go into the distinctions between the Torah and the Gospels in terms of historical origins, literary form, and theological message. As a Jew, he could not be a skeptic; but even for the Christian, skepticism is a deeply absurd option, a sort of theological suicide bombing, which only shows the utterly forlorn hope of any sort of Christology.

Toleration

The position according to which no religious authority can be proven (and therefore all of them need to be accepted) seemed like a sort of terrorism for Rabbi Mortera, but nonetheless it became, under the label of toleration, a sort of consensus position two generations later in the context of the early Enlightenment. The foremost Jewish polemicist of the early Enlightenment period in Amsterdam, Abraham Gómez Silveyra (1656–1741), claims for the Jewish observer the privileged position of an impartial judge in the deadlocked confessional struggle because he maintains only what is incontrovertible among all believers: the revealed truth of the Torah. This is how Gómez Silveyra opens the second book of the seven-volume collection that he produced between 1700 and 1738, still in Golden Age Spanish, under the title *Silveyradas*. It was begun as a refutation of the *Dissertations on the Messiah* of the Huguenot pastor Isaac Jacquelot (1647–1708), to whom he addresses the following warning:

> As I have to tell you before we start, I consider that we agree on the fact that God is the judge of the controversies and that His word is the foolproof rule of truth. As all errors are due to bad translation or bad explanation of texts, I will not make any comment upon the Hebrew words, nor will I deviate from their genuine sense. The Statue of Nebuchadnezzar was made of gold: pure gold is to be found in the clear verses that I quote and in the authority of the Sages that I repeat. Silver is in the natural glosses of the finest-tuned commentators. Clay and iron is everything that I may add to this. "Your word is the light of my foot" (Ps. 119:105): if I only follow God according to the tradition of the Sages, everything will be silver enameled with gold and cannot be false. . . . According to this, I pray you, and I pray the reader not to care about anything I say and to follow only what God and the Sages say.[51]

Gómez Silveyra, however, is quick to put Jacquelot out of mind. In the volumes that would follow, he is eager to discuss other major Christian controversists of his time. His reports from Christendom's theological and political battlefields transcend the generic limits of early modern religious controversy because the author attributes truth only to the exact wording of the scriptures and wishes to judge any man's words neutrally and critically. Indeed, Gómez Silveyra introduces the last volume, the *Mute Book*, in 1738, with the typical skeptic's dilemma that "there exist so many religions in the world and in each one there are so many and such diverse beliefs."[52] Believers, he mused in a book of humorous dialogues, look like a band of humpbacks walking in a circle: everyone sees the other's hump, but no one can see his own.[53] In his case, the Jew who joins the circle dance of the denominations is caught in the Pyrrhonian *isostenia*, the equivalence of antithetical arguments. The only legitimate belief is in a truth that is concretized in the Torah yet beyond institutional formulation and that leaves open the hope for a religious peace that antagonists would negotiate among themselves, respecting each other's inviolable individual conscience. In this way, the only method of ending religious controversies is by bringing them down to the ground zero of the Torah, which is recognized by all. In his fifth volume, published in 1725, Gómez Silveyra triumphantly insists on Calvin's recognition of prophetic authority and makes the following conclusion: "If the learned men considered well their own words, I would have nothing to say. All those biblical verses where true prophets reprehend false prophets, the Calvinists launch them at the papalists, and the papalists launch them at the Calvinists, everyone applying them to each other. All of them are right, because they all take away, augment and change what God has commanded in His law with the prohibition against taking away, augmenting or changing anything."[54]

Insofar as he represents the strict adherence to the Torah expressed in Judaism as the oldest monotheistic tradition, Gómez Silveyra claims the position of judge in the religious controversies of his time. He knows, however, that theology is not the only variable when it comes to religious politics. The pope and the king of France admit Jews but not Protestants; the king of England admits Jews but not Catholics. The Jews are inevitably loyal to their sovereign—they pray for their princes and have never revolted against any of them—because the strength and well-being of political authority is always in their best interest. The Socinians are persecuted everywhere, even though they believe in creation, providence, and retribution.[55] Mutual self-interest, not religion, is the basis of interstate alliances. France supported the Netherlands in their rebellion against Spain, but after the Peace of

Westphalia, when France became too powerful, Catholic Spain and Calvinist Holland joined forces to fight against France. According to Gómez Silveyra, "This happens every day, and it is very reasonable that one changes interests according to the occasion."[56]

Toleration of other creeds is not so much a maxim of philosophical skepticism as it is a simple political and economic necessity. Gómez Silveyra remembers that when the Spanish ambassador came to Amsterdam and was received by the Jews, he said that he then understood why the Dutch were so powerful and prosperous: "Liberty of Conscience is the strongest artillery with which these people, though they are heretics, liberated themselves from the dominion of my lord the King of Spain." And Gómez Silveyra concludes thus: "Charity and tolerance, justice and neighborly love are the foundations on which states are based, and if these are lacking, Divine Providence will not spare them their ruin."[57] What someone detests most in others, one does not notice in one's own personality, and very often a person accuses another slanderously of his own flaws. Toleration as a political rule is a corrective to man's natural egotism and narrow-mindedness. It promises a provisional truce in the permanent conflict that will find its solution only in the messianic age.[58]

In conclusion, I want to summarize my arguments in several points. The first is the surprising involvement of non-Christians in the confessionalization process. The status of Jews in early modern European society should be attributed not (or at least not only) to a process of secularization and neutralization of the public sphere but to its organization according to confessional lines, which maintained the importance of the distinctive religious credo in social life but envisioned the politico-religious order according to a pluralized pattern. The Sephardim of the early modern period did not define Jewishness primarily as the social experience of exile among the nations; rather, they defined it largely in theological terms as a set of recognizable dogmas, texts, memories, symbols, and rituals, which were considered among a plurality of other religious communities possessing different though comparable dogmas, texts, memories, symbols, and rituals.

Second, a clear historical and literary chain of tradition leads from the initial debates within Christianity to the new theological self-definition expressed in the clandestine vernacular texts of Portuguese Jewish writers. In fact, the reception and deployment of Christian literary models is in some cases so obvious as to indicate pure imitation.

Third, Jews start becoming involved in theological controversies with the second wave of the Reformation, when the intraconfessional divisions and the proliferation of dissident opinions transformed what had been a dichotomous debate (Protestants vs. Catholics) into a pluralistic one.

Fourth, among all the theological positions, the most radical ones—namely, free thought and skepticism—played additional roles as wild cards with thoroughly ambivalent effects. Maintaining a position of religious skepticism allowed a society to tolerate, on a provisional basis, different theological opinions, as it was impossible to decide the winner of an argument; however, such a position could also justify political means of coercion.

Fifth, the mind-set of tolerance arose from this confessional structure and its subversion by the tendency toward skepticism. We have come across a skeptical formula for tolerance, which accepts all faiths because nothing certain can be known, but there is also an antiskeptical kind of tolerance, which calls on all faiths to accept one another in order to uphold and defend the commonly held belief in God, providence, revelation, and retribution against the attacks made by free thinkers. And finally, we have, as in Abraham Gómez Silveyra, a blend of both positions: the arguments for religious relativism are put forward in order to counter the claims of religious exclusivism, while a firm confidence in the full and exclusive certainty of scriptural revelation is maintained in order to define a set of religious beliefs that must be shared by all faiths for there to be peaceful interconfessional coexistence in the enlightened state. In Gómez Silveyra, a fervent embrace of liberty of conscience, leading to a call for religious peace among all Christians, Jews, and Muslims, thus accompanies an extremist insistence on biblical truth. One has the impression that the two complementary demands of Dutch Calvinism, *scriptura sola* and *conscientiae libertas*, were melded into a newly defined Jewish doctrine whose central principle of "Torah alone" is considered as the only theological tenet capable of offering a minimal religious consensus to a divided humanity.

Notes

This chapter was previously presented at the seminar of the research project "Conversion, Overlapping Religiosities, Polemics and Interaction: Early Modern Iberia and Beyond" (CORPI) / CCHS-CSIC Madrid, September 30, 2016. I thank the Maimonides Centre for Advanced

Studies at the University of Hamburg for supporting the work on this chapter with a research fellowship and the discussions at the MCAS workshop "Jewish-Christian Polemics in the Middle Ages and in the Early Modern Period" on June 15, 2016.

1. Ben-Sasson, "Reformation," 313, 315–16.
2. Ben-Sasson, 239.
3. For new research on the sixteenth century, see Siewert, *Isaak ben Abraham*; Voß, *Umstrittene Erlöser*.
4. Kaplan, *Alternative Path*, 23.
5. Bodian, "Cross-Currents"; Bodian, *Dying in the Law*, 24–25; Bodian, "Reformation and the Jews," 126; Bodian, "Crypto-Jewish Criticism of Tradition," 35–36.
6. Israel, *European Jewry*, 30.
7. García-Arenal, "Creating Conversos," 14.
8. Krstić, *Contested Conversions*, 13.
9. Lauer, "Konfessionalisierung des Judentums"; Bell, "Confessionalization and Social Discipline."
10. Kaplan, *Alternative Path*, 21.
11. Kaplan, "Between Christianity and Judaism," 340.
12. Presented at the conference "Jewish History and Culture in Early Modern Europe: The Eighteenth Century Reconsidered," Heinrich Heine University Düsseldorf, June 25, 2012.
13. Wilke, *Marrakesh Dialogues*.
14. Wilke, "Midrashim from Bordeaux"; Wilke, *Isaac Orobio*. The latter volume is the result of a workshop that I organized in February 2016 at the Maimonides Centre for Advanced Studies at the University of Hamburg. Abraham Gómez Silveyra, who will be studied here as well, was the research subject of my fellowship at the same center in 2015–16.
15. Barros, *Ropicapnefma*, 121: "Agora nouamente a [opinião] dos Lutheranos, que ée huma salada de todas estas passadas eruas, muy saborosa a jgnorantes & dissimulada dalguns doctos."
16. Wilke, *Marrakesh Dialogues*, 295: "¿No veis que dijo Cristo, 'no penséis que vine a meter paz en la tierra: no vine sino a meter guerra y cuchillo, fuego y separación'? Lo que, cierto, bien se ha cumplido, especialmente entre cristianos, que desque los hay, siempre ha habido continuas guerras, no sólo contra sus enemigos, mas empero contra los que tienen su agua del baptismo. Y sin temor del señal de la Cruz, contra quien van, hacen otro en la frente que los libre de aquel peligro."
17. Wilke, 296.
18. Wilke, 298–99: "Y hora nuevamente los luteranos, libertinos, calvinos, rebaptizados, los cuales afirman ser necesario creer primero que baptizar—lo que todo es salada de todas las pasadas hierbas, sabrosa a necios y disimulada de doctos. En la Santa Ley que nuestro Señor nos dio no ha habido nada desto. Aunque, como hombres, somos y hemos sido pecadores, fuimos siempre muy celosos della, trayéndola por escudo de nuestra defensión, en virtud de la cual tañendo aquellas celestiales trompas, los muros de la ciudad caían por tierra."
19. Ben-Sasson, "Reformation," 301.
20. Wilke, "New Christians of Tavira."
21. Wilke, *Marrakesh Dialogues*, 390–91. The later additions are conserved in MS heb. 240g, Staatsbibliothek, Hamburg.
22. Usque, *Consolation for the Tribulations*, 185, 193; Bodian, "Reformation and the Jews," 123–24.
23. Wilke, *Marrakesh Dialogues*, 361.
24. Wilke, 384–87.
25. Wilke, 486.
26. Bodian, "Portuguese Jews," 335–38, 357.
27. Wilke, *Marrakesh Dialogues*, 389–90.
28. Alonso de Valdés, *Diálogo de las cosas ocurridas*, 206: "Mirad como havemos repartido entre nuestros santos los officios que tenían los dioses de los gentiles. En lugar de dios Mars, han sucedido Sanctiago y Sanct Jorge; en lugar de Neptuno, Sanct Elmo; en lugar de Baco, Sanct Martín; en lugar de Eolo, Sancta Bárbola; en lugar de Venus, la Madalena."

29. Wilke, "Historicizing Christianity."
30. Wilke, *Marrakesh Dialogues*, 389–90: "Venían los gentiles, trayendo cada uno su ídolo que tenía, y llamándose cristiano lo adoraba como de antes. Y por Jano pusieron a Dios Padre; y en lugar de Júpiter al hijo Cristo, y por Mercurio al Espíritu Santo. Y por Marte pusieron unos Santiago, otros San Jorge; y por Juno pusieron a María; y por Venus a la Magdalena. Y ansí a cada uno de los otros que traían les apropriaban una virtud conforme a lo que en los gentiles lo tenían; y solamente les fueron mudando los nombres."
31. Wilke, 487.
32. Kaplan, *From Christianity to Judaism*, 253; Orobio, *Israël Vengé*, 197.
33. Brown and Boer, *Barroco sefardí*, 98: "Que es grande afrenta y agravio visto / no meter en este baile à Jesucristo, / y es necesario, siendo tan sublime / que como el mismo Júpiter se estime. / Su fábula no hacer, es darle cómo, / porque Cristo es un dios de tomo y lomo, / que no hagan caso del, mucho me admira: / son los otros acaso más mentira? / Mas como yo le soy aficionado, / su fábula he de hacerle de contado, / porque muy grande ingratitud parece / no tratar deste Dios como él lo merece."
34. Bodian, "Portuguese Jews," 347–48.
35. For the sixteenth century, see Friedman, "Reformation in Alien Eyes"; Friedman, "Unitarians and New Christians."
36. Méchoulan, "Menasseh ben Israel," 93. See also Rauschenbach, *Judentum für Christen*.
37. Ben Israel, *Fragilité humaine*, 95.
38. Ben Israel, 87–88.
39. Orobio, *Prevenciones divinas*, 1:191.
40. Van Rooden, "Dutch Adaptation."
41. Salomon, *Saul Levi Mortera*, 767.
42. Salomon, 449: "Quem naõ ue que Joaõ Caluino, como quem sajo da tenebrosa escuridade dos erores papisticos, tinha a uista turbada, e naõ podia sofrir muita claridade? E assim naõ enxergou mas que o entropeso das imagines, istrumentos da idolatria actual. Por em, se fora caminhado mas adiante por os mesmos pasos, tomando a sua uista mas forças para fisalos em major claridade, enxergaua taõ bem o erro da pluralidade na esencia deuina, e pellas mesmas rezons que as outras refutaria os libros que insinaõ tal doctrina, como istrumentos da idolatria mental."
43. Salomon, 1097.
44. Bodian, "Portuguese Jews," 351–52.
45. Méchoulan, "Morteira et Spinoza," 59.
46. Méchoulan, 59–60; Fischer, "Opening the Eyes," 137–38.
47. Salomon, *Saul Levi Mortera*, 3.
48. Salomon, 867.
49. Salomon, 7.
50. Salomon, 3.
51. MS 75-F-5, Koninklijke Bibliotheek, the Hague, fols. 2v–3r.
52. MS 48-B-18, Ets Haim, Amsterdam, fol. 1r.
53. Gómez Silveyra, *Entretenimientos gustosos o diálogos burlescos*, MS mic. 2535, JTS, New York, p. 12: "Una recua de corbados / en un círculo redondo / ninguno ve su corcova / cada cual ve la del otro."
54. MS 48-A-18, Ets Haim, Amsterdam, fol. 180v.
55. MS 48-A-18, fol. 226v.
56. MS 48-A-18, fol. 227r.
57. MS 48-A-18, fol. 227v.
58. MS mic. 2535, JTS, New York, p. 248.

Bibliography

Abarbanel, Isaac. *Yeshuʿot meshiḥo.* Koenigsberg: Gruber et Langrien, 1861.

Abner of Burgos [Alfonso de Valladolid]. *Mostrador de Justicia.* 2 vols. Edited by Walter Mettmann. Opladen: Westdeutscher Verlag, 1994–96.

Accurti, Tommaso. *Editiones saeculi XV pleraeque bibliographis ignotae: Annotationes ad opus quod inscribitur "Gesamtkatalog der Wiegendruke" (G. K. W., I–IV).* Florence: Leo S. Olschki, 1930.

Addas, Claude. *Quest for the Red Sulphur: The Life of Ibn ʿArabi.* Lahore: Suhail Academy, 2000.

Aguiló i Fuster, Marian. *Cançoner Catalá.* 1900. 2 vols., facsimile of the first edition. Palma de Mallorca: Mossén Alcover, 1951–52.

Aguirre, José Miguel. *José de Valdivielso y la poesía religiosa tradicional.* Toledo: Diputación Provincial de Toledo, 1965.

Alabrús Iglesias, Rosa María. "San Juan de Ribera y la legitimación de la Expulsión de los moriscos." In *El Patriarca Ribera y su tiempo. Religión, política y cultura en la Edad Moderna,* coordinated by Emilio Callado Estela and Miguel Navarro Sorní, 547–54. Valencia: Diputació de València, 2012.

Alamany, Joan. *Obra de fray Joan Alamany de la venguda de Antichrist e de les coses que se han de seguir, ab una reprobaciò de la secta mahometica.* Valencia: Juan Jofre, 1520.

Albarracín Navarro, Joaquina. "Actividades de un *faqīh* mudéjar." In *Actas del VI Simposio Internacional de Mudejarismo. Teruel 16–18 de septiembre de 1993,* 437–44. Teruel: Instituto de Estudios Mudéjares, 1995.

Albarracín Navarro, Joaquina, and Juan Martínez Ruiz. *Medicina, farmacopea y magia en el "Misceláneo de Salomon" (texto árabe, traducción, glosas aljamiadas, estudio y glosario).* Granada: Universidad de Granada, 1987.

Albera, Dionigi. "'Why Are You Mixing What Cannot Be Mixed?' Shared Devotions in the Monotheisms." *History and Anthropology* 19, no. 1 (2008): 37–59.

Albo, Joseph. *Sefer ha-ʿikkarim: Book of Principles.* 4 vols. Edited by Isaac Husik. Philadelphia: Jewish Publication Society of America, 1946.

Alcalá Galve, Ángel. "Herejía y jerarquía. La polémica sobre el Tribunal de Inquisición como desacato y usurpación de la jurisdicción episcopal." In *Perfiles jurídicos de la inquisición española*, coordinated by José Antonio Escudero López, 61–87. Madrid: Universidad Complutense–Instituto de Historia de la Inquisición, 1986.

Alcover, Antoni Maria, and Francesc de Borja Moll. *Diccionari català-valencià-balear*. 10 vols. Palma de Mallorca: Moll, 1968–79.

Aldea Vaquero, Quintín, Tomás Marín Martínez, and José Vives Gatell, eds. *Diccionario de Historia Eclesiástica de España*. 4 vols. Madrid: Consejo Superior de Investigaciones Científicas, 1972–75.

Alfonsi, Petrus. *Dialogue against the Jews*. Translated by Irven Michael Resnick. Washington, DC: Catholic University of America Press, 2006.

———. *Dialogus contra iudaeos*. In *Pedro Alfonso de Huesca, Diálogo contra los judíos*, coordinated by María Jeús Lacarra. Huesca: Instituto de Estudios Altoaragoneses, 1996.

Alfonso X el Sabio. *Cantigas de Santa María*. 3 vols., edited by Walter Mettmann. Madrid: Castalia, 1989. Translated by Kathleen Kulp-Hill as *Songs of Holy Mary of Alfonso X, the Wise: A Translation of the Cantigas de Santa María*. Tempe: Arizona Center for Medieval and Renaissance Studies, 2000.

Alfonso, Esperanza. *Islamic Culture through Jewish Eyes: Al-Andalus from the Tenth to Twelfth Century*. London: Routledge, 2008.

Alfonso, Esperanza, Javier del Barco, M. Teresa Ortega Monasterio, and Arturo Prats, eds. *Biblias de Sefarad / Bibles of Sepharad. Las vidas cruzadas del texto y sus lectores*. Madrid: Biblioteca Nacional de España, 2012.

Alonso, Carlos. *Los apócrifos del Sacromonte (Granada). Estudio histórico*. Valladolid: Ediciones Estudio Agustiniano, 1979.

Alonso, Dámaso. *La poesía de San Juan de la Cruz, desde esta ladera*. Madrid: Silverio Aguirre, 1942.

Alonso Acero, Beatriz. *Cisneros y la conquista española del norte de África. Cruzada, política y arte de la guerra*. Madrid: Ministerio de Defensa–Secretaría General Técnica, 2006.

Alpartil, Martín de. *Cronica actitatorum temporibus Benedicti XIII pape*. Edited by José Ángel Sesma Muño and María del Mar Agudo Romero. Zaragoza: Centro de Documentación Bibliográfica Aragonesa, 1994.

Álvarez Gracia, Andrés. "El Islam y los judíos en Caspe." In *Territorio 30*, coordinated by Miguel Caballú Albiac and Francisco Javier Cortés Borroy, 109–22. Zaragoza: Gobierno de Aragón, 2008.

Ambrose of Milan. *Hexameron, De paradiso, De Cain, De Noe, De Abraham, De Isaac, De bono mortis*. Edited by Caroli Schenkl. Corpus Scriptorum Ecclesiasticorum Latinorum 32. Vienna: F. Tempsky, 1897.

Ames, Christine Caldwell. *Medieval Heresies: Christianity, Judaism, and Islam*. Cambridge: Cambridge University Press, 2015.

Amran, Rica. *Judíos y conversos en el Reino de Castilla. Propaganda y mensajes políticos, sociales y religiosos (siglos XIV–XVI)*. Valladolid: Junta de Castilla y León–Consejería de Cultura y Turismo, 2009.

Andrés, Juan. *Confusión o confutación de la secta mahomética y del Alcorán*. Valencia: Juan Jofre, 1515. Modern edition by Elisa Ruiz García and M. Isabel García-Monge. Extremadura: Junta Regional, 2003.

Antist, Vicente Justiniano. *La vida e historia del apostólico predicador sant Vicent Ferrer*. Valencia: Pedro de Huete, 1575.

Antonio, Nicolás. *Bibliotheca hispana nova, sive hispanorum scriptorum qui ab anno MD ad MDCLXXXIV floruere notitia*. 2 vols. Madrid: Joaquín de Ibarra, 1783; Madrid: Visor Libros, 1996.

Antonio, Nicolás, and Francisco Pérez Bayer. *Bibliotheca hispana vetus, sive hispani*

scriptores qui ab Octaviani Augusti aevo ad annum Christi MD floruerunt. 2 vols. Madrid: Joaquín de Ibarra, 1788.
Antonio Ortí, Marco. *Siglo quarto de la conquista de Valencia.* Valencia: Juan Bautista Marçal, 1640.
Aquinas, Thomas. *Opera omnia iussu impensaque Leonis XIII P. M. edita.* 50 vols., V. 13, *Summa contra gentiles.* V. 40, *De rationibus fide.* Rome: Ex typographia polyglotta S. C. de Propaganda Fide, 1882.
Argelich Gutiérrez, María A. "El Pintor cristiano y erudito de Juan Interián de Ayal. Entre el moralismo post-tridentino y el racionalismo pre-ilustrado." PhD diss., Universitat de Lleida, 2014.
Arranz Roa, Íñigo. "Las Indias de aquí: misiones interiores en Castilla, siglos XVI–XVII." *Estudios eclesiásticos* 82, no. 321 (2007): 389–409.
Asad, Talal. *Genealogies of Religion: Discipline and Reasons of Power in Christianity and Islam.* Baltimore, MD: Johns Hopkins University Press, 1993.
———. "Medieval Heresy: An Anthropological View." *Social History* 11, no. 3 (1986): 345–62.
Asensio, Eugenio. "El erasmismo y las corrientes espirituales afines (Conversos, franciscanos, italianizantes)." *Revista de Filología Española* 36, no. 3 (1952): 31–99.
Asín Palacios, Miguel. "Un tratado morisco contra los judíos. (El códice arábigo n. XXXI de la colección Gayangos)." In *Mélanges Hartwig Derenbourg, 1844–1908. Recueil de travaux d'érudition dédiés à la mémoire d'Hartwig Derenbourg par ses amis et ses élèves*, 343–66. Paris: A. Boudin, 1909.
Assmann, Jan. *Of God and Gods: Egypt, Israel, and the Rise of Monotheism.* Madison: University of Wisconsin Press, 2008.
Astrain, Antonio. *Historia de la Compañía de Jesús en la asistencia de España.* 7 vols. Madrid: Razón y Fe, 1905–25.
Augustine of Hippo. *De Doctrina Christiana.* Edited and translated by R. P. H. Green. Oxford: Clarendon Press, 1995.
———. *Enarrationes in Psalmos I–L.* Edited by Eligius Dekkers and Johannes Fraipont. Corpus Christianorum Series Latina 38. Turnhout: Brepols, 1956.
———. *Sancti Aurelii Augustini. Sermones de vetere testamento.* Edited by Cyrillus Lambot. Corpus Christianorum Series Latina 41. Turnhout: Brepols, 1961.
Austen, Ralph. "The Mediterranean Slave Trade out of Africa: A Tentative Census." *Slavery and Abolition* 13, no. 1 (1992): 214–48.
Avalle-Arce, Juan Bautista. "Review of Hernando de Talavera, *Católica impugnación*, ed. Francisco Martín Hernández." *Romance Philology* 19, no. 2 (1965): 385–86.
Avenoza, Gemma, Lourdes Soriano, and Vicenç Beltran, eds. *Bibliografia de Textos Antics Catalans, Valencians i Balears (BITECA).* Berkeley: Bancroft Library, University of California, 1997–2016. http://vm136.lib.berkeley.edu/BANC/philobiblon/biteca_en.html.
Azcona, Tarsicio de. *Isabel la Católica. Estudio crítico de su vida y su reinado.* Madrid: Editorial Católica, 1964.
———. "El tipo ideal de obispo en la Iglesia española antes de la rebelión luterana." *Hispania sacra* 11 (1958): 34–40.
Babudri, Francesco. *La figura del rimatore barese Schiavo nell'ambiente sociale e letterario duecentesco di Puglia e d'Italia.* Bari: Società Editrice Tipografica, 1954.
Bade, Norman, and Bele Freudenberg, eds. *Von Sarazenen und Juden, Heiden und Häretikern: Die christlich-abendländischen Vorstellungen von Andersgläubigen im Früh- und Hochmittelalter in vergleichender Perspektive.* Bochum: Winkler, 2013.
Baer, Yitzhak. *Galut.* New York: Schocken, 1947.
———. *A History of the Jews in Christian Spain.* Vol. 2, *From the Fourteenth Century to the Expulsion.* Philadelphia: Jewish Publication Society of America, 1961–66.
Bagby, Albert I., Jr. "The Moslem in the *Cantigas* of Alfonso X, El Sabio." *Kentucky Romance Quarterly* 20, no. 2 (1973): 173–207.
Balabarca, Lisette. "La polémica cristiano-musulmana tras la expulsión

(1609–1614): la *Contradicción de los catorce artículos* de Ibrahim Taybili frente a la *Expulsión justificada de los moriscos* de Pedro Azar Cardona." PhD diss., Boston University, 2006.

Barceló Torres, Carmen. "La morería de Valencia en el reinado de Juan II." *Saitabi. Revista de la Facultat de Geografia i Història* 30 (1980): 49–72.

Barletta, Vincent. *Covert Gestures: Crypto-Islamic Literature as Cultural Practice in Early Modern Spain*. Minneapolis: University of Minnesota Press, 2005.

———, ed. and trans. *A Memorandum for the President of the Royal Audiencia and Chancery Court of the City and Kingdom of Granada by Francisco Núñez Muley*. Chicago: University of Chicago Press, 2007.

Barré, Henri. "Antienne et reponse de la Vierge." *Marianum* 29 (1967): 209–11.

Barrios Aguilera, Manuel. *La suerte de los vencidos. Estudios y reflexiones sobre la cuestión morisca*. Granada: Universidad de Granada, 2011.

Barros, João de. *Ropicapnefma. Reprodução fac-similada da ed. de 1532*. Edited by Israël S. Révah. Lisbon: Instituto de Alta Cultura, 1952.

Bartholomaeus ab Edessa. *Confutatio Hagareni*. Translated into Latin by Etienne Le Moine as *Varia sacra ceu sylloge uariorum opusculorum graecorum ad rem ecclesiasticam spectantium*, vol. 1. Leiden: Van Gaasbeeck, 1685.

Barton, Simon. *Conquerors, Brides, and Concubines: Interfaith Relations and Social Power in Medieval Iberia*. Philadelphia: University of Pennsylvania Press, 2015.

Baskin, Judith R., ed. *Jewish Women in Historical Perspective*. Detroit: Wayne State University Press, 1991.

Bearman, P., Th. Bianquis, C. E. Bosworth, E. van Donzel, and W. P. Heinrichs, eds. *Encyclopaedia of Islam*. 11 vols. 2nd ed. Leiden: Brill, 1960–2002.

Bell, Dean Philip. "Confessionalization and Social Discipline in Early Modern Germany: A Jewish Perspective." In *Politics and Reformations: Histories and Reformations: Essays in Honor of Thomas A. Brady, Jr.*, edited by Christopher Ocker, Michael Printy, Peter Starenko, and Peter Wallace, 345–72. Leiden: Brill, 2007.

Beltrán de Heredia, Vicente. *Bulario de la universidad de Salamanca 1219–1549*. 3 vols. Salamanca: Universidad de Salamanca, 1966–67.

———. "San Vicente Ferrer, predicador de las sinagogas." *Salmanticensis* 2, no. 3 (1955): 669–76.

Benítez Sánchez-Blanco, Rafael. *Heroicas decisiones. La Monarquía Católica y los moriscos valencianos*. Valencia: Institució Alfons el Magnànim, 2001.

Benito de Pedro, Ana. "Elementos de Reconquista. Moras y judías en las *Cantigas* de Alfonso X." *eHumanista: Journal of Iberian Studies* 12 (2009): 87–106. http://www.ehumanista.ucsb.edu/sites/secure.lsit.ucsb.edu.span.d7_eh/files/sitefiles/ehumanista/volume12/Benito%20de%20Pedro.pdf.

Benito Goerlich, Daniel. "L'herència artística dels dominics valencians." In *El Palau de la Saviesa. El reial convent de predicadors de València i la biblioteca universitària*, edited by Emilio Callado Estela and Alfonso Esponera Cerdán, 35–55. Valencia: Universitat de València, 2005.

———. "Parets que ensenyen. Els cicles pictòrics murals del Col·legi de Corpus Christi." In *Domus Speciosa. 400 años del Colegio del Patriarca*, edited by Antoni Vilaplana Molina, 61–131. Valencia: Universitat de València–Fundación General de la Universitat de València, 2006.

———. "Pintura recuperada. El cuadro de san Pedro Pascual de José Orient." In *Herencia pintada. Obras pictóricas restauradas de la Universitat de València*, edited by Norberto Piqueras Sánchez, A. Lluch Hurtado, and Daniel Benito Goerlich, 61–104. Valencia: Universitat de València, 2002.

———. "Visión de San Pedro Pascual." In *La Universitat de València y su patrimonio cultural. Materia Preciosa*, 2 vols., coordinated by David Sánchez Muñoz, 2:130–31. Valencia: Universitat de València, 2008.

Benjamin, Walter. *Illuminations: Essays and Reflections*. New York: Schocken, 1968.

Ben-Sasson, Hayim Hillel. "The Reformation in Contemporary Jewish Eyes." *Proceedings of the Israel Academy of Sciences and Humanities* 4, no. 12 (1970): 239–326.

Berger, David. *The Jewish-Christian Debate in the High Middle Ages*. Philadelphia: Jewish Publication Society of America, 1979.

———. *Persecution, Polemic, and Dialogue: Essays in Jewish-Christian Relations*. Boston: Academic Studies Press, 2010.

Berger, David, and Michael Wyschogrod. *Jews and Jewish Christianity*. New York: Ktav, 1978.

Bernabé Pons, Luis Fernando. "De aljamía lejana: la literatura de los moriscos en el exilio." In *Aljamías. In memoriam Álvaro Galmés de Fuentes y Iacob M. Hassán*, edited by Raquel Suárez and Ignacio Ceballos, 105–30. Gijón: Trea, 2012.

———. *Cántico islámico del morisco hispano-tunecino Taybili*. Zaragoza: Institución Fernando el Católico, 1988.

———. "Los mecanismos de una resistencia: Los libros plúmbeos del Sacromonte y el Evangelio de Bernabé." *Al-Qanṭara* 23, no. 2 (2002): 477–98.

———. *Los moriscos. Conflicto, expulsión y diáspora*. Madrid: Catarata, 2009.

Bernáldez, Andrés. *Memorias del reinado de los Reyes Católicos*. Edited by Manuel Gómez-Moreno and Juan de Mata Carriazo y Arroquia. Madrid: Real Academia de la Historia, 1962.

Bernard, Vincent. *Minorías y marginados en la España del siglo XVI*. Granada: Diputación Provincial de Granada, 1987.

Bernard of Clairvaux. *Opera*. 8 vols., edited by Jean Leclercq, C. H. Talbot, and Henri Rochais. Rome: Cistercienses, 1957–77.

Bevilacqua, Alexander. "The Qur'ān Translations of Marracci and Sale." *Journal of the Warburg and Courtauld Institutes* 76 (2013): 93–130.

Bianchi, Luca. *Christian Readings of Aristotle from the Middle Ages to the Renaissance*. Turnhout: Brepols, 2011.

Bibago, Abraham. *Derekh 'emunah*. 1522. London: Gregg International, 1969; Jerusalem: Makor, 1969–70.

Biddick, Kathleen. *The Typological Imaginary: Circumcision, Technology, History*. Philadelphia: University of Pennsylvania Press, 2003.

Biosca i Bas, Antoni. "The Anti-Muslim Discourse of Alfonso Buenhombre." In *Medieval Exegesis and Religious Difference: Commentary, Conflict, and Community in the Premodern Mediterranean*, edited by Ryan Szpiech, 87–100. New York: Fordham University Press, 2015.

Blaya Estrada, Nuria. "La imatge de l'orde de Predicadors. Iconografia dominicana en els gravats de la Universitat de València." In *El Palau de la Saviesa. El reial convent de predicadors de València i la biblioteca universitària*, edited by Emilio Callado Estela and Alfonso Esponera Cerdán, 73–94. Valencia: Universitat de València, 2005.

Bleda, Jaime. *Corónica de los moros de España*. 1618. Facsimile of the first edition. Valencia: Universitat de València, 2001.

———. *Libro de la Archicofradía de la Minerva, en la qual se escriven más de cien milagros del Sanctíssimo Sacramento del altar*. Valencia: Casa de los hermanos de Juan Navarro, 1592.

———. *Qvatrocientos milagros y mvchas alabanças de la santa crvz: Con vnos tratados de las cosas más notables desta diuina señal*. Valencia: Patricio Mey, 1600.

Bodian, Miriam. "Crypto-Jewish Criticism of Tradition and Its Echoes in Jewish Communities." In *Religion or Ethnicity? Jewish Identities in Evolution*, edited by Zvi Gitelman, 38–58. New Brunswick, NJ: Rutgers University Press, 2009.

———. *Dying in the Law of Moses: Crypto-Jewish Martyrdom in the Iberian World*. Bloomington: Indiana University Press, 2007.

———. *Hebrews of the Portuguese Nation.* Bloomington: Indiana University Press, 1999.
———. "In the Cross-Currents of the Reformation: Crypto-Jewish Martyrs of the Inquisition 1570–1670." *Past and Present* 176, no. 1 (2002): 66–104.
———. "The Portuguese Jews of Amsterdam and the Status of Christians." In *New Perspectives on Jewish-Christian Relations: In Honor of David Berger*, edited by Elisheva Carlebach and Jacob J. Schacter, 329–57. Leiden: Brill, 2012.
———. "The Reformation and the Jews." In *Rethinking European Jewish History*, edited by Jeremy Cohen and Moshe Rosman, 112–32. Oxford: Littman Library of Jewish Civilization, 2008.
Bono, Salvatore. *Schiavi: Una storia mediterranea (XVI–XIX secolo)*. Bologna: il Mulino, 2016.
———. *Schiavi musulmani nell'Italia moderna, galeotti, vu' cumprà, domestici.* Naples: Edizione scientifiche italiane, 1999.
———. "Slave Histories and Memories in the Mediterranean World." In *Trade and Cultural Exchange in the Early Modern Mediterrnean: Braudel's Maritime Legacy*, edited by Maria Fusaro, Colin Heywood, and Mohamed-Salah Omri, 97–116. New York: I. B. Tauris, 2010.
Borja de Medina, Francisco de. "La Compañía de Jesús y la minoría morisca (1545–1614)." *Archivum historicum Societatis Iesu* 113, no. 57 (1988): 1–136.
Boswell, John. *The Royal Treasure: Muslim Communities under the Crown of Aragon in the Fourteenth Century.* New Haven, CT: Yale University Press, 1977.
Braudel, Fernand. *The Mediterranean and the Mediterranean World in the Age of Phillip II.* 2 vols. Berkeley: University of California Press, 1972.
Brodman, James W. "Community, Identity and Redemption of Captives: Comparative Perspectives across the Mediterranean." *Anuario de estudios medievales* 36, no. 1 (2006): 241–52.
———. *L'orde de la Mercé. El rescat de captius a l'Espanya de les Croades.* Barcelona: Quaderns Crema, 1990.
———. *Ransoming Captives in Crusader Spain: The Order of Merced on the Christian-Islamic Frontier.* Philadelphia: University of Pennsylvania Press, 1986.
Broggio, Paolo. *Evangelizzare il mondo. Le missioni della Compagnia di Gesù tra Europa e America. Secoli XVI–XVII.* Rome: Aracne Editrice, 2004.
———. "Las órdenes religiosas y la expulsión de los moriscos: Entre controversias doctrinales y relaciones hispano-pontificias." In *Los moriscos: Expulsión y diáspora. Una perspectiva internacional*, edited by Mercedes García-Arenal and Gerard Wiegers, 149–71. Valencia etc.: Universitat de València etc., 2013.
Brown, Kenneth, and Harm den Boer. *El barroco sefardí. Abraham Gómez Silveira (Arévalo, prov. de Ávila, Castilla 1656–Amsterdam 1741): Estudio preliminar, obras líricas, vejámenes en prosa y verso, y documentación personal.* Kassel: Reichenberger, 2000.
Buenhombre, Alfonso / Alfonsus Bonihominis. *De aduentu Messiae praeterito (Epistola Samuelis)*. Edited by Jean-Paul Migne. Patrologia Latina 149. Paris: Garnier fratres, 1882.
———. *Disputatio Abutalib.* Edited by Santiago García-Jalón and Klaus Reinhardt. Madrid: Aben Ezra, 2006.
———. *Opera Omnia.* Edited by Antoni Biosca i Bas. Turnhout: Brepols, forthcoming.
Bunes Ibarra, Miguel Ángel de. "El enfrentamiento con el Islam en el Siglo de Oro. Los antialcoranes." *Edad de oro* 8 (1989): 41–58.
Burke, Peter. *The Historical Anthropology of Early Modern Italy: Essays on Perception and Communication.* Cambridge: Cambridge University Press, 1987.
Burman, Thomas E. "How an Italian Friar Read His Arabic Qur'ān." *Dante Studies* 125 (2007): 93–109.
———. "Ramon Martí, the Trinity, and the Limits of Dominican Mission." In *The Mendicants of Thirteenth-Century*

Iberia, edited by Damian Smith. Forthcoming.
———. *Reading the Qur'ān in Latin Christendom, 1140–1560*. Philadelphia: University of Pennsylvania Press, 2007.
———. *Religious Polemic and the Intellectual History of the Mozarabs, c. 1050–1200*. Leiden: Brill, 1994.
———. "Riccoldo da Monte di Croce." In *Christian-Muslim Relations: A Bibliographical History*, vol. 4, *1200–1350*, edited by David Thomas and Alex Mallett, 678–91. Leiden: Brill, 2012.
———. "*Via impugnandi* in the Age of Alfonso VIII: Iberian-Christian Kalām and a Latin Triad Revisited." In *Rex Nobilis: The Reign of Alfonso VIII of Castile (1158–1214)*, edited by Miguel Gómez. Forthcoming.
———. "William of Tripoli." In *Christian-Muslim Relations: A Bibliographical History*, vol. 4, *1200–1350*, edited by David Thomas and Alex Mallett, 515–20. Leiden: Brill, 2012.
Burman, Thomas E., and Lydia M. Walker. "Spain, Islam, and Thirteenth-Century Dominican Memory." In *Festschrift for Thomas F. Glick*, edited by Mark Abate. Forthcoming.
Burns, Robert I. "Christian-Islamic Confrontation in the West: The Thirteenth-Century Dream of Conversion." *American Historical Review* 76, no. 5 (1971): 1386–434.
———. *Moros, cristians i jueus en el Regne croat de València*. Valencia: Biblioteca d'Estudis i investigacions, 1987.
———. "Piracy as an Islamic-Christian Interface in the Thirteenth Century." *Viator* 11 (1980): 165–78.
Cabanelas, Darío. "El caíd marroquí Abd al-Karim Ibn Tuda, refugiado en la España de Felipe II." *Miscelánea de estudios árabes y hebraicos* 12 (1963): 75–88.
Cabrillana Ciézar, Nicolás. *Santiago Matamoros. Historia e imagen*. Málaga: Servicio de Publicaciones de la Diputación de Málaga, 1999.
Calvet, Agustín. *Fray Anselmo Turmeda: Heterodoxo español (1352–1423–32?)*. Barcelona: Casa Editorial Estudio, 1914.
Callado Estela, Emilio. "Dominicos y moriscos en el Reino de Valencia." *Revista de historia moderna* 27 (2009): 109–34.
———. "*Tota Pulchra es amica mea et macula non est in te.* San Pascual, la Inmaculada y Valencia." In *Herencia pintada. Obras pictóricas restauradas de la Universitat de València*, edited by Norberto Piqueras Sánchez, A. Lluch Hurtado, and Daniel Benito Goerlich, 39–59. Valencia: Universitat de València, 2002.
Callado Estela, Emilio, and Alfonso Esponera Cerdán. "San Luis Beltrán. Un dominico en tiempos de reforma." In *Valencianos en la Historia de la Iglesia*, coordinated by Emilio Callado Estela, 137–85. Valencia: Facultad de Teología San Vicente Ferrer, 2008.
———. "1239–1835: Crònica del Reial Convent de Predicadors de València." In *El Palau de la Saviesa. El reial convent de predicadors de València i la biblioteca universitària*, edited by Emilio Callado Estela and Alfonso Esponera Cerdán, 15–34. Valencia: Universitat de València, 2005.
Campaner i Fuertes, Álvaro. *Cronicon mayoricense. Noticias y relaciones históricas de Mallorca desde 1229 á 1800*. Palma de Mallorca: Juan Colomar y Salas, 1881.
Campbell, William S., Peter S. Hawkins, and Brenda Deen Schildgen, eds. *Medieval Readings of Romans*. New York: T&T Clark International, 2007.
Cantera Burgos, Francisco. "Fernando del Pulgar y los conversos." *Sefarad* 4, no. 2 (1944): 295–348.
Canty, Aaron. "Saint Paul in Augustine." In *A Companion to St. Paul in the Middle Ages*, edited by Steven R. Cartwright, 115–42. Leiden: Brill, 2013.
Cardaillac, Denise. "La polémique anti-chrétienne du manuscrit aljamiado no. 4944 de la Bibliothèque Nationale de Madrid." 2 vols., PhD diss., Université Paul Vallery, 1972.
Cardaillac, Louis. *Morisques et Chrétiens, un affrontement polémique*. Paris: Klinksieck, 1978. Translated into Spanish by Mercedes García-Arenal as *Moriscos y*

cristianos, un enfrentamiento polémico (1492–1640), 2nd ed. Madrid: Fondo de Cultura Económica, 2004.
Carmona Muela, Juan. *Iconografía de los santos*. Madrid: Istmo, 2003.
Cartwright, Steven R., ed. *A Companion to St. Paul in the Middle Ages*. Leiden: Brill, 2013.
Carvallo, Luis Alfonso de. *Cisne de Apolo*. Edited by Alberto Porqueras Mayo. Kassel: Reichenberger, 1997.
Catalán, Oriol. "La predicació a la Catalunya baixmedieval. Un instrument de transformació cultural entre oralitat, escriptura, imatge, narració, música i teatre." PhD diss., Universitat de Barcelona, 2013.
Cátedra, Pedro M. "La predicación castellana de Fray Vicente Ferrer." *Boletín de la Real Academia de Buenas Letras de Barcelona* 39 (1983–84): 235–309.
———. *Sermón, sociedad y literatura en la Edad media. San Vicente Ferrer en Castilla (1411–1412)*. Salamanca: Junta de Castilla y León, 1994.
Catlos, Brian. *Muslims of Medieval Latin Christendom, c.1050–1614*. Cambridge: Cambridge University Press, 2014.
Cavallero, Constanza. "La temporalidad del lenguaje de la herejía. El caso de la construcción de la herejía judaizante en el ocaso de la Edad Media." *Medievalismo. Revista de la Sociedad Española de Estudios Medievales* 22 (2012): 11–35.
Certeau, Michel de. *Heterologies: Discourse on the Other*. Minneapolis: University of Minnesota Press, 1986.
Cerulli, Enrico. *Il Libro della scala e la questione delle fonti arabo-spagnole della Divina Commedia*. Vatican City: Biblioteca Apostolica Vaticana, 1949.
Chazan, Robert. *Daggers of Faith: Thirteenth-Century Christian Missionizing and Jewish Response*. Berkeley: University of California Press, 1989.
Checa Cremades, Fernando. *Carlos V y la imagen del héroe en el Renacimiento*. Madrid: Taurus, 1987.
Chiesa, Bruno, and Wilfrid Lockwood. *Ya'qūb al-Qirqisānī on Jewish Sects and Christianity*. Frankfurt: Peter Lang, 1984.
Chorâo Lavajo, Joachim. "Cristianismo e islamismo na península ibérica: Raimundo Martí, um precursor do diálogo religioso." 3 vols., PhD diss., Universidade de Évora, 1988.
Christian, William. "De los santos a María. Panorama de las devociones a santuarios españoles desde el principio de la Edad Media hasta nuestros días." In *Temas de antropología española*, edited by María Cátedra Tomás and Carmelo Lisón Tolosana, 49–105. Madrid: Akal, 1976.
Chrysostom, John, Saint. *Discourses against Judaizing Christians*. Translated by Paul W. Harkins. Washington, DC: Catholic University of America Press, 1979.
———. *Homilies on the Epistles of Paul to the Corinthians*. 1889. Revised with additional notes by Talbot W. Chambers. Grand Rapids, MI: Eerdmans, 1975.
Cirac Estopañán, Sebastián. *Los sermones de Don Martín García, obispo de Barcelona, sobre los Reyes Católicos*. Zaragoza: La Académica, 1956.
Cohen, Jeremy. *"Living Letters of the Law": Ideas of the Jew in Medieval Christianity*. Berkeley: University of California Press, 1999.
———. "'Slay Them Not': Augustine and the Jews in Modern Scholarship." *Medieval Encounters* 4, no. 1 (1998): 78–92.
Collell, Jaume. *Nou Fra Anselm. Llibre de bons consells, compost per un estudiant de theologia*. Vic: Ramón Anglada, 1870.
———. *Novíssim Fra Anselm católic monárquich. Llibret de bonas máximas compost per un hermitá*. Gràcia: Gayetà Campins, 1871.
Collell Costa, Alberto. "Ayer de la Provincia dominicana de Aragón." *Analecta sacra tarraconensia* 39, no. 2 (1966): 217–55.
Colombo, Emanuele. "Jesuitas y musulmanes en la Europa del siglo XVII." In *Saberes de la conversión. Jesuitas, indígenas e imperios coloniales en las fronteras de la cristiandad*, edited by Guilllermo Wilde, 415–40. Buenos Aires: Grupo Editorial, 2011.
Colominas Aparicio, Mònica. "Disputa con los cristanos [MS BNE 4944, Aljamiado XVI (or XVII) century]." In *Christian-Muslim Relations: A Bibliographical History*,

vol. 6, *Western Europe (1500–1600)*, edited by David Thomas and John Chesworth, 43–48. Leiden: Brill, 2014.

———. "Disputes about Purity in Late Medieval Iberia: Interreligious Contacts and the Polemical Language of the Mudejars." *Journal of Transcultural Medieval Studies* 1, no. 1 (2014): 117–42.

———. *The Religious Polemics of the Muslims of Late Medieval Christian Iberia: Identity and Religious Authority in Mudejar Islam.* Leiden: Brill, 2018.

Contreras, Jaime, Ignacio Pulido, and Rafael Benítez. *Judíos y moriscos: Herejes.* Barcelona: Debolsillo, 2005.

Corbín Ferrer, Juan L. "San Luis Bertrán: evangelización de América." *Memoria ecclesiae* 5 (1994): 235–39.

Córdoba, Sebastián de. *Garcilaso a lo divino.* Edited by Glen R. Gale. Madrid: Castalia, 1971.

Cordubensis, Eulogius. *Liber apologeticus Martyrum* 16. In *Corpus scriptorum muzarabicorum*, 2 vols., edited by Juan Gil. Madrid: Consejo Superior de Investigaciones Científicas–Instituto Antonio de Nebrija, 1973.

Corriente, Federico. *A Dictionary of Andalusi Arabic.* Handbuch der Orientalistik, Band 29. Leiden: Brill, 1997.

Cortabarría Beitia, Ángel. "L'étude des langues au Moyen Âge chez les Dominicains: Espagne, Orient, Raymond Martin." *Mélanges de l'Institut Dominicaine des Études Orientales du Caire* 10 (1970): 189–248.

———. "San Ramón de Penyafort y las escuelas dominicanas de lenguas." *Escritos del Vedat* 7 (1977): 125–54.

———. "Los *Studia Linguarum* de los dominicos en los siglos XIII y XIV." In *La controversia judeocristiana en España (Desde los orígenes hasta el siglo XIII). Homenaje a Domingo Muñoz León*, edited by Carlos Del Valle Rodríguez, 255–76. Madrid: Consejo Superior de Investigaciones Científicas, 1998.

Cortés i Cortés, Gabriel, and Miquel Forteza Pinya. *Inquisición de Mallorca. Reconciliados y relajados 1488–1691.* Barcelona: M. Perdigó, 1946.

Cowe, S. Peter. "Kirakos Ganjakecʿi or Arewelcʿi." In *Christian-Muslim Relations: A Bibliographical History*, vol. 6, *Western Europe (1500–1600)*, edited by David Thomas and John Chesworth, with John Azumah, Stanisław Grodź, Andrew Newman, and Douglas Pratt, 438–42. Leiden: Brill, 2014.

Crosby, John. *A lo divino Lyric Poetry: An Alternative View.* Durham: University of Durham, 1989.

Cruz, Óscar de la. "La trascendencia de la primera traducción latina del Corán (Robert de Keton, 1142)." *Collatio* 7 (2002): 21–28.

Cueva, Juan de la. *Exemplar poético.* Edited by José María Reyes Cano. Seville: Alfar, 1986.

Cuffel, Alexandra. "From Practice to Polemic: Shared Saints and Festivals as 'Women's Religion' in the Medieval Mediterranean." *Bulletin of the School of Oriental and African Studies* 68, no. 3 (2005): 401–19.

Dahan, Gilbert. *Les intellectuels chrétiens et les juifs au moyen âge.* Paris: Éditions du Cerf, 1999.

Daiber, Hans. "Raimundus Lullus in der Auseinandersetzung mit dem Islam. Eine philosophiegeschichtliche Analyse des Liber disputationis Raimundi Christiani et Homeri Saraceni." In *Juden, Christen und Muslime: Religionsdialoge im Mittelalter*, edited by Alexander Fidora and Matthias Lutz-Bachmann, 136–72. Darmstadt: Wissenschaftliche Buchgesellschaft, 2004.

Daileader, Philip. *Saint Vincent Ferrer, His World and Life: Religion and Society in Late Medieval Europe.* New York: Palgrave Macmillan, 2015.

D'Alverny, Marie-Thérèse. "Deux traductions latines du Coran au Mogen Age." *Archives d'histoire doctrinale et littéraire du Moyen Age* 16 (1948): 69–131.

Damascenus, Johannes. *Liber de haeresibus. Opera polemica.* Berlin: De Gruyter, 1981.

———. *Sancti Patris Nostri Iohannis Damasceni Monachi et Presbyteri Hierosolymitani, Opera Omnia quae extant.* Edited by Michel Lequien. Paris: J. B. Delespine, 1712.

Dammen McAuliffe, Jane, Claude Gilliot, and William Graham, eds. *Encyclopaedia of the Qur'ān*. Leiden: Brill, 2011–16.
D'Arenys, Pere. *Chronicon*. Edited by José Hinojosa Montalvo. Valencia: Anubar, 1975.
Dascal, Marcelo. "On the Uses of Argumentative Reason in Religious Polemics." In *Religious Polemics in Context: Papers Presented to the Second International Conference of the Leiden Institute for the Study of Religions (LISOR)*, edited by Theo L. Hettema and Arie van der Kooij, 3–20. Leiden: Brill, 2005.
Davis, Robert C. *Christian Slaves, Muslim Masters: White Slavery in the Mediterranean, the Barbary Coast, and Italy, 1500–1800*. New York: Palgrave Macmillan, 2003.
———. "Counting European Slaves on the Barbary Coast." *Past and Present* 172, no. 1 (2001): 87–124.
Dedieu, Jean-Pierre. "Herejía y limpieza de sangre. La inhabilitación de los herejes y de sus descendientes en España en los primeros tiempos de la Inquisición." In *Inquisición y sociedad*, coordinated by Angel de Prado Moura, 139–56. Valladolid: Universidad de Valladolid, 1999.
Deimann, Wiebke. *Christen, Juden und Muslime im mittelalterlichen Sevilla: Religiöse Minderheiten unter muslimischer und christlicher Dominanz (12. bis 14. Jahrhundert)*. Berlin: LIT Verlag, 2012.
Delarruelle, Étienne, ed. *La Piété populaire au Moyen Âge (99e congrès national des sociétés savantes, Besançon, 1974)*. Turin: Bottega d'Erasmo, 1975.
Delgado Criado, Buenaventura, coord. *Historia de la educación en España y América*. Vol. 1, *La educación en la Hispania Antigua y Medieval*. Madrid: Fundación Santa María, 1992.
D'Elia, Pasquale M. "La prima diffusione nel mondo del'imagine di Maria 'Salus Populi Romani.'" *Fede e arte* 10 (1954): 1–11.
Del Pulgar, Fernando. *Crónica de los Reyes Católicos*. 2 vols. Edited by Juan de Mata Carriazo y Arroquia. Madrid: Espasa-Calpe, 1943.
Derrida, Jacques. *Acts of Literature*. New York: Routledge, 1992.
Diago, Francisco. *Historia de la Provincia de Aragón de la Orden de Predicadores, desde su origen y principio hasta el año de mil y seyscientos*. Barcelona: Sebastián de Cormellas, 1599.
———. *Historia de la vida, milagros, muerte y discípulos del bienaventurado predicador apostólico valenciano San Vicente Ferrer de la Orden de Predicadores*. Barcelona: Gabriel Graellsy, 1600.
Di Cesare, Michelina. "New Sources for the Legend of Muḥammad in the West." *East and West. A Quarterly Published by the Isituto Italiano per l'Africa e l'Oriente* 58, no. 1/4 (2008): 9–31.
———. *The Pseudo-historical Image of the Prophet Muḥammad in Medieval Latin Literature: A Repertory*. Berlin: De Gruyter, 2011.
Domínguez Bordona, Jesús. "Instrucción de fray Fernando de Talavera para el régimen interior de su palacio." *Boletín de la Real Academia de la Historia* 96, no. 2 (1930): 785–835.
Dozy, Reinhart. *Supplément aux Dictionnaires Arabes*. 2 vols. 2nd ed. Leiden: Brill, 1927.
Duran, Profiat. *Iggeret 'Al Tehi Ka-'Avotekha*. Edited by Adolf Posnanski. Jerusalem: Aqademon, 1969–70.
Durán Grau, Eulàlia. "El mil·lenarisme al servi del poder i del contrapoder." In *De la unión de coronas al Imperio de Carlos V*, edited by Ernest Belenguer Cebrià, 293–308. Madrid: Sociedad Estatal para la Conmemoración de los Centenarios de Felipe II y Carlos V, 2001.
———. "Una refutació valenciana de l'Islam (segle XV)." *Boletín de la Sociedad Castellonense de Cultura* 74, no. 1/2 (1988): 141–60.
Echevarría Arsuaga, Ana. "Better Muslim or Jew? The Controversy around Conversion across Minorities in Fifteenth-Century Castile." *Medieval Encounters* 24 (2018): 62–78.

———. *The Fortress of Faith: The Attitude towards Muslims in Fifteenth Century Spain.* Leiden: Brill, 1999.

Eixemenis, Francesc. *Colecció de sentencies y concells.* Manresa: Antón Esparbé, 1899.

———. *Dotzè llibre del Crestià.* Edited by Curt Wittlin, Arseni Pacheco, Jill Webster, Josep M. Pujol, Josefina Figuls, Bernat Joan, and August Bover. Girona: Collegi Universitari–Diputació de Girona, 1986–2005.

El Alaoui, Youssef. "Ignacio de las Casas, jesuita y morisco." *Sharq Al-Andalus* 14–15 (1997–98): 317–39.

———. *Jésuites, morisques et indiens. Étude comparative des méthodes d'évangélisation de la Compagnie de Jésus d'aprés les traités de José de Acosta (1588) et d'Ignacio de Las Casas (1605–1607).* 1998. Paris: Honoré Champion, 2006.

El Brocense, Francisco Sánchez. *Obras del excelente poeta Garci Lasso de la Vega. Con anotaciones y enmiendas del Licenciado Francisco Sanchez Cathedrático de rhetórica en Salamanca.* Salamanca: Pedro Lasso, 1574.

El-Kaisy-Friemuth, Maha. "Al-Ghazālī." In *Christian-Muslim Relations: A Bibliographical History*, vol. 3, *1050–1200*, edited by David Thomas and Alex Mallett, 363–69. Leiden: Brill, 2011.

Emmen, Aquilin. "Cunctas haereses sola intermisti." *Maria Ecclesia* 9 (1961): 93–151.

Engen, John van. "Dominic and the Brothers: Vitae as Life-Forming Exempla in the Order of Preachers." In *Christ among the Medieval Dominicans: Representations of Christ in the Texts and Images of the Order of Preachers*, edited by Kent Emery and Joseph Wawrykow, 7–25. South Bend, IN: University of Notre Dame Press, 1987.

Epalza, Mikel de. *Fray Anselm Turmeda ('Abdallah al-Taryuman) y su polémica islamo-cristiana. Edición, traducción y estudio de la Tuhfa.* 2nd ed. Madrid: Hiperión, 1994.

———. "A modo de introducción. El escritor Ybrahim Taybili y los escritores musulmanes aragoneses." In *El Cántico islámico del morisco hispanotunecino Taybili*, edited by Luis Fernando Bernabé Pons, 5–30. Zaragoza: Institución Fernando el Católico, 1988.

———. *Los moriscos antes y después de la expulsión.* Barcelona: Mapfre, 1992.

Epalza, Mikel de, and Ignasi Riera Gassiot, eds. *Anselm Turmeda. Autobiografia i atac als partidaris de la creu: Introducció, Traducció.* 2nd ed. Palma de Mallorca: Hora Nova, 2005.

Epistolae Mixtae ex variis Europae Locis ab anno 1537 ad 1556 scriptae. 5 vols. Madrid: Augustinus Avrial, 1898–1901.

Erpenius, Thomas. *Orationes tres de linguarum hebraeae atque arabicae dignitate.* Leiden: Ex Typographia auctoris, 1621.

Escolano, Gaspar. *Décadas de la Insigne y Coronada Ciudad y Reino de Valencia.* Valencia: Patricio Mey, 1610.

Escrivá, Francisco. *Vida del Venerable Siervo de Dios Don Joan de Ribera.* Rome: Antonio Rossi, 1696.

Espina, Alonso de. *Fortalitium fidei contra Iudeos, Sarracenos aliosq[ue] Christiane fidei inimicos.* Lyon: J. de Romoys, 1511.

Esponera Cerdán, Alfonso. "Ne nos fratres praedicatores, sed dominicanos appellent . . . Disputas entre dominicos y jesuitas en la Valencia del patriarca (1597)." In *El Patriarca Ribera y su tiempo. Religión, política y cultura en la Edad Moderna*, coordinated by Emilio Callado Estela and Miguel Navarro Sorní, 275–98. Valencia: Diputació de València, 2012.

———. "Uno de los focos de la presentación apocalíptica de la figura de San Vicente Ferrer." *Escritos del Vedat* 30 (2000): 351–94.

Eubel, Conrad. *Hierarchia catholica medii aevi, sive Summorum pontificum, S. R. E. cardinalium, ecclesiarum antistitum series ab anno 1198 usque ad annum perducta e documentis tabularii praesertim Vaticani collecta, digesta, edita per Conradum Eubel.* 6 vols. Monasterii: Sumptibus et typis Librariae Regensbergianae, 1913–67.

Eymerich, Nicolás. *Directorium inquisitorum.* Rome: Stamperia del Popolo Romano, 1587.

Fages, H. *Historia de San Vicente Ferrer.* 2 vols., translated by Antonio Polo de Bernabé. Valencia: A. García, 1903.

Falomir Faus, Miguel. "El Patriarca Ribera y la pintura. Devoción, persuasión e historia." In *Una religiosa urbanidad. San Juan de Ribera y el Colegio del Patriarca en la cultura artística de su tiempo*, edited by Joaquín Bérchez, and Mercedes Gómez-Ferrer, 103–16. Valencia: Real Academia de Bellas Artes de Valencia, 2013.

Farmer, Sharon. *Communities of Saint Martin: Legend and Ritual in Medieval Tours.* Ithaca, NY: Cornell University Press, 1991.

Faulhaber, Charles B., dir. *PhiloBiblon.* Berkeley: Bancroft Library, University of California, 1997–2016. http://vm136.lib.berkeley.edu/BANC/philobiblon/index.html.

Faulhaber, Charles B., Ángel Gómez Moreno, Nicasio Salvador Miguel, María Morrás, Óscar Perea Rodríguez, Álvaro Bustos Táuler, Elena González-Blanco, José Luis Gonzalo Sánchez-Molero, eds. *Bibliografía española de textos antiguos.* Berkeley: Bancroft Library, University of California, 1997–2016. http://vm136.lib.berkeley.edu/BANC/philobiblon/beta_en.html.

Fernández Serrano, Francisco. "Órdenes sagradas en Zaragoza: *De licentia Adriani Papae sexti* (1522)." *Cuadernos de historia Jerónimo Zurita* 10–11 (1960): 61–177.

Feros Carrasco, Antonio. "Retóricas de la Expulsión." In *Los moriscos: Expulsión y diáspora. Una perspectiva internacional,* edited by Mercedes García-Arenal and Gerard Wiegers, 67–101. Valencia etc.: Universitat de València etc., 2013.

Ferreiro, Alberto. "Simon Magnus, Dogs, and Simon Peter." In *The Devil, Heresy & Witchcraft in the Middle Ages: Essays in Honour of Jeffrey B. Russell*, edited by Alberto Ferreiro, 45–90. Leiden: Brill, 1998.

———. "St. Vicent Ferrer's Catalan Sermon on St. Martin of Tours." *Hispania sacra* 65, no. 132 (2013): 543–61.

Ferrer, Vicent. *Beati Vincentii: Natione Hispani, professioni sacri praedicatorum Ordinis.* Antwerp: Ioan Stelsij, 1572. English translation available online, Albert G. Judy, "Sermons of St. Vincent Ferrer, O.P., 1350–1419," http://www.svfsermons.org.

———. *Colección de sermones de Cuaresma y otros según el manuscrito de Ayora.* Edited by Adolfo Robles Sierra. Valencia: Ayuntament de València, 1995.

———. *Opera omni: Tomus primus.* Edited by Juan Tomás de Rocaberti. Valencia: Bordazar y Artazú, 1693.

———. *Sermons.* 6 vols. Edited by J. Sanchís Sivera (vols. 1–2) and Gret Schib (vols. 3–6). Barcelona: Barcino, 1932–98.

———. *Sermons de Quaresma.* 2 vols. Edited by Manuel Sanchís Guarner. Valencia: Classics Albatros, 1973.

Ferrer Abárzuza, Antoni. *Captius i senyors de captius a Eivissa. Una contribució al debat sobre l'esclavitud medieval (segles XIII–XVI).* Valencia: Universitat de València, 2015.

Ferrer i Mallol, Maria Teresa. "Las comunidades mudéjares de la Corona de Aragón en el siglo XV. La población." In *De mudéjares a moriscos, una conversión forzada. Actas del Simposio Internacional de Mudejarismo,* 2 vols., 1:27–154. Teruel: Centro de Estudios Mudéjares–Instituto de Estudios Turolenses, 2002.

———. "Frontera, convivencia y proselitismo entre cristianos y moros en los textos de Francesc Eiximenis y san Vicente Ferrer." In *Pensamiento medieval hispano. Homenaje a Horacio Santiago-Otero*, 2 vols., edited by José M. Soto Rábanos, 2:1579–1600. Madrid: Consejo Superior de Investigaciones Científicas, 1998.

———. "Els sarraïns del regne de Murcia durant la conquesta de Jaume II (1296–1304)." *Anales de la Universidad de Alicante. Historia medieval* 11 (1996–97): 173–200.

Fidora, Alexander, and Josep E. Rubio, eds. *Raimundus Lullus: An Introduction to his Life, Works and Thought. Opera latina. Supplementum Lullianum II.* Corpus Christianorum Continuatio Mediaevalis 214. Turnhout: Brepols, 2008.

Fierro Bello, Maribel. "Spiritual Alienation and Political Activism: The *ghurabāʾ* in Al-Andalus during the Sixth/Twelfth Century." *Arabica* 47, no. 2 (2000): 210–40.
Fisher, Benjamin. "Opening the Eyes of the Novos Reformados: Rabbi Saul Levi Morteira, Radical Christianity, and the Jewish Reclamation of Jesus, 1620–1660." *Studia Rosenthaliana* 44 (2012): 117–48.
Fita, Fidel. "Concilios españoles inéditos. Provincial de Braga en 1261 y nacional en Sevilla en 1478." *Boletín de la Real Academia de la Historia* 22 (1893): 209–57.
Floristán, José M. "Francisco de Gurmendi, intérprete de árabe, turco y persa en la corte de Felipe III." *Boletín de la Real Academia de la Historia* 211, no. 2 (2014): 357–76.
Folena, Gianfranco. "Duecento [Rassegna bibliografica]." *La Rassegna della letteratura italiana* 59 (1955): 104–10.
Fonseca, Damián. *Iusta expulsión de los moriscos de España. Con la instrucción, apostasía y trayción de ellos.* Rome: Iacomo Mascardo, 1612.
Fontcuberta Famadas, Cristina. *Imatges d'atac. Art i conflicte als segles XVI i XVII.* Barcelona: Universidad de Girona–Memoria Artium, 2011.
Fontenay, Michel. "Esclaves et/ou captifs. Préciser les concepts." In *Le commerce des captifs. Les intermédiaires dans l'échange et le rachat des prisonniers en Méditerranée, XVe–XVIIIe siècle*, edited by Wolfang Kaiser, 15–24. Rome: École Française de Rome, 2008.
Formisano, Luciano. "La più antica (?) traduzione italiana del 'Corano' e il 'Liber Habentometi' di Ibn Tumart in una compilazione di viaggi del primo Cinquecento." *Critica del testo* 7, no. 2 (2004): 651–96.
Fort i Cogul, Eufemià. *Catalunya i la inquisició.* Barcelona: Aedos, 1973.
Fox, Yaniv, and Yosi Yisraeli, eds. *Contesting Inter-religious Conversion in the Medieval World.* London: Routledge, 2017.
Franco Llopis, Borja. "Arte y misión. San Francisco de Borja y la difusión de la doctrina católica en las Indias interiores." In *Francisco de Borja y su tiempo. Política, religión y cultura en la Edad Moderna*, coordinated by Enrique García Hernán and María del Pilar Ryan, 698–741. Valencia: Albatros, 2011.
———. "Consideraciones sobre el uso y abuso de la imagen en la Península Ibérica en el siglo XVI a través de los procesos inquisitoriales. Una visión multicultural del arte: moriscos, protestantes y cristianos viejos." *Sharq Al-Andalus* 20 (2011–13): 129–52.
———. "Espiritualidad, reformas y arte en Valencia (1545–1609)." PhD diss., Universitat de Barcelona, 2009.
———. "Identidades reales, identidades creadas, identidades superpuestas. Algunas reflexiones artísticas sobre los moriscos, su representación visual y la concepción que los cristianos viejos tuvieron de ella." In *Identidades cuestionadas. Coexistencia y conflictos interreligiosos en el Mediterráneo (ss. XIV–XVIII)*, edited by Borja Franco Llopis and Bruno Pomara, 281–300. Valencia: Universitat de València, 2016.
———. "Ignacio de las Casas y el arte como método de evangelización." *Travaux et documents hispaniques* 3 (2012): 39–45.
———. "Mercédaires, musulmans et morisques. Usages artistiques de l'Ordre de la Merci et création d'une iconographie critique anti-islamique au XVIIe siècle." In *Morisques (1501–1614). Une histoire si familière*, edited by Youssef El Alaoui, 143–60. Rouen: Presses universitaires de Rouen et du Havre, 2017.
———. "Nuevas tendencias historiográficas en torno al uso del arte en los procesos de asimilación de la minorías morisca. Propuesta de studio." *eHumanista. Journal in Iberian Studies* 1 (2013): 63–75. http://www.ehumanista.ucsb.edu/sites/secure.lsit.ucsb.edu.span.d7_eh/files/sitefiles/conversos/volume1/ehumanconv.francollopis.pdf.

———. "Propaganda, misión y oración privada. Usos y funciones artísticas en torno a san Francisco de Borja." *Revista Borja. Revista de l'Institut Internacional d'Estudis Borgians* 4 (2013): 483–96.

Franke, Franz R. "Die freiwilligen Märtyrer von Cordova und das Verhältnis der Mozaraber zum Islam (Nach den Schriften des Speraindeo, Eulogius und Alvar)." *Spanische Forschungen* 1, no. 13 (1958): 1–170.

Fredriksen, Paula. *Augustine and the Jews: A Christian Defense of Jews and Judaism.* New Haven, CT: Yale University Press, 2008.

———. "Divine Justice and Human Freedom: Augustine on Jews and Judaism, 392–398." In *From Witness to Witchcraft: Jews and Judaism in Medieval Christian Thought*, edited by Jeremy Cohen, 29–57. Wiesbaden: Harrassowitz Verlag, 1996.

Friedman, Jerome. "The Reformation in Alien Eyes: Jewish Perceptions of Christian Troubles." *Sixteenth Century Journal* 14 (1983): 23–40.

———. "Unitarians and New Christians in Sixteenth-Century Europe." *Archiv für Reformationsgeschichte* 81 (1991): 216–38.

Friedman, Yvonne. "Captivity and Ransom: The Experience of Women." In *Gendering the Crusades*, edited by Susan B. Edgington and Sarah Lambert, 121–39. New York: Columbia University Press, 2012.

———. *Encounter between Enemies: Captivity and Ransom in the Latin Kingdom of Jerusalem.* Leiden: Brill, 2002.

Frimer, Norman E. "A Critical Edition of *Eben Bohan.*" PhD diss., Yeshiva University, 1953.

Frimer, Norman E., and Dov Schwartz. *Hagut be-Ṣeil ha-'Eimah.* Jerusalem: Ben-Zvi Institute, 1992.

Fuchs, Barbara. *Mimesis and Empire: The New World, Islam, and European Identities.* Cambridge: Cambridge University Press, 2001.

Fuente Pérez, María Jesús. *Identidad y convivencia. Musulmanas y judías en la España medieval.* Madrid: Ediciones Polifemo, 2010.

Fuster Perelló, Sebastián. *Timete Deum. El Anticristo y el final de la Historia según San Vicente Ferrer.* Valencia: Ajuntament de València, 2004.

Galmés Mas, Lorenzo. "La cuestión de los moriscos en la época de San Luis Bertrán." In *Corrientes espirituales en la Valencia del siglo XVI (1550–1600). Actas del II Symposio de Teología Histórica (20–22 abril 1982)*, 291–300. Valencia: Facultad de Teología San Vicente Ferrer, 1983.

Garcés, María Antonia. "Zoraida's Veil: The 'Other' Scene of the Captive's Tale." *Revista de Estudios Hispánicos* 23, no. 1 (1989): 65–98.

García-Arenal, Mercedes. "Los andalusíes en el ejército saadí: un intento de golpe de estado contra Ahmad al-Mansur al-Dahabi." *Al-Qanṭara* 5 (1984): 169–202.

———. "Creating Conversos: Genealogy and Identity as Historiographical Problems (after a Recent Book by Ángel Alcalá)." *Bulletin for Spanish and Portuguese Historical Studies* 38, no. 1 (2013): 1–19.

———. "Dreams and Reason: Autobiographies of Converts in Religious Polemics." In *Conversions islamiques. Identités religieuses en Islam méditerranéen*, edited by Mercedes García-Arenal, 89–118. Paris: Maisonneuve et Larose, 2001.

———. "Granada as a New Jerusalem: The Conversion of a City." In *Space and Conversion in Global Perspective*, edited by Giuseppe Marcocci, Wietse de Boer, Aliocha Maldavsky, and Ilaria Pavan, 15–43. Leiden: Brill, 2015.

———. "Jewish Converts to Islam in the Muslim West." *Israel Oriental Studies* 17 (1997): 95–118.

———. "Moriscos e indios: para un estudio comparado de métodos de conquista y evangelización." *Chronica nova* 20 (1992): 153–76.

———. "Rapports entre les groupes dans la péninsule Ibérique. La conversion de juifs à l'islam (XIIe–XIIe siècles)." *Revue du monde musulman et de la Méditarranée* 63–64 (1992): 91–101.

———. "'Un réconfort pour ceux qui sont dans l'attente'. Prophétie et millénarisme dans la péninsule Ibérique et au Maghreb (XVI–XVII siècles)." *Revue de l'histoire des religions* 220, no. 4 (2003): 445–86.

———. "Shurafa in the Last Years of al-Andalus and in the Morisco Period: *Laylat al–mawlid* and Genealogies of the Prophet Muhammad." In *Sayyids and Sharifs in Muslim Societies: The Living Links to the Prophet*, edited by Muto Kazuo, 161–85. London: Routledge, 2012.

———, coord. "*Taqiyya*: Legal Dissimulation." *Al-Qanṭara* 34, no. 2 (2013).

García-Arenal, Mercedes, and Béatrice Leroy. *Moros y judíos en Navarra en la baja Edad Media*. Madrid: Hiperión, 1984.

García-Arenal, Mercedes, and Fernando Rodríguez Mediano. "Los Libros de los Moriscos y los eruditos orientales." *Al-Qanṭara* 31, no. 2 (2010): 611–46.

———. *Un Oriente español. Los moriscos y el Sacromonte en tiempos de Contrarreforma*. Madrid: Marcial Pons, 2010. Translated by Consuelo López-Morillas as *The Orient in Spain: Converted Muslims, the Forged Lead Books of Granada, and the Rise of Orientalism*. Leiden: Brill, 2013.

García-Arenal, Mercedes, and Katarzyna K. Starczewska. "'The Law of Abraham the Catholic': Juan Gabriel as Qur'ān Translator for Martín de Figuerola and Egidio da Viterbo." *Al-Qanṭara* 35, no. 2 (2014): 409–59.

García-Arenal, Mercedes, and Gerard Wiegers, eds. *Los moriscos: Expulsión y diáspora. Una perspectiva internacional*. Valencia etc.: Universitat de València etc., 2013. English translation and updated ed., *The Expulsion of the Moriscos from Spain: A Mediterranean Diaspora*. Leiden: Brill, 2014.

García Gutiérrez, Pedro Francisco. *Iconografía mercedaria. Nolasco y su obra*. Madrid. Revista de Estudios, 1985.

García Herrero, María del Carmen. *Del nacer y el vivir. Fragmentos para una historia de la vida en la Baja Edad Media*. Zaragoza: Institución Fernando el Católico, 2005.

García Oliver, Ferrán. *La vall de les sis mesquites. El treball i la vida a la Valldigna medieval*. Valencia: Universitat de València, 2003.

García Páramo, Ana María. "La iconografía de Santiago en la pintura gótica castellana." *Cuadernos de arte e iconografía* 6, no. 11 (1993): 92–97.

García Puyazuelo, Martín. *Sermones eminentissimi totiusque Barchinonensis gregis tutatoris acerrimi, necnon imarcessibilis sacre theologie paludamento insigniti Martini Garsie*. Zaragoza: Jorge Cocio, 1520.

Garganta, José María de. "San Juan de Ribera y San Luis Bertrán." *Teología espiritual* 5 (1961): 63–104.

Garganta, José María de, and Vicente Forcada Comins. *Biografía y escritos de San Vicente Ferrer*. Madrid: Editorial Católica, 1956.

Garshowitz, Libby. "Shem Tov ben Isaac Ibn Shaprut's *Touchstone* (Even boḥan) Chapters 2–10, Based on MS Plut. 2.17 (Florence, Biblioteca medicea laurenziana), with Collations from Other Manuscripts." PhD diss., University of Toronto, 1974.

Gauthier, René-Antoine. *Introduction à la Somme contre les gentils de saint Thomas d'Aquin*. Paris: Éditions Universitaires, 1993.

George-Tvrtković, Rita. "The Ambivalence of Interreligious Experience: Riccoldo da Monte Croce's Theology of Islam." PhD diss., University of Notre Dame, 2007.

———. *A Christian Pilgrim in Medieval Iraq: Riccoldo da Montecroce's Encounter with Islam*. Turnhout: Brepols, 2012.

Gerli, Edmund Michael. "Social Crisis and Conversion: Apostasy and Inquisition in the Chronicles of Fernando del Pulgar and Andrés Bernáldez." *Hispanic Review* 70, no. 2 (2002): 147–67.

Géza, Dávid, and Pál Fodor, eds. *Ransom Slavery along the Ottoman Borders (Early Fifteenth–Early Eighteenth Centuries)*. Leiden: Brill, 2007.

Gil, Juan, ed. *Corpus scriptorum muzarabicorum*. 2 vols. Madrid: Instituto Antonio de Nebrija–Consejo Superior de Investigaciones Científicas, 1973.

Gimeno Blay, Francisco. *El Compromiso de Caspe (1412). Diario del proceso. Estudio introductorio, edición crítica y notas*. Zaragoza: Institución Fernando el Católico, 2012.

———. "El sermón 'fiet unum ouile et unus pastor' (Io 10.16) de San Vicente Ferrer en Caspe." *Escritos del Vedat* 42 (2012): 163–94.

Gimeno Blay, Francisco, and María Luz Mandingorra Llavata, eds. *Sermonario de san Vicente Ferrer*. Valencia: Ajuntament de València, 2002.

Girón-Negrón, Luis M., and Laura Minervini, eds. *Las coplas de Yosef. Entre la Biblia y el Midrash en la poesía judeoespañola*. Madrid: Gredos, 2006.

Glei, Reinhold F. "Religious Dialogues and Trialogues in the Middle Ages: A Preliminary Essay." *Medievalia et Humanistica* 38 (2012): 21–36.

Glei, Reinhold F., and Roberto Tottoli. *Ludovico Marracci at Work: The Evolution of His Latin Translation of the Qur'ān in the Light of His Newly Discovered Manuscripts; with an Edition and a Comparative Linguistic Analysis of Sura 18*. Wiesbaden: Harrassowitz Verlag, 2016.

Glossarium latino-arabicum ex unico qui exstat codice Leidensi undecimo saeculo in Hispania conscripto / nunc primum edidit praefatione notisque instruxit tabulam phototypicam adiecit Christianus Fredericus Seybold. Ergänzungshefte für Assyriologie. Semitische Studien, Heft 15–17. Berolini: Emil Felber, 1900.

Gomis Corell, Joan C. *L'obra pictòrica de Francesc Ribalta a Algemesí*. Algemesí: Ajuntament d'Algemesí, 2006.

Gonzalbo Aizpuru, Pilar. *La educación popular de los jesuitas*. Mexico, DF: Universidad Iberoamericana, 1989.

González-Casanovas, Roberto J. "Marian Devotion as Gendered Discourse in Berceo and Alfonso X: Popular Reception of the *Milagros* and *Cantigas*." *Bulletin of the Cantigueiros de Santa Maria* 4 (1992): 17–31.

González Jiménez, Manuel. "Esclavos andaluces en el reino de Granada." In *La sociedad medieval andaluza, grupos no privilegiados. Actas del III Coloquio de Historia Medieval Andaluza*, 327–38. Jaen: Diputación Provincial de Jaen, 1984.

González Muñoz, Fernando, ed. *Exposición y refutación del Islam. La versión latina de las epístolas de al-Hāšimī y al-Kindī*. A Coruña: Universidade da Coruña, 2005.

González Rolán, Tomás, and Pilar Saquero Suárez-Somonte. *De la sentencia-estatuto de Pero Sarmiento a la instrucción del relator: Estudio introductorio, edición crítica y notas de los textos contrarios y favorables a los judeoconversos a raíz de la rebelión de Toledo de 1449*. Madrid: Aben Ezra Ediciones, 2012.

Grieve, Patricia. Floire and Blancheflor *and the European Romance*. Cambridge: Cambridge University Press, 1997.

Griffith, Sidney H. "Arguing from Scripture: The Bible in the Christian/Muslim Encounter in the Middle Ages." In *Scripture and Pluralism: Reading the Bible in the Religiously Plural Worlds of the Middle Ages and Renaissance*, edited by Thomas J. Heffernan and Thomas E. Burman, 29–58. Leiden: Brill, 2005.

Grossman, Avraham. *Pious and Rebellious: Jewish Women in Europe in the Middle Ages*. Translated by Jonathan Chipman. Waltham: Brandeis University Press, 2004.

Guadalajara Medina, José. "La Edad del Anticristo y el año del fin del mundo, según Fray Vicente Ferrer." In *Pensamiento medieval hispano, homenaje a Horacio Santiago-Otero*, 2 vols., edited by Jose María Soto Rábanos, 2:321–42. Madrid: Consejo Superior de Investigaciones Científicas, 1998.

———. "La venida del Anticristo. Terror y moralidad en la Edad Media Hispánica." *Culturas Populares. Revista Electrónica* 4 (2007). http://www.culturaspopulares.org/textos4/articulos/guadalajara.htm.

Gui, Bernard. *Practica Inquisitionis Heretice Pravitatis*. Edited by C. Douais. Paris: Alphonse Picard, 1886.

Guibert, Joseph de. *La spiritualità della compagnia di Gesú. Saggio storico*. Rome: Città Nuova Editrice, 1992.

Guillén Robles, Francisco. *Leyendas de José hijo de Jacob y de Alejandro Magno sacadas de dos manuscritos moriscos de la Biblioteca Nacional de Madrid.* Zaragoza: Imprenta del Hospital Provincial, 1888.

Guimerán, Felipe de. *Breue historia de la Orden de Nuestra Señora de la Merced de Redempción de cautiuos christianos y de algunos santos y personas illustres della . . . trátase más en particular de la . . . casa de la madre de Dios del Puche de Valencia.* Valencia: herederos de Juan Navarro, 1591.

Hagerty, Miguel J., ed. *Los Libros Plúmbeos del Sacromonte.* Madrid: Editora Nacional, 1980; 2nd ed., Granada: Comares, 1997.

Ḥajarī, Aḥmad b. Qāsim al-. *Kitāb Nāṣir al-Dīn ʿalā ʾl-Qawm al-Kāfirīn* [*The Supporter of Religion against the Infidels*]. Edited by Pieter Sjoerd van Koningsveld, Qasim Al-Samarrai, and Gerard Wiegers. Madrid: Consejo Superior de Investigaciones Científicas, 2016.

Halberstam, Solomon J. "Vikkuaḥ Tortosa." *Jeschurun* 6 (1868): 45–55.

Hames, Harvey J. "'And on This Rock I Will Build My Community': Jewish Use of the Gospel in Fifteenth-Century Spain." In *Christlicher Norden—Muslimischer Süden: Ansprüche und Wirklichkeiten von Christen, Juden und Muslimen auf der iberischen Halbinsel in Hoch- und Spätmittelalter*, edited by Matthias M. Tischler and Alexander Fidora, 215–26. Münster: Aschendorff, 2011.

———. "Reason and Faith: Inter-religious Polemic and Christian Identity in the Thirteenth Century." In *Religious Apologetics-Philosophical Argumentation*, edited by Yossef Schwartz and Volkhard Krech, 267–84. Tübingen: Mohr Siebeck, 2004.

———. "Rethinking the Dynamics of Late Medieval Jewish-Christian Polemics: From Friar Paul to Alfonso de Valladolid." In *Cultural Hybridities: Christians, Muslims and Jews in the Medieval Mediterranean*, edited by Brian Catlos and Sharon Kinoshita. New York: Palgrave Macmillan, forthcoming.

Harris, A. Katie. *From Muslim to Christian Granada: Inventing a City's Past in Early Modern Spain.* Baltimore, MD: Johns Hopkins University Press, 2007.

Harvey, Leonard P. "A Second Morisco Manuscript at Wadham College, Oxford: A 18.15." *Al-Qanṭara* 10, no. 1 (1989): 461–65.

Harvey, Leonard P., and Gerard Wiegers. "The Translation from Arabic of the Sacromonte Tablets and the Archbishop of Granada: An Illuminating Correspondence." *Qurtuba. Estudios Andalusíes* 1 (1996): 59–78.

Hauf, Albert. "Anselm Turmeda." In *Panorama crític de la literatura catalana*, vol. 1, *Edat Mitjana; Dels incis a principis del segle XV*, edited by Albert Hauf, 354–89. Barcelona: Vicens Vives, 2010.

———. *L'home que riu: Entorn a la paròdia medieval.* Manacor: Patronat de l'Escola Municipal de Mallorquí, 2000.

Hayyim ibn Musa. *Magen va-Romaḥ.* Edited by Adolf Posnanski. Jerusalem: Aqademon, 1969–70.

Hebrera, Joseph Antonio de. *Vida prodigiosa del ilustrísimo y venerable D. Martín García, obispo de Barcelona, hijo de la fidelíssima y antigua villa de Caspe.* Zaragoza: Domingo Gascón, 1700.

Heimann, Claudia. *Nicolaus Eymerich (vor 1320–1399); predicator veridicus, inquisitor intrepidus, doctor egregius; Leben un Werk eines Inquisitors.* Münster: Aschendorff, 2001.

Hermosilla, María Jesús. "Una versión aljamiada sobre Job." *Sharq Al-Andalus* 8 (1991): 211–14.

Hernando, Josep. "Ramón Martí (s. XIII): *De seta Machometi* o *De origine, progressu et fine Machometi et quadrupli reprobatione prophetiae eius.*" *Acta historica et archaeologica mediaevalia* 4 (1983): 9–63.

Hershenzon, Daniel. "Early Modern Spain and the Creation of the Mediterranean: Captivity, Commerce, and Knowledge." PhD diss., University of Michigan, 2011.

———. "'Para que me saque abesa por cabesa': Exchanging Muslim and Christian Slaves across the Western

Mediterranean." *African Economic History* 42 (2014): 11–36.
———. "Plaintes et menaces: captivité et violences religieuses en Méditerranée au XVIIe siècle." In *Les Musulmans dans l'histoire de l'Europe*, vol. 2, *Passages et contacts en Méditerranée*, edited by Jocelyne Dakhlia and Wolfgang Kaiser, 441–60. Paris: Albin Michel, 2012.
———. "The Political Economy of Ransom in the Early Modern Mediterranean." *Past and Present* 231, no. 1 (2016): 61–95.
Hettema, Theo L., and Arie van der Kooij, eds. *Religious Polemics in Context: Papers Presented to the Second International Conference of the Leiden Institute for the Study of Religions (LISOR) Held at Leiden, 27–28 April 2000*. Leiden: Brill, 2004.
Hillenbrand, Carole. "The Imprisonment of Reynald of Châtillon." In *Texts, Documents and Artefacts: Islamic Studies in Honour of D. S. Richards*, edited by Chase F. Robinson, 79–102. Leiden: Brill, 2003.
Hinojosa Montalvo, José. "Los mudéjares de Aragón y Cataluña en el reino de Jaime I." In *La sociedad en Aragón y Cataluña en el reinado de Jaime I: 1213–1276*, edited by Esteban Sarasa Sánchez, 157–98. Zaragoza: Institución Fernando el Católico, 2009.
Hoover, Jon. "Ibn Taymīyah." In *Christian-Muslim Relations: A Bibliographical History*, vol. 4, *1200–1350*, edited by David Thomas and Alex Mallett, 824–78. Leiden: Brill, 2012.
Horace. *Satires. Epistles. Art of Poetry*. Translated by H. R. Fairclough. Cambridge: Loeb Classical Library, 1926.
Iannuzzi, Isabella. "La biografía del reformista fray Hernando de Talavera en tiempo de Carlos V." In *Carlos V, europeísmo y universalidad*, 5 vols., coordinated by Francisco Sánchez-Montes González and Juan Luis Castellano, 5:315–28. Madrid: Sociedad Estatal para la Conmemoración de los Centenarios de Felipe II y Carlos V, 2001.
———. "Educar a los cristianos: Fray Hernando de Talavera y su labor catequética dentro de la estructura familiar para homogeneizar la sociedad de los Reyes Católicos." *Nuevo Mundo Mundos Nuevos* (2008). http://nuevomundo.revues.org/19122.
———. *El poder de la palabra en el siglo XV. Fray Hernando de Talavera*. Salamanca: Junta de Castilla y León, 2009.
Ibn al-ʿArabī, Muḥyī al-Dīn. *Bezels of Wisdom*. Translated by R. W. J. Austin, preface by Titus Burckhardt. New York: Paulist Press, 1980.
Ibn Ḥazm, Abu Muḥammad ʿAli ibn Aḥmad ibn Saʿīd. *Kitāb al-Fiṣal fi al-milal wa-al-aḥwāʾ wa-al-niḥal*. 5 vols. Edited by Muḥammad ibn ʿAbd al-Karīm Shahrastānī. Cairo: al-Maṭbaʿah al-adabīyah, 1899–1903.
Ibn Taymīyah, Aḥmad ibn ʿAbd al-Ḥalīm. *Al-Jawāb al-ṣaḥīḥ li-man baddala dīn al-Masīḥ*. 6 vols. Edited by ʿAlī ibn Ḥasan Ibn Nāṣir, ʿAbd al-ʿAzīz ibn Ibrāhīm ʿAskar, and Ḥamdān ibn Muḥammad Ḥamdān. Riyadh: Dār al-ʿĀṣimah, 1999.
Ibn Verga, Solomon. *Shevet Yehudah*. Edited by Azriel Shohat and Yitzhak Baer. Jerusalem: Schocken, 1947.
Ilan, Nahem. "Between an Oral Sermon and a Written Commentary: A Consideration of Rabbi Joseph ben Shoshan's Polemic in His Avot Commentary." *Anuario de estudios medievales* 42, no. 1 (2012): 183–99.
Interián de Ayala, Juan. *El pintor christiano y erudito ó Tratado de los errores que suelen cometerse freqüentemente en pintar y esculpir imágenes sagradas*. Madrid: Joaquín Ibarra, 1782.
Israel, Jonathan I. *European Jewry in the Age of Mercantilism, 1550–1750*. 3rd ed. London: Littman Library of Jewish Civilization, 1998.
Israel, Menasseh ben. *De la fragilité humaine et de l'inclination de l'homme au péché*. Translated by Henry Méchoulan, notes by Carsten Wilke. Paris: Éditions du Cerf, 1996.
Jacob ben Reuben. *Milḥamot ha-shem*. Edited by Judah Rosenthal. Jerusalem: Mosad Ha-Rav Kook, 1963.

Jameson, Fredric. *The Prison-House of Language: A Critical Account of Structuralism and Russian Formalism.* Princeton, NJ: Princeton University Press, 1972.

Jones, John R. "Thomas Erpenius (1584–1624) on the Value of the Arabic Language." *Manuscripts of the Middle East* 1 (1986): 15–25.

Jones, Linda G. *The Power of Oratory in the Medieval Muslim World.* Cambridge: Cambridge University Press, 2012.

Jordan of Saxony. "Libellus de principiis ordinis praedicatorum." In *Monumenta ordinis fratrum praedicatorum historica,* MOPH 16, edited by H. C. Scheeben. Rome: Institutum Historicum Fratrum Praedicatorum, 1935.

Joseph ben Nathan Official. *Sefer Yosef ha-meqanne.* Edited by Judah Rosenthal. Jerusalem: Mekize Nirdamim, 1970.

Juwaynī Imām al-Ḥaramayn, 'Abd al-Malik ibn 'Abd Allāh al-. *Shifa' al-ghalīl: Fī bayān mā waqa'a fī al-Tawrāh wa-al-Injīl min al-tabdīl.* Edited by Aḥmad Hijāzī as-Saqqā. Cairo: Maktabat kullīyāt al-Azharīyah, 1979.

Kaddouri, Samir. "Identificación de 'al-Qurṭubī, autor de *Al-iʿlām bi-mā fī dīn al-Naṣārā min al-fasād wa-l-awhām.*" *Al-Qanṭara* 21, no. 1 (2000): 215–20.

———. "Riḥlāt Aḥmad ibn ʿAmr al-Anṣārī al-Qurṭubī (t. 656 H.) fī l-Maghrib wa-l-Mashriq wa-muʾallafātihi al-ʿilmiyya." *Majallat Maktabat al-Malik Fahd al-Waṭaniyya* 11 (2005): 207–60.

Kaeppeli, Thomas. *Scriptores Ordinis Praedicatorum Medii Aevi.* 4 vols. Rome: S. Sabinae, 1970–93.

Kahf, Mohja. *Western Representations of Muslim Women: From Termagant to Odalisque.* Austin: University of Texas Press, 1999.

Kaplan, Yosef. *An Alternative Path to Modernity: The Sephardi Diaspora in Western Europe.* Leiden: Brill, 2000.

———. "Between Christianity and Judaism in Early Modern Europe: The Confessionalization Process of the Western Sephardi Diaspora." In *Judaism, Christianity, and Islam in the Course of History: Exchange and Conflicts,* edited by Lothar Gall and Dietmar Willoweit, 307–41. Munich: Oldenbourg, 2011.

———. *From Christianity to Judaism: The Story of Isaac Orobio de Castro.* Translated by Raphael Loewe. Oxford: Littman Library of Jewish Civilization, 1989.

Kassin, Leon Jacob. "A Study of a Fourteenth-Century Polemical Treatise Adversus Judaeos." 2 vols., PhD diss., Columbia University, 1969.

Keating, S. Toenies. "Ḥabīb ibn Khidma Abū Rāʾiṭa al-Takrītī." In *Christian-Muslim Relations. A Bibliographical History,* vol. 1, *600–900,* edited by David Thomas and Barbara Roggema, 567–81. Leiden: Brill, 2009.

Kedar, Benjamin Z. *Crusade and Mission: European Approaches toward the Muslims.* Princeton, NJ: Princeton University Press, 1988.

Kendrick, Thomas. *St. James in Spain.* London: Methuen, 1960.

Klepper, Deeana C. "First in Knowledge of Divine Law: The Jews and the Old Law in Nicholas of Lyra's Romans Commentary." In *Medieval Readings of Romans,* edited by William S. Campbell, Peter S. Hawkins, and Brenda Deen Schildgen, 167–81. New York: T&T Clark International, 2007.

———. *The Insight of Unbelievers: Nicholas of Lyra and Christian Reading of Jewish Text in the Later Middle Ages.* Philadelphia: University of Pennsylvania Press, 2008.

Kobler, Franz. *Letters of Jews through the Ages: From Biblical Times to the Middle of the Eighteenth Century.* 2nd ed. London: Ararat, 1953.

Kosto, Adam J. *Hostages in the Middle Ages.* New York: Oxford University Press, 2012.

Kozodoy, Maud. *The Secret Faith of Maestre Honoratus: Profyat Duran and Jewish Identity in Late Medieval Iberia.* Philadelphia: University of Pennsylvania Press, 2015.

Kressel, Getzel. "Rimoch, Astruc." In *Encyclopaedia Judaica,* 2nd ed., 22 vols., edited by Michael Berenbaum and

Fred Skolnik, 17:334. Detroit: Thomson Gale, 2007.
Krstić, Tijana. *Contested Conversions to Islam: Narratives of Religious Change in the Early Modern Ottoman Empire.* Stanford, CA: Stanford University Press, 2011.
Lachter, Hartley. *Kabbalistic Revolution: Reimagining Judaism in Medieval Spain.* New Brunswick, NJ: Rutgers University Press, 2014.
Ladner, Gerhart B. *Images and Ideas in the Middle Ages: Selected Studies in History and Art.* 2 vols. Rome: Edizioni di Storia e Letteratura, 1983.
Lammens, Henry. *L'Arabie occidentale avant l'hégire.* Beirut: Imprimerie catholique, 1928.
Landau, Leo. *Das Apologetische Schreiben des Josua Lorki an den Abtrünnigen Don Salomon ha-Lewi (Paulus de Santa Maria).* Antwerp: Teitelbaum & Boxenbaum, 1906.
La Parra López, Santiago. "1609 en el Ducado de Gandía." *Estudis. Revista de historia moderna* 16 (1990): 217–32.
———. "Los moriscos y moriscas de los Borja." In *Disidencias y exilios en la España Moderna,* edited by Antonio Mestre and Enrique Giménez, 435–46. Alicante: Universitat d'Alacant, 1997.
Lara Olmo, Juan Carlos. "Edición crítica, traducción y comentario de la obra *Sefer 'Aḥiṭub we Ṣalmon.*" PhD diss., Universidad Complutense, 1998.
Larios Ramos, Antonio. "Los Dominicos y la Inquisición." *Clío & Crimen* 2 (2005): 81–126.
Lasarte López, José Antonio, ed. *Poemas de Mohamad Rabadán.* Zaragoza: Diputación General de Aragón, 1991.
Lascorz Arcas, Francisco Andreu. *La aljama judía de Monzón, la recordada.* Zaragoza: Ayuntamiento de Monzón-Libros Certeza, 2001.
Lasker, Daniel J. "Anti-Christian Polemics in Eighteenth-Century Italy." [In Hebrew.] In *Proceedings of the Eleventh World Congress of Jewish Studies,* div. B, vol. 1, 185–92. Jerusalem: World Union of Jewish Studies, 1994.
———. "Averroistic Trends in Jewish-Christian Polemics in the Late Middle Ages." *Speculum* 55, no. 2 (1980): 294–304.
———, ed. *Biṭṭul 'iqqarei ha-noṣerim.* Ramat Gan: Bar-Ilan University Press, 1990. Translated by Daniel J. Lasker as *The Refutation of the Christian Principles,* by Hasdai Crescas. Albany, NY: SUNY Press, 1992.
———. "The Impact of the Crusades on the Jewish-Christian Debate." *Jewish History* 13, no. 2 (1999): 23–26.
———. "Jewish Anti-Christian Polemics in the Early Modern Period: Change or Continuity?" In *Tradition, Heterodoxy and Religious Culture: Judaism and Christianity in the Early Modern Period,* edited by Chanita Goodblatt and Howard Kreisel, 469–88. Beer Sheva: Ben-Gurion University Press, 2006.
———. "Jewish-Christian Polemics in Light of the Expulsion from Spain." *Judaism* 41, no. 2 (Spring 1992): 148–55.
———. "The Jewish Critique of Christianity: In Search of a New Narrative." *Studies in Christian-Jewish Relations* 6, no. 1 (2011): 1–9.
———. "The Jewish Critique of Christianity under Islam in the Middle Ages." *Proceedings of the American Academy for Jewish Research* 57 (1991): 121–53.
———. *Jewish Philosophical Polemics against Christianity in the Middle Ages.* 2nd ed. Oxford: Littman Library of Jewish Civilization, 2007.
———. "Joseph ben Nathan's *Sefer Yosef Ha-Mekanné* and the Medieval Jewish Critique of Christianity." In *Jews and Christians in Thirteenth Century France,* edited by Judah D. Galinsky and Elisheva Baumgarten, 113–22. New York: Palgrave Macmillan, 2015.
———. "Popular Polemics and Philosophical Truth in the Medieval Jewish Critique of Christianity." *Journal of Jewish Thought and Philosophy* 8, no. 2 (1999): 243–59.
———. "R. Hasdai Crescas' Polemical Activity in Light of the Medieval Jewish-Christian Debate." [In Hebrew.] In *R. Hasdai Crescas: Philosopher and*

Leader, edited by Esti Eisenmann and Zev Harvey. Jerusalem: Zalman Shazar Institute, forthcoming.

———. "Saadya Gaon on Christianity and Islam." In *The Jews of Medieval Islam: Community, Society, and Identity*, edited by Daniel Frank, 165–77. Leiden: Brill, 1995.

Lasker, Daniel J., and Sarah Stroumsa. *The Polemic of Nestor the Priest*. 2 vols. Jerusalem: Ben-Zvi Institute, 1996.

Lauer, Gerhard. "Die Konfessionalisierung des Judentums: Zum Prozess der religiösen Ausdifferenzierung im Judentum am Übergang zur Neuzeit." In *Interkonfessionalität—Transkonfessionalität—binnenkonfessionelle Pluralität: Neue Forschungen zur Konfessionalisierungsthese*, edited by Kaspar von Greyerz, Manfred Jakubowski-Tiessen, Thomas Kaufmann, and Hartmut Lehmann, 250–83. Gütersloh: Gütersloher Verlagshaus, 2003.

Lawee, Eric. *Isaac Abarbanel's Stance toward Tradition*. Albany, NY: SUNY Press, 2001.

———. "The Messianism of Isaac Abarbanel, 'Father of the [Jewish] Messianic Movements of the Sixteenth and Seventeenth Centuries.'" In *Millenarianism and Messianism in Early Modern European Culture*, vol. 1, *Jewish Messianism in the Early Modern World*, edited by Matt D. Goldish and Richard H. Popkin, 1–39. Dordrecht: Kluwer Academic, 2001.

Lazarus-Yafeh, Hava. *Intertwined Worlds: Medieval Islam and Bible Criticism*. Princeton, NJ: Princeton University Press, 1992.

———. "Taḥrīf." In *Encyclopaedia of Islam*, 2nd ed., edited by P. Bearman, Th. Bianquis, C. E. Bosworth, E. van Donzel, and W. P. Heinrichs. Leiden: Brill, 1960–2007. http://dx.doi.org/10.1163/1573-3912_islam_SIM_7317.

Lea, Henry Charles. *A History of the Inquisition of the Middle Ages*. 3 vols. New York: Harper & Brothers, 1887.

———. *The Moriscos of Spain: Their Conversion and Expulsion*. London: Bernard Quaritch, 1901; New York: Greenwood Press, 1968.

Lerner, Ralph. *Maimonides' Empires of Light*. Translated by Joel L. Kraemer. Chicago: University of Chicago Press, 2000.

Levi della Vida, Giorgio. "Manoscritti arabi de origine spagnola nella Biblioteca Vaticana." In *Collectanea Vaticana in honore Anselmi M. Card*, 2 vols., 2:133–89. Vatican City: Albareda, 1962.

———. *Ricerche sulla formazione del più antico fondo dei manoscritti orientali della Biblioteca Vaticana*. Vatican City: Biblioteca Apostolica Vaticana, 1939.

Lévi-Provençal, Évariste. "Un 'zaŷal' hispanique sur l'expédition aragonaise de 1309 contre Alméria." *Al-Andalus* 6, no. 2 (1941): 377–99.

Levy, Ian Christopher. "Medieval Readings of Old and New Law: From *Sacra Pagina* to *Sacra Doctrina*." In *Medieval Readings of Romans*, edited by William S. Campbell, Peter S. Hawkins, and Brenda Deen Schildgen, 70–97. New York: T&T Clark International, 2007.

Lida, María Rosa. "La hipérbole sagrada en la poesía castellana del siglo XV." *Revista de filología hispánica* 8 (1946): 291–309.

———. "El romance de la misa de amor." *Revista de Filología Hispánica* 3 (1941): 24–42.

Limor, Ora. "The Epistle of Rabbi Samuel of Morocco: A Best-Seller in the World of Polemics." In *Contra Iudaeos: Ancient and Medieval Polemics between Christians and Jews*, edited by Ora Limor and Guy Stroumsa, 177–94. Tübingen: Mohr Siebeck, 1996.

Linares, Lidwine. "Les saints matamores en Espagne du Moyen Âge au Siècle d'Or (XIIe–XVIIe siècles). Histoire et représentations." PhD diss., Université de Toulouse, 2008.

Litterae Quadrimestres. 3 vols. Madrid: Augustinus Avrial, 1894–1932.

Llull, Ramon. *Ars mystica theologiae et philosophiae*. Edited by Helmut Riedlinger. Paris: ROL, 1967.

———. *Blaquerna*. Nova Edició de les obres de Ramon Llull 8. Palma de Mallorca: Patronat Ramon Llull, 2009.
———. *Doctor Illuminatus: A Ramon Llull Reader*. Edited and translated by Anthony Bonner. Princeton, NJ: Princeton University Press, 1993.
———. *Liber de gentili et tribus sapientibus*. Transcription by Óscar de la Cruz. Corpus Christianorum Continuatio Mediaevalis 264. Turnhout: Brepols, 2015.
———. *Liber de participatione christianorum et sarracenorum*. Corpus Christianorum Continuatio Mediaevalis 78. Edited by Antoni Oliver and Michel Senellart. Turnhout: Brepols, 1988.
———. *Liber disputations Raimundi christiani et Homeri saraceni*. Valencia: Juan Jofre, 1510.
———. *Opera Latina VIII*. Edited by Hermogenes Harada. Corpus Christianorum Continuatio Mediaevalis 34. Turnhout: Brepols, 1980.
———. *Opera Latina XXII*. Edited by Aloisius Madre. Corpus Christianorum Continuatio Mediaevalis 114. Turnhout: Brepols, 1998.
———. *Selected Works of Ramon Llull (1232–1316)*. 2 vols. Edited by Anthony Bonner. Princeton, NJ: Princeton University Press, 1985.
Lobera Serrano, Francisco Javier. "Los conversos sevillanos y la Inquisición: El 'Libello' perdido de 1480." *Cultura Neolatina* 49, no. 1 (1989): 7–53.
López, Atanasio. *Memoria histórica de los obispos de Marruecos desde el siglo XIII*. Madrid: San Bernardo, 1920.
López-Baralt, Luce, Álvaro Galmés de Fuentes, and Juan Carlos Villaverde Amieva. *Tratado de los dos caminos por un morisco refugiado en Túnez (Ms. S 2 de la colección Gayangos, Biblioteca de la Real Academia de la Historia)*. Madrid: Instituto Universitario Seminario Menéndez Pidal, Universidad Complutense de Madrid, 2005.
López de Coca, José Enrique. "The Making of Isabel de Solís." In *Medieval Spain: Culture, Conflict, and Coexistence*, edited by Roger Collins and Anthony Goodman, 225–41. New York: Palgrave Macmillan, 2002.
López Martínez, Nicolás. *Los judaizantes castellanos y la inquisición en tiempo de Isabel la Católica*. Burgos: Aldecoa, 1954.
Losada, Carolina. "Powerful Words: St. Vincent Ferrer's Preaching and the Jews of Medieval Castile." In *Spoken Word and Social Practice: Orality in Europe (1400–1700)*, edited by Thomas V. Cohen and Lesley K. Twomey, 206–27. Leiden: Brill, 2015.
Lourie, Elena. "Anatomy of Ambivalence: Muslims under the Crown of Aragon in the Late Thirteenth Century." In *Crusade and Colonisation: Muslims, Christians, and Jews in Medieval Aragon*, edited by Elena Lourie, 1–77. Aldershot: Variorum, 1990.
Louth, Andrew. *St. John Damascene: Tradition and Originality in Byzantine Theology*. New York: Oxford University Press, 2002.
Lubac, Henri de. *Exégèse médiévale. Les quatre sens de l'écriture*. 4 vols. Paris: Aubier, 1959–64.
Maciá Serrano, Antonio. *San Vicente Ferrer en su vida, actos y obras*. Madrid: Publicaciones Españolas, 1971.
Madroñal, Abraham. "Entre Cervantes y Lope: Toledo, hacia 1604." *eHumanista: Journal of Iberian Studies* 1 (2012): 300–332. http://www.ehumanista.ucsb.edu/sites/secure.lsit.ucsb.edu.span.d7_eh/files/sitefiles/cervantes/volume1/17%20madronal.pdf.
———. "La primera edición de la *Vida de San José* del Maestro Valdivielso." *Revista de Filología Española* 82, no. 3–4 (2002): 273–94.
Madurell Marimón, José María, and Jorge Rubió y Balaguer. *Documentos para la Historia de la imprenta y librería en Barcelona (1474–1553)*. Barcelona: Gremios de Editores, de Libreros y de Maestros Impresores, 1955.
Magnier, Grace. "Pedro de Valencia, Francisco de Gurmendi y los Plomos del Sacromonte." In *Los plomos*

del Sacromonte: Invención y tesoro, edited by Manuel Barrios Aguilera and Mercedes García-Arenal, 201–16. Valencia: Universitat de València, 2006.

Maimonides, Moses. *Epistle to Yemen: The Arabic Original and the Three Hebrew Versions*. Edited by Abraham S. Halkin and Boaz Cohen. New York: American Academy for Jewish Research, 1952.

Maíz Eleizegui, Luis. *La devoción al Apóstol Santiago en España y el arte jacobeo hispánico*. 2nd ed. Madrid: S. Aguirre Torre, 1953.

Marín Padilla, Encarnación. *Relación judeoconversa durante la segunda mitad del siglo XV en Aragón. La ley*. Madrid: self-published, 1986.

Márquez Villanueva, Francisco. "The Converso Problem: An Assessment." In *Collected Studies in Honour of Américo Castro's Eightieth Year*, edited by Marcel P. Hornik, 316–33. Oxford: Lincombe Lodge Research Library, 1965.

———. *De la España judeoconversa: Doce estudios*. Barcelona: Bellaterra, 2006.

———. "Estudio preliminar." In *Católica impugnación*, by Hernando de Talavera, edited by Francisco Martín Hernández, 1–55. Barcelona: Juan Flors, 1961.

———. "Ideas de la *Católica impugnación* de fray Hernando de Talavera." In *Católica impugnación*, by Hernando de Talavera, edited by Francisco Márquez Villanueva, Stefania Pastore, and Francisco Martín Hernández, 13–32. Córdoba: Almuzara, 2012.

———. *Personajes y temas del Quijote*. Madrid: Taurus, 1975.

———. "El problema de los conversos: cuatro puntos cardinales." In *Hispania Judaica: Studies on the History, Language, and Literature of the Jews in the Hispanic World*, vol. 1, *History*, edited by Josep M. Sola-Solé, Samuel G. Armistead, and Joseph H. Silverman, 49–75. Barcelona: Puvill, 1980.

Martí, Ramon. *Capistrum iudaeorum*. 2 vols., edited and translated by Adolfo Robles Sierra. Würzburg: Echter Verlag, 1990–93.

———. *Pugio fidei adversus Mauros et Iudaeos*. Leipzig: Lenckisch, 1687; Farnborough: Gregg, 1967.

Martín de la Hoz, José Carlos. "La conversión en la predicación de san Vicente Ferrer." *Anales valentinos* 24, no. 488 (1998): 363–69. http://www.mercaba.org/Enciclopedia/C/conversion_en_la_predicacion.htm.

Martínez Gázquez, José. "Vtrum ritus infidelium sint tolerandi?" In *Ritus infidelium. Miradas interconfesionales sobre las prácticas religiosas en la Edad Media*, coordinated by José Martínez Gázquez and John Tolan, 223–46. Madrid: Casa de Velázquez, 2013.

Martínez Medina, Francisco Javier, and Martin Biersack. *Fray Hernando de Talavera, primer arzobispo de Granada: Hombre de Iglesia, estado y letras*. Granada: Universidad de Granada–Facultad de Teología, 2011.

Martínez Naranjo, Francisco Javier. "Las congregaciones marianas de la Compañía de Jesús y su contribución a la práctica de la caridad (ss. XVI–XVIII)." *Revista de historia moderna. Anales de la Universidad de Alicante* 21 (2003): 211–38.

Mata Carriazo, Juan de, ed. *Crónica de Juan II de Castilla*. Madrid: Real Academia de la Historia, 1982.

Matar, Nabil. *British Captives from the Mediterranean to the Atlantic, 1563–1760*. Leiden: Brill, 2014.

———. *Europe through Christian Eyes, 1578–1727*. New York: Columbia University Press, 2009.

Mateu Ibars, María Dolors. "San Pedro Pascual en el arte." In *Homenajes de las Entidades Culturales de Valencia a San Pedro Pascual en el tercer centenario de su canonización*, 61–110. Valencia: Imprenta Ortiz, 1973.

Mayáns y Siscar, Gregorio. *Aesopi Fabulae Latiné, atque Hispané scriptae: Quaque fieri potuit diligentia fidelitateque è Graeca Lingua in duas has traductae, iisque, qui Latinas litteras ediscere incipiunt, collatione linguarum utilissimae*. Translated by

Pedro Simón Abril. Valencia: Joseph Thomas Lucas, 1760.
Mazur, Peter A. *Conversion to Catholicism in Early Modern Italy*. New York: Routledge, 2016.
McMichael, Steven J., and Susan E. Myers, eds. *The Friars and Jews in the Middle Ages and Renaissance*. Leiden: Brill, 2004.
McReynolds, Susan. *Redemption and the Merchant God: Dostoevsky's Economy of Salvation and Antisemitism*. Evanston, IL: Northwestern University Press, 2008.
Méchoulan, Henry. "Menasseh ben Israel and the World of the Non-Jew." In *Menasseh ben Israel and His World*, edited by Yosef Kaplan, Henry Méchoulan, and Richard H. Popkin, 83–97. Leiden: Brill, 1989.
———. "Morteira et Spinoza au carrefour du socinianisme." *Revue des études juives* 135 (1976): 51–65.
Medina Rojas, Francisco de Borja. "Ignacio de Loyola y la 'limpieza de sangre.'" In *Ignacio de Loyola y su tiempo. Congreso Internacional de Historia (9–13 Septiembre 1991)*, coordinated by Juan de Plazaola Artola, 579–615. Bilbao: Mensajero, 1992.
Meerseeman, Gilles G. "La chronologie des voyages et des oeuvres de Frère Alphonse Buenhombre O.P." *Archivum Fratrum Praedicatorum* 10 (1940): 77–108.
Meerson, Michael, and Peter Schäfer, eds. and trans. *Toledot Yeshu: The Life Story of Jesus*. 2 vols. Tübingen: Mohr Siebeck, 2014.
Meillassoux, Claude. "Esclaves, vénacles, captifs et serfs." In *Esclavage et dépendances serviles. Histoire comparée*, edited by Myriam Cottias, Alessandro Stella, and Bernard Vincent, 367–73. Paris: L'Harmattan, 2006.
Menéndez Pelayo, Marcelino. "De la poesía mística." 1881. In *Discursos*, edited by J. M. de Cossío, 3–68. Madrid: Espasa-Calpe, 1964.
Menéndez Pidal, Ramón, ed. *Flor nueva de romances viejos*. 7th ed. Madrid: Espasa-Calpe, 1985.
Mérigoux, Jean-Marie. "L'ouvrage d'un frère Prêcheur florentin en orient à la fin du XIIIe siècle. Le *Contra legem Sarracenorum* de Riccoldo da Monte di Croce." *Memorie domenicane* 17 (1986): 1–144.
Mestre Godes, Jesús. *El compromís de Casp. Un moment decisiu en la història de Catalunya*. Barcelona: Edicions 62, 1999.
Meyerson, Mark. *Jews in an Iberian Frontier Kingdom: Society, Economy, and Politics in Morvedre, 1248–1391*. Leiden: Brill, 2004.
Milhou, Alain. *Colón y su mentalidad mesiánica en el ambiente franciscanista español*. Valladolid: Casa-Museo de Colón-Seminario de Historia de América de la Universidad de Valladolid, 1983.
Miller, Kathryn A. *Guardians of Islam: Religious Authority and Muslim Communities of Late Medieval Spain*. New York: Columbia University Press, 2008.
Millet-Gérard, Dominique. *Chrétiens mozarabes et culture islamique dans l'Espagne des VIIIe–IXe siècles*. Paris: Études Augustiniennes, 1984.
Mira, Joan F. *San Vicente Ferrer. Vida y leyenda de un predicador*. Alzira: Algar, 2002.
Mir y Noguera, Miguel, ed. *Escritores místicos españoles: Hernando de Talavera, Alejo Venegas, Francisco de Osuna, Alfonso de Madrid*. Madrid: Bailly-Baillière, 1911.
Monferrer Sala, Juan Pedro. "Al-Imām al-Qurṭubī." In *Christian-Muslim Relations: A Bibliographical History*, vol. 4, *1200–1350*, edited by David Thomas and Alex Mallett, 391–94. Leiden: Brill, 2012.
———. "Siete citas hebreas, más una aramea, transcritas al árabe en el *I'lām* del Imām al-Qurṭubī." *Miscelánea de estudios árabes y hebraicos. Sección Árabe e Islam* 48 (1999): 393–403.
Monteira Arias, Inés. *El enemigo imaginado. La escultura románica hispana y la lucha contra el Islam*. Toulouse: Université de Toulouse, 2012.
Monteret de Villard, Hug. *Lo studio dell'Islam in Europa*. Vatican City: Biblioteca Apostolica Vaticana, 1961.
Montero, Antón de. *Poesía completa*. Edited by Marithelma Costa. Cleveland, OH: Cleveland State University Press, 1990.

Montoliu, Manuel de. *Eiximenis, Turmeda i l'inici de l'humanisme a Catalunya: Bernat Metge.* Vol. 4 of *Les grans personalitats de la literatura catalana.* Barcelona: Alpha, 1959.

Monumenta Borgia: Sanctus Franciscus Borgia. Quartus Gandiae Dux et Praepositus Generalis Tertius. 5 vols. Madrid: Augustinus Avrial, 1894–1911.

Morocho Gayo, Gaspar, ed. *Pedro de Valencia, Obras Completas.* 4 vols. León: Universidad de León, 2000.

Mulsow, Martin. "Socinianism, Islam and the Radical Uses of Arabic Scholarship." *Al-Qanṭara* 31, no. 2 (2010): 549–86.

Münzer, Hieronymus. "Relación del viaje por España y Portugal en los años 1494 y 1495." In *Viajes de extranjeros por España y Portugal,* 3 vols., edited by José García Mercadal, 1:328–417. Madrid: Aguilar, 1952–62.

Murciano, Prosper. "Simon ben Zemah Duran, Keshet u-Magen: A Critical Edition." PhD diss., New York University, 1975.

Murphy, Sean. "William of Auvergne." In *Christian-Muslim Relations: A Bibliographical History,* vol. 4, *1200–1350,* edited by David Thomas and Alex Mallett, 288–94. Leiden: Brill, 2012.

Nasi, Don David. *Hodaʾat Baʿal Din.* Frankfurt am Main: H. L. Brönner's Druckerei, 1866.

Netanyahu, Benzion. *The Origins of the Inquisition in Fifteenth Century Spain.* New York: Random House, 1995.

New Jewish Publication Society of America. *Tanakh: A New Translation of the Holy Scriptures According to the Traditional Hebrew Text.* 2nd ed. Philadelphia: New Jewish Publication Society of America, 1999.

Niclós Albarracín, José-Vicente. *Profiat Durán. Cinco cuestiones debatidas de polémica.* Madrid: Aben Ezra, 1999.

———. *Šem Ṭob Ibn Šaprut "La Piedra de Toque" (Eben Bohan). Una obra de controversia judeo-cristiana.* Madrid: Consejo Superior de Investigaciones Científicas, 1997.

Nirenberg, David. *Communities of Violence: Persecution of Minorities in the Middle Ages.* Princeton, NJ: Princeton University Press, 1996.

———. "Does the History of Anti-Judaism Have Anything to Do with the Present?" Paper presented at the Gravensteen Lecture, Leiden University, September 5, 2014.

———. "Love between Muslim and Jew in Medieval Spain: A Triangular Affair." In *Jews, Muslims, and Christians in and around the Crown of Aragon: Essays in Honour of Professor Elena Lourie,* edited by Harvey J. Hames, 127–55. Leiden: Brill, 2004.

———. "Muslim-Jewish Relations in the Fourteenth-Century Crown of Aragon." *Viator* 24 (1993): 249–68.

———. *Neighboring Faiths: Christianity, Islam and Judaism in the Middle Ages and Today.* Chicago: University of Chicago Press, 2014.

Novikoff, Alex J. "Dialogue and Disputation in Medieval Thought and Society, 1050–1350." PhD diss., University of Pennsylvania, 2007.

———. *The Medieval Culture of Disputation: Pedagogy, Practice and Performance.* Philadelphia: University of Pennsylvania Press, 2013.

Obregón, Lope de. *Confutación del alcorán y secta mahometana, sacado de sus propios libros y de la vida del mesmo Mahoma.* Granada, 1555.

O'Callaghan, Joseph. *Alfonso X and the Cantigas de Santa María: A Poetic Biography.* Leiden: Brill, 1998.

———. *Reconquest and Crusade in Medieval Spain.* Philadelphia: University of Pennsylvania Press, 2003.

Olds, Katrina B. *Forging the Past: Invented Histories in Counter-Reformation Spain.* New Haven, CT: Yale University Press, 2015.

Olivar, Marçal, ed. *Bernat Metge—Anselm Turmeda; Obres menors.* Barcelona: Els Nostres Clàssics, 1927.

Olivares Torres, Enric. "Nuevas lecturas en torno al retablo mayor de San Jaime apóstol de Algemesí." *Imago. Revista de emblemática y cultura visual* 2 (2010): 95–115.

Oliver Asín, Jaime. "Un morisco de Túnez, admirador de Lope." *Al-Andalus* 1 (1933): 409–50.

———. "El *Quijote* de 1604." *Boletín de la Real Academia Española* 28 (1948): 89–126.

———. *Vida de Don Felipe de África, príncipe de Fez y Marruecos.* Madrid: Consejo Superior de Investigaciones Científicas, 1955.

O'Malley, John W. *The First Jesuits.* Cambridge, MA: Harvard University Press, 1993.

———. "Sant'Ignazio e le missione della Compagnia di Gesú nella cultura." In *Ignacio e l'arte dei Gesuiti*, coordinated by Giovanni Sale, 17–30. Milan: Editoriale Jaca Book Spa, 2003.

Orfali Levi, Moises. "Jews and Conversos in Fifteenth-Century Spain: Christian Apologia and Polemic." In *From Witness to Witchcraft: Jews and Judaism in Medieval Christian Thought*, edited by Jeremy Cohen, 337–60. Wiesbaden: Harrassowitz Verlag, 1996.

Origen. *Commentary on the Epistle to the Romans.* Translated by Thomas P. Scheck. Washington, DC: Catholic University of America Press, 2001.

Orobio, Isaac. *Israël Vengé, ou: Exposition naturelle des Prophéties Hébraïques que les Chrétiens appliquent à Jésus leur prétendu Messie. Par Isaac Orobio.* London, 1770.

———. *Prevenciones divinas contra la vana idolatría de las gentes.* 2 vols. Edited by Myriam Silvera. Florence: Leo S. Olschki, 2013–16.

Oropesa, Fray Alonso de. *Luz para el conocimiento de los gentiles.* Translated by Luis A. Díaz y Díaz. Madrid: Universidad Pontificia de Salamanca–Fundación Universitaria Española, 1979.

Pacios López, Antonio. *La Disputa de Tortosa.* 2 vols. Madrid: Consejo Superior de Investigaciones Científicas, 1957.

Panella, Emilio. "Presentatione." In "Fede e Controversia, nel '300 e '400." Special issue, *Memorie domenicane* 17 (1986): v–xxxix.

———. "Ricerche su Riccoldo da Monte da Croce." *Archivum Fratrum Praedicatorum* 58 (1988): 77–85.

Parrilla, Carmen. *Hernando de Talavera. Dos escritos destinados a la reina Isabel: Colación muy provechosa, Tratado de loores de San Juan Evangelista.* Valencia: Universitat de València, 2014.

Pascual, Pseudo Pedro. *El Obispo de Jaén sobre la Seta mahometana.* Edited and translated by Pedro Armengol Velenzuela. Rome: Imprenta Salustiana, 1968.

———. *Obras de S. Pedro Pascual, Mártir: Obispo de Jaén y religioso de la Mercé.* 4 vols. Edited and translated by Pedro Armengol Valenzuela. Rome: F. Cuggiani, 1905 (vol. 1); Rome: Salustiana, 1907 (vols. 2–3); Rome: Salustiana, 1908 (vol. 4).

———. *Sobre la se[c]ta mahometana.* Edited by Fernando González Muñoz. Valencia: Universitat de València, 2011.

Pastore, Stefania. *Un'eresia spagnola: Spiritualità conversa, alumbradismo e inquisizione (1449–1559).* Florence: Leo S. Olschki, 2004.

———. "Presentación." In *Católica impugnación del herético libelo maldito y descomulgado, divulgado en la ciudad de Sevilla*, by Hernando de Talavera, edited by Francisco Márquez Villanueva. Cordoba: Almuzara, 2012.

Paulmier-Foucart, Monique, and Marie-Christine Duchenne. *Vincent de Beauvais et le Grand miroir du monde.* Turnhout: Brepols, 2004.

Pedretti, Marco. "Anselm Turmeda." In *Història de la Literatura Catalana; Literatura medieval (II); Segles XIV–XV*, edited by Lola Badía, 239–60. Barcelona: Enciclopedia Catalana-Barcino-Ajuntament de Barcelona, 2014.

———. "Letture politiche delle opere catalane di Anselm Turmeda." *Studi ispanici* 36 (2011): 11–50.

Pedro Alfonso. *Diálogo contra los judíos.* Edited by Klaus-Peter Mieth, translated by Esperanza Ducay. Huesca: Instituto de Estudios Altoaragoneses, 1996.

———. *Dialogue against the Jews.* Translated by Irven M. Resnick. Washington, DC: Catholic University of America Press, 2006.

Perarnau i Espelt, Josep. "Aportació a un inventari de sermons de Sant Vicenç Ferrer. Temes bíblics, títols i divisions esquemàtiques." *Arxiu de textos catalans antics* 18 (1999): 479–811.

———. "Cent anys d'estudis dedicats als sermons de Sant Vicent Ferrer." *Arxiu de textos catalans antics* 18 (1999): 9–62.

Perceval, José María. *Todos son uno. Arquetipos, xenofobia y racismo. La imagen del morisco en la Monarquía española durante los siglos XVI y XVII*. Almería: Instituto de Estudios Almerienses, 1997.

Pereda, Felipe. *Las imágenes de la discordia. Política y poética de la imagen sagrada en la España del 400*. Madrid: Marcial Pons, 2007.

Pérez, Quintín S. I. *Fr. Hernando de Santiago. Predicador del Siglo de Oro (1575–1639)*. Madrid: Instituto Miguel de Cervantes, 1949.

Pérez Collados, José María. *Las Indias en el pensamiento político de Fernando el Católico*. Borja: Centro de Estudios Borjanos–Institución Fernando el Católico, 1992.

Pérez de Chinchón, Bernardo. *Libro llamado Alcorán, qve qviere dezir contra el Alcorán de Mahoma, repartido en veynte y seys sermones*. Salamanca: Juan and Andrés Renault, 1595.

Pérez García, Rafael, and Manuel Fernández Chaves. "La infancia morisca, entre la educación y la explotación." In *La infancia en España y Portugal. Siglos XVI–XVII*, coordinated by Francisco Núñez Roldán, 149–86. Madrid: Sílex, 2010.

Pérez Ruiz, Pedro Antonio. *La fe, la historia y el arte en el antiguo Convento de Predicadores de Valencia*. Valencia: Real Academia de la Historia, 1952.

Perry, Craig. "Slave Women Converts to Judaism and Their Supporters in Medieval Egypt." In *Contesting Inter-religious Conversion in the Medieval World*, edited by Yaniv Fox and Yosi Yisraeli, 135–59. London: Routledge, 2017.

Peter of Ferrand. *Legenda Sancti Dominici*. In *Monumenta historia sancti patris nostri Dominici*, MOPH 16, edited by Angelus Walz, 209–60. Rome: Institutum Historicum Fratrum Praedicatorum, 1935.

Peter the Venerable. *Adversus iudeorum inveteratam duritiem*. Edited by Yvonne Friedman. Turnhout: Brepols, 1985.

———. *Against the Inveterate Obduracy of the Jews*. Translated by Irven Michael Resnick. Washington, DC: Catholic University of America Press, 2013.

Pfandl, Ludwig. "Itinerarium hispanicum Hieronymi Monetarii (1494–1495)." *Revue Hispanique* 48, no. 113 (1920): 1–179.

Phelan, John L. *The Millennial Kingdom of the Franciscans in the New World: A Study of the Writings of Geronimo de Mendieta (1525–1604)*. 2nd ed. Berkeley: University of California Press, 1970.

Phillips, William D., Jr. *Slavery in Medieval and Early Modern Iberia*. Philadelphia: University of Pennsylvania Press, 2014.

Pierce, Frank. *La poesía épica del siglo de Oro*. Madrid: Gredos, 1968.

Pines, Shlomo. "Al-ʿĪsāwiyya." In *Encyclopaedia of Islam Online*, 2nd ed., edited by P. Bearman, Th. Bianquis, C. E. Bosworth, E. van Donzel, and W. P. Heinrichs. http://dx.doi.org/10.1163/1573-3912_islam_SIM_3608.

———. "The Jewish Christians of the Early Centuries of Christianity According to a New Source [Abd al-Jabbar]." *Proceedings of the Israel Academy of Sciences and Humanities* 2 (1969): 237–310.

Piquer Jover, Josep J. *La vida i els miracles de San Raimon de Penyafort segons un grabador flamenc. Contribució a la iconografia raimondina*. Barcelona: Fimagraf, 1980.

Platti, Emilio. "L'image de l'Islam chez le dominicain Vincent de Beauvais (m. 1264)." *Mideo: Mélanges de l'Institut dominicain d'études orientales du Caire* 25–26 (2004): 65–139.

Plinius Secundus, Gaius. *Historia Natural*. Translated by Francisco Hernández. Mexico, DF: Universidad Nacional Autónoma de México, 1966–76.

Postel, Guillaume. *Grammatica Arabica*. Paris: Petrum Gromorsum, n.d.

———. *De orbis terrae concordia*. Edited by Johannes Oporinus. Basel: Oporinus, 1543–44.

Potthast, Daniel. *Christen und Muslime im Andalus: Andalusiche Christen und ihre Literatur nach religionspolemischen Texte des zehnten bis zwölften Jahrhunderts*. Wiesbaden: Harrassowitz Verlag, 2013.

Poutrin, Isabelle. *Convertir les musulmans. Espagne, 1491–1609*. Paris: Presses Universitaires de France, 2012.

———. "The Jewish Precedent in the Spanish Politics of Conversion of Muslims and Moriscos." *Journal of Levantine Studies* 6 (2016): 71–87.

Pradei, Andrew. *St. Vincent Ferrer: The Angel of the Judgment*. Charlotte, NC: TAN Books, 1974.

Praedicatores Inquisitores: The Dominicans and the Medieval Inquisition. Acts of the 1st International Seminar on the Dominicans and the Inquisition; 23–25 February 2002. Edited by Wolfram Hoyer. Dissertationes Historicae Fasciculus 29. Rome: Insituto Storico Domenicano, 2004.

Prudentius Clemens, Aurelius. *Aurelii Prudentii Clementis Carmina*. Edited by Ioannes Bergman. Corpus Scriptorum Ecclesiasticorum Latinorum 61. Vienna: Hoelder-Pichler-Tempsky, 1926.

———. *Preface. Daily Round. Divinity of Christ. Origin of Sin. Fight for Mansoul. Against Symmachus 1*. Translated by H. J. Thomson. Loeb Classical Library 387. Cambridge, MA: Harvard University Press, 1949.

Puig Sanchís, Isidro, and Borja Franco Llopis. "Juan de Sariñena y Luis Beltrán, dos iconos de la espiritualidad en el arte valenciano. Apreciaciones a propósito del lienzo conservado en el Museo Ibercaja-Camón Aznar de Zaragoza." *Archivo de arte valenciano* 95 (2014): 31–46.

Quevedo y Villegas, Francisco de. *Obras completas*. Edited by Felicidad Buendía. Madrid: Aguilar, 1986.

Qurṭubī, Aḥmad ibn ʿUmar ibn Ibrāhīm ibn ʿUmar al-Anṣārī al-. *Kitāb al-Iʿlām bi-mā fī dīn al-Naṣārā min al-fasād wa-l-awhām wa-iẓhār maḥāsin dīn al-Islām wa-ithbāt nubuwwat nabiyyinā* Muḥammad. Edited by Aḥmad Hijāzī as-Saqqā. Cairo: Dār al-Turāth al-ʿArabī, 1980.

Raimon and Anselm Turmeda. "Elogi dels diners." In *Catalan Protest Songs*. Smithsonian Folkways Recordings, FW05410 / FD 5410, 1971.

Rauschenbach, Sina. *Judentum für Christen: Vermittlung und Selbstbehauptung Menasseh ben Israels in den gelehrten Debatten des 17. Jahrhunderts*. Berlin: De Gruyter, 2012.

Redondo, Agustín. *Antonio de Guevara (1480–1545) et l'Espagne de son temps. De la carrière officielle aux oeuvres politico-morales*. Geneva: Droz, 1976.

Reeves, Marjorie. *The Influence of Prophecy in the Later Middle Ages: A Study in Joachimism*. 1969. Reprint, Oxford: Clarendon Press, 2000.

Regev, Shaul. "*Sefeiqot . . . ʿal maʿaseh Yeshu ha-Noṣeri*." *Kiryat Sefer* 63, no. 1 (1989–90): 263–69.

Remensnyder, Amy G. *La Conquistadora: The Virgin Mary at War and Peace in the Old and New Worlds*. New York: Oxford University Press, 2014.

Requesens i Piquer, Joan. "La poesía política de Jaume Collell (1868–1871)." *Anuari verdaguer* 12 (2004): 117–79.

Resines, Luis. *Hernando de Talavera: Prior del Monasterio de Prado*. Salamanca: Junta de Castilla y León, 1993.

Riera i Sans, Jaume. "La invenció literària de Sant Pere Pasqual." *Caplletra. Revista Internacional de Filología* 1 (1986): 45–60.

———. "Les llicènces reials per predicar als jueus i als sarraïns (segles XIII–XIV)." *Calls* 2 (1987): 113–43.

———. *Sodomites catalans. Història i vida (segles XIII–XVIII)*. Barcelona: Editorial Base, 2014.

Ringbom, Sixten. "Devotional Images and Imaginative Devotions: Notes on the Place of Art in Late Medieval Private Piety." *Gazette des beaux-arts* 73 (1969): 159–70.

———. *Les images des dévotion XIIe–XVe siècle*. Paris: Gérard Monfort Èditeur, 1995.

Riquer, Martí de. *Història de la literatura catalana; Part antiga*. 3 vols. 3rd ed. Barcelona: Ariel, 1982.

Robbins, Joel. "Crypto Religion and the Study of Cultural Mixtures: Anthropology, Value and the Nature of Syncretism." *Journal of the American Academy of Religion* 79, no. 2 (2011): 408–24.

Robinson, Cynthia. *Imagining the Passion in a Multiconfessional Castile: The Virgin, Christ, Devotions and Images in the Fourteenth and Fifteenth Centuries*. University Park: Pennsylvania State University Press, 2013.

———. "Preaching to the Converted: Valladolid's *Cristianos nuevos* and the *Retablo de Don Sancho de Rojas*." *Speculum* 81, no. 1 (2000): 112–63.

Robles, Laureano. *Escritores dominicos de la Corona de Aragón. Siglos XIII–XV*. Salamanca: Imprenta Calatrava, 1972.

Robles Sierra, Adolfo. "Correspondencia de San Luis Bertrán." In *San Luis Bertrán. Reforma y Contrarreforma española*, 335–74. Valencia: Artes Gráficas Soler, 1973.

———. "Manuscritos del Archivo del Real Convento de Predicadores de Valencia." *Escritos del Vedat* 15 (1984): 349–402.

———, ed. *Obras y escritos de san Vicente Ferrer*. Valencia: Ajuntament de València, 1996.

———. "La reforma entre los dominicos de Valencia en el siglo XVI." In *Corrientes espirituales en la Valencia del siglo XVI (1550–1600). Actas del II Symposio de Teología Histórica (20–22 abril 1982)*, 183–209. Valencia: Facultad de Teología San Vicente Ferrer, 1983.

———. "San Vicente Ferrer en el contexto del diálogo. Las minorías religiosas." *Escritos del Vedat* 26 (1996): 143–76.

Rocabertí, Juan Tomás de. *Sancti Vincentii Ferrarii . . . Opera: Complectens sermones totius temporis Paschalis et solemnitatum S.S. Trinitatis et Corporis Christi*. 1694. Madrid: Universidad Complutense, 2009.

Roca Traver, Francisco A. "San Vicente Ferrer y los judíos. La 'Disputa' de Tortosa." *Boletín de la Sociedad Castellonense de Cultura* 85 (2009): 203–27.

Rodríguez, Jarbel. *Captives and Their Saviors in the Medieval Crown of Aragon*. Washington, DC: Catholic University of America Press, 2007.

Rodríguez Barral, Paulino. *La imagen del judío en la España medieval. El conflicto entre el cristianismo y el judaísmo en las artes visuales góticas*. Bellaterra: Universitat Autònoma de Barcelona, 2009.

Rodríguez de Gracia, Hilario. "Un censo de moriscos de finales del siglo XVI." *Toletum: Boletín de la Real Academia de Bellas Artes y Ciencias Históricas de Toledo* 11 (1981): 521–42.

Rodríguez de la Flor, Fernando. *Barroco. Representación e ideología en el mundo hispánico (1580–1680)*. Madrid: Cátedra, 2002.

———. *La península metafísica: Arte, literatura y pensamiento en la España de la Contrarreforma*. Madrid: Biblioteca Nueva, 1999.

Rodríguez Paniagua, Luis. "Recursos sintácticos destinados al adoctrinamiento en los textos sapienciales castellanos y árabes." *Res Diachronicae* 2 (2003): 303–11.

Roggema, Barbara. "To Mār Naṣr, Letter 36." In *Christian-Muslim Relations: A Bibliographical History*, vol. 1, *600–900*, edited by David Thomas and Barbara Roggema, 530–31. Leiden: Brill, 2009.

Röhricht, Reinhold. "Lettres de Ricoldo de Monte-Croce sur la prise d'Acre (1291)." *Archives de l'Orient latin* 2, no. 2 (1884): 258–96.

Romagnoli, Gaetano. *Dottrina dello schiavo di Bari Secondo la lezione di tre antichi testi a penna*. Bologna: Presso Gaetano Romagnoli, 1865.

Romano, David. "Conversión de judíos al Islam. Corona de Aragón, 1280 y 1284." *Sefarad* 36, no. 2 (1976): 333–37.

Rosa-Rodríguez, María del Mar. "Simulation and Dissimulation: Religious Hybridity in a Morisco Fatwa." *Medieval Encounters* 16, no. 1 (2010): 143–80.

Rosenstock, Bruce. *New Men: "Conversos," Christian Theology, and Society in Fifteenth-Century Castile*. London:

Queen Mary University of London Press, 2002.

Roth, Norman. "Anti-Converso Riots of the Fifteenth Century, Pulgar and the Inquisition." *En la España medieval* 15 (1992): 367–94.

———. *Conversos, Inquisition, and the Expulsion of the Jews from Spain.* Madison: University of Wisconsin Press, 2002.

Rotman, Youval. "Captif ou esclave? Entre marché d'esclaves et marché de captifs en Méditérranée médiévale." In *Les esclavages en Méditerranée. Espaces et dynamiques économiques*, edited by Fabienne P. Guillén and Salah Trabelsi, 25–46. Madrid: Casa de Velázquez, 2012.

———. "Forms of Slavery." In *A Companion to Mediterranean History*, edited by Peregrine Horden and Sharon Kinoshita, 263–78. Chichester: Wiley Blackwell, 2014.

Rubio, Diego. "La *taqiyya* en las fuentes cristianas: indicios de su presencia entre los moriscos." *Al-Qanṭara* 34, no. 2 (2013): 529–46.

Rubió i Balaguer, Jordi. *Història de la literatura catalana.* Vol. 1. Barcelona: Abadía de Montserrat, 1984.

Ruel, Malcolm. *Belief, Ritual and the Securing of Life: Reflective Essays on a Bantu Religion.* Leiden: Brill, 1997.

Ruiz, Juan. *The Book of True Love.* Edited by Anthony N. Zahareas, translated by Saralyn R. Daly. University Park: Pennsylvania State University Press, 1978.

Ruiz García, Elisa. "La 'criptobiblioteca' de un polemista cristiano." In *Bibliotecas y librerías en la España de Carlos V*, coordinated by José María Díez Borque, 225–49. Barcelona: Calambur, 2015.

———. "Joan Martí Figuerola." In *Christian-Muslim Relations: A Bibliographical History*, vol. 6, *Western Europe (1500–1600)*, edited by David Thomas and John Chesworth, 89–92. Leiden: Brill, 2014.

Rumeu de Armas, Antonio. *Itinerario de los Reyes Católicos: 1474–1516.* Madrid: Instituto Jerónimo Zurita–Consejo Superior de Investigaciones Científicas, 1974.

———. *La política indigenista de Isabel la Católica.* Valladolid: Instituto Isabel la Católica de Historia Eclesiástica, 1969.

Russell, Josiah C. *Late Ancient and Medieval Population.* Transactions of the American Philosophical Society 48. Philadelphia: American Philosophical Society, 1958.

Rustomji, Nerina. *The Garden and the Fire: Heaven and Hell in Islamic Culture.* New York: Columbia University Press, 2009.

Ryan, Michael A. "Byzantium, Islam, and the Great Western Schism." In *A Companion to the Great Western Schism (1378–1417)*, edited by Joëlle Rollo-Koster and Thomas M. Izbicki, 197–238. Leiden: Brill, 2009.

Saadia Gaon. *Kitāb al-'amānāt wal-'i'tiqādāt.* Edited by Yosef Kafih. Jerusalem: Sura Institute, 1969–70. English translation from the Arabic and the Hebrew by Samuel Rosenblatt, *The Book of Beliefs and Opinions.* 2nd ed. New Haven, CT: Yale University Press, 1967.

Saborit, Vicente. *Historia de la vida, virtudes y milagros del Beato Luis Bertrán, de la Orden de Predicadores.* Valencia: Casa de los herederos de Chrysóstomo Gárriz, 1651.

Sadan, Joseph. "Some Literary Problems Concerning Judaism and Jewry in Medieval Arabic Sources." In *Studies in Islamic History and Civilization in Honour of Professor David Ayalon*, edited by Moshe Sharon, 353–98. Jerusalem: Cana, 1986.

Sadik, Shalom. "Between Ashkenaz and Sefarad: The Ideological Apostate." *Hebrew Union College Annual* 82–83 (2011–12): 61–78.

Saffioti, Tito. *I giullari in Italia; La storia, lo spettacolo, i testi.* Milan: Xenia Edizioni, 1990.

Salinas, Miguel de. *Rhetórica en lengua castellana.* Edited by Encarnación Sánchez García. Naples: L'Orientale Editrice, 1999.

Salomon, Herman P. *Saul Levi Mortera en zijn "Traktaat betreffende de Waarheid van de Wet van Mozes," eigenhandig geschreven in de Portugese taal te Amsterdam 1659–1660*. Braga: Barbosa & Xavier, 1988.

Salomons, Carolyn. "A Church United in Itself: Hernando de Talavera and the Religious Culture of Fifteenth-Century Castile." *Catholic Historical Review* 103 (2017): 639–62.

Samsó Moya, Julio. "Turmediana: I. Trasfondo cultural islámico en la obra catalana de Anselmo Turmeda. II. En torno a la *Tuḥfa* y al *Libre de bons amonestaments*." *Boletín de la Real Academia de Buenas Letras de Barcelona* 34 (1971–72): 51–85.

San Cecilio, Pedro de. *Annales de la Orden de Descalzos de Nuestra Señora de la Merced. Redempción de Cautivos Christianos*. Barcelona: Dionisio Hidalgo, 1669.

Sánchez López, Juan Francisco. "Martín García Puyazuelo y su papel en el establecimiento de la Inquisición en Aragón." *Anuario del Centro de la Universidad Nacional de Educación a Distancia en Calatayud* 13, no. 1 (2005): 233–44.

Sánchez Martínez, Francisco Javier. *Historia y crítica de la poesía lírica culta 'A lo divino' en la España del siglo de oro*. Vol. 1, *Técnicas de divinización de textos líricos y otros fundamentos teóricos*. Alicante: self-published, 1995.

Sánchez Sánchez, Manuel A. *Un sermonario castellano medieval. El Ms. 1854 de la Biblioteca Universitaria de Salamanca*. 2 vols. Salamanca: Universidad de Salamanca, 1999.

Sanchís Sivera, Josep, trans. *Quaresma de Sant Vicent Ferrer*. Barcelona: Institut Patxot, 1927.

Sans i Roselló, Elvir. "Fra AnselmTurmeda en 1402." *Estudis Universitaris Catalans* 22 (1936): 405–8.

Santonja Hernández, Pedro. "La Disputa de Tortosa. Jerónimo de Santa Fe y san Vicente Ferrer." *Helmantica: Revista de filología clásica y hebrea* 63, no. 189 (2012): 133–52.

———. "Sobre judíos y judeoconversos en la baja Edad Media. Textos de controversia." *Helmantica: Revista de filología clásica y hebrea* 60, no. 181 (2009): 177–203.

Sapir Abulafia, Anna. "The Bible in Jewish-Christian Dialogue." In *The New Cambridge History of the Bible*, vol. 2, *From 600 to 1450*, edited by Richard Marsden and E. Ann Matter, 616–37. Cambridge: Cambridge University Press, 2012.

Saquero Suárez-Somonte, Pilar. *De la sentencia-estatuto de Pero Sarmiento a la instrucción del relator. Estudio introductorio, edición crítica y notas de los textos contrarios y favorables a los judeoconversos a raíz de la rebelión de Toledo de 1449*. Madrid: Aben Ezra Ediciones, 2012.

Schiaparelli, Celestino, ed. *Vocabulista in Arabico. Pubblicato per la prima volta sopra un codice della Biblioteca Riccardiana di Firenze*. Firenze: Tipografia dei Successori Le Monnier, 1871.

Schmid, Beatrice. "La lengua sefardí en su plenitud." In *Sefardíes: Literatura y lengua de una nación dispersa. XV Curso de Cultura Hispanojudía y Sefardí de la Universidad de Castilla-La Mancha organizado por la Asociación de Amigos del Museo Sefardí in memoriam Ana Riaño y Iacob M. Hassan*, coordinated by Iacob M. Hassan and Ricardo Izquierdo Benito, 51–79. Cuenca: Universidad de Castilla–La Mancha, 2008.

Schmidtke, Sabine. "The Rightly Guiding Epistle (*al-Risāla al-Hādiya*) by ʿAbd al-Salām al-Muhtadī al-Muḥammadī: A Critical Edition." *Jerusalem Studies in Arabic and Islam* 36 (2009): 439–70.

Schreckenberg, Heinz. *Die christlichen Adversus—Iudaeos—Texte und ihr literarisches und historisches Umfeld (13–20 Jh.)*. Frankfurt am Main: Peter Lang, 1994.

Scotto, Davide. "'Como en un resplandeciente y terso espejo': Hernando de Talavera tra i musulmani nelle vite della prima età moderna." *Rivista di storia e letteratura religiosa* 51 (2015): 431–64.

———. "'Neither by Habits, nor Solely by Will, but by Infused Faith': Hernando de Talavera's Understanding of Conversion between Judaism and Islam." In *Coming to Terms with Forced Conversion: Coercion and Faith in Premodern Iberia and Beyond*, edited by Mercedes García-Arenal and Yonatan Glazer-Eytan. Leiden: Brill, forthcoming.

Segesvary, Victor. *L'Islam et la réforme. Étude sur l'attitude des réformateurs zurichois envers l'Islam (1510–1550)*. Geneva: Éditions L'Age d'homme, 1978.

Seguí Cantos, José. "Presencia de la Orden de Predicadores en la vida social y cultural de la Valencia del siglo XVI." *Archivo Dominicano* 17 (1996): 157–86.

Shagrir, Iris. "The Fall of Acre as a Spiritual Crisis: The Letters of Riccoldo of Monte Croce." *Revue belge de philologie et d'histoire / Belgisch Tijdschrift voor Filologie en Geschiedenis* 90 (2012): 1107–20.

Shamir, Yehuda, ed. *Rabbi Moses Ha-Kohen of Tordesillas and His Book 'Ezer Ha-Emunah: A Chapter in the History of the Judeo-Christian Controversy*. 2 vols. Coconut Grove, FL: Field Research Projects, 1972.

Shirman, Ḥaim. *Ha-Shirah Ha-'Ivrit Be-Sefarad u-Provance*. 2 vols. Jerusalem: Bialik, 1954.

Sicroff, Albert A. "El caso del judaizante jerónimo Fray Diego de Marchena." In *Homenaje a Rodríguez-Moñino. Estudios de erudición que le ofrecen sus amigos o discípulos hispanistas norteamericanos*, 2 vols., 2:227–33. Madrid: Castalia, 1966.

———. *Les controverses des statuts de pureté de sang en Espagne du XV au XVII siècle*. Paris: Didier, 1960.

Siebald, Manfred. "Lazarus of Bethany." In *A Dictionary of Biblical Literature in English Literature*, edited by David Lyle Jeffrey, 438–40. Grand Rapids, MI: Eerdmans, 1992.

Siewert, Rosemarie. *Isaak ben Abraham aus Troki im christlich-jüdischen Gespräch der Reformationszeit*. Münster: Lit, 2005.

Skottki, Kristin. "Medieval Western Perceptions of Islam and the Scholars: What Went Wrong?" In *Cultural Transfers in Dispute: Representations in Asia, Europe and the Arab World since the Middle Ages*, edited by Jörg Feuchter, Friedhelm Hoffmann, and Bee Yun, 107–34. Frankfurt: Campus, 2011.

S. M. C. *Angel of the Judgment: A Life of Vincent Ferrer*. Notre Dame, IN: Ave Maria Press, 1954. http://www.svfsermons.org/Letter%20to%20Benedict%20XIII.htm.

Smith, Macklin. *Prudentius' Psychomachia: A Reexamination*. Princeton, NJ: Princeton University Press, 1976.

Soldevila, Ferrán. *El Compromís de Casp (resposta al Sr. Menéndez Pidal)*. 1965. Barcelona: Rafael Dalmau, 1994.

Soto González, Teresa, and Katarzyna K. Starczewska. "Authority, Philology and Conversion under the Aegis of Martín García." In *After Conversion: Iberia and the Emergence of Modernity*, edited by Mercedes García-Arenal, 199–228. Leiden: Brill, 2016.

Southern, Richard W. *Western Views of Islam in the Middle Ages*. Cambridge, MA: Harvard University Press, 1962.

Soyer, François. "'All One in Christ Jesus'? Spiritual Closeness, Genealogical Determinism and the Conversion of Jews in Alonso de Espina's *Fortalitium Fidei*." *Journal of Spanish Cultural Studies* 17, no. 3 (2016): 239–54.

Starczewska, Katarzyna K. "Apologetic Glosses-Venues for Encounters: Annotations on Abraham in the Latin Translations of the Qur'ān." *Medieval Encounters* 24 (2018): 252–85.

———. "Latin Translation of the Qur'ān (1518/1621) Commissioned by Egidio da Viterbo: Critical Edition and Introductory Study." PhD diss., Universitat Autònoma de Barcelona, 2012. Reprint, Wiesbaden: Harrasowitz, 2018.

Starr-LeBeau, Gretchen D. *In the Shadow of the Virgin: Inquisitors, Friars, and Conversos in Guadalupe, Spain*. Princeton, NJ: Princeton University Press, 2003.

Stewart, Devin. "Dissimulation in Sunni Islam and Morisco Taqiyya." *Al-Qanṭara* 34, no. 2 (2013): 439–90.

———. "The Identity of 'the *Muftī* of Oran,' Abū l-ʿAbbās Aḥmad b. Abī Jumʿah al-Maghrāwī al-Wahrānī (d. 917/1511)." *Al-Qanṭara* 27, no. 2 (2006): 265–301.
St. Jerome. *Commentary of Galatians.* Translated by Andrew Cain. Washington, DC: Catholic University of America Press, 2010.
Stow, Kenneth R. *Popes, Church and Jews in the Middle Ages: Confrontation and Response.* Aldershot: Ashgate, 2007.
Stroumsa, Sarah. *Dāwūd Ibn Marwān al-Muqammiṣ's Twenty Chapters (ʿIshrūn Maqāla).* Leiden: Brill, 1989.
Suárez Fernández, Luis. *Política internacional de Isabel la Católica. Estudio y documentos.* Valladolid: Instituto Isabel la Católica de Historia Eclesiástica, 1965–71.
Sullivan, Karen. *The Inner Lives of Medieval Inquisitors.* Chicago: University of Chicago Press, 2011.
Szpiech, Ryan. *Conversion and Narrative: Reading and Religious Authority in Medieval Polemic.* Philadelphia: University of Pennsylvania Press, 2013.
———. "Conversion as a Historiographical Problem: The Case of Zoraya/Isabel de Solís." In *Contesting Inter-religious Conversion in the Medieval World,* edited by Yaniv Fox and Yosi Yisraeli, 24–38. London: Routledge, 2017.
———. "Converting the Queen: Gender and Polemic in the *Book of 'Aḥiṭub and Ṣalmon.*" *Journal of Medieval Iberian Studies* 3, no. 2 (2011): 203–17.
———. "Introduction." In *Medieval Exegesis and Religious Difference. Commentary, Conflict, and Community in the Premodern Mediterranean,* edited by Ryan Szpiech, 1–26. New York: Fordham University Press, 2015.
———. "Latin as a Language of Authoritative Tradition." In *Oxford Handbook of Medieval Latin Literature,* edited by Ralph J. Hexter and David Townsend, 63–85. New York: Oxford University Press, 2012.
———, ed. *Medieval Exegesis and Religious Difference: Commentary, Conflict and Community in the Premodern Mediterranean.* New York: Fordham University Press, 2015.
———. "The Original Is Unfaithful to the Translation: Conversion and Authenticity in Abner of Burgos and Anselm Turmeda." *eHumanista: Journal in Iberian Studies* 14 (2010): 146–77. http://hdl.handle.net/2027.42/64932.
———. "Preaching Paul to the Moriscos in the *Confusión o confutación de la secta Mahomética y del Alcorán* (1515) by Juan Andrés." *La corónica* 41, no. 1 (2012): 317–44.
———. "Rhetorical Muslims: Islam as Witness in Western Christian Anti-Jewish Polemic." *Al-Qanṭara* 34, no. 1 (2013): 153–85.
———. "A Witness of Their Own Nation: On the Influence of Juan Andrés." In *After Conversion: Iberia and the Emergence of Modernity,* edited by Mercedes García-Arenal, 174–98. Leiden: Brill, 2016.
Ta'labi, Aḥmad b. Muḥammad al-. *Ara'is al-Majalis fi Qisas al-Anbiya', or Lives of the Prophets.* Edited by William M. Brinner. Leiden: Brill, 2002.
Talmage, Frank. "The Francesc de Sant Jordi-Solomon Bonafed Letters." In *Studies in Medieval Jewish History and Literature,* edited by Isadore Twersky, 337–64. Cambridge, MA: Harvard University Press, 1979.
Tarjumān, ʿAbd Allāh al-. *Libre de bons amonestaments i altres obres.* Introduction by Mikel de Epalza. Palma de Mallorca: Moll, 1987.
———. "Libre de bons amonestaments." In *Bernat Metge—Anselm Turmeda. Obres menors,* edited by Marçal Olivar, 144–59. Barcelona: Els Nostres Clàssics, 1927.
———. *Polemical Writings of Profiat Duran.* [In Hebrew.] Jerusalem: Zalman Shazar Center and Dinur Center, 1981.
Tartakoff, Paola. *Between Christian and Jew: Conversion and Inquisition in the Crown of Aragon, 1250–1391.* Philadelphia: University of Pennsylvania Press, 2012.
Taylor, Bruce. *Structures of Reform: The Mercedarian Order in the Spanish Golden Age.* Leiden: Brill, 2000.

Téllez, Gabriel (Tirso de Molina). *Historia General de la Orden de Nuestra Señora de las Mercedes*. 1640. 2 vols. Madrid: Provincia de la Merced de Castilla, 1973.
Thomas, David. "Al-Qaysī." In *Christian-Muslim Relations: A Bibliographical History*, vol. 4, *1200–1350*, edited by David Thomas and Alex Mallett, 732–36. Leiden: Brill, 2012.
Tinti, Amadio M. *Maria debellatrice delle eresie*. Pistoia: Tipografia Pistoiese, 1960.
Tolan, John V. "Royal Policy and Conversion of Jews to Christianity in Thirteenth-Century Europe." In *Contesting Inter-religious Conversion in the Medieval World*, edited by Yaniv Fox and Yosi Yisraeli, 96–110. London: Routledge, 2017.
———. *Saracens: Islam in the European Medieval Imagination*. New York: Columbia University Press, 2002. Translated into Spanish by Jose Ramón Gutiérrez and Salustiano Moreta Velayos, *Sarracenos. El Islam en la imaginación medieval europea*. Valencia: Universitat de València, 2007.
Tommasino, Pier Mattia. "Textual Agnogenesis and the Polysemy of the Reader: Early Modern European Reading of Qur'anic Embryology." In *After Conversion: Iberia and the Emergence of Modernity*, edited by Mercedes García-Arenal, 155–73. Leiden: Brill, 2016.
Tornberg, Carl J. *Codices arabici, persici et turcici. Bibliothecae reglae Universitatis Upsaliensis*. Upsala: Universitatis Upsaliensis, 1849.
Torras i Bages, Joseph. *La tradició catalana: Estudi del valor étich y racional del regionalisme catalá*. Barcelona: Estampa "La Ilustración," 1892.
Torres, Gaspar. *Regula et constitutiones fratrum sacri ordinis beatae Mariae de Merced redemptionis captivatum*. Salamanca, 1565.
Tottoli, Roberto. *Biblical Prophets in the Qur'an and Muslim Literature*. Curzon Studies in the Qur'an Series. Richmond: Curzon Press, 2002.
Trautner-Kromann, Hanne. *Shield and Sword: Jewish Polemics against Christianity and Christians in France and Spain from 1100–1500*. Tübingen: Mohr Siebeck, 1993.
Tripolitanus, Guillelmus. *Wilhelm von Tripolis, Notitia de Machometo / De statu Sarracenorum*. Edited by Peter Engels. Würzburg: Corpus Islamo-Christianum, 1992.
Unterseher, Lisa A. *The Mark of Cain and the Jews: Augustine's Theology of Jews and Judaism*. Piscataway: Gorgias Press, 2009.
Usque, Samuel. *Consolation for the Tribulations of Israel*. Translated by Martin Cohen. Philadelphia: Jewish Publication Society of America, 1965.
Valcárcel Martínez, Vitalino. "La *Vita Mahometi* del códice 10 de Uncastillo, s. XIII: estudio y edición." In *Actas del III Congreso Hispánico de Latín Medieval (León, 26–29 de septiembre de 2001)*, edited by Maurilio Pérez González, 1:211–45. León: Universidad de León, 2002.
Valdés, Alonso de. *Diálogo de las cosas ocurridas en Roma*. Edited by José F. Montesinos. Madrid: La Lectura, 1928.
Valdés, Fernando de. *Cathalogus librorum, qui prohibentur mandato illustrissimi et reverend. d. Ferdinandi de Valdes Hispalensis, archiepiscopus, inquisitoris Generalis Hispaniae*. Valladolid: Sebastián Martínez, 1559. Reprint by Archer M. Huntington, New York: De Vinne Press, 1896.
Valdivielso, José de. *Vida, excelencias y muerte del Gloriosíssimo patriarca y esposo de nuestra Señora S. Joseph*. Lisbon: Francisco de Lyra, 1609.
Valkenberg, Pim. "Polemics, Apologetics, and Dialogue as Forms of Interreligious Communication between Jews, Christians and Muslims in the Middle Ages." In *Religious Polemics in Context: Papers presented to the Second International Conference of the Leiden Institute for the Study of Religions (LISOR) Held at Leiden, 27–28 April 2000*, edited by Theo L. Hettema and Arie van der Kooij, 376–83. Leiden: Brill, 2004.

———. *Sharing Lights on the Way to God: Muslim-Christian Dialogue and Theology in the Context of Abrahamic Partnership.* New York: Rodopi-Brill, 2006.
Valle Rodríguez, Carlos del. "Atalaya del judaísmo hispano VI." *Iberia Judaica* 9 (2017): 145–68.
Vallés Borrás, Vicent J. *La Germanía.* Valencia: Institució Alfons el Magnànim, 2000.
Van Koningsveld, Pieter S. "Andalusian-Arabic Manuscripts from Christian Spain: A Comparative Intercultural Approach." In *Israel Oriental Studies* 12, edited by Joel L. Kraemer, 75–110. Leiden: Brill, 1992.
———. "Muslims Slaves and Captives in Western Europe during the Late Middle Ages." *Islam and Christian-Muslim Relations* 6 (1995): 5–23.
———. "Le parchemin et les livres de plomb de Grenade. Écriture, langue et origine d'une falsification." In *Nuevas aportaciones al conocimiento y estudio del Sacro Monte: IV Centenario Fundacional (1610–2010)*, edited by María Julieta Vega García-Ferrer, María Luisa García Valverde, and Antonio López Carmona, 171–96. Granada: Fundación Euroárabe, 2011.
Van Koningsveld, Pieter S., and Gerard Wiegers. "Five Documents Illustrating the Early Activities of Miguel de Luna and Alonso del Castillo in Deciphering and Translating the Arabic Passages of the Parchment Found in the Torre Turpiana in Granada." In *Nuevas aportaciones al conocimiento y estudio del Sacro Monte: IV Centenario Fundacional (1610–2010)*, edited by María Julieta Vega García-Ferrer, María Luisa García Valverde, and Antonio López Carmona, 215–58. Granada: Fundación Euroárabe, 2011.
———. "The Parchment of the 'Torre Turpiana': The Original Document and Its Early Interpreters." *Al-Qanṭara* 24, no. 2 (2003): 327–58.
———. "The Polemical Works of Muhammad al-Qaysī (fl. 1309) and Their Circulation in Arabic and Aljamiado among the Mudejars in the Fourteenth Century." *Al-Qanṭara* 15, no. 1 (1994): 163–99.
Van Rooden, Peter T. "A Dutch Adaptation of Elias Montalto's *Tratado sobre o princípio do Capítulo 53 de Jesaias*: Text, Introduction and Commentary." *Lias* 16 (1989): 189–238.
Vega García-Ferrer, María Julieta. *Fray Hernando de Talavera y Granada.* Granada: Universidad de Granada, 2007.
Vendrell, Francisca. "La actividad proselitista de san Vicente Ferrer durante el reinado de Fernando I de Aragón." *Sefarad* 13, no. 1 (1953): 87–104.
Verlinden, Charles. *L'esclavage dans l'Europe médiévale.* 2 vols. Bruges: Rijksuniversiteit te Gent, De Tempel, 1955 [vol. 1]; Gent: Rijksuniversiteit te Gent, 1977 [vol. 2].
Vespertino Rodríguez, Antonio. *Leyendas aljamiadas y moriscas sobre personajes bíblicos.* Madrid: Gredos, 1983.
Vidal Doval, Rosa. "La matriz medieval de la disidencia en Castilla: la herejía judaizante y la controversia sobre los conversos." In *Disidencia religiosa en Castilla la Nueva en el siglo XVI*, edited by Ignacio J. García Pinilla. Toledo: Almud, 2013.
———. *Misera Hispania: Jews and Conversos in Alonso de Espina's Fortalitium Fidei.* Oxford: Society for the Study of Medieval Languages and Literature, 2013.
Viera, David J. "The Treatment of the Jews in Vincent Ferrer's Vernacular Sermons." *Fifteenth-Century Studies* 26 (2001): 215–24.
Viguera Molins, María Jesús. "Una glosa aljamiada de la historia de Jonás (J. LXIV, 12)." In *Mélanges María Soledad Carrasco Urgoiti*, 2 vols., edited by Abdeljelil Temimi, 1:203–8. Zaghouan: Tunis, 1999.
Villaverde Amieva, Juan Carlos. "Los manuscritos aljamiado-moriscos: hallazgos, colecciones, inventarios y otras noticias." In *La Memoria de los Moriscos. Escritos y relatos de una diáspora cultural*, coordinated by Alfredo Mateos Paramio, 91–128. Madrid: Sociedad Estatal de Conmemoraciones Culturales, 2010.

Vincent of Beauvais. *Bibliotheca mundi. Vincentii Burgundi, ex ordine Praedicatorum venerabilis episcopi Bellovacensis, Speculum Quadruplex, Naturale, Doctrinale, Morale, Historiale.* 4 vols. Douai: Balthazar Bellère, 1624.

Vincke, Johannes. *Zur Vorgeschichte der Spanischen Inquisition die Inquisition in Aragon, Katalonien, Mallorca und Valencia während des 13. und 14. Jahrhunderts.* Bonn: P. Hanstein, 1941.

Vitoria, Francisco de. *Comentarios a la Secunda Secundae de Santo Tomás.* 5 vols., edited by Vicente Beltrán de Heredia. Salamanca: Biblioteca de Teólogos Españoles, 1932–56.

Vitry, Jacques de. *Iacobi de Vitriaco, libri duo, quorum prior Orientalis siue Hierosolymitanae, alter Occidentalis Historia nomine inscribitur.* Douai: Balthazar Bellère, 1597.

Vives-Ferrándiz Sánchez, Luis. *Vanitas: Retórica visual de la mirada.* Madrid: Ediciones Encuentro, 2011.

Vorágine, Santiago de la. *La legenda dorada.* 2 vols., translated by Fray J. Manuel Macías. Madrid: Alianza, 1982. Reprint, 2016.

Vose, Robin. *Dominicans, Muslims and Jews in the Medieval Crown of Aragon.* Cambridge: Cambridge University Press, 2009.

Voß, Rebekka. *Umstrittene Erlöser: Politik, Ideologie und jüdisch-christlicher Messianismus in Deutschland, 1500–1600.* Göttingen: Vandenhoeck & Ruprecht, 2011.

Walfish, Barry Dov, with Mikhail Kizilov. *Bibliographia Karaitica: An Annotated Bibliography of Karaites and Karaism.* Leiden: Brill, 2011.

Wardropper, Bruce W. *Historia de la poesía lírica a lo divino en la cristiandad occidental.* Madrid: Revista de Occidente, 1958.

Wasserstrom, Steven. *Between Muslim and Jew: The Problem of Symbiosis under Early Islam.* Princeton, NJ: Princeton University Press, 1995.

Wensinck, Arent J. *Concordance et indices de la tradition musulmane. Les Six Livres, le Musnad d'al-Darimi, le Muwatta' de Malik, le Musnad de Ahmad b. Hanbal.* 8 vols. Leiden: Brill, 1936–88.

Wiegers, Gerard. "The Andalusi Heritage in the Maghrib: The Polemical Work of Muhammad Alguazir (fl. 1610)." In *Poetry, Politics and Polemics: Cultural Transfer between the Iberian Peninsula and North Africa*, edited by Otto Zwartjes, G. J. Van Gelder, and E. De Moor, 107–32. Amsterdam: Rodopi, 1996.

———. "Biographical Elements in Arabic and Spanish Anti-Christian and Anti-Jewish Mudéjar Writings." In *Biografías mudéjares o la experiencia de ser minoría. Biografías islámicas en la España cristiana*, edited by Ana Echevarría Arsuaga, 497–515. Madrid: Consejo Superior de Investigaciones Científicas, 2008.

———. *Islamic Literature in Spanish and Aljamiado: Yça of Segovia (FL. 1450), His Antecedents and Successors.* Leiden: Brill, 1994.

———. "Jean de Roquetaillade's Prophecies among the Muslim Minorities of Medieval and Early-Modern Christian Spain: An Islamic Version of the *Vademecum in tribulatione*." In *The Transmission and Dynamics of the Textual Sources of Islam: Essays in Honour of Harald Motzki*, edited by Nicolet Boekhoff-van der Voort, Kees Versteegh, and Joas Wagemakers, 229–47. Leiden: Brill, 2011.

———. "Moriscos and Arabic Studies in Europe." *Al-Qanṭara* 31, no. 2 (2010): 587–610.

———. "Muhammad as the Messiah: A Comparison of the Polemical Works of Juan Alonso with the Gospel of Barnabas." *Bibliotheca orientalis* 52, no. 3–4 (April–June 1995): 245–91.

———. "Las obras de polémica religiosa escritas por los moriscos fuera de España." In *Los moriscos: Expulsión y diáspora. Una perspectiva internacional*, edited by Mercedes García-Arenal and Gerard Wiegers, 391–413. Valencia etc.: Universitat de València etc., 2013.

———. "Polemical Transfers: Iberian Muslim Polemics and Their Impact in Northern Europe in the Seventeenth Century." In *After Conversion: Iberia and the Emergence of Modernity*, edited by Mercedes García-Arenal, 229–50. Leiden: Brill, 2016.

Wieland, George M. *The Significance of Salvation: A Study of Salvation Language in the Pastoral Epistles*. Milton Keynes: Paternoster, 2006.

Wilke, Carsten. "Historicizing Christianity and Profiat Duran's 'Kelimat ha-Goyim' (1397)." *Medieval Encounters* 22 (2016): 140–64.

———, ed. *Isaac Orobio: The Jewish Argument with Dogma and Doubt*. Berlin: De Gruyter, forthcoming.

———. *The Marrakesh Dialogues: A Gospel Critique and Jewish Apology from the Spanish Renaissance*. Leiden: Brill, 2014.

———. "Midrashim from Bordeaux: A Theological Controversy inside the Portuguese Jewish Diaspora at the Time of Spinoza's Excommunication." *European Journal of Jewish Studies* 6, no. 2 (2012): 207–47.

———. "New Christians of Tavira in the Sixteenth Century: Trade Diaspora and Religious Heterodoxy between Morocco and the Low Countries." Paper presented at the international congress Judeus e Cristãos-Novos no Mundo Lusófono, Instituto Superior de Ciências Sociais e Políticas, Universidade de Lisboa, December 2, 2015.

———. "'That Devilish Invention Called Faith': Seventeenth-Century Free-Thought and Its Use in Sephardic Apologetics." In *Conversos, marrani e nuove comunità ebraiche in età moderna*, edited by Myriam Silvera, 131–44. Firenze: Casa Editrice Giuntina, 2015.

Yeves, Juan Antonio. *Manuscritos españoles de la Biblioteca Lazaro Galdiano*. 2 vols. Madrid: Ollero-Ramón-Fundación Lázaro Galdiano, 1998.

Zetterstéen, Kart Vilhem. "Notice sur un rituel musulman en langue espagnole, en caractères arabes et latins." In *Centenario della nascita di Michele Amari. Scritti di filologia e storia araba*, 2 vols., edited by Enrico Besta, Gaetano M. Columba, Carlo A. Nallino, Antonio Salinas, Giambattista Siragusa, and Carlo O. Zuretti, 1:277–91. Palermo: Virzi, 1910.

Zubillaga, Félix. "Métodos misionales de la primera instrucción de San Francisco de Borja para la América Española (1567)." *Archivum historicum Societatis Iesu* 12 (1943): 58–66.

Zuili, Marc. "L'Itinerarium . . . de Jérôme Münzer ou le témoignage d'un Allemand dans l'Espagne de la fin du XVe siècle: une écriture entre littérature de voyage et histoire." *e-Spania* (2016). http://e-spania.revues.org/25260.

Zumel, Francisco. *Regula et constitutiones fratrum sacri ordinis beatae Mariae de Merced redemptionis captivatum*. Salamanca, 1588.

Zuriaga Senent, Vicent Francesc. *La imagen devocional en la orden de la Merced. Tradición, formación, continuidad y variantes*. Valencia: Institució Alfons el Magnànim, 2007.

Notes on Contributors

Antoni Biosca i Bas is an associate professor of Latin philology at the University of Alicante (Spain). He has focused his research on the edition and study of medieval Latin texts, especially those related to the Crown of Aragon and religious controversies among Muslims, Jews, and Christians. Among other works, he has edited and studied the *Opera Omnia* of the Spanish Dominicans Pere Marsili and Alfonso Buenhombre (fourteenth century) as well as the medieval Latin version of the apocryphal *History of Joseph and Asenath* (twelfth century).

Thomas E. Burman is a professor and Robert M. Conway Director at the Medieval Institute of the University of Notre Dame. His research and teaching focus is on the intellectual and cultural interactions among Jews, Christians, and Muslims in the medieval Mediterranean, especially as revealed in Arabic-to-Latin translations, religious polemical literature, and scriptural commentary (particularly Latin biblical and Arabic Qur'an commentaries). His publications include *Religious Polemic and the Intellectual History of the Mozarabs, c. 1050–1200* (Brill, 1994) and *Reading the Qur'ān in Latin Christendom, 1140–1560* (University of Pennsylvania Press, 2007).

Mònica Colominas Aparicio holds a doctorate from the Department of Religious Studies at the University of Amsterdam and received the 2015–16

Dissertation Award of the Amsterdam School of Historical Studies. She is, as of April 2016, Research Fellow at Department I of the Max Planck Institute for the History of Science in Berlin and core member of the Max Planck interdisciplinary project "Convivencia: Iberia to Global Dynamics, 500–1750."

John Dagenais is a professor of medieval Iberian literatures and cultures at the University of California, Los Angeles. His publications include *The Ethics of Reading in Manuscript Culture: Glossing the "Libro de buen amor"* (Princeton, 1994); a special issue of the *Journal of Medieval and Renaissance Studies,* coedited with Margaret Greer, "Decolonizing the Middle Ages" (2000); and "Medieval Spanish Literature in the Twenty-First Century" for the *Cambridge History of Spanish Literature,* edited by David Gies (2004). He is currently at work on Anselm Turmeda / ʿAbd Allāh al-Tarjumān, on an English translation of Ramon Llull's *Doctrina pueril* (Támesis, 2018), and on research into Junípero Serra's study and teaching in Mallorca prior to his missionary journey to the New World.

Óscar de la Cruz is a professor of Latin philology at the Universitat Autònoma de Barcelona. He has published and continues to work on editions of various Latin texts from the medieval and early modern periods that reflect the intellectual relations between the Latin and the Byzantine worlds, paying particular attention to the Western perception of Islam. His research interests focus on editing Latin texts translated from Greek, Arabic, and, more recently, Hebrew/Aramaic.

Borja Franco Llopis is a Ramón y Cajal researcher in the History of Art Department at the Universidad Nacional de Educación a Distancia, Madrid. His research interests lie in the uses of art in the indoctrination of Moriscos in Iberia as well as the visual representations of Muslims in Hispanic artworks during the early modern period. He is the principal investigator of the research group titled "Before Orientalism: The Images of Islam in Iberia and Their Mediterranean Connections."

Mercedes García-Arenal is the principal investigator of the CORPI project at CCHS-CSIC, Madrid. Her research focuses on the religious history of Iberia and the Muslim West, mainly regarding the conversion, polemics, messianism, religious dissidence, and dissimulation of religious minorities. Her publications include *After Conversion: Iberia and the Emergence of Modernity* (Brill, 2016); with G. Wiegers, *A Mediterranean Diaspora: The Expulsion of the Moriscos from Spain* (Brill, 2014); and with F. Rodríguez Mediano, *The Orient in Spain: Converted Muslims, the Forged Lead Books of Granada and the Beginnings of Orientalism* (Brill, 2013).

Linda G. Jones is the Investigadora Ramón y Cajal in the History Department at the Universitat Pompeu Fabra. She obtained her PhD at the University of California, Santa Barbara, Department of Religious Studies, in 2004 with "The Boundaries of Sin and Communal Identity: Muslim and Christian Preaching and the Transmission of Cultural Identity in Medieval Iberia and the Maghreb (12 Cent.)." Among her publications are *The Power of Oratory in the Medieval Muslim World* (Cambridge University Press, 2012) and "The Preaching of the Almohads: Loyalty and Resistance across the Strait of Gibraltar," *Medieval Encounters* 19 (2013).

Daniel J. Lasker is the Norbert Blechner Professor of Jewish Values (emeritus) in the Goldstein-Goren Department of Jewish Thought at Ben-Gurion University of the Negev, Beer Sheva, Israel. He is the author of more than two hundred publications in the fields of medieval Jewish philosophy, especially on the thought of Rabbi Judah Halevi; the Jewish-Christian debate, including the edition of a number of central Jewish polemical texts; and Karaism. His most recent books are *From Judah Hadassi to Elijah Bashyatchi: Studies in Late Medieval Karaite Philosophy* (Brill, 2008) and *The Sage Simhah Isaac Lutski: An Eighteenth-Century Karaite Rabbi; Selected Writings* (Ben-Zvi Institute, 2015 [Hebrew]).

Davide Scotto has published a number of essays and scholarly reviews on Christian understandings of Judaism and Islam in fifteenth-century Europe and coedited four books on the history of Christianity in the Middle Ages and the early modern times. Since 2010, he has been a member of the editorial board of the *Rivista di Storia e Letteratura Religiosa* (Turin/Florence), and as of 2013, he lectures and works as a postdoctoral research fellow at the University of Tübingen, Centre for Islamic Theology. He is an external member of the CORPI project, CCHS-CSIC, Madrid, where he has been developing a monograph project on Hernando de Talavera (1428–1507) and his interreligious thinking in the premodern Mediterranean.

Teresa Soto is an early stage researcher of CORPI at CCHS-CSIC and a PhD candidate in the Department of Spanish and Arabic at the University of Salamanca, where she is currently working on her dissertation on Morisco poetry. She has received a Fulbright grant to pursue graduate studies in the United States at the University of Colorado Boulder and a MEDASTAR European grant at the American University of Beirut. Her research focuses on literature and poetics, cultural transfer, and intellectual networks in Europe and the Islamic world.

Ryan Szpiech is an associate professor in the Departments of Romance Languages and Literatures and Judaic Studies and an affiliate of the Department of Comparative Literature at the University of Michigan. He studies the cultures and literatures of medieval Iberia, focusing especially on cultural interaction, exchange, and conflict. He participates in different international research projects. His publications include *Conversion and Narrative: Reading and Religious Authority in Medieval Polemic* (2013) and, as editor, *Medieval Exegesis and Religious Difference: Commentary, Conflict, and Community in the Premodern Mediterranean* (Fordham University Press, 2015).

Pieter Sjoerd van Koningsveld is an emeritus professor of Islamic studies at Leiden University. His work focuses, first of all, on Christians in al-Andalus and their Latin-Arabic manuscripts and texts. His most recent study in this field is *The Arabic Psalter of Ḥafṣ ibn Albar al-Qûṭî: Prolegomena for a Critical Edition* (Aurora, 2016). He also has various publications on the circulation of Arabic manuscripts in Christian Spain. Together with Gerard Wiegers, he has published various studies and editions of Arabic texts related to Muslim minorities in Spain. One of these is a second, improved, and enlarged edition of a study and translation of Al-Hajarî's *Kitâb Nâṣir al-Dîn ʿalâ al-Qawm al-Kâfirîn*. At present, again together with Wiegers, he is preparing a critical edition and English translation of the Granadan Lead Books.

Gerard Wiegers is a professor of religious studies with the faculty of humanities at the University of Amsterdam. He has published on the relations between Islam and other religions in Europe and the Muslim West, the history of Islamic and Jewish minorities in Europe, and issues of method and theory in the study of religion. He is the project leader of the now-funded

"Project Delicate Relations: Muslims and Jews in Amsterdam and London." With Van Koningsveld, he is preparing a critical edition of the Granadan Sacromonte Lead Books. His most recent books are, with M. García-Arenal, *The Expulsion of the Moriscos of Spain: A Mediterranean Diaspora* (Brill, 2014); and with Van Koningsveld and Q. al-Samarrai, *Aḥmad Ibn Qâsim Al-Ḥajarî: Kitâb Nâṣir al-Dîn ʿalâ ʾl-Qawm al-Kâfirîn* (*The Supporter of Religion against the Infidel*; CSIC, 2015).

Carsten Wilke is a professor in the History and Medieval Studies Departments of Central European University Budapest, where he serves as the director of the Center for Religious Studies. He has authored studies on the religious history of European Jewry from the Middle Ages to the Emancipation era, with focus areas in Jewish-Christian controversy, Iberian crypto-Judaism, Christian Hebraism, Jewish historiography, and the modern history of the rabbinate. His latest publications include *The Marrakesh Dialogues: A Gospel Critique and Jewish Apology from the Spanish Renaissance* (2014), *Histoire des juifs portugais* (Chandeigne, 2nd ed., 2015), and *Farewell to Shulamit: Spatial and Social Diversity in the Song of Songs* (De Gruyter, 2017), as well as the conference volumes *Modern Jewish Scholarship in Hungary: The "Science of Judaism" between East and West*, edited with Tomás Turán (De Gruyter, 2016), and *Isaac Orobio: The Jewish Argument with Dogma and Doubt* (De Gruyter, forthcoming).

Index

Page numbers in italics refer to figures.

Abarbanel, Isaac, 106
Abbasid Caliphate, 5
ʿAbdallāh al-Asīr, 273–74, 277
ʿAbd al-Mālik b. Marwān, 277
Abner of Burgos / Alfonso de Valladolid, 104, 290
Abraham, 55, 56, 129, 179, 234, 287–88, 293
  Abrahamic religions, 149 n. 80
Absalom, 332
Abū Maʿshar, 174
Acre, 281–82
Africa, 170, 223 n. 6, 279, 341
  North Africa, 8, 14, 16, 17, 39, 55, 161, 168, 203, 271, 272, 274, 276, 278, 281, 284, 293, 307, 314, 321, 334, 345, 350 n. 2
Agermanados. See *Germanías*
Agnesio, Juan Bautista, 183
Ahasuerus, 332
Alamany, Joan, 167
Albo, Joseph, 105, 113
Albuixec, 186
Alcorán. *See* Qurʾān
Aleppo, 205, 277
Alfandech, 82, 89
alfaquí. See *faqīh*
Alfonsi, Petrus, 46, 48, 289, 299 n. 37
Alfonso V de Aragón, 162–63, 170, 307, 325 n. 27
Alfonso X, 277
algaribos, 61, 172–73
Algemesí, 189, 199 n. 31
Algeria, 105
Alguazir, Mohammad, 16, 265, 331, 333, 340, 344–49, 350 n. 2
Aliaga, Luis de, 184
aljama, 13, 54, 55, 57–61, 63, 65–69, 169, 176 n. 10
aljamía / *aljamiado*, 10, 18, 54, 55, 58, 60–64, 66, 157, 171–72, 174, 225 n. 14, 272–73
Almería, 278, 297 n. 9
Alphonse the Magnanimous. *See* Alfonso V de Aragón
America, 167, 182, 186
Amsterdam, 16, 18, 360–61, 367–69, 371, 373
Anabaptism, 362, 368
Andalus, al-, 10, 36, 40, 57, 58, 60, 69 n. 18, 172, 208, 223 n. 2, 292
Anglicus, Bartholomeus, 129

Anṣārī al-Andalusī, Muḥammad al-, 294
Anslo, Gherbrand van, 368
Antequera, Ferdinand of, 74, 83, 325 n. 27
Antichrist, 75, 79, 87, 167
Antonio, Nicolás, 118, 144 n. 7
apocalypse, 75, 167, 362, 364
    apocalyptic sermons, 85, 93, 95
apostasy, 12, 18, 19, 67, 69 n. 28, 113, 136–37, 148 n. 50, 152 n. 114, 165, 168, 311, 328 n. 51
    apostate, 19, 69 n. 18, 104, 106, 136, 137, 187, 195, 200, 305, 306, 310, 326 n. 33, 339
    Muslim apostates, 54, 63, 65, 67, 313, 314, 320
Aquinas, Thomas, 38, 43 n. 55, 74, 92, 93, 130, 132, 148 n. 57, 149 n. 80, 164–65
Arab-Christian
    authors, 8, 26, 29, 30, 33, 34
    texts, 26–30, 34–36, 211, 217
Arabic
    Judaeo-Arabic, 105–9
    language, 13–15, 20, 26–27, 36–38, 40, 54–55, 58–62, 112, 155–78, 203–68, 272–75, 279, 287, 307–8, 346, 351 n. 16, 353 n. 38, 355 n. 58
    school, 184
    script, 10, 18, 28, 35, 63–65, 156–57, 171
    studies, 7, 67, 74, 94, 158, 183, 205–6, 278, 280, 299 n. 35
    translation from, 45–52, 62, 285–86
    translation into, 9, 28, 30–32, 34, 60
    translator, 15, 173, 205–6, 208
Arabists, 7, 204, 206–7, 218
Aragon, 27, 71, 74, 83, 95, 167, 273, 307, 310, 314, 323 n. 11, 325 n. 27, 326 n. 34, 327 n. 34
    Consejo de, 164
    Justicia de, 169
    Muslims in, 10, 13, 55, 58–60, 82, 86, 92, 155–63, 168, 170–75
Aramaic, 8–9, 25–43
Arenys, Pere d', 74
Arias Montano, Benito, 141
Aristotle, 133, 149 n. 70
    anti-Aristotelian, 105
    Aristotelian, 11, 113
Arminians, 277
Arot and Marot, 169
Asín Palacios, Miguel, 55
Aucassin, 292
Augustine of Hippo, 81, 124, 131–32, 136, 140, 148 n. 57, 149 n. 66, 289, 291, 302 n. 66
Auvergne, William of, 38, 131
Averroism, 112–13
Avignon, 75
Ayyub. *See* Job

Babylon, 284, 287, 289, 293
Bacchus, 365
Baeza, Hernando de, 292
Baghdad, 281–82
Bakrī, Abū l-Ḥasan Aḥmad b. ʿAbdallāh al-, 53, 209, 234 n. 57, 235 n. 69, 237 n. 75
baptism, 80–87, 93–94, 164–66, 187, 212, 239, 317
    forced, 13, 165, 168, 314, 320, 326 n. 33
    rite of, 87, 121, 138, 375 n. 16
Barbara, Saint, 365
Barbary / Berbería, 97 n. 34, 184, 187, 191, 200 n. 42, 275, 328 n. 51, 332
Barcelona, 58, 74, 75, 96 n. 16, 108, 156–57, 309
Bar Hiyya, Abraham, 54
Barros, João de, 361–62
Bartholomaeus ab Edessa, 46
Beauvais, Vincent of, 39–40, 47, 48
Bedwell, Thomas, 207
Béjaïa. *See* Bougie
Beltrán, Luis, 184, 186–88, 191, 197, 200 n. 30
Ben Nathan Official, Joseph, 108
Ben-Sasson, Hayim Hillel, 357, 360, 362
Berber / Berbería / *berberisco*. *See* Barbary
Bernáldez, Andrés, 121, 137, 145 n. 19
Bibago, Abraham, 106
Bible / Tenach
    biblical themes, 74–89, 98 n. 67, 99 n. 80, 117, 129, 232 n. 49, 283, 287, 332, 349
    biblical times, 139–40
    bilingual, 180, 182

Hebrew, 6–9, 26, 28–30, 33–36, 39, 63, 99 n. 104, 105, 273, 289
literal reading of the, 125, 149 n. 64
popular reading of the, 364
Sacra Biblia Arabica, 218
translations of the, 64, 176 n. 12, 337
Vulgate, 39, 99 n. 104, 148 n. 57
Bibliander, Theodore, 45
Black Plague, 276
blasphemy, 13, 18, 19, 49, 75, 79, 94, 155, 160, 164, 166, 169, 174, 277, 280, 297 n. 14, 328 n. 51, 353 n. 38
Bleda, Jaime, 184, 186, 188–90, 192
Boabdil, 292
Bodian, Miriam, 20, 358
Bologna, 25, 26, 27, 38, 40, 307, 320
Bonafed, Solomon, 106
Bonafide, Honoratus. *See* Duran, Profiat
Bonjorn, David, 104
Bono, Salvatore, 275
Borgia y Aragón, Francis. *See* Duke of Gandía
Borja, 55
Borja de Medina, Francisco de, 181
Borriana, 186
Boswell, John, 58
Bougie, 40, 271
Breen, Daniel de, 368
Brocense, Francisco Sánchez de las Brozas el, 337
Broggio, Paolo, 179
Buenhombre, Alfonso, 9, 46, 48–50, 95, 284–87
Buluqiyyā, 53
Bunyol, 186
Burns, Robert I., 5, 277
Byzantium, 167, 275, 278, 298 n. 29

Cádiz, 122, 333
Calahorra, 185
Calvinism, 361–64, 367–69, 372–74
Canaan, 55
Cantiga, 277–79
captives, 8, 15, 191, 193, 195, 197, 201 n. 60, 271–95
Cardaillac, Louis, 20, 322 n. 1, 334
Cartagena, Alonso de, 12, 128
Carthusians, 271
Carvallo, Luis Alfonso de, 337–43, 349
Casas, Ignacio de las, 182–83
Casaubon, Isaac, 206
Caspe, 83
Castile, 71–78, 92, 119–21, 133, 138, 146 n. 28, 189, 191, 209, 344, 349
Castilian language, 87, 117, 141, 292, 305, 309, 313. *See also* Romance
Inquisition in, 119, 121–22, 127, 136
Jews in, 6, 56, 106
Muslims in, 10, 13, 58, 61, 95, 158, 168
Castillo, Alonso del, 208, 215, 217, 220, 264 n. 20
Castro, Pedro de. *See* Vaca de Castro y Quiñones, Pedro
Catalán, Oriol, 72
Catalonia, 15, 58, 72, 95, 161, 167, 168, 274, 305, 310
Catalan language, 105, 165, 167, 271, 274, 279, 305, 307–15, 320–22
Cátedra, Pedro, 73, 75, 92, 99 n. 104
Catholic Monarchs, 13, 119–23, 133, 136, 141–43, 144 n. 13, 157–58, 164
Catlos, Brian, 57
Cecilio, 203–4, 213, 225 n. 12
Centelles, 182
Centurión, Juan Bautista, 210
Certeau, Michel de, 18–19
Cervantes, Miguel de, 292
Cervera, 72, 98 n. 67
Charles I / Charles V, 13, 155–56, 161, 163–64, 166, 168, 177 n. 47, 184
Chebar river, 281
Christian
anti-Christian, 8, 11, 15–18, 53, 65, 68 n. 1, 70 n. 30, 86–87, 93, 103–13, 137, 166, 192, 212, 272–74, 280, 311, 321, 331–56, 361–62, 366, 370
authorities, 10, 19, 136, 158, 168, 321, 325 n. 27, 361
heretics, 10, 317
New, 17, 119, 122, 137, 139, 165, 187, 198 n. 11, 305–29, 361
non-Christian, 27, 72–73, 77, 89, 92–93, 108, 119, 124, 149 n. 80, 152 n. 105, 164, 193, 201 n. 64, 312, 319, 362, 373

Christian (*continued*)
Old, 122, 125, 137, 139, 179, 181, 187, 196–97, 305–29
Cilicia, 32
Cisneros, Francisco Jiménez de, 161, 165
Ciudad Rodrigo, 185
Clairvaux, Bernard of, 289
Clavijo, battle of, 190
Clement VI, 284
Clement VIII, 211, 216
Clement X, 282
Cocentaina, 166–67
coercion, 143, 165, 374
indirect coercion, 88, 156, 160, 164
Cohen, Jeremy, 9
Colegio del Corpus Christi, 76, 186
Colegio del Emperador, 184
Colegio de San Pablo, 183, 196
Collell, Jaume, 310
compulsion, 39, 140
indirect compulsion, 13, 160–61, 163–64, 174
conversion
Buluqiyyā, 53
converts / *conversos* / new converts, 2, 6, 8, 10–12, 14, 18–20, 117–43, 191, 195–97, 312, 317, 343, 360
decree of, 6, 13, 155, 158–61, 165, 175
forced, 3–5, 13, 15, 161–65, 175, 179, 313–14
to Islam, 107, 283, 292, 308, 314, 320–21
Jewish, 10, 12, 18, 20, 34–35, 104–6, 112, 114 n. 1, 122, 126, 160, 290, 317, 365
mass, 103, 108, 111, 113
Muslims, 155, 157–60, 166–69, 174, 180–88, 192, 205, 278, 292–95, 305–7
problem, 6, 53–70
sermons, 71–100
Cordoba, 36, 37, 120, 144 n. 13
Córdoba, Sebastián de, 344
Council
of Jerusalem, 131
Royal, 161–62
of Seville, 120
of State, 144 n. 13, 216
of Tarragona, 58
of Toledo, 165
of Trent, 136, 338
Count-Duke of Olivares, Gaspar de Guzmán, 209
Counter-Reformation, 2, 358
Count of Aranda, Miguel Ximénez de Urrea y Toledo, 164
Count of Humanes, Francisco de Eraso, 208
Count of Ribagorza, Martín de Gurrea y Aragón, 163
Counts of Oliva, Centelles family, 182
Crescas, Hasdai ben Judah, 105, 106, 109, 111–13
Crispin, Gilbert, 131, 134
Crusades, 5, 39, 122, 161, 167–68, 170, 277, 281
Cueva, Juan de la, 350 n. 6
Cyprus, 219

Dahan, Gilbert, 38
Daileader, Philip, 75
Damascenus, John, 46, 192, 277
Damascus, 277
Dante Alighieri, 141
David ha-Nasi, 106
Derrotarán y Mendiola, Martín, 216, 220
devil, 129, 224, 278, 288, 291, 363
Deza, Diego de, 121
dhimma, 57, 107
Diago, Francisco, 190
Dias, Estêvão, 361, 364–65
Diaspora, 17, 287, 290, 360, 366
Disputation, 28, 53, 60, 159–60, 163, *209*, 271–73, 278, 281, 284, *286*, 331, 345
of Barcelona, 108, 110
inter-Christian, 3
against Muslims, 35, 156
of Paris, 108
public, 1, 88, 103, 106
of Tortosa, 88, 105–6, 115 n. 16
Dobelio, Marcos / al-Du'ābilī al-Kurdī, Murquṣ, 7, 14, 203–63
Dominic, Saint, 25–27, 37–38, 40 n. 7, 72, 75–76, 148 n. 64
Duns Scotus, John, 160, 164–65
Duran, Profiat, 104, 106, 110–11, 113, 361, 365
Duran, Simeon ben Zemah, 105, 113
Duran, Solomon ben Simeon, 105

Durandarte, 337, 339
Dutch Republic, 20
Calvinism, 374
language, 116 n. 39
Rebellion, 359
Reformed Church, 367
society, 17, 206, 364–74

Echevarría Arsuaga, Ana, 88
Edom, 290, 301 n. 51
Egypt, 30–31, 113, 236–37, 285, 287, 289, 291
Eiximenis, Francesc, 141, 165, 167, 200 n. 37, 310
El Escorial, 198 n. 7, 210, 218, 278
Elmo, Saint, 323 n. 11, 365
England, 38, 206, 363–64, 372
Enlightenment, 8, 367, 371
Eolus, 365
Erpenius, Thomas, 45, 206
Escolano, Gaspar, 179
Espina, Alonso de, 12, 129, 149 n. 80, 165, 291
Eulogius Cordubensis, 46
Eusebius of Caesarea, 192
evangelization, 75, 118–20, 142, 167, 182, 193, 197, 200
of Muslims, 6, 12, 13, 156, 158, 181, 183–88
exegesis
biblical, 74, 81, 87, 110, 291
Qurʾānic, 7, 156. See also *tafsīr*
rabbinic, 110
explorers, 276, 284
expulsion
decree of, 168
of Jews, 4, 6, 20, 63, 68, 103, 106
of Muslims, 14, 16, 20, 88, 155, 168, 179, 183–84, 187–90, 195–97, 272, 332–34, 349
Ezekiel, 135

faqīh / *alfaquí*, 13, 61, 66, 81, 82, 83, 89, 98 n. 58, 157, 160, 163, 167, 169–73, 175 n. 5, 181
Farissol, Abraham, 362
fatwā, 172, 265 n. 37, 327 n. 47
Feast of Sacrifice / *Pascua del degüello*, 171
Fernández Solís, Pedro, 122, 144 n. 13
Feros, Antonio, 195
Ferrand, Peter of, 25–27, 38
Ferrer, Vincent, 5, 10–11, 71–100, 138, 185–87, 199 n. 31, 200 n. 37
Figuerola, Johan Martín de, 12–13, 82–83, 94, 155–78, 210
Fitzsimon, Simon, 47
Flanders, 163, 363. *See also* Dutch Republic
Florence, 282
Fonseca, Damian, 184, 186, 188–89
Fraga, 55, 59
France, 38, 70 n. 39, 75, 141, 167, 273–74, 276, 362–63, 365, 372–73
Francis, Saint, 75, 148 n. 64
Franke, Franz R., 46
Fratello, Nicolas / Nicolas Myrtle, 329 n. 52

Galip, Muḥammad, 169
Gandía, 166, 180
Duke of, Francis Borgia y Aragón, 180–85, 187, 193, 198 n. 7, 202 n. 75
García, Martín, 13, 156–63, 171, 173–74
García-Arenal, Mercedes, 12–13, 19, 58, 69 n. 18, 83, 142, 205–7, 209–10, 359
Garcilaso de la Vega, 337, 353 n. 28
Gener, Josep, 313
Gentiles, 362, 365–67, 375 n. 28, 376 n. 30
George, Saint, 365–66
Georgians, 277
Germanías, revolt of / *Agermanados*, 13, 166–68
Germany, 13, 141, 166, 359–60, 363–64
gharīb. See *algaribos*
Gharīb, ʿAlī al-, 61–64, 66–67, 297 n. 11
Ghazālī, Muḥammad al-, 38, 214, 225 n. 11, 237 n. 75, 238 n. 79, 243 n. 113
ghuraba. See *algaribos*
Girón-Negrón, Luis, 64
glosadores / glosses, 156–57, 346, 363, 371
Gómez Silveyra, Abraham, 366, 371–74
González de Mendoza, Pedro, 122, 145 n. 18
Gospel, 12, 26–28, 37, 65, 75, 81, 83, 89, 123–42, 213–14, 221, 228, 242–43, 245, 345, 347–48, 365, 369–70
of Jesus, 133
of John, 143, 161, 307
of Matthew, 126, 130
gōyim, 33

Granada, 6, 11–12, 14, 20, 78, 82, 118–19, 126, 143, 156, 159, 161, 163, 165, 181, 183, 203–68, 282–83, 291–92, 299 n. 41
Cathedral, 117
Greek language, 124, 133, 139, 203, 275–77, 291, 342
Gregory, Saint, 188
Grigor, 277
Gui, Bernard, 317–18
Guimerán, Felipe, 192–93, 197
Gurmendi, Francisco de, 206, 215–18, 220, 265 n. 41

Habsburg, 167, 196, 219, 359
Hadith, 7, 74, 85, 94, 171, 173, 227 n. 22, 243 n. 111
Hagar, 55, 64
Hagerty, Miguel, 209
Hales, Alexander of, 132
Halevi, Solomon, 105
Hamburg, 359
Hames, Harvey, 3, 115 n. 16
Hannaxa, Ahmad, 82, 89, 94
Hauf, Albert, 311–12, 319
Hebraica veritas, 39
Hebrew, 7–8, 10, 25–43, 63–65, 70 n. 43, 74, 96 n. 16, 104–9, 112, 115 n. 17, 141, 203, 209, 212, 227, 290, 293, 371
Henry III, 138
Henry IV, 120
Heraclius, 39
herces, 181
heresy, 19, 88, 119, 121–22, 127, 135–38, 184, 265 n. 41, 328 n. 51, 332, 334
and apostasy, 12, 18, 148 n. 50
heretics, 12, 18–19, 72, 75, 124, 127, 132, 136–39, 187, 195, 291, 306, 318, 344, 347, 362, 373
Judaizing, 118, 143
Heterodoxy, 6, 11, 66, 88, 119, 126–27, 135, 137, 211, 214
Hohenstaufen, 167
Holy Land, 90–91, 167, 224, 227, 233, 238, 281
Holy Office. *See* Inquisition
Huesca, 55, 69 n. 22

Ibiza, 320, 328 n. 51
Iblis, 174
Ibn al-ʿArabī, Muḥammad, 172
Ibn Daud, Abraham, 54
Ibn Ḥazm, Aḥmad, 35, 54
Ibn Musa, Hayyim, 105
Ibn Shaprut, Shem Tov, 104, 109
Ibn Sīnā, Abū-ʿAlī al-Ḥusayn ibn ʿAbdallāh, 272
Ibn Taymīyah, Taqī al-Dīn Ahmad, 38
Ibn Tuda, ʿAbd al-Karim, 335
Idiáquez, Juan de, 215–16, 267 n. 63
Idolatry, 94, 125, 190, 345, 363–66, 369
Ignatius, Saint, 180, 191
Illescas, 77
images, 2, 6, 14, 18, 19, 146 n. 26, 162, 180–81, 188–89, 191, 195, 197, 277, 294, 366–69
for evangelization, 119, 122, 126–27, 182, 186–94, 196
imām, 36–37, 70 n. 33, 176 n. 10
Immaculate Conception, 194
Imola, Benvenuto da, 47
Incarnation, 27, 43 n. 39, 113, 273, 283
Indies, 180, 182, 187, 197
infidels, 28, 73, 75, 78–81, 84–85, 88, 90–91, 164–67, 183–84, 189–96, 204, 234, 241, 288–89, 354 n. 44
Inquisition, 15–16, 19, 147 n. 45, 152 n. 105, 157, 160, 162, 168–69, 176 n. 8, 182–83, 189, 206, 209, 215, 267, 305–6, 308, 312–15, 318–19, 326 n. 33, 334–35, 364, 369
in Castile, 12, 119, 121–22, 127, 136
Council, 162, 176 n. 25, 209, 215, 305
prohibited books, 118
Interián de Ayala, Juan, 192, 193, 195, 197
Iraq, 109
Isabel I of Castile, 11, 117, 122–24, 128–30, 144 n. 13, 145 n. 15, 150 n. 83, 157, 165. *See also* Catholic Monarchs
Isabella of Portugal, 181
Isawiyya, 64
Iṣfahānī, Abū ʿĪsā al-, 64
Ishmael, 55–56
Isidore, Saint, 32, 361
Islamic

anti-Islamic, 9, 45, 47, 50, 73–74, 79, 85, 92, 129, 181
crypto-Muslim, 6, 180, 182, 185, 221, 320, 329
doctrine, 54, 60, 66, 157, 168, 173, 182–83, 192, 205, 361, 368
sources, 14
studies, 7
territories, 5–6, 10, 282–83, 321
texts, 15, 125, 194, 208, 211–19, 221, 331, 333, 338
traditions, 16, 18, 47, 56, 94, 118, 279, 332, 342, 346
world, 26, 38, 40, 45, 107, 115 n. 21, 196, 275–77, 292
Ismail, sacrifice of, 171–72
Israel, 28, 30–32, 56, 139–40, 227, 236, 240, 242–43, 287, 289
Israel, Jonathan, 358–59
Israel, Menasseh ben, 367–68
Italian, 14, 112, 218, 308, 315, 317
Italy, 45, 75, 106, 108–9, 141, 298 n. 29, 308, 324 n. 17

James, Saint, 14, 32, 131, 203, 223, 225, 227, 365–66
James I, 58, 190–91, 194
Jansenist, 367
Javierre, Jerónimo, 184
Jerome, Saint, 126, 136
Jerusalem, 131, 134, 160–1, 167, 289
Jews
anti-Jewish riots, 103–5, 109
biblical, 12, 120, 135–38, 140, 142
crypto-Jewish, 6, 358, 362
Italian, 108, 115 n. 26, 358
Portuguese, 17–18, 358, 360, 364, 367, 373
Sephardi, 8, 16–18, 63, 301 n. 51, 357–76
Jiménez de Rada, Rodrigo, 37, 286
Job / Ayyub, 129, 173–74, 369
John, Saint, 203
John Damascenus, Saint, 46, 192, 277
John the Baptist, Saint, 173, 212, 347
Jonas / Yunus, 172–73
Joseph, Saint, 227, 230–31, 233–34, 236–38, 243, 284–85, 287, 332, 336, 339–40
Joseph ben Shalom Ashkenazi, 54
Joseph ben Shem Tov, 105–6, 110
Joseph ben Shoshan of Toledo, 56
Juan Alonso Aragonés, 235 n. 65, 265 n. 30
Juan Andrés, 129, 159, 171, 297 n. 12
Juan Gabriel / Ioanes Gabrielis Terrolensis, 13, 45, 157, 171, 173
Judaeo-Arabic, 108–9
Judah, 28, 30, 33–34
Judith, 332
Juno, 366
Jupiter, 366
Juwaynī, ʿAbd al-Malik, Imām al-Ḥaramayn- al-, 35

Kabbalah, 141
Kaddouri, Samir, 36–37
Kalām, 26–27, 113
Kaplan, Yosef, 358, 360
Karaism, 108, 116 n. 36, 116 n. 39
Kassin, Jacob Leon, 55
Ketton, Robert of, 9, 39, 45–46
Khazrajī, al-, 294
Kindi, Abū Yūsuf Yaʿqūb b. Isḥāq al-, 46–48
Kohen of Tordesillas, Moses ha-, 104, 112
Krstić, Tijana, 17, 359
Kurdī al-Duʿābilī, Murquṣ al-. *See* Dobelio, Marcos

Laínez, Diego, 183
La Parra, Santiago, 182
La Sapienza, University of, 205, 218
Latin
language, 84, 87, 106, 203, 207, 264 n. 16, 275, 289, 319, 323 n. 11, 358, 368
polemical literature in, 9, 27, 272
Scholasticism, 9, 27, 38
Sermons, 79
translations, 29–31, 33–34, 37–39, 45–52, 73, 74, 116 n. 39, 157, 285–86, 345
Lauer, Gerhard, 360
Lazarus, 81, 83, 94
Lead Books, 14, 203–68
Leo Africanus, Joannes, 45
Lepanto, Battle of, 359
Leroy, Béatrice, 142

Lleida, 58, 74, 272–73, 307
Lliria, 186
Llombai, 185, 187
Llull, Ramon, 15, 46, 167, 271–74, 277–82, 284, 286, 293, 295, 297 n. 13
Lombard, Peter, 132
Lomellini, Ignazio, 45
London, 359
Lorki, Joshua, 105, 110
Los Palacios, 121
Lucaris, Cyril, 45
Luna, Miguel de, 209, 215, 217, 220, 224–25 nn. 9–12, 226–46 nn. 17–123, 254 n. 322, 265 n. 32, 266 n. 56, 267 n. 64
Luther, Martin, 357, 365
  Lutherans, 362–63
Lyra, Nicholas of, 9, 39, 48–49, 106, 134, 286

Madrid, 162, 168, 206, 209, 265 n. 35, 306
Madrid, Jerónimo de, 117
Maghreb, 15, 57, 60, 294
Maghribī, Samau'al al-, 212
mahdī. *See* messiah
Mahoma. *See* Muḥammad
Maimonides, 111
  anti-Maimonidean, 105
majūsī. *See* pagan
Mallorca, 190, 274, 305–7, 309, 311–14, 317–20
Malta, Ludovico de, 215
Manresa, 310
Marchena, Diego de, 128
Mardones, Diego de, 184
María del Puig, Santa, 191–96
María de Uncastillo, Santa, 46
Maria Maggiore, Santa, 180
Marién, 59
Maronite, 175 n. 4, 209, 221
Márquez Villanueva, Francisco, 119, 127, 144 n. 7, 147 n. 45, 148 n. 50, 152 n. 110
Marquis of Estepa, Adán Centurión y Fernández de Córdoba, 209–10, 221, 265 n. 33
Marracci, Ludovico, 45, 218–19, 221, 225 n. 11, 226 n. 15, 228 n. 27, 232 n. 49, 233 n. 53, 234 n. 57, 252 n. 255
marranos, 141
Martí, Ramon, 3, 7–9, 25–40, 46–50, 64, 72–74, 88, 92, 93, 95, 147 n. 14, 223 n. 1, 224 n. 10, 236 n. 72
Martí de Riquer, 309
Martin, Saint, 84–86, 93, 365
Martínez Romeros, Tomás, 75
Martin I, 83
Martyr, Justin, 32
Mary Magdalene, Saint, 365–66
mashiha. *See* messiah
Matar, Nabil, 275, 294–95
Matarana, Bartolomé de, 186
Mawlid, 173
Méchoulan, Henry, 367, 369
Medina del Campo, 77
Mendicants. *See* Mendicant *under* order, religious
Menorca, 313
messiah / *mahdī*, 8, 11, 25–43, 87–88, 106, 110, 113, 130, 173, 212, 357, 362, 364, 369–71
  messianic ideology, 160, 164, 167, 174, 215, 332, 373
Michael, Saint, 309
Michelangelo, 192
Micó, Juan, 185–86, 188
Middle Ages, 1, 5, 11, 20, 39, 45, 64, 149 n. 67, 161, 171, 189, 191, 275–76, 280, 286, 291, 328 n. 50, 353 n. 32
millenarianism, 161, 167, 173–75
Millet-Gérard, Dominique, 46
Minervini, Laura, 64
Mir, Gaspar, 309
miracles
  of Jesus, 75, 89, 90, 173, 204, 222–46
  of Muḥammad, 56, 65
  of St. Martin, 85
  tales, 93, 95 n. 1, 99 n. 80, 186, 188, 286
  of the Virgin, 191–92, 277–78
Mirandola, Pico della, 141
Moncada, Raymond of, 45
Mongols, 5, 277
Montaigne, Michel de, 358
Montcada, 186
Montcada, Roger de, 325 n. 27
Monte di Croce, Riccoldo da, 38, 46–47, 88, 281
Monteira Arias, Inés, 189

Montoliu, Manuel de, 311
Mordechai, 332
morería / Muslim quarter, 13, 74, 82, 157–58, 164, 170, 326 n. 33
Morillo, Gregorio, 208
Morisco, 4, 13–14, 16–18, 20, 55, 61–64, 172, 179–97, 204, 208–10, 213, 215, 217–20, 320, 332–35, 339–40, 343, 344, 352 n. 18
    anti-Morisco, 297 n. 12
    Arabophone, 159
    expulsion of the, 16, 183, 195–97, 332–33, 349
    literature, 171, 220, 334, 354 n. 51
    polemical writings, 17, 63, 331, 349, 350 n. 2
    school for, 180
Morocco, 20, 284, 286, 350 n. 2, 352 n. 18
Mortera, Saul Levi, 368–71
Morverdre, 57
Moses ha-Yitzhari, Mattathias ben, 115 n. 16
Moshe, Mattityahu ben, 68 n. 2
Mozarab, 46, 332
Mudejar
    communities, 10–13, 86, 88–89, 92, 159, 162, 164, 168–69, 175, 297 n. 12
    conversion, 83, 157, 159, 174, 326 n. 33
    polemical writings, 53–70, 72–74, 78, 80, 82, 210
    preacher, 86
Muḥammad, Prophet, 28–29, 35, 38–39, 46, 55, 65, 73, 77, 82, 85, 87, 94, 141, 178 n. 64, 213, 216, 235 n. 69, 237 n. 75, 243 n. 113, 307
    genealogy, 53
    life, 39, 173, 211, 214, 238 n. 80
    prophecy, 56, 64, 211
Mulay Ḥasan, Abū al-Ḥasan ʿAlī, 291
Muntaner, Bernat, 319
Muqammaṣ, Dāwūd al-, 107, 111
Museros, 185–86
Muslim quarter. *See morería*
Mutawakkil, Mulay Muḥammad al-, 352 n. 18

Nahmanides, Moses ben Nahman, 110
Naironi, Nicola, 175 n. 4
Navarra, Francisco de, 182, 185
Nebuchadnezzar, 371
Neptune, 365
Netherlands, 345, 357–76
Nikephoros, Saint, 192
Nirenberg, David, 59, 63, 68, 69 n. 25
Niwālī, ʿAlī al-, 350 n. 3
Novikoff, Alex, 3
Nuestra Señora de Prado monastery, 118, 123
Núñez Muley, Francisco, 20

Obregón, Lope de, 159
Ocaña, 76
Ojeda, Alonso de, 121
Oldradus de Ponte, 69 n. 28
Oran, 161, 172
order, religious
    Dominican, 5, 7, 9–10, 13–14, 25–27, 34, 38–40, 71–74, 78–79, 81–83, 85, 88, 91–95, 96 n. 16, 121, 139, 166, 179–202, 281, 284, 326 n. 34
    Franciscan, 5, 15, 139, 161, 164–65, 167, 174, 179, 305–6, 310, 312, 320–21, 323 n. 11, 326 n. 34
    Hieronymite, 82, 117–18, 128, 136, 142
    Jesuit, 13–14, 82, 179–202, 216
    Mendicant, 5, 8, 72
    Mercedarian, 13–14, 83, 179–202, 276, 282–83
    Preachers, 25, 27
Orient, José, 194
Orobio de Castro, Isaac, 366, 368
Oropesa, Alonso de, 12, 128
Ottoman Empire, 184, 191, 196–97, 219, 303 n. 76, 359
    of North Africa, 17, 20, 35, 331
Oviedo, Ebía de, 305

pagan / *majūsī*, 28, 85–86, 88, 93, 124, 165, 291, 332, 338, 365–67
Paradise, 85–86, 212, 226, 228, 241, 246
Paris, 25, 27, 74, 271, 297 n. 13
Parrilla, Carmen, 123
Pascua del degüello. See Feast of Sacrifice
Pascual, Pedro, 92, 192–97, 282–83, 285–87
Pastore, Stefania, 119, 122, 127

Pastrana, 344
manuscripts, 61, 209, 211–12, 218, 220–21, 265 n. 26
Pati, 163, 170
Paul, Saint, 12, 32, 77, 111, 117–53, 288, 337, 339
Epistles, 12, 119–20, 124, 129, 131–32, 134, 136, 139, 141, 288, 293
Pedrola, 70 n. 33
Pelagianism, 368
Penyafort, Raymond of, 92, 189–90
Pereda, Felipe, 119, 146 n. 28
Pérez, Juan. *See* Taybili, Ibrahim
Perpignan, 186
Persia, 277–78
Persian, 215, 225 n. 14
Peter the Venerable, 47, 88, 135, 147 n. 42
Petrarch, Francesco, 141
Pharaoh, 242, 293
Pharisees, 138, 244
Philip II, 216, 335, 352 n. 18
Philip III, 195, 205, 332, 339
Philip IV, 195, 197
pilgrimage, 90, 204–5
pirates, 184, 191, 196–97
Pisa, 271–72, 277, 359
Poitiers, Peter of, 47
polygamy, 79, 94
polytheism, 55, 67, 365
popes, 150, 179, 182, 200, 218, 220, 299, 364, 368, 372
Benedict XIII, 74, 75, 82, 96 n. 23
Gregory IX, 326 n. 34
Innocent VIII, 122
Innocent XI, 204, 218
John Paul II, 204
nuncio, 157, 175 n. 4
papal bull, 121–22, 268 n. 75
Paul V, 210, 263 n. 8
Pius V, 136
Utrecht, Adriaan of, 155, 161, 163
Portugal, 106, 120, 181, 361–62
Postel, Guillaume, 45–46, 141
Prado, Miguel del, 186
Prague, 359
proselytism, 11, 17, 66, 71–73, 75, 82–83, 93, 96 n. 16, 106, 157, 159, 162, 180, 187, 196
Protestantism, 17, 19–20, 186–88, 197, 357–76
Prudentius, Aurelius, 288
Pulgar, Fernando del, 121, 145 n. 18
Purgatory, 84, 188

Qaysī, Muḥammad al-, 61, 272–74, 277, 279–80, 282, 284, 293–95, 297 n. 9
Quevedo, Francisco de, 339, 355 n. 53
Qur'ān / *Alcorán*, 28–29, 85, 166, 169, 181, *210*, 221, 273, 295, 332
attacks on, 35, 156
knowledge of, 73–74, 87, 94, 157–60, 171, 205, 209, 211
quotations, 9, 45–52, 157, 346
translation of, 7, 9, 13, 39, 142, 217, 219, 224 n. 9
Qurṭubī, Aḥmad ibn ʿUmar al-Anṣārī al-, 35–38

Ramah, 174
Ramírez de Haro, Antonio, 185
Randa, Mount, 281
Raqilī, Abū Zakariyyā Yaḥyā b. Ibrāhīm al-, 61, 70 n. 33
Rashi, Rabbi Shlomo Yitzhak, 39
Reconquest, 118, 196, 292
Red Sea, 113
Reformation, 19, 21, 357–64, 367, 374
Counter-Reformation, 2, 358
Reinhard, Wolfgang, 359
Resurrection, 81, 83, 90, 94, 98 n. 67, 242
Reuben, Jacob ben, 104, 109–10
Reuchlin, Johann, 141
Reynald, 277
Ribalta, Francisco, 189
Ribera, Juan de, 182, 184–86
Rimoch, Astruch, 59
Riquer, Martí de, 309–14, 328 n. 51
Roa, 161
Robles Sierra, Adolfo, 73, 79
Rocabertí, Thomas, 79, 92
Rodríguez Mediano, Fernando, 205–10
Roggema, Barbara, 35

Romance, 18, 54, 64, 157, 176 n. 10, 216, 273, 275, 292. *See also* Castilian language *under* Castile
Romancero, 336–37, 342–43
Rome, 14, 115 n. 26, 162, 175 n. 4, 180–82, 205, 207, 210, 218, 221, 244, 265 n. 35, 278, 365
Roque, Saint, 309

Saadia Gaon, 107
Sabbath, 121
Sacromonte, 14, 203–4, 207–8, 213, 216, 222
Saint Bartholomew, massacre of, 359
Saint Onofre monastery, 185
Saint Victor, Andrew of, 39
Sala, Francisco, 190
Saladin, 277
Salamanca, 118, 166
Salazar, Juan de, 195
Saldaña, Toribio de, 162
Sánchez Sánchez, Manuel, 72
Sanchís Sivera, Josep, 73, 92
San Donnino, monastery of, 272
Sanhedrin, 31
Santa Fe, Gerónimo de, 105
Santa María, Pablo de. *See* Halevi, Solomon
Santa María de Guadalupe, monastery of, 128
Santiago, 189–90
Santiago, Hernando de, 335
Sant Jordi, Franciscus de, 59, 106
Saracens, 25, 39, 46, 69 n. 28, 76–77, 79, 86–87, 93–94, 97 n. 35, 177 n. 39, 271–72, 280–82, 285–86, 292, 317
Sarah, 64
Saxony, Jordan of, 25, 40 n. 7
Schilling, Heinz, 359
Schmidtke, Sabine, 35
Sebastian, Saint, 309
Segovia, Juan de, 45, 142
Semitic, 40, 48
Sergio, 209–15, 221, 265 n. 35
Serrah Mahomet, Lopello de, 58
Seville, 12, 119–25, 130, 134, 136, 141, 205, 207
  riots, 120–21, 124, 129
Shalom Ashkenazi, Joseph ben, 54
Shem Tov, Joseph ben, 105–6, 110
Shoshan of Toledo, Joseph ben, 56
Silesia, Herman of, 45
Sinai, Mount, 231 n. 45
Sisebut, 165
Sistine Chapel, 192
skepticism, 4, 20, 358, 370, 373–74
slavery, 15, 236, 275–76, 278, 280–82, 288–89, 293–94, 313, 328 n. 51
Society of Jesus. *See* Jesuit *under* order, religious
Socinianism, 367, 369–70, 372
Sodom and Gomorrah, 288
Solís, Isabel de, 291–92
Soria, 59
Spanish language, 10, 13, 16–18, 64, 112, 157, 171, 203, 209, 211–16, 219, 221, 265 n. 37, 333–34, 348, 350 n. 2, 354 n. 42, 355 n. 58, 361, 371. *See also* Castilian language *under* Castile
Spinoza, Baruch, 8
  Spinozist, 367
sunna, 84–85, 93–94
syncretism, 20, 64, 120, 131, 135, 141
Szpiech, Ryan, 2, 62–63

tafsīr, 156–57
taḥrīf, 18, 35
Talavera, Hernando de, 11–12, 20, 82, 117–53, 181, 183
Talavera de la Reina, 58, 65
Talmud, 9, 27, 39, 96 n. 16, 111, 115 n. 17, 141, 147 n. 42
Tarjumān, ʿAbdallāh al- / Anselm Turmeda, 15, 305–29
Tavira, 362
Taybili, Ibrahim, 16–18, 331–56
Terrolensis, Ioanes Gabrielis. *See* Juan Gabriel
Testament, 32, 126, 134, 235 n. 65
  First (Old), 29, 35, 39, 126, 129–30, 132–35, 160, 174, 227 n. 21, 291
  New, 104, 109–11, 132, 212, 244 n. 115, 273, 288
Tigris, 281
Tirso de Molina, Gabriel Téllez, 192, 202 n. 74
Tolan, John, 5, 9, 88
Toledano, Pedro, 46

Toledo, 18, 74, 76, 86, 95 n. 12, 97 n. 41, 98 n. 80, 120, 165, 205, 220, 263 n. 5, 332–36
Cortes of, 120
riots, 12, 129, 145 n. 16, 151 n. 93
Toledo, Mark of, 45
Toledo, Peter of, 48
Torah, 11, 35, 56, 58, 63, 65–67, 113, 357–76
Torquemada, Juan de, 12, 128
Torras i Bages, Josep, 309
Tortosa, 162
Disputation of, 11, 88, 105–6, 115 n. 16
Toulouse, 74
Tribaldos de Toledo, Luis, 210
Trinitarianism, 8, 26–27, 35–37, 43 n. 39, 79, 87, 113, 125, 214, 272, 276, 316–17, 347, 363, 366, 369
anti-Trinitarian, 16, 217, 225 n. 11
Tripoli, 161
Tripoli, William of, 38, 46–47
Tudela, 104
Tunis, 16–18, 20, 271–73, 300 n. 43, 305, 307–8, 311, 325 n. 27
Tunisia, 15, 307, 323 n. 11, 324 n. 17, 331, 334, 336, 350 n. 2
Turmeda, Anselm. *See* Tarjumān, ʿAbdallāh al-
Tvrtković, Rita G., 88

unbelief, 81, 90, 273
Unitarianism, 368, 370
Usque, Samuel, 364

Vaca de Castro y Quiñones, Pedro, 205–6, 208–10, 215–17, 220
Valdés, Alonso de, 365
Valdés, Fernando de, 118
Valdivielso, José de, 331–49
Valencia, 13–14, 57, 74–76, 78, 81–83, 88–89, 94, 155, 159, 161, 166–68, 175, 179–202, 282, 297 n. 12, 305, 309–10, 312, 325 n. 22
riots, 13, 166
Valencia, Pedro de, 215, 220
Valladolid, 78, 118, 123, 161
Valladolid, Alfonso de. *See* Abner of Burgos
Vatican, 14, 204, 206–8, 211, 215, 218–19, 221
Veneto, Paolino, 48
Venus, 365–66
Vergara, José, 195
Vernet, Antoni, 309
Vilanova, Arnau de, 167
Vinalesa, 186
Viterbo, Egidio da, 13, 45, 48, 141, 157
Vitoria, Francisco de, 166, 184
Vitry, Jacques de, 47–48
Voragine, Jacobo de, 84–86, 93

Wasserstrom, Steven, 65
Westphalia, Peace of, 372–73

Xàtiva, 59, 71, 166

Yiddish, 112
Yunus. *See* Jonas
Yusuf Dey, 331
Yuza de Bedmar, 169

Zaidan, Muley, 350 n. 2
Zaragoza, 13, 59, 65, 71, 83, 161–62
mosque, 155, 157, 169–70
Zaynab, 46, 173
Zaytūna mosque, al-, 273
Zechariah, 173
Zion, 31, 301 n. 51
Zoilus, 342

www.ingramcontent.com/pod-product-compliance
Lightning Source LLC
Chambersburg PA
CBHW021927290426
44108CB00012B/752
* 9 7 8 0 2 7 1 0 8 1 2 2 9 *